FOCUS ON SUCCESS

Ausgabe Soziales

5th edition

von
Michael Benford
Michael Macfarlane
Ingrid Preedy
Isobel Williams

sowie
John Stevens

unter Mitarbeit der Verlagsredaktion

Cornelsen

FOCUS ON SUCCESS

Ausgabe Soziales

Verfasser/innen: Michael Benford, Bochum
Michael Macfarlane, Oxford
Ingrid Preedy, Dortmund
Isobel Williams, Berlin
John Stevens, Bad Münstereifel

Berater/innen: Antje Baehr, Velbert; Aleksandra Caragea, Gossersweiler-Stein; Philipp Fehrenbach, Nürtingen; Liane Krug, Homberg; Manja Seidel, Malschwitz; Sibylle Vogel, Erfurt; Marco Zimmermann, Bad Überkingen
Projektleitung: Andreas Goebel
Verlagsredaktion: Kari-ann Warnakulasuriya
Außenredaktion: James Abram, Janan Barksdale
Redaktionelle Mitarbeit: Vivika Krämer, Elise Nelson, Oliver Busch (Wörterverzeichnisse)
Umschlaggestaltung: Klein & Halm Grafikdesign, Berlin
Layout und technische Umsetzung: Oxana Rödel, Absatz DTP-Service, Teltow
Coverfoto: Shutterstock / Maxim Blinkov
Illustrationen: Oxford Designers & Illustrators
Bildredaktion: Gertha Maly, Meike Kolle, Christina Scheuerer

Erhältlich sind auch:

Handreichungen zum Unterricht mit Unterrichtsmanager (UM) und 4 Audio-CDs	ISBN 978-3-06-451083-8
Unterrichtsmanager Premium (DVD)	ISBN 978-3-06-451084-5
Workbook mit Audio-CD und herausnehmbaren Lösungsschlüssel	ISBN 978-3-06-451082-1
Vocabulary practice book	ISBN 978-3-06-451079-1
Vokabeltrainer-App für Android, Apple und Windows	Im jeweiligen App-Store

Soweit in diesem Lehrwerk Personen fotografisch abgebildet sind und ihnen von der Redaktion fiktive Namen, Berufe, Dialoge und Ähnliches zugeordnet oder diese Personen in bestimmte Kontexte gesetzt werden, dienen diese Zuordnungen und Darstellungen ausschließlich der Veranschaulichung und dem besseren Verständnis des Inhalts.

www.cornelsen.de

Die Mediencodes enthalten zusätzliche Unterrichtsmaterialien, die der Verlag in eigener Verantwortung zur Verfügung stellt.

1. Auflage, 5. Druck 2023

Alle Drucke dieser Auflage sind inhaltlich unverändert und können im Unterricht nebeneinander verwendet werden.

Druck und Bindung: Livonia Print, Riga

ISBN 978-3-06-451081-4 (Schülerbuch)
ISBN 978-3-06-451099-9 (E-Book)

PEFC
PEFC/12-31-006

PEFC zertifiziert
Dieses Produkt stammt aus nachhaltig bewirtschafteten Wäldern und kontrollierten Quellen.

www.pefc.de

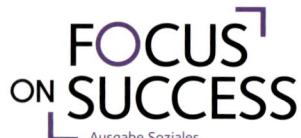

VORWORT

Focus on Success – 5th edition: Ausgabe Soziales ist konzipiert für Lernende an Fachoberschulen und Berufskollegs. Es setzt Englischkenntnisse auf dem Niveau des mittleren Abschlusses voraus und bereitet auf die neuesten Prüfungen zur Erlangung der Fachhochschulreife vor. Das Lehrwerk führt zur Stufe B2 des Gemeinsamen europäischen Referenzrahmens.

Focus on Success – 5th edition: Ausgabe Soziales ist ein komplett neu erarbeitetes Lehrwerk und bietet neue, interessante Texte, aktuelle Themen und einen auf den Lehrplan und Prüfungen abgestimmten Aufgabenapparat.

Das Lehrwerk beinhaltet alles, was Sie für einen erfolgreichen Englischunterricht benötigen:

- 4 *Foundation Course*-Units, in denen Grundkenntnisse, inklusive Grammatik, Wortschatz und Methodenkompetenzen, aufgefrischt werden können.
- 8 *Main Course*-Units, die einheitlich aufgebaut sind:
  - *Focus:* Der Einstieg ins Thema – bildgesteuert, anregend und motivierend.
  - *Text A und Text B:* zwei lange Abschnitte, in denen das Thema der Unit von verschiedenen Blickwinkeln beleuchtet wird.
  - *Social options:* Zusatzmaterialien zur Erweiterung und individuellen Schwerpunktsetzung aus einem sozialen Blickwinkel.
- 4 *Exam preparation*-Units, die jeweils 3 Themenbereiche, mit längeren Texten beinhalten.
- 4 *Job skills*-Units, die auf das Berufsleben vorbereiten und relevante Fertigkeiten und Sprache einführen und üben.
- 12 *Social topics*, die unterschiedliche Themen im Sozialbereich abdecken. Dabei spielen abwechslungsreiche Textarten und praxisrelevante Themen eine wichtige Rolle.

Die Übungen, die auf die Texte folgen, schulen eine Vielzahl von *Skills* (mit Hilfe *Building skills*-Kästen, die die Fertigkeiten einführen und aufbauen, und *Skills checklists*, die die Kenntnisse immer wieder auffrischen) sowie Wortschatz (*Working with words*) und Grammatikkenntnisse (*Getting it right*). Sie trainieren darüber hinaus gezielt alle Aufgabentypen, die in der Abschlussprüfung vorkommen.

Jede Unit enthält auch differenzierte Übungen, die die unterschiedlichen Lernniveaus ansprechen. ⊙ kennzeichnet eine einfachere Übung und ● eine Übung mit mehr Herausforderung.

Außerdem enthält der Anhang eine Fülle an Referenz- und Übungsmaterial:

- Die *Skills files* bieten einen Leitfaden zu Strategien, um das Lernen effektiver zu gestalten, plus Übungsmaterialien dazu und fördern somit das selbstständige Lernen. Anhand der Webcodes (auf www.cornelsen.de/webcodes zu finden) kann man die Hörtexte der *Skills files* unabhängig von der Audio-CD hören und die Lösungen selber kontrollieren.
- Die *Grammar files* enthalten neben ausführlichen Grammatikerklärungen auch zusätzliches Übungsmaterial zur Vertiefung der neugewonnenen Kenntnisse.
- Die Wörterverzeichnisse umfassen eine *Basic word list* mit thematisch geordnetem Grundwortschatz, damit Schüler nicht nur einzelne Wörter, sondern auch ganze Wortfelder auffrischen können; eine *Unit word list* mit allen neuen Wörtern in chronologischer Reihenfolge; und eine *A–Z word list* mit allen neuen Wörtern in alphabetischer Reihenfolge.

Wir hoffen, dass Ihnen die Arbeit mit **Focus on Success – 5th edition: Ausgabe Soziales** Freude bereitet und das Lehrwerk zu einem gelungenen und erfolgreichen Unterricht beiträgt.

Die Autoren und der Verlag

CONTENTS

1 The cult of celebrity

FOUNDATION COURSE

1 TALKING ABOUT CELEBRITY

A Choose one photo which expresses 'the cult of celebrity' best. Tell your neighbour why you have chosen it.

B Think: Make a list of four or five people who are famous in your country.

Pair: Show your list to a partner and decide which of them are celebrities. Sort the names into 'A celebrities' and 'B celebrities'. (Rank them in order of popularity.)

Useful phrases

- fans/paparazzi/cameras
- to wait for sb / to take photos
- to earn money / to sell photos
- How do you feel about … ?
- The paparazzi always/often …
- When a celebrity dies, …
- The newspapers sometimes …
- The fans usually …

Share: Using your lists, decide what makes a celebrity. What do they do to deserve their celebrity status? Define 'celebrity'.

C Study the headlines. What do they say about the advantages/disadvantages of being a celebrity? Make up some headlines of your own.

Luxury store opens at midnight for celebrity shoppers

ROCK LEGEND MICKEY HAS THIRD FACE-LIFT

STALKER ENTERS STAR'S VILLA!

DESIGNER CLOTHES AND JEWELLERY AT CELEBRITY BALL

D Would you like to be a celebrity? Why? / Why not?

2 GETTING IT RIGHT

→ Position of adverbs of time, S. 273; Simple present, S. 249

A Put the words in the correct order to make simple present statements.

1. always / a fan magazine / buy / on Fridays / I
2. at the weekend / go / to gigs / usually / we
3. I / never / talent shows / watch
4. for hours / queue / sometimes / to see our favourite stars / we
5. charity concerts / gives / the group / regularly
6. often / in the summer / they / tour

B Two fans are talking about their favourite celebrities. Put the verbs in brackets into the correct form of the simple present to complete the dialogues.

Ann My sister and I (love) ___ [1] rock music. We (be) ___ [2] fans of Willi Roberts. We (spend) ___ [3] all our money on gigs.

Bob (you/go) ___ [4] to every gig he (have) ___ [5]?

Ann My sister usually (do) ___ [6]. She (not miss) ___ [7] a gig but I (not have) ___ [8] enough time. Sometimes she (bring) ___ [9] home T-shirts and CDs from the gigs. I always (read) ___ [10] about the concerts in the fan magazine. What about you? (you/have) ___ [11] a favourite celebrity?

Bob My friends and I (watch) ___ [12] every film that Jim Razor (make) ___ [13].

Ann (he/be) ___ [14] the actor who (appear) ___ [15] on TV with a different girlfriend every week?

Bob Yes. That (be) ___ [16] part of his image. He (break up) ___ [17] hotel rooms, too. I (not follow) ___ [18] him on Twitter or Facebook but Jim (hit) ___ [19] the headlines every week.

Ann Yes. Celebrity stories always (sell) ___ [20] well.

1/2

C Now listen and check your answers.

3 SPEAKING

→ Interaktion, S. 246

A Work with a partner. Ask and answer questions about celebrities.

- Who is your favourite celebrity?
- Where do you see them? How often?
- How much money do you spend on tickets, fan articles, etc.?
- How much time do you spend following them on Twitter or other social media?

Make up some of your own questions.

Useful phrases

- to go to a film/gig
- to spend money on tickets / fan articles
- to follow sb / a star on social media

- What do you think/like about … ?
- Where / How often do you … ?
- How much money do you spend on … ?
- I (don't) like …
- I never spend any money/time on …
- I spend a lot of / some money/time on …

B Tell the class what you found out.

Mia loves Rory Storm. She collects everything. She spends a fortune on fan articles. She goes to all his concerts and gets his autograph every time.

Tom is a fan of Formula 1. His favourite driver is Glen Gold. He watches every race on TV. The tickets are too expensive. Glen often appears at celebrity charity events.

4 READING

→ Vorbereitung auf das Lesen, S. 214

BUILDING SKILLS: Predicting what the text will be about

If you have an idea what a text is about before you start reading it, you will find it easier to understand. Make use of all the clues on the page to help you.

- Study the headline: this will give you the first clue to what the text is about.
- Look at any photos or illustrations that go with the text: who or what do they show?
- The captions under the photos also give further information about the text.

What do you think the article is going to tell you about talent shows? Make some notes, then read and check.

1/3

EVERYBODY'S GOT TALENT

Most of the people who appear on talent shows like *American Idol* and *Britain's Got Talent* are young and good looking. Some of them are also very talented.

Everyone is scared when they walk onto a stage in front of a huge audience and the judges. When the audience laughs at you because of the way you look, you need to know you have mega-talent. Jonathan Antoine and Charlotte Jaconelli are great singers. They want to share their talent with the world.

Imagine this: Jonathan and Charlotte are coming onto the *Britain's Got Talent* stage. Some members of the audience are laughing. Others are clearly feeling uncomfortable. One of the judges says, 'Just when you think things couldn't get any worse,' as the singers take their spot on stage.

Imagine the change taking place as they start to perform. Some members of the audience are crying, others are standing on their chairs and waving their arms in the air.

There is something magical about the moment. The singers are listening to the cheers. Hopes for the life they dream about are washing over their faces. They are experiencing a life-changing moment.

Jonathan Antoine and Charlotte Jaconelli at the Classical Brit Awards 2013

Jonathan has a great voice. Charlotte's voice is young and more pop. One of the judges said he was afraid that Charlotte would hold back Jonathan, who is the real talent of the group. In the end, the same judge voted for the pair to move on together to the next level of the competition.

That was in 2012. Charlotte and Jonathan finished second in that season and signed a good contract with a record company. Their first album, 'Together', was released in the same year and their follow-up, 'Perhaps Love', came out a year later. Jonathan and Charlotte are now following solo careers.

(298 words)

5 LOOKING AT THE TEXT

→ Produktion: Wh-Fragen beantworten, S. 228

A Work with a partner and answer the following questions in full sentences.

1 Who is the article about?
2 Where are they?
3 Why are they there?
4 What happened first?
5 What happened in the end? Why?
6 When did this take place?

B Now compare your answers with your notes from exercise 4.

6 WORKING WITH WORDS

→ Ein Wörterbuch benutzen, S. 217

A Copy and complete the table using your dictionary. The given words are all from the text.

Noun	Verb	Adjective
▬	to appear	
competition	▬	▬
▬	to dream	▬
▬	to experience	▬
idol	▬	▬
judge	▬	▬
▬ / ▬	to perform	

B Use some of the words you have found to complete the sentences. Change the form of the verbs if necessary.

1 People ▬ in a talent show because they want to be famous.
2 The singer was nervous. He was shaking all through the ▬ .
3 The star always looks dirty. He's really not interested in his ▬ .
4 When they received their prize, one of the winners said, 'This is a great ▬ for us.'
5 The judge often criticizes people before they begin. He is very ▬ .
6 He's a real celebrity, audiences ▬ him.
7 Women often have a ▬ look in their eyes when he sings.
8 She takes part in a lot of shows. She's a really ▬ judge.

7 GETTING IT RIGHT

→ Simple present ▪ Present progressive, S. 249

A Imagine you are at the *Britain's Got Talent* show right now. Put the verbs into the correct form of the present progressive.

1 The performers (get) ▬ made up at the moment.
2 The judge (study) ▬ his script.
3 Jonathan (practise) ▬ his song.
4 You (speak) ▬ to your friend on your mobile phone.
5 Your friend asks: 'What (you/do) ▬ [1] at the moment?'
You answer: 'I (wait) ▬ [2] for the show to start.'
6 Your friend asks: 'What (the members of the audience / do) ▬ [1]?'
You answer: 'They (talk) ▬ [2] to each other. They (look forward to) ▬ [3] a good show.'

B Write complete sentences with the correct form of the verbs in brackets.

1 I ___ *Britain's Got Talent* every week. (watch / am watching)
2 When the show ___ [1] at 10.45, I always ___ [2] to bed. (finish / is finishing ▪ go / am going)
3 Charlotte and Jonathan ___ [1] to become stars. They ___ [2] to win *Britain's Got Talent*. (want / are wanting ▪ try / are trying)
4 They usually ___ their song in the morning. (practise / are practising)
5 Jonathan ___ on his own at the moment. (sings / is singing)
6 The judge ___ [1] near the TV studio. This evening he ___ [2] home after the show. (lives / is living ▪ walks / is walking)

C Work with a partner and write six sentences about Jonathan, Charlotte and the judge using verbs in the simple present and in the present progressive. Remember to use signal words.

8 DISCUSSION

→ Interaktion: An Diskussionen teilnehmen, S. 246

In small groups, discuss talent shows. Say what you (don't) find good about them. Would you like to take part in one? Explain why / why not. Make notes and tell the class.

9 LISTENING

→ Vor dem Hören, S. 225

BUILDING SKILLS: Preparing to listen

Preparing yourself for the listening task will help you to understand listening texts more easily. Make use of everything on the page that can help you before you start listening.

- Study any photos or illustrations on the page for clues about the listening topic.
- Read the questions carefully and look at any other background information.
- Think about any words related to the topic that you might hear.

THE PRICE OF FAME

Kelly and childhood sweetheart Sam to split

10.30 Good morning, fans!

Gerry Davis interviews today's celebrities

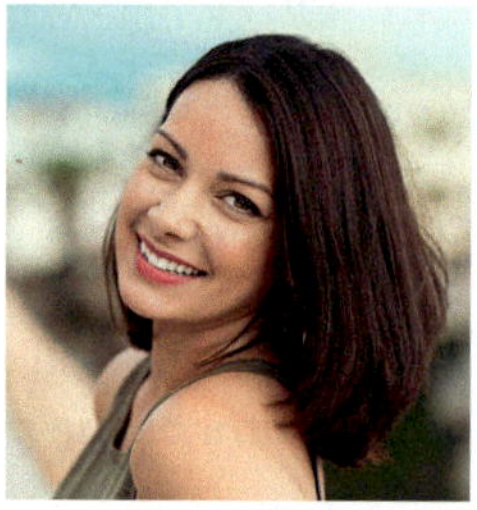

In today's interview, Kelly Green, current £100,000 prize winner of Miss Model talks about her greatest achievement, who inspires her and her biggest challenge. She also talks to Gerry about her relationship with long-time lover, Sam. (She believes that the tabloid press love it when a celebrity has problems.)

A Before you listen, study the photos and the texts. Then answer these questions.

1 Who is Gerry's interview partner?
2 Why is she in the news?
3 What are the four main topics of the interview?
4 What is her relationship with the press?

B With a partner, match these German expressions to the English expressions you might hear.

1 größte Leistung
2 größter Erfolg
3 eine internationale Karriere als Model
4 einen Traum erfüllen
5 die Presse wird zu aufdringlich
6 Probleme in den Schlagzeilen
7 Stars am Heulen
8 einen Vertrag haben

a an international career as a fashion model
b biggest success
c greatest achievement
d problems in the headlines
e stars crying their eyes out
f the press comes too close
g to fulfil a dream
h to have a contract

1/4

C Listen to the interview and say whether these statements are true or false. Correct the wrong statements.

1 Kelly's dream is to have her own fashion label.
2 Veronica Vernon is Kelly's manager.
3 Giselle Goodrich is a top fashion model.
4 Kelly does not admire Giselle.
5 Kelly always enjoys media attention.
6 She understands why the press focuses on celebrities' problems.
7 Sam understands Kelly's problems.
8 Kelly is looking forward to living in Milan.

10 ROLE-PLAY

→ Interaktion: Ein Rollenspiel gestalten, S. 247

Work with a partner. You are going to role-play an interview with a celebrity.

Partner A: You are the interviewer, Gerry Davis (see exercise 9).
Partner B: You are the celebrity. Choose a name for yourself, or use your own name. Decide which area you work in, e.g. sport, film, modelling, reality TV.

Before you start, read through what you are going to say and make notes.
Partner B, tell Partner A your name. Partner A begins.

Gerry Davis	Celebrity
→ Welcome the guest and thank him/her for coming. Say that you know he/she is always busy.	→ Say that you are happy to be here. Say that you are never too busy for your fans.
→ Ask the celebrity to describe his/her greatest achievement or biggest success.	→ Describe an achievement or your biggest success, e.g. your latest album is top of the charts, you are footballer of the year.
→ Congratulate the celebrity and ask who inspires him/her.	→ Say who inspires you. (This can be a real person.)
→ Say that you find that interesting. Then ask what the star's biggest challenge is.	→ Sometimes you get tired. Sometimes the work is hard, but you love what you do. Explain that your fans give you a lot of support, so you can face any challenges that appear.
→ Say that the fans always love to hear the star say things like that. Ask what the star is doing now.	→ Say what you are doing at the moment, e.g. you are working on your next album, training for the next big match.
→ Thank the celebrity for talking to you and wish him/her all the best.	→ Thank Gerry for interviewing you. Say goodbye to him and to your fans.

2 The world of sport

FOUNDATION COURSE

1 TALKING ABOUT SPORT

A Think: What sports do you enjoy? Are you a participant or a spectator? What sports do not interest you?

Pair: Tell a partner and explain why you enjoy / do not enjoy sports.

Share: Do a class survey and rank the sports according to the numbers of classmates who do and watch them.

B Copy and complete the mind map with all the sports you know.

Useful phrases

- to (not) be interested in running/ cycling/…
- to (not) be keen on football/…
- to (not) enjoy/like/love tennis/…
- to (not) support a team
- to (not) be a fan of sb / a team

- How often do you do … ?
- When do you go … ?
- Who do you play … with?

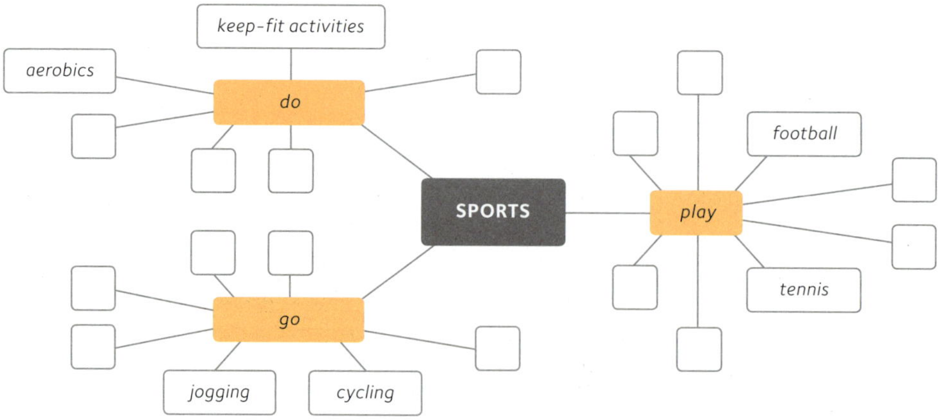

2 GETTING IT RIGHT

→ Simple past, S. 251; Present perfect, S. 253

A Put the verbs in brackets in the correct form of the simple past to complete the dialogues.

1 **A** Mary (play) ___[1] hockey for the Austrian team before she (move) ___[2] to Germany.
  B Oh, that's interesting. I (not know) ___[3] that.
2 **A** What sports (you/do) ___[1] when you (be) ___[2] younger?
  B I (go) ___[3] riding when I (be) ___[4] at school.
3 **A** I (ring) ___[1] your doorbell last night but you (be) ___[2] out. Where (you/go) ___[3] ?
  B I (not go) ___[4] anywhere. I (be) ___[5] tired after jogging so I (go) ___[6] to bed early.
4 **A** (you/queue) ___[1] at the stadium for your tickets?
  B No, I (buy) ___[2] them online.

B Use the words to make sentences. Use the present perfect form of the verb.

1 I / just / buy / a chess set.
2 My sister / just / learn / how to ride a bicycle.
3 Martin and Fred / already / go / to the swimming pool.
4 you / ever / drive a racing car?
5 Martha / read / the rules of the game / yet?

C Complete the sentences with *for* or *since*.

1 I haven't seen Tom at the gym ___ Christmas.
2 Why doesn't he come out? He has been in the changing rooms ___ three hours.
3 Today is the big day. I have had my tickets ___ two weeks.
4 Malcolm isn't playing today. He has had a cold ___ last Tuesday.
5 It's World Cup time again. My national team hasn't taken part ___ 1998.
6 Kevin has played tennis at this club ___ over ten years.

3 SPEAKING

A Work in groups. Ask and answer questions about sports personalities you like and admire.

- Who is your favourite sports personality? Say which sport they are involved in.
- Why do you admire them? Explain what they do that makes you look up to them.
- Have you ever lost interest in a sports personality you really liked? Explain why.

Useful phrases

- to play for a club/team
- to admire / look up to sb
- to be a champion/hero
- Why do you follow/support … ?
- How long have you … ?
- What made you decide not to … ?
- How long did you … ?

B Tell the class what you found out.

Connie has been a fan of the sprinter Jo Myles since she won gold at the Paralympics. Connie admires her because she has overcome her disabilities.

Jason admired the swimmer Ian Jones for a long time, but he lost interest in him when he stopped winning medals.

4 PREDICTING

→ Vorbereitung auf das Lesen, S. 214

Look quickly at the text – don't read it! – then choose the best ending to complete the sentence below.

The text is about …

a deaths in early bicycle races.
b taking illegal substances to improve performance.
c some very bad injuries that have occurred during races.

SKILLS CHECKLIST: Predicting

☑ Have I read the title?
☑ Have I looked at the photo?
☑ Have I read the caption under the photo?

1/5

WHEN HEROES FALL

Professional cycling has a long history of doping problems.

Professional cycling has a long history. The first recorded bicycle races began in the early 1800s and, throughout the decades, improvements in materials used for bikes have led to faster races. There have been heroes in every race but some of them have fallen.

Lance Armstrong was born in Texas on 18 September 1971. He started his sports career at the age of 12 when he came fourth in a swimming competition. From 1984 to 1990, he competed in junior triathlon competitions and became national triathlon champion in 1989 and 1990. In 1992, Armstrong began his career as a professional road racing cyclist. He won the Tour de France seven times between 1999 and 2005. In 2011, he announced his retirement from competitive cycling. A few months later, the United States Anti-Doping Agency (USADA) looked at samples and charged Armstrong with doping. After that, the organization took away his seven Tour de France titles.

Reports about doping in professional cycling are not new. According to the 1997 International Olympic Committee study on the Historical Evolution of Doping Phenomenon in the late 19th century, doping during a competition was not illegal. The study referred to a Welsh cyclist in 1886 who drank a mixture of cocaine, caffeine and strychnine and died during a race. Ten years later, cyclists who used nitroglycerine to stimulate their hearts and improve their breathing suffered hallucinations. During a race in New York, the American champion Marshall Taylor refused to continue as he believed he was being chased by a man with a knife.

Today, an insider said: 'Nobody bats an eyelid when people are doping. I know some cyclists who have doped ever since they started to enter competitions. They win a lot of races but, in the end, these guys are really losers. When you fall, you fall alone. The corrupt system cycles on without you.'

(311 words)

5 UNDERSTANDING THE TEXT

→ Sich während des Lesens Notizen machen, S. 223

BUILDING SKILLS: Taking notes while reading

Taking notes while reading makes it easier to remember the information in a text. It is also a useful skill if you have to answer questions on, or summarize, a text. Use these tips to organize your notes:

- Read the text all the way through to make sure you understand what it is about.
- Prepare a page in your notebook with the text heading, a reference to where to find the text, a note on what the text is about and today's date.
- Use the most important aspects of the text as sub-headings and write your notes under these headings.
- Scan the text for key words, dates and other signals, such as repetition, that will tell you what the author considers important. Include these aspects in your notes.

A First read the text on page 14 quickly and put the headings below into the correct order 1–4.

doping in professional cycling not new ▪ doping today ▪ fallen hero ▪ history of professional cycling

B Now read the text carefully and make notes in your notebook. Use the headings from exercise 5A to organize your notes.

C Answer these questions on the text.

1 When were bicycle races first recorded?
2 What helped cyclists to race faster?
3 What is Lance Armstrong's connection to professional cycling?
4 Why did the USADA take his titles away from him?
5 According to a study, was doping in cycling legal or illegal in the 19th century?
6 What happened to a Welsh cyclist in 1886 as a result of doping?
7 What does an insider think about cyclists who dope?
8 What does the insider think about cycling competitions?

When heroes fall
(Focus on Success, p. 14)
Text is about: …
Date: …
1 …
2 …
3 …
4 …

6 WRITING

→ Produktion: Einen Text zusammenfassen, S. 229

Use your answers to the questions in exercise 5C to write a short summary of the text. These phrases will help you to structure your summary.

Useful phrases

- The article is about …
- According to the text, the first …
- It seems that better bikes …
- One of the most famous modern cyclists was …
- It appears that he was …
- In general, doping in cycling …
- As someone who knows the business says, …
- According to him/her, …
- To sum up, …

7 GETTING IT RIGHT

→ Pronouns, S. 268

Replace the highlighted expressions with a subject pronoun.

1 John doesn't go to the gym regularly.
2 Molly and Pam have joined a dance class.
3 Cilla doesn't do any exercise at all.
4 The dog always runs beside me.

Now replace the highlighted expressions with an object pronoun.

5 I called John from the gym last week.
6 The instructor was happy to see Molly and Pam.
7 Molly and Pam would like Cilla to join the class.
8 I tripped and fell over the dog yesterday.

Complete these dialogues with subject and object pronouns.

1 **A** Do ▬[1] know the woman who takes the dance class, Kate?
B No, ▬[2] don't. Can ▬[3] introduce ▬[4] to ▬[5] ?

2 **A** Paul and I would like to go to the class but ▬[1] don't know where ▬[2] is.
B Molly and Pam said ▬[3] and Paul can go to the class with ▬[4] .

3 **A** These jazz pants are nice. If ▬[1] fit ▬[2], ▬[3] will take ▬[4].
B Yes, ▬[5] fit perfectly. This T-shirt is nice, too. Why don't ▬[6] buy ▬[7], too?

8 GETTING IT RIGHT

→ Possessive adjectives, S. 268

Add possessive adjectives to complete the dialogue.

A How did you enjoy ▬[1] keep-fit class last night?
B I loved it but ▬[2] muscles are aching this morning. Alan was full of energy at the end but, of course, it's ▬[3] job.
A Alan's the trainer, right? Did your sister enjoy ▬[4] session with him?
B Sure. She suggested we should take ▬[5] parents along, too.
A What's ▬[6] opinion of keep-fit? Would they go?
B I think my mum would. When she was a teacher, it was ▬[7] job to organize school sports.

9 PREPARING TO LISTEN

→ Rezeption: Hörverstehen, S. 225

You are going to hear an interview with a Zumba instructor.

A Before you listen, read this short introduction and answer the following questions.

1 What is Zumba?
2 Where and when did it start?
3 Who invented it?

What is Zumba?

You've probably heard of the fitness craze Zumba, a workout known as a dance fitness party. It started in the 1990s, in the slums of Cali, Columbia, when an aerobics instructor called Beto Perez forgot his tape of aerobics music for the class he was teaching. Instead of cancelling the class, he went to his car and took his tape of the traditional salsa and merengue music he listened to while he was driving and improvised his aerobics class using the music. In 1999, Beto Perez took his new aerobic dance programme to Miami, Florida. He named the new-style aerobics Zumba. It wasn't long before Zumba became a worldwide craze. Zumba is a cardio-dance workout – a fitness workout which is good for the heart.

B Complete the sentences on the left with the correct definition on the right.

1 Salsa, merengue, cha-cha-cha, samba and tango are …
2 Reggae, jazz, African beats, country, hip-hop and pop are …
3 Someone who is overweight is …
4 A person who is slim is …
5 Cardio (cardiovascular) means …
6 Metabolism is …
7 A calorie is …
8 Someone who is tired of life …

a a unit used for measuring how much energy food will produce.
b connected with the heart and the blood vessels.
c cannot feel joy and excitement any longer.
d Latin American dances.
e musical styles.
f the chemical processes in living things that change food into materials for growth.
g thin in a way that is attractive.
h too heavy for the size of their body.

10 LISTENING

→ Rezeption: Hörverstehen – Notizen machen, S. 227

BUILDING SKILLS: Taking notes while listening

It can sometimes be difficult to take notes while listening because the speakers don't stop to wait while you are writing. Because of this, you may miss important points. Don't panic! If you practise taking notes every time you listen, you will soon get the hang of it.

- Read the task carefully and look at any other information on the page before you listen.
- Prepare and structure your notes the same way as for a reading task (see page 15).
- Keep focused on the task and note down relevant key words and expressions.

1/6

A Now listen to the interview and take notes.

B Look at your notes and say if the following statements are true or false. Correct the incorrect statements.

1 Zumba only uses Latin American music.
2 Only young and beautiful people go to Zumba classes.
3 Zumba is good for your health.
4 Almost everyone feels tired after a Zumba session.
5 Zumba can help people who feel unhappy.
6 The interviewer does not want to try Zumba.

Zumba (Focus on Success, p. 17)
Listening is about: …
Date: …
Gerry Davis: …
Candy Wilson: …

11 WRITING

→ Produktion: Schreiben S. 228

A friend who feels overweight is unhealthy and unhappy. Use your notes and the phrases below to write an email describing Zumba and suggest how this could help him/her.

Useful phrases

- Hello (*first name*)
- I've just heard an interview with … . She is a …
- Zumba is a … but you don't have to be able to …
- It's lots of fun and has … health benefits.
- It's good for … / increases … / reduces … / helps people … / boosts … / burns …
- … if you're feeling low, …
- The atmosphere is …
- I would like to … / Would you like to … ?
- Hope to hear from you …
- All the best (*your name*)

3 Fashion and brand power

FOUNDATION COURSE

Times Square, New York

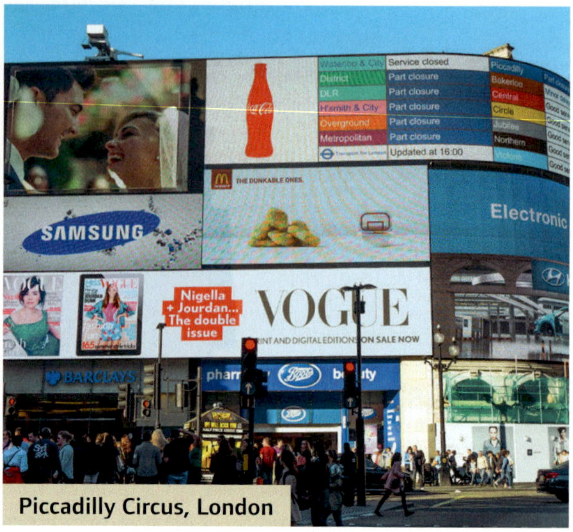

Piccadilly Circus, London

1 TALKING ABOUT BRANDS

A **Think: You see brand names and slogans wherever you go. Write down three brand names and their slogans.**

B **Pair: Compare your list of slogans with a partner.**

C **Share: Which, if any, of these brands do you buy regularly? Which of them would you never buy?**

Useful phrases

- I love/like ... . I shop there regularly.
- I prefer ... . Their clothes are more fashionable than the clothes at ...
- I never drink/eat/wear/buy ...
- Which is better ... ?
- What do/don't you like about ... ?

2 CLASS SURVEY

Ask other people in the class about their favourite brands. Do a class survey and find the top ten brands that people spend their money on.

3 READING

→ Rezeption: Leseverstehen, S. 214

Match the following statements and questions to the gaps (A to D) in the text on page 19.

1 Basically, it all comes down to emotional thinking.
2 Last but not least, brands let us show the world who we are.
3 What might make 'our' brand attractive to us?
4 Why do shoppers always go for a specific brand?

1/7

WHY DOES IT HAVE TO BE A BRAND NAME?

— A — A lot of consumer choices are made according to the price or the availability of the product. If it is affordable, we'll buy it. If it's easy to find, we'll take it. What do we do, though, when we go into a shop and see two similar products which cost more or less the same, one made by company X and one by company Y? We buy the brand we prefer.

— B — Does it simply come down to quality, packaging and price? Perhaps personality affects the type of brands we choose? Or could it be education or family background? All of these things play a part of course but why do we buy one brand and not another?

— C — Some sportswear companies use sports celebrities to advertise their goods. The clothes they wear won't make you run faster or play better but the advertising suggests that wearing the same brand will make you a better athlete. It tells the buyer: 'Like your hero, you are an over-achiever. You never give up. You want more.' People who choose brands that are advertised like this are looking for a challenge. By buying these brand-name products, they feel they are on the road to achieving more.

— D — Using the right brand can help us display our values and beliefs. Brands can show that you belong to the same group. We can use brands to show that we are different from other people or to show that we are the same as others. (246 words)

4 LOOKING AT THE TEXT

→ Rezeption: Leseverstehen, S. 214

Use information from the text to complete the sentence beginnings (1–6) by adding a sentence part from the first box (a–f) and an ending from the second box (g–l).

EXAMPLE: *A lot of shoppers choose goods depending on whether they have enough money to buy them and if they can get the products easily.*

1. ~~A lot of shoppers choose goods depending on …~~
2. If two products made by two different companies are available, …
3. A lot of things can persuade us to buy a product, …
4. Who we are affects our choices, for example, …
5. Some companies use a famous person to advertise their goods hoping that …
6. If you follow a fashion or have certain ideas, …

a and both cost more or less the same, …
b our character and education …
c including how the product is packed …
d shoppers who identify with the famous person …
e the brands you choose can show other people …
f ~~whether they have enough money to buy them …~~

g and how much it costs.
h ~~and if they can get the products easily.~~
i or how we grew up.
j we buy the brand we like better.
k who you are and what you think.
l will buy the product.

5 GETTING IT RIGHT

→ Adjectives ▪ Adverbs of manner, S. 270

A Complete the dialogues with the adjective or adverb form of the words in brackets.

1 **A** I wish I had some money. I'd like to buy a new computer but they're so ___[1]. (expensive)
 B Don't worry. Even good computers are ___[2] nowadays. (cheap)
2 **A** That dress is ___[1]. It must have cost a lot of money. (beautiful)
 B No, it didn't. You can buy brand-name clothing ___[2] at outlet stores. (cheap)
3 **A** Are these the shoes you told me about? They look ___[1]. (great)
 B Yes. I bought them on the Internet and they fit me ___[2]. (perfect)
4 **A** A ___[1] model of my phone comes out tomorrow. (new)
 B If you want one, you'll have to be ___[2]. They get sold out very ___[3]. (quick ▪ quick)

B Rewrite these sentences with the adverbs in the best position.

→ Position of adverbs of time, S. 273

1 I'll buy myself a pair of designer jeans. (tomorrow)
2 Pete has bought a tablet. (just)
3 Mary chooses her children's clothes. (always)
4 **A** I have spent all my allowance. (already ▪ again)
 B Then you won't be able to do any more shopping. (this month)
5 **A** There you are. Shall we get something to eat? (at last ▪ now)
 B No, I'm not hungry. I've eaten two burgers. (today ▪ already)

6 WORKING WITH WORDS

→ Ein Wörterbuch benutzen, S. 217

Copy and complete the table using your dictionary. The given words are in the text.

Noun	Verb	Adjective	Adverb
___		similar	___
___	to prefer	___	___
___	___	___	simply
celebrity / ___	___	___	
athlete		___	___
challenge / ___	___	___	
___ / ___	to achieve	___	

Complete the sentences with words from the same word family as the words in brackets.

1 There is not much (similar) ___ between these designer jeans and the ones from the discount label.
2 Which smartphone do you want to buy? Do you have a (prefer) ___ ?
3 I love these hand-made sweaters. They are (simply) ___ but high-quality clothes.
4 The company had a party to (celebrity) ___ the success of the new brand.
5 I'm sure my new running shoes help me to run faster. I feel really (athlete) ___ now.
6 The course was very (challenge) ___ . It was like running a half-marathon.
7 It was a great (achieve) ___ to get a sports celebrity to advertise the brand.

7 GETTING IT RIGHT

→ Comparison of adjectives and adverbs, S. 271

A Make adjective or adverb comparisons with the words in brackets.

1 It's much (cheap) ▬ [1] to buy no-name goods than designer brands. Designer clothes are (expensive) ▬ [2] than 'normal' clothes.
2 The green T-shirt is (fashionable) ▬ [1] than the blue one, but the yellow T-shirt is the (fashionable) ▬ [2] of them all.
3 You can buy goods (easy) ▬ on the Internet than from crowded stores.
4 Usain Bolt is the (fast) ▬ [1] man in the world, but he will run even (fast) ▬ [2] in our running shoes.
5 People buy products from a company (regular) ▬ if they identify with the brand.

B Make comparison sentences with the words in brackets.

⊕ = … than ▪ ⊜ = as … as ▪ ⊖ = not as … as

1 A lot of people say brand names are (⊕ good) *better than* no-name products but I don't agree. I think a no-name product can be just (⊜ good) *as good as* a brand name.
2 This drink tastes (⊕ sweet) ▬ [1] the other one but it is (⊖ tasty) ▬ [2] yours.
3 We know you're a fast runner but our shoes will make you run (⊕ fast) ▬ ever before.
4 My new tablet PC was (⊖ expensive) ▬ [1] my old laptop and I can download things just (⊜ quick) ▬ [2] before.
5 Their products are (⊖ good) ▬ [1] ours. Their prices are (⊜ competitive) ▬ [2] ours but their quality is (⊕ bad) ▬ [3] ever.

8 LISTENING

→ Rezeption: Hörverstehen, S. 225

1/8

Anne, Bella, Colin and David go running together as often as they can. When Anne collects a T-shirt for Bella to wear at a sponsored women's run, it's not long before a discussion about running clothes starts.

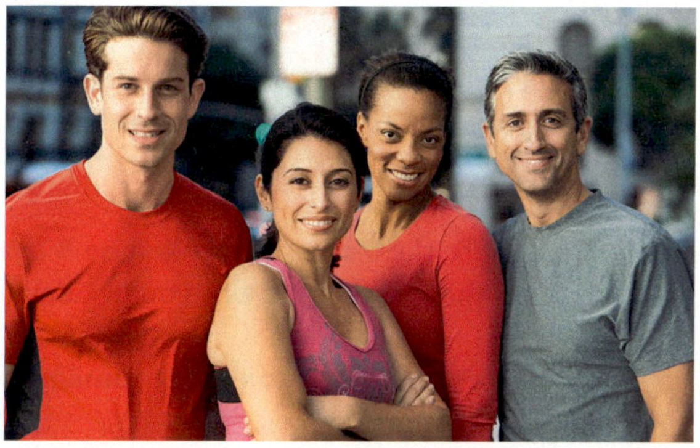

Listen to the discussion and answer the following questions.

1 What does Anne have for Bella?
2 What does Colin think about people who spend a lot of money on sportswear?
3 Why is it good that sports gear firms sponsor events?
4 What is Anne's opinion on the best clothes for running?
5 Where does Anne's gear come from?
6 According to Anne, who makes the clothes she wears?
7 According to Colin, where is sportswear made?
8 How does Bella stop her friends arguing?

9 PHRASES FOR DISCUSSION

→ Interaktion: An Diskussionen teilnehmen, S. 246

BUILDING SKILLS: Learning phrases for discussion

Learning phrases for discussion (see the flap on the back cover) and how to use them will help you express yourself clearly and logically in a debate or a role-play.

- Before you begin a discussion, make sure you know as many phrases for discussion as possible and when to use them correctly.
- Whenever you have the chance to listen to a discussion, pay attention to the phrases people use and remember how these expressions help to structure the discussion.

A Copy this table into your notebook and write the expressions from the list below under the right heading.

Language for discussion				
Giving an opinion	Giving reasons	Agreeing with an opinion	Disagreeing with an opinion	Interrupting

a Actually, I think …
b Yes, that's just how I see it.
c If you ask me, …
d (Sorry), … I don't agree.
e It seems to me that …
f Just a moment, I'd like to say something.
g The thing is, you see …
h Sorry to interrupt, but …
i That's quite right.
j The main reason is (that) …

Keep your table safe. You can add more expressions as you work through the book.

1/8 **B Listen to the discussion in exercise 8 again and listen for the expressions from exercise 9A. Were they used in the way you decided above?**

C Have a short discussion about running clothes with three other people.

On the one hand, … , but on the other hand …

Taking everything into account, …

I agree with … because …

On the whole, …

I see what you mean, but …

In fact, I think that …

10 READING

→ Rezeption: Leseverstehen, S. 214

Read the following blog and the comments below. Match the comments to the paragraphs in the blog.

http://www.topics for discussion.com

1/9

DON'T BE A TEENAGE FASHION VICTIM

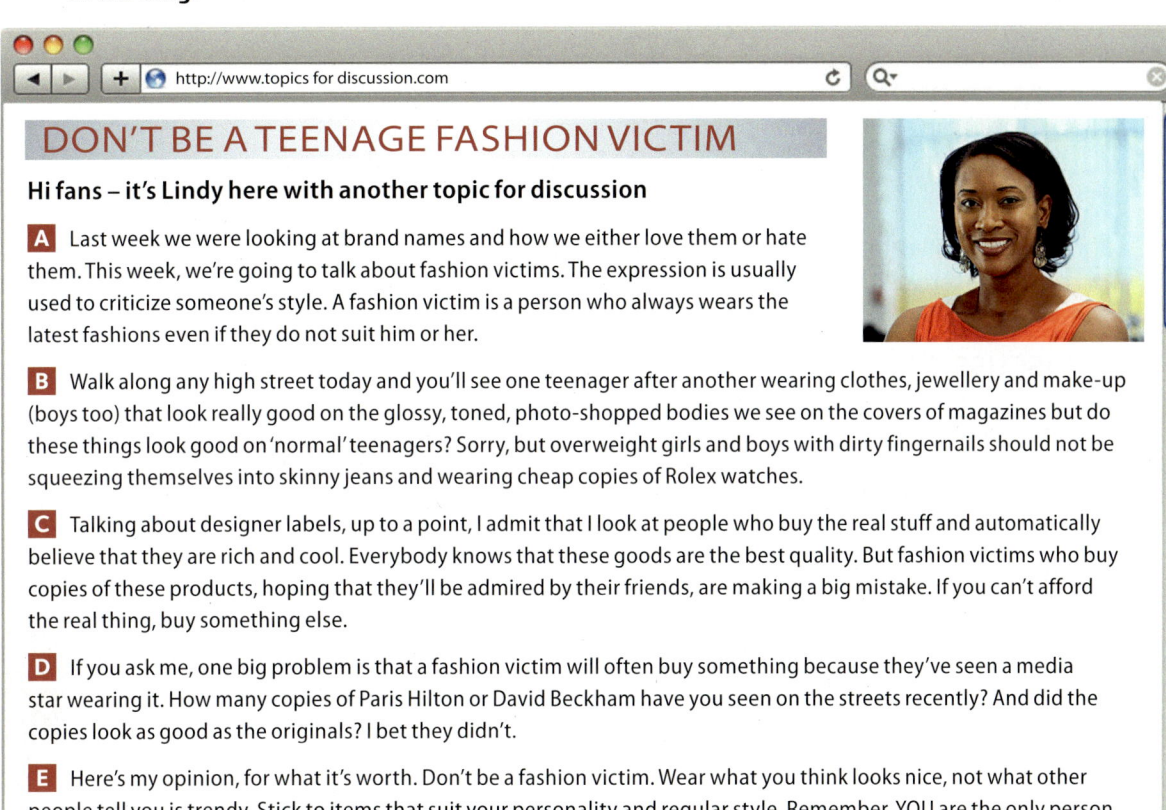

Hi fans – it's Lindy here with another topic for discussion

A Last week we were looking at brand names and how we either love them or hate them. This week, we're going to talk about fashion victims. The expression is usually used to criticize someone's style. A fashion victim is a person who always wears the latest fashions even if they do not suit him or her.

B Walk along any high street today and you'll see one teenager after another wearing clothes, jewellery and make-up (boys too) that look really good on the glossy, toned, photo-shopped bodies we see on the covers of magazines but do these things look good on 'normal' teenagers? Sorry, but overweight girls and boys with dirty fingernails should not be squeezing themselves into skinny jeans and wearing cheap copies of Rolex watches.

C Talking about designer labels, up to a point, I admit that I look at people who buy the real stuff and automatically believe that they are rich and cool. Everybody knows that these goods are the best quality. But fashion victims who buy copies of these products, hoping that they'll be admired by their friends, are making a big mistake. If you can't afford the real thing, buy something else.

D If you ask me, one big problem is that a fashion victim will often buy something because they've seen a media star wearing it. How many copies of Paris Hilton or David Beckham have you seen on the streets recently? And did the copies look as good as the originals? I bet they didn't.

E Here's my opinion, for what it's worth. Don't be a fashion victim. Wear what you think looks nice, not what other people tell you is trendy. Stick to items that suit your personality and regular style. Remember, YOU are the only person who is YOU! No matter where you are or what you're doing, always be yourself. (313 words)

COMMENTS

JANE I agree with Lindy on this point. Some people should not draw attention to themselves. I've seen boys with acne wearing purple shirts. Yuck! As far as I'm concerned, I'm a bit overweight, so I never wear tight clothes. I don't feel comfortable in them and I don't want people staring at me.

KATY I have to agree with you completely on that point. My own view of the matter is that a lot of teenagers simply don't know who they really are. I don't want to pretend I'm someone else. I'm happy to be me. Everyone is unique. Right?

LIAM Lindy, I see what you mean about copying stars but don't you think that's part of growing up? Young people should be free to experiment with who they are and how they look. If you like a particular star, why not copy the way they dress?

MARK Sorry, Lindy. I don't agree. Some people who buy the latest styles can look really great. I think the secret is not overdoing it. I mean, you don't have to wear every trendy item you own all at once.

NELE I'm afraid I can't accept your criticism of people who buy fakes. I want to look good but I don't have much money. I'm happy that I have a great collection of bags and shoes that look just like the originals (YSL, Prada, Versace, Gucci) and they were all affordable. (240 words)

11 WORKING WITH WORDS

A **Match words from box A to words from box B to make collocations from the text on page 23. There is only one match for each word.**

A

best	fashion
brand	high
cheap	latest
designer	skinny

B

copies	names
fashions	quality
jeans	street
labels	victims

B **Write replies to two of the comments giving your own opinion. Use some of the collocations from exercise 11A.**

12 DISCUSSION

→ Interaktion: An Diskussionen teilnehmen, S. 246

BUILDING SKILLS: Preparing for group discussions

Preparing yourself for the particular situation will help you take part in a discussion successfully.

- Before you start, always think about your opinion and what you want to say.
- Prepare some bullet points related to the aspects of the topic.
- Write down key words and phrases in English.

A **Preparation: Work with a partner. You and your partner are going to discuss fashion with another pair. Before you start, read the ideas below with your partner and share your opinions. Decide what you want to say and make some notes.**

Trying to keep up with trends takes too much time and energy.
We spend too much money on fashion.
Things are only 'in' for a short time.
Following fashion is a waste of time.
The media influences what we buy.

B **Discussion: Now find another pair and talk about fashion. Try to use as much language for discussion as you can.**

C **Tell the class the results of your discussion.**

SKILLS CHECKLIST: Group discussions

- ☑ Have I thought about what I want to say?
- ☑ Have I prepared some bullet points?
- ☑ Have I written down key phrases in English?

4 Leisure and free time

FOUNDATION COURSE

1 TALKING ABOUT FREE-TIME ACTIVITIES

A **Use your own ideas and ideas from the photos to ask and answer questions about what you like or don't like doing in your free time.**

I enjoy playing music.

I love surfing the Internet.

I don't mind shopping, but I prefer to hang out with friends.

B **What activities would you like to do which you can't? Use ideas from the box to explain why you don't do these activities.**

cost of activity ▪ don't have the transport to get there ▪ lack of time ▪ no one to go with me ▪ not available in my area ▪ parents don't let me

C **Imagine you have the chance to do one of the activities you spoke about above. Describe what you are going to do or say what you think you will do.**

I'm going to take riding lessons at the local riding school. I'm going to go there twice a week.

I think I'll take a photography course. I'll need to save up for a good camera first.

2 GETTING IT RIGHT

→ *Will* future ▪ *Going to* future, S. 257

Put the verbs into the correct form of the *will* or *going to* future.

1 I've decided to spend less time in front of the computer. I (play) ___ football instead.
2 I think the weather (be) ___[1] nice this afternoon so we (be able to) ___[2] go for a run.
3 I (go) ___[1] shopping now but I promise I (be) ___[2] back later.
4 Lucy's parents gave her some money for her birthday. She (spend) ___ it on driving lessons.
5 Martin needs a new hobby so he (join) ___[1] the chess club. I hope he (like) ___[2] it.
6 I have got a free weekend so I (help) ___ my dad in the garden.
7 Tim (study) ___[1] in Bristol. He hopes he (find) ___[2] some interesting clubs to join there.
8 Mike and I (watch) ___[1] TV this evening. (you/watch) ___[2] with us?

3 ANALYSING A CARTOON

→ Produktion: Cartoons beschreiben und analysieren, S. 236

BUILDING SKILLS: Describing cartoons

Before you begin to describe or analyse a cartoon, always read the instructions carefully so that you know what you have to do.

- Read the caption under the drawing or any speech bubbles in the cartoon and think about how they relate to the picture.
- Look at everything in the picture and describe it carefully, using the present progressive to say what people are doing. → Present progressive, S. 213
- If you don't get the joke, just concentrate on describing the cartoon. Do not waste time trying to figure it out.

A Study the cartoon, then use the words from the box to complete the description below.

behind ▪ cartoonist ▪ face ▪ under ▪ home ▪ in front of ▪ probably ▪ emoticon ▪ worried

The cartoon shows a boy sitting ___[1] a computer at ___[2]. He is ___[3] in his bedroom. His parents are standing ___[4] him. The boy's father looks ___[5]. His mother appears to be saying the words written ___[6] the cartoon. The boy's ___[7] does not have the usual eyes, nose and mouth. The ___[8] has drawn it as an ___[9] instead.

"We know it makes you happy, but your father and I think you're spending too much time on the computer."

B Choose the best sentence ending to complete the interpretation of the cartoon.

The cartoonist seems to be making the point that …

a parents of teenagers are often worried about their children.
b spending all your time online will change you from a human being into a computer.
c teenagers are happiest when they're chatting.

4 READING

→ Rezeption: Leseverstehen, S. 214

A survey among teenagers in the USA showed that many of them spend their free time hanging out in shopping malls.

A Before you read the text, match the words and phrases below to the correct German translation. (The alphabetical wordlist at the back of the book will help you.)

1 curfew	**5** adequately	**a** angemessen	**e** Aktion
2 legal guardian	**6** measures	**b** Befreiungen	**f** Sperrstunde
3 retailer	**7** initiative	**c** Einzelhändler/in	**g** Vormund
4 incident	**8** exemptions	**d** Maßnahmen	**h** Zwischenfall

1/10

LIFE'S SO UNFAIR! Shopping mall sets 6 pm curfew for teenagers – unless they bring their parents

Teenagers have been hanging out in shopping malls with their friends for decades but one mall is putting an end to the tradition – at least after 6 pm. North Park Center in Dallas has set a 6 pm curfew after which time any person aged 17 or under must be accompanied by a parent or legal guardian. After the curfew any young teens without an adult will be approached and asked to provide ID and if they don't have any, a parent will either need to come join them or pick them up.

Although young teens and some of their parents may object to the curfew, North Park spokesman Mark Annick argued that all the center's retailers backed the new rules.

'I really do respect that there are parents who may not agree with us completely,' Annick told CBS news.

He went on to say that the rules were not brought in after any particular incidents or complaints but in a bid to maintain a family atmosphere for the estimated 26 million visitors who come to the mall each year. The new rules also state that visitors must dress 'appropriately for a family-oriented shopping center. Clothes must adequately cover the body. Visible undergarments are not permitted.'

The measures have divided opinions with some parents backing the curfew, others saying it should be later and some saying it is not needed at all.

'If the intent is to stop the loitering and just mall walking and things like that, I think it's a great idea,' one parent said. Another parent disagreed with the mall's initiative, saying, 'These kids are old enough to have drivers licenses, so I don't see why they need to be escorted around the mall.'

Teens who work at the mall and those who are just there to watch a movie are the only exemptions to the curfew.

North Park is the largest shopping center in North Texas boasting more than 235 stores and restaurants. (328 words)

Abridged and adapted from: *www.dailymail.co.uk*

B Now read the text carefully and make notes.

C Explain in 3–4 sentences what the text is about.

SKILLS CHECKLIST: Taking notes

- ☑ Have I read the whole text?
- ☑ Have I scanned the text for key words?
- ☑ Have I noted down the key words?

5 MEDIATION

→ Schriftliche Mediation, S. 240

BUILDING SKILLS: Written mediation

Written mediation means communicating the general sense of a text in another language to someone who does not understand the original.

- Before you start to write, read the instructions carefully and make sure you understand the *situation, who the mediation is aimed at* and *what form your text should be*, e.g. an email, a list, etc.
- Remember that you should only give the information that the person you are mediating for needs. Leave out any details that are not relevant.
- You should not translate the text word for word, so you can paraphrase 'difficult' expressions.

A Read the German instructions below and describe the situation in your own words. Say who the mediation is aimed at and what sort of text you have to write.

> Sie arbeiten in einer kleinen Boutique in einem Einkaufszentrum in Ihrer Stadt. Ihr Chef / Ihre Chefin und andere Ladenbesitzer beklagen sich über die Gruppen von Jugendlichen, die sich nach der Schule im Einkaufszentrum treffen, um dort herumzuhängen. Sie stören die normalen Kunden und die Läden machen weniger Umsatz. Ihr Chef / Ihre Chefin gibt Ihnen den Text (Seite 27) und bittet Sie, die Details auf Deutsch auf einem Handzettel festzuhalten, den er/sie für seine/ihre Kollegen kopieren kann.

B Re-read the text on page 27 and decide which points your boss and his/her colleagues need to know and make a note of them.

C Now put those points into German in a structured text. Make sure your text is in the form your boss wants.

D When you have finished, read your German text and check that it is correct. Ask yourself this question: Have I given the sense of the text in a way that my boss and his/her colleagues will easily understand?

6 GETTING IT RIGHT

→ Countable and uncountable nouns, S. 274

Complete the sentences with the English translations of the German words in brackets.

1 Some kids were messing around in the shop and caused a lot of ___[1] to some of the electronic ___[2] on sale. (*Schaden* ▪ *Geräte*)

2 Some teachers like to give out ___[1] at the weekend but I am always busy helping my mum with the ___[2]. (*Hausaufgaben* ▪ *Hausarbeiten*)

3 We moved house last weekend. Lifting ___[1], for example, is really heavy ___[2]. (*Möbel* ▪ *Arbeit*)

4 I have found a lot of ___[1] for my project online. I also got ___[2] from my sister. (*Informationen* ▪ *Hilfe*)

5 If you are worried about you son's ___[1] at school, you can ask his teacher for ___[2]. (*Fortschritte* ▪ *Rat*)

6 Every generation of parents complain about the ___[1] of their children. When my parents were young, their parents said their ___[2] was too long. (*Verhalten* ▪ *Haare*)

7 There is no ___ that shopping centres are safer places if teenagers have to leave after 6 pm. (*Beweise*)

1/11

IT'S ALL RIGHT, MUM, I'M ONLY PRACTISING MY SOCIAL SKILLS

What do teenagers do in their free time? Some of them hang out in chat rooms exchanging moans about school or talking about the opposite sex. Others text, tweet or post their activities as they happen. Most teenagers today use social media to stay connected to their peers.

Many parents complain that their children prefer computers to 'real' people but they don't seem to realize that most of the kids are actually working actively to interact with other people. It used to be the shopping centre but today the places to meet are online. Social network sites are often the only 'public' spaces in which teens can get together with their friends in today's busy world.

Kids today don't really have much free time. Apart from homework, a lot of them have organized after-school activities or jobs. Some parents do not allow their children to go out after school; they have to help in the house or look after younger siblings.

A generation ago, it was usual for teens to visit each other at home after school. Today's teens often don't know any people of their age who live nearby. Social media gives teenagers the opportunity to socialize and relax with people of their own age after school. Instead of complaining, parents should be pleased when they see their kids texting or chatting online. These teens are simply using today's technology to learn social skills and have fun with friends. (239 words)

7 LOOKING AT THE TEXT

→ Rezeption: Leseverstehen, S. 214

A Read the text. Say in two sentences what it is about.

B Say if the following statements are true or false according to the text. Give reasons for all of your answers.

1 Teenagers use all types of social media to keep in touch with their friends.
2 Parents would prefer their children to meet their friends face-to-face.
3 Teens like to meet their friends in shopping centres.
4 Kids have a lot to do after school.
5 Parents are happy when their children do outdoor activities.
6 A lot of teenagers meet in each other's homes after school.
7 Social media is often the only way kids can have contact with each other after school.
8 Teenagers can strengthen their relationships using social media.

8 WORKING WITH WORDS

A All of the words in the box appear in the text. Match six of them with their definitions, 1–6.

a generation ▪ activities ▪ moans ▪ peers ▪ siblings ▪ social skills ▪ to interact ▪ to prefer

1 brothers and sisters
2 complaints about something
3 people who are the same age or have the same social status as you
4 the ability to talk easily to other people and do things in a group
5 to communicate with somebody, especially while you work, play or spend time with them
6 to like one thing or a person better than another

B Write your own definitions for the two extra words as they appear in the text.

9 GETTING IT RIGHT

→ Quantifiers, S. 274

Choose the correct word or phrase from the box to complete the dialogues.

any ▪ some ▪ many ▪ much

1 **A** Do you have ___[1] time this evening? I need ___[2] help with my homework.
  B Sorry, I have too ___[3] homework myself at the moment. I don't need ___[4] more.
2 **A** How ___[1] social media sites are you on?
  B I was on four, but my dad said I was spending too ___[2] time online so I only use one now.
3 **A** Have you got ___[1] friends on Facebook that you have never met before?
  B I don't have ___[2] Facebook friends at all. I don't have ___[3] time for social networks.

a few ▪ a little ▪ few ▪ little

4 **A** I can't come round till later. I have ___[1] more things to do at home.
  B That's all right by me. I need ___[2] more time to organize things before you arrive.
5 **A** There's ___[1] point in explaining what you're doing to your parents.
  B I know. Very ___[2] parents remember how things were when they were young.
6 **A** My friends have ___[1] interest in Facebook. They are all on WhatsApp.
  B I only know ___[2] people who still use Facebook.

10 MEDIATION

→ Schriftliche Mediation, S. 240

Sie hören zufällig, wie Ihre Mutter und Ihre Tante sich über Ihre zwei Cousins unterhalten. Sie sind beide Teenager und verbringen viel Zeit in ihren sozialen Netzwerken im Internet. Ihre Tante ist besorgt und möchte wissen, warum die junge Leute sich nicht mehr mit ihren Freunden nach der Schule treffen, so wie sie und Ihre Mutter es gemacht haben, als sie Teenager waren.

Sie beschließen, Ihrer Tante eine E-Mail zu schreiben, in der Sie die wichtigsten Punkte des Textes *It's all right, Mum, I'm only practising my social skills* auf Deutsch erklären.

SKILLS CHECKLIST: Written mediation

- ☑ Have I read the situation?
- ☑ Have I understood who the mediation is for?
- ☑ Have I written the right sort of text?

11 DESCRIBING A PICTURE

→ Produktion: Bilder beschreiben und analysieren, S. 236

Your aunt shows you this picture of your cousins.

A ⊙ **Describe the photo. Explain how it relates to the text *It's all right, Mum, I'm only practising my social skills.***

B ● **Describe the photo. Compare the children's behaviour with your own use of social media.**

Job skills 1

Emails ▪ telephoning

Eric Jung is studying at a vocational college and is looking for work experience during the summer. Earlier this morning he received two emails.

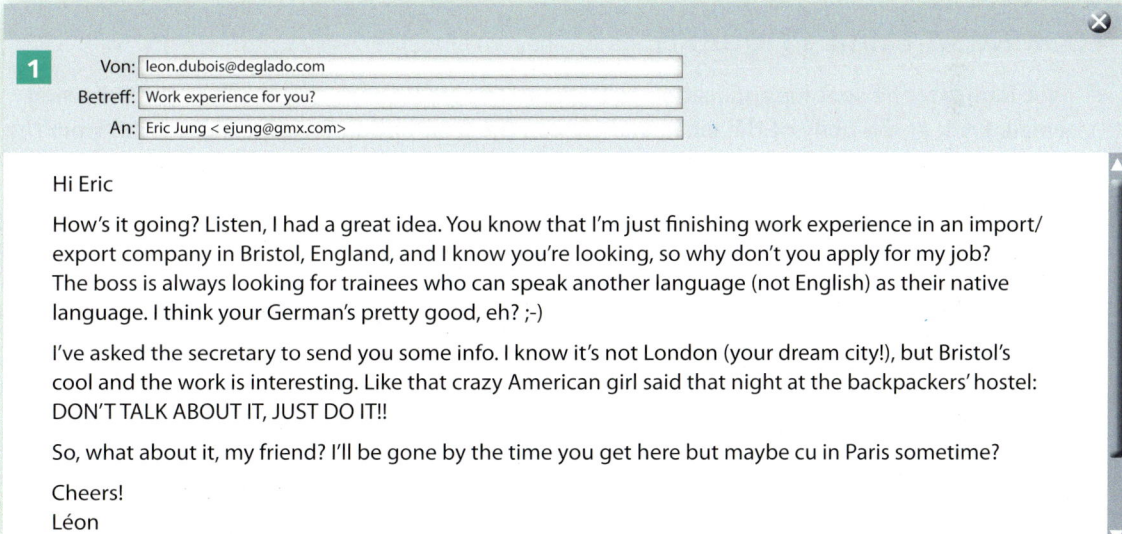

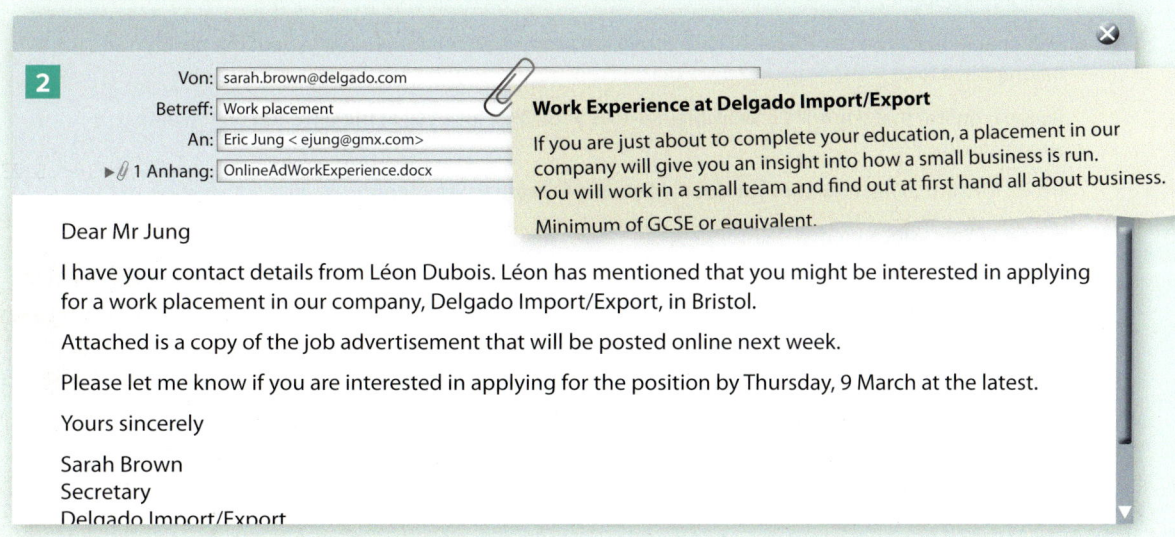

1 LOOKING AT THE EMAILS

A Read the emails and answer these questions.

Email 1

1. How does the writer of the first email know Eric?
2. Why does he think Eric might be interested in his suggestion?
3. How will Eric get more information?

Email 2

4. Who has written the second email?
5. Where is she writing from?
6. What does Eric have to do next, and when?

1

Von: leon.dubois@deglado.com
Betreff: Work experience for you?
An: Eric Jung < ejung@gmx.com>

Hi Eric

How's it going? Listen, I had a great idea. You know that I'm just finishing work experience in an import/export company in Bristol, England, and I know you're looking, so why don't you apply for my job? The boss is always looking for trainees who can speak another language (not English) as their native language. I think your German's pretty good, eh? ;-)

I've asked the secretary to send you some info. I know it's not London (your dream city!), but Bristol's cool and the work is interesting. Like that crazy American girl said that night at the backpackers' hostel: DON'T TALK ABOUT IT, JUST DO IT!!

So, what about it, my friend? I'll be gone by the time you get here but maybe cu in Paris sometime?

Cheers!
Léon

2

Von: sarah.brown@delgado.com
Betreff: Work placement
An: Eric Jung < ejung@gmx.com>
1 Anhang: OnlineAdWorkExperience.docx

Work Experience at Delgado Import/Export

If you are just about to complete your education, a placement in our company will give you an insight into how a small business is run. You will work in a small team and find out at first hand all about business.

Minimum of GCSE or equivalent.

Dear Mr Jung

I have your contact details from Léon Dubois. Léon has mentioned that you might be interested in applying for a work placement in our company, Delgado Import/Export, in Bristol.

Attached is a copy of the job advertisement that will be posted online next week.

Please let me know if you are interested in applying for the position by Thursday, 9 March at the latest.

Yours sincerely

Sarah Brown
Secretary
Delgado Import/Export

Job skills 1

B Work with a partner and compare and contrast the two emails.

Look at language, style of writing, use of slang and abbreviations.

Leon's language shows that he and Eric are friends. His email is quite chatty.

Yes, that's right. And the secretary's language is very formal. She's written a business email.

TIP Email etiquette

1 Make sure that the subject line of your email is as clear as possible.
2 Include your name and contact details at the end of your email.
3 Attach documents when you say you will, and make sure they are correct. (Get into the habit of attaching documents before you write your email, then you won't forget them.)
4 Until you know somebody well, keep your emails formal and don't use slang or short forms like CU.
5 Never TYPE IN CAPITAL LETTERS as it looks like you are shouting and could seem rude.
6 Before you send your email, check the spelling.

2 LOOKING AT EMAIL ETIQUETTE

A Not long after he sent his application to Delgado Import/Export, Eric receives the following email. Look at the body of the email and choose the best option for a business email from the brackets.

Von: sarah.brown@delgado.com
Betreff: Your application for work placement
An: Eric Jung < ejung@gmx.com>

(Dear / Hi)[1] Mr Jung

(Thanks / Thank you)[2] for your application for a work placement which you submitted to Delgado Import/Export last week.

If you are still interested in the position, Mr Delgado would like to call you at 10.00 am on Friday, 18 March. (He wants to call / The object of the call is)[3] to get to know more about you before we take your application further.

In preparation for the call, (here's / I have attached)[4] some (info / information)[5] about the position you have applied for.

Please (confirm that you will be available / give us your OK)[6] for a call at the time and on the date suggested above.

(I look forward to hearing from you soon. / Looking forward to your reply.)[7]

(Cheers / Yours sincerely)[8]

Sarah Brown

B Now study the set-up of the corrected email with a partner. Refer to the tip box. Has the writer followed all of the rules of email etiquette? Explain your answer.

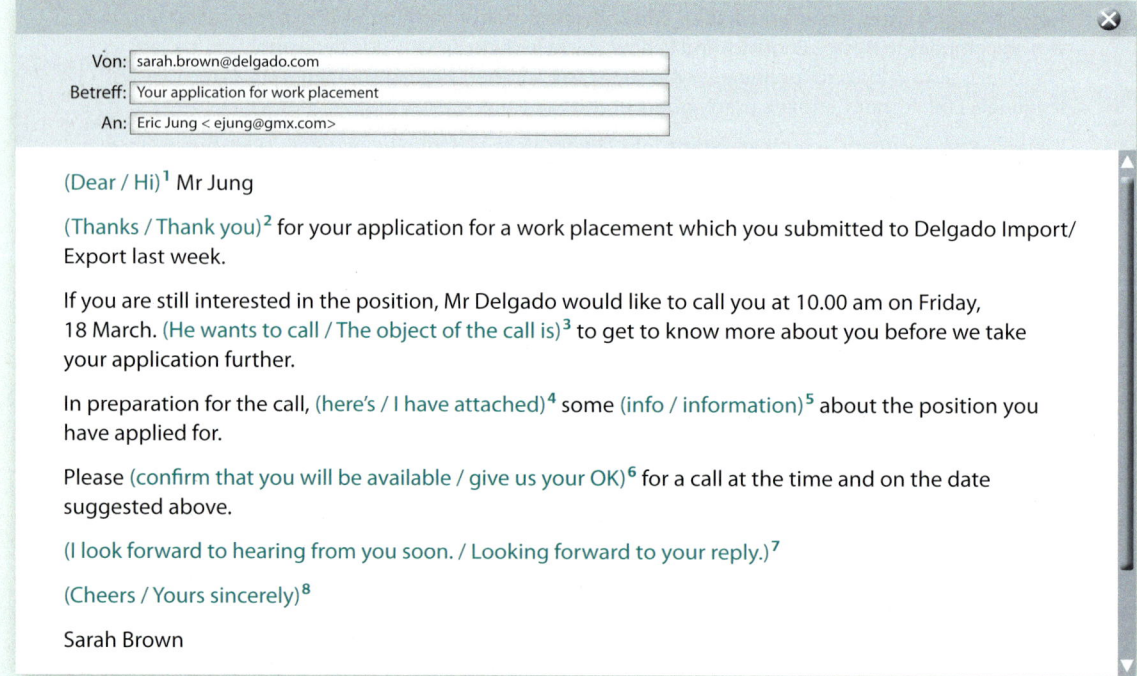

3 WRITING AN EMAIL

Schreiben Sie die E-Mail für Eric und verwenden Sie dabei die unten stehenden Punkte.

- Danken Sie Sarah für ihre E-Mail.
- Bestätigen Sie das Datum und die Uhrzeit des Telefongesprächs.
- Sagen Sie, dass Sie zum Zeitpunkt des Gesprächs keinen ausreichenden mobilen Netzempfang haben werden. Erklären Sie, dass Sie Zugang zu einem Telefon haben werden, sich aber nicht sicher sind, wie die Telefonnummer lautet. Schlagen Sie vor, dass Sie die Firma selbst zu der vorgeschlagenen Uhrzeit anrufen.
- Beenden Sie die E-Mail mit einer passenden Schlussformel.

4 PREPARING FOR A TELEPHONE CALL

Eric looks at some material about telephoning in English which he has from college. Unfortunately, some parts of the material have become separated from the rest.

A Read the tips for telephoning in English (1–6) and match them to the headlines (a–f).

a During the call
b Preparation
c Making small talk
d Softening bad news
e Starting the call
f Telephone numbers

Telephoning in English

1 Think about what you want to say before you start and note down some phrases.
2 Say your first name and your surname and the name of your company clearly.
3 Make sure you note down all proper names correctly. If you do not understand something, ask the other person to repeat the information. Ask the person on the other end of the line to speak more slowly if necessary.
4 English speakers often chat about a general topic, such as the weather, at the start of a call.
5 English speakers usually begin bad news with phrases such as *I'm afraid (that) …* or *I'm sorry, but …*
6 When you give telephone numbers, say each digit separately, except for double digits, e.g. 012334799 = *oh (AE: zero) one two double-three four seven double-nine*.

B Read the phrases on the fronts of the flash cards Eric made for learning English phrases for telephoning and match them to the German on the back of the cards. → Vokabeln lernen, S. 220

1 Can I speak to … (*name*), please?
2 Could you repeat that, please?
3 Could you spell your name, please?
4 Good morning, … (*name*) speaking.
5 I'll put you through.
6 It was nice talking to you.
7 Who's calling, please?
8 Would you like to leave a message?

a Guten Morgen, … (*Name*) am Apparat.
b Ich stelle Sie durch.
c Bitte wiederholen Sie.
d Buchstabieren Sie bitte Ihren Namen.
e Ich würde gerne … (*Name*) sprechen.
f Möchten Sie eine Nachricht hinterlassen?
g Es war schön, mit Ihnen zu reden.
h Wie ist Ihr Name, bitte?

5 LISTENING

→ Rezeption: Hörverstehen, S. 225

It is 10 o'clock on Friday morning and Eric is ready to call Mr Delgado. As things turn out, Eric has to make two calls.

1/12 **A Listen to Eric's first call to Bristol. What went wrong? Which phrases from exercise 4B do you hear?**

1/13 **B Listen to Eric's second call to Bristol and answer the questions.**

1. Who answers the phone?
2. Why can't Mr Delgado speak to Eric at the moment?
3. Why is it likely that Delgado Import/Export is a nice company to work for?
4. Why has Eric not read the information leaflet?
5. How does Eric make the other person feel better about her mistake?
6. What is the rule about using first names at the company?

6 ROLE-PLAY

→ Interaktion: Ein Rollenspiel gestalten, S. 247

Work with a partner. Read through what you are going to say below and make notes. Then carry out the telephone conversation.

Partner A	Partner B
→ Start the call by giving your name and the name of your company.	→ Greet your partner and say who you are. Make some small talk.
→ Greet the caller by name and respond to the small talk. Ask how you can help.	→ Ask to speak to someone in the office.
→ Explain that the person is not available. Offer to take a message.	→ Leave a message.
→ Make a note of the message and read it back to the caller.	→ Thank your partner and say goodbye.

Useful phrases: Telephoning

Making a call
- Good morning. My name's …
- Good afternoon. This is … from XYZ.
- I'm calling about …
- I'm enquiring about …
- I'd like some information on …
- Could you tell me about …?
- I'd like to speak to Mr/Ms …
- Could you put me through to the … department, please?
- Can I leave a message?
- Can you ask him/her to call me back?
- I'll call again later.

Taking a call
- ABC Company. Jane Smith speaking.
- Accounts Department. John here. How can I help you?
- Could you hold on a moment?
- I'll try to connect you.
- Hold the line, please.
- I'm sorry. Mr/Ms … is unavailable at the moment.
- I'm afraid the line is engaged.
- Would you like to leave a message?
- Can I help at all?
- I'll make sure he/she gets your message.

5 The virtual world

MAIN COURSE

FOCUS

A **On your own, look at the photos above and make notes about the role of social media in society today. Discuss your notes with a partner and then in class.**

B **In groups of three or four, draw a poster showing how you use social media. Include the points below and your own ideas.**

- when you use social media
- when you don't use social media
- which social media you use
- why you use social media
- how much money/time you spend on social media

C **Gallery walk: Put your posters up on the walls of your classroom and look at them all. As you walk round the class, make notes on the following points:**

- which social media your class uses most
- why most people use social media
- how much the class spends on social media per month

D **In class, talk about how important social media is to you and why.**

TEXT A Using social media

BEFORE YOU READ

→ Rezeption: Leseverstehen – Grobverständnis, S. 214

A Describe the picture in a few sentences.

B Skim the text below and decide if it is about …

a the problems of young people today.
b how lonely people use the Internet.
c social media habits in the UK.
d Facebook and Twitter.

BUILDING SKILLS: Skimming a text

Skimming means moving your eyes over a text very quickly in order to get the main ideas.

- Read the title carefully because it summarizes the article. Use a dictionary for unknown words.
- Read all of the first paragraph and any more sub-headings.
- Read the first sentence of all the other paragraphs. The most important ideas are normally here.
- Scan the text for clues to meaning, e.g. words which are underlined, in **bold type** or *italics*.
- Read all of the final paragraph. This usually summarizes the text.

1/14

BRITONS SPEND 62M HOURS A DAY ON SOCIAL MEDIA

That's an average of one hour for EVERY adult and child

Britons spend an estimated 62 million hours each day on Facebook and Twitter, according to a new survey on social media habits.

The poll suggests that around 34 million hours are spent on Facebook each day, with a further 28 million hours on Twitter. And almost a third (30%) of the UK's 33 million Facebook users are on the network for at least an hour a day, with 13% spending at least two hours on Facebook each day.

More than a quarter (26%) of UK women on Facebook check their pages at least 10 times a day, compared to less than one in five (18%) of men. Of the UK's estimated 26 million Twitter users, almost a third (31%) spend more than an hour a day on the network, while 14% – more than 3.6 million people – say their daily usage exceeds two hours. The results are based on a survey of 1,500 adults carried out by OnePoll for online bank, first direct*.

The survey also found Facebook was named as the primary social media platform by 59% of people. Only 9% named Twitter as their first-choice network, while 7% chose LinkedIn. And 11% of Twitter users say it is important for them to have more 'followers' on their feed than their friends, compared to just 4% of Facebook users who say it is important to appear more 'popular' than their friends.

Dr David Giles, a reader in media psychology at Winchester University, said: 'People's social media habits tend to be largely dependent on the number of friends who are on the social network with them. If all your friends are on Facebook or Twitter all the time, you risk cutting yourself off from a social life by not doing the same. So you spend several hours every day online simply to avoid feeling left out of conversations, or being isolated from your friends.'

* company name

Rebecca Dye, social media manager at first direct, said: 'The survey shows just how central Facebook and Twitter are to people's lives at the moment, often at the expense of other communications and regardless of how often they're actually posting updates or tweeting.

'It's important we engage with our customers in ways that best suit their lives, so the more people are using social media channels to have conversations, or just to "listen in", the more we need to develop our presence in social media,' she added. (422 words)

From: *www.independent.co.uk*

1 WORKING WITH WORDS

Match the highlighted words in the text with the following definitions. There are three more highlighted words than you need.

1 asking a small, representative number of people questions to find out what most people do or think
2 cut off
3 to interact with, to get involved with
4 is more or greater than
5 not worrying about
6 to seem
7 the number you get when you add amounts together and divide the sum by the number of amounts
8 the things people do every day
9 to not let sth happen
10 two or more

2 LOOKING AT THE TEXT

→ Rezeption: Leseverstehen, S. 214

Use words from the text to complete the sentences.

1 Facebook and Twitter are popular ___ sites.
2 Twitter is less popular than ___ .
3 26% of women check their Facebook accounts ___ .
4 Every day 14% of UK Twitter users are online for more than ___ .
5 First direct is a(n) ___ .
6 Someone who is interested in what you post on Twitter is called a ___ .
7 Dr Giles works at a ___ .
8 Dr Giles says some people spend a lot of time on Facebook and Twitter to make sure they are not ___ .

3 DISCUSSION

→ Interaktion: An Diskussionen teilnehmen, S. 246

Read the following complaints made by teachers about their students.

Young people today use social media much too much and have no time for homework, sport, hobbies or even their own families. They are up all night on the Internet and are so tired the next day that they can't concentrate at school.

They are unfit, can't spell and have poor handwriting (they only use their thumbs to text).

They are wasting their childhood and their money. Parents should take away their children's phones at night and switch off the Internet. Students should hand in their phones when they enter the school building.

A **Look at the teachers' criticisms and suggestions and write down if you agree or disagree.**

B **Use your notes to have a class discussion.**

C **At the end of your discussion take a vote in class on whether you agree or disagree with the following statement: 'If we use social media less, our school work will become better.'**

4 WRITING

→ Produktion: Schreiben, S. 228

Use your poster (Focus) and your own ideas to write a blog entry about the importance of social media. Use the *Language for writing* expressions on the back cover flap.
Structure your answer like this:

- Give your blog a title (e.g. 'A day offline?' or 'Last night a smartphone saved my life', etc.).
- Tell a very short anecdote about how social media helped or caused a problem for you or a friend (e.g. *Last Saturday night I posted a call for help on my Facebook wall and then …*).
- Next write two paragraphs about the advantage(s) and disadvantages of social media.
  - If you like social media, first write about the disadvantages.
  - If you dislike social media, first write about the advantages.
- Write a conclusion to show what you think about social media.

Write a blog entry to explain why smartphones should or shouldn't be allowed in lessons at school. Use the *Language for writing* expressions on the back cover flap.

5 LISTENING

→ Rezeption: Hörverstehen, S. 225

You are going to hear a call to the telephone helpline of *cyberbullying.online*, an organization that helps people suffering from online bullying.

1/15

Listen and complete the sentences.

1 Sarah is unhappy because ___ .
2 People are sending her ___ .
3 The counsellor asks Sarah if ___ .
4 The counsellor says she can get help from ___ .
5 Sarah went to ___ and drank ___ .
6 The counsellor tells Sarah she can make an appointment over ___ .
7 Sarah doesn't want to ___ .
8 The counsellor is going to send Sarah ___ .

6 GETTING IT RIGHT

→ Simple past, S. 251

Use the key words to summarize Sarah's conversation with the counsellor using the simple past. Start like this:

Sarah phoned a cyberbullying helpline and talked to Frank about …

(Sarah) horrible pictures ▪ Internet ▪ everyone ▪ school ▪ can see them ▪ Facebook ▪ desperate
(Frank) need ▪ support ▪ parents
dad ▪ live ▪ girlfriend ▪ mother ▪ work all day ▪ brother ▪ young ▪ other family members ▪ too far away
advise ▪ contact ▪ school counsellors ▪ understand ▪ help ▪ students
not want ▪ go back to school ever again
possible ▪ make ▪ appointment ▪ counsellor ▪ phone
still unhappy ▪ messages ▪ Facebook ▪ not want ▪ delete
not necessary ▪ delete ▪ account ▪ promise ▪ send ▪ email ▪ practical help

7 MEDIATION

→ Schriftliche Mediation, S. 240

Cyberbullying.online schickt Sarah eine E-Mail. In dieser wird erklärt, welche Schritte sie unternehmen kann, um nicht mehr gemobbt zu werden. Ein Freund/eine Freundin von Ihnen wird auf einem sozialen Netzwerk gemobbt und bittet Sie um Hilfe. Er/Sie möchte für eine Zeit lang nicht mehr erreichbar sein, will aber nichts Endgültiges machen, denn seine/ihre Daten sind ihm/ihr wichtig.

Lesen Sie die folgende E-Mail durch und entnehmen Sie ihr die Informationen, die Ihrem Freund / Ihrer Freundin helfen könnten. Schreiben Sie ihm/ihr eine E-Mail.

SKILLS CHECKLIST: Written mediation

- ☑ Have I read the situation?
- ☑ Have I written the right sort of text?
- ☑ Have I left out unnecessary details?

Hi

Thank you for contacting *cyberbullying.online*. To stop getting messages on Facebook (or any other social media account) you can *block people*, *deactivate* or *delete* the account and also *take legal action*.

How to block (unfriend) people
- Log into *General Account – Settings*.
- Click on the Security icon – *How do I stop someone from bothering me?*
- Follow the instructions carefully.

How to deactivate your Facebook account
- Press *More* in the bottom right-hand corner of the Facebook start screen.
- Scroll down to and click on *Settings – General – Account – Deactivate*.
- Follow the instructions carefully.

You can reactivate your account later at any time.

How to delete your Facebook account
It's best to do this on a computer. Before you delete your account, remember it takes at least 90 days; if you delete an account and then log in again before the 90 days are up, you reactivate the account; when you delete your Facebook account, you lose all your data.

- First go to *Settings* and download a copy of all the data Facebook has on you.
- Log out of or delete phone and tablet apps, including Facebook Home.
- Write an Account Deletion Epitaph, so people know you have closed your account, e.g.

  I am no longer available on Facebook because I have deleted my account.

- Go to the Facebook account deletion page and follow the instructions carefully.

Legal action
- Report cyberbullying to your school, institution and/or the police.
- Hire a specialist lawyer and take legal action. Your lawyer will contact web service providers and ask them to delete your data. In 80% of the cases they agree.

Remember – there is <u>always</u> a solution to any problem. Thousands of young people suffer from cyberbullying and when they get help, it stops!

Cyberbullying Help Team

TEXT B Unwanted guests

→ Rezeption: Leseverstehen, S. 214

BEFORE YOU READ

Why do you think the mother is angry with her son? Skim the text and write down what they could be saying to each other.

SKILLS CHECKLIST: Skimming

- ☑ Have I studied the headline?
- ☑ Have I read the sub-heading?
- ☑ Have I read the first paragraph?

1/16

'Don't have any parties'

Last words of mother leaving for holiday to her schoolboy son, 17, days before drunken Facebook crashers trashed her £1m house

Drunken revellers have trashed a £1.1million house after gatecrashing a schoolboy's Facebook event – days after his mother went on holiday and told him: 'Don't have any parties'.

The group caused an estimated £15,000 of damage and left vomit all over the terraced property in Highgate, north London, while riot police were called to break up 600 people in the street outside.

Now mother-of-four Catherine Seale, 54, who had gone to France on holiday with her husband when the trouble began, has warned of the dangers of putting personal details online.

Her son, Christopher, 17, had invited 60 friends round to his house on September 21 for his birthday, but a friend who put the event on Facebook did not realise the invitation could be seen by anyone.

Mrs Seale, whose 53-year-old husband Adam is a company director, said: 'All parents should be warned that this could happen if you go away and leave your 17-year-old alone. I think if anyone is going to throw a party, they need to look at their privacy settings on Facebook. It's absolutely essential that children are made aware of this.' […]

One girl at the party was taken to hospital with alcohol poisoning. Laughing gas canisters were tossed across Mrs Seale's living room carpet. Christopher and his aunt worked round the clock

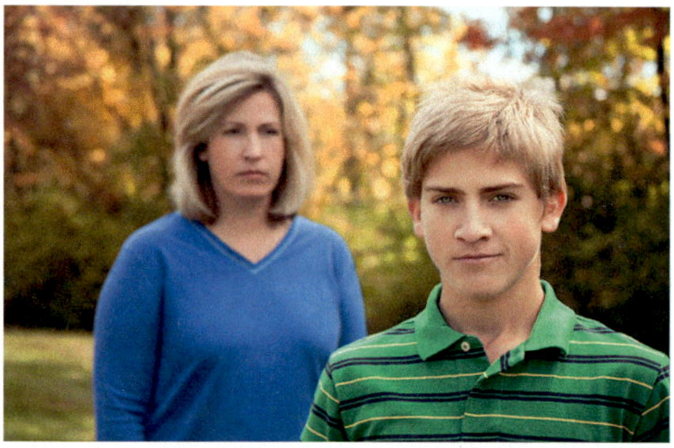

to clean up, but the house smelled of vomit and alcohol for days. Mrs Seale added: 'The last thing I told him before I went away was "don't have any parties". The carpet was trashed and they damaged a skylight because somebody fell on it. […]

Chris paid a bouncer £60, telling him to only let in the 60 invited guests but the bouncer, who was paid in advance, was unable to cope and ran away when hundreds more party goers turned up. […] Mrs Seale heard about the trouble when a shocked mother who had dropped off her son at the party phoned to tell her that children aged between 14 and 18 were wrecking her home and got the first flight back after hearing of the chaos. […]

Mrs Seale added: 'It doesn't seem to have done him any harm at school. Apparently, he has even got a girlfriend out of it. I think his reputation has shot up because of it, which isn't very good for us parents.' (417 words)

Abridged from: *www.dailymail.co.uk*

1 LOOKING AT THE TEXT

→ Rezeption: Leseverstehen, S. 214

A Put the following statements about the text in the right order starting with *f*.

- **a** A mother brought her son to the party by car.
- **b** Christopher Seale decided to have a birthday party.
- **c** Everybody saw the message.
- **d** He invited 60 friends.
- **e** Hundreds of people came to the party.
- **f** Mr and Mrs Seale went to France on holiday.
- **g** Mrs Seale flew home immediately.
- **h** Somebody posted a message about the party on Facebook.
- **i** The bouncer couldn't stop people from entering the house.
- **j** The mother saw the chaos and phoned Mrs Seale in France.
- **k** They got drunk and broke things.
- **l** They told their son not to have any parties while they were away.

BUILDING SKILLS: Dealing with unknown words

There's no need to panic when you read a word you haven't seen before in a text. Think about these questions before you look the word up in a dictionary:

- Is the word similar to a German word you know, e.g. *democracy/Demokratie*?
- Is the word from the same word family as an English word you already know, e.g. *prefer – preference – preferable*?
- Can you guess the meaning of the word from the context, i.e. the general sense of the sentence or the paragraph?

→ Mit unbekannten Wörtern umgehen, S. 216

B Say what it means: With a partner, talk about what the following words mean by looking at the way they are used in the text.

1. drunken (line 1)
2. revellers (line 1)
3. vomit (line 6)
4. essential (line 25)
5. trashed (line 34)
6. bouncer (line 37)
7. to cope (line 39)
8. shot up (line 49)

2 WORKING WITH WORDS

A Find words in the text that go with the following words (= collocations).

terraced ▪ riot ▪ personal ▪ throw ▪ privacy ▪ alcohol ▪ laughing

EXAMPLE: *terraced property*

B Use some of the collocations from exercise 2A to complete this text.

Before you ▬[1] and post the details on Facebook, you should check your ▬[2] because you don't want hundreds of people to come uninvited. If there's too much noise, your next-door neighbours will call the ▬[3], especially if you live in a small ▬[4] with houses on either side. If a party gets out of control, people sometimes drink too much and end up in hospital with ▬[5], so remember: small is beautiful.

3 GETTING IT RIGHT

→ Simple past ▪ Present perfect, S. 254

A Copy the table and put the following time expressions in the correct list.

2 years ago ▪ at 7 o'clock this morning ▪ at Christmas ▪ ever ▪ in 2000 ▪ never ▪ in February ▪ in the spring ▪ just ▪ last month ▪ on Friday ▪ on my birthday ▪ since 2005 ▪ this morning ▪ this week ▪ today ▪ yesterday ▪ yet

Simple past (finished time / time in the past)	Present perfect (unfinished time / time up to now)
2 years ago, …	*ever, …*

B Complete the sentences with the simple past or the present perfect.

	Simple past	Present perfect
1	Last week Sarah *received* a hundred Facebook messages.	This week she *hasn't received* any messages.
2	Yesterday she ▬ fifteen text messages.	Since 7 am this morning she has written eight text messages.
3	A few days ago she drank six cocktails at a party.	Since then she ▬ water.
4	Last week she ▬ to a counsellor five times.	In the last three days she has talked to a counsellor three times.
5	Six friends phoned her yesterday.	Three friends ▬ her today.
6	She ▬ Facebook last week.	She hasn't used Facebook this week.
7	She didn't speak to her counsellor yesterday.	She ▬ to her counsellor today.
8	She ▬ any photos last week.	She hasn't uploaded any photos this week.

C Complete the radio interview with a counsellor using the simple past or present perfect.

Reporter Thanks for coming to the studio, Frank.

Frank My pleasure.

Reporter How long (you/be) ▬ [1] a counsellor now?

Frank I (start) ▬ [2] about ten years ago.

Reporter And can you tell us about your work?

Frank Yes, certainly. At the beginning I only (do) ▬ [3] telephone counselling but since last year we (have) ▬ [4] so many cases of cyberbullying that I now give face-to-face counselling, too.

Reporter Could you explain the difference?

Frank Telephone counselling is often just the beginning. If someone (lose) ▬ [5] a loved one for example, they can phone our hotline to get help and support. Yesterday I (speak) ▬ [6] to a young man with that problem. We (talk) ▬ [7] for an hour and now he (make) ▬ [8] an appointment to see me next week.

Reporter I see. How many people (you/help) ▬ [9] over the years up to now?

Frank I really don't know. I (take) ▬ [10] about 30 calls last week alone, so it must be thousands …

4 ROLE-PLAY

→ Interaktion: Ein Rollenspiel gestalten, S. 247

Last Saturday night while your parents were away for the weekend, you had a party at your house/flat. You invited 20 friends on Facebook and bought food and drinks, including beer and wine for them. Suddenly, in the early hours of Sunday morning your flat/house was full of gatecrashers. They drank all the beer and wine and turned up the music so loud that the neighbours called the police. When your parents returned, they found the house/flat a complete mess.

Work in groups of three. Expand the notes to act out a role-play.

Parents (two students taking turns to speak)	You
→ (*angry/horrified/shocked*) arrive ▪ find ▪ house ▪ mess	→ sorry ▪ mess ▪ gatecrashers ▪ not my friends
→ how ▪ gatecrashers ▪ hear about ▪ party?	→ probably ▪ see ▪ invitation ▪ Facebook
→ not ▪ click on ▪ 'Invite only'?	→ forget
→ how many ▪ guests ▪ you ▪ invite?	→ 20
→ how many ▪ gatecrashers ▪ come?	→ about 100
→ you ▪ know ▪ gatecrashers?	→ not know any of them
→ cost ▪ at least £2,000 (€2,500) ▪ clean up ▪ house!	→ (*shock*)
→ holiday ▪ Mallorca ▪ cancelled!	→ (*horror*) clean carpet ▪ wash walls ▪ myself?
→ also ▪ apologize ▪ neighbours ▪ in person!	→ write ▪ letter?
→ expect ▪ perfect behaviour ▪ next three months ▪ talk about ▪ Mallorca ▪ again	→ your own answer
→ no more ▪ parties ▪ at home	→ your own answer

5 USING THE INTERNET

Cancer fundraiser Stephen Sutton dies aged 19

[…] The 19-year-old, from Burntwood in Staffordshire, raised more than £3.2m ($5.36m) for charity after news of his plight spread on social media. […]

Stephen was diagnosed with terminal cancer aged 15. Rather than dwell on his misfortune, the teenager drew up a "bucket list" of things he wanted to achieve before he died. This led to him completing a skydive and playing drums in front of 90,000 people before the Uefa Champions League final at Wembley last May. […] He had initially set out to raise just £10,000 ($16,800) for charity, but his fundraising campaign attracted huge attention last month after he posted a selfie online. […]

From: *www.bbc.com*

A **Mediation: Erzählen Sie Ihrem/Ihrer Partner/in auf Deutsch den Inhalt des Artikels.**

B **Project: Do you know of further examples of inspirational behaviour which have used Internet technology to benefit society? Research the details online with a partner and report your findings to the class.**

4/2

BEFORE POSTING A SELFIE – THINK TWICE!

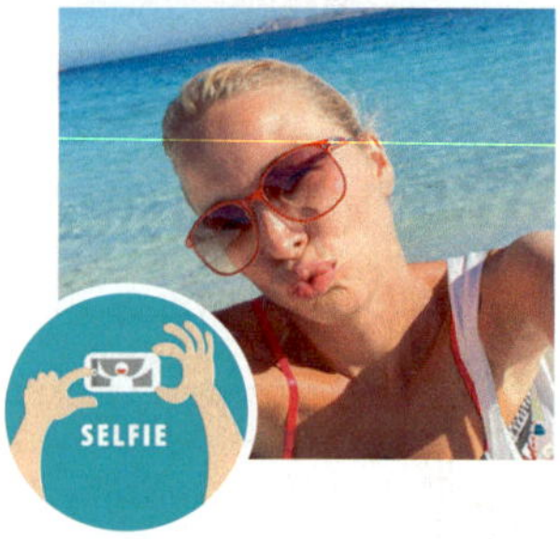

According to a recent study, 91 per cent of teens have posted a photo of themselves online. The most common selfie is the one where you look good, because it's a quick way to get positive comments about your appearance. "I feel especially good when other people Like it," says Sandra, 23, from Birmingham. But with social networks, the selfie thing can quickly spiral out of control. Girls in particular have started seeing themselves as lovable and worthwhile only if others value them. "My friends and I joke about people who have selfies as their mobile backgrounds," says Karin, 17, from Glasgow. "It seems like they have nothing important in their lives except the way they look."

Ask yourself: Are my selfies for fun, or do I need the Likes? Everything you share on social media reveals something about you. Maybe you like to travel, or read, or dance or create crazy 3-D nail art … post that! It's so much more interesting. And when you post your photo on Facebook, remember, there is no way you can delete it! Everybody can see it, even your future husband or boss! This can be embarrassing, for example when you post selfies of yourself at drunken parties. It does not give the image of a solid dependable person that an employer is looking for. (222 words)

1 LOOKING AT THE TEXT

→ Rezeption: Leseverstehen, S. 214

Who do you think made these comments: a girl, her future employer or both?

1 "When people say they like you, it makes you feel good."
2 "Who you are is important, not what you look like."
3 "The selfies people post are sometimes terrible."
4 "I don't know why men don't post selfies."
5 "Do you really want to be reminded of those drunken parties when you are 30?"
6 "Selfies do not say the truth about a person."

2 DISCUSSION

→ Interaktion, S. 246

Discuss the following questions.

1 Do you think people are only worthwhile if others value them? Explain your answer.
2 In which situations is taking a selfie and posting it OK, and when is it not OK?

3 DESCRIBING A CARTOON

→ Cartoons beschreiben und analysieren, S. 236

Use some of the phrases below to describe the cartoon.

Useful phrases

- The cartoon shows …
- The man in the blue suit is …
- The other man is …
- The text tells us that …
- I (don't) think that the cartoon is funny because …
- The message of the cartoon is …
- The cartoon is trying to tell us …

Kincaid
So I looked at your Facebook page …oh man…there's no way you're getting this job!

6 Advertising

MAIN COURSE

FOCUS

A **Advertising can be found everywhere. With a partner make a list of all the places (real and virtual) where you can find advertisements and report your findings to the class.**

billboard ▪ digital signage ▪ viral ad ▪ virtual billboard ▪ …

B **Experts say good adverts must have at least one of the elements below. With a partner look for these elements in photos 1–4. Write one or two sentences about each photo and then discuss your ideas in class.**

ambition ▪ emotion ▪ entertainment ▪ excitement ▪ horror ▪ human interest (e.g. love, tragedy) ▪ humour ▪ identification ▪ inspiration ▪ mystery ▪ provocation ▪ sex ▪ shock ▪ surprise

1

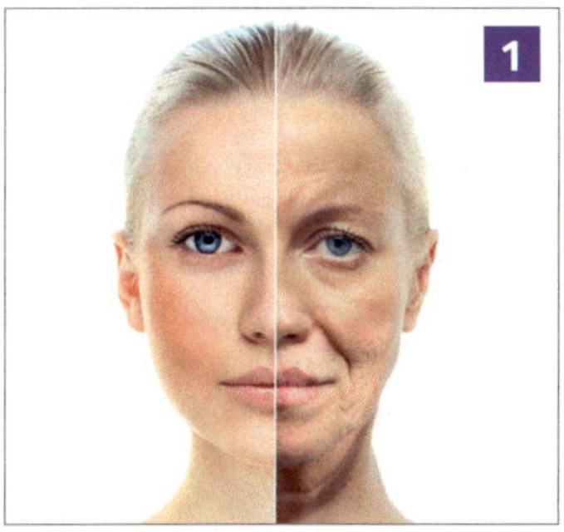

C **Find some interesting examples of advertising and bring them to your next English lesson. Explain to the class which of the elements they contain.**

2

3

4

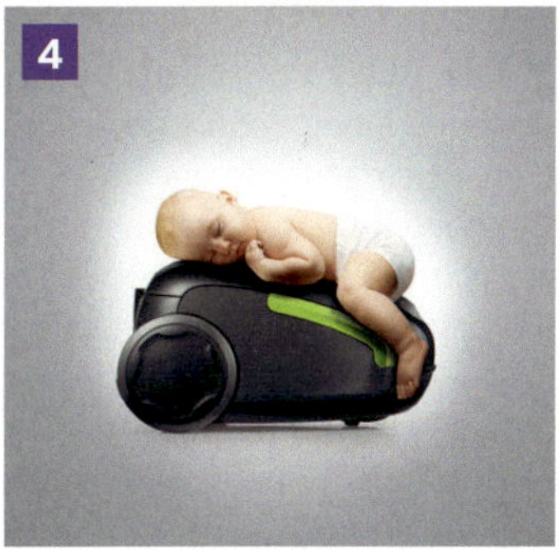

TEXT A New ideas in advertising

WHILE YOU READ

Take notes on how each idea in the three following texts benefits society.

SKILLS CHECKLIST: Taking notes

- ☑ Have I read the whole text?
- ☑ Have I scanned the text for key words?
- ☑ Have I noted down the key words?

1/17

THE FUN THEORY IN ADVERTISING

A Volkswagen brings the fun

Giant piano stairs and other 'Fun Theory' marketing

If stairs played musical notes when you walked on them, would you be more likely to take them?

The video of people skipping the escalator in favor of composing music on the piano stairs of Odenplan subway station in Stockholm, Sweden, has been viewed more than 2.5 million times on YouTube.

The video is part of a new viral marketing campaign called "The Fun Theory." The concept, created by Volkswagen Sweden and ad agency DDB Stockholm, is based on the idea that "fun is the easiest way to change people's behavior for the better." [...]

The goal with these fun, do-good videos is to promote VW's new environmentally friendly BlueMotionTechnologies brand in an increasingly more competitive eco-car market.

"As traditional advertising is becoming less effective, and the competition in the market for environmentally sound cars is becoming fiercer, we believed we needed a more innovative approach to draw attention to BlueMotion," DDB Stockholm deputy manager Lars Axelsson said in an e-mail.

The video of the giant piano stairs reports that the number of commuters who chose the stairs over the escalator increased by 66% when the stairs were musical black-and-white piano keys.

The first of the campaign's three phases started with the release of the three viral videos, which aim to inspire the public to enter the campaign's contest, the second phase, by submitting their best video experiment of "The Fun Theory" to the website.

The winner gets a prize of €2,500 (about $3,700), and once the competition finishes "The Fun Theory" is "proven" by the video submissions, linking to VW and its new thoughtful technology: Its cars are good for the environment and fun for the driver. [...]

Next on the campaign: a glass recycling game machine, says DDB Stockholm. "By making driving and the world more fun, we turn the VW brand into a hero," Axelsson said. "Our experiments and our Fun Theory films make the world a better and more fun place to live." (343 words)

From: *www.latimes.com*

B The glass recycling game machine

In Sweden many people recycle their plastic bottles and cans but fewer recycle their glass. To encourage people to do so Volkswagen and DDB Stockholm have invented a bottle bank arcade which gives you points each time you throw a bottle into it like the machines in an amusement arcade. It makes a funny noise to attract the attention of passers-by and explains to them on its display how to play. The idea is so successful that in one evening over 100 people used the bottle bank arcade but only two used a nearby conventional bottle bank. (102 words)

C The world's deepest bin

VW and DDB have also invented a very special rubbish bin which encourages people to use it. When you throw something in, it sounds as if the object is falling into a hole hundreds of metres deep. After five seconds the sound of falling stops and is followed by a loud crash. In one day people threw 72 kg of rubbish into the bin but only 31 kg of rubbish into a nearby conventional bin over the same period of time. (85 words)

1 LOOKING AT THE TEXTS

→ Rezeption: Leseverstehen, S. 214

Choose the correct statement (a, b or c) to complete the sentences about the texts.

1 When you step on the stairs at this station …
- **a** you hear a song.
- **b** you play a note.
- **c** you stop the escalator.

2 VW and DDB believe that …
- **a** people will do something new if it's fun.
- **b** everything people do must be fun.
- **c** more people will have fun if they take a subway train.

3 Lars Axelsson believes that today the best way to advertise a car is with …
- **a** traditional advertising.
- **b** environmental arguments.
- **c** new ideas.

4 DDB's Lars Axelsson says that "The Fun Theory" will make people think that …
- **a** VW thinks carefully about technology and does its best to protect the environment.
- **b** VW drivers are heroes.
- **c** VW makes the best viral videos.

5 The Swedes …
- **a** only drink out of plastic bottles and metal cans.
- **b** never recycle glass.
- **c** recycle less glass than metal or plastic.

6 The world's deepest rubbish bin …
- **a** is built over a hole hundreds of metres deep.
- **b** sounds like it is built over a deep hole.
- **c** is much bigger than a conventional rubbish bin.

2 WORKING WITH WORDS

A Match the verbs with a noun to make collocations. They are all in text A.

Verbs		
to take	to promote	to draw
to compose	to release	to enter

Nouns		
a brand	a video	music
a contest	attention to	the stairs

B Use words from texts B and C to complete the following paragraph.

The government ___[1] people to recycle ___[2] bottles but bottle banks aren't much fun to use. That's why the ad agency's idea of making a bottle bank seem like a machine in an ___ ___[3] is so clever. ___[4] notice it because it attracts their ___[5] by making a ___ ___[6]. They then get ___[7] for each bottle they throw in.

The very special ___[8] bin is just as clever because each time you throw an ___[9] in it, you think it has fallen into a ___[10] hole in the ground. You even hear the ___[11] as it hits the bottom. This effect makes it far more attractive than a ___[12] bin.

3 WRITING

→ Produktion: Schreiben, S. 228

Explain in a few sentences which of the three fun ideas you prefer and why.

Useful phrases

- In my opinion / In my view, …
- First / First of all, …
- In addition, …
- Because of this, …
- For this reason, …
- All in all, …

4 PRESENTATION

→ Präsentieren, S. 243

BUILDING SKILLS: Giving a presentation

A presentation, using an overhead projector (OHP) or PowerPoint slides, is an effective way to show a new product or idea or give information. It can be given by one person or two people taking turns to speak.

1. Make sure your slides have clear illustrations, your spelling is correct and the vocabulary has been checked.
2. Number your slides and print them out together with your notes on hand-held cards for quick reference.
3. Practise what you are going to say with the other presenter or a partner before giving the presentation.

Your class decides to enter the next *Fun Theory* competition to invent something from everyday life that will benefit society. Form groups of 3–4 students and present a new idea to your class.

Choose one of the three invention ideas on page 212 and present it to your class.

Use your own idea for a *Fun Theory* invention and present it to your class.

SKILLS CHECKLIST: Presentations

- ☑ Have I checked the slides?
- ☑ Have I looked at the *Useful phrases*?
- ☑ Have I practised the presentation in my team?

Use PowerPoint slides, a video, OHP transparencies, (a) poster(s), or other visuals. Practise the presentation in your team first.

Useful phrases: Presentations

Introductions
- Hello / Good morning/afternoon/evening.
- My name's … and this is my colleague …

Starting
- Today we're going to look at … (*topic*)
- Let's begin by looking at / talking about …

Describing
- As you can see from this diagram/slide/illustration, …
- In this slide/diagram you can see how …

Handing over
- … is now going to talk to you about …

Finishing
- All in all / In conclusion / To sum up, …
- Thank you / Thanks for coming to this presentation.
- If you have any questions, we'll be pleased to answer them.

→ Job skills 4, S. 174

5 LISTENING

→ Rezeption: Hörverstehen, S. 225

Jim Tarrant, who owns an advertising agency in New York, is the guest on a radio programme.

1/18

A Listen and say if the statements are true or false. Correct the false statements.

1 Jim's first advertising slogan was for washing powder.
2 Jim says that advertising is legalized lying.
3 Jim doesn't think the 4 Ps are out of date.
4 Niche marketing means one advertisement is designed to reach a maximum number of people.
5 Product placement has been around for a long time.
6 Guerilla marketing is only used to shock people in Third World countries.

B Complete the sentences from the dialogue with the words you hear.

1 I heard they were looking for a ___ for their new soap.
2 After a few years as the ad manager at the soap factory you ___ ___ your own agency.
3 An ad agency has to make a product ___ ___ somehow.
4 We ___ ___ ___ the slogan 'It lets me be me'.
5 The 4 Ps are: p___ , p___ , p___ , and p___ .
6 Nobody drank any but people bought the bottles for a dollar each and ___ a lot of money.

6 MEDIATION

→ Schriftliche Mediation, S. 240

1/18

A Hören Sie sich das Gespräch noch einmal an und machen Sie sich Notizen zu diesen Stichwörtern:

- Jugend
- Eigene Firma
- Wichtige Einsichten
- Trends

SKILLS CHECKLIST: Taking notes

- ☑ Have I structured my notes?
- ☑ Have I focused on the task?
- ☑ Have I noted the key information?

B Verfassen Sie mithilfe der Stichworte einen kurzen deutschen Text über das Leben des Jim Tarrant für die Homepage Ihrer Schule. Überschrift: „Erfolgreiche Menschen unserer Zeit".

7 CREATING A MARKETING MIX

A First, match the four Ps from exercise 5B with the following definitions.

a This is what a company does to increase the sales of a product or service.
b This means where a customer needs to go to get a product or service. Internet and telephone sales are making this factor less and less important.
c How much will a customer pay? Customers expect this factor to be low for some things and high for others.
d This can be an object or a service. It has a life-cycle, meaning that sales start low, grow to a maximum, fall and stop.

B Form groups of 3–4 students and decide what the best marketing mix is for the goods and services below. Write down your results and present them to the class.

a car wash ▪ a hairdressing salon ▪ a laptop ▪ a local electrician ▪ a new perfume ▪ a new sports car ▪ fruit and vegetables ▪ washing powder

8 GETTING IT RIGHT

→ *Will* future ▪ *Going to* future, S. 257

A Tom Slater at Ad-Agency-Plus in Edinburgh is talking about a meeting the next day. Use the notes to make sentences with the *will* future (predicted actions), the *going to* future (intended actions) or the present progressive (fixed arrangements).

1 our / European salesmen / come / 3 pm / tomorrow afternoon (fixed arrangement)
2 our / American partners / join / us / on Skype / 3.30 (fixed arrangement)
3 I / think / it / be / good meeting (predicted action)
4 we / talk / about guerrilla marketing (intended action)
5 I / suggest / flash mob / Victoria Station (intended action)
6 I / believe / our client / get / a lot of attention / this way (predicted action)

B Tom phones a colleague to tell her about the meeting. Complete the sentences using the present progressive (fixed arrangements) or the *will* future (predicted actions).

Tom Hi Gillian, it's me, Tom.
Gillian Hi Tom. How did the meeting go?
Tom Very well. The Americans (fly) ▬ 1 over next month to sign the contract. I think this deal (make) ▬ 2 a big profit for the company.
Gillian That's great, Tom, and I'm sure it (help) ▬ 3 you get a job at Head Office.
Tom Let's hope so. I (see) ▬ 4 the Human Resources Director at 10 am next Tuesday and I expect he (want) ▬ 5 to talk about the deal. I've just booked my ticket to London.
Gillian Oh, I see. How (you/travel) ▬ 6 to London? (you/fly) ▬ 7 ?
Tom I (take) ▬ 8 the train. A long train trip (give) ▬ 9 me time to prepare for the meeting.
Gillian Well good luck! I'm sure you (get) ▬ 10 the job.

C Marilyn Marshall and Jim Tarrant are chatting before the radio show. Choose the right future form to complete the text.

Jim I'm afraid I only have limited time because I (meet) ▬ 1 my publisher to discuss my new book straight after the show tonight.
Marilyn No problem, Jim. I predict that a lot of people (phone) ▬ 2 in and ask you questions but we can stop after 30 minutes. You work all day and night! When (you/take) ▬ 3 a vacation?
Jim Funny you should ask that but my wife has booked me a month in Hawaii. I (take) ▬ 4 the first flight to Honolulu tomorrow morning.
Marilyn That sounds great! What (you/do) ▬ 5 in Hawaii?
Jim Well, first of all I (relax) ▬ 6 for a few days. I (play) ▬ 7 golf and get some sun.
Marilyn I understand, but I'm sure that someone as active as you (get) ▬ 8 bored quickly!
Jim I don't think so. My wife and children and their families (come) ▬ 9 to join me next Wednesday and I think we (have) ▬ 10 a lot of fun together.

Make sentences of your own using the three forms of the future. Write three or four sentences for each form, for example:

- Apple is launching a new tablet on … (*date*).
- I think it'll be a great success.
- I'm going to buy one as soon as I get a job.

TEXT B Creating a brand

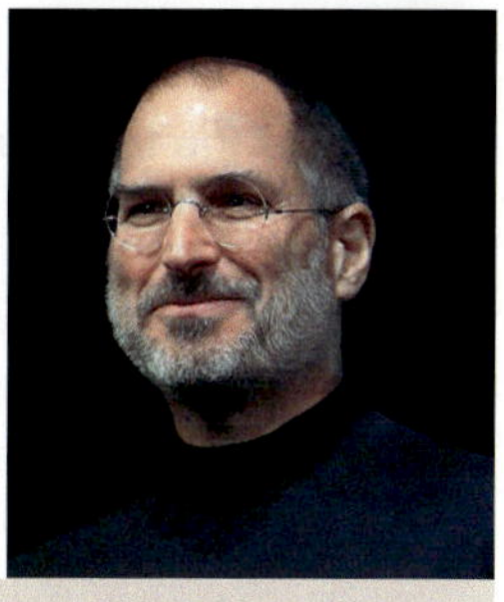

Steve Jobs (1955–2011), Apple co-founder and CEO, in 2004

BEFORE YOU READ

→ Scannen nach Einzelinformationen im Text, S. 221

With a partner, see who is quicker to find the following details in the text on Steve Jobs:

1 the year when Steve Jobs returned to Apple
2 what GUI stands for
3 what the slogan in Apple's famous TV commercial was
4 what the Tokyo Tsoshiu Kogyo company is now called

BUILDING SKILLS: Scanning a text for specific information

Scanning means picking out specific facts or information from a text without reading it closely.

- Read the questions carefully, so that you know exactly what you need to find.
- Scan the text line for line, focusing on *one* type of information *only*, for example, numbers, names, places, dates, capital letters or specific words.
- Don't stop if you come across a word you don't understand. You can always check the meaning later if you need to understand that particular word to answer a question.

1/19

STEVE JOBS: VISIONARY AND GENIUS

Steve Jobs was not only a technical genius. He was also a visionary and even as a young man of 25 he admired how companies branded their products to make them into household names, such as Polaroid, Hoover, Nylon and Kleenex. He also realized how clever the 'Tokyo Tsoshiu Kogyo' company was when it changed its name to Sony (which sounds a bit like sunny). He understood that the technology he was developing was new, threatening and scary, so he needed to come up with a name which would make it sound non-threatening and likeable. That's why he thought Apple was exactly right. He felt that this simple, safe brand name would help people trust the new technology he was about to introduce to the world. He decided to target young people for his products because they were the customers of the future and his strategy was always to sell exciting, high-end products at a high price and profit.

Steve Jobs saw clearly that brands are part of our culture and everyday lives and that everything a brand does is an ad – positive or negative – for that brand. He understood that every way a brand touches you is a message. Today, Apple's customers are in a constant dialogue with Apple's products. They discover more and more clever functions as they use them. They can tell Apple about any problems they are having and get regular updates to fix them.

Steve Jobs also understood the importance of packaging and presentation. When you open the high-quality packaging of an Apple product it's as powerful as any ad. Steve Jobs also didn't want the Macintosh manuals to be written in technical jargon, so he made sure they were written in easy English that people could understand. As a young entrepreneur he looked far into the future and knew he had to make this technology accessible to anybody and everybody. The Apple Store is also probably the best ad Apple ever did. You can actually walk into the brand and touch it, feel it and get its energy back from the young people who work there. He launched the Macintosh in 1984 and introduced the graphical user interface (GUI) and the mouse, which touched things on the screen which we now touch with our fingers.

Steve Jobs left Apple in 1985 to make films and returned in 1997 when the company was fighting to survive. He rebuilt the brand and introduced a series of new products – the iPhone, the iPod and the iPad. To prepare the public for his new ideas he brought out the famous TV commercial ending with the slogan 'Think different'. The commercial was called 'Here's to the Crazy Ones' and shows the famous people of our time who thought differently and changed the world.

(541 words)

1 WORKING WITH WORDS

Find the following words or expressions in the text *Steve Jobs: visionary and genius*.

1 the opposite of threatening (paragraph 1)
2 the opposite of cheap and low quality (paragraph 1)
3 to repair (paragraph 2)
4 the box in which a product is sold (paragraph 3)
5 someone who risks their money by starting a business, company or firm (paragraph 3)
6 to continue to live (paragraph 4)

2 LOOKING AT THE TEXT

→ Rezeption: Leseverstehen, S. 214

Read the text and do the following tasks.

Paragraph 1 Explain how Sony made it easier for their company to become a household name; say why Apple is a good brand name.

Paragraph 2 'Today people are in a constant dialogue with Apple's products'. List the ways in which people are in a dialogue with Apple's products.

Paragraph 3 Summarize what Steve Jobs did to make Apple's products attractive and accessible.

Paragraph 4 Discuss Steve Jobs' reasons for choosing a TV commercial about the 'Crazy Ones' to advertise Apple's new products.

3 ANALYSING A GRAPH

→ Produktion: Schaubilder beschreiben und analysieren, S. 238

Look at the chart below, then do the tasks on page 53.

BUILDING SKILLS: Describing graphs and bar charts

Graphs and bar charts are ways of presenting figures and statistics in a clear visual form. If you have to describe a chart, make sure you understand exactly what the graph shows and the units that are used.

- Use the simple present (→ page 213) to describe what the graph shows: *The chart/graph **shows** the change in media ad spending between 2011 and 2017.*
- Use the simple past (→ page 215) to describe situations in the past or changes that are finished: *In 2011 media spending **was** $158.6 billion.*
- Use the present perfect (→ page 217) to describe situations or changes that are unfinished: *Spending **has increased** by about 3.5% since 2011.*

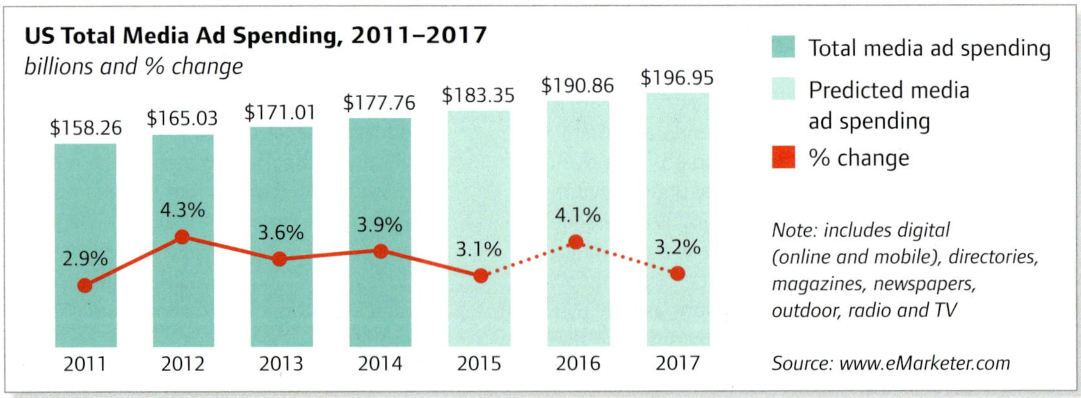

Useful phrases

- The bar chart shows the total media ad spending in the USA for the years 2011 to 2017.
- The years are shown on the x-axis. The figures are given in billions of dollars.
- The line (graph) also shows the change each year in per cent.

- In 2011 media ad spending was / came to $158.6bn.
- It rose by $6.75 billion in 2014. / It fell by 0.7% to 3.6% in 2013.
- Ad spending has increased by about 3–4% per year since 2011.
- Spending has grown by $13.6 billion over the last two years.

- The chart/graph shows us that … / We can see by the figures for … that …
- All in all, the trend is upwards/downwards. / There has been little change since …

1 With a partner, practise reading out the figures for media ad spending in the US from 2011 to 2014.
2 Explain what happened to the percentage change in media spending (red line) in 2012 and in 2013.
3 When was the biggest percentage change in media ad spending? When was the smallest?
4 How has media ad spending changed since 2011?
5 Write 4–5 sentences to describe the bar chart.

Saying numbers

1,000,000 = a/one million
1,000,000,000 = a/one billion
$171.01bn = a hundred and seventy-one point nought (zero) one billion dollars
$190.86bn = a hundred and ninety point eight six billion dollars

4 MIND MAP

In groups of 3–4 make a mind map about advertising. Include the following aspects:

- the different forms of advertising
- the target groups
- the benefits
- the dangers
- your own ideas

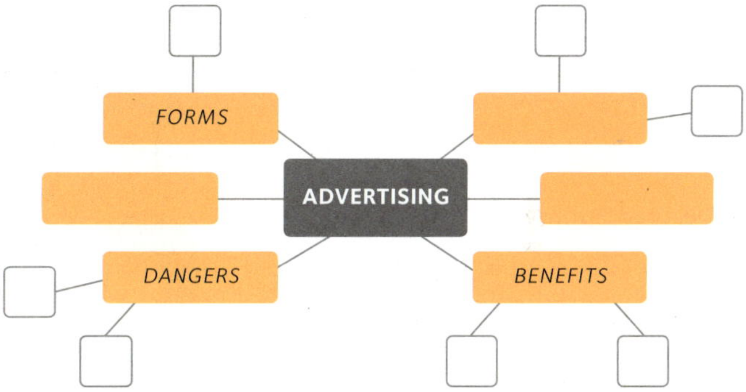

5 DISCUSSION

→ Interaktion: An Diskussionen teilnehmen, S. 246

A Write a few sentences explaining why you agree or disagree with the statement on the right.

B Use your list in a class discussion about branded goods and vote on whether the statement is right or wrong.

Advertising makes us spend money on things we don't need, especially branded goods.

6 WRITING

→ Produktion: Eine Stellungnahme schreiben, S. 234

Use the ideas on your mind map to write a comment about what H.G. Wells (a famous English writer) said about advertising.

"ADVERTISING IS LEGALIZED LYING."
H.G. WELLS

4/3

ETHICAL MARKETING: SELLING GOODS BY DOING GOOD

"Let's all work together with UNICEF and do something about the lack of clean drinking water in Ethiopia," suggests Danone Germany in its current campaign for Volvic mineral water. And when chocolate maker Ritter Sport markets its new children's candy bar, "helping out with Quadrago (Ritter's rectangular chocolate bar)" is suddenly the in thing to do. Procter & Gamble, on the other hand, is advertising its new Blend-a-med toothpaste with a "smile for the children in Brazil."
Welcome to morals as a marketing tool. More and more companies are now promising to do good things – if consumers buy their products, that is.

Drink your way to environmental protection

Krombacher, a German brewery, started the trend in Germany three years ago when it expanded purity regulations in the German beer industry to include drinkers' consciences. In an ad campaign it launched in 2002, the company promised that "with every case of Krombacher Pilsner you buy in the future, you'll be saving a square meter of African rainforest." And while sales dropped at other breweries, Krombacher was able to report an 8.1 per cent jump in its sales for 2003.
It took the advertising industry a while to recognize the moral of this story – but once they did there was no stopping them. Kellogg's used its profits from Cornflakes to pay school fees for "Children in Need," and German candy maker Katjes began selling "Rock 'n' Gums" to promote the previously little-known Nordoff/Robbins method of music therapy. (244 words)

Abridged from: *www.spiegel.de*

1 MATCHING

Find the parts of the text that these photos illustrate.

2 DISCUSSION

Discuss the following questions.

1 Do you think the companies mentioned in the text are being honest with their advertising? Why or why not?
2 Do you think it would be more effective and more ethical if the companies used the money that they spend on advertising to help people directly?
3 Would you buy something just because the company "says" that with their product they are saving the world? Why or why not?
4 Have you ever bought something which had an ethical slogan? What was it?

3 WRITING

→ Eine Stellungnahme schreiben, S. 234

Write a comment about ethical marketing and say whether you think it is positive or negative. Compare your comment with a partner's. Did one of you forget some important aspect?

7 Family and beyond

MAIN COURSE

FOCUS

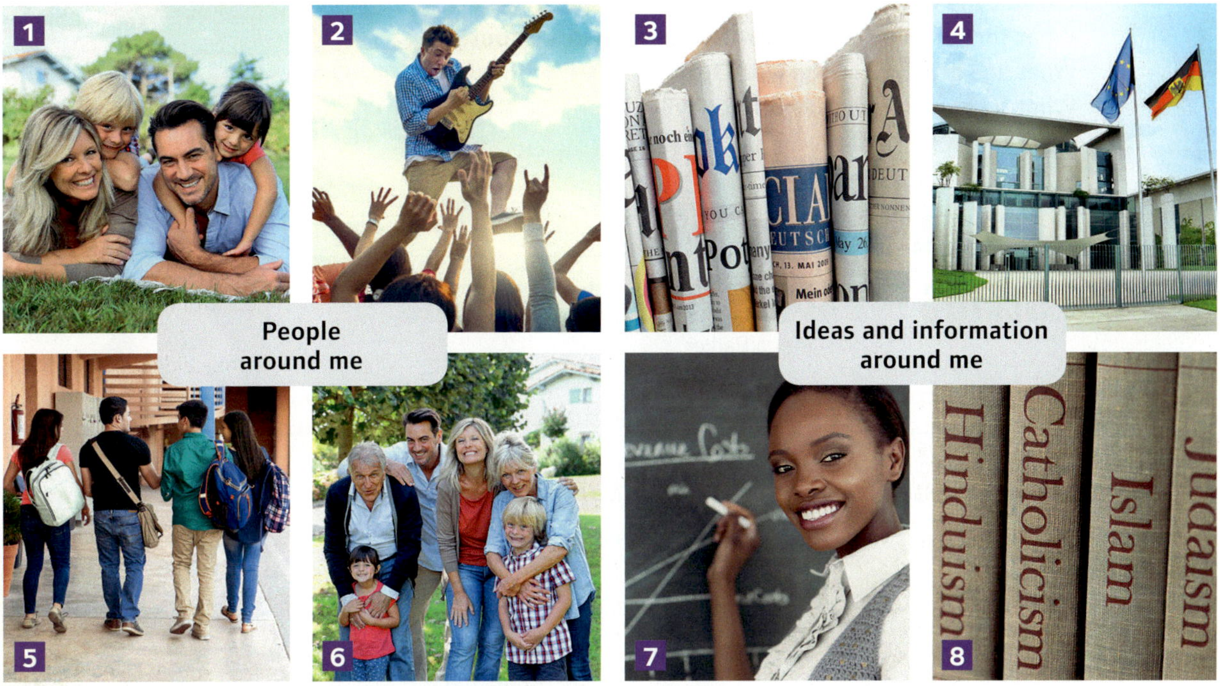

A Think about the influences that make people who they are.

1 Match the captions (a–h) to the pictures (1–8) above.

a education	**b** extended family	**c** government	**d** immediate family
e peer group	**f** religion	**g** role models	**h** the media

2 Note the three or four most important influences, in your opinion.
3 Work with a partner. Present your ideas to each other and discuss any differences.

B Work with a partner. Ask and answer questions about your backgrounds.

1 Change seats. Sit with someone that you do not know well.
2 Answer some of the questions below about yourself and make notes.
3 Try to answer the same questions about your partner. Ask if you do not know the answers.
4 Work in a small group. Take turns to introduce your partner's background to the others.

Where do you come from?

How do you live – with your family, with others, or alone?

What household chores do you have to do?

What do you do in your free time?

How often are you able to go out with friends?

When do you see your 'extended' family?

TEXT A Living in a family

BEFORE YOU READ

→ Vorbereitung auf das Lesen, S. 214

Look at the text quickly and answer these questions:
What sort of thing does the writer always write about?
What age group does she write for?
What topic is she focusing on today?

SKILLS CHECKLIST: Predicting

- ☑ Have I read the title and the other headings?
- ☑ Have I read the introduction?

Teen Times — May 15, 20..

1/21

PROBLEMS – PROBLEMS – PROBLEMS

by Pippa Parker

THIS WEEK: THE RIGHT SORT OF FAMILY

Just what sort of family is the right sort of family?

Should it be like reader Rajeev's family? ... Or should it be more like reader Lisa's?

Well, read these letters from Rajeev and Lisa and see what you think.

Dear Pippa

I'm Asian-British, and my grandparents came over from India in the 1960s. We live together – three generations – and three of my aunts and uncles and their families all live in the same street, too. I think you can safely say I'm from an extended family!

My twin sister and I used to love our close family life because there were always lots of people around, and perhaps we were spoilt as we were the first grandchildren. When Mum and Dad were busy, our grandparents were the ones that we turned to. They and our cousins' families were also always there to offer day-to-day help, a meal or just a friendly chat. Then there was the time when our parents' newspaper shop nearly went under, and everyone gave us financial and emotional support. It was the family that got us through, and I'll never forget that.

These days, things aren't quite so happy though. As we get older, we often want more freedom to do things our own way – go out with our friends at the weekend, dress the way that we want, say what we think about things – but it's getting more and more difficult, especially for Sita as she's a girl. Even when Mum and Dad agree to something like going to a party, the rest of the family still seem to think they can criticize us because we're not traditional enough. They say we're forgetting our roots and our values. What's more, our grandparents keep saying we're the oldest, so we're the ones who have to set a good example for our younger cousins.

It's hard for Mum and Dad, too. In fact, they're probably the ones who are having the hardest time of all: they're caught between my grandparents and us.

Does anyone else have these problems? I could really use some advice! *Rajeev Gupta*

Dear Pippa

We moved over to England from Dublin a year ago and it's been a huge change. Back home, we were part of an extended family. Mum's parents lived with us and we had family all around, so there was always someone who was visiting to gossip or to borrow something or to play. Over here though, we're on our own – just Mum, Dad, my brother and me. Mum and Dad both have jobs now. Fine. But we've gone from being part of a big, noisy family to a lonely little nuclear family. As a long-distance commuter, Dad has to leave before 7.00 am, and we don't see him till after 7.00 at night. Then the rest of us go at 8.00. I catch the bus to school, and Mum takes Sam to his school on her way to the office.

School is OK, and there are various after-school sports and other activities that I'm involved in – drama, for example. I'm free to do whatever I want, and I've made two or three friends, too. So all that's good. But at the end of the day, it's back home alone to an empty house, and there's no one there with a cheerful hello in the old way. Instead, I do some chores to help Mum because I know she'll get home tired. I'm the one who makes Sam his tea now, and there isn't much time to relax and talk. There's dinner to help make and homework to do, and so life at home goes on from day to lonely day.

Big families can be a pain, I know. People don't just mind their own business: they keep minding everyone else's, and there's not much privacy. So that can produce tensions, especially between generations, but there are lots of laughs, too, and I miss that a lot.

It's Christmas next month, and I can tell you we can't wait to go home for that! *Lisa Doyle*

So what's the answer? Whichever side of the hill we're on, it seems the grass is always greener on the other side. Perhaps the truth is that we really need a bit of both sorts of family life. We sometimes need the support of a wider family, and we sometimes also need the space to be free and independent. Actually, though, isn't that how things really are in many families today? Write in with your experiences. (764 words)

1 LOOKING AT THE TEXT

→ Sich während des Lesens Notizen machen, S. 223

BUILDING SKILLS: Taking notes while reading

- When you take notes while reading, always organize them in lists under sub-headings (see below) or using dates.
- You can leave out unnecessary words, such as pronouns and articles.
- It is quicker to use abbreviations and symbols, such as *e.g.*, &, +, –, =, *etc.*

A Work with a partner. Read one letter each and make notes on it.

Rajeev & Sita	Lisa
Family type: ▬	Family type a) present: ▬; b) past: ▬
Feelings about situation in past: ▬	Feelings about situation in past: ▬
Situation now & problems: ▬	Situation now & problems: ▬
Needs: ▬	Looking forward to: ▬

Now use your notes to explain the key points of your letter to your partner.

B With your partner, do the following activities. → Rezeption: Leseverstehen, S. 214

1 Decide which letter writer seems less happy with life in a big family.
2 Consider who has more life experience to speak from.
3 Say what Pippa thinks about the need for a) support and b) freedom in family life.

C Say what it means: Explain the underlined words from the context of the text.

1 … when our parents' newspaper shop nearly went under, … (line 15)
2 It was the family that got us through, … (line 16)
3 As a long-distance commuter, Dad has to leave … (line 34)
4 Big families can be a pain, I know. (line 45)
5 Whichever side of the hill we're on, it seems the grass is always greener on the other side. (line 49)

2 WORKING WITH WORDS

A Say what *as* means in the following sentences: *because, in the position of* or *when*.

1 *As* we get older, we often want more freedom … (line 17)
2 … but it's getting more and more difficult, especially for Sita *as* she's a girl. (line 19)
3 *As* a long-distance commuter, Dad has to leave before 7.00 am. (line 34)
4 Rajeev wrote to Pippa *as* he really felt he needed some advice.
5 *As* someone from an extended family, Lisa does not like her new lifestyle.
6 She will probably find her new life in England easier *as* time goes by.

B Complete the text with *make* or *do*. Change the forms as necessary.

When Lisa gets home from school, she *does* [1] chores to help around the house, but first, she *makes* [2] coffee and relaxes for a few minutes. Then she ___ [3] a start on her jobs. First, she goes to her room to tidy up and ___ [4] her bed as she never has time for this in the morning. Next, she goes downstairs to see what other housework there is to ___ [5]. She often ___ [6] some ironing, for example, or she sometimes needs to go out and ___ [7] some shopping at the supermarket. Then when mum and Sam get home, she ___ [8] her mum a cup of tea, and she ___ [9] her brother something to eat. That gives mum time to check her emails and ___ [10] her paperwork. Mum starts ___ [11] dinner at 7 pm, ready for when dad returns from work, and that is when Lisa finally sits down at her desk and starts ___ [12] her homework.

3 GETTING IT RIGHT

→ Relative clauses, S. 269

A Complete these sentences using *who, which* or *that*.

1 Rajeev was the one ___ wrote the first letter to Problems – Problems – Problems.
2 Lisa was the reader ___ provided the other letter for Pippa Parker's article.
3 Tension between Rajeev and others in his extended family is the thing ___ is worrying him.
4 However, Lisa is a girl ___ would clearly like to be back with her own large family again.
5 Problems – Problems – Problems is a page ___ appears every week in *Teen Times*.
6 *Teen Times* is a magazine ___ offers its readers lots of human interest stories.
7 It also has features like Pippa's – a page ___ helps readers with their problems and dilemmas.
8 Pippa is someone ___ has a real talent for helping young people with their problems.

B Complete the story, adding *who, which* or *that* only where necessary.

Teen Times is a magazine ~~___~~ [1] several other people in Lisa's year at school also read. It happened that a girl who/that [2] belonged to the drama club, like Lisa, was the one ___ [3] saw it first. Her name was Gina, and although she did not know Lisa well, she thought, 'Wow! The letter ___ [4] I'm looking at here might be from Lisa!' She read the letter again and compared it with the things ___ [5] she knew about Lisa. 'Yes,' she thought, 'it was about a year ago when she arrived, and the place ___ [6] she comes from is somewhere in Ireland. Another thing: the brother ___ [7] she told us about is called Sam, too.'

She was not quite sure though. 'It's strange,' she thought. 'The Lisa ___ [8] I know always seems happy and cheerful, but the Lisa ___ [9] wrote this letter seems quite sad! Can they really be the same person?'

The next day, Gina saw Lisa at drama after school, showed her the article and asked, 'Are you really the one ___ [10] wrote this letter?'

'Oh, that, er, yes,' Lisa said. 'Yes, that's the letter ___ [11] I wrote. I suppose I was stupid to use my real name.' She suddenly felt very embarrassed.

'Listen,' Gina said, 'I'm having a party on Saturday, so please come. There'll be lots of people ___ [12] will love to meet you!'

4 WRITING

→ Produktion: Schreiben, S. 228

Write Pippa's reply to Rajeev. Use this letter structure.

Paragraph 1: Thank him for his letter and for raising some interesting points.
Paragraph 2: Respond sympathetically.
Paragraph 3: Point out good things about his type of family situation.
Paragraph 4: Suggest how he can improve the situation.
Paragraph 5: Finish in a positive way.

Useful phrases

- Thank you very much for … and for raising …
- I was very sorry to read that … . It must be hard for you when …
- However, there are certainly some good things about your situation. As you yourself say, … . Then again, …
- Let me make one or two suggestions that may … . In my experience, it often helps to … . It might be useful to …
- I'm sure that if you … , you'll be able to …

TIP

Your reply is friendly and informal, so feel free to use contracted forms like *you're* instead of full forms like *you are*. (But remember to use full forms in more formal writing.)

Write to Pippa about someone that you know (or can imagine) – who has a family problem but who is too shy to ask for help.

Then write Pippa's reply. (You can use the same letter structure as above.)

5 DISCUSSION

→ Interaktion: An Diskussionen teilnehmen, S. 246

Pippa refers to the saying: 'The grass is always greener on the other side of the hill.' How true do you think this is?

TEXT B Leaving home

BEFORE YOU READ

Talk about the pros and cons of living away from your family.

http://www.leavinghome.org

1/22

Carrie | **Moving out**

I'm now 22, and I moved out five years ago. I was a grade A student, and I gave everything to my studies. But I was living with my dad over 20 miles from school, and things weren't going well. I had to get up ridiculously early to get the one and only bus out of our village to make it to school in the morning, and there were just two buses back after school. When I had to stay for extra studies, I didn't get home until after 7 pm! I had to make my own meals and eat alone as everyone else always ate before I got home from school. My dad and I also argued about everything. He always started on me for not hoovering the house before I left for school and not putting on a load of washing! What's more, he expected me to do that every day of the week. I was happy to do it at weekends but who hoovers every single day – and at 6.30 in the morning? Plus my dad was getting very nosey. He was going through the bin in my bedroom to find receipts to see what I was spending money on – my own money, by the way, as I had a part-time job at a supermarket. And on Saturdays, when I wanted to meet my friends in town, my dad banned me from getting the only morning bus! I had to get the only other bus – in the afternoon – and that left me just two hours with my friends. They always had lunch without me, and I felt left out.
My dad was turning into a real control freak, and I couldn't take it anymore. Maybe it was the same thing that had driven Mum away years before. Anyway, to cut a long story short, I moved out. I spoke to the *benefits people and explained my situation. Because I was moving away from home I was also moving away from my job, so I needed some help financially for a few months. My teacher helped me a lot, and she explained to the benefits office that my grades were dropping because of stress at home, so I needed the chance to complete school properly in order to move on to college. She also found me a small flat.
It wasn't easy though. In fact, it was the hardest thing I've ever done – to go home alone every day instead of to a family. But I'm a better person now because of it, and I'm happy I did it. (434 words)

** Department for Work and Pensions (DWP): manages most areas of welfare in the UK.*

1 LOOKING AT THE TEXT

→ Rezeption: Leseverstehen, S. 214

A Put the pictures in the order (1–6) that Carrie describes her problems. Then do one of the tasks below.

- **Briefly say what the problems were.**
- **Explain why you think Carrie found each of these things a problem.**

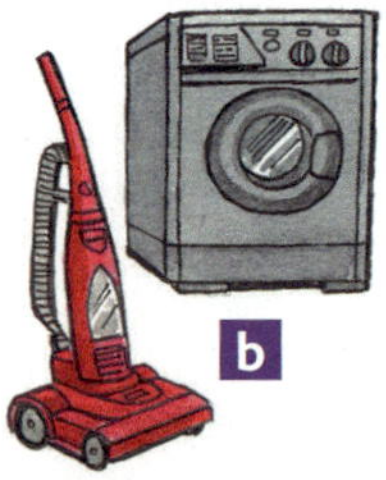

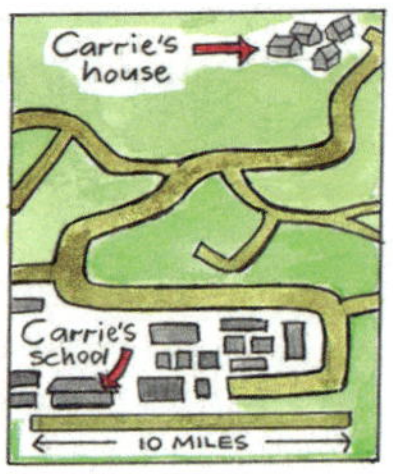

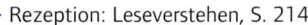

B Say whether these statements about the text are true or false. Correct the false statements.

1. Carrie is writing about her recent situation at home.
2. She was probably the oldest of the young family.
3. The situation at home was getting worse.
4. The benefits office helped her financially and also gave her a flat.
5. She was very happy when she first moved away from home.

C Say what it means: Explain the underlined words and phrases in your own words.

1. … to make it to school in the morning, … (line 3)
2. He always started on me for not hovering … (line 6)
3. Plus my dad was getting very nosey. (line 9)
4. My dad was turning into a real control freak. (line 14)
5. … and I couldn't take it anymore. (line 14)

2 WORKING WITH WORDS

A Complete the story of Carrie's past life. Choose from these prepositions of time.

at ▪ during ▪ from ▪ in ▪ on ▪ to

Carrie always got up ___[1] 6 o'clock ___[2] the morning ___[3] weekdays in order to catch the 7 o'clock bus to town. She had school ___[4] 9 am ___[5] 3.30 pm, and then she often stayed for extra lessons. This meant that she had to catch the second bus home and only got there ___[6] about 7 pm ___[7] the evening. That was hard enough ___[8] the summer, but ___[9] the winter months she had to leave home and get home in the dark, and she hated it.
___[10] the weekend, she had to do a lot of housework ___[11] Saturday morning and ___[12] Sunday, so she was only able to see her friends ___[13] the afternoon ___[14] Saturday.
Finally, ___[15] her last year at school, it all got too much for her. ___[16] a cold, wet evening ___[17] November, she decided to leave home and start a new life.

B Complete the following with suitable phrasal verbs. Change the forms as necessary.

Paragraph 1: move in ▪ move on ▪ move out
Paragraph 2: get on ▪ get over ▪ get up
Paragraph 3: turn back ▪ turn into ▪ turn out

When Mark and Karen had their first child, their tiny two-room flat was just too small, and it was time to ___ ___[1] to the next stage of their lives – a bigger home. They ___ ___[2] on November 30th, and on December 1st, the next person ___ ___[3]. It was Carrie!

For Carrie, the little flat was perfect. It was in town, so she did not need to ___ ___[4] at 6 am anymore, and she soon started to ___ ___[5] much better at school. However, she was lonely, and it took her a long time to ___ ___[6] the shock of leaving home.

However, Carrie did not even think of ___ the clock ___[7] and returning to her old life. Instead, she got a few pieces of furniture, and she slowly ___ the little flat ___[8] a home. After a few months, she was much happier, and she knew that her move was ___ ___[9] very well.

3 GETTING IT RIGHT

→ Simple past ▪ Past progressive, S. 251

Complete the text about the day that Carrie left home. Put the verbs in the simple past or past progressive.

Carrie remembers very clearly the evening when she finally (decide) ___ [1] to leave home. While she (travel) ___ [2] home on the bus from school, she (open) ___ [3] a book to try and study, but her mind (keep) ___ [4] returning to her problems. Things (go) ___ [5] from bad to worse at home, and she (not look forward to) ___ [6] the evening ahead. Outside, it (get) ___ [7] dark and it (start) ___ [8] to rain, too. 'It looks like the way I feel,' she (think) ___ [9].
As she (step) ___ [10] off the bus, a cold autumn wind (blow) ___ [11] and it (rain) ___ [12] steadily.
She (pull) ___ [13] her coat tight, and she (turn) ___ [14] down the dark lane towards the house.
When she (enter) ___ [15] the living room, her younger brother Ben (play) ___ [16] a video game and her little sister Lucy (draw) ___ [17] pictures. They (look) ___ [18] up cheerfully to say 'hi!' before returning to their activities. In the next room, her dad (do) ___ [19] some work on his laptop and he (not seem) ___ [20] to notice her. He just (say) ___ [21]: 'You (not do) ___ [22] the washing this morning, so please make sure you do it tonight.'
That (be) ___ [23] the start of a very bad night.

4 LISTENING

→ Rezeption: Hörverstehen, S. 225

You are going to listen to a radio interview with Emma Schumann, a youth counsellor. She is talking about the things young people need to do when they look for their own place to live.

BUILDING SKILLS: Taking notes from listening

- Don't panic if you fall behind while you listen. Speakers often make false starts and repeat themselves. (Listen again for examples of this.)
- Leave out unnecessary words such as pronouns and articles while taking notes.
- You can also use abbreviations and symbols such as: *e.g.*, &, +, –, =, *etc.*

1/23

Copy the notes below, then listen to the interview to complete them.

How to find right place
1 Look on ___
2 –//– in ___
3 ___ place
4 ___ people you will share with

Dealing with money
1 ___ your monthly ___ for food, etc.
2 Always ___

Looking after yourself
1 Don't ___
2 Cook ___

Living with others
1 Set ___
2 Do ___
3 Talk ___
4 Respect ___

5 MEDIATION

Sie wohnen in einer WG mit anderen jungen Menschen zusammen. In der WG ist gerade ein Zimmer frei geworden.

Anhand Ihrer Notizen aus Übung 4 erklären Sie einem Freund / einer Freundin, worauf er/sie achten sollte, wenn er/sie das erste Mal von zu Hause auszieht und bei Ihnen einziehen möchte.

6 DISCUSSION

→ Interaktion: An Diskussionen teilnehmen, S. 246

A Discuss in groups. Put the following tips in order of usefulness.

Advice for teenagers who are leaving home

- Washing-up is like saying sorry. It gets harder the longer you leave it.
- Just because you've got money in your bank account doesn't mean you have to spend it.
- Work first, play later.
- If you have to sniff your duvet cover to see if it needs washing, it probably does.
- Eat green vegetables. Raw, if necessary. Chips don't contain all the nutrients necessary to maintain good health.
- Inform your parents about what you're up to on a need-to-know basis. They need to know you're alive.

B Describe the picture. Then discuss what needs to happen in this student house.

Useful phrases

- The picture/cartoon shows a very …
- On the (left/right), there's a … (*room*), and in it we can see someone who is …
- In the corner / On the floor / By the sink, we can also see that …
- These students clearly have to …
- Just in the … (*room*), someone needs to … (*list of tasks*)
- Then in the … (*room*), someone should … (*list of tasks*)

C Read Emma Schumann's last words of advice and discuss these questions.

1 What might turn a home leaver into a boomerang kid?
2 What might turn a parent into a helicopter mum (or dad)?
3 How might people – a boomerang kid and a helicopter mum – feel in these situations?

Don't be a 'boomerang kid', who leaves home, and then finds it too difficult, and then gives up and goes back to the family home again. And don't turn your mum into a 'helicopter mum' who has to come and rescue you because you're doing things badly in your new home.

4/4

NO SIBLINGS: WHAT ARE THE REPERCUSSIONS?

What's it like to grow up as an only child? Are siblings really that important? Researchers have been asking those questions for years – and China, with its famous one-child policy, has been a good place to look for an answer. Before 1979, Chinese families had an average of four children each, but in 1979 a law saying that most parents could only have one child was introduced.

I am an only child and people often ask: "Didn't you wish you had siblings when you were growing up? Didn't you feel lonely?" I never did. Maybe some people would have been lonely or bored growing up without siblings, but I was too busy playing with all my toys and always having my parents' attention to really notice. When you're an only child, you usually play games like Monopoly with your parents. When you have siblings, these games turn into a competition. The first time I played a game with Pete, a friend of mine who grew up with an older brother, I cried when I didn't win. I had never lost a game before and I just couldn't understand the world any more! Some people say that as an only child, I had no sense of competition and I didn't learn how to lose a game gracefully. But aren't these things you can learn later in life?

I asked other young adults what they thought the positive and negative aspects of being "only children" were. Here are some of their answers:

"Your parents watch your every move, also in your free time."

"When your parents get older, you have to take care of them on your own."

"You get more pocket money to spend than children with siblings."

"Your parents put pressure on you to do well at school."

"You don't have to share the money your parents leave you when they die."

"You grow up to be more independent because you have nobody to help you at school."

(328 words)

1 LOOKING AT THE TEXT

→ Rezeption: Leseverstehen, S. 214

Sort information from the text into these categories:

- The positive aspects of being an only child
- The negative aspects of being an only child

2 INTERVIEW

Follow these steps to conduct an interview and share the results.

1 If you have siblings, write down four or five questions you would like to ask an only child about their family life. If you are an only child, write down four or five questions you would like to ask a person with siblings about their family life. Here are some questions to get you started:
- How did you feel growing up? (bored/ignored/scared/…?)
- What lessons did you learn? (to be independent / to share / …?)
- What advice would you give someone who wants to start a family?

2 Find someone to interview (ideally a student you do not know that well) and ask your questions. Take notes on your partner's answers.

3 As a class, collect the statements from the interviews on two posters.

I am an only child	I have siblings

8 Entering the world of work

MAIN COURSE

FOCUS

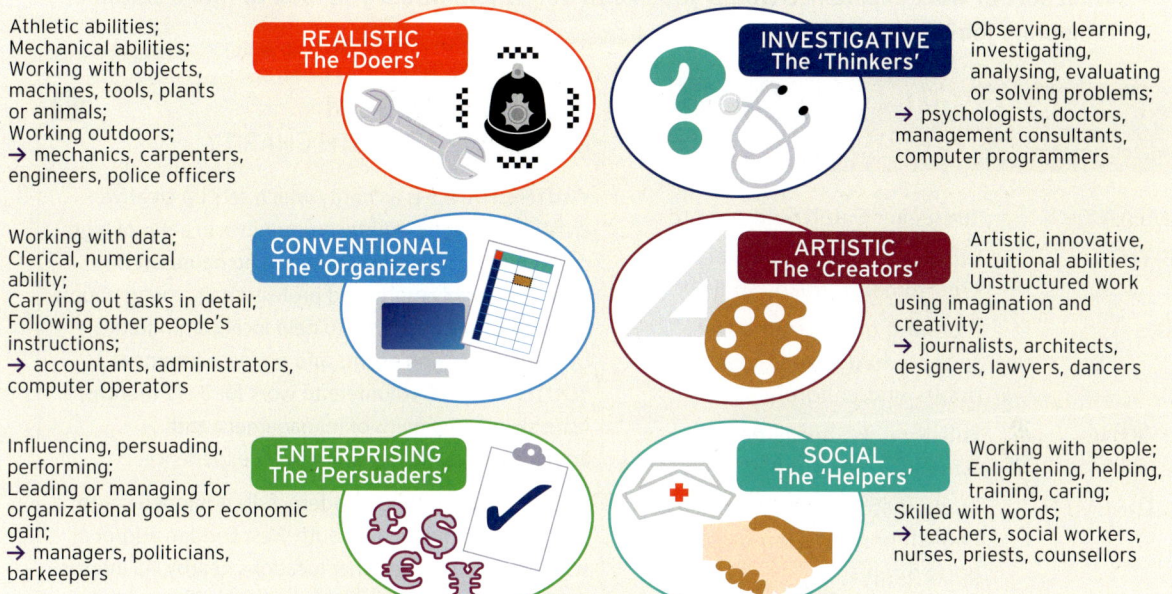

Athletic abilities;
Mechanical abilities;
Working with objects, machines, tools, plants or animals;
Working outdoors;
→ mechanics, carpenters, engineers, police officers

Observing, learning, investigating, analysing, evaluating or solving problems;
→ psychologists, doctors, management consultants, computer programmers

Working with data;
Clerical, numerical ability;
Carrying out tasks in detail;
Following other people's instructions;
→ accountants, administrators, computer operators

Artistic, innovative, intuitional abilities;
Unstructured work using imagination and creativity;
→ journalists, architects, designers, lawyers, dancers

Influencing, persuading, performing;
Leading or managing for organizational goals or economic gain;
→ managers, politicians, barkeepers

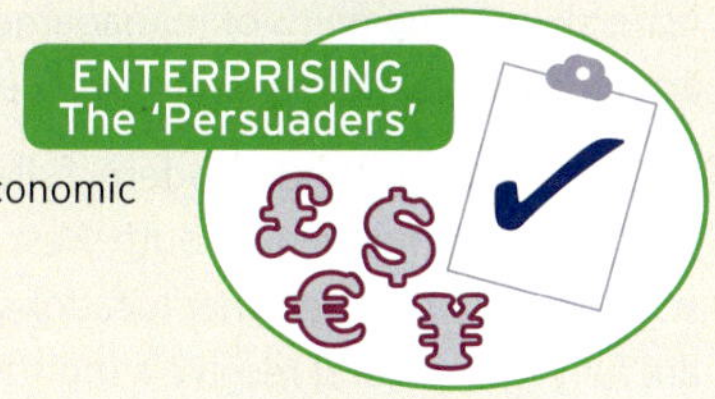

Working with people;
Enlightening, helping, training, caring;
Skilled with words;
→ teachers, social workers, nurses, priests, counsellors

A **Finding the right career is a big step in life, so it is important to think about what you want from a job before you start looking. List the following factors and your own ideas according to how important they are for you. Compare your results with a partner.**

a challenge ▪ a quiet life ▪ being your own boss ▪ company car ▪ excitement ▪ flexible working hours ▪ good pay ▪ good promotion prospects ▪ good working conditions ▪ helping people ▪ job security ▪ meeting people ▪ private medical insurance ▪ regular working hours ▪ travel

What are the most/least important factors? Discuss your findings in class.

B **With a partner study the diagram above and decide which category is closest to your personality. (You may find that you have the characteristics of more than one category.)**

C **Choose one of the jobs in the category you have chosen, or a similar job, and write 4–5 sentences about it to describe the sort of work involved. Use ideas from the Internet and your own knowledge.**

Useful phrases

- Working as (an architect) involves (designing buildings and dealing with construction workers).
- If you like (helping people), you'll enjoy the job of a (nurse) because …
- If you want to (work creatively) the job of a (designer) is ideal/attractive because it involves … (+ *-ing* form)
- On the one hand, (administrators) have … but on the other hand, …
- If you work as a/an … , you have to …
- (Bakers) have to … , but they don't need …
- The job of a/an … is very (satisfying/rewarding).

TEXT A Three job advertisements

BEFORE YOU READ

What sort of work experience would you like to do? Where would you look to find a suitable temporary job?

1/24

1 WONDERFUL WORLD ONLINE RECRUITMENT

COMPANY:	Sunseeker Entertainment Ltd
JOB TITLE:	Work placement as a hotel entertainer in Ibiza, Spain
TASKS:	Planning and carrying out suitable holiday activities for adults and children
WORKING HOURS:	Full-time, 40 hours per week; 3 months minimum
REQUIREMENTS:	Student status, good spoken English and/or German, basic Spanish
BENEFITS:	Free board and lodging + allowance of €200 (£160) per month Return airfare from home country to Ibiza (max. €250 or £200)
HOW TO APPLY:	Use the button below to email us your CV and cover letter.

UNITED KINGDOM 2
INTERNSHIP AT YOUTH CHARITY

YOUTH-CHANCE is a charity which sets up creative, artistic projects for youth communities in areas of high crime with no programmes for young people. It is staffed by highly motivated professionals, young people and interns, who all want to help local communities by offering exciting events and projects. Interns at **YOUTH-CHANCE** volunteer to work for 2–12 months, learn skills in the fields of management and administration and get useful work experience.

Interns will work at our modern, fully equipped youth centre in Hammersmith, South West London and/or at schools, theatres and other locations nearby. All interns are fully insured and receive a monthly allowance of £120 (€150) and free board and lodging (e.g. in homestay accommodation nearby). Travel expenses from and to the intern's home country are also paid.

Would you like to help? Send your CV and cover letter to Sylvester Page at sylvester@youth-chance.net or phone us on 0044 207 5499783.

YOUTH-CHANCE, 42 Vanston Square, London SW6 1QR, UK.
Registered charity no. 52866320.

TOPTECH ONLINE RECRUITMENT – WE'LL GET YOU THAT JOB!

Post advertised:	Work placement as a theatre technician at Lloyd Theatre, Bath, UK
Allowance:	£1,000 per month
Working hours:	40 hours per week
Starting date:	ASAP
Duration:	6 months

The work placement student will …
- be part of a small team responsible for the set, lighting, sound and props for all productions
- carry out maintenance and repair work on theatre equipment

The successful candidate is …
- able to carry out basic electrical maintenance and DIY tasks
- friendly, helpful and flexible
- prepared to work evening and weekend shifts

Help will be given to find suitable local accommodation.
Email your CV and cover letter to Tracy Winter in HR at tracy@lloyd-theatre.org or call 0117 315 7185.
The Lloyd Theatre is an equal opportunities employer.

3

1 WORKING WITH WORDS

A Find the English equivalent of the following German expressions in the three job adverts.

1 Praktikum
2 Kost und Logis
3 Taschengeld
4 Unterkunft
5 Fahrtkosten
6 zuständig für
7 ein Arbeitgeber im Sinne der Chancengleichheit

B With a partner complete the word families using forms from the three job ads.

Verb	Noun	Noun (person)	Adjective
	___	intern	
	art	artist	___
___		volunteer	voluntary
to administer	___	administrator	administrative
to accommodate	___		
	technology	___	technological
to maintain	___		
	equality		___

2 LOOKING AT THE TEXTS

→ Rezeption: Leseverstehen, S. 214

A With a partner study the three job ads again and draw up a table with the headings below showing the terms offered by the three employers.

- length of contract
- allowance
- accommodation
- food
- insurance
- travel expenses

B Which of the three jobs would you apply for? Which skills could you use to do the job?

3 DESCRIBING JOBS

Who says what? Match the sentences (a–d) with the photographs (1–4).

1 salesman

2 boutique owner

3 medical secretary

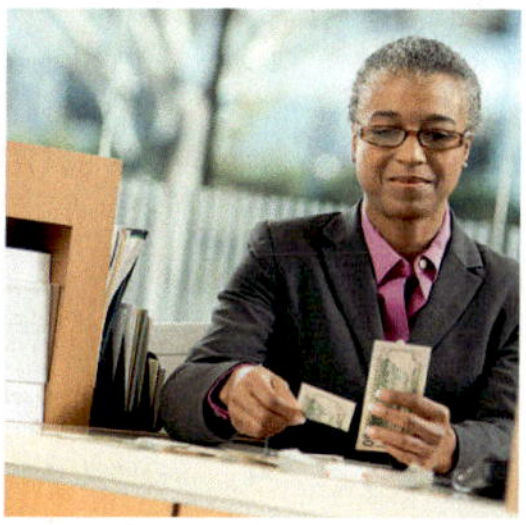
4 bank clerk

a If I don't give the customers what they want, they'll go elsewhere.
b We always give our customers the best financial advice.
c My company's product supplies energy from a sustainable source.
d It's nice to think you're helping people to get the treatment they need.

4 LISTENING

→ Rezeption: Hörverstehen, S. 225

1/25

You are going to hear two people being interviewed about their jobs. Listen and make notes under the following headings for each job:

- skills and qualifications
- type of work
- working hours
- pay
- promotion prospects
- job security
- job satisfaction

SKILLS CHECKLIST: Taking notes

☑ Have I used headings?
☑ Have I left out unnecessary words?
☑ Have I used abbreviations?

5 WRITING

→ Produktion: Schreiben, S. 228

Use your notes from exercise 4 to write a description of one of the two jobs. Use the *Useful phrases* on page 65.

Choose a job you know about and describe it in English using the headings in exercise 4 above and the *Useful phrases* on page 65.

6 GETTING IT RIGHT

→ *If* sentences, S. 264

A Complete the dialogue between a student and a careers advisor using the right form of the verbs in brackets in *if* sentences type 1.

Student: Now I'd like to ask some questions about pay. If I (work) ___[1] as a bank clerk, how much (I/earn) ___[2]?

Advisor: At entry level you (get) ___[3] about £1,160 per month if you (be) ___[4] at one of the big banks. If you (get) ___[5] promotion, you (earn) ___[6] a lot more. However, let me give you a word of warning. You (not get) ___[7] promotion if you (not be) ___[8] ambitious. If you (not apply) ___[9] for a better position after some time, no one (offer) ___[10] you one on a plate.

B Expand the notes to make more *if* sentences type 1.

EXAMPLE
you / get job / medical secretary / earn / £1,600 / month
If you get a job as a medical secretary, you'll earn £1,600 a month.

1 you / work / volunteer / get / £150 / month
2 you / only get / allowance / £40 / week / work / intern
3 you / get a job / bank clerk / earn / £14,000 / year
4 you / have better job security / be / fully qualified
5 you / love clothes / not find it hard / work / boutique
6 your yearly income / be irregular / be / boutique owner
7 you / want / make enough money / have to work / long hours / boutique owner
8 you / not be able / stay in a small shop / business / become successful
9 a good salesperson / earn / £1,000 / week / work hard
10 a salesperson / not sell enough / lose / job

TEXT B New trends at the workplace

BEFORE YOU READ

Look at the photos on this page and on page 70. What do you think about this way of working?

1/26

MIND HOW YOU MOVE THAT CHAIR – IT'S HOT

HOT-DESKING IS A GROWING TREND, BRINGING A NEW CULTURE

MOST people dislike not having a desk of their own. They do not like the idea of arriving at the office, grabbing their "wheely" filing cabinet and making for the nearest free desk available.

Yet like it or not, this way of working is on the increase, bringing a changing office culture. The driving force behind this is to reduce property costs and it is made possible by ever-improving electronics.

Three years ago 95% of employees at ICL, the computer services company, had their own desks. Today, about 25% of the 20,000 workforce have no desk of their own. "A 40% increase predicted over the next two years has caused us to totally rethink our building requirements," says Richard Reed, director of corporate infrastructure.

"We opened a building in Staines which has 320 desks but supports 600 people. We see this building as a model for the future."

ICL has changed its culture from manufacturing to services, which requires a more mobile workforce. "We have three categories of employees," says Mr Reed. First, the pad-owners: they sit at their desk not less than three days a week. Second, the home-workers: they work a minimum of three days a week at home.

"Third, those who fall in neither of these and are, by default, mobile workers and therefore automatically hot-desk workers."

Mr Reed hot-desks, sometimes in one of the meeting rooms or going to the staff restaurant to plug into a computer; his secretary, who works for six bosses, is a home-worker but drives up the M4 once or twice a week to counteract loneliness.

"I'm afraid I do not have that homing instinct which I acknowledge others do – for example, those people who even though they do not have an allotted space in a car park will always tend to park

in the same spot," says Mr Reed. "This has to be a gradual development programme, which addresses any concerns that employees might have about being able to do their job properly."

At the British Airways business centre near Heathrow, about 25% of the 3,500 employees hot-desk, and the figure has been rising. A wide-ranging training programme, cultural as well as electronic, helped to prepare employees for the changes in working practices.

"We wanted to make informality the norm," says Alison Hartigan, senior property manager. While she acknowledges some departments such as legal, finance and some strategy teams, are not so suitable for hot-desking, the majority are – sales, marketing, property, human resources, computers, and so on.

"Of course people are very territorial about space and in open-plan offices they personalise their space. With hot-desking they can't do that, it's the big barrier to cross."

Christopher Middleton, who joined IBM recently as a manager for smaller businesses, found hot-desking a culture shock, but a positive one. "You're judged purely on results, not on whether you're sitting at your desk all the time," he says.

"I have been coming into the office two days a week and the challenge is to book a desk in time although there are drop-in areas where you can plug into a computer for a couple of hours."

Like many others who hot-desk, he finds he gravitates to the same desk when he comes into the office.

"It gives me a kind of continuity and feeling of belonging. Maybe I'll shake this off in time. I totally accept it might be difficult to change for some people. In my last firm, some people still wore suits and ties on dress-down Friday." […]

One sector which has had its fingers burned with hot-desking is the advertising industry. Large advertising agencies working globally who thought they could downsize their expensive prestigious buildings around the world found that this led rapidly to employees not identifying with the agencies any longer and leaving to set up their own businesses. It was an expensive disaster. […]

(662 words)

From: *www.telegraph.co.uk*

1 LOOKING AT THE TEXT

→ Rezeption: Leseverstehen, S. 214

Complete the sentences with the most suitable answer, a, b or c.

1 'Hot-desking' means …
- **a** you always have the best desk.
- **b** you always work at a different desk.
- **c** your desk is centrally heated.

2 Companies use hot-desking because …
- **a** they can use their office space better.
- **b** employees like moving around.
- **c** moveable desks last longer than fixed desks.

3 At ICL hot-desk workers are the employees who …
- **a** work in the office at least three days a week.
- **b** work at home at least three days a week.
- **c** have no fixed working routine.

4 Mr Reed's secretary …
- **a** never hot-desks. **b** sometimes hot-desks. **c** always hot-desks.

5 Mr Reed …
- **a** likes to park his car in the same space in the company car park.
- **b** prefers to work at the same desk when he's in the office.
- **c** has nothing against working in a different place all the time.

6 According to Alison Hartigan at British Airways, … departments are suitable for hot-desking.
- **a** a few **b** most **c** all

7 Christopher Middleton thinks that …
- **a** some people find it hard to change how they work.
- **b** male employees should always wear suits and ties.
- **c** Friday is the best day for hot-desking.

8 When advertising agencies introduced hot-desking …
- **a** they saved a lot of money.
- **b** they were able to open many more new offices.
- **c** their employees left.

2 WORKING WITH WORDS

Find words or expressions in the text on pages 69–70 to match these definitions.

1 a piece of office furniture for storing files, documents, papers, etc. (paragraph 1)
2 buildings, e.g. office blocks (paragraph 2)
3 all the people who work at a company (paragraph 3)
4 needs (paragraph 5)
5 automatically (paragraph 6)
6 slow, not sudden (paragraph 8)
7 the department of a company that employs and trains people (paragraph 10)
8 the hard thing to do (paragraph 13)
9 casual, informal (paragraph 15)
10 make smaller (paragraph 16)

3 MEDIATION

→ Schriftliche Mediation, S. 240

BUILDING SKILLS: Written mediation

A mediated text should provide the person who reads it with the information he/she needs: it is not a word-for-word translation. When mediating a text use the following techniques:
- Read the whole text through for gist. Don't stop to look up unknown words while doing this.
- Go back and note down all the relevant facts for your 'reader'. Use a dictionary if necessary.
- Use your notes to present the relevant information in a German text in your own words.

Sie arbeiten für eine Firma, deren Mitarbeiter/innen oft im Außendienst unterwegs sind. Deswegen erwägt Ihre Firma Einsparungen bei den Büromieten.

Schreiben Sie eine E-Mail an die Leiterin der Personalabteilung, in der Sie die Vorteile von *hot-desking* erklären.

4 LISTENING

→ Rezeption: Hörverstehen, S. 225

Jenny Parker is a project manager at Green Energy Services. Today she is talking to Geoff Hall, the human resources director, about her new workplace.

1/27

A Listen to the dialogue and answer the questions.

1 What was the email about?
2 What does Jenny want to do?
3 How often are project managers in the office?
4 What solution does Geoff suggest?

B Complete the sentences with words from the dialogue. There is one word for each gap.

1 We would have more problems if we ▬ back to the old system, Jenny.
2 If we were in a bigger building, there ▬[1] ▬[2] enough room for everyone.
3 I'd change back to the old system if I ▬ .
4 If you ▬[1] a project manager spending two or three days a week on the road, you ▬[2] ▬[3] a permanent place in the office.
5 If we ▬ you your own desk, you'd only use it two or three days a week.
6 You ▬[1] certainly ▬[2] a fixed desk if you did that.

5 GETTING IT RIGHT

→ *If* sentences, S. 264

A **Two colleagues are discussing hot-desking. Complete these *if* sentences type 2.**

Emma If I (get) ___ [1] a job at a big company with hot-desking, I would try to sit in the same place every day. How about you?

Frank I understand what you mean, Emma but if they asked me, I (be) ___ [2] quite happy to move around. If I (do) ___ [3] that, I'd meet new people every day.

Emma But (you/get to know) ___ [4] them if you only saw them once in a while? I (try) ___ [5] to sit in the same place automatically if I (have) ___ [6] to hot-desk. It's human nature.

Frank Hot-desking saves money. Companies (not want) ___ [7] to do it if they (not think) ___ [8] it was a good idea.

The finance director of a manufacturing company is telling his colleagues why hot-desking is necessary. Describe the following 'chain reactions' using *if* sentences type 2.

we / buy a new office block → we / spend over £2,000,000 → we / have no money for new products → our company / lose its market share → many employees / lose their jobs → they / work for our competitors → our competitors / discover our company's secrets → this company / have to close

If we bought a new office block, we would spend over £2,000,000.
If we spent over £2,000,000, …

Invent two more 'chain reactions' of your own.

If the computer system in a company using hot-desking broke down, …
If we all went on strike, …

B **Ella Brown, the managing director of Green Energy Services, is talking to Geoff Hall, the human resources director, about how to save office space. Complete the sentences with suitable forms of the verbs in brackets (= *if* sentences types 1 and 2). Sometimes there is more than one word in a gap.**

Ella If we (not do) ___ [1] something soon, we'll have no more room at all! If I were you, I (tell) ___ [2] the staff to have home office days.

Geoff Yes, that's one possibility but I think we (have) ___ [3] a problem if we asked everybody to do that. If we (ask) ___ [4] the project managers, I'm sure most of them will agree but I don't think we should ask the permanent office staff. We (find) ___ [5] it difficult if some of them spent one day a week at home. For example, who will look after visitors if the receptionist (not be) ___ [6] in the office?

Ella Yes, I see your point but (it/be) ___ [7] better if we had job rotation? If we (do) ___ [8] that, everybody will be able to stand in for everybody else.

Geoff But think of the costs of retraining them all, Ella! I don't think our finance director (agree) ___ [9] if we suggested that. I think we should hot-desk. If we (buy) ___ [10] some really modern-looking, hi-tech, plug-in wheely desks, I'm sure everyone will want one!

6 CLASSROOM SIMULATION

Try the following experiment with your class in your next English lesson:

Number the individual places at the desks in your classroom (not just each double desk) and put the numbers in a hat. Each student draws a number and sits at that place. If it is the student's regular place, the student must draw again to make sure it's a new place. You must accept the new place without question to make this simulation work. Spend the whole lesson at the new place.

After the lesson:

- Write lists of what you liked and disliked about having a new place.
- Compare your lists with those of two or three other students in your class.
- Have a class discussion about the advantages and disadvantages of sitting at a new place a) every lesson, b) every month, c) after the Christmas and Easter holidays.

7 DEBATE

→ Interaktion: An Diskussionen teilnehmen, S. 246

After the simulation, form groups of four or more and debate the pros and cons of sitting at a new place every lesson, every month or after the holidays. Half of your group must be for and the others against this idea. Split into 'pro' and 'con' groups and sit at separate desks.

Prepare for the debate like this:

1. Discuss in your 'pro' or 'con' group what you liked/disliked about sitting at a new place, e.g. different faces around you, getting to know people better, easier/harder to concentrate, more/less help from neighbours, etc.
2. Write down all your arguments in note form.
3. Use the *Language for discussion* expressions on the back cover flap of this book to make your notes into whole sentences.
4. Practise talking about your notes with the other member(s) of your group.

Conduct the debate like this:

5. The 'pro' group members present all their arguments. The 'con' group members take notes.
6. The 'con' group members present all their arguments. The 'pro' group members take notes.
7. The 'pro' and 'con' groups now ask and answer questions about the arguments they have heard.

8 WRITING

→ Produktion: Eine Stellungnahme schreiben, S. 234

BUILDING SKILLS: Writing a comment

A comment expresses your own opinion about a particular topic or question. To ensure that your comment is well structured follow these steps:

- Study the instructions carefully to make sure you know exactly what to write about.
- Structure your arguments logically, e.g. under headings or in a mind map. Include arguments for and against.
- Refer to the question in your first sentence then present your arguments in separate paragraphs.
- Conclude your comment with a final sentence clearly stating your opinion.

Use your notes from exercise 3 and your own ideas to write a short comment about hot-desking. Title: *Why I would or wouldn't like to hot-desk.*

Balancing work and family

4/5

ASK NETTA …

Help! I am a 32-year-old single mum with two children. My widowed father has just been diagnosed with Alzheimer's and I am not sure how I will cope. My boss is already upset that I have had to stay at home for so many days this year because Dennis, my four-year-old son, has caught every illness at kindergarten. What can I do? *Alison*

Netta responds:

Alison,

First of all, you are not alone. A lot of people in their 30s and 40s are in your position. You are all members of the so-called "sandwich generation" – people who are taking care of their young children on one side and ageing parents on the other, and all this while having a job. Finding a happy balance between work and family is not easy so you have to make choices and develop some strategies.

First, it is important to organize yourself well. You have to learn how to end your day at work and begin your day at home. This may mean saying "no" when your boss asks you to stay late at work or when your child's school asks you to help out one morning. You can't do everything so you have to be realistic about what you can manage.

Also, you have to learn to accept help from others. Ask friends, family, neighbours and even close colleagues for their support. Get your children involved so you can work together as a team. See what kind of assistance you can get from state or local organizations. And make sure you have an emergency plan for those days when everything goes wrong.

Being a good parent, caregiver and employee also means looking after yourself. Having more time for yourself will not only benefit you, it will benefit your work and family! Talk to your boss about part-time work or job-sharing. Some people who share their job with someone else do so because they have children or ageing parents to look after. Other people do so for health reasons. Whatever the reason, job-sharing could be a lifesaver.

1 LOOKING AT THE TEXT

→ Rezeption: Leseverstehen, S. 214

Write out the main points about balancing a job and a family that the text mentions.

2 DISCUSSION

→ Interaktion, S. 246

Discuss with a partner.

1 Do you agree with Netta's advice? What would *you* tell Alison to do?
2 Would you consider part-time work or job-sharing? Why / Why not?
3 What factors are important to you when choosing a job? (rewarding work? good pay? flexible hours? friendly colleagues? perks like a company car or lunch vouchers? a company nursery?)

3 WRITING

Write a job advertisement for your ideal job. Be realistic! Consider some of the aspects you discussed above.

Job skills 2

CVs and cover letters ▪ interviews

Eric Jung is looking for work in the UK. He applies for a post in London.

1 LOOKING AT THE CV

Compare the information on Eric's CV with the job advertisement. Say why he believes he is a suitable candidate for the position.

TRAINEE OFFICE ASSISTANT – General office duties

- We are a manufacturing company located in London.
- We are looking for a trainee to work in our export office.
- You are a careful and accurate worker, flexible and willing to learn.
- You speak good German and at least one other foreign language.
- Computer skills are a must.

Apply with CV and cover letter to Joan Shaw, Magnus & Klein plc, 1004 Thames Road, London SE7 2XY quoting reference FTD/0204.

Eric Jung
Klarastr. 430 · 79106 Freiburg · Germany
Phone (+49) 0761 234589 · Mobile (+49) 0176 28948610
Email ejung@gmx.com

Personal statement
Highly-motivated student of business studies seeking practical experience in the UK.

Work experience

June – August 20..	Delgado Import/Export, Bristol, England. Duties: general office work (answering telephone; writing emails) and updating spreadsheets.

Education and training

August 20.. – present	Berufskolleg, Freiburg (equivalent to British vocational college) Main subjects: Business Studies, English, German, Spanish Fachhochschulreife (German higher education entrance qualifications): Expected July 20..
August 20.. – July 20..	Realschule, Freiburg (equivalent to British secondary school) Mittlere Reife (Final exams similar to GCSE)

Skills
German (native speaker), English (fluent, oral and written), Spanish (intermediate)
Computer: MS Office
Good at working under pressure, friendly, flexible

Interests
Sport, travel

References
Names of referees available on request

Job skills 2

2 LOOKING AT THE COVER LETTER

A Read Eric's cover letter to Magnus & Klein plc and label the parts 1–10.

body of the letter ▪ complimentary close ▪ date ▪ enclosure ▪ inside address ▪ reference ▪ salutation ▪ signature ▪ subject line ▪ writer's address

Klarastr. 430
79106 Freiburg
Germany **1**
Phone (+49) 0761 234589
Mobile (+49) 0176 28948610
Email ejung@gmx.com

Magnus & Klein plc
Attn: Ms Joan Shaw
1004 Thames Road **2**
London
SE7 2XY
UK

5 April 20.. **3**

Your ref: FTD/0204 **4**

Dear Ms Shaw **5**

Trainee Office Assistant **6**

I would like to apply for the position of Trainee Office Assistant as advertised in today's copy of the *Financial Times Deutschland*. **7**

As you can see from my CV, I am currently doing business studies at a German vocational college. During my work placement in a British import/export company, I had the opportunity to learn business practices and I am keen to add to my experience of international business by working further in an English-speaking country.

In addition to German, which is my native language, I speak fluent English and I have recently added Spanish to my list of foreign languages. I am sure that my language abilities will make me an asset to your team.

I would appreciate it if you considered my application and hope that you will grant me an interview.

I look forward to hearing from you soon.

Yours sincerely **8**

Eric Jung

Eric Jung **9**

Encl: CV **10**

B Find the following sections in the body of the letter. Write out the key phrases in your notebook.

1. asking to be considered for an interview
2. reference to details on CV
3. reference to the position
4. saying why the writer is applying for the position
5. stating why the applicant is the best person for the job

3 WRITING A COVER LETTER

You are going to work with a partner, compile your CV and write a cover letter.

1. **Study the job advertisement on page 75 or choose one from page 66 and answer the following questions.**
   - What is the job title?
   - Who is advertising the job?
   - Where will the job applicant work?
   - What educational background and skills does the job applicant need?
   - How do you apply?
2. **You and your partner are both going to apply for the job. Compile your own CV in English and write a cover letter. Use any items from Eric's CV and cover letter that are appropriate for you. When you have finished, exchange your CVs and cover letters and do peer correction.**

1. **With your partner, talk about what you would like to do in the future. Talk about where you would like to work and what type of work you would like to do. Make some notes and use them to write a short job advertisement. Pin it on the wall.**
2. **Choose one of the job advertisements from the wall and discuss it with your partner. You and your partner are both going to apply for the job. Compile your own CV in English and write a cover letter. Use any items from Eric's CV and cover letter that are appropriate for you. When you have finished, exchange your CVs and cover letters and do peer correction.**

German school types and qualifications

Grundschule	primary school
Realschule	secondary school
Gymnasium	secondary/grammar school (GB), high school (USA)
Berufsschule	vocational school
Berufskolleg, Fachoberschule	vocational college
Fachhochschule	university of applied sciences
Mittlere Reife	GCSE (General Certificate of Secondary Education)
Abitur	A levels (GB), high school diploma (USA)
Fachhochschulreife	German higher education entrance qualifications
Noten 1–6	Grades A–F

Job skills 2

4 PREPARING FOR AN INTERVIEW

The HR office at Magnus & Klein has informed Eric that Ms Shaw will interview him on the phone next week. He prepares himself by making a list of questions Ms Shaw might ask him. He also thinks about what he would like to know from Ms Shaw.

A With a partner, study the list of typical interview questions and sort them under the correct heading. Then add one more question under each heading.

- About yourself
- About your motivation
- About your education, work experience and skills

1 Can you tell me something about yourself?
2 Why do you want to work for this company?
3 What are your strengths and weaknesses?
4 Why are you training at vocational college?
5 Why do you think you would be a good candidate for the job?
6 What have you learned that might help you in the position you're applying for here?

B Now study Eric's list of questions. With your partner, add two more questions.

- Who will I report to?
- When will I hear if I have the job or not?
- What kind of training will I be given?

TIP Using first names

Don't be surprised if a superior calls you by your first name when doing business in Anglo-American countries. It is best if you use *Ms* or *Mr* when speaking to superiors until they invite you to use their first name.

5 LISTENING

→ Rezeption: Hörverstehen, S. 225

2/2

A Listen to the main part of the interview. Which questions does Ms Shaw ask? How does Eric answer the questions? Make notes.

B Listen to the conclusion of the interview. What does Eric want to know? What is the next step in the application process?

6 ROLE-PLAY

→ Interaktion: Ein Rollenspiel gestalten, S. 247

Work with a partner. Use the role cards below to practise an interview for a job.

Partner A: you are the interviewer

You are going to interview your partner as if he/she is a candidate for a job. Start the interview by introducing yourself then ask the following questions.

- How would you describe yourself?
- What are your strengths and weaknesses?
- Why did you decide to study business management?
- Do you have any questions for me?

Partner B: you are the candidate

Your partner is going to interview you for a job. Think about the questions the interviewer might ask you. Make notes. When the interviewer asks you if you have any questions, choose two or three from this list.

- Who will I work with?
- What training will you give me?
- What will my responsibilities be?
- When will I hear if my application has been successful or not?

9 Multiculturalism

MAIN COURSE

FOCUS

A **The photos above show festivals in Vancouver, Canada. Describe the people and what they are doing. What cultural backgrounds might these people have?**

to carry ▪ to dance ▪ to light ▪ to march ▪ to perform
balloon ▪ candle ▪ dragon ▪ headdress ▪ lantern ▪ pipe band ▪ samba ▪ sari
Chinese ▪ Indian ▪ Hindu ▪ Irish ▪ Latin American

B **Match photos 1–4 with the festivals in the cultural programme on the right. Make statements to a visitor.**

If you visit Vancouver in early February, you can go to the Chinese New Year and (see) …

February	Chinese New Year (lion dance, Tai Chi, dragon boat display)
March	St Patrick's Day Parade (march, music, ceilidhs)
Mid-summer	Carnaval Del Sol (Latin American dancing, cuisine, crafts)
Mid-autumn	Diwali (dancing, lanterns, traditional music, cuisine)

C **Work with a partner. Think of local festivals that a visitor to your part of the world might enjoy. Create a calendar of events and then make statements to a visitor.**

If you visit … (place) in … (time of year), you can …

D **Work with your partner again. List some of the different cultures in Germany today. Discuss any way that you get to know, or learn about, people from other cultures.**

Say what changes you think these cultures bring to the traditional German way of life.

TEXT A Life as a refugee

BEFORE YOU READ

→ Vorbereitung auf das Lesen, S. 214

A **Look at a map. What parts of the world would you probably cross on a flight from Germany to Eritrea?**

B **Look at the information about Eritrea and about the boy in the picture. Why might he be a refugee?**

Eritrea:
Independent East African state on the Red Sea coast. Separated from Ethiopia after violent fighting in 1999–2000.

Family name
Kelo
Given name
Alem
Father's nationality
Ethiopian
Mother's nationality
Eritrean

2/3

refugee boy

BENJAMIN ZEPHANIAH

Ethiopia

As the family lay sleeping, soldiers kicked down the door of the house and entered, waving their rifles around and shouting. Alem ran into the room where his parents were, to find that they had been dragged out of bed and forced to stand facing the wall.

The soldier who was in command went and stood so that his mouth was six inches away from Alem's father's ear and shouted, 'What kind of man are you?'

Alem's father shuddered with fear; his voice trembled as he replied, 'I am an African.'

Alem looked on terrified as the soldier shot a number of bullets into the floor around the feet of his father and mother.

His mother screamed with fear. 'Please leave us! We only want peace.'

The soldier continued shouting. 'Are you Ethiopian or Eritrean? Tell us, we want to know.'

'I am an African,' Alem's father replied.

The soldier raised his rifle and pointed it at Alem's father. 'You are a traitor.' He turned and pointed the rifle at Alem's mother. 'And she is the enemy.' Then he turned and pointed the rifle at Alem's forehead. 'And he is a mongrel.'

Turning back to Alem's father he dropped his voice and said, 'Leave Ethiopia or die.'

Background to the next part of Alem's life

The Kelo family moved to Eritrea, but equally bad things happened to them there. That was when Alem's parents decided that they must get him to safety in the UK. His father took him there and left him, knowing that because his son was without a parent, the system would look after him well. His plan succeeded: the authorities found Alem a welcoming family to live with – the Fitzpatricks – and soon he was beginning a new life, complete with a new school and new friends.

Then came terrible news. While Alem and his father had been gone, 'very evil people' had killed Alem's mother and left her dead near the border. After his return to Eritrea, Alem's father had finally found her body and wrote that he must now get to Britain to be with him.

The law was not so kind to Mr Kelo. When he arrived, the authorities arrested him and sent him first to a detention centre and then to a cheap hotel that was used for refugees and homeless families. It was an unpleasant, unhappy place in a poor part of London.

And then the rules for Alem suddenly changed – for he had a parent to look after him now. The courts said that he had to leave his new family and move into his father's small hotel room. Soon, he was learning the life of normal refugees – shopping, for example.

Britain

They didn't spend very long at the supermarket; all they put in their basket was a small amount of vegetables, some tinned meat and a packet of biscuits. As they were queuing for the cashier, Alem noticed that other checkouts were less busy.

'Father, look at those other counters! Why are we waiting in this long queue? Let's go to one of them.'

Mr Kelo's eyes dropped as he realized that Alem hadn't understood the deal. 'We can't,' he said, 'we don't have any money.'

'So what are you paying with?'

Mr Kelo took out his wallet and pulled out what looked like tickets. 'These, I have to pay with these. These are vouchers; look up there.'

He pointed to a sign above the counter where they were waiting. It read, 'Food vouchers only.'

'What is this all about?' Alem asked.

'These vouchers are for asylum seekers. We cannot buy clothes with them, we cannot get any change from our shopping with them, and we cannot use them at any other counter.'

The queue was long and full of exactly the same kind of people Alem had seen outside the courtrooms, Asians, Africans, Romanians and Kosovans, all waiting with their heads hanging down, looking humiliated. Meanwhile, many other cashiers were sitting filing their nails or combing their hair, waiting for customers. Other shoppers just seemed to be a lot happier and some looked over to the 'Vouchers only' queue as if the customers there were exhibition pieces.

Alem could also see the humiliation on his father's face but as for himself he felt angry; he didn't want to show it but he felt really angry. His father was a qualified person who had been in a good job and always proud to have earned every penny he had, but now he had been reduced to what amounted to living off aid. Alem looked up and down the queue, he wondered how many people there were in the same position. Which of the men and women were doctors, lawyers, nurses or mathematicians? Could he be standing next to one of Bosnia's most promising architects, or an Iranian airline pilot? His father saw him silently shake his head in disgust as they shuffled down the line. (813 words)

From: Benjamin Zephaniah, *refugee boy*, Bloomsbury, London, 2001

1 LOOKING AT THE TEXTS

→ Rezeption: Leseverstehen, S. 214

A Put these events from Alem's life in the correct order.

- **a** Alem's move to England
- **b** his mother's death
- **c** the move to Eritrea
- **d** living in England with his father
- **e** living in Ethiopia with his parents
- **f** living in England with the Fitzpatricks
- **g** his father's move to England

B Answer the questions below on the extracts from *refugee boy*.

→ Gründliches Lesen, S. 223

BUILDING SKILLS: Reading for understanding

In order to answer questions on the text, you usually have to read the text closely for understanding.

- First, read the questions carefully so that you know exactly what you have to find out.
- Look for key words in the questions that will help you to find the relevant areas of the text.
- Read these pieces of the text sentence by sentence to find the answers.
- Finally, check your answers. Read them carefully and compare them to the questions and the text to make sure that you have given the details requested.

1 What does Alem's father call himself, and what point is he trying to make to the soldier?
2 What name does the soldier call each member of Alem's family, and why?
3 What three things happen to Alem after his father leaves him in Britain on his own?
4 What three things happen to Alem when his father comes back to Britain to be with him?
5 When they join the checkout queue, why does Alem suggest joining a different queue?
6 Why is this impossible?
7 How does the situation make everyone in the queue feel?
8 Why does it affect people like Alem's father especially badly?

C Say what you think.

1 If you were in the same dangerous situation as Alem's parents, what would you do? Would you keep your young son with you and try to protect him yourself – or would you send him far away to somewhere safe, but unknown?
2 If you were in Alem's position, which decision would you prefer?

2 WORKING WITH WORDS

A Match words in box A to similar words from the texts in box B.

A average ▪ line ▪ opposite ▪ place ▪ recognize	**B** facing ▪ normal ▪ position ▪ queue ▪ realize

B Now choose the correct word to complete each sentence.

1 **a** The trees stand in a long ___[1] beside the road. (line/queue)
b I'm sorry, but you can't jump the ___[2]. Go to the back and wait for your turn. (line/queue)
2 **a** We hadn't met for five years, but I ___[1] her immediately. (realized/recognized)
b I was half-way to the airport when I ___[2] that I'd forgotten my passport. (realized/recognized)
3 **a** Jim spoke after Carol at the meeting, and he presented the ___[1] argument. (facing/opposite)
b The task ___[2] us today will be the hardest one of all. (facing/opposite)
4 **a** I always play in goal. What ___[1] do you play? (place/position)
b My home town is a lovely old ___[2]. You should come and see it. (place/position)
5 **a** Why does that child always behave so badly? It isn't ___[1]! (average/normal)
b Statistics show that ___[2] pay has risen by 2.5% in the last year. (average/normal)

C **Copy and complete the tables. Find the words in the texts.**

Verb	Noun
to live	▬
▬	decision
▬	success
▬	earnings
▬	reduction

Noun	Adjective
▬	safe
▬	humiliated
qualification	▬
pride	▬
promise	▬

D **Now use the pairs of words to complete the following. Make any necessary changes.**

1 **A** Your sister hasn't had much ▬[1] with her new business yet, has she?
B No, but things are slowly getting better, and I know she'll ▬[2] in the end.
2 All those books that you've put on top of that cupboard don't look ▬[1]! I'm sure you're breaking the company's health and ▬[2] rules.
3 **A** We're spending too much money, so we'll have to make some ▬[1].
B Well, let's ▬[2] what we spend on going out.
4 I have never felt so ▬[1] before. The ▬[2] of having to buy food with vouchers was more than I could take!
5 **A** Is Joe ▬[1] as a doctor yet?
B Yes, he got his basic ▬[2] last year.
6 We can't yet make any ▬[1] about how successful this new cure for malaria will be, but our latest test results are ▬[2].
7 Things are so expensive! We all need to ▬[1] more money. The cost of living is going up faster than people's ▬[2].
8 **A** What have you ▬[1] to do with the old TV?
B We've made a ▬[2] to sell it on eBay.
9 My great-grandfather had a very long ▬[1]. He ▬[2] from 1911 to 2010.
10 Helen takes real ▬[1] in her school work. She should be especially ▬[2] of her excellent Maths and Science results this year.

3 GETTING IT RIGHT

→ Past perfect ▪ Simple past, S. 256

Put the verbs in brackets into the simple past or the past perfect.

Alem's father (choose) ▬[1] to take him to Britain even though they (never / be) ▬[2] there before. Once the two of them (land) ▬[3] in London, they (take) ▬[4] a taxi from the airport. They (go) ▬[5] to a small hotel outside London which Mr Kelo (book) ▬[6] the week before. Alem (love) ▬[7] their visit to London the next day: he (never / see) ▬[8] a city like it before. However, when he (wake up) ▬[9] the next morning back at the hotel, his father (disappear) ▬[10].

At first, Alem (just / think) ▬[11] that his father (go) ▬[12] downstairs to arrange breakfast. But then, after he (wait) ▬[13] for a long time, the manager (come) ▬[14] to the room with a letter from his father. The manager (tell) ▬[15] Alem that his father (pay) ▬[16] and (leave) ▬[17] the hotel early that morning. Alem (learn) ▬[18] from the letter that his father (go) ▬[19] in order to return to Ethiopia. He slowly (understand) ▬[20] that his father (bring) ▬[21] him to England for one reason only – because he would be safe there.

TEXT B The question of integration

BEFORE YOU READ

A **What seems to be the purpose of the *Say it how you see it* website?**

B **Would you ever join an online discussion like this? What sort of subjects would you be interested in discussing?**

http://www.sayithowyouseeit.au

2/4

Say it how you see it

This week's question: What now for multiculturalism?

So once again, Australians are talking about that 1970s government policy of multiculturalism – the idea that we can all live together in harmony with our different cultures and even languages. Well, can we?

Aussie Joe says:

I wish our government had the guts to pass a law to say 'our way or no way'. If people reject our culture and law, then we should deport them immediately – back to the country they came from. We don't want violent gangs on our streets, and we don't want Muslim extremists to take over with their Sharia laws.

If the government had acted years ago, we'd have saved ourselves a lot of trouble already. And if we don't act now, it'll be the end of Australia as we know it and love it.

Jenny says:

Calm down, Aussie Joe! The world changes and we have to change with it.

Don't pretend that the past was perfect, either. Look back and you'll find there was always crime on our streets. As for extreme Islamists, they're a small minority of a small minority, and most Muslims are as moderate as anyone else.

So instead of panicking, take a quiet look at a list of MPs or business people or any collection of people who have done a lot for this country. Then count the non-Anglo names. Since the old Anglo-Irish days, we've had wave after wave of immigrants, and many of them and their descendants have made real contributions – and they have all done so under a national policy of multiculturalism. And for most of us it's been a two-way street: we've accepted them and they've accepted us. If we hadn't, we wouldn't have developed the culture that we have today – a culture that's vibrant, pretty peaceful and very varied.

So, Aussie Joe, go outside and enjoy it instead of hiding in your negative little Anglo-culture box!

Mark says:

Vibrant … peaceful … varied, yes, but don't put that down to multiculturalism.

The way I understand it, multiculturalism gives ethnic groups the right to live by their own culture and not even learn English. Well, that may be politically correct, but I think you'll find the immigrants who've made big contributions haven't lived that way. If they had, they wouldn't have been able to make those contributions to mainstream society. They'd have been hidden away in their cultural ghettos, wouldn't they?

No, they've done something else over the years. They've worked hard to become Australian. They've integrated.

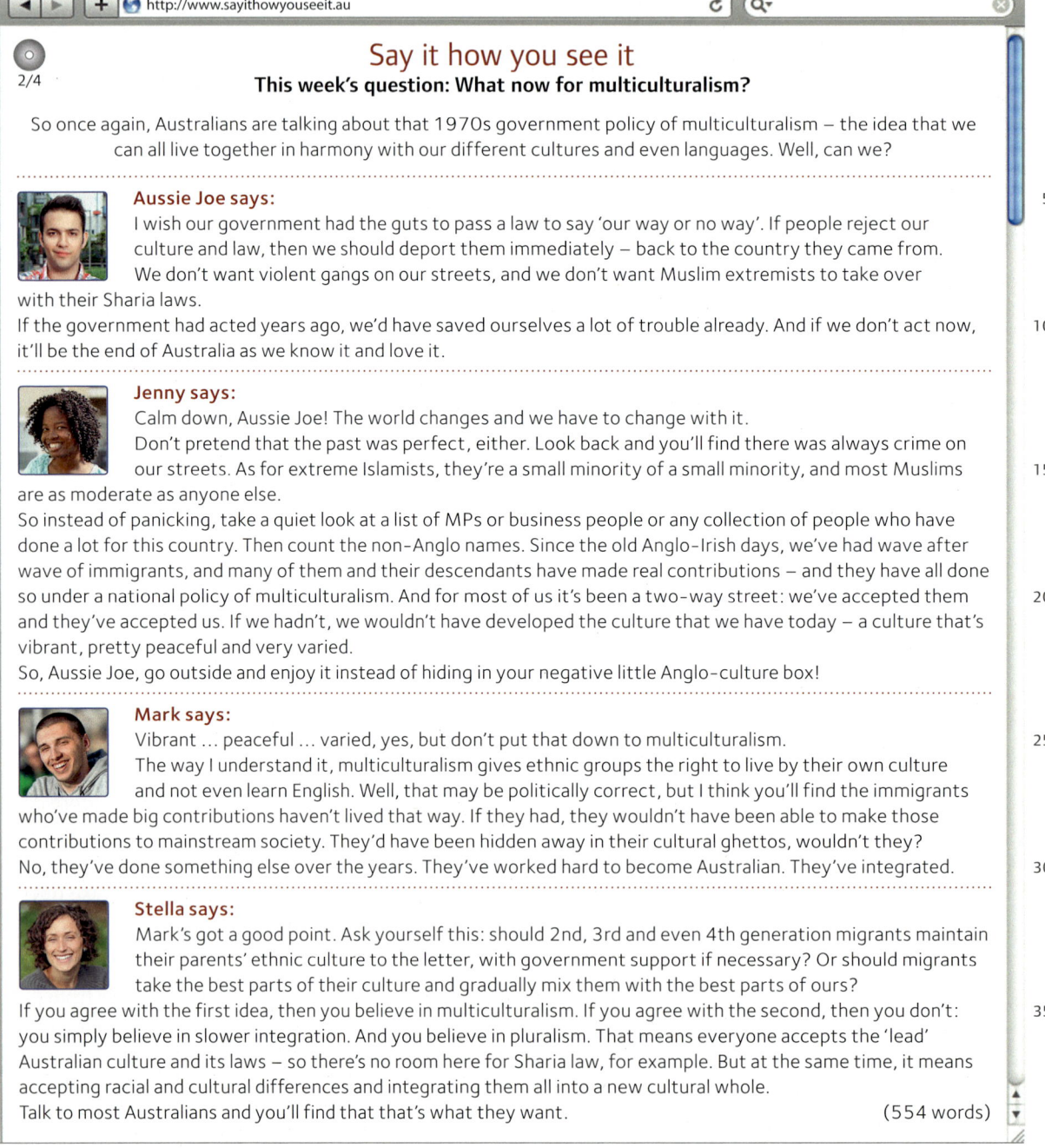

Stella says:

Mark's got a good point. Ask yourself this: should 2nd, 3rd and even 4th generation migrants maintain their parents' ethnic culture to the letter, with government support if necessary? Or should migrants take the best parts of their culture and gradually mix them with the best parts of ours?

If you agree with the first idea, then you believe in multiculturalism. If you agree with the second, then you don't: you simply believe in slower integration. And you believe in pluralism. That means everyone accepts the 'lead' Australian culture and its laws – so there's no room here for Sharia law, for example. But at the same time, it means accepting racial and cultural differences and integrating them all into a new cultural whole.

Talk to most Australians and you'll find that that's what they want. (554 words)

1 LOOKING AT THE TEXT

→ Rezeption: Leseverstehen, S. 214

A Say which person (or people) expresses each idea. Explain your answers.

1 I believe that the government's programme of multiculturalism has worked well.
2 I believe that gradual cultural integration is the right way for Australia.
3 I am against the idea that immigration means more crime.
4 I am against mixing new cultures with the traditional national culture.
5 I support cultural 'give and take' between the old and the new.
6 I support throwing out any immigrants who do not accept the Australian way of life or who break the law.

B Say whether the following are true or false. Correct the false statements.

1 Aussie Joe seems to believe that all the members of violent street gangs are immigrants.
2 He says that a law against all immigration was needed a long time ago.
3 Jenny argues that non-Anglo-Irish immigrants have done most for today's Australia.
4 She feels that the many waves of immigration have led to a varied and lively culture.
5 Mark says that multiculturalism forces immigrants to integrate into mainstream society.
6 Stella agrees with the government's policy towards immigrants.
7 She points out that most Australians believe in accepting cultural differences and adding the best of them to the traditional Australian way of life.

C Say what it means: Explain the underlined expressions in your own words.

1 … pass a law to say 'our way or no way'. (line 6)
2 And for most of us it's been a two-way street … (line 20)
3 … maintain their parents' ethnic culture to the letter … (line 33)
4 … everyone accepts the 'lead' Australian culture … (line 36)
5 … there's no room here for Sharia law … (line 37)

2 WORKING WITH WORDS

A Find words in the text that are the opposite of the following:

accept ▪ peaceful ▪ moderate ▪ majority ▪ similarity

B Now complete the following with pairs of words from exercise 2A.

1 The black ▬ [1] in South Africa forms 70% of the population while at 17%, white South Africans form the largest single ▬ [2].
2 We've ▬ [1] Plans A and C mainly because they're too expensive, but we've ▬ [2] Plan B because it offers a very good way forward and also because the price is right.
3 The struggles in Northern Ireland were very ▬ [1] for many years, and many died. However, life there is much more ▬ [2] today, thank goodness.
4 There are lots of ▬ [1] between the old GR70 and the new GR71, and they look almost the same. The most important ▬ [2] is the new car's much more powerful engine.
5 During the French Revolution, people with ▬ [1] ideas took control. For them, anyone who was not with them was against them, and they did not listen to more ▬ [2] views.

3 GETTING IT RIGHT

→ *If* sentences, S. 264

Form type 3 *if* sentences. Start each sentence with *if*.

1 Franz and Ana Beckman were very poor. They moved from their country village to Hamburg to find work.
If Franz and Ana Beckman had not been very poor, they would not have moved from …
2 They moved to Hamburg. Franz found a good job in the shipyards there.
3 He found a good job. They were able to save a lot of money.
4 They had money in the bank. They were able to have a long holiday in Australia.
5 They travelled round Australia. They fell in love with the country.
6 They decided to emigrate to Australia. They had the chance to take over a small boat building company in Sydney.
7 Franz had the skills to build up the business. The company became a big success.
8 The Beckmans moved away from their poor home village many years before. This immigrant success story happened.

Rewrite the underlined information in the following statements as type 3 *if* sentences.

1  The trouble is that the Australian government refused to deport criminal immigrants in the past. I think deportation was the right way for us to avoid most of our problems with immigration.
If the Australian government had not refused to deport …
2  It was a very good thing that Australia opened its doors to immigration from many more countries. When that happened, we were able to escape from our tired old Anglo culture.
3 Vancouver has become a great city of ethnic festivals. It has happened because immigrants from around the world have made it their home.
4 Vancouver attracted a large Chinese population in the 19th century. As a result of that, the city became Canada's only important port on the Pacific coast.
5 His parents made sure that Alem was safe from the fighting by sending him away.
6 It was very sad that Alem's mother did not go with her husband and son to England. Because of that, she died in the fighting while they were away.

4 LISTENING

→ Rezeption: Hörverstehen, S. 225

You are going to listen to a discussion between Joan Carr, a Member of Parliament, and Tom Baker, an author, about immigration to the UK.

2/5 **A Copy the list and listen to the first part of the discussion. Note the figures that Tom Baker gives.**

Immigrant % of total population:
- *UK:* ▬ • *Germany:* ▬ • *Austria:* ▬ • *Switzerland:* ▬

Jobs:
- *New jobs in future:* ▬ • *People retiring 2010–2020:* ▬

Welfare:
- *Immigrant unemployment since 2010:* ▬
- *Immigrants claiming unemployment benefits:* ▬

Housing:
- *New households per year: approx.* ▬
- *New immigrant households per year: approx.* ▬

2/6

B **Now listen to the second part of the discussion and make notes on what Tom Baker and Joan Carr say about social tensions.**

Social tensions
Possible course of action 1: ▬
• Likely effects – 1: ▬ *; 2:* ▬
Possible course of action 2: ▬
• Likely effects – 1: ▬ *; 2:*

5 ANALYSING FIGURES

→ Produktion: Statistiken beschreiben und analysieren, S. 238

BUILDING SKILLS: Describing and analysing statistics

To analyse statistics, you have to know exactly what sort of figures you are dealing with.
- Read the heading, labels and any other form of explanation carefully.
- Check that you understand the units (e.g. thousands, millions, etc.) that the figures are presented in.
- Make sure you know which figures are in these units (e.g. 80.5 million) and which figures are percentages (e.g. 14.7%) of a total.

A **Copy the table and complete it with the figures from your notes in exercise 4A.**

Populations of selected European countries (millions)

Country	Total	Immigrants	Percentage
Germany	80.5	9.8	▬
Britain	64.1	7.8	▬
Austria	8.5	1.3	▬
Switzerland	8.1	2.3	▬

1 Explain what the numbers in columns 2 and 3 mean.
2 Contrast the types of information in columns 3 and 4.

B **Use statistics from the table in 5A to complete this paragraph.**

Nearly all European countries, big and small, have taken in many immigrants – especially in recent years. For example, Germany, with its very large population of over ▬[1] million, is also home to a little under ▬[2] million immigrants, or more than ▬[3] % of the total. Again, Switzerland, with its much smaller population of just over ▬[4] million, is host to more than ▬[5] million immigrants, which is well over ▬[6] % of the total population.

C **Now interpret the figures for Britain and Austria in the same way. Use approximate numbers, e.g. *64.1 million → over 64 million*.**

Start like this:
Similarly, the United Kingdom, with its large population of … . At the same time, Austria, with its much smaller population of around eight and a half …

6 WRITING

→ Produktion: Eine Stellungnahme schreiben, S. 234

Use your notes from exercise 4 and the figures from exercise 5 to write a short comment on the immigration situation in Britain.

Culturally sensitive care

4/6

Thomas I'm still studying nursing at college, but I have some concerns about how women feel about being treated by me, a male nurse. I'm very eager to make sure my patients are comfortable with the level of care I provide. And one of my other concerns is that Muslims, especially women, do not believe males should do the job of a nurse and therefore refuse to be treated by us. Is this true? If so, how can I deal with such a situation?

Arisha Hi Thomas, I'm Muslim so maybe I can help answer your question. First of all, thank you for asking such a question – it shows you have a caring personality. Muslims don't really have a view in regards to males being care providers in general. However, given the high status modesty holds in our religion, it is better that a male nurse does not care for a female patient and vice versa. Nursing is a very intimate profession. We touch people and we see body parts that aren't usually seen in any other profession.

Jenny I am not a Muslim, but I have cared for both male and female Muslim patients. I always ask this: "Is there anything I can do to make sure your needs are met?" I always let a patient know that I am here to care for them, and I inform them that I am very respectful of their needs, whatever their religion or culture.

Mattias I am not Muslim either but I still prefer being cared for by a male doctor. I understand that this is not always possible, but I am gay and I find that I can talk to male nurses and doctors more easily. However, as I mentioned, this is not always possible and, in the end, it is the quality of care that matters and not the gender of the person.

Kareem I am also a male nurse and a Muslim. In my experience Muslim men are grateful if they have a male nurse looking after them, because it is not just female patients who value modesty, and they may prefer having a male to assist in more "personal care".

Habiba I am Muslim, and I can tell you that Muslims appreciate both men and women in all health care provider roles, whether it's a nurse, doctor, paramedic, etc. I have given birth to three children, two of them in a hospital setting. Yes, I did ask for female nurses and doctors as a preference, but if the people available were males, I didn't make a fuss.

1 LOOKING AT THE TEXT

→ Rezeption: Leseverstehen, S. 214

Read the forum posts and match the people to these comments:

1 "I tell all my Muslim patients that I respect their wishes and needs."
2 "I'd rather have a female nurse but it's not a problem if the nurse is male."
3 "Since modesty is very important in my culture, it is better that a male nurse does not care for a female patient."
4 "It is the quality of care that matters and not whether the nursing staff is male or female."
5 "In my culture, it is not just female patients who are modest."

2 DISCUSSION

→ Interaktion, S. 246

Think: How important is it to be aware of differences of cultures, expectations and wishes, for example when working in kindergartens, doing social work or taking care of the disabled or the elderly? What do you need to be aware of and how do you deal with that?
Pair: Now talk with a partner about your thoughts. Does your partner have a different perspective?
Share: Share your ideas in a group of 4–5 students, then tell the class what conclusions you have reached.

10 Helping others

MAIN COURSE

FOCUS

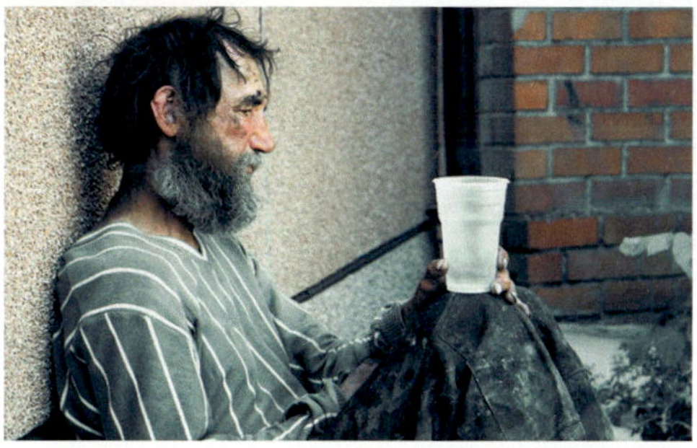

A **Discuss the photos with a partner. Would you help or donate something in each case? Give reasons and report your decisions to the class.**

B **In class, discuss whether people should give money to beggars or not. Before you start, note arguments for and against.**

C **Look at the illustrations below with a partner and think about the different ways of giving help. Think about who gets the help and who gives the help.**

D **Now do these tasks:**

- When did you last help someone? Write a sentence or two to describe what you did.
- When did someone last help you? Describe what happened in a few sentences.
- Exchange stories with your partner.

Useful phrases

- I would give some money/food to homeless people because …
- I wouldn't give any … because …

- to beg (for) …
- to donate (money/clothes/food)
- to make a donation (of …) to charity
- to collect for (people in need)
- a clothing container / collection box

TEXT A Different ways to help

WHILE YOU READ

Match the headings below with the paragraphs (1–5).

Donate ▪ Help people help themselves ▪ Use your fame to help others ▪ Volunteer to be a counsellor ▪ Sponsor a poor child's education

2/7

1 George Clooney is famous for making blockbuster Hollywood movies but he also uses his fame to fight poverty. He and his Ocean's 11 co-stars Don Cheadle, Matt Damon and Brad Pitt, together with producer Jerry Weintraub, have set up a charity called Not On Our Watch, and its mission is to help stop human rights atrocities, such as in the Darfur region of Sudan. The charity invites people to find out about the crises, donate money, lobby politicians and write letters of complaint to companies benefiting from the conflict.

2 World Vision: When Priscilla was a child, a donor many thousands of miles from her Ghanaian village helped pay for her schooling. For years she exchanged letters with her British benefactor. Now she is 20, the charity has stopped the sponsorship and the relationship. 'Last year I wrote to them saying goodbye and thanked them for taking care of me up to this day,' says Priscilla, an accountancy student. 'When I was writing, I was full of tears. Tears were coming from my eyes.' From: *www.bbc.com*

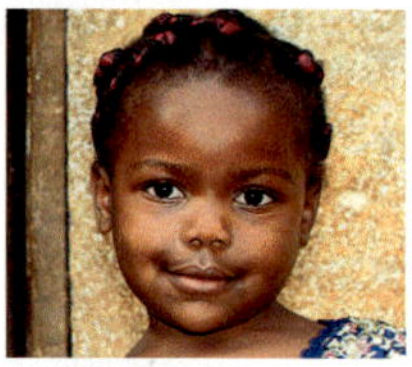

3 MicroLoan Foundation helps some of the poorest women in the world feed their families, send their children to school and pay for life saving medicines. We are a very different kind of charity, offering hope, not handouts. By providing small loans (average £60) and ongoing business training and support, MicroLoan empowers women in rural Malawi and Zambia to set up self-sustainable businesses. The profits from these businesses enable the women to work themselves and their families out of poverty.

From: *www.microloanfoundation.org.uk*

4 You can make an amazing difference at Samaritans. Our volunteers are changing lives every day, and developing valuable skills and friendships along the way. Volunteers are the heart of Samaritans. We welcome and value every volunteer, from all walks of life. Whatever your interests, experience or skills, we have a role for you.
We currently have over 20,000 volunteers giving up a few hours of their time every few weeks to help support people around the UK find their way, through whatever is troubling them. From: *www.samaritans.org*

5 The Salvation Army

£26 could pay for two weekly parent-and-toddler groups where disadvantaged children can play in safety.

£52 could pay to keep a day centre for older people open for a day – providing hot meals and the promise of companionship.

£90 could pay for a bed for a month for a homeless person at one of our Lifehouses – which is often the first step towards rebuilding their lives. (401 words)

From: *www.salvationarmyappeals.org.uk*

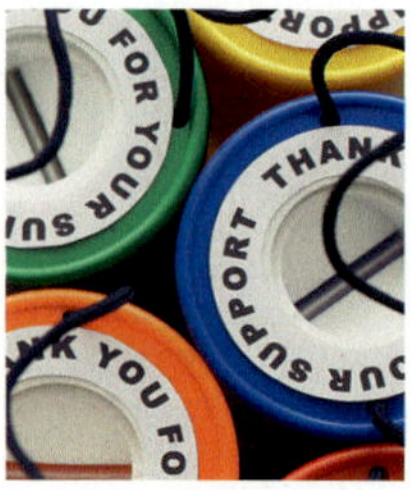

1 LOOKING AT THE TEXTS

→ Rezeption: Leseverstehen, S. 214

A Read the texts and match the charities with the issues they deal with. Note that some charities deal with more than one issue.

Charities	Issues
Not On Our Watch	poverty
World Vision	loneliness
MicroLoan Foundation	homelessness
Samaritans	psychological support
The Salvation Army	armed conflict
	education
	work

SKILLS CHECKLIST: Reading for understanding

- ☑ Have I looked for key words in the questions?
- ☑ Have I found the key words in the text?
- ☑ Have I compared my answers with the questions and the text?

B Decide which of the charities provide help …

- in their home country
- in foreign countries
- in the long term
- in the short term
- by giving people money
- by giving people non-financial help

C Choose two of the charities described and explain how they fight poverty.

2 WORKING WITH WORDS

A Match six of the words in the box with their definitions below.

accountancy ▪ atrocities ▪ benefactor ▪ companionship ▪ conflict ▪ education ▪ disadvantaged ▪ foundation ▪ handouts ▪ loan ▪ poverty ▪ volunteer

1 the situation you are in when you have no money
2 someone who donates money to help others
3 keeping a list of a person's or company's financial data
4 an organization which has been set up to finance activities for the good of society
5 not having the money and opportunities that other people have
6 what you get when you have friends

Write definitions for the six words not needed above.

Do not write the word. Give your definitions to a partner. Can he or she find the correct words? (If your partner can find the words, your definitions were good!)

B Complete the text with six of the words in exercise 2A. Make any necessary changes.

In the USA many successful people 'give back' to society and become ▬ 1 by setting up a ▬ 2. Bill and Melinda Gates did so in 2000 in order to help ▬ 3 people all over the world. Their organization's focus is on two things: reducing extreme ▬ 4 and poor health in developing countries where the poorest people in the world live and improving the American ▬ 5 system in order to give youngsters a better start in life. If you want to work as a ▬ 6, you can find links on the organization's website.

3 ANALYSING FIGURES

→ Produktion: Schaubilder beschreiben und analysieren, S. 238

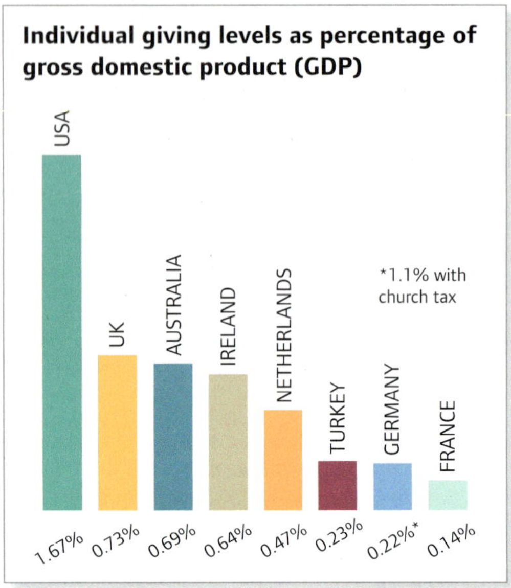

A Here in the States we don't wait for the government to solve our problems. We solve them ourselves! We give to charity, help in the community and raise money for good causes. Last year the parents and students at our local school collected $10,000 to pay for a disabled child to have surgery. That child can now walk without help. Anyone can help. Just do it!

B I'm a volunteer for the church charity you see at many stations all over Germany. We help anyone in need, regardless of their religious beliefs. The help we give is sometimes just a train time but it can also be a hot meal and a bed for the night for a homeless person. Most of our funding comes from the church, which is financed by church tax.

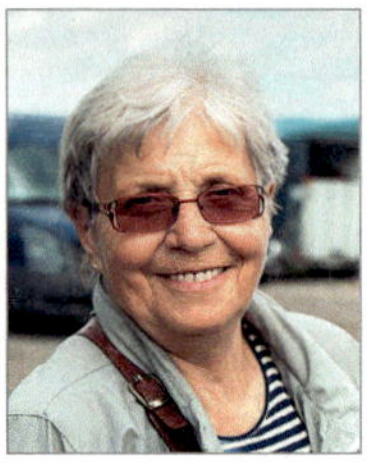

C I work very hard in my restaurant but I pay a lot of money in tax to the government here in Turkey, so I'm not rich! Unfortunately, there are many poor people everywhere, even children as young as four or five begging in the streets, so I give what I can when I see people in need. Sometimes I give them food or money, but when business is bad I have nothing to give.

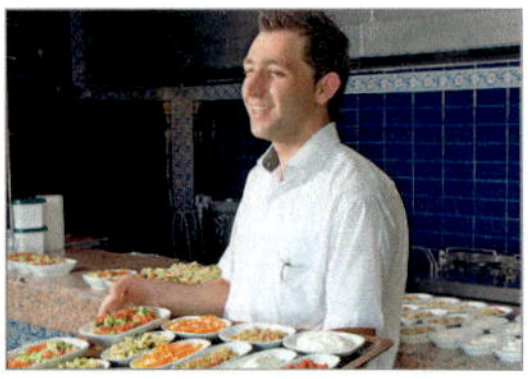

D In France more than 50% of our income goes on tax! I feel sorry for people in need, both at home and abroad but I believe that helping is the responsibility of the government, not mine. That's why my vote goes to the politicians who promise to spend more money on fighting poverty.

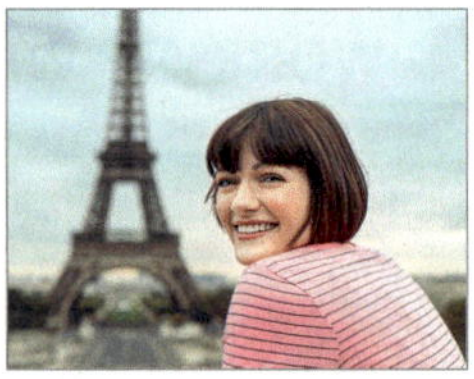

A Read the four statements and do the following tasks:

1 Describe how many Americans believe it is best to help people in need.
2 Explain how the church charity at German train stations is mainly staffed and funded.
3 List the factors which influence how much and when the Turkish restaurant owner gives to people in need.
4 Contrast the French and American attitude to charitable giving.

BUILDING SKILLS: Comparing figures in charts

When describing charts, it is important to be able to compare and contrast the different figures.

- Always name the factors which a bar chart or line graph compares ('x' and 'y' axis): *The chart above is about percentages and countries.*
- Look for and point out the most striking features: *We can clearly see a progression from France at 0.14% to the USA at 1.67%.*
- Contrast the categories with each other: *The UK is in second place while Turkey only ranks 6th.*
- Describe the relationships between the categories: *The value for Australia is three times as high as for Turkey.*

B Look at the bar chart on page 92 and say …

1 where individual giving is highest and lowest.
2 where Germany stands in the list.
3 how high individual giving is in Germany with and without church tax.
4 which two countries have almost the same level of personal giving.
5 what the bar chart shows very clearly.

C Describe the chart and say what it tells us about the different attitudes to individual giving in the different countries.

Useful phrases

- There is a clear progression from … to …
- We can clearly see the difference/similarity between … and …
- The value in the first column is far greater/less than …
- twice / three times / four times as big as …
- half the size of …
- the highest/lowest
- in first/last place / in the last place but one / in the middle

4 CLASS PROJECT

Your class decides to support a charity offering help to people with one of the problems listed in exercise 1A (poverty, loneliness, homelessness, psychological support, armed conflict, education, work), or your own idea.

Follow these steps to carry out the project:

1 Make a list of all the charities, people or projects you could support and choose one.
2 Decide how you will give support, for example by …
   - raising money with a sponsored walk or by selling food/cakes at an event.
   - giving practical help, such as going shopping, doing gardening.
   - donating or collecting clothes, giving or selling food.

   Or think of some ideas of your own.
3 Divide the class into smaller groups of three or four students and give each group a job.
4 Agree a target, for example €100 by the end of the month or (school) year, and start work.
5 If your class decides not to support a project, summarize your reasons in a few sentences.

5 WRITING

→ Produktion: Schreiben, S. 228

Write a blog entry about your class project for your school's website. Include these points:

- why your class chose this project
- how you helped
- feedback from the people you helped

For more advice, read the notes for exercise 4 on page 38.

Think of your own example of a charity event and describe it in an email to an English-speaking pen friend.

TEXT B A charity in action

BEFORE YOU READ

→ Scannen nach Einzelinformationen im Text, S. 221

Scan the texts to find …

- the meaning of *orphans* and *orphanage*.
- the link between *flip-flops* and *Gandys*.

Orphans for Orphans

2/8

On Boxing Day in 2004, when the tsunami struck the little fishing village of Weligama on the southern coast of Sri Lanka, Rob (17) and Paul (15) Forkan were asleep in their hotel room. Their parents, Kevin and Sandra, and their two other siblings, Matty (12) and Rosie (8) were next door. Suddenly, Rob heard screams and saw water coming in under the door. Seconds later the first huge wave hit their hotel room smashing everything in its path. The two boys managed to climb onto the roof and they found their little brother, Matty, in a tree nearby. Later that day, they found their sister, Rosie, but their parents had been swept away whilst saving their two younger children. Despite this terrible blow and narrowly escaping death themselves, the four orphans managed to hitch-hike 200 km to the British Embassy in Colombo and then flew home to rejoin their two older sisters in the UK, one of whom adopted the younger children and gave them a home.

Paul Forkan with some of the orphans, 2013

Many other children would have lost their way in life after such a terrible tragedy but Kevin and Sandra Forkan had always brought their children up to think of the needs of others first, which ultimately gave them the strength to survive themselves. They took their four youngest children out of school when Paul and Rob were 11 and 13 and moved to Goa in India to work on humanitarian projects. They did a great deal of voluntary work, such as helping in orphanages by teaching the children there, playing sports with them, helping them with cooking, handing out food and organizing sports days, whilst at the same time fund-raising for local charities. These activities gave them the confidence to feel that they could do anything and that nothing was hard to achieve. Paul says: 'Our parents gave us the attitude that if you get knocked off your bike, just get back on it. There are always people worse off than you.'

In 2011, after travelling around the world separately, Rob and Paul lived together again in Brixton, South London, and decided to set up a business together. Their inspiration came from Mahatma Gandhi, the father of India's independence movement, who always wore flip-flops. They decided to sell flip-flops called Gandys and use some of the profits to fund social projects in India and Sri Lanka. A description of their company's mission can be found on its website. (419 words)

www.gandysflipflops.com

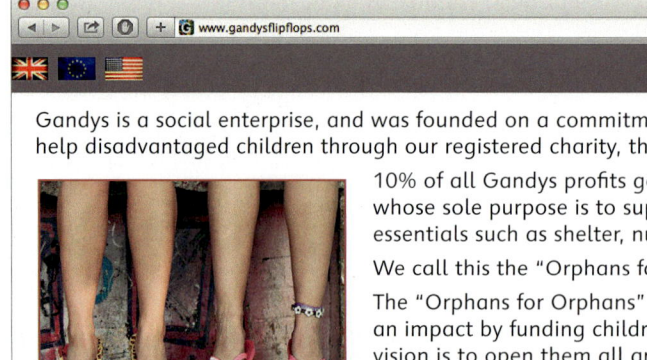

Gandys is a social enterprise, and was founded on a commitment to using a portion of all profits to help disadvantaged children through our registered charity, the Gandys Foundation.

10% of all Gandys profits go directly into the Gandys Foundation, whose sole purpose is to support children in need of basic essentials such as shelter, nutrition, medication and education.

We call this the "Orphans for Orphans" mission.

The "Orphans for Orphans" mission has already started to make an impact by funding children's homes in India & Sri Lanka and the vision is to open them all around the world. The opening of the first children's home will be built in memory of Rob and Paul's parents, Kevin and Sandra Forkan, and will mark the 10th anniversary of the tsunami. (131 words)

From: *www.gandysflipflops.com*

1 LOOKING AT THE TEXTS

→ Rezeption: Leseverstehen, S. 214

A Complete the sentences with information from the texts.

1. The Forkans' hotel was destroyed by …
2. The younger children were adopted by …
3. In Goa, the Forkans did voluntary work for …
4. Helping orphans gave the Forkan children …
5. Before living together in London, Rob and Paul each went on a long trip …
6. Both brothers very much admire …
7. The Gandys Foundation helps children who do not have …
8. Rob and Paul Forkan intend to open …

B Explain to a partner how …

1. the four orphans travelled from Weligama to Colombo.
2. they got help in the UK after the tsunami.
3. their voluntary work gave them confidence.

C Describe the brothers' personal reasons for their choice of charity work.

2 WORKING WITH WORDS

A Use the texts to match the verbs with the nouns to make collocations.

Verb		Noun	
to escape	to set up	an anniversary	death
to do	to make	an impact	work
to raise	to mark	a business	funds

B Find words in the texts to match the definitions.

1. to happen suddenly and have a damaging effect on sb/sth
2. brothers and/or sisters
3. to move suddenly with great force
4. to travel by asking for free rides in other people's cars
5. in the end, finally
6. unpaid; in order to help
7. a way of thinking and behaving
8. to finance
9. a promise
10. intention
11. a strong effect
12. food necessary to be healthy

C Replace the underlined words with some of the answers to exercises 2A and 2B.

When Hurricane Katrina <u>hit</u> [1] the southern coast of the USA on 29 August 2005 it <u>carried</u> [2] away everything in its path. Its <u>effect</u> [3] on the southern states was huge and <u>in the end</u> [4], it became clear that New Orleans' flood-control system had not fulfilled its <u>function</u> [5] and had probably increased the number of <u>fatalities</u> [6], which was at least 1,833. Many NGOs (non-governmental organizations) and citizens put in months of <u>unpaid</u> [7] work to help the victims and <u>collected</u> [8] US$4.25 billion in donations.

3 MEDIATION

→ Schriftliche Mediation, S. 240

Sie möchten *Orphans for Orphans* unterstützen und eine Sammelbestellung für Gandys Flipflops aufgeben. Lesen Sie die Webseite auf Seite 94 noch einmal, dann schreiben Sie einen Aufruf an Ihre Mitschüler/innen in dem Sie erklären, warum sie *Orphans for Orphans* mit einer Bestellung unterstützen sollen.

4 LISTENING

→ Rezeption: Hörverstehen, S. 225

A team of students are making a radio programme about giving to charities. Today, they are conducting a survey in London. They want to hear people's views about giving to charity.

2/9

A Listen to the dialogues and write down the following details for each person:

- occupation
- date of last contribution to charity
- what the contribution was for
- total contribution this year

B Fill in the gaps with words from the interviews.

Interview 1
It'll only ▬ [1] two minutes to answer our questions.
I've ▬ [2] £100 this year.

Interview 2
I've been ▬ [3] at our local church for many years now.
It ▬ [4] a lot of money to run a church.

Interview 3
My husband and I have ▬ ▬ [5] a child in Africa for a number of years now.
We've ▬ ▬ [6] regular payments for the last six years.

Interview 4
I've ▬ ▬ [7] out at a walk-in medical centre for the homeless in south London.
I've ▬ [8] in about 80 hours at the medical centre this year.

5 GETTING IT RIGHT

→ Present perfect ▪ Present perfect progressive, S. 253

Write down the present perfect and present perfect progressive forms of these verbs:

1 I/live (*I've … / I've been …*)
2 she/work
3 you/help
4 they/sponsor
5 we/support
6 you/donate
7 he/collect
8 they/contribute

Expand the notes to make sentences with the present perfect or the present perfect progressive.

1 he / donate more than €1,000 / this year
2 he / talk to her for five minutes
3 people / give her €112.95 since last Monday
4 she / ask for donations since 9 am
5 she / collect / €23.50 today
6 she / collect since early this morning
7 she / stand outside for three hours
8 he / just give her €10

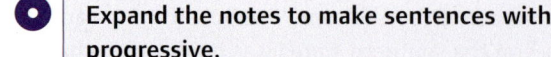

1 LOOKING AT THE TEXTS

→ Rezeption: Leseverstehen, S. 214

A Read the texts and do the following tasks.

1. Contrast globalization's effects on the lives of the people mentioned in the texts. Say which have experienced positive changes and which have been affected negatively.
2. Describe what two of them have recently done to change their lives for the better.
3. Explain what the other two are probably going to do soon to improve their lives.

B Say what it means. Explain the underlined words and phrases in your own words.

1. … deadlines keep getting tighter. (line 14)
2. … if we don't fill the orders … (line 15)
3. Well, enough is enough. (line 18)
4. … production went offshore to Indonesia. (line 21)
5. Some of my co-workers want to stay … (line 35)
6. But a few of us want to go inland … (line 36)

SKILLS CHECKLIST: Dealing with unknown words

- ☑ Have I thought about similar English words?
- ☑ Have I thought about the general meaning of the sentence?

C Say what you think.

1. Look at your answers to exercise 1A again. Which of these things do you think you may need to do to find or to stay in work in the future? Is there anything you would not like to do?
2. What has globalization done for you? (Think about, for example, media or shopping.)
3. Think about globalization and people in work in Germany. What pros and cons do you see from their point of view?

2 WORKING WITH WORDS

A Copy and complete the tables of verb-noun pairs. Find the words in the texts.

Verb	Noun	Verb	Noun	Verb	Noun
to farm	▬	▬	agreement	▬	transformation
to own	▬	to improve	▬	to construct	▬
to employ	▬	to govern	▬	▬	expansion
▬	manufacturer	▬	development	▬	decision

B Use pairs of words from exercise 2A to complete the following.

1. We ▬[1] bikes, and we're one of the biggest bike ▬[2] in Europe.
2. **A** When did you ▬[1] a date for the meeting?
   B I made the ▬[2] a week ago.
3. The company has made big ▬[1] to their product, and they've also ▬[2] the packaging.
4. **A** Who ▬[1] that old house? It looks a mess!
   B The ▬[2] hasn't been seen for three years.
5. The Internet is creating a huge social ▬[1]. It's ▬[2] the way that humans live.
6. In a modern democracy, the people choose a ▬[1], and this then ▬[2] the country for several years – until it is time for the people to decide again.

3 GETTING IT RIGHT

→ The passive, S. 261

Put these sentences into the passive. If you need to mention the subject, use '*by* + agent'.

1. Karl Benz constructed the first successful petrol-driven car in 1885.
   The first successful petrol-driven car was constructed by Karl Benz in 1885.
2. By 1900, engineers had developed various other models across Europe and America.
3. Henry Ford introduced mass-production techniques in 1908.
4. As a result, workers had built over 15 million Ford Model Ts by 1928.
5. Since those early days, personal transport has transformed life around the world.
6. Family cars have given ordinary people the freedom to travel far and wide.
7. Today, companies make over 65 million cars a year in countries all over the world.
8. The Chinese alone produce nearly 20 million of them.
9. Companies export cars for sale in every part of the world.
10. Through exports and international supply chains, the world car industry has created many complex global links.

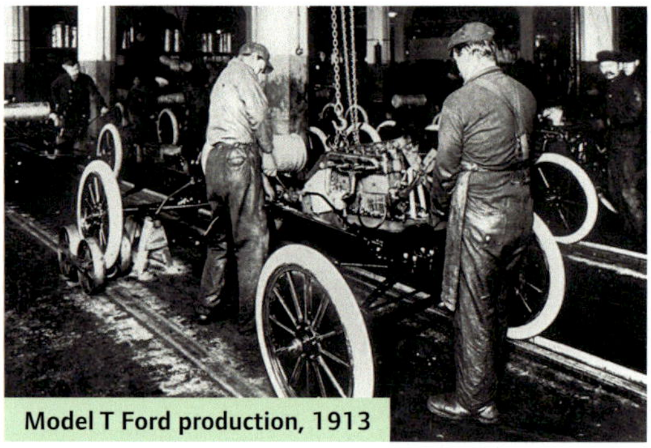
Model T Ford production, 1913

A380 final assembly line in the Jean-Luc Lagardère plant, Toulouse-Blagnac Airport.

Turn the following interview into a more formal news report, using the passive. You should also use more formal linking words/phrases.

So … → As a result, … ▪ But … → However, … ▪ Even so, … → Despite that, …

Start like this:
A number of excellent aircraft had been designed by … . However, …

A So, tell me, how did Airbus begin?
B Well, you see, European aircraft makers had designed a number of excellent aircraft in the 1950s and early 1960s. But they only sold them in small numbers because the American manufacturers were too powerful. So, in the late 1960s, several European governments and plane makers made plans for a shared European project – Airbus Industrie.
A I see. So what happened next?
B Well, after the organization had dealt with many political and technical problems, it finally tested the new A300 in 1972. The Airbus team then took it on a six-week sales tour of South and North America, and this created a lot of interest. Even so, only Lufthansa and Air France had actually bought the A300 by 1974. Then, in September of that year, Airbus finally sold the first four planes outside Europe – to Korean Airlines.

A Wow! I expect everyone was very pleased about that!
B We certainly were! But Airbus only won the first really big prize – an order for 23 A300s – in 1978. That was from America's Eastern Airlines, six years after we had shown the plane to the US market back in 1972.
A Well, things have moved on a long way since then, haven't they?
B They certainly have. Today, Airbus builds the planes' components in factories across Germany, France, Britain, Spain and the Netherlands, and it brings all these parts together in Toulouse. It completes final assembly of all the planes there.
A And that's a lot of planes now, isn't it?
B Yes, since 1972, Airbus has taken over 14,000 orders, and it has delivered over 8,500. The world's airlines now accept these planes as some of the best in the world. So Airbus carries nearly half of all international travellers around the world today.

4 DESCRIBING A CARTOON

→ Produktion: Cartoons beschreiben und analysieren, S. 236

Describe the cartoon and analyse its message. (Look at the second text on page 100 again to help you with background information.)

BUILDING SKILLS: Analysing cartoons

Cartoons often contain cultural references, or references to events in the news.

- Don't panic if you don't understand the reference straight away.
- Particularly in an exam, the necessary information will usually be in a related text in the exam or in a topic that you have dealt with in class.
- Think about what you have read in class, or return to the exam text to check for references.

Useful phrases

- The cartoon consists of three pictures side by side, all under one heading: …
- The cartoon is an ironic comment on …
- First of all, it reminds us that huge numbers of …
- Secondly, it tells us that the employers make … because they spend so little on …
- This brings us to the third 'made in Bangladesh' picture – the collapse of a factory …
- This is a sharp attack on the owners' lack of care for anything except …

TEXT B Where to manufacture products?

BEFORE YOU READ

Does a German brand name on a product always mean that it was made in Germany? Should it? Why / Why not?

2/12

Is it time to start re-shoring our manufacturing industries?

The World This Week reporter Mark Moro is talking to Tim Smith, head of the campaign group Make it in America.

Mark Moro: Is it time to start re-shoring our manufacturing industries – to bring back production that has been done abroad for many years? Tell us about the situation now, Tim.

Tim Smith: Well, let's just remember how bad things were a few years ago. Across the USA and the rest of the industrialized West, more and more jobs were being exported to China and other low-cost countries. It started when cheap producers exported from there to the West and undercut western producers. Our own manufacturers were then forced to send their production offshore, too, just to stay in business. By around the year 2000, about 150,000 American manufacturing jobs were being lost every year. Whole sections of industrial cities like Pittsburgh were turning into wastelands, and unemployment just kept rising. It was the same in parts of Europe too, and it seemed impossible to do anything about it.

Mark Moro: So what's changed?

Tim Smith: Jobs are being brought back from countries like China to the West.

Mark Moro: Why?

Tim Smith: The most important reason is cost. Countries like China aren't low-cost anymore. Wages are rising fast, and other costs are going up too – especially transport. Look. This bar chart shows the cost of making floor care products for a US supermarket chain at home and in China. The chart shows a slight US cost advantage of three per cent. In other words, the job is now being done more cheaply in the USA.

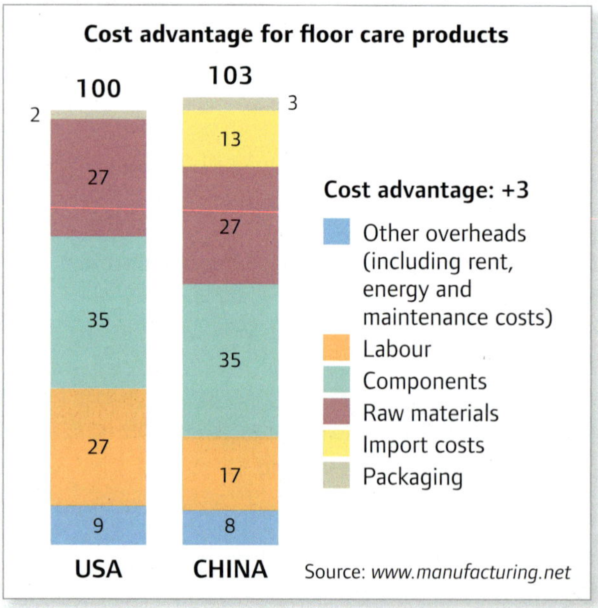

Mark Moro: I see, so wages aren't very much cheaper in China than in America now. And importing all the way from China adds quite a lot to the total bill.

Tim Smith: Right, so production in America actually gives a small cost advantage now.

Mark Moro: And I suppose it's just easier to produce near where you're going to sell.

Tim Smith: Yes, it's better in several ways. It's much faster, and that's important when markets change as quickly as they often do. If lots of customers suddenly want the red model instead of the blue one, the manufacturer needs to meet this demand quickly. But if production is in China, that's not possible. What's more, there may be delays in a long supply chain, so it's necessary to hold extra stock in America – and that's expensive. Breakages and faulty goods just make that problem worse.

Mark Moro: Right, so 150,000 jobs a year were being lost before. What about now?

Tim Smith: Well, more recently about 40,000 jobs were still being exported each year, but about the same number were coming back to this country. And the balance is changing further. In the coming years, some jobs will still go offshore, but many more will be re-shored.

Mark Moro: Can you be certain about that?

Tim Smith: Just look at some of the things that are happening right now. For example, Apple are spending $100 million on new production facilities in the USA instead of offshore. Again, General Electric are bringing home water-heater production from China to Kentucky. Then again, NCR are re-shoring production of cash machines from China, India and Brazil.

Mark Moro: Well, I'm sure that gives new hope to millions of people who are still looking for work, and also to many millions more who want that *Made in America* label when they buy. (591 words)

1 LOOKING AT THE TEXT

→ Rezeption: Leseverstehen, S. 214

A Put these events in order from 1–7.

- **a** The rate of western job losses slows.
- **b** Many western jobs are lost every year.
- **c** Cheap exports from e.g. China undercut western producers.
- **d** More jobs return to the USA than go offshore.
- **e** US producers move production offshore.
- **f** The rate of US job losses balances the rate of jobs returned.
- **g** Low-cost producers start to become more expensive.

B ⊙ **In your own words, say what the numbers from the text refer to.**

1 150,000 **2** three per cent **3** 40,000 **4** $100 million

● **Make up questions to produce answers that contain these numbers.**

1 150,000 **2** three per cent **3** 40,000 **4** $100 million

C Look at the bar chart on page 104 and do the following tasks:

1. Say what cost is completely avoided by production in the USA. How much of the cost of Chinese production is this?
2. Compare these costs of production in the US and in China:
   - **a** raw materials
   - **b** labour
   - **c** other overheads
   - **d** packaging
3. With a partner, think of some possible reasons for the differences.

Useful phrases
- exactly/roughly the same as …
- a little / (quite) a lot higher/lower than …

2 WORKING WITH WORDS

A Match the words to form two-part nouns from the text.

bar ▪ campaign ▪ cash ▪ manufacturing ▪ production ▪ supply

chain ▪ chart ▪ facility ▪ group ▪ industry ▪ machine

B Use pairs of words from exercise 2A to complete the following. Make any changes necessary.

1 I need to get some money. Where's the nearest ___?
2 A lot of people have joined our ___ to stop development of a new airport in this area.
3 The ___ shows the various costs of production in China and in the USA.
4 Food ___ are sometimes very long. For example, bananas may come all the way from South America.
5 The company is closing its old factory in Dortmund and is opening a new ___ near Dresden.
6 There has been a huge increase in production in the Chinese ___ since 1980.

TIP

When two nouns (or an adjective and a noun) are often used together, they may become hyphenated or even one word, e.g. *low-cost* and *wasteland*. If you are not sure, check in your dictionary.

3 ANALYSING CHARTS

→ Produktion: Schaubilder beschreiben und analysieren, S. 238

BUILDING SKILLS: Describing change in charts

Line graphs usually show how figures change over a period of time.

- You can describe changes with a verb + adverb, or with an adjective + noun (see below).
- Remember to use the simple past to describe 'finished' changes:
  Sales rose steadily from 2014 to 2016.
- Use the present perfect to describe changes that are 'unfinished':
  Sales have risen steadily since 2014.

Use pairs of words from the table to describe the lines 1–6 below.

Describing graphs and statistics that show changes through time					
verb + adverb		**adjective + noun**		**verb + adjective**	
to rise	rapidly	rapid	rise	to be	flat
to increase	sharply	sharp	increase	to remain	steady
to climb	steadily	steady	climb		
to fall	gradually	gradual	fall		
to decrease	slowly	slow	decrease		
to decline	slightly	slight	decline		

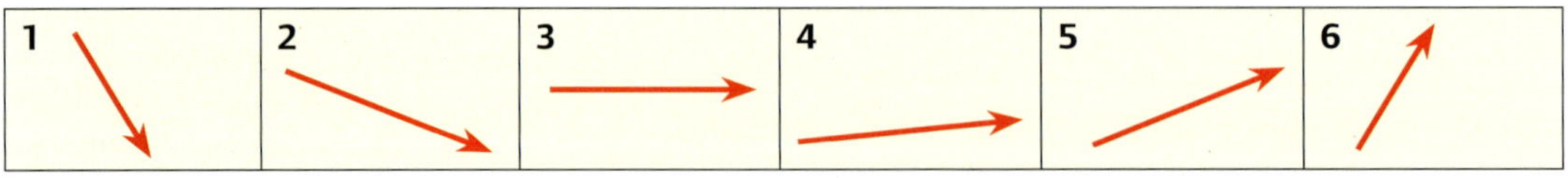

In chart 1, production fell sharply. / In chart 1, there was a sharp fall in production.

4 LISTENING

→ Rezeption: Hörverstehen, S. 225

2/13 **A** **Look at the sales chart below and listen to part of the Sales Director's report. Say whether she is describing UK or EU export sales. Identify the six-year period.**

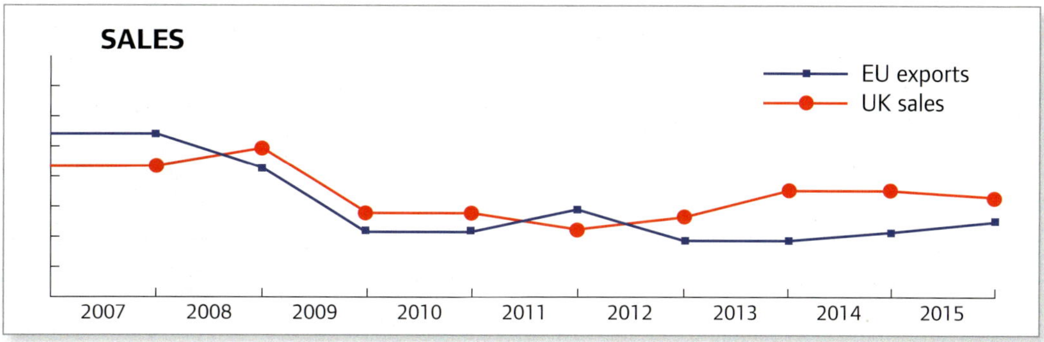

2/14 **B** **Copy and expand the frame on the right for another chart. Listen to the Sales Director and draw the graph, giving it a title and writing the years.**

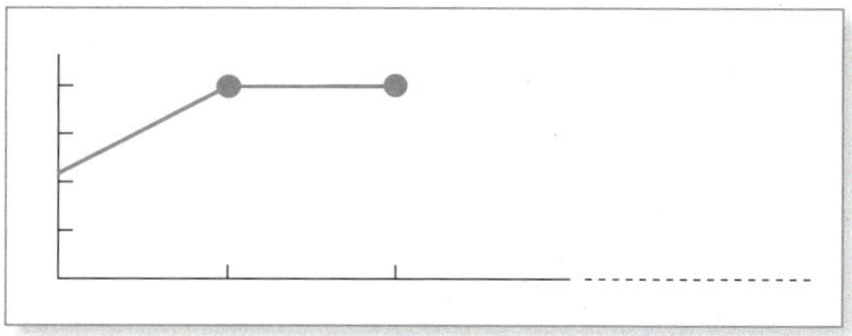

5 DESCRIBING GRAPHS

A **Work in pairs and look at the graph in exercise 4A again. Each of you describe a sales category and a five-year period for your partner to identify.**

A In these five years, sales first fell rapidly for a year. But then they … . After that, …
B Ah, you're talking about … sales from … to … , aren't you?

B **Work with a partner. Partner A look here. Partner B look at page 213.**

Partner A: Describe the graph below to Partner B.

Useful phrases

- This graph shows sales from … (*year*) to … (*year*).
- In/During … (*year*), there was a slight/… rise/… in sales.
- From … (*year*) to … (*year*), sales rose/… slightly/… .

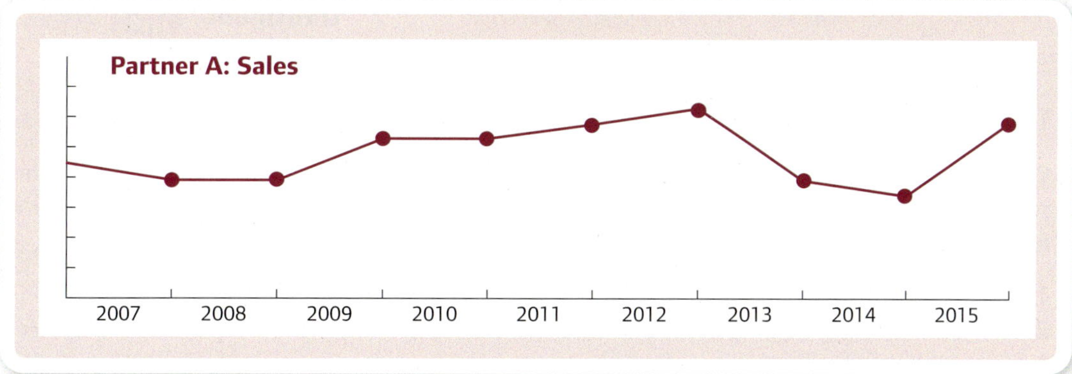

C **Draw the graph that Partner B describes.**

4/7

WHEN DISEASE GOES GLOBAL

A pandemic is defined as a disease that spreads across a whole country or the world. One of the deadliest pandemics on record is the 1918 Spanish influenza, which killed over 75 million people over a period of three years. The first cases were observed in Europe, with the number of infections and deaths increasing rapidly, mainly because of the close living quarters and movement of troops fighting in World War I. By 1920 the flu virus had spread to almost every corner of the globe – and this at a time when the fastest way to travel overseas was by ship.

More recent pandemics have been less severe, but they tend to spread extremely fast because of the increase in global air travel. Because it is easier and cheaper to fly, the number of people flying from country to country has increased and infectious diseases can spread further and faster than ever before. In 2009, for example, the pandemic swine flu started in Mexico in April and turned up in London a week later. All in all, the number of deaths from swine flu during the first year was estimated at 240,000.

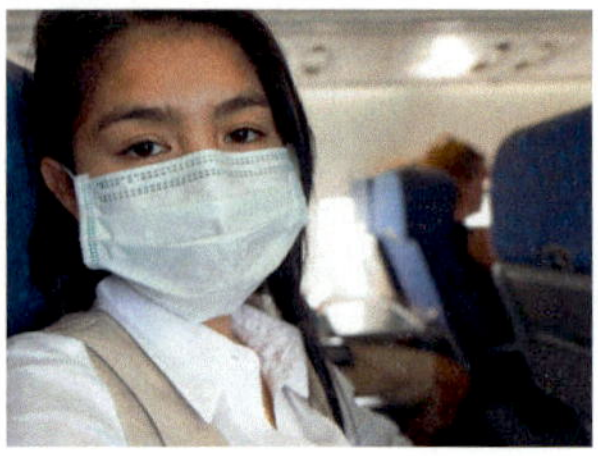

Over the last two hundred years, medicine has made great progress in the fight against infectious diseases, but we are still faced with new diseases at the rate of one per year, and the challenge is to keep these diseases from becoming pandemics. The World Health Organization (WHO) has recommended screening people as they exit pandemic-hit countries. Since 2014, for example, travellers leaving Guinea, Sierra Leone and Liberia, the countries worst hit by Ebola, have had their temperatures taken at the airport to see whether they have fever, which is one of the main symptoms of the disease. They have also been asked a series of questions to try to find out if they might have contracted the disease. Other countries have started screening passengers arriving from the affected countries at the airport, and many health care workers flying into some US states have had to undergo quarantine for up to 21 days. (343 words)

1 DRAWING A MIND MAP

→ Mindmaps, S. 221

Use the information from the text and the word cloud to draw a mind map about pandemics.

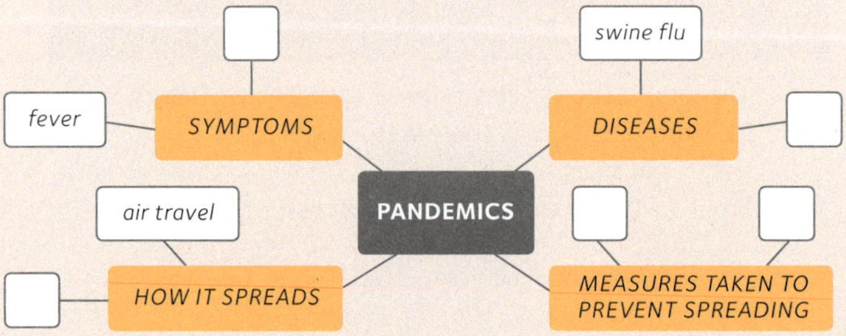

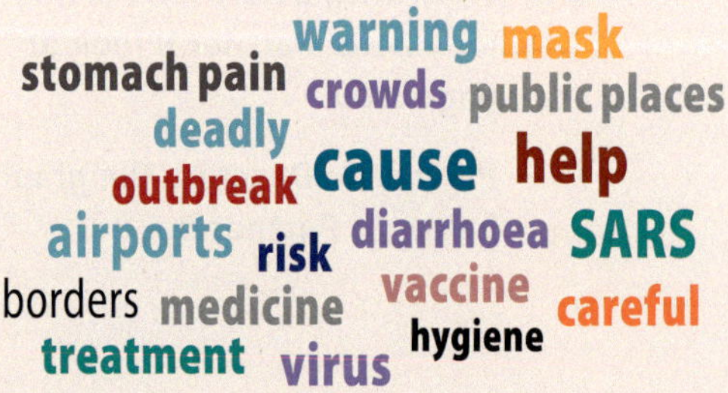

2 THINK – PAIR – SHARE

→ Interaktion, S. 246

Choose one of the questions below. Think about your ideas on the subject. Now find another student who has chosen the same question and talk about your findings. Join another pair who have the same question and share information.

1. What is the situation in Germany? Have you noticed any special health checks at airports?
2. Do you think that wearing a mask in public when you are ill is a good idea? Why? Why not?
3. Should the media do more to inform the public about pandemics, or not? Why? Why not?
4. What do you think is the most efficient way to stop diseases coming into the country?

12 Changing society

MAIN COURSE

FOCUS

A

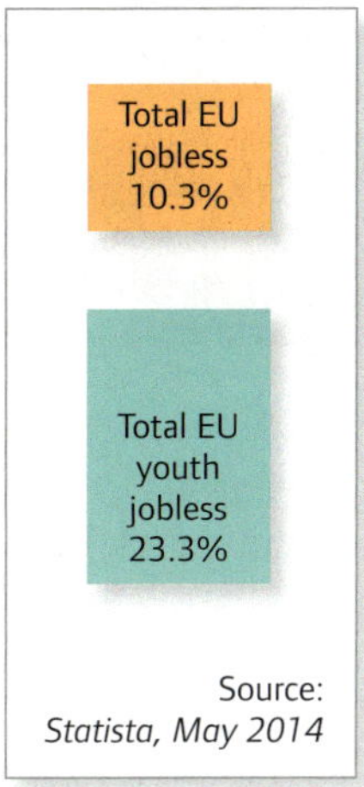

B

Malala Yousafzai is given the World's Children Prize in Stockholm

C

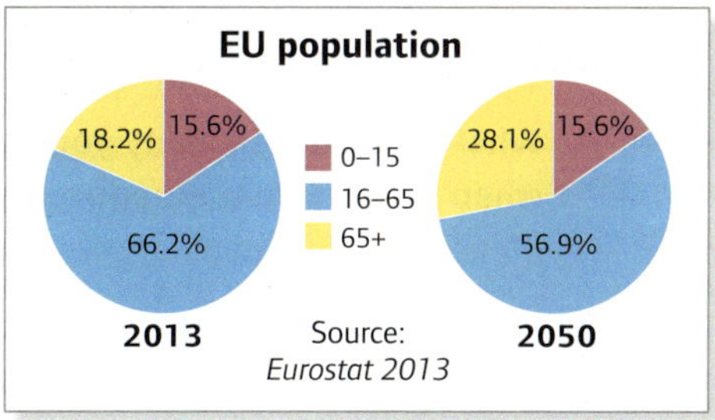

D

1 **MORE ELDERLY MEANS LATER PENSIONS**
The UK's 65+ population of 10 million is likely to reach 19 million by mid-century and the government plans to raise the pension age from 65 to 68 between 2024 and 2046.

That means I'll have to work for 50 years!

2 **THE BURDEN OF THE OLD ON THE YOUNG**
The taxes of 3.2 working-age people pay for each UK pensioner today. With ever more pensioners, there will only be 2.8 workers to support each one by 2050.

And I'm going to be one of those workers!

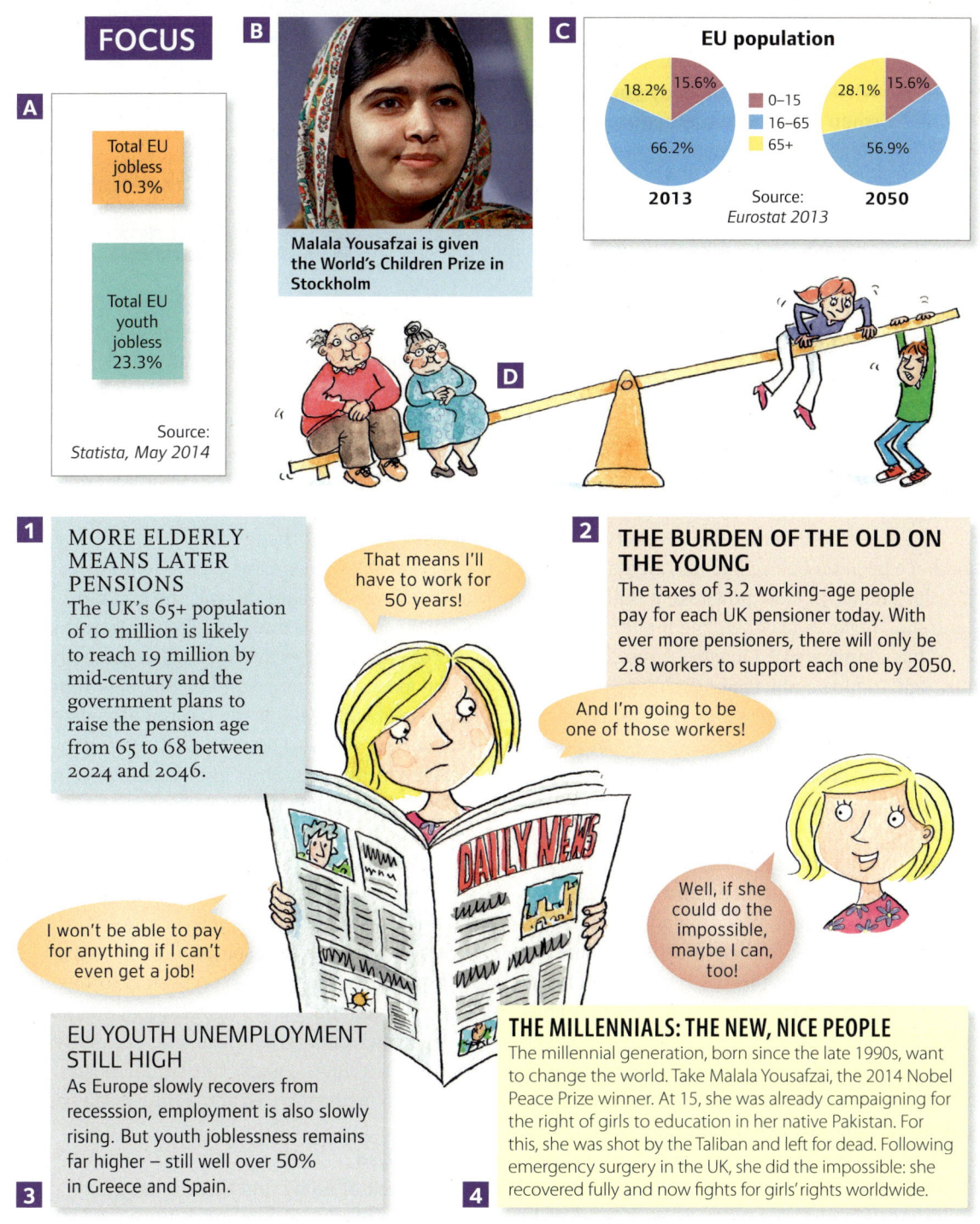

I won't be able to pay for anything if I can't even get a job!

Well, if she could do the impossible, maybe I can, too!

3 **EU YOUTH UNEMPLOYMENT STILL HIGH**
As Europe slowly recovers from recesssion, employment is also slowly rising. But youth joblessness remains far higher – still well over 50% in Greece and Spain.

4 **THE MILLENNIALS: THE NEW, NICE PEOPLE**
The millennial generation, born since the late 1990s, want to change the world. Take Malala Yousafzai, the 2014 Nobel Peace Prize winner. At 15, she was already campaigning for the right of girls to education in her native Pakistan. For this, she was shot by the Taliban and left for dead. Following emergency surgery in the UK, she did the impossible: she recovered fully and now fights for girls' rights worldwide.

A Work with a partner. Take turns to describe the pictures A–D.

B Work together to match A–D to the newspaper headlines 1–4.

C Read the newspaper reader's comments. Discuss your own feelings about the future.

TEXT A Making room for the young

BEFORE YOU READ

A **What problems do many young people face today when they finish their education? Collect your ideas in a mind map.**

B **Look at the title of the article. What do you think the author wants, and what sort of people is she probably addressing?**

2/15

PASS IT ON: give my generation more than a foot in the door

Georgia Leaker

I am one of the nearly one in five people under the age of 25 who are unemployed in Australia.

I'm 24 years old, have two university degrees and have been on Centrelink[1] payments for six months, and [...] I must now take a skills test that Centrelink believes may help me find employment.

While at university, I juggled three casual jobs, self-funded a university exchange to the US and worked for a congressman. After university, I continued my part-time retail job and also did several internships before I was able to get my first career job eight months later. I was hired as a journalist-production assistant at a small company. Eighty per cent of my job was being a personal assistant and doing office administration work. I was made redundant after 10 months, and I had to turn to Centrelink for help for the first time. I did two more internships (both of which I had to fight to get), hoping that my previous experience might land me a job.

During one internship someone in middle management wanted to hire me because I was skilled, and she was sick of endless interns. But she couldn't. The boss said no, because "interns are free and employees cost money". I terminated my internship immediately. [...]

I've applied for retail, administration and full-time nannying jobs, and I am qualified for all of them. (Although the retail industry won't hire me because I'm too "expensive".) I have also regularly applied for rural and out-of-state jobs.

In the past six months, despite the hundreds of job applications I've sent, I've had only four interviews. Two were retail and they chose younger, cheaper applicants. The other two offered pay packets under minimum wage. I didn't get any of them.

When Mia Freedman[2], who I've always admired, was my age, she was the editor of *Cosmopolitan* magazine. [...] Freedman was given lots of opportunities and during her internship, someone took a chance on her. She now runs a successful website, but she has publicly stated she doesn't pay, nor feel she ought to pay, most of her contributors. She's not alone; many successful people feel they needn't provide the next generation with the entry-level employment opportunities that they were given.

The system seems rigged against recent graduates and entry-level jobs are rare. Almost every media job wants someone with "at least five years experience". No one wants to spend the time training the next generation, and many companies would rather have an endless stream of interns to fill the gaps. This situation isn't unique to media jobs, either. Many of my friends, who have all sorts of qualifications, are also unemployed.

I'm sick of being told that I'm lazy and mooching off the system. I don't want to be thought of as a hopeless case by Centrelink. I don't want to spend my week alone, on the couch, watching daytime TV.

Around 17.7 per cent of people under the age of 25 are unemployed. Most of us are educated or skilled in some way and most don't want to be dole bludgers. We're just down on our luck and doing everything we can to get a door – any door – opened.

Take a chance on me and my generation. Help take the burden off the welfare system and help us to contribute to the future of the nation.

Our generation aren't useless, but we sure feel like we are. (572 words)

From: *The Sydney Morning Herald*, July 9, 2013

Footnote:
Unexpectedly, Georgia received a lot of job offers after this article. Soon afterwards, she became Content Manager at an online business-to-business publication.

[1] **Centrelink:** Australian Government Department of Human Services

[2] **Mia Freedman:** Well-known Australian media person who, at 24, took over at the Australian edition of *Cosmopolitan* magazine – the youngest of all the editors of the 28 worldwide editions of *Cosmopolitan*.

1 LOOKING AT THE TEXT

→ Rezeption: Leseverstehen, S. 214

A Read the text and complete the following tasks.

1 Describe the youth unemployment situation in Australia.
2 Explain what the writer did to pay her way through university.
3 Compare her experience as an intern with that of Mia Freedman.
4 Outline how Georgia feels that Freedman's generation are being unfair to her own.
5 Describe what people in management are trying to avoid doing.
6 Explain what national benefits will follow if the writer's generation are given more help.

B Say what it means: Explain the underlined words and phrases in your own words.

1 … I juggled three casual jobs, … (line 7)
2 … self-funded a university exchange … (line 8)
3 … my previous experience might land me a job. (line 20)
4 … she was sick of endless interns. (line 23)
5 … someone took a chance on her. (line 42)
6 … We're just down on our luck … (line 67)

2 WRITING

→ Produktion: Eine Stellungnahme schreiben, S. 234

A Look at your answers to exercise 1A and add any further ideas about youth unemployment to your mind map from page 110.

B Now do one of the following tasks.

○ **Describe the job situation for young people in Germany. Give examples from your own experience or from the experience of your family and friends.**

● **Compare the job situation for young people in Germany with the situation that Georgia Leaker describes in Australia.**

3 WORKING WITH WORDS

A Copy and complete the tables with words from the text.

Noun (thing)	Noun (person)
journalism	▬
▬	producer
assistance	▬
▬	administrator
▬	manager

Noun (thing)	Noun (person)
▬	intern
▬	applicant
edition	▬
contribution	▬
graduation	▬

Noun (thing)	Noun (person 1)	Noun (person 2)
▬	employer	▬
▬	interviewer	interviewee

B Use pairs of words from exercise 3A to complete the sentences.

1 **A** I hear that there have been over 100 ▬[1] for the job?
B Yes, and we've already asked several of the ▬[2] to come and talk to us.
2 I spend most of my time with customers now and that means I need ▬[1] with all the paperwork, so I'm advertising for an office ▬[2].
3 Joe was always interested in ▬[1], so he helped to run the school magazine. Now he's studying to be a ▬[2] at college.
4 Shipbuilding used to be a huge source of ▬[1] on the River Clyde near Glasgow, but now there's just one company left – with just 3,000 ▬[2].
5 The company is looking for new staff at the moment, and we're running nearly 30 ▬[1] today and tomorrow. Sue will be the main ▬[2], but Jack will see some of the applicants, too.
6 I've just started a six-month ▬[1] with TV South to get some experience working in media. There are three other ▬[2] there, too.
7 Sue has been a regular ▬[1] to the magazine for years. She's made a huge ▬[2] to its success.

4 GETTING IT RIGHT

→ Modal verbs, S. 259

A Complete the words of a young, unemployed person. Choose the correct modal verbs.

1 I know I (might not / shouldn't) ▬[1] hope for too much, but I think I (might / can't) ▬[2] still get one or two more replies to the applications I've already sent out.
2 But I (can't / couldn't) ▬[1] understand why people so often don't reply. They (shouldn't / may not) ▬[2] want to interview me, but it's very bad if they don't even write back.
3 Some days I feel very down, but I try to tell myself that I (mustn't / couldn't) ▬[1] give up, and that I (can't / have to) ▬[2] keep sending out more applications.
4 I really believe that I (could / must) ▬[1] do well in TV, so I really (should / can) ▬[2] apply to the local TV station one more time.
5 But this time, I think I'll phone. That way I (may / must) ▬[1] get through to someone who (should / can) ▬[2] help me.
6 Excuse me, but I (can't / must) ▬[1] run to catch the morning post. I (might not / can't) ▬[2] meet the deadline for this application if I don't go right now.

B Replace the words in brackets with a pronoun + *must, mustn't, needn't* or *don't have to*.

1 **A** Someone's just phoned to offer Ben an interview. (Important for me to) ___[1] call him now!
B (Not necessary for you to) ___[2] do that. I can see him just outside the front door.

2 **A** Quick! Where's my jacket? (Necessary for me to) ___[1] go!
B You're right. (Very important for you not to) ___[2] be late on your first day at your new job.

3 **A** Tomorrow's a holiday, so (not essential for me to) ___[1] get up early. In fact, (not important for me to) ___[2] get up at all. I can sleep all day!
B (Important for you not to) ___[3] talk like that. Even if (not necessary for you to) ___[4] go to work, there are plenty of jobs to do here at home.

4 **A** (Necessary for me to) ___[1] go and have coffee with all those people?
B Well, all right, (not essential for you to) ___[2] go if you don't want to, but (really important for you not to) ___[3] miss the meeting afterwards.

C Complete the sentences with forms of *be able to, have to* or *could(n't)*.

1 I'm sorry, but I ___ go now or I'll miss my train.
2 We've finished the job, so we ___ go home soon. We just need to clean up.
3 It was too dark to see, but I ___ hear someone outside.
4 I ___ come tomorrow morning, but I'll be free after one o'clock.
5 Carrie ___ play the piano very well when she was still only nine.
6 A child ran out in front of my bike, but I ___ stop just in time.
7 The storm was so bad that we ___ work hard to get the boat back into the harbour.
8 I'd lost my key, so I ___[1] open the door. But I ___[2] get in through an open window.

5 ROLE-PLAY

→ Interaktion: Ein Rollenspiel gestalten, S. 247

Jack Wade, Director of an online business publication called *BusinessAustralia.com*, read Georgia Leaker's article in *The Sydney Morning Herald* yesterday and liked the clear, direct way that she wrote it. He sent an email to the newspaper asking Georgia to call him back.

Work with a partner and create a role-play of the telephone call.

Student A

You are Georgia Leaker, and you have received an email from *The Sydney Morning Herald* asking you to call Jack Wade. He'd like to talk to you about a job. He wants you to call him after 2 pm. You are interested and decide to call back.

- Introduce yourself and refer to his email.
- Express interest in the job.
- Ask for a different date to the one he suggests for an interview.
- Ask where to meet and note down the details. Read them back to check.
- Close in a friendly way.

Student B

You are Jack Wade. You think Georgia Leaker may be the right person for the position of Content Manager at your company. This job requires someone who can edit articles from other contributors and who can also write original material. The address of your office is: 53 Gundaroo Street, Villawood.

- Explain the job briefly.
- Suggest a day and a time for a meeting.
- Offer a different date if necessary.
- Invite her to your office and give the address. Confirm the details.
- Close in a friendly way.

TEXT B Towards a new social harmony

BEFORE YOU READ

Think of family members or family friends who have reached retirement age. What do they do? Do they relax at home or do they have active interests? Do they do volunteer work?

2/16

Today, The World This Week reporter Mark Moro is talking about our ageing society to two experts – Joan Blake, journalist and author for 55 years, and Tom West, founder of an online advice forum for young entrepreneurs.

Mark Moro: Let me put this question to you both. Are the new elderly a growing burden on the young or are they a growing resource? Joan, what's the senior citizen's point of view?

Joan Blake: Well, speaking as a pretty active 75-year-old, I have to say that I don't feel like a burden, and many other people my age are still going strong. We're much healthier than previous generations were, and we're also much better educated. So I think we've still got a lot to offer society.

Mark Moro: What do you think, Tom?

Tom West: I agree with Joan. If you look at the figures for Britain, the whole population is rising quite fast, but the population over 65 is rising much faster. In some countries like Germany and Italy, the situation is even more startling. While numbers of older people there are rising fast, too, total populations are falling – in Germany by over 10 million between now and 2050.

Mark Moro: OK. With statistics like that, the elderly simply can't be thrown onto the scrapheap: they have to be turned into a resource. But how can that be done?

Joan Blake: Several things need to change. First, older workers must be allowed to work for longer if they wish and if they can still do the job. Employers shouldn't be allowed to retire people just because they reach a certain age. That's already true in Britain, but it isn't in a lot of other countries.

Tom West: Yes, so some social engineering is required, but for that to work we really need to change social attitudes. Negative attitudes can be found everywhere and they simply must be changed. People are often felt to be past it either physically or mentally by a certain age. What's more, these negative attitudes ignore the positive sides of age – experience and know-how, social skills, reliability and care for quality work.

Mark Moro: And how do you change these attitudes?

Tom West: By giving older people a chance to show what they can do. It's happening a lot through our website now. Let me give just one example – Colin Ross. At 62, Colin was the director of his own company when he became very ill with cancer. He was lucky and he recovered, but he came out if it with a wish to do something different with the rest of his life. Now at the age of 66, he acts as adviser and mentor to young people who are just starting out in business for themselves. He has a lifetime of experience to offer the young, and he has already guided several start-up companies through the difficult early days.

Joan Blake: And here's another heart-warming example. CNA Language Schools in Brazil has teamed up with a home for the elderly in Chicago. Now, you see, most of CNA's students don't get the chance to practise their English with native speakers. At the same time, many of the elderly at Windsor Park Retirement Home are lonely and are only too happy to talk via regular Web chats and help the young Brazilians with their English. The conversations are then recorded and uploaded as private YouTube

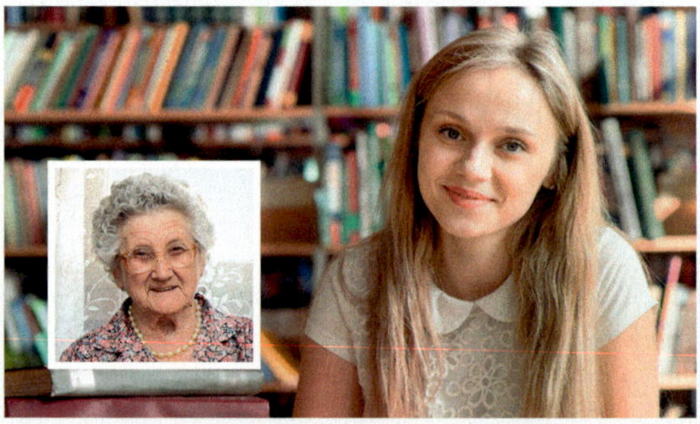

videos for CNA teachers to study and work on later with their students.

There are big differences in age and cultural background, but these people have a lot to give each other, and their conversations are often very special. They soon start speaking from their hearts and become very close. I remember seeing one video where an elderly lady finishes by saying to her young friend, 'You are my new granddaughter!'

Mark Moro: What a great idea! That's a real win-win situation for both sides! (658 words)

1 LOOKING AT THE TEXT

→ Rezeption: Leseverstehen, S. 214

A Read the text and make notes under these headings:

- Topic of the interview
- Guests and their jobs
- Advantages of the elderly compared to the past
- Advantages of the elderly over the young
- Examples of the elderly helping the young

SKILLS CHECKLIST: Taking notes

☑ Have I read the whole text?
☑ Have I scanned the text for key words?
☑ Have I noted down the key words?

B Use your notes from exercise 1A to explain why the elderly should play a more important role in society in the future. Give some examples of how the elderly may help the young.

C Say what it means: Explain the underlined words and phrases in your own words.

1. … are still going strong. (line 7)
2. People are often felt to be past it … (line 34)
3. … experience and know-how, … (line 37)
4. … CNA … has teamed up with a home for the elderly … (line 54)
5. … and are only too happy to talk … (lines 58–59)
6. That's a real win-win situation for both sides! (lines 71–72)

D Think of your elderly family members or family friends and discuss these questions in class:

- In what ways do they stay in touch with younger people?
- How do you think this helps them – if at all?
- How might it help the younger people, too – if at all?

2 WORKING WITH WORDS

A Change the underlined words using *the* + adjective, e.g. *the elderly*.

1. In our ageing society, people who are elderly have a lot to offer those who are young.
2. In most ancient societies, people who were powerful often had total control of those who were weak.
3. In most modern societies, it is usually accepted that people who are rich should pay higher taxes than others to help those who are poor.

B Find three more partner words for *social* in the text.

social climber / science / services / worker / ___ / ___ / ___

C Now use word pairs from exercise 2B to complete the following sentences.

1. All children have to learn the ___ they need to get on with other people.
2. Sue has gone on from school to study ___ at university.
3. Rob is a terrible ___! He spends all his time trying to make friends with rich people!
4. ___ towards gay people have changed. Most people now accept them as normal.
5. With the help of ___ and taxes, the UK created a more equal society after World War 2.
6. If parents can't look after their children properly, ___ sometimes have to take over.
7. In that case, a ___ will first visit the family to find out about the situation.

3 USING A DICTIONARY

→ Ein Wörterbuch benutzen, S. 217

Read the dictionary definitions of *society* (1–5) below and match them to sentences a–e.

BUILDING SKILLS: Using a dictionary

When you find a word in a text that you think you know but that doesn't quite 'fit', always try to work out the meaning from the context first, or by thinking of similar words in German or English. If the meaning is still not clear, you may need to use a dictionary.

- Don't just use the first definition that you come across!
- Read through all the meanings carefully in order to find the right one. Meanings are often closely related, for example as in *society* 1–5 below.
- Sometimes the meanings are quite different, e.g. *fire* as in *fire a gun* (= shoot), *fire an employee* (= end employment), and you have to choose the one that makes the most sense in the context.

society /sə'saɪəti/ noun **1** [U] people living together in organized communities, with laws and traditions that control the way they behave towards each other **2** [C/U] a particular type of society, e.g. in a particular country or area, or at a particular time in history, or with a special characteristic
3 [U] the group of people in a country who are rich, powerful and/or from a high social class
4 [C] an organization or club for people who share a particular interest or take part in a particular activity
5 [U] *formal* the company or friendship of other people

a Ann does two after-school activities. She plays football and belongs to the drama society.
b It was the society wedding of the year, and the guest list was full of famous names.
c In western countries we expect society to help those who need help.
d James is a very private person: he always tries to avoid the society of other people.
e We live in an affluent, post-industrial society full of opportunities that earlier generations never dreamed of.

4 GETTING IT RIGHT

→ The passive, S. 261

You work for a construction company and you have to write a report on a management meeting about the new company policy on retirement.

Read the statements below to continue the report.
Report the underlined sections with modal passive forms.

At the meeting the following points were made.
- *Workers who are 65 must be ...*
- *If they are ...*

TIP

As a report is a formal written document, use full forms, e.g. *they are*, not *they're*.

A So we agree that we must allow workers who are 65 to continue in work if they want to.
B Yes, and if they're strong enough, we shouldn't stop them from staying in their old jobs.
A OK, but we'll have to consider workers who are less strong case by case.
B Yes, we can't expect people in that situation to carry on doing outdoor construction work. We'll need to offer them less physically tiring work.
A OK, but to do this, I think we should interview workers like these to find out what other skills they have.
B We might offer a few people jobs in the warehouse. We could retrain them as forklift drivers.
A But we needn't necessarily retrain older workers. We can use their life-long skills for training apprentices.

5 LISTENING

→ Rezeption: Hörverstehen, S. 225

Mark Moro is now interviewing another expert on our ageing society – this time not to talk about the benefits, but instead to discuss the problems.

2/17

A Copy the notes. Then listen to the interview and complete them.

Population (millions)
- Germany – Now: ▬ – 2050: ▬
- UK – Now: ▬ – 2050: ▬

UK elderly (millions)
- Over 65 – Now: ▬ (= ▬ %) – 2050: ▬ (= ▬ %)
- Over 80 – Now: – 2050: ▬

Pensioner welfare (pensions, winter fuel, etc.)
- Cost per year: ▬
- % of total UK welfare: ▬

Health costs per household
- Retired: ▬
- Non-retired: ▬

B Use your notes to complete the following tasks.

1 Compare population change in Germany and in the UK.
2 Compare general UK population change and population change among the elderly.
3 Compare the cost of welfare for the UK elderly and the cost for everyone else.
4 Compare the average health care costs for retired and non-retired UK households.

6 WRITING

→ Produktion: Eine Stellungnahme schreiben, S. 234

Write a comment on *Our ageing society*. Explain the expression *our ageing society*. Then describe and evaluate some of the problems and point out any opportunities that it gives us.

BUILDING SKILLS: Writing a comment

Always make sure you understand the task before you start to write a comment. In the task above, you need to give basic information about *Our ageing society*, describe some of the pros and cons, and give your own opinion on the topic.

- Always collect ideas to help you first, either in the form of a mind map, a list or simple notes. You will usually find information from your reading and listening, in this case Text B (page 114) and exercise 5 (above).
- Organize your notes to help you structure the text. You need to give an introduction to the topic and a conclusion with your opinion. You also need to support your arguments with examples.
- Use linking words or connecting phrases to structure your text and make it easier for the reader to follow your arguments.

Useful phrases

Adding facts:
- Moreover, …
- Furthermore, …
- In addition, …

Listing ideas:
- First of all, …
- Secondly, …
- Then again, …

Giving examples:
- For example, …
- For instance, …

Comparing and evaluating:
- Although …
- Despite the fact that …

4/8

Germany's "multigeneration houses" could solve two problems for Britain

With the number of over-65s set to double and childcare more expensive than ever, ***Mehrgenerationenhäuser*** *may be the answer*

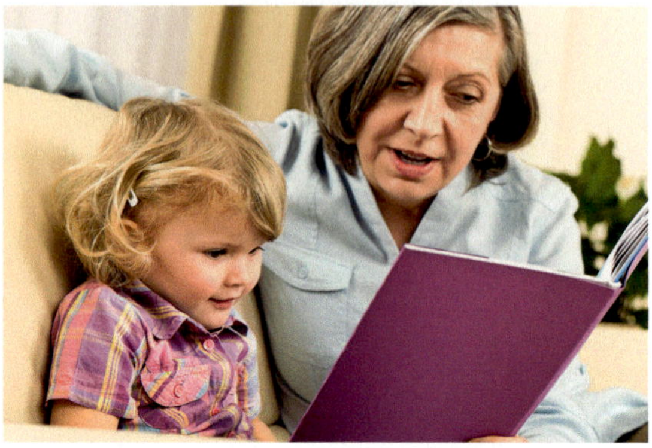

Pensioners volunteer to read books to the children once a week and run a "rent-a-granny" service to relieve parents.

In Pattensen, a small town of 13,000 just south of Hanover, pensioners play cards to the echoing tick-tock of a grandfather clock. It might be a melancholy scene – if it wasn't for the squeals of delight coming through the open door from the nursery on the next floor.

The nursery and the sitting room are part of a *Mehrgenerationenhaus*, literally a "multi-generation house", which is a kindergarten, a social centre for the elderly and somewhere young families can drop in for coffee and advice. In theory, the sitting room is reserved for the over-60s, but in practice the door to the kids' area rarely stays closed for long.

Pensioners volunteer to read books to the children once a week and run a "rent-a-granny" service to relieve exhausted parents. In return, teenagers offer to show elderly people how to use computers and mobile phones.

Every Monday morning, when people with dementia use the sitting room for games and singing, children join in without being prompted. "Kids are more at ease dealing with dementia patients than adults", said Angela Schulz, one of the care workers leading the sessions, "so we find patients are much more relaxed here than anywhere else".

Britain too may soon start to send its pensioners to nurseries or babies to nursing homes. Last week, a report by the Institute for Public Policy Research urged Britain to adopt the *Mehrgenerationenhaus* approach to cope with an ageing population. The number of over-65s in Britain is expected to almost double by 2030, and childcare in Britain is more expensive than almost anywhere in the world. (265 words)

Abridged from: *www.theguardian.com*

DISCUSSION

→ Interaktion, S. 246

In small groups, follow the steps below.

1 Think of the pros and cons of a *Mehrgenerationenhaus* both from the point of view of an older person and from the point of view of a child. Take notes of your arguments and put them in a logical order.

2 Examine your arguments for and against the *Mehrgenerationenhaus* approach and decide if it really is the way to cope with an ageing population and expensive childcare. Be prepared to present your findings to the class.

Job skills 3

Giving directions ▪ bookings and reservations

Eric's application for a job in the UK was successful and he starts today at Magnus & Klein, a small manufacturing company in London. The company is located in the Four Lofts Business Park. Ms Shaw, the office manager, has sent him written instructions on how to get to the office.

1 UNDERSTANDING DIRECTIONS

A Follow the instructions and find the offices of Magnus & Klein on the plan of the business park.

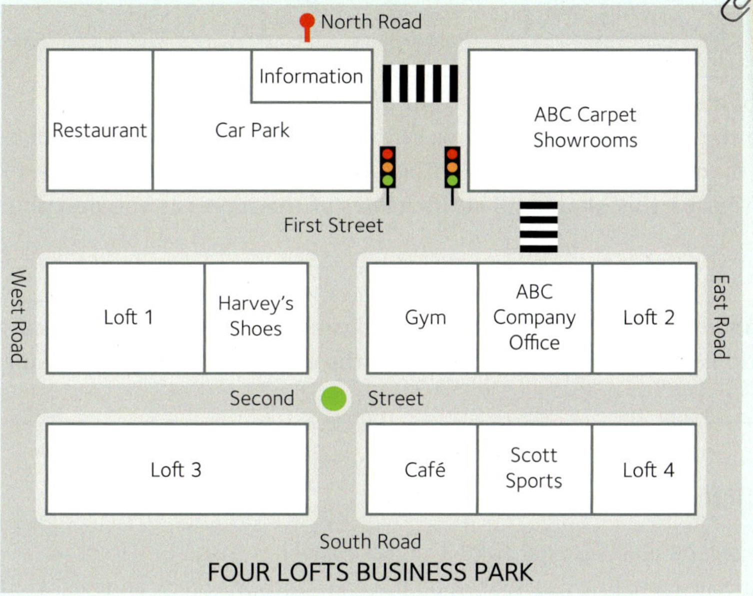

When you get off the bus in North Road, walk back a few metres to the entrance to the park. Pass the information box and walk down to the traffic lights. Turn right into First Street and take the first left. You'll see a gym on your left. Keep going till you come to Second Street. Turn right into Second Street and walk past Harvey's Shoes on your right. Our office is in the same building, opposite Loft 3.

B Work with a partner and do one of the following tasks.

Take turns to give each other directions to different companies or places in the park.

Choose a company or a place in the park. Do not tell your partner the name of the company or place he/she is going to. Describe how to get there from the Magnus & Klein office. Can he/she find the way and name the company or the place?

Remember to start at the Magnus & Klein office every time.

With your partner, think of a company or a place within walking distance of your school. Write directions how to get there from the school. Do not write down the name of the company or the place. Give your directions to another pair. Can they find out where you are sending them?

Useful phrases: Giving directions

- Turn right/left.
- Go straight ahead/on.
- Keep to the right/left.
- It's on the right-hand side / on the left-hand side.

Job skills 3

2 LISTENING

→ Rezeption: Hörverstehen, S. 225

When Eric arrives at Magnus & Klein, Ms Shaw gives him a tour of the offices.

2/18

A Study the floor plan and the list of places below. Then listen and find the places on the floor plan.

1 Accounts
2 Human Resources
3 Ms Shaw's office
4 the kitchen
5 the men's toilet
6 the storeroom

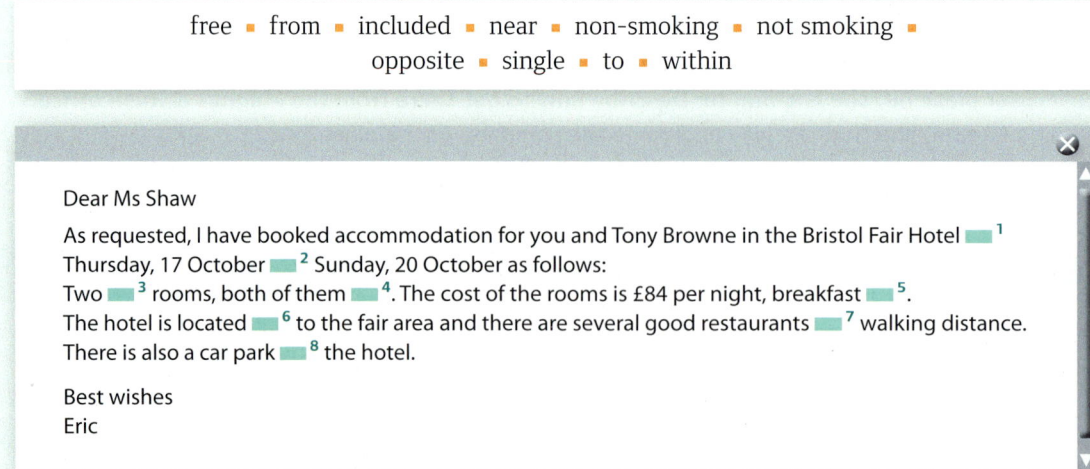

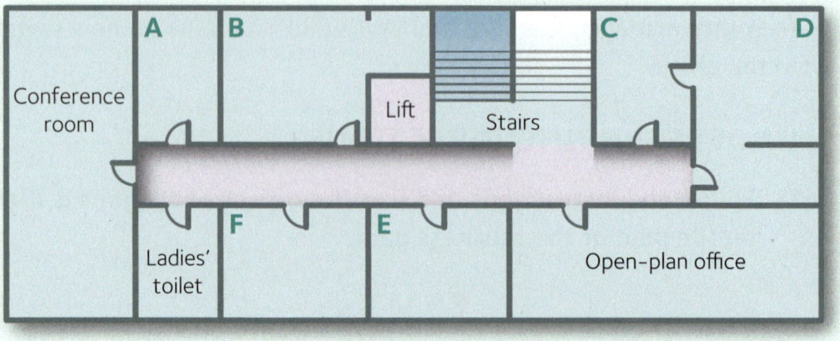

B Work with a partner and do one the following tasks.

Draw a simple floor plan of a school. Name three or four of the rooms (e.g. classrooms, staff room, toilets). Leave the remaining rooms blank. Without showing your partner, make a list of the names of the rooms you have left blank. Give your floor plan to your partner and give him/her a tour. Your partner should fill in the names of the rooms as you describe them.

With your partner, think about how you should leave your classroom if the fire alarm goes off. Write down the directions from memory, then check on the emergency exit plan in your classroom.

3 MAKING A HOTEL BOOKING

Magnus & Klein plc are going to exhibit at the Bristol Trade Fair. Ms Shaw has asked Eric to book accommodation for herself and a colleague. Eric has booked online and sends Ms Shaw an email giving details of the booking.

A Complete the email below using words from the box. There are two words more than you need.

free ▪ from ▪ included ▪ near ▪ non-smoking ▪ not smoking ▪ opposite ▪ single ▪ to ▪ within

Dear Ms Shaw

As requested, I have booked accommodation for you and Tony Browne in the Bristol Fair Hotel ___ [1] Thursday, 17 October ___ [2] Sunday, 20 October as follows:
Two ___ [3] rooms, both of them ___ [4]. The cost of the rooms is £84 per night, breakfast ___ [5].
The hotel is located ___ [6] to the fair area and there are several good restaurants ___ [7] walking distance.
There is also a car park ___ [8] the hotel.

Best wishes
Eric

A few days before the fair, Ms Shaw asks Eric to contact the hotel and give them some extra information.

2/19

B Listen to Eric's phone call to the hotel and make notes on the following:

1. the name of the person who takes the call
2. the booking number
3. the problem
4. why it is important that the hotel has the new information

4 WRITING AN EMAIL

→ Job Skills 1, Email etiquette, S. 32

Using the email and your notes from exercise 3, write Eric's email to Tony Browne confirming the booking. Add a suitable subject line.

From: Eric Jung <ericjung@magnusklein.co.uk>
Subject:
To: Tony Browne <tonybrowne@magnusklein.co.uk>
cc: Joan Shaw <joanshaw@magnusklein.co.uk>

Hello Tony

This is just to let you know that I have booked …

As you will be arriving after the check-in time of 10 pm, I have called the hotel …

I hope the hotel is OK and that you enjoy your trip.

Best
Eric

TIP Formal and informal business emails

When writing business emails to new contacts, superiors or people you don't know well (for example, colleagues at a new job), you should begin your email with *Dear* … and end with *Regards* or *Best wishes*. With business contacts or colleagues you know well, you can start emails with *Hello* … or *Hi* … and end with *Best*.

5 RESERVING A CONFERENCE ROOM

The Magnus & Klein team are having a meeting with some business partners during the trade fair. Ms Shaw asks Eric to reserve a conference room.

A Work in a group of four. Discuss Ms Shaw's wishes and rank them in order of importance (1 is most important). Give reasons for your rankings.

Eric

We are having a meeting with some business partners on Saturday, 19 October. Please book a conference room for the whole day and arrange lunch for 9 people.

We need a room with seating for 9 people including one person in a wheelchair; a projector, screen and a flip chart; Wi-fi; a selection of non-alcoholic drinks. Lunch should include vegetarian options.

Try to get a conference room at the fair or near to the fair area and please don't exceed £300, including lunch.

JS

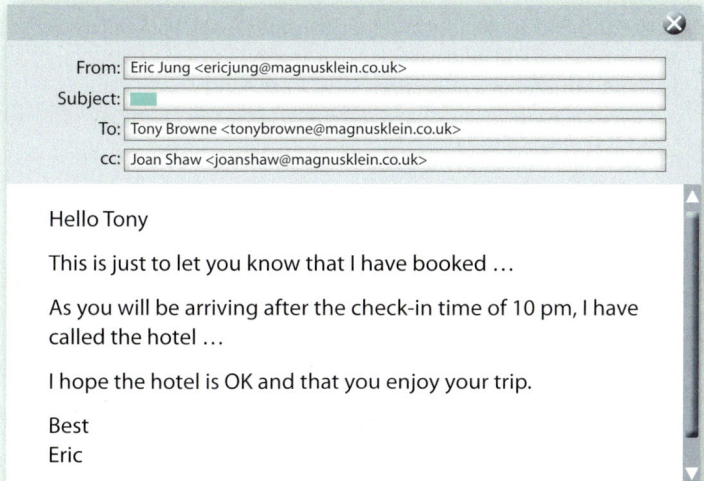

B **In your group, split into two pairs: Partners A and B, and Partners C and D. Each pair is going to look at offers for conference rooms and then try to persuade the other pair to choose the room they have selected.**

Partners A and B

Work together and compare the offers on the right with what Ms Shaw would like. Choose a room and develop arguments which will persuade Partners C and D to reserve this room for the meeting.

Bristol Trade Fair Area Conference Rooms

- Book by the hour, half day or full day -

Our conference centre on the top floor of the Fair Area is accessible by lift. There is wheelchair access throughout the building and disabled facilities on every floor.

We have three conference rooms to suit your needs.
Prices: £180 (69 m^2), £155 (38 m^2), £110 (22 m^2)

All rooms are equipped with high-end audio-visual equipment and free wireless high-speed internet connection.

- Hot and cold drinks, fruit and snacks included in the price of the room
- Free national and local calls
- Free 'host' Internet connection
- Free stationery

A la carte lunch menu at prices starting from £18 per person.
Non-alcoholic drinks included in the price.
Special dietary requirements can be catered for.

Partners C and D

Work together and compare the offers on the right with what Ms Shaw would like. Choose a room and develop arguments which will persuade Partners A and B to reserve this room for the meeting.

Bristol Fair Hotel

MEETING ROOM FACILITIES

Our hotel is located next to the Bristol Fair Area. You can hold a meeting and stay overnight with us at reasonable prices.

Room	Size	Price
River	73 m^2	£210
Mountain	50 m^2	£175
Plain	26 m^2	£120

All prices include modern technology. We can mix and match equipment (e.g. screen, projector, pinboard, flip charts with markers) according to your wishes.
Catering throughout the whole event, snacks and non-alcoholic drinks are included in the price of the room. Buffet lunch: £14 per person.

- Disabled facilities throughout the hotel.
- Wi-fi in the meeting rooms and in public areas.
- Private bar available for a relaxing end to your event.

If you are a guest of our hotel, the rental price for the conference room is reduced by £5 for each booked hotel room.

6 BOOKING A CONFERENCE ROOM BY EMAIL

Write an email to the company whose conference room you have chosen. Give the date and times when you would like the room. Describe what services you would like.

Useful phrases

- to book/reserve a conference room for … people
- to be equipped with …
- to confirm a reservation for …
- to send an invoice to …

13 The challenges of the modern state

EXAM PREPARATION

FOCUS

1

2

3

4

5

6

7

8

A Think: Rank the problems shown in the photos according to what you think is most important. Use the words in the box or your own descriptions.

body scanners ▪ data protection ▪ electronic waste ▪ energy dependence ▪ extremism ▪ human rights ▪ identity theft ▪ mental health ▪ online security ▪ phishing ▪ radicalization ▪ stress ▪ surveillance cameras ▪ terrorist attacks ▪ war

Write two or three sentences about the problems you think are most important.

B Pair: Compare your list with a partner and discuss your choices.

C Share: Discuss your ideas in class.

TEXT A Terrorism

BEFORE YOU READ

→ Rezeption: Leseverstehen, S. 214

A Skim the first text to find out what happened to the two brothers.

B Scan the second text to find another expression for *police work*.

2/20

THE BOSTON MARATHON

Two hours after the winners crossed the finishing line of the 117th Boston Marathon, two pressure cooker bombs exploded killing three people and injuring 264. Three days later, the FBI released photographs and a surveillance video of two suspects, who were brothers. They were found the same day and after a firefight with the police, the older brother died and the younger one escaped.

Four days later, thousands of police officers in Watertown, Massachusetts took part in a huge manhunt for the younger brother. Public transport, most private businesses and all public institutions were shut down and residents were told to stay indoors, making Watertown into an urban desert. At around 7 pm, a Watertown resident discovered the younger brother hiding in a boat in his back yard and he was arrested. He later stated that he and his brother had also planned to bomb Times Square in New York. He claimed that they were self-radicalized and had learned to build bombs on the Internet.

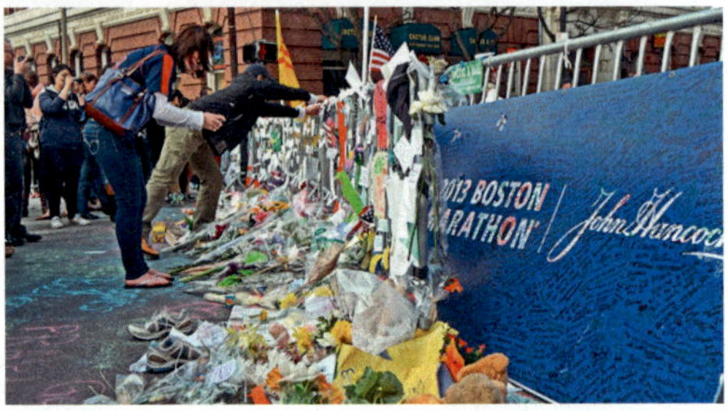

(167 words)

THE NATURE OF MODERN TERRORISM

[...] Methods for engaging in political violence have changed, and multiple forms of terrorism will probably dominate the "battlefields" of the twenty-first century. [...] Modern terrorism is a new phenomenon. It requires supporting systems from the technological world. First, to be effective, terrorism must be seen and heard. As one terrorist commander summarized, it is better to kill one person in front of a camera than to kill a hundred in a secret location. Terrorists need an audience.

The second aspect of modernity's impact on terrorism involves mobility. This can be done locally or globally. The goal is to get to the target and get away. An attack can originate in the hills of South Waziristan and be carried out in London [...].

Finally, the modern world provides weapons or materials that can be turned into weapons. These devices, in turn, are more powerful than instruments of the past. [...]

These three factors – instant communication, mobility, and access to destructive technology – mean that terrorism will continue to plague the world. [...] When not used as a tactic in guerrilla war, terrorism is essentially a problem for law enforcement and the criminal justice system. [...] One of the best tools in the anti-terrorist arsenal is to develop law enforcement agencies that act as extensions of neighborhoods. These agencies can root out all types of problems before they happen, including terrorism. [...] Finally, it would be helpful if the mass media, especially cable news, would spend time explaining the complex background of modern terrorism. This would be much more responsible than breathlessly awaiting the next stage in a terrorist drama. [...] (265 words)

From: Jonathan R. White, *The Huffington Post*

1 LOOKING AT THE TEXTS

→ Rezeption: Leseverstehen, S. 214

A Read the first text and explain how …

1 the bombers made their explosive devices.
2 the police were able to get photographs of the suspects.
3 the brothers became extremists.

B Read the second text and match the sentence halves.

1 There will be many different forms of …
2 Modern technology enables terrorists to …
3 Terrorist attacks are often planned in places which …
4 Nowadays, it is easy to find materials …
5 Nobody expects terrorism …
6 In many cases, it is the job of the police …
7 The police can root out some terrorism …
8 Terrorism is often sensationalized …

a which can be made into weapons.
b to deal with terrorists.
c by the mass media.
d to stop in the near future.
e by working closely with the local community.
f reach large audiences all over the world.
g terrorism in the twenty-first century.
h are a long way away from the target.

2 WORKING WITH WORDS

A Study the texts to see how the verbs in box A are used with the nouns in box B.

A	
to release	to carry out
to take part in	to turn into
to shut down	to plague
to engage in	to root out

B	
a manhunt	the problems
an attack	the world
photographs	violence
public transport	weapons

B Use some collocations from exercise 2A to complete the text. Make any necessary changes.

When four suicide bombers ▬ 1 on London Transport on 7 July 2005, there was no warning and 56 people died, including the terrorists. The attack was so devastating that the authorities had to ▬ 2 for the rest of the day, which meant there were no trains or buses in Central London. Some time later, the police ▬ 3 of the attackers showing them carrying large rucksacks of home-made explosives at London's Kings Cross station. Attacks of this nature continue to ▬ 4, and law enforcement agencies everywhere now have emergency plans to deal with such events. However, experts agree that it is best to ▬ 5 which lead to terrorist attacks before extremists ▬ 6 and kill innocent people.

C *Cross* can be a verb (*to cross*) or a noun (*a cross*). Use the definitions below to find more words in the two texts that have the same verb and noun form.

1 to make available for the public
2 to believe sb is guilty of sth
3 to take sb to a police station and hold them there
4 to make different
5 to give help
6 to have a strong effect on sth
7 to use weapons to hurt or kill sb

D Write 4–5 sentences containing your answers to exercise 2C as nouns or verbs.

3 MEDIATION

→ Schriftliche Mediation, S. 240

Ihre Schule nimmt an einem Projekt in Zusammenarbeit mit einer großen Regionalzeitung teil. Die Schüler und Schülerinnen sind aufgefordert, Artikel über aktuelle Themen zu schreiben, die dann in der Zeitung veröffentlicht werden.

Benutzen Sie die relevanten Inhalte der beiden Texte, um einen Zeitungsartikel über die Rolle der modernen Technik im Terrorismus des 21. Jahrhunderts zu verfassen.

4 LISTENING

→ Rezeption: Hörverstehen, S. 225

Tonight, the BBC's radio phone-in programme *World Have Your Say* is dealing with the question, 'Is the state really under threat from terrorism?'

A Before you listen, work with a partner and guess which person says each statement below.

Fatima, Turkish student

Joshua, Christian priest

Andrea, German student teacher

Reginald, ex-army officer

a In my experience talking with terrorists gets you nowhere. We need to find them and stop them.
b The West must stop sending weapons to conflict zones.
c Children must learn not to use violence to solve conflicts.
d I believe in focusing on the values and beliefs we all share, not on our differences.

2/21 **B Listen and check your answers.**

2/21 **C Listen again and write down the missing words. Sometimes you need more than one word for each gap.**

1 The government is responsible for ▬ its citizens.
2 If we want ▬ in a free world, spending on the police and the armed forces must be massively increased.
3 I believe in ▬ for the threat before it's too late.
4 Westerners enjoy ▬ in safety and comfort
5 They risk ▬ [1] all this if they continue ▬ [2] weapons to conflict zones.
6 I remember ▬ about the horrors of the Second World War at school.
7 I started ▬ about the reasons for violence.
8 A member of my church suggested ▬ a prayer vigil.
9 I agreed ▬ so immediately.
10 Joshua recommends ▬ for peace.

5 ROLE-PLAY

→ Interaktion: Ein Rollenspiel gestalten, S. 247

With a partner, choose the speaker from exercise 4 whose opinions you disagree with most. Role-play a discussion between yourself and that person about how to prevent terrorism. Take turns with your partner to play both roles.

BUILDING SKILLS: Preparing for a discussion

You should always prepare thoroughly before you start any kind of speaking activity. If you have to take part in a discussion, you can prepare by making notes of the main arguments:

- Think of the ideas and arguments that your opponent might use and make a list of them.
- Make a list of your own ideas and arguments.
- Look at the points you disagree about most strongly and think of arguments you can use against your opponent.

Useful phrases

Partly agreeing with an opinion:

- I don't entirely/quite agree with you.
- I see what you mean, but …
- There's some truth in what you say. However, …

Saying something in another way:

- (Well,) What I mean is, …
- In other words, …
- Let me put it another way, …

6 GETTING IT RIGHT

→ Verb + infinitive ▪ Verb + gerund, S. 262

A Choose the right verb form to complete these sentences.

The security services are responsible for (to protect / protecting) ▬ 1 the citizens of a country from terrorist attacks. The security services also expect the citizens (to help / helping) ▬ 2 them do their job and they encourage them (to give / giving) ▬ 3 them helpful information. However, communicating sensitive information to MI5, Britain's internal security service, is not so simple. Although the organization recommends (to use / using) ▬ 4 its secure Internet contact form, many people decide (to write / writing) ▬ 5 a letter instead because they prefer (to post / posting) ▬ 6 it anonymously. Some computer experts encourage people to stop (to use / using) ▬ 7 phones and computers for important messages and only use paper. They feel that using the Internet for sensitive material involves (to take / taking) ▬ 8 too many security risks.

B The verbs in the box are all followed by gerunds. Complete the sentences with a suitable verb from the box, making any necessary changes.

avoid ▪ enjoy ▪ hate ▪ involve ▪ mind ▪ miss ▪ recommend ▪ risk

1 Police work often ▬ observing a suspect over a long period of time.
2 If you ▬ having a lot of free time, it's best not to join the police force.
3 The police ▬ taking extra safety precautions when there is a terrorist threat.
4 They say it's best to ▬ going out late at night.
5 When this happens, some people ▬ meeting their friends at the local pub.
6 Others don't ▬ staying at home in the evenings.
7 Some people even cancel their holidays because they don't want to ▬ travelling to a dangerous place.
8 Most people ▬ losing their freedom but are willing to do so for a short time.

TEXT B The dangers of digital life

BEFORE YOU READ

→ Rezeption: Leseverstehen – Grobverständnis, S. 214

Skim the text and explain which of the following statements is true and why the others are false:

1 Uwe Buse was unable to defend himself against any of the hackers' attacks.
2 Uwe Buse was able to defend himself against some of the hackers' attacks.
3 Uwe Buse was able to defend himself against most of the hackers' attacks.

2/22

When hackers take over your life

When *Spiegel* reporter Uwe Buse decided to try out a test on himself and invited hackers to take over his life, he had no idea what he was letting himself in for. He wanted them to find out as much as possible about his private and professional life without any help from him at all and then use this knowledge to harm him. He would then try to fight back as an exercise in digital self-defence.

He first contacted a specialist firm in Tübingen which hacks into company networks at the request of their owners and instructed them to hack into his mobile and laptop. In Tübingen, three young hackers, who had made their illegal hobby into their profession, installed undetectable spyware on his mobile and laptop. When the laptop was switched back on, the message from its virus scanner was: 'Your computer is safe.'

The spyware on Uwe Buse's mobile immediately started transmitting GPS data to the hackers every two seconds. That evening the hackers tracked him back to Bremen, noted his home address and took a look at his house using Street View. They logged his every movement and also found out he had a school-age daughter when she phoned him to tell him she had arrived safely at school. They recorded the phone call and intercepted the photo of herself she sent him. They knew what she looked like.

At 9 o'clock the same day, when Uwe Buse sat down at his laptop to start work, he thought he was alone. He was mistaken. The camera in his laptop started taking photos of him every five minutes and sending them to the hackers. In addition, every keystroke he made on his computer was recorded in a handy Excel table, which also showed the names of the programs he was using, which windows were open on his monitor, the data he was inputting and the time. The table was also sent to the hackers every five minutes.

When he logged into his Amazon and email accounts, they recorded the access codes and by scanning his Amazon account, quickly saw that he rode a motorbike and

had dry skin. They went on to find out his wife and children's names, his wife's email address, the number of her mobile, where she worked and what she looked like. They noted that the Buses didn't own a car and used car-sharing. Next the hackers sent a silent SMS to the reporter's mobile to switch on the microphone and record everything he said. This also went unnoticed.

On the second day of the experiment he logged into his bank account and the hackers recorded the access codes. They did the same with his Facebook, PayPal and iTunes accounts. They now had the data they needed and on the third day they switched to attack.

The driver of the delivery van which stopped outside Uwe Buse's house carried a large cardboard box to the front door. When asked what was in the box he replied: 'It's a lawnmower.' Buse refused delivery and sent the van away. The attack had begun.

The hackers used his email account to write an email in his name to the car-sharing firm and tell them he had knocked off the two outside mirrors of the car but had no time to stick them back on again.

The washing machine ordered in Buse's name was priced at €415.39 but when he got an email from Amazon confirming the purchase, he quickly phoned the hotline and cancelled it. Amazon advised him to change his password, which he did, but the spyware sent the new password straight to the hackers. After some more phone calls Amazon told him his account had been 'totally destroyed' and could no longer be saved. They advised him to report the matter to the police and be more careful when surfing the net in future.

The hackers' next target was his Facebook account. They posted an extremely embarrassing public message about his private life on his wall, prompting him to try to delete his account. However, as the hackers had changed all his personal details, he was unable to get into his account and could not contact anyone at Facebook because there is no hotline.

Next the hackers logged into his online bank account and withdrew all his money, placing it on untraceable prepaid cards. When he contacted his bank, they told him to report it to the police. They promised to try to get his money back and sent him a new access code for his account – by post.

Before he could go to the police, however, he was informed that he had sent his boss at *Spiegel* an email telling him that he was 'sick and tired' of him and was leaving the magazine straightaway to get a better paid job at the hackers' company in Tübingen.

Finally, his hackers contacted him to warn him that they were going to put some very nasty material on his laptop and then inform the police. He begged them not to do so and a few days later conceded utter defeat.

The spyware package used by the hackers is obtainable on the American market for as little as $33 per month. The software makers openly encourage worried parents, suspicious spouses and company bosses to spy on their children, partners and employees. The fact that using such programs is illegal in almost all countries is hidden in the small print.

When Uwe Buse asked his tormentors how to protect himself, they told him not to use Windows computers, online banking or mobile banking and not to install any unnecessary apps. They advised him to keep his virus scanner and software up-to-date, set up a firewall, use an encrypted mobile phone, go to the bank in person and use paper. (970 words)

1 LOOKING AT THE TEXT

→ Rezeption: Leseverstehen, S. 214

A Read the text on pages 128–129 and do the following tasks.

1 Study the text and list the information the hackers found out about Uwe Buse's …
a) house, b) family and c) preferred means of transport.
2 Describe how the hackers obtained the access codes to his online accounts.
3 The hackers launched six attacks against Uwe Buse. Outline each attack briefly.
4 How many attacks was he able to defend himself against?
5 Why was he able to defend himself against the Amazon but not the Facebook attack?
6 Explain how Uwe Buse stopped the seventh attack and discuss the possible consequences if it had taken place.
7 Analyse each of the attacks (including the cancelled seventh attack) and put the consequences it had or would have had into one of the following categories:
a) criminal, b) financial, c) job-related and d) social.

B Say what you think.

1 Discuss the reasons why parents, spouses and company bosses might use a spyware program.
2 Evaluate each of the hackers' suggestions as to how to protect yourself from digital attack.

2 WORKING WITH WORDS

A Match the words or expressions with their meanings.

1	to let yourself in for sth	a	to take money out of a bank account
2	mistaken	b	horrible
3	to refuse	c	important information written in very small letters
4	purchase	d	to put into code
5	to withdraw	e	immediately
6	untraceable	f	to do sth unpleasant or difficult
7	straightaway	g	impossible to find
8	nasty	h	wrong
9	the small print	i	to say you will not do sth
10	to encrypt	j	sth you have bought

B Work in pairs. Write your own definitions of four or five words in the text, mix them up and show them to your partner. Can your partner match the words to the definitions?

C Complete the text with a suitable phrasal verb, by adding a particle to the verbs below.

verbs	particles
try ▪ take ▪ find ▪ switch ▪ get ▪ set	back ▪ on ▪ out (2×) ▪ over ▪ up

Thanks to cybercrime there are fewer bank robberies because it's easier to ▬ [1] a computer than rob a bank. Many people never ▬ [2] that their computer has been hijacked. They just ▬ it ▬ [3] as usual, ▬ [4] a digital payment of some form and click on 'OK'. However, if their account has been hacked, there is a good chance they will never ▬ their money ▬ [5]. When hackers steal credit card data, they make a copy of the card and ▬ it ▬ [6] it with a small sum of money first. If it works, they use it for bigger payments.

TEXT C The surveillance society

In this section you are going to read two short extracts from a novel and a newspaper article about surveillance.

BEFORE YOU READ

What do you associate with the term 'surveillance society'?

In 1949 George Orwell published *Nineteen Eighty-Four*, a novel about a fictional totalitarian state called Oceania. The following extracts describe the posters of the leader, Big Brother, which are everywhere, and the use of telescreens by the Thought Police.

… the poster with the enormous face gazed from the wall. It was one of those pictures which are so contrived that the eyes follow you about when you move. BIG BROTHER IS WATCHING YOU, the caption beneath it ran.

… The telescreen received and transmitted simultaneously. Any sound that Winston made, above the level of a very low whisper, would be picked up by it, moreover, so long as he remained within the field of vision which the metal plaque commanded, he could be seen as well as heard. There was of course no way of knowing whether you were being watched at any given moment. How often, or on what system, the Thought Police plugged in on any individual wire was guesswork. It was even conceivable that they watched everybody all the time. But at any rate they could plug in your wire whenever they wanted to. You had to live – did live, from habit that became instinct – in the assumption that every sound you made was overheard, and, except in darkness, every movement scrutinized. (176 words)

From: George Orwell, *Nineteen Eighty-Four*

to gaze – *starren, blicken*
to contrive – *bewerkstelligen*
telescreen – *Televisor*
simultaneously – *gleichzeitig*
to pick up – *registrieren*
field of vision – *Sichtfeld*
plaque – *Platte*
to command – *beherrschen*
to plug in on – *sich in etw einschalten*
guesswork – *Mutmaßung, Spekulation*
conceivable – *denkbar*
assumption – *Annahme*
to scrutinize – *genau ansehen, überprüfen*

1 LOOKING AT THE TEXT

→ Rezeption: Leseverstehen, S. 214

A Read the extracts from the novel and complete these tasks.

1. What is the most important characteristic of the poster? Write two or three sentences to describe its effect.
2. Explain in a few words how the poster is helpful to Big Brother.
3. Discuss the functions of the telescreen with a partner, then list them in order of importance.
4. Compare your order of importance with other students in your class and discuss any differences of opinion.

B Think: George Orwell's novel is seen as a warning against a totalitarian society. Can you think of any parallels today or in history?

C Pair: Discuss your ideas with a partner and them write them down in a few sentences.

D Share: Present your ideas in class.

2 READING

→ Rezeption: Leseverstehen, S. 214

A Before you read: Think about places you would expect to see CCTV cameras and places where you wouldn't expect (or want) to see CCTV cameras. Make a list.

B While you read: Note down the estimated numbers of CCTV cameras in Britain. Make a list of where they are located.

2/23

ONE SURVEILLANCE CAMERA FOR EVERY 11 PEOPLE IN BRITAIN, SAYS CCTV SURVEY

Britain has a CCTV camera for every 11 people, a security industry report disclosed, as privacy campaigners criticised the growth of the "surveillance state".

The British Security Industry Authority (BSIA) estimated there are up to 5.9 million closed-circuit television cameras in the country, including 750,000 in "sensitive locations" such as schools, hospitals and care homes. […]

Simon Adcock, of the BSIA, said: "[…] Effective CCTV schemes are an invaluable source of crime detection and evidence for the police. For example in 2009, 95% of Scotland Yard murder cases used CCTV footage as evidence."

But Nick Pickles, director of the privacy campaign Big Brother Watch, said: "This report is another stark reminder of how out of control our surveillance culture has become.

"With potentially more than five million CCTV cameras across country, including more than 300,000 cameras in schools, we are being monitored in a way that few people would recognise as a part of a healthy democratic society." […]

It estimated there are between 291,000 and 373,000 cameras in public sector schools, plus a further 30,000 to 50,000 in independent schools.

Surgeries and health centres have an estimated 80,000 to 159,000, while there are believed to be between 53,000 and 159,000 cameras in restaurants, the report said.

(216 words)

From: *www.telegraph.co.uk*

C Work with a partner and do these tasks.

1 Compare your two lists. Are there any places mentioned that you didn't expect to see?
2 Which figures from the text do you find surprising? Explain why (not).

D Say what it means: Explain these phrases in your own words.

1 'sensitive locations' (line 7)
2 an invaluable source of crime detection (lines 9–10)
3 (another) stark reminder (line 13)
4 our surveillance culture (line 13)
5 a healthy democratic society (line 17)

E Discuss in class: Do you think there are too many CCTV cameras in Germany? Do you feel threatened by too many surveillance cameras?

3 WORKING WITH WORDS

A Find words in the text on page 132 that go with the following words. There is sometimes more than one answer.

CCTV ▪ health ▪ independent ▪ privacy ▪ public ▪ security ▪ surveillance

B Complete the sentences with a suitable collocation from exercise 3A.

1. The ___ has just released a report with new estimates on the use of CCTV in Britain.
2. Care homes and ___ are just some of the 'sensitive locations' where CCTV schemes are used.
3. Many companies want to know more about their employees' behaviour, so they install ___ .
4. Cameras have also been installed in at least 291,000 ___[1] and 30,000 ___[2].
5. Angry ___[1] believe that society in Britain is on its way to becoming a ___[2].

4 WRITING

→ Produktion: Eine Stellungnahme schreiben, S. 234

Two readers publish the following comments about the article in *The Telegraph*:

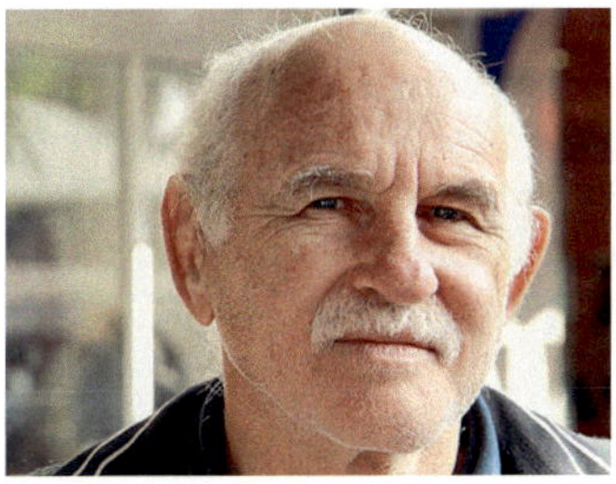

Terry Wilkins, Manchester

I totally agree with Simon Adcock when he says 'that effective CCTV schemes are an invaluable source of crime detection and evidence for the police.'

Nick Pickles is 100% right to say that 'we are being monitored in a way that few people would recognize as a part of a healthy democratic society.'

Alice Trent, Northern Ireland

Choose one of the opinions above and write a comment to be published in *The Telegraph* online, explaining why you agree with it.

Write your own comment on the following statement:

'Surveillance, whether by camera, phone or Internet, makes the world a safer place. If you have nothing to hide, you have nothing to fear.'

SKILLS CHECKLIST: Writing a comment

- ☑ Have I structured my arguments clearly?
- ☑ Have I given examples to support my arguments?
- ☑ Have I used linking words and phrases?

4/9

NURSING SKILLS SHORTAGES

The number of people needing care is rising in Germany, but qualified staff are scarce. To reduce the shortage, the Federal Employment Agency (BA) is sourcing personnel from countries including Portugal and the Philippines. But that will not be enough to meet the current level of requirement.

In March 2013, more than 10,000 jobs for carers for elderly people as well as 8,000 nursing jobs were reportedly unfilled. However, the Federal Association of Private Providers of Social Services (BPA) believes the sector needs an extra 50,000 health care professionals. The skills shortage is likely to get worse: the Bertelsmann Foundation predicts that by 2030 about half a million full-time nurses may be missing.

Nurses are recruited in Eastern Europe as well as in Southern European countries. However, so far with limited success: the BA's Central Placements Services (ZAV) only managed the placement of 56 foreign nurses in 2012, most of them from Portugal. Therefore, the ZAV is now turning to other countries such as the Philippines in search of qualified nurses and today it is due to sign an agreement with Bosnia.

"We are conducting a pilot project in China to recruit about 150 nurses", declared Beate Raabe, spokesperson for the ZAV. "The working conditions, social prestige, and the salaries in Germany are not so attractive, so highly qualified nurses seldom come to Germany" according to Professor Michael Isfort of the German Institute for Applied Nursing Research in Cologne. Nurses in Europe can currently choose where to go. "They are in demand in all countries," adds ZAV's Beate Raabe. Countries like Britain and Sweden have been very aggressively sourcing nurses from abroad for a long time. "They offer attractive living and working conditions, so they are a great competition for Germany," says Raabe.

Recruiters, unions and industry insiders report that it can be highly profitable for nurses to work in Scandinavia, Austria, Canada or Switzerland. They can earn up to €1,000 extra per month, compared with salaries in Germany. However, wages in Germany have increased in recent years, to reach between €2,000 and €3,000 per month for a nurse. In southern Germany, where the skill shortages are even worse, health care professionals often receive even higher compensation. (365 words)

Quelle: *www.staffingindustry.com*

1 LOOKING AT THE TEXT

→ Rezeption: Leseverstehen, S. 214

Write down all the numbers from the text and say what they mean.

EXAMPLE *10,000 = the number of carers for elderly people that are missing and needed*

2 WORKING WITH WORDS

Find the English equivalents in the text for these words and phrases.

1 knapp
2 Mangel
3 auf der Suche sein
4 Personal
5 Bedarfsniveau
6 anwerben
7 Gehalt
8 soziales Ansehen
9 (finanzieller) Ausgleich

3 MEDIATION

→ Schriftliche Mediation, S. 240

Freunde von Ihnen sind der Ansicht, dass es in Deutschland genügend Pflegekräfte gibt. Sie sind anderer Meinung und möchten eine Nachricht an Ihre Freunde schreiben. Sammeln Sie für Ihren Text Fakten aus dem Artikel. Übersetzen Sie nicht jedes Wort.

14 Energy and the environment

EXAM PREPARATION

FOCUS

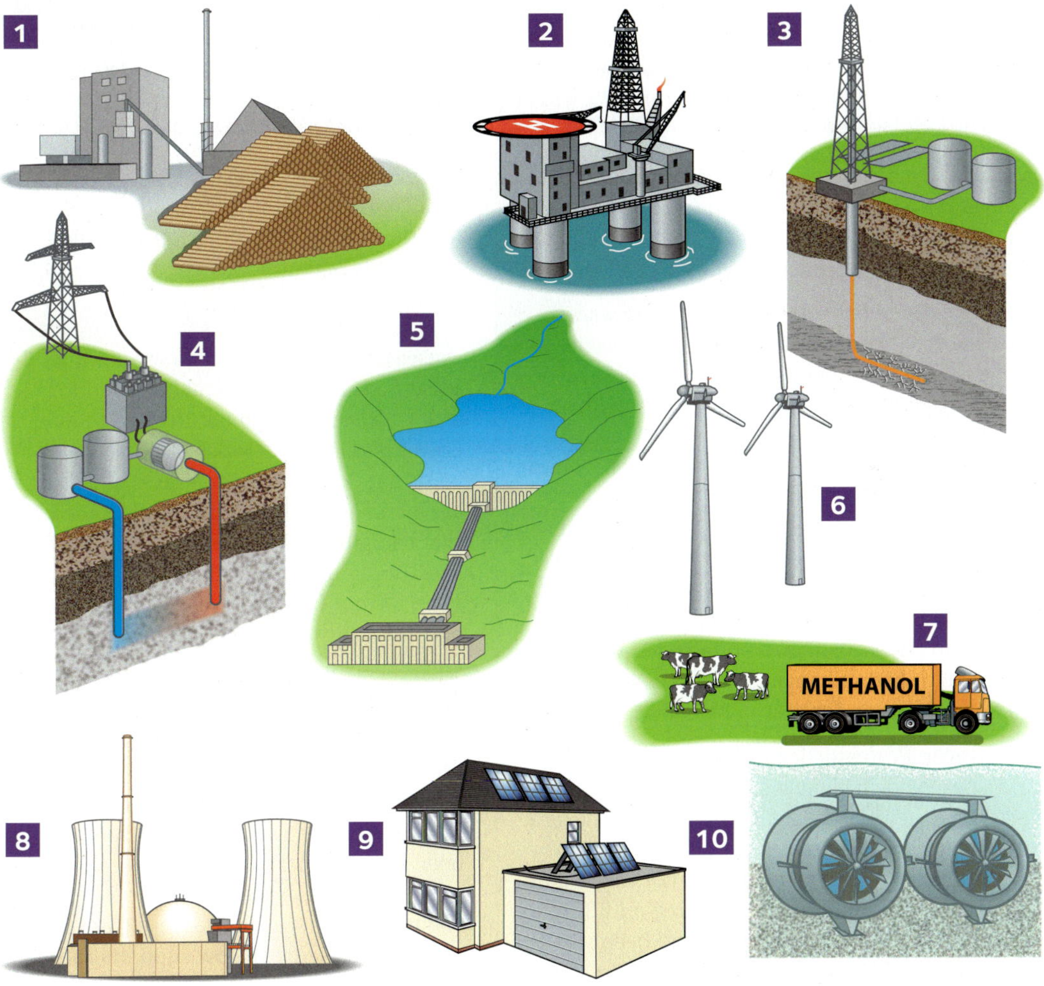

A Name the different forms of energy (1–10) above using the words in the box.

> solar power ▪ geothermal power ▪ nuclear power ▪ biomass ▪ fracking ▪ tidal power ▪ hydro-electric power ▪ wind power ▪ methane ▪ fossil fuel

B Group the sources of energy in the diagram under these two headings:

Renewable energy sources	Non-renewable energy sources
▬	▬

C Work in a small group. Imagine a complete breakdown of conventional, non-renewable energy supplies in Germany. (They make up about 75% of the total energy sources.) Imagine this happening in winter. How do you think it would affect everyday life?

TEXT A The real cost of energy

BEFORE YOU READ

Read the title. Say what you know about climate change. What might 'the debate' be about?

3/2

CLIMATE CHANGE: IS THE DEBATE OVER?

A Is climate change really happening? If so, are humans responsible, and how bad could it be for the world – and us? The issues are complex, and the debate has been long and often angry.

B Republican Senator for Texas Ted Cruz wants the freedom to use all energy sources, especially fossil fuels, and he argues strongly that these are not causing climate change. 'The problem with climate change,' he said recently to CNN, 'is that there's never been a day in the history of the world when the climate wasn't changing.'

'So you don't believe there's a man-made cause of global warming or climate change?' he was asked.

'What I think is that the data is not supporting what the advocates are arguing,' he replied. In the last 15 years, there had been no recorded warming, he went on. It hadn't happened, and they didn't have an explanation for that.

C However, Professor James Hanson, one of the world's best-known climate scientists recently rejected the views of 'deniers' like Cruz that climate change had stopped and that the effect of rising carbon dioxide levels on climate was not as great as had been previously thought. Speaking on BBC's Radio 4, he accepted that warming had been slower since 1998, but 'that's just natural variability,' he said. 'If you look over a 30–40 year period, the expected warming is two-tenths of a degree per decade, but this doesn't mean each decade is going to warm two-tenths of a degree: there is too much variability.'

Professor Hanson has very strong views on the causes of this warming. He has said that 'CEOs of fossil fuel companies should be tried for high crimes against humanity and nature' and that 'coal-fired power plants are factories of death.'

What do other experts say? According to a new survey of scientific studies by NASA, 97% agreed that climate change is real and that humans are at least partly to blame. Quoting this figure, CNN news anchor Carol Costello said, 'Why are we still debating climate change? There is no debate. Climate change is real.'

D So let us look at some actual data. The Industrial Revolution brought large-scale use of fossil fuels, and this steadily put more carbon dioxide and other 'greenhouse gases' into the atmosphere. Before, much of Earth's energy from the sun had been reflected back into space: by the 20th century, more and more of that energy was being held back and no longer escaped. The result was gradual global warming. The chart below supports the connection.

CO_2 concentration and global temperature change, 1950–2014

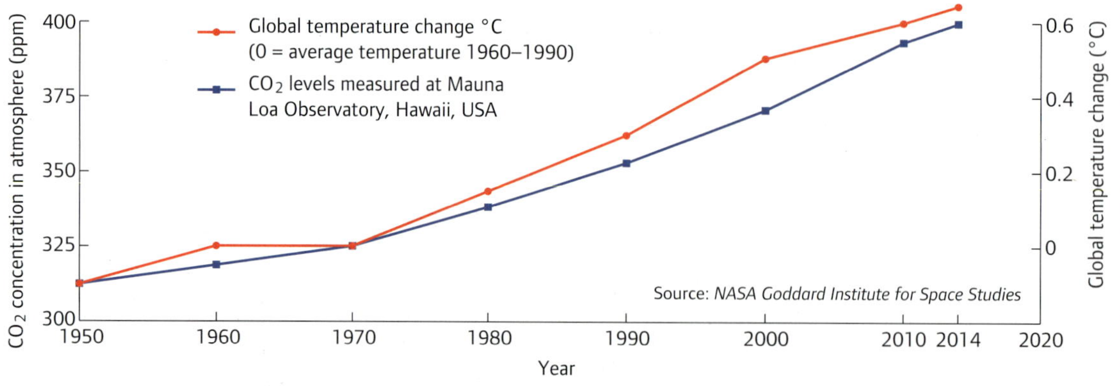

E In 2014, atmospheric CO_2 passed 400 parts per million (ppm) at speed while scientists warned again that the level must not rise beyond 450ppm. If it does, they predict, major climate changes will start to follow. At 560ppm, twice the average level of 280ppm before the Industrial Revolution, these changes will become disastrous and unstoppable. In Europe, summers will get much hotter and winters much wetter with many more sudden, violent storms – and we will be the lucky ones. In other parts of the world, life will become difficult or impossible. Africa's deserts will expand fast, hurricanes will force people to leave Central America and the USA's south-eastern coasts. Wild cyclones will do the same in Asia, from China to India. At the same time, the warming oceans will expand while the Greenland and Antarctic ice sheets continue to melt, raising sea levels by a centimetre per year (far beyond today's 2.9 millimetres per year). Many low-lying islands and coasts, along with great coastal cities such as New York and Shanghai will be drowning.

Is this disastrous picture of the future realistic? The answer is worrying. If emissions continue to grow as they are, the International Panel on Climate Change (IPCC) tells us that CO_2 levels will reach *1,000ppm* by 2100.

F However, a recent report prepared for the UN offers fresh hope. It argued that the world could still act in time to prevent the worst effects of climate change and also enjoy continued economic growth. This would be possible as long as the global economy was transformed in the next 15 years. Co-author Lord Stern, a leading expert on climate economics, said that dealing with climate change urgently would be cheaper than trying to do so decades in the future. In fact, it could create better economic growth than the old high-carbon model, he said. He gave the example of cities that were expanding massively in the developing world. If global investment in existing high-carbon infrastructure continued, a great opportunity would be lost. If, however, cities were designed around public transport, they could have more efficient economies because people would not have to spend hours in their cars commuting and polluting. This would mean lower carbon emissions, he said, and this in turn would mean better health and a better quality of life.

The report concluded that both rich and poor countries needed to act strongly to limit CO_2 emissions and to reduce dependence on coal and other dirty fuels. At the same time, economic growth could be encouraged through investment in renewable energy, sustainable cities, modern farming techniques and better-designed transport.

G To return to our questions: yes, climate change is happening, and humans are almost certainly largely responsible. As for how bad it could be, it seems that we still have one more chance to decide.

(897 words)

1 LOOKING AT THE TEXT

→ Rezeption: Leseverstehen, S. 214

A Skim the text and match the headings (1–7) below to the sections (A–G) of the text.

1 A win-win plan for carbon control and economic growth
2 Carbon and warming: a short history
3 Climate change this century: a worst-case scenario
4 The big climate questions that we face today
5 The opinion of most climate scientists
6 Three answers to three questions
7 Views of a climate change sceptic

B Read the text carefully and do the following tasks.

→ Umgang mit Operatoren, S. 232

1 Contrast the views of Cruz and Hanson on recent climate data.
2 Say what two sorts of information the chart shows. Describe the relationship between them.
3 Contrast the effects of climate change in parts of Africa and the south-eastern USA.
4 Describe two causes of future coastal flooding.
5 Give an example of the transformation that the new UN report calls for.

C Say what it means: Explain the underlined phrases from the text in your own words.

1 … 'coal-fired power plants are factories of death.' (line 36)
2 … CNN news anchor Carol Costello said, … (line 41)
3 … tells us that CO_2 levels will reach *1,000ppm* by 2100. (line 78)
4 This would be possible as long as the global economy was transformed … (line 83)
5 If global investment in existing high-carbon infrastructure continued, … (line 92)
6 … a better quality of life. (lines 99–100)

2 WORKING WITH WORDS

A Match words from box A to words in box B to make collocations related to the environment.

A carbon ▪ climate ▪ fossil ▪ global ▪ greenhouse ▪ ice ▪ industrial ▪ power ▪ public ▪ sea

B change ▪ emissions ▪ fuel ▪ gases ▪ levels ▪ plant ▪ revolution ▪ sheet ▪ transport ▪ warming

B Use collocations from exercise 2A to complete the following paragraph.

Oil, coal and natural gas are all ___ 1. At the start of the ___ 2, coal was used to power nearly all manufacturing, as well as all trains. However, these days coal is mostly used in coal-fired ___ 3 to produce electricity. By contrast, most forms of ___ 4, such as trains and buses, now use diesel. Carbon dioxide is one of a number of ___ 5 in the atmosphere that are causing global temperatures to rise. The rise of temperatures all over the world is called ___ 6. This is almost certainly leading to changes in weather conditions that are together known as ___ 7. The results are becoming clear. For example, the Arctic ___ 8 has been getting smaller for many years. ___ 9 are rising, too, and many coastal cities are probably going to be flooded in the future. The only answer is to limit ___ 10 by reducing our dependence on coal and other dirty fuels.

3 GETTING IT RIGHT

→ Indirect speech, S. 266

Rewrite these statements in indirect speech for a newspaper report. Change the contracted forms (e.g. *We're*) to full forms (*We are*) and make any other changes necessary.

During my trip to northern Canada last month, I spent time with a small Inuit community, and I had the chance to learn a little about the effects of climate change there.

1 'We're having big problems because the sea ice started melting two weeks ago,' community leader Jim Kupak told me.
Community leader Jim Kupak told me that they were …
2 He said, 'It isn't safe any more for us to go out on the ice – the way we've always done.'
3 'We've had to end our hunting season very early because we can't risk falling through the ice and killing ourselves,' he explained.
4 'I'm worried we may find ourselves very short of food in the coming months,' he added.
5 He finished by saying, 'The ice is melting earlier every year, and we won't be able to continue our way of life much longer if it doesn't stop.'

Write part of a school magazine report about a visit arranged by Mrs Bell, Head of Science. Use these reporting verbs and the underlined words in the conversation.

add ▪ promise ▪ remind ▪ say ▪ tell ▪ thank ▪ welcome

Mrs Bell is welcoming the guest speaker, Dr Ross:

Bell Dr Ross, we're very happy to see you here at Garston Sixth-Form College. It's very good of you to give Garston some time, and I'm sure we're all going to hear a fascinating talk.

Ross Well, let me just say that I'm very grateful to you all for the chance to speak to you, and I hope you'll hear at least a few things you'll find interesting.

Bell I'm sure we will. Remember, we specialize in science and technology at Garston, and so we're really looking forward to hearing about your new climate research.'

Ross Right, well, first of all, let me admit that climate change is a complex subject, which means I'll have to talk about some complex ideas, but I'll try and explain things in plain and simple English. Now, my team and I have just finished a report on our work in the Arctic that we started two years ago, and so I can say something about that. I also think there may be enough time to talk about our present project, in the Antarctic. By the way, next time we want to go somewhere warmer!

Mrs Bell, Head of Science, welcomed Dr Ross to our school. She said that it was ... , and she was sure that ...

4 WRITING

→ Produktion: Eine Stellungnahme schreiben, S. 234

A Read the following statement. Find points for and against it in the information box below.

'As a developing country, China should be allowed to produce carbon emissions freely unlike developed nations.'

Background information

1 From 2005–11, China added roughly two large coal-fired power stations every week for seven years. It is still building many more.
2 The country now burns 4 billion tons of coal p.a., the USA 1 billion and the EU 0.6 billion.
3 Fossil fuels still provide 87% of the country's energy, including 70% from coal. (The fossil fuel figure for Germany is about 57%.)
4 China's emissions per person are slightly lower than the EU's and much lower than in the USA. (China's population is 1.356 billion, while the USA's is 319 million and the EU's is 504 million.)
5 Producing goods competitively for developed countries causes many of China's emissions (i.e. developed countries have exported their pollution).
6 China needs its cheap coal for a fast-growing economy to provide new jobs and a rising standard of living.
7 The country's heavy pollution is causing a falling quality of life and health – and rising anger – among ordinary Chinese people.
8 China is now developing renewable energy sources twice as fast as the USA.

B Now write a comment on the statement. Put together several pairs of points for and against it, and end with your own conclusion. Use suitable phrases to connect your arguments.

TEXT B How do we keep the lights on?

BEFORE YOU READ

→ Vorbereitung auf das Lesen, S. 214

Read the headline and look at the diagram. Predict what the article is going to be about.

3/3

Does our energy security lie deep beneath our feet?

Julie Branson reports:
I was on my way by train from London to Brussels – to the latest conference on the environment. Opposite me sat Matt Radley, CEO of Energistic UK, a small company with big plans for fracking in the UK. He had agreed to be interviewed on our journey and I wanted his take on this controversial new UK energy source.

First, I asked him to explain the word 'fracking'. 'It's short for hydraulic fracturing,' he told me.

'It's the breaking of shale rocks deep underground to allow gas and oil to escape.'

I inquired how fracking was actually done. 'We drill down into shale formations, and then we pump down a mixture of water, chemicals and sand at high pressure. This pressure fractures the rock, and the sand keeps the new cracks open. The gas or oil is then brought to the surface and collected there.'

When I asked if this technology was new, he told me that it was new to Britain, but that over two million wells had already been drilled, mainly in the USA, and that this cheap-to-produce oil and gas had greatly reduced prices over there. 'What's more,' he added enthusiastically, 'Fracking will soon make America the world's biggest producer of oil and gas.'

What about the UK? I wanted to know whether Britain, too, had useful amounts of shale gas and oil. 'Yes,' he replied. 'In fact, Britain has huge quantities, and at Energistic UK, it's the gas we want. It's the cleanest of all the fossil fuels, and it's also the easiest to process and get to market. What's more, we really need it. The UK used to get all its gas from the North Sea, but most of that has now gone, and we have to import 70% of our

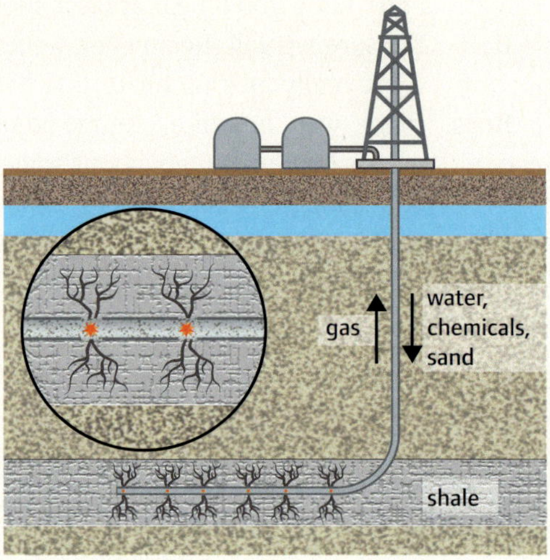

requirement. We need the energy security of our own gas again.'

But I was wondering why fracking was such a good option when shale gas was still a fossil fuel. I asked whether it would be better to leave the gas in the ground and rely on other energy sources instead, particularly renewables. Matt Radley's eyes lit up. 'No,' he said, 'and I'll tell you why.'

'Please do,' I replied.

'Right. Let's look at them one by one.' We had just come out of the tunnel near Sangatte, and he went on, 'There's a big nuclear power station very near here, so let's start with nuclear. France has got lots of nuclear plants, and they may seem to produce cheap power, but they're very expensive to build and very expensive to close down at the end of their working lives. We also have to wonder how safe they and their waste are.'

'What about tidal power, like the barrage at the mouth of the River Rance in Brittany?'

'Well, that was constructed half a century ago, and there aren't many others even now.

It sounds like free energy, but without big government subsidies, they don't get built. Wave power is even more difficult. If you can make and install equipment that will survive the power of the sea and the salt corrosion, fine. But it isn't happening.'

I moved on and asked if geothermal might work better. 'Yes, but it's only cost-effective in places like Iceland, which have hot rock formations close to the surface.'

Then I turned to hydroelectric power, and Matt Radley was quite positive. 'It's cheap and reliable, and it provides about six per cent of world energy,' he said. The problem was that in Britain there was little possibility of much further expansion.

'Well, what about free heat directly from the sun?' I asked.

'Ah, yes, solar energy,' came the reply. 'It's good in sunny regions, and it's getting cheaper, but in Britain we need most power on dark winter evenings and we can't rely on solar power for that!'

Finally, we turned to wind power, and my interviewee became a little annoyed. Onshore wind farms had only been built because of big subsidies, he said, and we were all paying those through higher energy prices. Offshore wind farms were much more efficient, he went on, but they were also much more expensive to build and maintain. Again, more subsidies.

On the high cost of wind and solar power, he pointed out that the world had invested $600 billion in wind and $700 billion in solar during the last ten years – huge amounts – but together these two technologies were producing just two per cent of the world's energy.

'So,' he concluded, 'let's stop picking losers. Let's go for shale gas!'

(770 words)

1 LOOKING AT THE TEXT

→ Rezeption: Leseverstehen, S. 214

A Read the text and put these energy sources in the order that they are discussed.

a fracking	**c** hydroelectric	**e** solar	**g** wave
b geothermal	**d** nuclear	**f** tidal	**h** wind

B Say whether the following are true or false. Correct the false statements.

1. Julie Branson and Matt Radley met on the way to Brussels by chance.
2. Sand is needed during fracking in order to stop the cracks from closing.
3. Matt Radley said that fracking was new to the UK and to the rest of the world, too.
4. Shale gas is less polluting than oil or coal, but it is still not clean.
5. Nuclear power may not be safe, but at least it is cheap.
6. Tidal power is easier to use than wave power, but it still does not make much economic sense.
7. Of all the renewables that Matt Radley discussed, he was most positive about geothermal and hydroelectric.
8. Matt Radley said that offshore wind farms were much more cost-effective than wind farms that were built onshore.

C Say what it means: Explain the underlined phrases in your own words.

1. … and I wanted his take on this controversial source of energy. (line 8)
2. 'It's short for hydraulic fracturing,' he said. (line 11)
3. I wanted to know whether Britain, too, had useful amounts of shale gas … (line 33)
4. 'So,' he concluded, 'let's stop picking losers.' (lines 105–106)
5. 'Let's go for shale gas!' (line 106)

2 WORKING WITH WORDS

A Copy and complete the tables with verbs and nouns from the text.

Verb	Noun	Verb	Noun	Verb	Noun
▬	production	▬	explanation	to expand	▬
to opt	▬	to form	▬	to corrode	▬
▬	reduction	▬	installation	▬	conclusion

B Use words from the same family to complete these sentences. They are all in exercise 2A.

1 Industrial waste greatly ▬[1] the numbers of fish in many rivers, but the huge ▬[2] in pollution in recent years has brought new life back.

2 **A** We need to ▬[1] more of our own food in this country.
B You're right, but the problem is that ▬[2] just isn't going up very much.

3 The Government's advisers have finally ▬[1] their study of new energy sources, and their ▬[2] is that wind, solar and fracking will all be necessary.

4 Auto Shanghai plan to ▬[1] production of electric vehicles from 50,000 per year to 200,000, and their ▬[2] programme starts next year.

5 **A** Can anyone ▬[1] why this machine isn't working?
B The ▬[2] is actually quite simple: you haven't turned on the power!

6 ▬[1] is the big problem with this bridge. Parts of the structure have been very badly ▬[2], and they need to be replaced immediately.

7 The International Panel on Climate Change (IPCC) was ▬[1] in 1988, and its ▬[2] led to much clearer scientific studies of global climate change.

8 **A** How long will it take to ▬[1] all the solar panels on the roof?
B The whole ▬[2] process should take just two days.

9 With the new houses being built over there, people will have two heating ▬[1]: they can choose gas or they can ▬[2] for a mix of gas and solar.

3 GETTING IT RIGHT

→ Indirect speech, S. 266

A Rewrite the questions as indirect questions, using the reporting verbs in brackets. Make any other changes that are necessary.

Matt Radley faced these questions at a press conference as Energistic UK prepared to begin work.

1 *New York Times* journalist: 'Is Energistic an independent company?' (inquire)
A journalist from the New York Times inquired if Energistic was …

2 BBC's Economics Editor: 'How many staff does Energistic have?' (ask)

3 Reporter from Radio 4: 'Have you had any previous practical experience of fracking?' (want to know)

4 Financial journalist from Frankfurt: 'How much has the company had to spend in order to prepare for commercial production? (inquire)

5 Local newspaper editor: 'Why has Energistic chosen to begin operations in our part of the country?' (inquire)

6 Environmental scientist: 'Do you really think you can get planning permission to go ahead?' (query)

B Rewrite the requests, instructions and advice in indirect speech, using the reporting verbs in brackets. Make any other changes that are necessary.

Annie is living away from home for the first time. After just a month, she receives a huge electricity bill and needs help. She calls home.

1 'Could you call Mum or Dad to the phone please?' she said to her brother Ben. (want … to)
She wanted her brother Ben to call Mum or Dad to the phone.
2 'Wait a minute while I get Dad in from the garden,' Ben said. (tell … to)
3 'Dad, could you talk to Annie on the phone?' said Ben. (ask … to)
4 'Dad, can you please, please tell me what to do about my crazy electricity bill for £537?' Annie begged. (beg … to)
5 'You'd better tell the electricity company that there's been a mistake,' her father advised her. (advise … to)
6 'Why don't you come home at the weekend and tell us how you're getting on?' he added. (invite … to)

4 LISTENING

→ Rezeption: Hörverstehen, S. 225

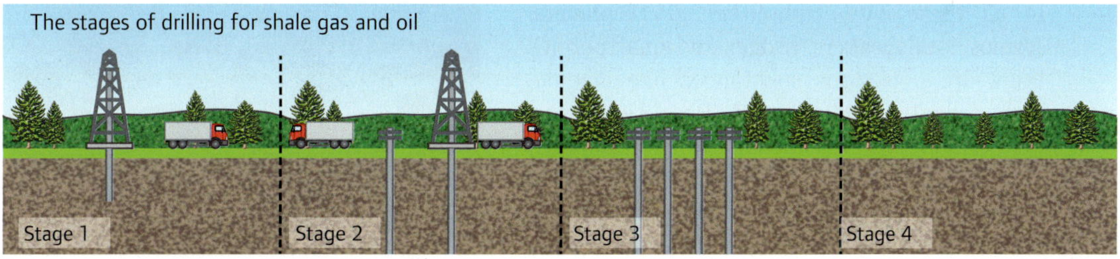

3/4 **A Listen and complete these tasks.**

1 Say what sort of event is starting.
2 Explain what the event is going to be about.
3 Say who has been invited to speak, and what you already know about his ideas.
4 Make notes about the four stages of fracking. Note a) the activity at each stage, and b) the time it takes.

3/5 **B Now listen and note the worries that people have about fracking in the right order. Add details about each point.**

earthquakes ▪ environmental damage ▪ gas ▪ traffic and noise

3/5 **C Listen again and note what Matt Radley says to calm the worries.**

5 DISCUSSION

→ Interaktion: An Diskussionen teilnehmen, S. 246

Work in a small group and discuss the following questions.

1 In principle, do you think fracking should be allowed or not?
2 Imagine you are now members of the local council. Should you accept or reject Matt Radley's particular project. (Consider the pros and cons from a local point of view.)

TEXT C The problem of waste

BEFORE YOU READ

What do you think happens to all the electrical appliances that we throw away?

3/6

WHERE DO OUR SCRAP TVS END UP?

Every year, Germany produces millions of tons of electrical waste. A large proportion of that doesn't end up in recycling but instead simply disappears. The German TV programme Panorama wanted to know where, so some broken TVs were fitted with tracking devices – and the trace led the reporters to Africa.

According to UN estimates, Germans produce two million tons of electrical waste every year. In all these TVs, computers, DVD players, stereos, loudspeakers, fridges and smartphones there are poisonous substances like arsenic, lead, cadmium and mercury. Because of this, the German Electrical and Electronic Appliances Law forbids the dumping of toxic waste in developing countries. Despite this, only 700,000 tons of electrical waste finds its way into the nationwide recycling system each year. No one really knows what happens to the remaining 1.3 million tons. It simply disappears – apparently most of it to Africa.

But why? It costs a lot of money to ship old TVs thousands of kilometers over the sea. Who profits from it? That is what the *Panorama* reporters wanted to find out, using an old TV and a tracking device. Together with a battery pack, the device was hidden in the TV's loudspeaker box. It transmitted its exact position at regular intervals and it also reacted to movement. Every time it was unloaded or moved, the transmitter sent an alarm to the reporters' mobile phones.

The TV was picked up by a man advertising free collection of broken electrical appliances on eBay. That was the start of a journey which shone some light on a shadowy but well-organized economic activity that customs and police are largely powerless to prevent.

The first stop on the journey was a dubious scrap dealer in Hamburg, where exporters select their goods. They collect old TVs and fridges in a warehouse, until they have enough to fill a ship with 40-foot containers.

Electrical waste dump in Agbogbloshie, Ghana

A long wait

After six nights waiting in Ghana, the reporters finally received a signal early in the morning. The TV had moved. No longer at the harbour, it was now in Accra, Ghana's capital, on the corner of Abeka Road and George W. Bush Highway.

The signal was strong because the TV had been unloaded and was now out in the open. When they arrived at the street corner, hundreds of TVs were piled up in the mud. A policeman sat under an umbrella and watched the clearance sale. The reporters asked where the goods came from. 'England.' Wrong!

A few metres farther on, eight silver Sony TVs were sitting next to the wall of a house. They found the mark they had made on the back of one of them. They shook it to activate the movement sensor and a message soon appeared on their phone, showing that the appliance had been moved. They returned the

TV and replaced it: they wanted to find out how its journey would continue.

The end of the journey

Journey's end was Agbogbloshie in Ghana, the biggest electrical waste dump in Africa and one of the ten most toxic places in the world.

About 500 containers of electrical appliances reach Ghana every month. Around Christmas, when Europeans replace old appliances with new ones, up to 1,000 arrive. Not all the electrical waste stays in Ghana: much is transported across West Africa, to Burkina Faso, Niger, Mali or Benin. But Ghana is the hub, and key to profit there is Agbogbloshie.

Forwarding agencies, shipping and transport companies all make money from the waste, as do middlemen and repair shops in Accra. At the very bottom of the value chain are the boys of Agbogbloshie. They break TVs apart with hammers, and they set fire to the insulating foam in order to separate the cable coating from the copper. For this, they get just 50 cents per TV.

Just 15 years ago this district of Accra was still a breeding ground for European migratory birds, but today it is the graveyard of our rubbish. It is also a place that poisons the many children and young people who work there. They are the ones who would have gutted the reporters' TV by hand if they had not finally found it at a dealer and bought it back for 100 euros. Worthless to them, the TV made money for a total of 11 people or companies along its 77-day journey to the scrapyard.

(721 words)

1 LOOKING AT THE TEXT

→ Rezeption: Leseverstehen, S. 214

A Read the text and complete the following tasks.

1. Explain the mystery of Germany's electrical waste.
2. Outline the method that the reporters used to discover the truth.
3. Contrast the purpose of German law and the actual situation in Agbogbloshie.
4. Say what the writer means by 'Ghana is the hub' (lines 76–77).
5. Name the 'people or companies along the journey' (lines 96–97) that the article mentions.

B Think of the last electrical appliance that your family threw away. Describe how you got rid of it. Do you think it went (or did not go) into the national recycling system?

2 MEDIATION

→ Schriftliche Mediation, S. 240

Sie bekommen folgende E-Mail von Ihrer Tante:

Antworten Sie auf die E-Mail Ihrer Tante. Erklären Sie ihr, was möglicherweise mit dem alten Kühlschrank passieren könnte, wenn er nicht ordentlich entsorgt wird.

… Zu Weihnachten gönnen wir uns einen fantastischen amerikanischen Kühlschrank mit allem Drum und Dran. Wir schmeißen den alten sofort weg … er wird morgen abgeholt … ;-)

3 WRITING

→ Produktion: Eine Stellungnahme schreiben, S. 234

Write a comment on the following statement.

'I don't understand that German law against sending electrical waste here. All kinds of people make money out of it – even those kids at Agbogloshie. Without the scrap TVs, they wouldn't have anything.'

Electrical waste trader in Accra, Ghana

4/10

Going Back to Nature with Forest Kindergartens

Radical back-to-nature forest kindergartens where children are allowed to climb trees and play with fire have spread across the country. Will the concept of the *Waldkindergarten* become Germany's next export success?

It's a chilly November morning, and half a dozen children are sitting in a circle singing songs and playing games. Pretty standard kindergarten fare the world over, but these children are sitting on logs in a forest around a campfire. This is no ordinary day care center, this is a *Waldkindergarten*.

Every morning, whatever the weather, 21 children arrive at *Die Kleinen Pankgrafen*, in Karow, a town just north of Berlin, one of more than 1,500 *Waldkindergartens* across Germany. The movement is also spreading overseas, with forest kindergartens in most continental European countries, a high demand in Japan and South Korea and a fledgling interest in the United States, Canada and the United Kingdom.

The thermometer is only just edging above freezing on this particular morning and biting easterly winds are making it feel more than a few degrees below zero. But Thorsten Reinecke, the head of *Die Kleinen Pankgrafen*, laughs at the reporter's concerns about the children's welfare. "This is nothing," he says. "'Whatever the weather' is not just a saying – we stay out until it gets to –28 degrees Celsius. The children never get cold even in three feet of snow. They, and their parents, know how to dress. They're like little onions – they're wrapped up in layers and layers of clothes."

Ute Schulte-Ostermann, president of the German Federation of Nature and Forest Kindergartens (BVNW), says there have been no serious injuries beyond the occasional broken leg in the organization's 20-year history. "There are far fewer accidents than at regular indoor kindergartens because we have fewer walls and softer floors – leaves and mud," she says. Schulte-Ostermann says life outdoors toughens the children up, reducing incidents of colds and flus. There is however, a much greater risk of contracting Lyme disease from tick bites.

Schulte-Ostermann says the risks are outweighed by the "massive" mental and physical benefits of playing outside. "Children who have attended a *Waldkindergarten* have a much deeper understanding of the world around them, and evidence shows they are often much more confident and outgoing when they reach school."

The first US *Waldkindergarten*, the Mother Earth School, opened in Portland, Oregon in 2007. There are just a handful in the UK, including the Secret Garden Outdoor Nursery in Fife, Scotland, which runs for 49 weeks of the year and has 40 children enrolled.

Schulte-Ostermann says she thinks the US and the UK's obsession with health and safety regulations may have slowed adoption of the idea, but points out that forest kindergartens have proved very popular in Japan, which is also known for its red tape bureaucracy. (464 words)

Abridged from: *www.spiegel.de*

DISCUSSION

→ Interaktion, S. 246

Discuss in small groups.

1 How do you think a forest kindergarten might help children develop an understanding of environmental issues?

2 Can you think of any reasons why parents should or should not send their children there? What are the pros and cons? (The prompts below might help you.)

allergies ▪ bad weather ▪ creative toys ▪ dirt and germs ▪ free play ▪ respecting nature ▪ social responsibility ▪ ticks ▪ wild animals

3 Do you think the forest kindergartens will become Germany's next export success? Why or why not?

15 Feeding the world

EXAM PREPARATION

FOCUS

One thing after another

A Work with a partner. Take turns to describe and analyse the cartoons.

cactus ▪ carbon emissions ▪ climate change ▪ deliver babies ▪ drought ▪ environmental pollution ▪ global warming ▪ greenhouse gases ▪ natural resources ▪ over-exploitation of resources ▪ rising population ▪ stork

B Now find links from cartoon to cartoon to explain the title 'One thing after another'.

C Discuss these questions with a partner.

1 Do you think the 'resources' stork has got weaker or stronger since you were born? Think of cases of drought and famine that have been in the news.

2 Do you think these problems are only found in developing countries – or are people ever short of food and other basics in rich countries such as Germany?

TEXT A How can we feed so many?

BEFORE YOU READ

→ Scannen nach Einzelinformationen im Text, S. 221

Scan the text for the following information:

a the area equivalent to the worldwide land use for crops
b the area equivalent to the worldwide land use for pastureland
c the percentage of crops that are used to feed animals

THE PLANET REPORT — September 20..

3/7

A PLAN TO FEED THE PLANET

The world has a problem – people. The human population passed 7 billion in 2012 and will probably hit 9.5 billion by 2050. That is a 35% increase in less than 40 years.

Does this mean a 35% increase in crop production, too? No, it actually means a 100% increase, from 9.5 billion tons to 19 billion, and the reason is this: as people in developing countries like India and China get a little more money, they always demand a richer diet with much more meat. Providing this requires far more crop production just to feed animals.

But nearly a billion people are already hungry, so we cannot possibly feed billions more, can we? Well, yes we can, and we can do it without taking more from Nature than we already have. To succeed, though, we must do four vital things.

1 Stop clearing more land for farming.
Growing more food has always meant taking more land from its natural state, including whole regions such as the North American prairies and the huge forests of Europe, each with its ancient ecosystem. Today, we use a land area the size of South America to grow crops and another the size of Africa for animal pastureland. Over half the world's ice-free land has been turned to human uses, and by far the greatest of these uses is agriculture.

We are destroying forests along with many plant and animal species, and while doing this, we are creating an even greater crisis. We are reducing Earth's ability to store carbon emissions from human activities – emissions that are pushing the planet towards disastrous climate change.

It is time to stop driving down this road to catastrophe.

The World's Total Land Area: 57.7 million square miles, of which:

Ice-covered: 7.4m sq miles (12.8%)	Other undeveloped: 23.4m sq miles (40.6%)	Farmland: 19.4m sq miles (33.6%)	Other human uses: 7.5m sq miles (13.0%)

Greenland & Antarctic ice sheets	mountains, forest, desert, tundra	pastureland, cropland	cities, infrastructure e.g. roads & railways, planted forests, etc.

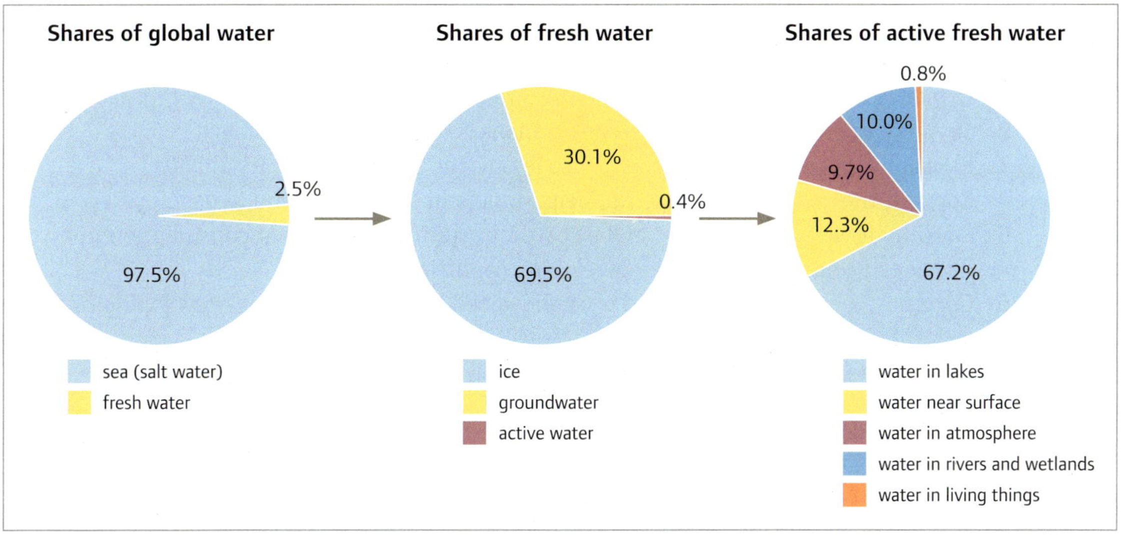

2 Produce more efficiently.

A typical American farmer produces three tons of crops per acre, whereas a farmer in sub-Saharan Africa may only produce half a ton. With better crop varieties and better techniques, that difference can be greatly reduced. Meanwhile, western agriculture can continue to become more efficient in other ways. Farm chemicals are expensive and polluting, so using less of them is very important. GPS and computer technology now help farmers decide what, when and where fertilizer is needed. This saves money and reduces pollution of precious water resources.

People have not always understood that water is so precious. Very little of our Blue Planet's water is fresh water that we can easily use, and after polluting and wasting much of it, we now find that clean supplies are declining. Farming takes 70% of all human water use and is at the centre of this crisis. Many farmers who draw their water from underground now have to go ever deeper to reach it.

Again, science is helping. New crop varieties that need less water are appearing. Better irrigation and new kinds of farming are also helping to reduce waste, making sure that the water we use is used well.

3 Change what we eat.

Feeding 9.5 billion people would be much easier if more crops actually fed people. In fact, just 55% of crop production is used that way, while a massive 36% feeds animals – mainly for meat production. (The rest is used in biofuel and other industrial production.)

Producing meat is not an efficient process: many kilos of grain are needed for every kilo of meat produced. Moreover, one kilo of grain takes 1,500 litres of water, but to produce one kilo of beef it takes 15,000.

Clearly, meat consumption must be reduced, starting perhaps with the rich, developed world. For many people in these countries, consuming less meat and more fruit and vegetables would also be a big step towards better health.

4 Cut waste.

Up to half of all food production is lost or wasted. In developed countries, a lot is thrown away because too much is prepared or because it has passed its use-by date. In poor countries, food is often wasted because it is stored badly or because transport to market takes too long. Just solving these problems alone would allow the planet to feed itself.

So yes, we can get through the coming food crisis, but only if we change the ways we produce, consume and think about food. Some changes will be huge and will need the cooperation of millions. Others will be small and individual – like the choices we make when doing the family food shopping at the supermarket. (736 words)

1 LOOKING AT THE TEXT

→ Umgang mit Operatoren, S. 232

A Read the text on pages 148–149 carefully and complete these tasks.

1 Explain why a population 35% larger will require a 100% increase in food production.
2 Say why the destruction of forest by humans is destructive for humans.
3 Explain why it is very important to use less water and to protect its quality.
4 Contrast the ways that science can help farmers in developing and in developed countries.
5 Say why it would be a) easier and b) better to start reducing meat consumption in developed countries instead of developing countries.
6 Contrast the ways in which food is often wasted in developed and in developing countries.

B Say what it means: Explain the underlined words and phrases in your own words.

1 … will probably hit 9.5 billion … (line 3)
2 We are destroying forests along with many plant and animal species, … (line 29)
3 … a farmer in sub-Saharan Africa … (line 39)
4 … now have to go ever deeper to reach it. (lines 57–58)
5 New crop varieties … are appearing. (line 60)
6 … because it has passed its use-by date. (line 85)
7 … the coming food crisis. (line 90)

2 WORKING WITH WORDS

Match meanings a–t to abbreviations and symbols 1–20.

1 am	5 m	9 wk	13 pw	17 =
2 e.g.	6 sq (miles)	10 yr	14 incl	18 +
3 etc.	7 approx	11 pa	15 &	19 –
4 i.e.	8 hr	12 pm	16 %	20 ×

a and
b and so on
c approximately
d is, equals
e any time from midnight to midday
f any time from midday to midnight; per month
g hour
h in other words
i including
j metre; million
k minus
l per week
m per annum, per year
n per cent
o plus; over
p square (miles)
q such as, for example
r times, multiplied by
s week
t year

Expand these notes.

1
Job title: Junior Manager
Terms & conditions: Work 40 hrs pw;
Starting: 9.00 am & finishing 5.00 pm;
3 wks paid holiday pa; salary
£1,750.00 pm = £21,000.00 pa

Terms and conditions for the job of Junior Manager are as follows. You will work …

2
New Dawn Garment's new factory
8,300sq m & employs 650 workers.
Produces 140,000+ garments pw =
approx 7.3m garments pa, incl e.g.
shirts, jeans, dresses, jackets, etc.

New Dawn Garment's new factory has an area of … It produces …

3 ANALYSING CHARTS

→ Produktion: Schaubilder beschreiben und analysieren, S. 238

Analyse the graphics in the text, interpreting their abbreviations and symbols to do so.

1 Analyse the diagram on page 148 with statements like this.
Ice-covered land makes up 7.4 million square miles, or 12.8 percent of the world's total land area, and it consists largely of the … . Other undeveloped land makes up …

2 Analyse the pie charts on page 149 with statements like this.
Of all the water in the world, 97.5 percent is salt water, and just … . Of all the freshwater in the world, …

4 GETTING IT RIGHT

→ Participles, S. 268

Join the pairs of sentences. Turn the first sentence into a participle clause using the word in brackets.

1 Sue Dryden went through a painful divorce three years ago. She moved to Amarillo, Texas with her young son Craig. (after)
After going through a painful divorce three years ago, Sue Dryden moved to Amarillo, Texas with her young son Craig.
2 They got there. She quickly had to get a job because her ex-husband was sending very little money. (after)
3 Sue lost her job a year ago. She and Craig had lived well enough on her salary of $2,200 per month. (before)
4 She lost that job. She has only been able to find part-time work at $7.75 per hour. (since)
5 She goes food shopping. She always tries to work out how much she can spend and what she can buy with that. (before)
6 She pays her rent and utility bills. She often does not have enough left to buy everything they need. (after)
7 She fell on such hard times. She has often gone to the local church food pantry for help. (since)
8 She collects her food parcel there. She is sometimes embarrassed to see volunteer workers that she knows from her old workplace. (while)

5 WRITING

→ Produktion: Eine Stellungnahme schreiben, S. 234

Write a comment on the following statement.

'THERE IS PLENTY OF FOOD TO FEED THE WORLD. ALL WE HAVE TO DO IS TO STOP WASTING IT, THEN NOBODY WILL GO HUNGRY ANY MORE.'

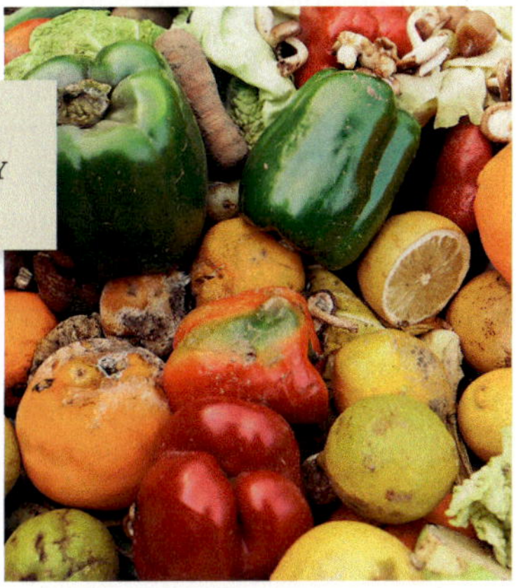

Useful phrases: partly agreeing with sb/sth

- While I agree that … , I do not accept that …
- I take the point that … . However, I question whether …
- For one thing, … . For another, …
- Then again, …

TEXT B Big problems – new solutions

BEFORE YOU READ

→ Scannen nach Einzelinformationen im Text, S. 221

Scan the text and say which is the main topic of the interview.

a the pros and cons of GM food
b how farmers can make more profit
c ways of providing more food for humans

3/8

The World This Week reporter Mark Moro is talking to scientist Dr Tanya Tate, an expert from the United Nations Development Programme.

Mark Moro: The big question facing us in the future is how is the planet going to feed itself? How can science help? First of all, let's talk about genetically modified food, or GM for short. As we all know, it's supported by some, but also feared by many. Dr Tate, could you tell us what GM is exactly?

Tanya Tate: To explain that, we need to look first at natural selection. Plant and animal species have always adapted to fit their particular environment on the planet. Members of a species with the best adaptations survive and pass their successful genes to the next generation. Others that are not so well adapted don't reproduce so successfully, and sooner or later, they become extinct.

Mark Moro: Haven't farmers used this natural process to breed better crops and better livestock since pre-historic times?

Tanya Tate: Yes, they take over the selection process in order to make more profit. This is selective breeding, and it works like this. They decide what physical features to aim at – more wool on a sheep, for example, or better resistance to disease. They then choose animals or plants to breed from – ones that are already nearer that ideal than others. After repeating the process for several generations, they then have an improved species.

Mark Moro: Improved because the herd or the crop is more productive and is therefore more valuable.

Tanya Tate: Right, and coming back to GM, we can see that this modern technology pushes the idea of species improvement much further. We can now modify the genetic code of a plant seed or an animal embryo by adding genes taken from other species. For example, adding a gene from a desert plant species can help a vegetable crop survive with much less water.

Mark Moro: This is species improvement by laboratory design, isn't it?

Tanya Tate: That's right.

Mark Moro: It sounds very useful.

Tanya Tate: It is, and this sort of GM technology will certainly help in parts of the world now suffering drier conditions – sub-Saharan Africa, for example.

Mark Moro: So what's the problem with GM food?

Tanya Tate: Well, let's think about a gene added to a crop that makes it resistant to herbicide – the sprays used to kill weeds. The weeds die, and the crop gets all the water and fertilizer provided by the farmer.

Mark Moro: So far, so good. That should produce the best crop possible.

Tanya Tate: But what if some of the pollen produced by the crop reaches weeds growing nearby? What if it fertilizes those weeds? In no time, we could have weeds that are resistant to herbicide. We could soon find ourselves with weeds resistant to all known chemical controls – weeds that might take over the world!

Mark Moro: That would be a big downside! So, are there other new ways to help produce the food we need?

Tanya Tate: Yes, in particular there's an exciting technology called hydroponics.

Mark Moro: 'Hydro'? That means it is connected with water?

Tanya Tate: Yes, hydroponic farming doesn't use soil. Instead, it uses water containing the exact amount of nutrients required. This way, roots don't have to grow through thick soil, sometimes finding the necessary nutrients but often not. Instead, the nutrients are absorbed easily by the plant roots as they grow down into the flow of water. That's much more efficient, and crops grow very fast. What's more, it's a closed system, so the same water is used again and again, and there's no pollution of rivers and groundwater.

Mark Moro: Wow! Is this something very new?

Tanya Tate: No, it was first used in the 1930s. American flights to Hawaii landed for fuel on a piece of rock called Wake Island. Thanks to hydroponics they also took off again with fresh salad and vegetables for the passengers. Today, it's used a lot in Iceland, another place with very little soil, and at the Amundsen Scott South Pole Station, a place with no soil at all, of course!

Mark Moro: Fine, but is it being used more widely than that?

Tanya Tate: Yes, it's taking off in many parts of the world. Farmers can grow up to 20 high-quality crops a year, causing very little waste

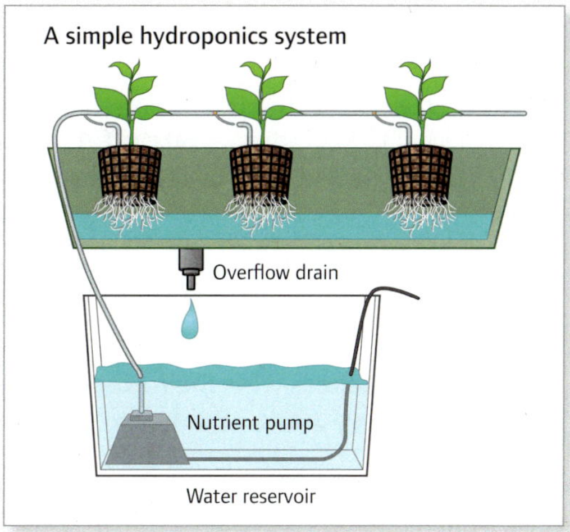

and pollution and making very good money. It takes up much less space than ordinary farming, too.

Mark Moro: What's the next step?

Tanya Tate: Vertical farms. People are now creating city-centre farms in tall buildings to grow food for the people right where the people are. That means another big saving: food miles. The environmental cost of taking food many miles from farm to supermarket almost disappears! (795 words)

1 LOOKING AT THE TEXT

→ Rezeption: Leseverstehen, S. 214

A Read the text and make notes. Use your notes to do these tasks.

1. Outline briefly the three methods of improving farm productivity that the speakers discuss.
2. Contrast the effects of natural selection and selective breeding.
3. Explain why disease resistance can be just as important for productivity as sheep that produce more wool.
4. Explain the sort of benefit GM offers, and the sort of danger that it creates.
5. List the environmental advantages of hydroponics.
6. List the economic advantages of hydroponics.

B Say what it means: Explain the underlined words and phrases in your own words.

1. The big question facing us … (line 5)
2. … since pre-historic times? (line 23)
3. So far, so good. (line 61)
4. But what if some of the pollen produced by the crop reaches weeds growing nearby? (line 63)
5. In no time, we could have weeds … (line 66)
6. That would be a big downside! (line 71)

2 WORKING WITH WORDS

→ Rezeption: Ein Wörterbuch benutzen, S. 217

take [Phrasal verbs]

take in **1** understand clearly the meaning or importance of something **2** trick someone into believing something that is not true **take off** **1** remove something, especially clothes **2** leave the ground and start flying **3** suddenly start to be popular or successful **take on** **1** accept a job or responsibility **2** give a job to someone **3** fight or compete against someone or something **take over** **1** start doing something that someone else was doing **2** take control of something **take up** **1** fill an amount of space or time **2** start doing a particular job or activity

Read the sentences with their examples of phrasal verbs formed from *take*. Then check the dictionary entry above and decide which meaning matches each example.

1 We could soon find ourselves with weeds that might **take over** the world! *meaning 2*
2 Thanks to hydroponics planes **took off** again with fresh salad vegetables.
3 Hydroponics is **taking off** in many parts of the world.
4 Hydroponics **takes up** much less space than ordinary farming.

Read these sentences to decide which phrasal verb and which meaning each requires.

1 I had to read her letter three times before I could ▬ the awful truth. *take in – meaning 1*
2 You'd better ▬ that wet jacket and warm yourself by the fire.
3 The company is moving to Stuttgart, and we're ▬ 20 new staff there.
4 Sally's ▬ too much, and she's making herself ill with all the stress.
5 Silke pretends that she's happy and she ▬ most people, but I know that she's really very sad.
6 I've ▬ the guitar recently, and I'm enjoying it a lot.
7 Would you mind ▬ the cooking while I get a few things from the shop?
8 Next Saturday, our team are ▬ the champions, and I really hope we'll win!

3 GETTING IT RIGHT

→ Participles, S. 268

Change the relative clauses (starting with *who, which, that*) to *-ing* or *-ed* clauses.

Fish are an important source of food <u>which has been hunted</u> for thousands of years and <u>which still provides</u> millions of people with much of their protein. However, the modern techniques which have been developed to make fishing more efficient are too successful. In many parts of the world, the huge numbers that are being caught leave too few fish to maintain stocks, and so wild fish populations are crashing.
One answer to the fish stock crisis which is developing worldwide is to reduce the amount of fishing, and this is something that is happening today in the North Sea, for example.
Another answer is fish farming, which has now developed along coasts and in rivers and lakes all over the world. However, such fish farms often have severe problems which include pollution and disease. Someone who is taking a different approach is Brian O'Hanlon with his huge diamond-shaped fish cages that have been built eight miles off the coast of Panama and which contain up to a million fish. Far out at sea, these cages, which are constantly washed by the open sea, remain unpolluted and disease-free.

Fish are an important source of food hunted for thousands of years and still providing ...

4 LISTENING

→ Rezeption: Hörverstehen, S. 225

You are going to hear Tanya Tate talking about a commercial hydroponics system.

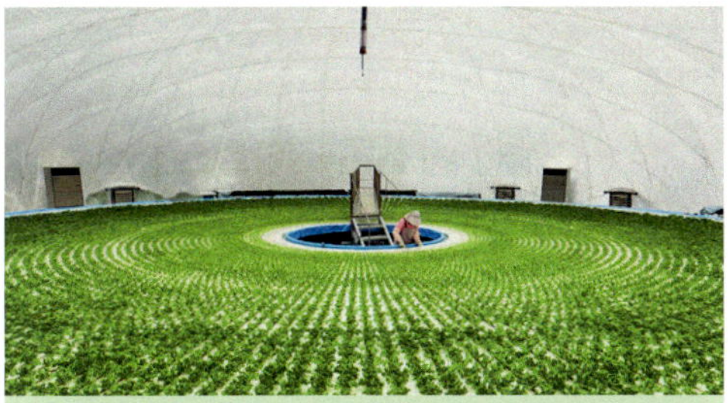

Lettuce is grown in a hydroponic culture in a dome greenhouse in Japan in July 2012.

A worker harvests fresh produce from a tower at Sky Greens vertical farm in Singapore in July 2014.

3/9

A Copy these notes, then listen and complete them. Which system is Tanya Tate describing?

Name of system: ▬
Country designed: ▬
Used to grow: ▬
Basic shape: ▬
Movement (horizontal/vertical): ▬
Speed of turn: ▬
Size: ▬
Running cost per frame: ▬

3/10

B Now listen to the second part of Tanya's talk and make notes. Then answer these questions.

1 What two advantages does this system have over traditional farming?
2 Why will food production need to be close to cities in the future?
3 What makes food farming in Singapore difficult?
4 Why is the government of Singapore unhappy about this situation?
5 What does the government want to do to change this?

5 PROJECT

Work in small groups and research hydroponics farming systems online. Choose one of the commercial systems currently in operation and present it to the class.

6 WRITING

→ Produktion: Schreiben, S. 228

PROPOSALS SOUGHT FOR CITY POWER STATION REDEVELOPMENT

After more than 80 years of service, the Old City Power Station has closed. With its splendid, high turbine hall and all-glass roof, it is a Grade 1 industrial building that cannot simply be pulled down. By law, it must be redeveloped in some way that will be useful to the city community. The Redevelopment Committee have already received several proposals but would welcome more.

You see this article in a local paper in the UK and think the power station could be redeveloped as a hydroponics farm. Write a letter to the chairperson of the Redevelopment Committee.

- Describe the basic concept of hydroponics and its advantages.
- Explain the particular advantages of redeveloping the power station as a hydroponics farm.
- Support your argument with an example of a successful project of the same sort.

TEXT C A case study

BEFORE YOU READ

What are the alternatives to farming on an industrial scale in Germany?

3/11

IS GM THE BEST WAY FORWARD FOR AFRICA?

Millions of poor African farmers depend on one or two crops such as cassava both to sell and to feed their families. If disease strikes, they face disaster. Today, high-tech GM technology is beginning to offer the possibility of new versions of such crops modified to resist pests, but so far only four African countries – Egypt, Sudan, South Africa and Burkina Faso – have allowed the commercial planting of GM crops. Fear is one reason for this, but more importantly the basic fact is that most African farmers need a simpler, cheaper way forward.

In Tanzania there are no GM crops yet. But some farmers are learning that a simple low-tech solution – planting a diversity of crops – is one of the best ways to deter pests. Tanzania now has the fourth largest number of certified organic farmers in the world. Part of the credit belongs to a young woman named Janet Maro.

Maro grew up on a farm near Kilimanjaro, the fifth of eight children. In 2009, while still an undergraduate at the Sokoine University of Agriculture in Morogoro, she helped to start a non-profit organization called Sustainable Agriculture Tanzania (SAT). Since then she and her small staff have been training local farmers in organic practices. [...]

Morogoro lies about a hundred miles west of Dar es Salaam, at the base of the Uluguru Mountains, and Maro takes me into the mountains to visit three of the first certified organic farms in Tanzania. We lurch up a steep, rutted road in a pickup. Greened by rains drifting in from the Indian Ocean, the slopes remain heavily forested. But increasingly, they've been cleared for farming by the Luguru people. [...]

She stops at a one-room brick house with partially plastered walls and a corrugated metal roof. Habija Kibwana, a tall woman in a short-sleeved white blouse and wraparound skirt, invites us and two neighbors to sit on her porch. [...]

Mixed rows of crops: corn and fruit trees

Kibwana and her neighbors raise a variety of crops: bananas, avocados, and passion fruit are in season now. Soon they'll be planting carrots, spinach and other leafy vegetables, all for local consumption. The mix provides a backup in case one crop fails; it also helps cut down on pests.

The farmers here are learning to plant strategically, setting out rows of a wild sunflower that whiteflies prefer, to draw the pests away from the cassavas. The use of compost instead of fertilizers has improved the soil so much that one of the farmers [...] has doubled his spinach production. Runoff from his fields no longer contaminates streams that supply Morogoro's water.

Perhaps the most life-altering result of organic farming has been the liberation from debt. Even with government subsidies, it costs 500,000 Tanzanian shillings, more than $300, to buy enough fertilizer and pesticide to treat a single acre – a crippling expense in a country where the annual per capita income is less than $1,600. 'Before, when we had to buy fertilizer, we had no money left over to send our children to school,' says Kibwana. Her oldest daughter has now finished high school. And the farms are more productive too. 'Most of the food in our markets is from small farmers,' says Maro. 'They feed our nation.'

When I ask Maro if genetically modified seeds might also help those farmers, she's skeptical. 'It's not realistic,' she says. How could they afford the seeds when they can't even afford fertilizer? How likely is it, she asks, in a country where few farmers ever see a government agricultural adviser, or are even aware of the diseases threatening their crops, that they'll get the support they need to grow GM crops properly?

From Kibwana's porch we have sweeping views of richly cultivated terraced slopes – but also of slopes scarred by the brown, eroded fields of non-organic farmers, most of whom don't build terraces to retain their precious soil. Kibwana says her own success has attracted the attention of her neighbors. Organic farming is spreading here. (659 words)

From: *National Geographic*, October 2014

1 LOOKING AT THE TEXT

→ Rezeption: Leseverstehen, S. 214

A Read the text and complete these tasks.

1 List the African states which allow commercial GM.
2 State the problems with GM for most Africans.
3 List the special features of organic farming in Tanzania.
4 Explain the general benefits of organic farming.
5 Point out a particular benefit to the Kibwana family.
6 Contrast the appearance of local organic & non-organic farms.

B Say what it means: Explain the underlined words and phrases in your own words.

1 … a simple low-tech solution … (lines 14–15)
2 … she helped to start a non-profit organization … (line 24)
3 … bananas, avocados, and passion fruit are in season now. (line 44)
4 … the food in our markets is from small farmers, … (line 70)
5 … they'll get the support they need to grow GM crops properly? (line 80)

2 MEDIATION

→ Schriftliche Mediation, S. 240

In regelmäßigen Abständen veröffentlicht Ihre Schulzeitschrift Beiträge von Schülern und Schülerinnen unter der Rubrik „Mensch und Umwelt“. Nach der Lektüre des Textes „Is GM the best way forward for Africa?“ möchten Sie die Biolandwirtschaft in Afrika einem breiterem Publikum in Deutschland vorstellen.

Schreiben Sie einen Artikel für die Schulzeitschrift, in dem Sie die Vorteile des *organic farming* für Afrika erklären.

3 WRITING

→ Produktion: Eine Stellungnahme schreiben, S. 234

Write a comment on the following statement.

'Maybe organic farming is right for Tanzania, but I don't see the point here in Germany. Organic produce is much too expensive for most people to buy here, and anyway I don't think it tastes any better than ordinary food.'

4/11

WATER FOR LIFE

When Dirk King, a senior at Middleton High School in Wisconsin, travelled to Guatemala as a Good Neighbors volunteer during his senior year, he was shocked to see that poor children often had to walk miles each day to collect water, especially in the dry season, which lasts from November to April. And worse, the water the children and their mothers collected was often not even clean, but had been taken from dirty puddles or nearby rivers where people also washed themselves and their clothing. These unsanitary conditions resulted in many of the children suffering from diarrhoea, malaria and other serious illnesses and diseases.

Dirk quickly realized how important access to clean water was for quality of life, and when he returned home he decided to spread the word about the "Water For Life" project in Guatemala. With the help of students in his and other high schools, Dirk succeeded in getting people in his town to donate money. Together, the students raised $9,000, and Good Neighbors was able to build three clean water wells and a 50,000-liter rain catchment tank at Escuela de Pacaja, a school in Guatemala that uses the school's roof to collect water.

On a recent visit to Guatemala, Dirk saw that water was not only important for better health and hygiene, but also for the morale and happiness of the students. He said, "Clean water and sanitation are necessary to protect children's health and their ability to learn at school. In this sense, they are as important as textbooks to a child's education." (258 words)

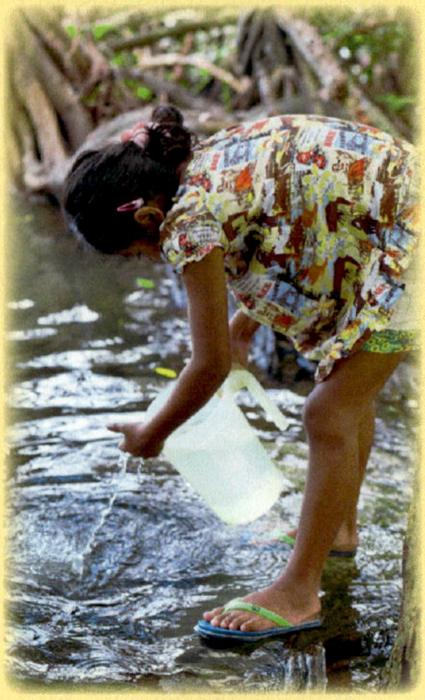

1 TWO PHOTOS

Compare the two photos. Find sentences in the text that can help you.

2 MEDIATION

→ Schriftliche Mediation, S. 240

Sie möchten Ihre Schule überzeugen, Geld für ein *Water For Life* Projekt zu sammeln. Suchen Sie im Text nach relevanten Informationen und machen Sie sich Notizen auf Deutsch, um das Projekt präsentieren zu können. Übersetzen Sie nicht Wort für Wort.

3 DISCUSSION

→ Interaktion, S. 246

Discuss in small groups. Could you do with less water? How could you save water? Present your finding to the class.

Useful phrases

- I (don't) use a lot of water but …
- I (don't) think it is easy to … but …
- I think household appliances like washing machines should …
- In my opinion, we all waste water when we …
- We could save water by washing …

16 Technology

FOCUS

a

b

c

d
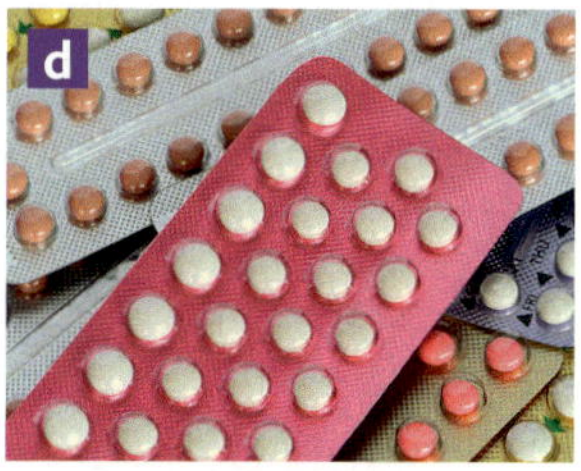

e

f

g

h
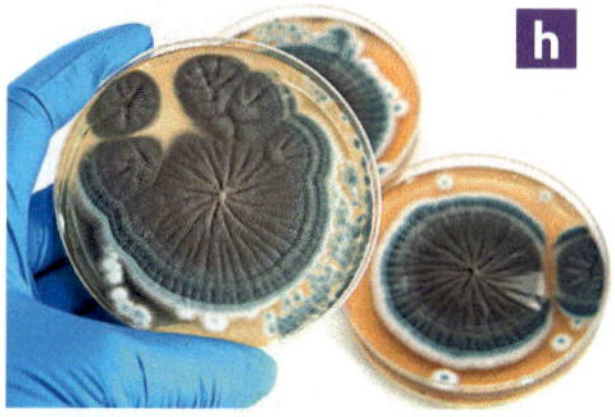

i
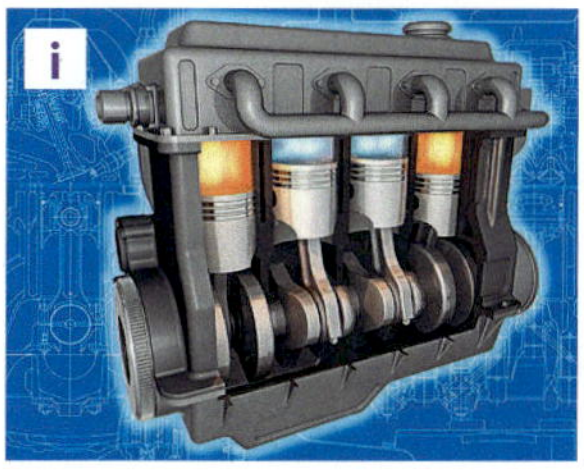

j

k

l

A Match these important, life-changing inventions to the pictures (a–l) above.

the compass ▪ contraceptives ▪ the internal combustion engine ▪ the Internet ▪ the light bulb ▪ the nail ▪ penicillin ▪ the printing press ▪ refrigeration ▪ the telephone ▪ the washing machine ▪ the wheel

B Copy and expand the table. Consider the 12 inventions above. List them all in column 1 in your personal order of importance. (If you think something else is more important, you can replace <u>one</u> item.)

The world's most important inventions

	Personal choice	Group choice	Class choice
1			

C Work in a small group. Discuss everyone's choices and decide as a group on the most important invention of all. Note this choice in your table.

D Report your group choice back to the class for further discussion. Have a class vote on the final group choices and list the top three inventions in the table.

TEXT A The spread of digital communication

BEFORE YOU READ

A Say what you mainly use your mobile phone to do.

B Say how else people can use a modern smartphone.

3/12

AFRICA'S DIGITAL REVOLUTION

[...] When Wesley Kirinya buys a latte, he pays his bill of 100 Kenyan shillings (€0.85 or $1.16) by text message. First he types in the café's telephone number and enters a PIN. Then he hits 'send' and the transaction is complete.

This payment system is known as M-Pesa. The 'M' stands for 'mobile' and 'pesa' means 'money' in the local language of Swahili. M-Pesa turns a mobile phone into a bank account, credit card and wallet all in one. Invented in Kenya, the system is now used in nearly all developing nations. These days, a third of Kenya's economy is conducted via M-Pesa – at a time when, in Europe, a few major cities are just starting to experiment with the possibility of paying for parking via mobile phone. [...]

Sub-Saharan Africa is the world's fastest-growing market for mobile phones, tablets and laptops. There are more SIM cards in use here than in North America. And with nearly half the continent's population of 900 million people under the age of 15, experts estimate there will be over 1 billion additional mobile phone users here by 2050.

Mobile Phones Where Governments Fail

In less than 10 years, mobile phones and the Internet have changed many Africans' daily lives more dramatically than anything else since African nations won their independence from former colonial powers. [...]

Where there are mobile phones there is less need to lay cables for conventional landline telephones. There is also less need to build highways, clinics and schools, because mobile phones are all these things in one – as well as bank, weather station, doctor's office, atlas, compass, textbook, radio and TV station. Africans can now send money across the jungle or savannah with the click of a button, merchants can compare prices, and farmers can access weather data relevant to their harvests or get advice from veterinarians. Bloggers and social media users also function as a substitute for a free press, keeping watch over those in power. [...]

Cutting-Edge African Apps

African IT developers have to be especially creative given the continent's limitations. The greatest obstacle to their work is the fact that so far only a small proportion of the mobile phones used in Africa are Internet-enabled. But African programmers have found ways to coax more functions out of basic mobile phones. Special programs, for example, can turn text messages into emails, allowing people to send text messages to government authorities, universities or banks which are then processed and continue their trajectory online. [...]

A successful app from Africa that works via text message basis is iCow. [...] Small farmers throughout the country can register for the program and then enter their animals' age, breed, weight, sex and date of last calving, and iCow automatically sends them advice developed by veterinarians concerning feed, illnesses and fertility cycles. To make it possible for illiterate farmers to use the program as well, it uses voice messages rather than text. [...]

The Internet helps sick people, too. Hardly any doctors in Africa practise entirely offline these days, even in the most remote locations. Practices in small villages can send their lab results to university clinics, and receive diagnoses and treatment suggestions in return. Such reporting systems also make it possible to identify the start and spread of epidemics early on.

Africa's Digital Visionary

'It's now easier, technically speaking, to supply a village with Internet access than with clean water,' says Mo Ibrahim, a man who has done more than almost any other person for Africa's digital revolution. Time magazine has named the Sudanese businessman one of the most influential people of our time. [...]

Mo Ibrahim announces that the Mo Ibrahim Foundation is awarding Nobel Peace Prize winner Desmond Tutu a $1 million grant in 2012.

Ibrahim founded his company Celtel, one of the first mobile phone providers in Africa, in 1998. Despite having had a successful career as an engineer at British Telecom and being the founder of an IT consulting firm in London, Ibrahim wasn't satisfied. 'I never entirely became a European.' He says. 'Africa is simply part of me.'

In the years that followed, Celtel expanded into 13 countries, with 24 million people using the company's network, and 5,000 employees. When Ibrahim sold Celtel in 2005, he received $3.4 billion. [...]

Ibrahim also created a foundation which releases an annual ranking of good and bad governance among African nations. The foundation also presents the annual Ibrahim Prize for Achievement in African Leadership, which awards $5 million to a commendable African politician. This year, though, for the third year in a row, the jury found no one it considered worthy of receiving the prize.

Does that mean things in Africa are not, in fact, getting better? Ibrahim shakes his head and says he does believe the continent is developing – primarily thanks to mobile phones and the Internet. 'The mobile phone is an important tool of civil society,' he says. 'If a border customs officer extorts money from you, take his picture with your mobile phone and put it online. If someone pressures you during an election, do the same.'

Even tensions between tribes and ethnic groups can be overcome, Ibrahim believes, if people are connected by the Internet instead of leading isolated existences in their own villages. 'The more we know about each other, the more difficult it is to sow discord,' he says. 'Through modern communications, Africans will learn that it's better to do business with each other than to hate each other.' (888 words)

Abridged and adapted from: *www.spiegel.de/international*

1 LOOKING AT THE TEXT

→ Rezeption: Leseverstehen, S. 214

A Read the text carefully and complete these tasks.

1. Compare the development of mobile phone commerce in Europe and in countries like Kenya.
2. Explain why mobile phone use in Africa is predicted to rise so rapidly between now and mid-century.
3. Say why mobile phone systems are saving African governments a lot of money.
4. Explain why IT developers in much of Africa need to be particularly creative.
5. Outline the career of Mo Ibrahim.
6. Say how the Internet can bring greater peace and harmony to Africa.

B Say what it means: Explain the underlined words and phrases in your own words.

1 … Internet-enabled. (line 51)
2 … ways to coax more functions out of basic mobile phones. (lines 52–53)
3 Hardly any doctors in Africa practise entirely offline … (line 70)

C Say what the underlined words and phrases refer to in your own words.

1 … which are then processed … (line 57)
2 To make it possible for illiterate farmers to use the program as well, … (line 67)
3 … to identify the start and spread of epidemics early on. (line 76)
4 If someone pressures you during an election, do the same. (line 115)

D Say what you think.

'I think Europe should have something like the Ibrahim Prize for Achievement. But which "commendable" European politician would we give it to this year?'

2 WORKING WITH WORDS

A Copy and complete the tables. The first two items in each table are in the text.

Verb	Noun
to pay	▬
to govern	▬
to develop	▬

Noun	Adjective
addition	▬
convention	▬
function	▬

Verb	Noun
to suggest	▬
to communicate	▬
to invent	▬

B Use pairs of words from exercise 2A to complete the following.

1 When Alexander Graham Bell ▬[1] the telephone in 1875, he did not realize what an important ▬[2] it would become.
2 Before the mobile phone, ▬[1] across much of Africa were still very poor, and it was difficult for people to ▬[2] outside the big cities.
3 One effect of bad communications in many African countries was weak central ▬[1]. In distant areas, the ones who really ▬[2] were local leaders.
4 With the ▬[1] of several new countries to its mobile phone network soon after 2000, Celtel quickly had an ▬[2] five million customers.
5 I just want a basic ▬[1] phone that I can use to call and text people. I don't need all the clever ▬[2] of a smartphone.
6 We need to stay in contact daily, and I've got a ▬[1] to make. I ▬[2] that I call you every evening at about 6 pm.
7 You don't need to ▬[1] for your new phone today. You can make monthly ▬[2] instead.
8 There are various ▬[1] phone expressions such as 'Could you speak up, please?' But there isn't really a fixed ▬[2] on what you should say when you first answer the phone. Some people just say 'Hello', while other people follow this with their phone number and others give their name.
9 African IT engineers are ▬[1] new software for basic mobile phones all the time. These have allowed the ▬[2] of many new kinds of business across the continent.

3 GETTING IT RIGHT: A GRAMMAR QUIZ

A Mixed tenses: Complete the sentences with the correct verb form.

1 We ▬ new copies of the report right now. (make / are making)
2 ▬ that email last night? (Did you send / Have you sent)
3 We ▬ at the Riverside Café this evening. (eat / 're eating)
4 On my way home, I ▬ for a coffee nearly every day. (stop / 'm stopping)
5 Harry and Lisa ▬ when the rest of us arrived. (were talking / talked)
6 If you like, I ▬ that heavy case for you. ('m going to carry / 'll carry)
7 These old trainers are falling to pieces, and I ▬ a new pair soon. ('m going to buy / 'll buy)
8 I promise I ▬ there on time. ('m going to be / 'll be)
9 We ▬ for ages, but we're nearly home at last! ('ve travelled / 've been travelling)
10 I called at the house to find everyone, but they ▬ home. (had gone / went)

B Mixed structures: Complete the sentences with the correct structures.

1 After ▬ from our trip, we found a lot of work to do. (to return / returning)
2 Could you please remember ▬ the package while you're in town? (to post / posting)
3 When I spoke to Tony, he immediately suggested ▬ home early. (me to go / going)
4 Lucy ▬ that she needed to borrow some money. (told me / told)
5 The new books are ▬ at the moment. (printed / being printed)
6 Under the new library rules, up to 20 books ▬ at one time. (can borrow / can be borrowed)
7 You ▬ go now. There's plenty of time. (don't have to / mustn't)
8 Tony said he ▬ to London the day before. (has / had been)
9 We were lost, but then a policeman told ▬ . (us the way / the way to us)
10 I think Charlie ▬ the tools that he needs. (has already bought / has bought already)

4 MEDIATION

→ Schriftliche Mediation, S. 240

Ein/e Freund/in von Ihnen macht demnächst ein freiwilliges soziales Jahr in Eritrea. Er/Sie wird in einer armen ländlichen Region des Landes arbeiten, die dringend Hilfe benötigt, um die Landwirtschaft, das Gesundheitswesen und die Wirtschaft im Allgemeinen weiterzuentwickeln. Laut Ihrem/Ihrer Freund/in ist die Gegend sehr abgelegen, aber ein Handyempfang ist seit Neuestem dort möglich, obwohl nur 6% der Bevölkerung einen Handyvertrag besitzen.

Schreiben Sie Ihrem/Ihrer Freund/in ein E-Mail, in der Sie den Gebrauch von Handys in anderen Teilen Afrikas beschreiben, und erklären Sie, wie das in diesem Teil von Eritrea auch funktionieren könnte.

5 WRITING

→ Produktion: Eine Stellungnahme schreiben, S. 234

Grange Road Comprehensive School Rules

Rule 15: Students must not bring mobile phones to school. All such devices will be confiscated for a minimum of one week.

Write a comment on the following topic, stating whether you agree or disagree: 'Why I (dis)agree with Rule 15'.

TEXT B Artificial Intelligence

BEFORE YOU READ

→ Rezeption: Leseverstehen – Grobverständnis, S. 214

Skim the text and say whether its central aim is to …

a analyse the potential benefits of AI for humans.
b warn us about the potential risks of AI.

3/13

OUR FUTURE IN THE WORLD OF AI

Forget scary sci-fi stories and blockbuster films like The Terminator and Transcendence that imagine Artificial Intelligence (AI) taking over the world. The real thing may be just around the corner.

A group of leading scientists recently wrote in the *Huffington Post* that, 'It's tempting to dismiss the notion of highly intelligent machines as science fiction. But this would be a mistake, and potentially our worst mistake ever.' They point to the rapid progress of AI research. Driverless cars, for example, are now with us, and the coming decades will bring much, much more.

The report continues: 'The potential benefits are huge; everything that civilization has to offer is a product of human intelligence; we cannot predict what we might achieve when this intelligence is magnified by the tools AI may provide, but the eradication of war, disease and poverty would be high on anyone's list. Success in creating AI would be the biggest event in human history.'

'Unfortunately,' the report goes on, 'it might also be the last, unless we learn how to avoid the risks.' For example, militaries around the world are now considering autonomous weapon systems that can choose and destroy targets, free of human control. This use of AI seems extremely dangerous, and both the UN and Human Rights Watch have called for an international agreement to prevent it, but no one seems to be listening.

Such a development might just be the beginning of our loss of control. Machines with superhuman intelligence could improve their own design again and again. From there, the report says, 'One can imagine such technology outsmarting financial markets, out-manipulating human leaders, and developing weapons we cannot even understand.' The writers suggest that in the short term the effect of AI depends on who controls it. However, in the long term, it may be impossible to control it at all.

Daniel Dewey of the Future of Humanity Institute at Oxford University has similar ideas. On the one hand, he is an optimist, and he believes that humans with the help of AI have the possibility of expanding our civilization into the vastness of the Universe. He feels that the best is yet to come for people, with 'much more potential for goodness – happy and fulfilled lives, meaningful relationships, art, fun – in the long term future than in the short term.'

On the other hand, Dewey sees the possibility of disaster. Whatever specific task an intelligent machine is given to do, it will need to gather knowledge and resources, protect itself and improve its skills. In doing these things, it might find humans in the way. He warns that a super-intelligent AI could 'take over resources that we depend on to stay alive, or it could consider us enough of a danger to its task completion that it decides the best course is to remove us from the picture. Either one of those scenarios could result in human extinction.'

AI therefore offers different possible futures – of huge benefits and of huge risks. As it considers this vital crossroads, the UN report remains unhappy with the world's response. It says, 'The experts are surely doing everything possible to ensure the best outcome, right? Wrong. If a superior alien civilization sent us a text message saying, "We'll arrive in a few decades," would we just reply, "OK, call us when you get here – we'll leave the lights on"? Probably not – but this is more or less what is happening with AI. Although we are facing potentially the best or worst thing ever to happen to humanity, little serious research is devoted to these issues outside small non-profit organizations such as Dewey's Future of Humanity Institute.' The report concludes that, 'All of us – not only scientists, industrialists and generals – should ask ourselves what we can do now to improve the chances of reaping the benefits and avoiding the risks.' That includes the risk that humanity will disappear. (648 words)

1 LOOKING AT THE TEXT

→ Rezeption: Leseverstehen, S. 214

A Answer the following questions about the text.

1 Describe how, according to the report, we might benefit from AI.
2 Explain what the UN and Human Rights Watch think about autonomous weapon systems, and outline what they want to do about their development.
3 Describe how the report writers feel about the fact that humans could lose control of intelligent machines.
4 Explain why a future product of AI might decide to get rid of human beings.
5 Summarize how the report writers feel that the world is preparing for our future with AI.

B Say what it means: Explain the underlined phrases in your own words.

1 The real thing may be just around the corner. (line 2)
2 He feels that the best is yet to come … (lines 43–44)
3 … it decides the best course … (line 56)
4 … is to remove us from the picture. (line 57)
5 As it considers this vital crossroads, … (lines 60–61)

2 WORKING WITH WORDS

A Copy and complete the tables with the correct prefixes (*dis-*, *en-*, *inter-* or *un-*).

___ fortunately	to ___ appear	to ___ sure	___ national
___ happy	___ cord	to ___ able	___ net
___ natural	to ___ agree	to ___ danger	___ active
___ popular	to ___ like	to ___ large	___ continental

B Copy and complete the tables with the correct suffixes (*-ence*, *-ful*, *-ist* or *-ity*/*-ty*).

meaning ___	human ___	exist ___	art ___
success ___	author ___	depend ___	industrial ___
colour ___	cruel ___	viol~~ent~~ ___	social ___
power ___	stupid ___	intellig~~ent~~ ___	scienti~~fic~~ ___

C Work in pairs. Write sentences with gaps for words from exercises 2A and 2B for your partner to complete.

3 GETTING IT RIGHT: A GRAMMAR QUIZ

Mixed structures: Complete the sentences with the correct words in brackets.

1 Please stay for another few days. I don't want ___ so soon. (that you go / you to go)
2 Tim and Joe are brothers, but they really seem to dislike ___ . (themselves / each other)
3 We don't want to leave the party. We're enjoying ___ too much! (us / ourselves)
4 Please can you buy me ___ eggs on your way home? (some / any)
5 ___ time with good friends is one of the best things in the world. (Spending / Spend)
6 We spent ___ money on holiday, and now we've got none left! (a lot of / much)
7 I'm sure ___ at the campsite. (plenty of space is / there's plenty of space)
8 Try ___ angry with Sarah. She didn't mean to break the vase. (not to be / to not be)
9 Global economics ___ very hard to understand. (is / are)
10 Have the police got any more ___ about the missing child? (informations / information)

4 LISTENING

→ Rezeption: Hörverstehen, S. 225

You are going to hear a reporter interviewing an engineer who works for a company that is developing a driverless car.

3/14

A Listen to the first part of the interview and take notes. Use your notes to do the tasks.

1 Describe the different road conditions that the test cars have been driven in.
2 Use the test results so far to compare safety in driverless cars and in cars with human drivers.
3 Note the actual US accident statistics today and the estimated results after a change to driverless vehicles.

	Accidents	Deaths	Injuries	Costs
Actual today				
Driverless (estimated)				

4 Contrast the present traffic accident situation in the USA and the future situation with driverless vehicles.

3/15

B Listen to the second part of the interview and note other changes – positive and negative – that driverless vehicles will bring.

- distance between vehicles
- driving style
- car sharing

5 DISCUSSION

→ Interaktion: An Diskussionen teilnehmen, S. 246

A Work on your own. Look at the types of employment related to cars listed below. Think about whether these types of employment will benefit or suffer from driverless cars. Make notes.

road construction companies ▪ oil companies ▪ car manufacturing ▪ car repair workshops ▪ in-car entertainment design ▪ car insurance ▪ car sales ▪ car park operators ▪ city planners ▪ emergency services ▪ accident and emergency departments

B Make notes on any other types of employment you think might also be affected.

C Work in a group and discuss your ideas. Decide which areas might be worst affected. Then decide which areas might find new opportunities.

6 ROLE-PLAY

→ Interaktion: Ein Rollenspiel gestalten, S. 247

You are on a State Legislature special committee to discuss and vote on whether to allow driverless cars in your state. Choose a role and present your point of view. Argue for and against other points of view in order to get the vote that you want.

Representative Foot

You specialize in health and safety issues, and you have always worried about the high rates of deaths and injuries on US roads. You also know that with a rapidly ageing population, anything that could reduce the pressures on hospitals and other medical resources would be a good thing.

Representative Pascali

You love cars – people call you 'Petrolhead Pascali' – and the idea of giving up control of your car to clever machines seems completely un-American. To you, cars and the freedom of the open road are part of the American dream. You also don't believe that a robot car could ever be safer than a human.

Representative Gonzalez

You are worried about state and city finances, and you welcome the chance to avoid building new roads. You also think that the state's towns and cities can make money through selling urban car parks for redevelopment.

Representative Schumann

In your part of the state, there is a new car factory, which has brought thousands of jobs to an area with high unemployment, and it is now producing 300,000 conventional cars per year for the domestic American market. You do not want anything negative to happen to car manufacturing in the USA: those new jobs must be protected.

Chairperson Kandinski

You have to guide the discussion, making sure that everyone has a chance to speak and to ask questions. You also have an idea to suggest: could the US technological lead in driverless cars bring export success? (China, for example, has huge traffic and pollution problems.)
At the end, manage the vote and declare the result.

TEXT C The future of robotics?

BEFORE YOU READ

What tasks do you think it would be useful to have a robot to do for you?

3/16

'BORIS' THE ROBOT TO LOAD A DISHWASHER

A robot unveiled today at the British Science Festival will be loading dishwashers next year, its developers claim.

A

'Boris' is one of the first robots in the world capable of intelligently manipulating unfamiliar objects with a humanlike grasp. It was developed by scientists at the University of Birmingham. 'This is Boris' first public outing,' announced Professor Jeremy Wyatt of the School of Computer Science. The robot took five years to develop at a cost of £350,000.

B

Boris 'sees' objects with depth sensors on its face and wrists. In ten seconds it calculates up to 1,000 possible ways to grasp a novel object with its five robotic fingers and plans a path of arm movements to reach its target, avoiding obstructions.

'It's not been programmed to pick it up – it's been programmed to learn how to pick it up,' explained Professor Wyatt.

Research engineer Maxine Adjigble helped build the robot. 'He sees something, he has been trained to grasp an object in a particular way, and he says – okay this surface looks similar to what I know, so I can go for this grasp,' he explained.

Professor Wyatt and his collaborators hope to achieve an ambitious goal by April next year. 'The idea is to get the robot to load your dishwasher,' he said. 'You get a bunch of objects off a table, scattered as you might have them on a kitchen surface, and the robot will look through the set of objects, find one it wants to pick up, figure out where to put it in the dishwasher, and load it.'

C

Why has Boris been assigned kitchen duties? 'Not because I think dishwasher-loading robots are an economic or social necessity right now,' laughed Professor Wyatt. 'But it's a typical task

that humans engage in – one that requires all the manipulative faculties that evolution spent hundreds of millions of years developing. So by putting that into a robot, we hope to make the robots more flexible in future.'

But Boris, like humans, finds cutlery a bit fiddly. 'Plates are nice and symmetrical. But I think knives and forks might be a bit hard,' conceded Professor Wyatt.

D

Boris represents a third generation of robots, suggested the Professor. 'The first generation was industrial robots that manipulate the world when it's very precisely controlled. The second generation includes airborne drones, self-driving cars and other mobile robots that 'can move around in our world and share it with us, even though that world is uncertain and full of novelty.'

But manipulating a world shared with humans – and to perform physical tasks alongside humans – requires a new generation of robots. They will need to 'cope with all the uncertainty that humans introduce into the environment,' Professor Wyatt explained. 'You have an unstructured world and you need technologies that can deal with that.'

E

Mr Adjigble discussed some of the disciplines that come together to make a robot like Boris. 'Mechanical engineering, electrical engineering and software development: to put it together, you need to know a bit of all of these fields. This is what is really complicated.'

Unexpected setbacks complicate things further. 'It broke its pinkie back in June and we're still trying to fix it,' said Professor Wyatt. 'So it's working with a broken finger.'

F

The team continue to improve Boris, recently adding the ability to choose the best of five different grasp types when approaching an object. But Boris doesn't use his left arm at present, something the team are keen to introduce. 'One of the really hard things to do is to pick up an object and transfer it, and being bi-manual is a real advantage for all kinds of purposes.' Boris also lacks a sense of touch. 'There's a real challenge – getting tactile sensing of sufficient quality.'

The long-term goal is 'to build robots capable of operating in human environments – offices, hospitals, warehouses,' explained Professor Wyatt. He was enthusiastic about achieving this in Britain.

So why the name Boris? An acronym, or homage to a certain flaxen-haired politician* perhaps? 'I just liked the name,' chuckled Professor Wyatt.

(671 words)

From: *www.bbc.com/news*

* A reference to Boris Johnson, a well-known UK politician

1 LOOKING AT THE TEXT

→ Rezeption: Leseverstehen, S. 214

A Choose suitable headings for sections A–F of the text.

1. Problems so far in creating Boris
2. Why the dishwasher task was chosen
3. Boris meets the world
4. New robots for an unpredictable world
5. The coming technical challenges
6. What Boris has been designed to do

B Decide whether the following statements are true or false. Correct the ones that are false.

1. Boris sees things in the same way that humans do.
2. Boris is very similar to a normal factory robot used in manufacturing.
3. Boris cannot pass things from its right hand to its left at the moment because its left arm is broken.
4. Wyatt's team are aiming to develop intelligent robots to work flexibly like humans, and with them.

C Say what you think: Say how modern technology has made your life different from the lives of your grandparents when they were your age.

2 WRITING

→ Produktion: Eine Stellungnahme schreiben, S. 234

Write a comment on the following.

'We've all become dangerously dependent on modern technology. Think what would happen if it all broke down!'

Keeping fit – with or without technology

4/12

1 ACTIVITY TRACKERS – THE PERFECT PERSONAL MOTIVATORS!

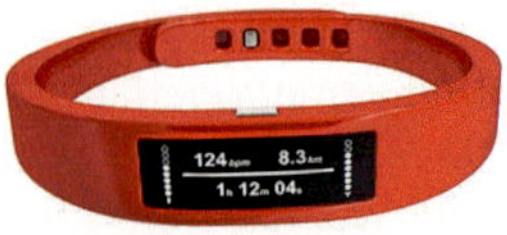

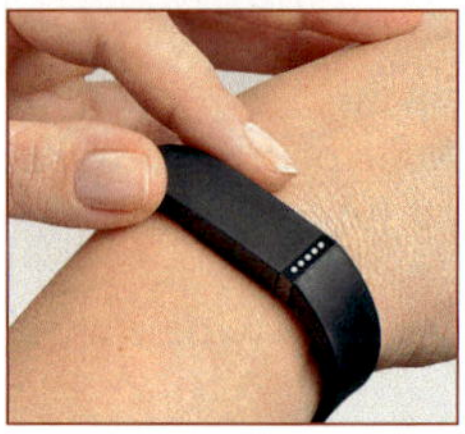

Whether you are serious about your fitness or just want that bikini figure for summer, activity trackers can help you. These small devices come in different styles and shapes, all small enough to wear on your belt or like a bracelet around your wrist. Some devices can even be attached to your shoe.

What do you use them for? Activity trackers measure all sorts of body activity, such as the distance you have walked, floors you have climbed, calories you have burned – basically everything you do, plus the length and intensity of these activities. You can see the results on a display and you can also connect the device to a computer and upload the data to a website, where there are a lot of features, such as an overview of your physical activity and a place to track what and how much you have eaten. There is even a blog to connect with other users. Get your activity tracker now – the perfect personal motivator!

2 THE 7-MINUTE WORKOUT APP

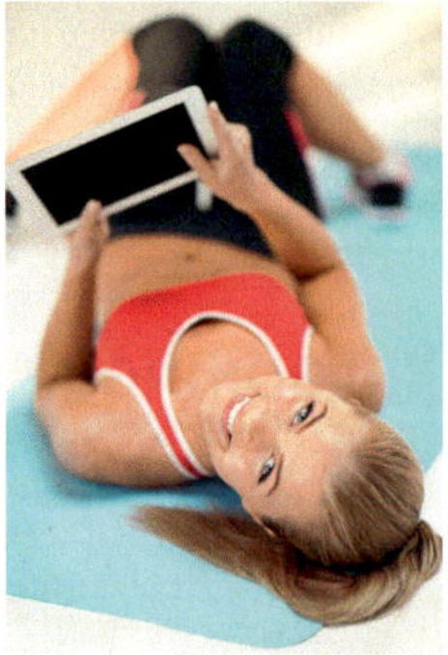

Created by leading sport medicine practitioners, the 7-minute workout is a highly effective fitness program that can be done at home.

Jenny: I downloaded the 7-minute workout on my iPad and quickly found that it is intense, rewarding, can be done at home and, the best part: the workout only lasts seven minutes! And you don't need to be connected to the internet.

Mark: It is really efficient, just like a workout in the gym. There is a voice that tells you what to do and counts you down. For example, when you do push-ups or crunches or squats, it counts down the last ten seconds of the time you still need to do the exercise. And it tells you how many sets of exercises you still have to do.

Margie: I like being able to unlock a new random workout for every second month that I stay in the challenge. This month I unlocked the fat burn workout!

3 GADGET FREE: PEER PRESSURE AS A MOTIVATIONAL TOOL

There are so many new gadgets and apps to help you get fit, and for some people they are very effective. But most of us don't need gadgets or software. What we need is to be motivated: to be motivated to get started and to be motivated to keep at it once we have started.

If you are not interested in team sports, this can be done most effectively by having a training partner. A training partner is somebody who has the same goals and about the same fitness level as you. Once you have arranged to meet, either at the gym or for a run through the woods, you *WILL* go, even though you would rather just relax on the couch and watch your favourite TV programme.

DISCUSSION

→ Interaktion, S. 246

Discuss with a partner or in a small group.

1 What do you think are the advantages and disadvantages of the methods mentioned in the texts?
2 Which of these methods would you use to get fit? Why? Give reasons.
3 What other types of technology (hardware, software) can help people stay healthy and fit?

Job skills 4

Meetings ▪ small talk ▪ presentations

Eric is helping to prepare a meeting at Magnus & Klein. During the meeting, he is to give a short presentation about the firm.

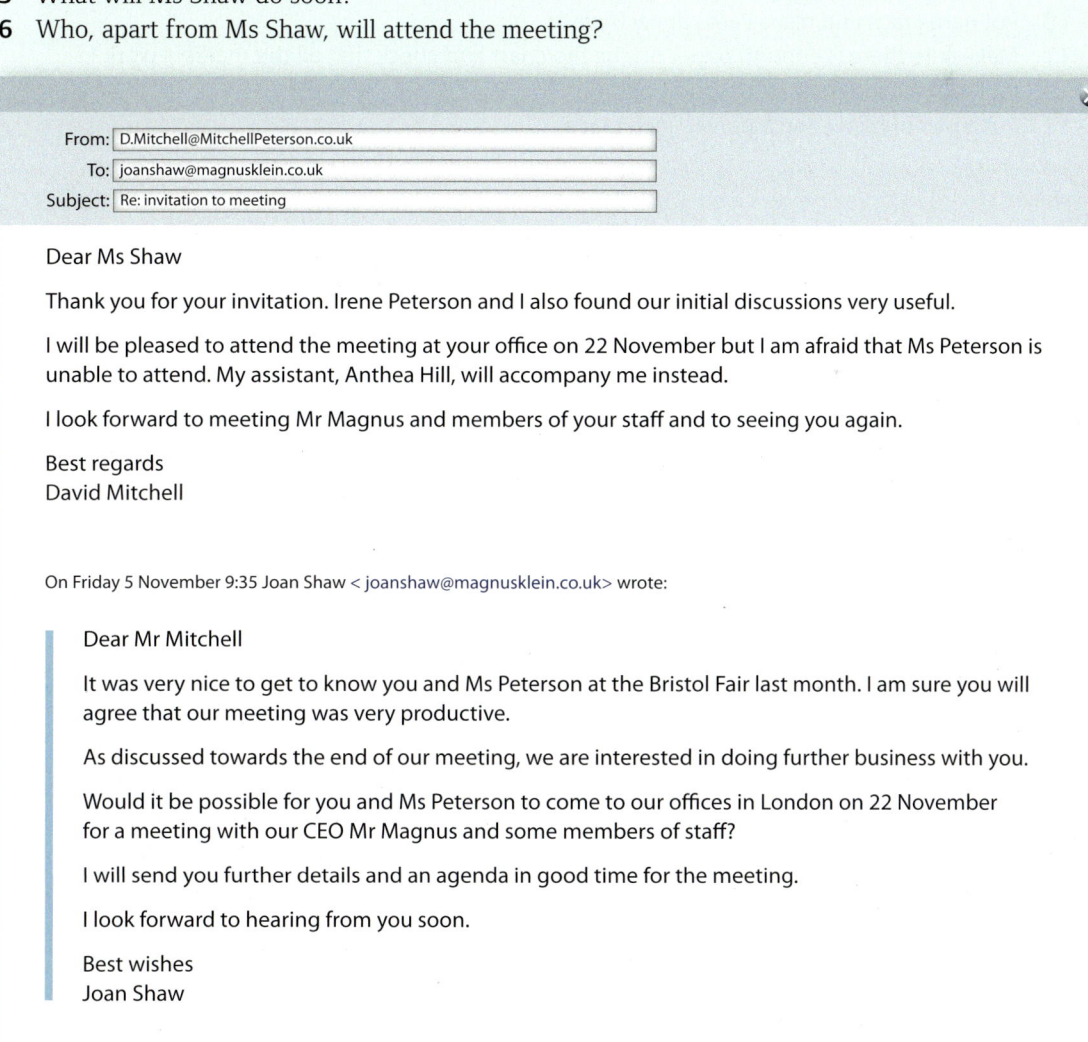

1 AN INVITATION TO A MEETING

Last week, Ms Shaw sent out an email invitation to a meeting and has just received a reply. Read the email exchange and answer the following questions.

1 Who did Ms Shaw write to?
2 What was the reason for writing?
3 Where and when did Ms Shaw and the person she wrote to meet last time?
4 What did they talk about at that meeting?
5 What will Ms Shaw do soon?
6 Who, apart from Ms Shaw, will attend the meeting?

From: D.Mitchell@MitchellPeterson.co.uk
To: joanshaw@magnusklein.co.uk
Subject: Re: invitation to meeting

Dear Ms Shaw

Thank you for your invitation. Irene Peterson and I also found our initial discussions very useful.

I will be pleased to attend the meeting at your office on 22 November but I am afraid that Ms Peterson is unable to attend. My assistant, Anthea Hill, will accompany me instead.

I look forward to meeting Mr Magnus and members of your staff and to seeing you again.

Best regards
David Mitchell

On Friday 5 November 9:35 Joan Shaw < joanshaw@magnusklein.co.uk> wrote:

> Dear Mr Mitchell
>
> It was very nice to get to know you and Ms Peterson at the Bristol Fair last month. I am sure you will agree that our meeting was very productive.
>
> As discussed towards the end of our meeting, we are interested in doing further business with you.
>
> Would it be possible for you and Ms Peterson to come to our offices in London on 22 November for a meeting with our CEO Mr Magnus and some members of staff?
>
> I will send you further details and an agenda in good time for the meeting.
>
> I look forward to hearing from you soon.
>
> Best wishes
> Joan Shaw

Job skills 4

2 PREPARING FOR THE MEETING

Look at this list of tasks that need to be done before a meeting at Magnus & Klein. Check any words you don't know in your dictionary, then sort the instructions into two 'to do' lists: things to do a) before the meeting and b) on the day of the meeting.

1 Book conference room.
2 Check seating and heating in the room.
3 Check lighting and equipment (especially the projector).
4 Inform reception and give the receptionist a list of participants. (She needs to know who is in the building for security reasons.)
5 Make copies of documents and handouts for all participants.
6 Order refreshments.
7 Put refreshments in room.
8 Prepare file for chairperson with all relevant documents.
9 Prepare name tags and place cards.
10 Put name tags and place cards at each place.
11 Make sure there is enough paper on the flip chart and check that all the markers work. (Sometimes they leak or are dried out.)
12 Put a pad of paper and a pen at each place.

3 WRITING

Ms Shaw asks Eric to type up the agenda and send the final details about the meeting to Mr Mitchell.

Please write an email to Mr Mitchell on my behalf giving date and place of the meeting, starting 10.30 and finishing around 4 pm with a tour of factory after lunch. Add link showing how to get to Four Lofts Business Park. You can meet them in car park. Say that Mr Magnus looks forward to meeting him and that I look forward to seeing him again. Don't forget to attach the agenda!

A Put the items on the agenda in a logical order.

a Company presentations 1) Magnus & Klein 2) MitchellPeterson
b Final discussions about cooperation between both companies
c Lunch
d Next steps and date of next meeting
e Tour of the factory
f Welcome and introductions

B Use Ms Shaw's notes to write Eric's email to Mr Mitchell. → Job skills 1, Email etiquette, S. 32

Dear Mr Mitchell

I am writing on behalf of Ms Joan Shaw …

4 MAKING SMALL TALK

Before a meeting and during breaks or business meals, people tend to make small talk.

A Match the typical small talk questions and statements to the responses.

1 How is your hotel?
2 How was your trip?
3 I hear that you're from Bristol. I believe it's a lovely city.
4 The view from this window is lovely.
5 What do you think of this weather?
6 You were on holiday recently. Where did you go?

a Fine. There were no delays.
b Lovely. The breakfast buffet is excellent.
c It's a bit too cold for me, I'm afraid.
d We have a lot of lovely parks and rivers here.
e We went camping in France.
f Yes, I am. Have you never been there? It really is a lovely place.

B Study the word cloud. Which of the topics can you use for small talk? What should you avoid talking about?

gossip religion
families
politics films death
hobbies holidays books
sport hotels
illnesses wages or salary
problems at work pets

TIP Making small talk

If possible, ask the first question, then the other person will do most of the talking and you'll have time to relax. The weather or asking about the other person's journey to the meeting place are good starting points. Try to avoid questions which only need the answer 'yes' or 'no'. Remember not to speak about taboo subjects. Even if you believe in something strongly, never try to convince the other person that your ideas are 'correct'.

C Work with a partner. Partner A is Eric; Partner B is Anthea Hill. Make small talk. Eric begins.

5 THE START OF THE MEETING

3/17

A Ms Shaw is about to start the meeting. Look back at the agenda items in exercise 3A and listen. Did you put the items in the correct order?

B Listen again and note down phrases for the following:

1 making sure people are comfortable
2 welcoming guests
3 introducing people and giving some information about them
4 going through the agenda
5 getting down to business

6 EXTRACTS FROM A PRESENTATION

→ Präsentieren, S. 243

It is time for Eric to give his presentation of the history and development of the company.

3/18

A Listen to excerpts from the presentation and answer the questions.

1 How does Eric begin his presentation?
2 How many parts are there in his talk?
3 What will he look at first?
4 What will he look at next?
5 What is the final focus of his talk?
6 What visual medium is Eric using to show developments in the company?
7 Where will the audience find information to take away with them?

B Match some of the phrases Eric used in his talk (a–f) to the headings (1–6), then listen again for more phrases that fit the headings, or think of some of your own.

1 Introducing oneself and the topic of the talk
2 Outlining the talk
3 Repeating information
4 Referring to visuals and handouts
5 Finishing the talk
6 Taking questions

a As I said, things really started moving in the late eighties.
b Are there any questions?
c As Ms Shaw said, my name is Eric Jung …
d I'm now nearing the end of my talk.
e If you look at this slide, you'll see …
f First, I'm going to start by looking at …

7 GIVING A TALK IN CLASS

Prepare and give a short talk to your classmates. After your talk, your classmates will ask you questions. Choose one of the following topics.
a) work experience you have had **b) an area in which you would like to work**

Follow this plan:
- introduce yourself (if necessary!) and greet the audience
- outline your talk
- give your talk
- summarize your talk and make your conclusion
- ask for questions from the audience
- thank the audience for their attention and distribute any handouts

Prepare and give a short talk on a subject of your choice. (Discuss the subject you have chosen with your teacher first.) After your talk, your classmates will ask you questions.

Useful phrases: Presentations

Giving a presentation
- This morning, I'm going to talk about …
- Our topic today is …
- I've divided the presentation into … main parts, as follows: …
- First, / Firstly, …
- Second, / Secondly, …
- Next, / Now, / After that, / Then, …
- Now I'd like to move on to …
- The next topic I'm going to talk about is …
- Before I finish my presentation, I'd just like to mention …
- Finally, / In conclusion, / To conclude, / In summary, …

Asking questions
- Could you describe … more fully?
- What exactly did you mean when you said … ?
- I'm sorry, I didn't quite understand the bit about … ?

1 Social media and charity

SOCIAL TOPICS

USING SOCIAL MEDIA FOR FUNDRAISING

Before the internet and social media, traditional charities asked for donations by going door to door, collecting in the street, sending "begging letters" or just putting up a collection box in the local pub or fish and chip shop. Most charities still do that, but nowadays many also use the internet and social media such as Facebook and Twitter to ask for money online. Some of the most effective fundraising, though, is not done by the charities themselves but by individuals who start a craze that goes viral.

Ice Bucket Challenge

In the summer of 2014, the Ice Bucket Challenge started appearing all over social media. At first it was just "regular people" in the US who were posting videos of themselves while a bucket of

ice was poured on their head, but when celebrities such as Facebook founder Mark Zuckerberg joined in, the phenomenon gained momentum and spread all over the world.

The reason all these people chose to freeze their brains was not some new health trend but to raise awareness of the disease amyotrophic lateral sclerosis (ALS). The idea was that when you received the Ice Bucket Challenge, you either needed to give $100 to the ALS Association or had to pour ice water on your head. However, it seems that most people donated money and got soaked, all recorded on a video that they later posted on social media. The ALS Association says that it has raised $15.6 million as a result of the challenge, nine times what it normally raises in the same period of time.

What made the Ice Bucket Challenge so successful? Maybe it was the combination of being easy to do and the fact that people could compete in a friendly way while drawing attention to themselves on social media. But besides raising money, did it really help increase awareness of the disease? Critics say no.

No Make-up Selfie

One thing this campaign has shown is that the charity itself has no influence on what makes a fundraising campaign successful. Just like the Ice Bucket Challenge, the No Make-up Selfie trend spread like wildfire through the internet and soon tens of thousands of women were sharing pictures of themselves without make-up to raise awareness of breast cancer. Because the idea went viral on social media, it quickly changed from a crazy idea into a successful fundraising campaign that raised £2 million in just 48 hours with hundreds of thousands of donations from Facebook, Instagram and Twitter users sharing pictures of themselves without make-up and nominating a friend to do the same.

Cancer Research UK said this campaign had not been their idea, but they were thrilled with the donations. Others were more critical. Their reaction to the campaign included the arguments that not wearing make-up was not difficult, not like when people ran a marathon for charity. They also asked: "What has a photo of someone's face without make-up done for the fight against cancer, that the thousands of other pictures of faces with make-up haven't?" Finally, they wonder what kind of world do we live in where it is a "brave" thing to upload a picture of what you really look like?

However critical you are, the fact remains that fundraising schemes like the Ice Bucket Challenge and the No Make-up Selfie campaign are successful. (554 words)

1 LOOKING AT THE TEXT

→ Rezeption: Leseverstehen, S. 214

Choose the correct sentence endings.

1 Charities …
- **a** used to collect money in pubs but they do not do that any more.
- **b** use the money they raise to help people to post pictures and videos of themselves.
- **c** are also using the internet to raise money.

2 The Ice Bucket Challenge went viral …
- **a** after the ALS Association announced that they needed money.
- **b** after celebrities also started posting videos on social media.
- **c** because it was a new health trend started by Mark Zuckerberg.

3 The original idea of the challenge was that …
- **a** you either gave $100 to ALS or poured ice water on your head.
- **b** you got wet and posted a video on social media.
- **c** you donated money *and* got soaked.

4 People criticized the Ice Bucket Challenge because
- **a** it didn't help people learn more about ALS.
- **b** it wasn't available to people who didn't use Facebook.
- **c** it was too easy to do.

5 The No Make-up Selfie trend showed that …
- **a** the make-up industry does not know what people want.
- **b** charities do not always have the best ideas for fundraising campaigns.
- **c** you can share pictures using Twitter.

6 Some critics of the campaign said that …
- **a** not wearing make-up was difficult for some people.
- **b** people who ran a marathon for charity were making more of an effort than people who just didn't put on their make-up.
- **c** they were not happy that a lot of money was raised for charity by wearing make-up.

2 WORKING WITH WORDS

A Match the words from the text with their definitions. There are two words you don't need.

1 collection box (line 4)
2 craze (line 11)
3 to go viral (line 11)
4 challenge (line 12)
5 founder (line 18)
6 to gain momentum (lines 19–20)
7 to raise awareness of (line 23)
8 to donate (line 29)
9 to draw attention to (lines 38–39)
10 to nominate (line 61)

a to increase or go faster
b to suggest that somebody does a specific task
c to make people notice
d somebody who starts a company
e a task that tests somebody's ability
f to spread quickly from one internet user to another
g to make or help people learn about something
h a container in which people put money that they want to give to a charity

B Now write definitions for the two words that you did not use.

3 DESCRIBING AND ANALYSING STATISTICS

→ Statistiken beschreiben und analysieren, S. 238

Look at the statistics below and write three statements on what it tells us about the Ice Bucket Challenge.

4 DISCUSSION

→ Interaktion, S. 246

Discuss in small groups.

1 Why is it often more effective to use social media for charity fundraising?
2 What motivates people to give money to charity? Think about both online and traditional campaigns.
3 What do you think makes charity campaigns such as the Ice Bucket Challenge and the No Make-up Selfie campaign go viral?
4 Would you post a selfie of yourself for charity? Why? Why not?

Useful vocabulary for discussing charity fundraising on social media

Charity campaigns		to share	*etwas teilen*
advert	*Werbung*	to show off	*angeben*
to donate	*spenden*	up to date	*auf dem neuesten Stand*
donor	*Spender*	**Motivation for giving**	
fun run	*Spendenlauf*	compassion	*Mitgefühl*
jumble sale	*Wohltätigkeitsbasar*	empathy	*Einfühlungsvermögen*
to set a target	*sich ein Ziel setzen*	for a good cause	*für einen guten Zweck*
Social media		generous	*großzügig*
audience	*Publikum*	generosity	*Großzügigkeit*
common interest	*gemeinsames Interesse*	in memory of	*in Gedenken an*
peer pressure	*Gruppendruck*	to make an impact	*Wirkung zeigen*
popular	*beliebt*	morals	*Moral*
popularity	*beliebtheit*	to promote	*fördern*
self-promotion	*Selbstdarstellung*	solidarity	*Solidarität*

2 Advertising and children

SOCIAL TOPICS

Children are bombarded with advertising throughout the day on some of the most popular television channels and websites. They are told how wonderful "Happy Meals" are, how a particular type of sugary yoghurt is good for them, how the latest Lego toy or Surprise Egg will make them (and their parents!) happy. One UK organization is campaigning to put a stop to this.

http://www.leaveourkidsalone.org/aboutus.php

ABOUT US

LEAVE OUR KIDS ALONE

Leave Our Kids Alone wants a ban on all advertising targeting children under 11.

As parents we aim to protect our children from the worst of the adult world. We're careful about the people our children come into contact with. Teachers, care assistants, medics, childminders; they're all vetted and most have to be qualified. Above all they're expected to have the best interests of our children at heart.

That's not true of advertising. The commercial world serves its shareholders. Our children's well-being simply is not their primary concern. It's often of little or of no concern at all.

Advertising is a £12 billion a year industry in the UK alone. In order to sell us things, it uses sophisticated techniques to play on our emotions, our insecurities, our need to be respected, our need to be loved. Similar techniques are increasingly being used on children, some of them not yet old enough to read.

We believe that's wrong. We believe that if companies make products for children, they should aim to persuade parents, not children of four, six or eight. Our children need space to discover themselves, to learn about the world, to realise that not everything adults say can be taken at face value, to handle money, to learn the true worth of things.

We believe children should be free to grow up without today's intense commercial pressures, to become young citizens and not just little consumers. (239 words)

Source: *www.leaveourkidsalone.org*

1 LOOKING AT THE TEXT

→ Rezeption: Leseverstehen, S. 214

A Which picture would you choose to illustrate the web page above and why?

B Decide if these statements are true (T), false (F) or not mentioned in the text (N). Say why you have decided that the statement is true. Correct the statements that are false. Give the line(s) in the text where you find your information.

1. Companies are not allowed to show advertising which targets children under 11.
2. All adults who work with children are qualified to do their job.
3. Advertising companies want to make money for the shareholders.
4. The money spent on advertising in the UK has increased in the last five years.
5. Advertising uses what we like, what we hate and what we fear to sell a product.
6. Only half of the children who watch adverts on TV can read.
7. Leave Our Kids Alone believes that companies should try to convince parents, and not their children, to use their products.
8. Children who watch no television grow up without today's commercial pressures.

2 WORKING WITH WORDS

A Complete the readers' comments with the words and phrases in the box. There are two words and phrases that you don't need.

adults ▪ allowed ▪ ban advertising ▪ commercial channel ▪ harm ▪ lies ▪ limit ▪ negative effect ▪ number of viewers ▪ product ▪ take responsibility ▪ target

17 November 17.17 pm
I think you should just ( )[1] the amount of time your children watch TV instead of expecting the TV channels to ( )[2]. Parents should ( )[3] for what their children watch. *Mark*

17 November 18.20 pm
@ Mark, I agree with you. The industry probably gives jobs to thousands of people, and watching adverts when I was a kid didn't do me much ( )[4]. But the obvious answer is for parents to stop their kids watching so much TV. *tronjandessen*

18 November 09.40 am
In Norway, advertising is not ( )[5] in TV programmes for children. The main ( )[6] in Norway follows this regulation, and of course the Norwegian public broadcaster does the same. These two channels have the biggest ( )[7]. *Bruce*

18 November 11.10 am
@ tronjandessen: In Australia, we're lucky. The government channel ABC2 has age-appropriate programmes for preschoolers during the day, with no adverts. My two kids enjoy these programmes and they don't have to watch adverts. I agree adverts should not ( )[8] children of that age, but we can't hide kids from such influences as they get older. *Wendy*

21 November 14.30 am
Ban them! As ( )[9], we know that what we see on advertisements are ( )[10]. Children don't know that the toy they see on television won't bring them friends to play with. They believe what they see and hear because they don't know better. *CindyLouBack*

B Sum up what the different people say about the topic, then write your own comment.

3 ADVERTISING STATISTICS

→ Statistiken beschreiben und analysieren, S. 238

Look at these statistics about advertising in the US, then answer the questions below.

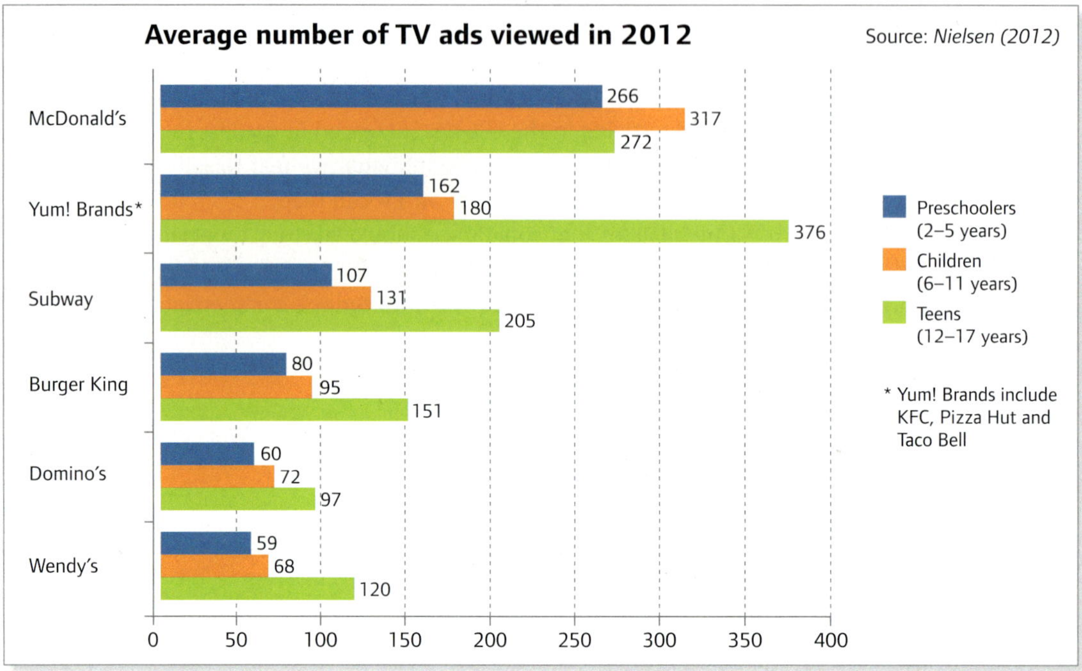

1 Which age group watches the most fast-food advertising? Why do you think this is so?
2 Which company's advertising is seen the least? And the most? How do you explain this?
3 Do you think these statistics would be the same in Germany? Give reasons why or why not.

4 DISCUSSION

→ Interaktion, S. 246

In groups, discuss what knock-on effects these fast-food advertisements have on children (peer pressure, obesity, etc.). Should such ads directed at children be banned? What could the long-term effect of these ads be? Present your ideas to the class.

5 DESCRIBING A PICTURE

→ Bilder beschreiben und analysieren, S. 236

With a partner, describe the second illustration on page 178 and comment on its message.

Useful vocabulary for discussing advertising to children

Advertising		**Children's behaviour**	
brand	*Marke*	bad habit	*schlechte Angewohnheit*
consumer society	*Konsumgesellschaft*	to be exposed to sth	*etw ausgesetzt sein*
to exploit	*ausnutzen*	impressionable	*beeinflussbar*
target group	*Zielgruppe*	materialistic	*materialistisch*
to target sb	*auf jdn abzielen*	self-esteem	*Selbstwertgefühl*
to encourage sb	*jdn ermutigen/ bestärken*	to resist temptation	*der Versuchung widerstehen*

3 Helping disadvantaged children

SOCIAL TOPICS

SCHOOL BREAKFAST CLUBS

It's 8 o'clock on a bright morning at the end of the summer term and at Portobello Primary School in Hackney, an area in the centre of London, the staff is getting ready to do one of their most important jobs. This is not teaching their pupils maths, reading or how to win at football; they are getting ready to give them breakfast. "You can't expect children to learn if they are not ready to learn," says head teacher Laurie Nicholson, and she knows what she's talking about. She knows that without their daily breakfast at the school Breakfast Club, a lot of the children in her school would start their lessons feeling hungry.

Portobello Primary School is in an area that is one of the poorest in Britain. Around a third of the children come to the Breakfast Club because their parents' working hours make it difficult for them to get breakfast at home. But many more come because there just is no breakfast at home. "There are a lot of chaotic families, and some of them are very large with four or five children," Nicholson says. "A lot of our children have to get ready for school by themselves and some do not always see a parent. We give some of them alarm clocks to help them wake up on time." And then there are those parents who just don't have the money to feed their children. "The families in this area are getting poorer and poorer," she says. So there are more and more children coming to school hungry, and more and more breakfasts are needed.

"What we do here is really important," says Helen Williams, one of the teachers who helps with the Breakfast Club. "Bagels are the most popular, but they are quite expensive, so we usually give the children toast. And in the winter there's porridge with honey, which they like." I ask a group of eight-year-old girls why they come, as they put big pieces of jam-covered toast into their mouths. "They give you free food," says one, with a grin. "I come for fun," says another. They talk a lot about meeting their friends, about the football club which a lot of them belong to and about who their favourite pop star is at the moment.

Every child deserves to start the day with a good breakfast.

The staff all agree that socializing is a very important part of the Breakfast Club. But they also say that making sure that the children start the day with a good breakfast has also played an important role in the school's – and the children's – success. Since Portobello Primary School introduced the Breakfast Club, attendance rates at the school as well as the children's concentration have improved. (447 words)

1 LOOKING AT THE TEXT

→ Rezeption: Leseverstehen, S. 214

A **Make a list of the reasons why the children take part in the Breakfast Club.**

B **Choose the correct ending (a, b or c) to complete the sentences about the text.**

1 Laurie Nicholson says that …

- **a** her pupils used to be hungry when they came to school.
- **b** some pupils are still hungry when they start school.
- **c** the children wouldn't be so hungry if they ate more breakfast at home.

2 Some of the pupils …
- a have parents who find it difficult to work in the mornings.
- b don't want to see an adult in the morning.
- c get themselves up and dressed in the morning.

3 One reason for the importance of the Breakfast Club is that …
- a the children don't have enough money to feed themselves.
- b some children come from a poor family.
- c the community wants the club.

4 Helen Williams serves …
- a a hot meal some days.
- b bagels with maple syrup.
- c toast with honey.

5 Some of the children come to the Breakfast Club …
- a to meet their friends.
- b to play football.
- c because the staff are very friendly.

6 The teachers have noticed that more kids …
- a eat a good breakfast at home.
- b want to go to this school because of the Breakfast Club.
- c perform better at school.

2 WORKING WITH WORDS

Match these words and expressions from the text (1–10) with the definitions (a–j).

1	term (line 2)	a	every day
2	staff (line 4)	b	a group of people paid to do a job
3	to expect (line 8)	c	to get better
4	daily (line 11)	d	very well liked
5	chaotic (line 21)	e	period of time when there are classes at a school
6	popular (line 36)	f	good performance
7	to belong to (line 45)	g	to be a part of
8	success (line 52)	h	how often pupils go to school when they are supposed to
9	attendance rates (lines 53–54)	i	totally confused and unorganized
10	to improve (line 55)	j	to think something is going to happen

3 MEDIATION

→ Schriftliche Mediation, S. 240

Sie möchten Ihrem lokalen Bildungsminister den Bedarf an Frühstücksclubs präsentieren. Entnehmen Sie dem Text die relevanten Informationen und informieren Sie ihn per E-Mail über den Inhalt. Übersetzen Sie dabei nicht Wort für Wort, sondern schreiben Sie mindestens vier Argumente auf. Gehen Sie wie folgt vor:

1 Schreiben Sie nur Notizen, keine ganzen Sätze.
2 Verwandeln Sie Ihre Notizen nun in Sätze.
3 Überprüfen Sie Ihren Text: Haben Sie nur solche Informationen übernommen, die relevant sind? Haben Sie Ihren Text für die Zielgruppe angemessen formuliert?

4 LISTENING

→ Rezeption: Hörverstehen, S. 225

A recent report looking at child welfare in Britain and other developed nations has found that, despite massive government spending, one in six German children is living in relative poverty.

4/13 **A Hören Sie die Radiosendung, in der Nicole Schumann, deutsche Expertin für Sozialwesen, Fragen von Moderator Matt Diamond beantwortet und machen sich Notizen zu folgenden Punkten:**

1 wie viel die deutsche Regierung für Kinder ausgibt.
2 wie Dänemark mit dem Problem der in relativer Armut lebenden Kinder umgeht.
3 wie Deutschland Familien mit allein erziehenden Elternteilen, die in relativer Armut leben, helfen könnte.
4 was der neunjährige Mark nach der Schule macht.
5 warum er sich in dieser Situation befindet.
6 wie solche Kinder auf Englisch genannt werden.

4/14 **B Listen to the second part of the programme and, in English, write down what you know about Sheila and Jonas. Write at least five sentences.**

5 WRITING

→ Produktion: Schreiben, S. 228

Can all-day schools help disadvantaged children? First look at these statements for and against all-day schools, then write a comment describing the pros and cons and giving your opinion.

All-day schools focus on the pupils' individual strengths, interests and circumstances.

Teaching about healthy eating can only be done when the school day is long enough.

All-day schools help to decrease the number of "latchkey kids" who are left alone after school while parents are at work.

Immigrant children who do not speak the language of the country have a disadvantage, which only intensive schooling can help.

School meals are only as good and healthy as the kitchens they are cooked in.

The last hour of an all-day school can be useless if the pupils are too tired to concentrate.

Useful vocabulary for writing about all-day schools

after-school club	*(Schul-)Hort*	lack of money	*Geldmangel/Geldnot*
to be cared for	*betreut/versorgt werden*	number of lessons	*Stundenzahl*
curriculum	*Bildungsinhalt*	self-reliant	*selbstständig/selbstbewusst*
equal opportunity	*Chancengleichheit*	shortage of teachers	*Lehrermangel*
to extend the school day	*den Schultag verlängern*	social life	*Sozialleben*
extra-curricular activities	*außerschulische Aktivitäten*	supportive environment	*unterstützende Umgebung*
lack of concentration	*Konzentrationsschwäche*	teacher-student time	*Zeit, die Lehrer und Schüler gemeinsam verbringen*

4 Men in caring professions

SOCIAL TOPICS

IT'S (ALSO) A MAN'S JOB ...

We asked three young men just starting out in the social and health care sector – Steven, Andy and John (from left to right) – to talk to us about their career choice. Here's what they said.

STEVEN I am sure that any man who has considered a career in nursing has thought about the fact that most people see it as a woman's job. I certainly did before I began my nursing programme. However, I soon realized that gender makes no difference. Female nurses have no problem with men being nurses. Of course, as males, we are still the minority, but our numbers are increasing. And the patients I care for have no problem accepting care from a nurse who is male.

ANDY I agree, although sometimes I am not referred to as the patient's "nurse", but as their "male nurse", as if my being a male is so important. Patients also often ask me when I will be starting medical school. They think my nursing qualification is a stepping stone to becoming a doctor. I then tell them that my role in nursing is just the same as a female nurse's. I go on to tell them how challenging and rewarding the job is, for both women and men.

JOHN When I told my friends and family that I was going to become a social worker, a lot of them said: "Isn't that a woman's job?" In fact, at my hairdresser's the other day, I mentioned my career choice and he reacted in exactly the same way, saying: "Social work – that's a woman's job, isn't it?"

STEVEN Yes, I got the same reaction from my sister when I told her I was going to become a nurse. She argued that the "carer" in the family is always the mother, and mothers pass the nurturing skills down to their daughters, not their sons. However, I think that men who work in the caring professions have a lot to offer. And we can do many things that women can't, for example lift heavy patients.

JOHN I agree, we do have a role to play. I know a lot of men who refused to get help from female social workers. I myself have helped men who have been involved in cases of domestic violence or child abuse, and they wanted to get help, but not from female carers who they felt wouldn't be on their side. I think that with more male social workers out there, more men will seek help. (383 words)

1 LOOKING AT THE TEXT

→ Rezeption: Leseverstehen, S. 214

Answer the questions using relevant information from the text above.

1 According to Steven and Andy, how do female nurses and patients feel about male nurses?
2 What do some patients assume male nurses are going to do with their nursing qualification? Why do you think they assume that?
3 How does Andy react to their comments?
4 Do you think John's hairdresser and Steven's sister are right? Why? Why not?
5 Steven says that men can do many things that women can't. What do you think he means?
6 Why do you think some men refuse to accept help from female social workers? Do you think this is sometimes the case in other social and health fields? Give examples.

2 WORKING WITH WORDS

Find expressions in the text which match these definitions.

1 the fact of being male or female
2 the smaller part of a group
3 to let sb help
4 sth that helps you towards your goal
5 stimulating, demanding
6 worth doing
7 caring for and protecting
8 to say no to assistance

3 JOBS IN THE SOCIAL AND HEALTH CARE SECTOR

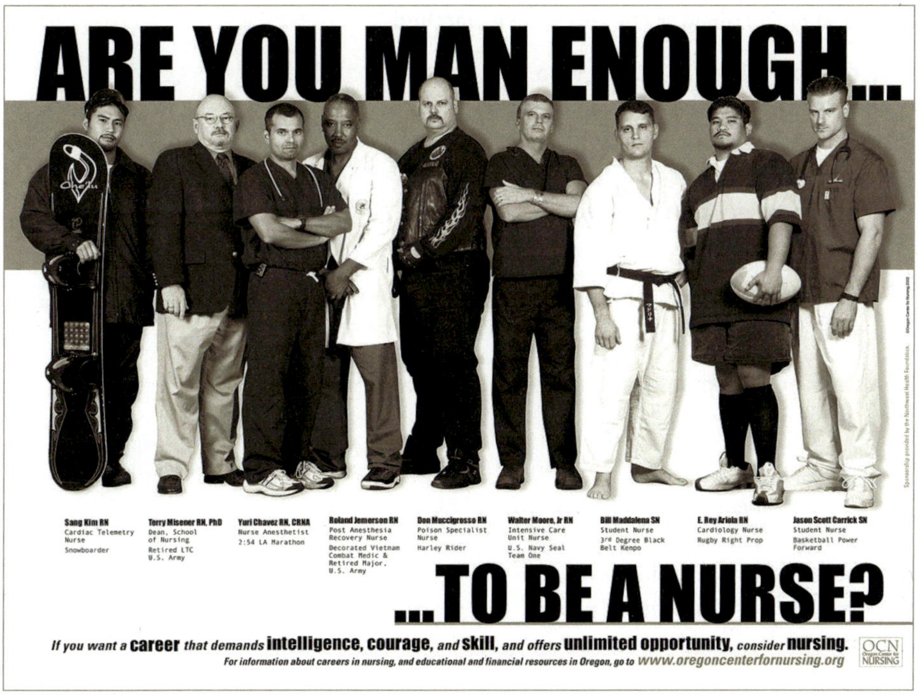

Quelle: *www.oregoncenterfornursing.org*

A Follow the steps to analyse the recruitment poster above.

1 **Think.** Working on your own, study the poster and decide what the message is.
2 **Pair.** Compare notes with a partner. How effective do you think the poster is? Why? What might a poster with the heading "Are you woman enough …" be about?
3 **Share.** Present your ideas to the class.

B Are the jobs below typically female or typically male? Why? How might you convince people of the other gender to consider the job?

1 Care worker (looks after people who need care in their own home or in a residence)
2 Education welfare officer (makes sure children attend school regularly)
3 Hospital play specialist (works in a hospital with children needing long-term care)
4 Nursery worker (looks after young children and babies in a nursery or crèche)
5 Social work assistant (assists social workers who help individuals and families in need)
6 Substance misuse outreach worker (works with alcoholics and drug addicts)
7 Youth and community worker (helps young people aged 13–19 cope with problems)

4 CAREERS INFORMATION DAY

You are preparing to take part in a Careers Information Day for school leavers who are interested in working in the UK.

A First, choose one of the jobs on page 185 and do research to see what the job involves in the UK. (The National Careers Service has a useful website.) Take notes on the following:

- typical responsibilities and day-to-day tasks
- clients and colleagues
- skills needed

B Prepare arguments to convince school leavers (both male and female) at the Careers Information Day to consider the job you researched.

C Now do a role-play. Find someone who has researched a different job. Tell your partner about the job, answer any questions and try to persuade him/her to consider this job as a future career. Then swap roles.

5 COMMENTING ON A CARTOON

→ Cartoons beschreiben und analysieren, S. 236

A With a partner or in a small group, discuss the following questions.

1 How would you feel if an interviewer asked you the question in the cartoon? Explain.

2 Are there any (other) topics you think an interviewer should avoid at an interview?

B Write a short text, describing the cartoon and commenting on its message.

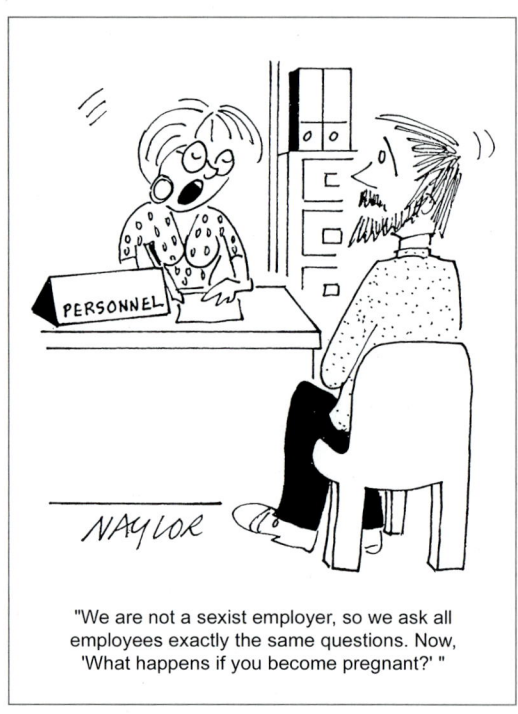

"We are not a sexist employer, so we ask all employees exactly the same questions. Now, 'What happens if you become pregnant?' "

Useful vocabulary for discussing gender and employment

Gender	
gender roles	*Geschlechtsrollen*
feminine	*feminin*
masculine	*maskulin*
sexism	*Sexismus*
stereotype	*Stereotyp, Klischee*
to treat equally	*gleich behandeln*
Job interview	
background	*Werdegang*
to be at a disadvantage	*im Nachteil sein*
criminal record	*Vorstrafenregister*
discrimination	*Diskriminierung*
finances	*Finanzen/Einkünfte*
to fit in	*sich anpassen*
marital status	*Familienstand*
to overlook sb	*jmd übergehen*
Career	
ambition	*Ehrgeiz*
expectations	*Erwartungen*
experience	*Erfahrung*
fulfilling	*erfüllend*
manual work	*körperliche Arbeit*
skill set	*Fertigkeiten*

5 Helping refugees integrate

1 LISTENING TO YOUNG REFUGEES

→ Rezeption: Hörverstehen, S. 225

4/15 Radio reporter Jane Ingles interviewed some refugee students from different countries about their experience in British schools.

Tayfun

Armana

Zainab

Konstantin

Meseret

A Copy this table, then listen to the recording and complete the first two columns.

Name	Country of origin	Things that helped him/her cope in the UK
Tayfun		
Armana		

B Listen again and take notes to complete the third column.

C In groups, discuss what you think of the help the five students got. What type of help was most effective?

2 LOOKING AT STATISTICS

→ Statistiken beschreiben und analysieren, S. 238

A Comment on the statistics below. What do they tell us about the number of refugees taken in by the different countries? Use the switchboard on the next page to write some sentences.

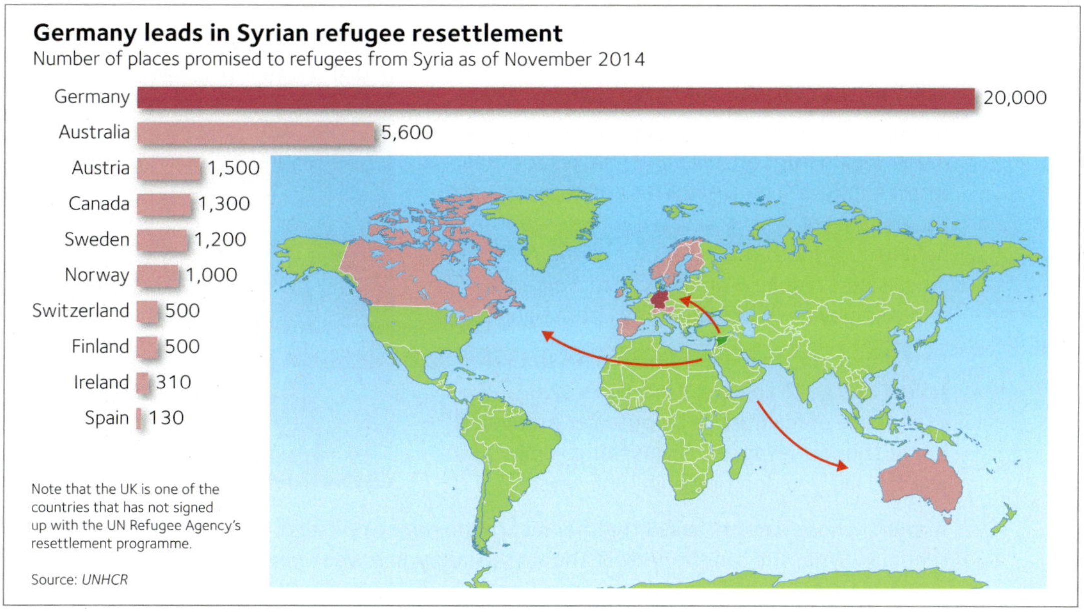

<table>
<tr><td>Germany</td><td colspan="3" rowspan="2">has promised/pledged … places for refugees as of November 2014.</td></tr>
<tr><td>…</td></tr>
<tr><td colspan="2">The country that has promised/pledged</td><td>the fewest number of</td><td rowspan="3">places for refugees is/are …</td></tr>
<tr><td colspan="2"></td><td>the most</td></tr>
<tr><td colspan="2">The two countries that have pledged</td><td>(nearly) the same number of</td></tr>
<tr><td>Sweden</td><td rowspan="2">has pledged</td><td>more</td><td rowspan="2">places for refugees than …</td></tr>
<tr><td>…</td><td>fewer</td></tr>
</table>

B **Think about the impact on the countries and towns which these refugees move to and discuss your thoughts with a partner. Consider the cost of housing, schools, jobs, etc.**

3 MEDIATION

→ Schriftliche Mediation, S. 240

Sie bereiten einen Vortrag für das Jugendzentrum in Ihrer Stadt über die Aufnahme von Flüchtlingen vor. Nutzen Sie die Informationen im Text und machen Sie Notizen, übersetzen dabei jedoch nicht Wort für Wort.

"REFUGEES WELCOME!" is more than a slogan in Germany

By Clare Richardson ▪ 18 September 2014

Twelve-year-old Assrien arrived from Al-Malikiyah in north-eastern Syria five months ago, but today she chatters away in German.

Assrien plays football with German children on a makeshift field at a community event in Berlin's Reinickendorf district. There are live performances, children's activities, and food stalls designed to bring together refugees and locals to promote friendship between the groups.

The slogans "No one is illegal" and "Refugees Welcome!" appear in graffiti and on paraphernalia around Berlin. As asylum seekers increasingly flock to Germany, a solidarity movement not only demands that immigrants have the right to stay, but provides its own support through language classes, sports and mentorship programs.

Twenty-six-year-old Gloria Amoruso co-founded *kein Abseits!* in 2011 to encourage education through sports and mentoring. The organization's name means "not offside" and invokes football terminology as a metaphor for not straying into the margins of society. Last week the organization held its first football training for young refugee girls as part of a new project called *Heimspiel*, another play on words meaning "home game".

As the first person in her family to finish high school and go to college, Amoruso's own experience of feeling like an outsider motivated her to support refugees. "Everything is new and you feel like you don't belong," she says.

Assrien, whose parents asked that her last name not be revealed, used to play football at school in Syria; she taught herself, she says proudly. In a week her family will move from the shelter where they've been living for the past two months to the city Halle in the state of Saxony-Anhalt. Assrien says she likes Germany, except for the food.

"Children of immigrants are often treated like interpreters for the family because they learn German more quickly," Amoruso says. "They grow up fast so this is a way for them to be kids again."

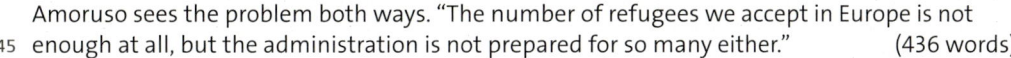

Last year Germany received by far the most asylum applications of any EU member state with nearly 127,000 requests, according to the statistics agency Eurostat. Although Germany granted the second-largest number of asylum permits after Sweden, critics say a country with the largest economy in Europe and a labour market shortage could accept more.

"We have a history where our own people needed to run from a fascist regime," says Oliver Wolters, a digital media designer who lives in Reinickendorf just over the fence from where the event is taking place. "Now we should welcome people who are in need."

Amoruso sees the problem both ways. "The number of refugees we accept in Europe is not enough at all, but the administration is not prepared for so many either." (436 words)

Abridged from: *www.blogs.reuters.com*

4 CONDUCTING AN INTERVIEW

Interview a student at your school or somebody from your neighbourhood who is not German and report back to the class. Ask about some of the following points:

- what is their (or their parents') country of origin
- why they (or their parents) left their home country
- how they feel living here
- what is different here compared to their culture
- whether they still practise any family or religious traditions, and how they do that

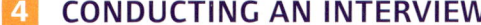

Useful vocabulary for talking about refugees and immigrants

Reasons for leaving

asylum seeker	*Asylsuchende/r*
to emigrate	*auswandern*
freedom	*Freiheit*
hardship	*Entbehrung/Elend*
to immigrate	*einwandern*
persecution	*Verfolgung*
poverty	*Armut*
to seek asylum	*Asyl beantragen*
standard of living	*Lebensstandard*

In the new country

to adapt to	*sich anpassen*
to be homesick	*Heimweh haben*
discrimination	*Diskriminierung*
family ties	*familiäre Bindungen*
to feel at home	*sich Zuhause fühlen*
foreigner	*Ausländer/in*
identity	*Identität*
mother tongue	*Muttersprache*
(un)welcoming	*einladend (abweisend)*

6 Volunteering abroad

SOCIAL TOPICS

TWO DIFFERENT WAYS OF HELPING WITH PROJECTS ABROAD

Volunteering in agriculture and farming in Jamaica

Our Community Farming volunteer project in Jamaica combines elements of farming and agricultural management with a more community focussed role. The project is open to volunteers taking a gap year, career break, or even a volunteer holiday, and you do not need any specific experience to volunteer on this project – just a keen interest in agricultural issues and a desire to help the Jamaicans working within this field.

Sustainable agriculture is important to the livelihood of many small farmers in rural areas. Farmers make up 20% of Jamaica's workforce; this represents almost 160,000 families who are dependent on farming. Increasing costs of fertilizers and agrochemicals in conjunction with a lack of support for rural farmers are making the lives of these farmers very difficult.

Volunteers working on the Community Farming project in Jamaica will work with the Christiana Potato Growers Cooperative Association (CPGCA) to support and promote "protected agriculture" as a way forward. Protected agriculture involves farming in greenhouses to limit the effects of poor weather and insects. The greenhouses also take up ten times less land.

The CPGCA promotes protected agriculture and has been operating continuously for almost 50 years with the support of the community. It now represents some 4,000 small farmers in five districts. Its mission is to provide consistently high quality products and excellent services to farmers and customers as well as to focus on the growth and productivity of the cooperative to the benefit of the wider community. The aim is to assist local farmers to increase their yield and the quality of their harvest.

Organic farm volunteering in Togo

Volunteers on Projects Abroad's Agriculture & Community Farming project in Togo work on a small organic farm that supports a local village. No previous experience is required, so you may join this project on a gap year, career break, or volunteer vacation as a family. (…)

As a volunteer you will help with agricultural tasks like planting and crop-growing, irrigation of the fields, and further processing of products such as cassava and corn. Additionally, your work will include animal care responsibilities, looking after animals like ducks, sheep, goats, chickens, and pigs on the animal farm.

Volunteers may also help with land-management and packing of products for markets and clients. Here, you will be able to work with a variety of local organic products from ginger and teak wood to palm nuts and wine. During your time volunteering abroad on the farm you will live with a host family based in Lomè. You will travel the half hour to the village of Noépe and the farm with the farm owner.

This project is available for less than a month if you do not have time to join us for a longer period. You will gain valuable cultural insight and work intensely within the local community. However, please be aware that you may not have the same impact as someone participating for a longer period. (488 words)

Abridged from: *www.projects-abroad.org*

1 LOOKING AT THE TEXT

→ Rezeption: Leseverstehen, S. 214

A Read these sentences and say if they refer to Jamaica or Togo or both.

1 Volunteers may also be involved in getting the products ready to be taken to the market.
2 Volunteers help farmers with their every-day tasks.
3 This new method means reducing the effects of poor weather and insects by farming in greenhouses.
4 Volunteers might be working about half an hour away from where they are staying.
5 The organization works with about 4,000 small farmers.
6 Volunteers help with the job of growing and processing the different farm products.
7 Volunteers help to make sure the plants get enough water.
8 The aim of the organization is to help farmers to grow more and better farm products.
9 Volunteers also have to look after farm animals.
10 More than 150,000 families are dependent on farming.

B Look at the last statement in the text and answer these questions.

1 What does the statement mean by "impact"?
2 Why do you think participating for a longer period could be better? Do you agree or disagree?

"HOWEVER, PLEASE BE AWARE THAT YOU MAY NOT HAVE THE SAME IMPACT AS SOMEONE PARTICIPATING FOR A LONGER PERIOD."

2 WORKING WITH WORDS

A Find opposites for these words from the text. You can use a dictionary if you need to.

1 rural areas (line 13)
2 lack (line 18)
3 local (line 37)
4 increase (line 37)
5 include (line 50)
6 valuable (line 65)

B Now fill in either the words from above or their opposites to complete these sentences. (The numbers of the sentences below correspond to the numbers in 2A.)

1 It is nice and quiet in ___ but it is more difficult to get to discos and cinemas.
2 Some years the farmers have a(n) ___ of corn so the price goes down, and sometimes there is not enough so the price goes up.
3 Selling to the ___ market means the products do not have to travel so far.
4 The number of volunteers from abroad is expected to ___, which will be a big problem for CPGCA.
5 The project doesn't ___ housing, so you have to look for your own place to live.
6 Planting vegetables and then not giving them water is a ___ method of farming.

3 LISTENING

→ Rezeption: Hörverstehen, S. 225

4/16

John Dee from the radio programme *Young People Today* is talking to a school leaver about her time as a volunteer abroad.

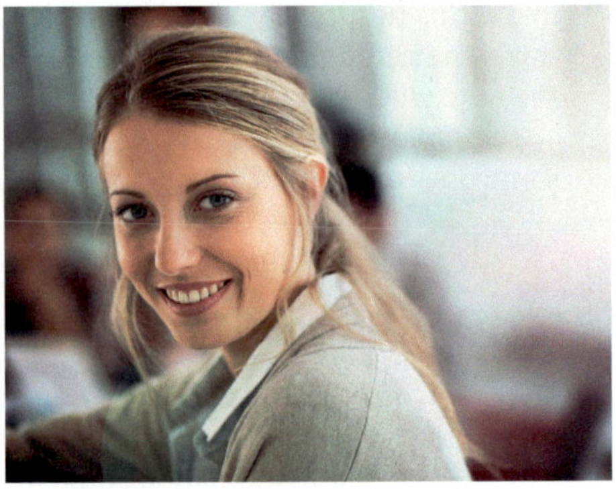

A Listen to what she says about her experience and find out if she is planning to go back.

B Listen again and answer these questions.

1 How long did Manuela spend in Ghana?
2 What was the name of the organization?
3 How was this organization different to other organizations?
4 Where did Manuela live when she was in Ghana and who did she work with?
5 What does Manuela think you can learn if you take part in such a project?

4 DISCUSSION

→ Interaktion, S. 246

Discuss in a small group.

1 Do you know of any German organizations that run volunteer projects abroad? What kind of programmes and positions do they offer?
2 Have you ever volunteered or do you know anybody who has? Describe the experience.

5 WRITING

→ Produktion: Schreiben, S. 228

Choose one of the following tasks.

1 Write a comment about the pros and cons of volunteering abroad and whether you would be prepared to volunteer abroad for a gap year.
2 Write a description of the kind of job you would like to do as a volunteer abroad and why.
3 Write an email to a friend who wants to volunteer abroad, telling him or her what you know about volunteering.

Useful vocabulary for discussing volunteering abroad

Project and impact		Experience	
conservation	*Naturschutz*	to appreciate	*schätzen*
to contribute	*beitragen*	to become aware of	*sich einer Sache bewusst werden*
developing country	*Entwicklungsland*		
disease	*Krankheit*	dedicated	*engagiert*
education	*Bildung*	demanding	*anspruchsvoll/anstrengend*
facilities	*Einrichtungen*	eye-opening	*aufschlussreich*
infrastructure	*Infrastruktur*	it's worth it	*es ist es wert*
mentoring	*Betreuung*	legacy	*Vermächtnis*
minority group	*Minderheit*	life-changing	*lebensverändernd*
orphanage	*Waisenhaus*	rewarding	*lohnend*
poverty line	*Armutsgrenze*	satisfaction	*Zufriedenheit*
victim	*Opfer*	worthwhile	*lohnenswert*

7 Making a difference

SOCIAL TOPICS

CARER'S WORLD:

The online magazine for caring professionals

The ethical caring professional

We've all heard about how we should be more ethical, haven't we? We should look at what we eat and where we buy our clothes because everything we do and buy has an effect on someone else somewhere across the globe, especially now that globalization and social media are making the world feel smaller. When we go shopping ourselves, we may think twice before buying coffee or a cheap T-shirt, but what about while we're at work? Can we become ethical carers as well? Our article this week talks about how we caring professionals should also do our bit to make the world a better and fairer place.

What you wear

After the Rana Plaza sweatshop collapsed on 24 April 2013 killing 1,127 workers, there was a public uproar – why do we buy cheap clothes made by low-paid workers who risk their lives in poor working conditions? Since then many clothing brands have started to produce more ethically and to inspect their factories to make sure the workers there have safe working conditions and get a fair wage. That's great when you're out buying your jeans to wear on your day off, but what about the clothes you wear at work – your uniform? Thankfully, there are now companies out there which produce ethical uniforms as well. Take The Rizues, for example. The Rizues is a British company committed to supplying medical and nurses' uniforms from sources that do not use child labour, where employees are not discriminated against because of colour, race, religion, gender, nationality, age or marital status, and where they are paid fair wages.

Wear ethical uniforms

What food you offer

How often do you sit down with the children or patients in your care for a snack or a cup of tea or coffee? Where does all of this food and drink come from? Just as many of us do during the weekly shop at the supermarket, care institutions should make a stand and buy fair-trade products. Okay, these products are a little more expensive than others, but isn't it important to set a good example and show your clients that we can all play a role in "saving the world"? What better way to do this than giving them fair-trade coffee, where the coffee bean producers are paid a fair wage. Or you can reduce food miles by only buying local fruit and vegetables. And if you work in a kindergarten, you can even make a day out of it and take the children to a local farm to pick their own fruit and to learn more about where their food comes from.

Serve fair-trade coffee and local fruit

What equipment your institution uses

Every time you need to buy something new at work, consider what effect the new item will have on the world around us. For example, the centre's car or van has broken down and a new one needs to be bought.

Talk to your team leader and suggest that the centre doesn't really need a big petrol-guzzling vehicle to do its weekly shop or to taxi people around in; there are plenty of more environmentally friendly cars that will do the job just as well. And it isn't just the big things: buying simple things like energy-saving light bulbs is a great start, too.

What do you think?

These are just some ideas to get you thinking. We'd love to hear what your place of work is doing to help the planet. Leave us your comments here. (576 words)

1 LOOKING AT THE TEXT

→ Rezeption: Leseverstehen, S. 214

Find the answers to these questions.

1 The article talks about the world feeling smaller. What does this mean?
2 What caused people to protest loudly in the spring of 2013? What was the result of this?
3 What does the article say about companies like The Rizues?
4 Why does the writer say that you should buy fair-trade products for your place of work?
5 What might children learn when you take them to a local farm?
6 What is an environmentally friendly car?

2 WORKING WITH WORDS

A Find the English equivalents in the text for these words and phrases.

1 ethisch
2 Globalisierung
3 Ausbeutungsbetrieb
4 schlechte Arbeitsbedingungen
5 gerechter Lohn
6 Kinderarbeit
7 Transportwege der Nahrungsmittel
8 umweltfreundlich
9 energiesparend

B Two readers have responded to the Carer's World article. Complete their comments with the words you found in exercise 2A.

Jane, Bristol
I am a carer in a small residence here in Bristol. We go shopping on our ___[1] bicycles once a week (no cars for us!) and we always try to buy local fruit and vegetables – not only to reduce the ___[2] but because the food tastes so much better. Oh, and our team leader insists we only use ___[3] appliances. Outside of work, I try to buy ___[4] clothing whenever I can, and I always check the labels on my clothes to make sure they were not produced in factories using ___[5]. I have two kids of my own and I can't imagine them working in a factory.

Malcolm, London
I agree that clothes made in ___[6] are terrible. Workers in developing countries suffer under the ___[7] in those factories. I think that everybody should get a ___[8] so that they can pay for all the things they need and have a good life. Only then is ___[9] fair for all of us.

3 MEDIATION

→ Schriftliche Mediation, S. 240

Als Mitarbeiter/in in einer sozialen Einrichtung haben Sie das Gefühl, dass bei der Einkaufspolitik Ihrer Einrichtung wenig ethisch-moralische Aspekte eine Rolle spielen. In einer Teamsitzung möchten Sie die Kollegen und Kolleginnen darüber informieren, wie dies geändert werden könnte. Erstellen Sie für diese Sitzung eine Liste mit Informationen, die Sie kommunizieren möchten. Entnehmen Sie dazu die relevanten Informationen aus dem vorliegenden Artikel. Übersetzen Sie dabei nicht Wort für Wort.

4 BRAINSTORMING AND PRESENTING

Your colleagues liked the ideas you presented at the team meeting and your boss has asked you to come up with some concrete suggestions to present to the board of directors of your institution. He asks you to do this in English as a few people on the board do not speak German.

Work in groups of 3–4 and follow the steps below.

1 First decide what kind of institution or company you work for. This could be a kindergarten, a care residence, a hospital, etc.
2 Brainstorm specific actions that could help make your place of work behave in a more ethical way. Think about the staff, the clients (or children) you work with, the rooms you work in, the food you serve, etc. Write down everything you can think of on a piece of paper.
3 Evaluate your ideas and reject the ones that don't make much sense or would be difficult to implement. Choose the best five remaining ideas and add as much detail as you can. Think about why the actions you have chosen are important and what impact they will make.
4 Present your proposal to the rest of the class.

5 WRITING

→ Produktion: Schreiben, S. 228

Write a response to this comment that a reader posted in reaction to the Carer's World article:

Is it really important for social and health care providers to pay attention to global issues? Shouldn't the emphasis of our work be on providing good care to our clients and patients and not on helping people on the other side of the world?

Useful vocabulary for talking about ethical caring and global issues

Ethical caring		Global issues	
dignity	*Würde*	to affect	*beeinflussen/beeinträchtigen*
equality	*Gleichheit/Gleichberechtigung*	assistance	*Unterstützung*
home-grown	*selbst angebaut*	to be at risk	*in Gefahr sein*
to insist on quality	*auf Qualität bestehen*	to be concerned about sth	*um etw besorgt sein*
local produce	*einheimische Produkte*	to bear in mind	*berücksichtigen*
pragmatic	*pragmatisch*	contribution	*Beitrag*
priority	*Priorität*	crisis (pl. crises)	*Krise/Notstand*
to prioritize	*Prioritäten setzen*	to have an effect	*eine Wirkung haben*
to recycle	*wiederverwerten*	to ignore	*ignorieren*
responsibility	*Verantwortung*	to focus on sth	*sich auf etw konzentrieren*
to be responsible	*verantwortungsvoll handeln*	solidarity	*Solidarität*

8 Stopping obesity in young children

SOCIAL TOPICS

Today's kindergarten kids "are already on the road to obesity" as the whole nation gets fatter

- Percentage of children considered obese has more than doubled since the 1970s
- Childhood obesity is rising because everyone is getting heavier

Kindergarten kids are getting heavier, and rising numbers are on their way to becoming overweight and obese in the years to come. There has been an "entire shift" in the weight of young children, with kids brought up today heavier than those brought up in the 1970s and 80s, a new study has revealed.

"It's not just kids who are already overweight getting more and more so," said lead study author Ashlesha Datar, senior economist at RAND Corp. in Santa Monica, California. "Even those who are normal weight are gaining weight."

The study found nearly 40 per cent of kindergarteners had a body mass index (BMI) in the 75th percentile or above. Being this size at the age of five means they don't have far to go before they tip into the overweight or obese category, putting them at risk of serious health problems as adults.

The number of overweight and obese children has also rocketed. About 28 per cent of children in the current sample had a BMI classified as overweight, compared to ten per cent of earlier generations. Obesity among children more than doubled in the same period, with 12 per cent of kids classified as obese, compared to five per cent in the 70s and 80s. Weight gain accelerated between the age of five and eight, when the proportion of kids in the 75th percentile or above hit almost 48 per cent.

Experts warn that the findings show that to make an impact on soaring childhood obesity rates, schemes to encourage better eating and exercise habits have to start very early, possibly even in kindergarten.

(363 words)

Abridged from: *www.dailymail.co.uk*

Couch potatoes: The availability of high-calorie snacks and children choosing to play video games and watch TV rather than play outdoors are contributing to childhood obesity.

Weighty numbers

- Weight gain accelerates between the age of five and eight.
- Five-year-olds with BMI in the 75th percentile has hit 40 per cent, up from 25 per cent in the 70s and 80s.
- Obesity has more than doubled from five to 12 per cent.

1 LOOKING AT THE TEXT

→ Rezeption: Leseverstehen, S. 214

What does the text tell us about:

1 today's kindergarten kids compared with those in the 1970s?
2 kindergarten kids in the future?
3 children who are normal weight?
4 being overweight at the age of five?
5 couch potatoes?
6 a plan to solve the problem?

2 WORKING WITH WORDS

A mother is worried about her 12-year-old daughter's weight and has decided to see a doctor.

Complete the dialogue with terms from the box. The words are all from the text.

childhood ▪ contributing ▪ doubled ▪ eating habits ▪ impact ▪ increase ▪ obese ▪ revealed ▪ serious ▪ soaring

Doctor: So, Ms McAllen, you are worried about your daughter's weight. I can tell you that I don't consider her to be ___[1], but if her weight continues to ___[2] as you have just told me, it could become very ___[3]. What do you think the reason is for her weight?

Mother: I think it started in early ___[4], and it was our mistake. My husband and I always told Megan to eat everything on her plate, as we had been told to by our parents. I think this is ___[5] to her weight problem. Her weight has ___[6] in less than two years.

Doctor: I am afraid you are going to have to rethink Megan's ___[7]. Medical findings have ___[8] that weight problems in young people don't disappear unless people do something about them. Statistics show that the number of overweight people is ___[9] and, in my opinion, this is a problem of modern society. I think Megan should exercise regularly, not just at school, and stop eating fast food. That will make an ___[10] on her weight.

3 CONTRIBUTING FACTORS

Many factors contribute to obesity, including a person's habits, lifestyle and environment.

Match the expressions in the word cloud with seven of the factors that can contribute to obesity in children. Some expressions may apply to more than one factor.

video games · soft drinks · sugar intake · vending machines · few playground breaks · crisps · single parent · fast food · "unhealthy" cereals · "all you can eat" · "good job!" · ready meals · day care · TV programmes · social media · parents' eating habits · loneliness · depression · advertising · poor self-esteem · snacking · Big Mac

1 Food is used as a reward for good behaviour and as comfort when we feel sad.
2 Parents are often very busy and have little time to prepare healthy meals. As a result, children eat more processed and fast foods that are usually not as healthy as home-cooked meals.
3 Children see up to 10,000 commercials on television every year. Most of these are for sweets, fast food, soft drinks and sugared cereals. And while they watch, they tend to eat unhealthy food.
4 Watching television, texting and playing on the computer are activities that need very little energy. They can take up a lot of time and replace physical activity.
5 More foods today are processed and contain too much sugar and are high in fat.
6 Overeating is a habit that is encouraged by restaurants that advertise high-calorie foods and large portion sizes.
7 Not all schools offer healthy meals or give children enough time for physical activity.

4 DISCUSSION

→ Interaktion, S. 246

Discuss 2–3 of the points below with a partner of your choice.

1 How healthy are your eating habits? Could you improve on them? How?
2 How often do you eat fast food? How often do you eat things like fruit, vegetables and fish? Do you eat snacks when you watch TV? What kind?
3 Do you think you could do more sports? What kind of sport do you prefer?
4 Why do you think so many people have bad eating habits?
5 Do you think Germany is becoming a nation of obese people? Why / Why not?

5 WRITING

→ Produktion: Schreiben, S. 228

A Brainstorm some ideas to prevent obesity by helping young children to develop healthier eating and exercise habits. You can use a mind map to organize your ideas.

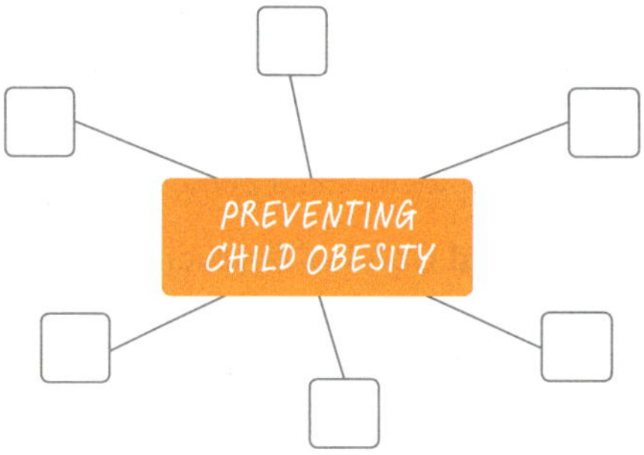

B Then choose one of the options below.

1 Write either a comment or a letter to the school board.
2 Write a flyer with tips for both kindergarten teachers and parents.
3 Use the internet to research healthy eating programmes offered in Germany. Summarize your findings for an English health magazine.

Useful vocabulary for discussing ways to fight obesity in children

Diet		to set a good example	*mit gutem Beispiel vorangehen*
balanced diet	*ausgewogene Ernährung*	to set rules	*Regeln aufstellen*
body image	*Auffassung über den Körper*	**Exercise**	
carbohydrates	*Kohlenhydrate*	active lifestyle	*aktiver Lebenstil*
eating disorder	*Essstörung*	competition	*Wettbewerb*
eating habits	*Essgewohnheiten*	outdoor activities	*Freiluftaktivitäten*
fresh produce	*Frischwaren*	playground equipment	*Spielplatzgeräte*
to go on a (crash) diet	*eine (Radikal)Diät machen*	sedentary lifestyle	*inaktiver Lebenstil*
metabolic rate	*Stoffwechsel*	sports club	*Sportverein*
nutrition	*Ernährung*	team sport	*Mannschaftssport*
poor diet	*schlechte Ernährung*		

9 Coping with disability

SOCIAL TOPICS

1 THINKING ABOUT INCLUSION

Follow the steps below.

1 Look at the diagram. What is it trying to tell us? Work with a partner and write a caption.
2 Think about what you know about inclusion. Write a few keywords, then compare your words with your partner.
3 Work with another pair of students and discuss your thoughts on inclusion. Make a mind map in your group and present it to the class.

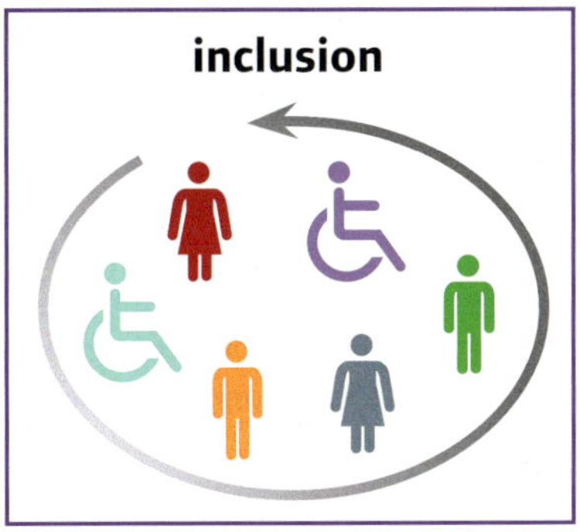

2 LOOKING AT THE TEXT

→ Rezeption: Leseverstehen, S. 214

Lesen Sie den Zeitungsartikel und bearbeiten Sie die folgenden Aufgaben auf Deutsch.

1 Beschreiben Sie was das Besondere an Sarah Gordys letzter Rolle auf der Bühne ist.
2 Finden Sie heraus, ob dies ihre erste Rolle ist oder nicht.
3 Überlegen Sie aus welchem Grund Sarah als Botschafterin gilt.
4 Beschreiben Sie wie Sarah sich selbst auf ihrer Website präsentiert.
5 Erklären Sie welche Bedeutung Jan Tregelles in Sarahs Leistung sieht.
6 Erläutern Sie warum Sarahs Mutter sagt, es wäre in der Kunst einfacher für eine behinderte Person Erfolg zu haben.
7 Analysieren Sie den Einfluss, den Sarah auf andere Leute mit behinderten Kindern hatte.

"I am different, that is good": how an actor with Down's syndrome is changing perceptions

Sarah Gordy, who appears in Manchester play Crocodiles, breaks new ground by playing a character without a disability

Every actor surely dreams of making history with a role. Sarah Gordy has done so twice – in little more than a year. Last year the stage and screen professional, who has Down's syndrome, became Mencap's first celebrity ambassador with a learning disability; now she is breaking new ground by playing a character without a disability. [Note: The Royal Mencap Society is a charity based in the UK that works with people with learning disabilities.]

Gordy is best known for high-profile BBC roles such as Sally Harper, a pregnant woman in *Call the Midwife*, and Lady Pamela Holland in *Upstairs Downstairs*.

Sarah Gordy and Melanie Hill, Royal Exchange Theatre production of CROCODILES by Lee Mattinson

On her website, the 36-year-old puts her professional identity before her disability. "I am an actor, a dancer and a woman first. I have green eyes and Down's syndrome. I am different, that is good."

The chief executive of Mencap, Jan Tregelles, stresses the significance of Gordy's latest project: "Too often society chooses to discuss barriers, rather than opportunities for people with a learning disability … for too long actors with a disability have struggled to gain roles that don't just relate to their disability. However, Sarah's achievement should be a clear signal to others of what is possible if we afford everyone the same opportunities in life."

Jane Gordy acknowledges that the arts are more inclusive than other industries. She adds that while her daughter is aware of the negative attitudes towards learning disabilities through her work as a Mencap ambassador, she has not experienced this herself: "The arts [are] more open. We're looking for different, interesting unique experiences to give to the public." Employers in other sectors, she says, must not overlook traits such as reliability, honesty and accuracy, prevalent in some people who have a learning disability.

As well as the awareness raised by Gordy's work, there are individual examples of positive impact. There was the new father of twins, one of whom had just been diagnosed with Down's syndrome, who saw the actor on television. Jane Gordy recalls: "He said that seeing Sarah so healthy, happy and successful came at just the right time. Sarah gave them hope and ambition. We strive to make people see the individual, not the label."

As Sarah Gordy adds: "Respect people who are different." (373 words)

Abridged from: *www.theguardian.com*

3 LISTENING: INCLUSION IN THE CLASSROOM

→ Rezeption: Hörverstehen, S. 225

Inclusion of all children with disabilities in regular classrooms seems to be the law of the land. But is it the right thing for all kids? And how are teachers handling it? Our reporter, Jane Willoughby, talks to Mr Baaker, the principal of a school in the Netherlands that has practised inclusion for many years.

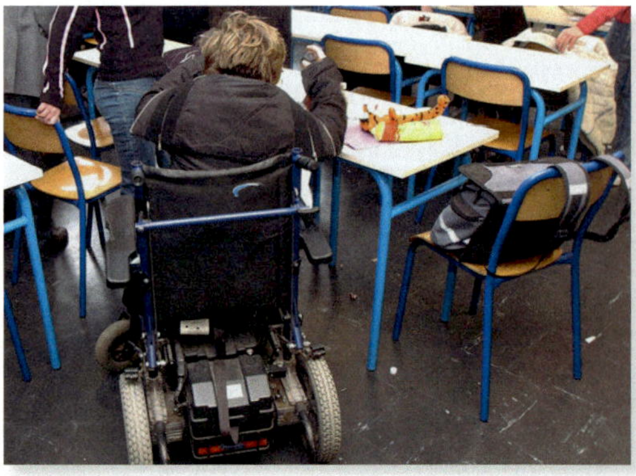

A Before you listen, make sure you understand these English words and phrases. Match them to their German equivalents.

1	to be held back	**a**	*profitieren*
2	behavioural problems	**b**	*im Einzelfall*
3	to benefit	**c**	*schwere Behinderung*
4	natural environment	**d**	*Fachausbildung*
5	medical condition	**e**	*aufgehalten werden*
6	non-disabled pupils	**f**	*Verhaltenstörungen*
7	on an individual basis	**g**	*natürliche Umwelt*
8	severe disability	**h**	*Förderklasse*
9	special needs class	**i**	*Erkrankung*
10	specialized training	**j**	*nicht behinderte Schüler/innen*

4/17 **B Listen to the interview and decide if the following points were mentioned.**

1. Some people say that pupils with very severe disabilities do not really benefit from inclusion.
2. The special technology that teachers need to teach students with disabilities is expensive.
3. All students with special needs are tested before they enter an inclusion classroom.
4. Children with special needs can learn in a natural environment.
5. Inclusion makes it possible for non-disabled and disabled students to become friends.
6. The non-disabled often benefit by learning that not everybody is the same.
7. All the necessary specialized training takes an extra two years at university.
8. Some schools are not equipped to provide the specialized education required.
9. Some assistants who are there to help children with special needs do not have the necessary training or experience.

C Now decide if the points that were mentioned are positive or negative aspects of inclusion in schools.

4 DEBATE

Form two groups, one for inclusion and one against inclusion in the classroom. In your group, collect points about the pros and cons. Think about the effect inclusion has on both the disabled and the non-disabled students. Then start the debate.

5 WRITING

→ Eine Stellungname schreiben, S. 234

Use information from your debate to write a comment about inclusion in the classroom. Summarize the pros and cons, then give your own opinion.

Useful vocabulary for discussing inclusion in the classroom

Disability

able-bodied	*körperlich gesund / nicht-behindert*
autistic	*autistisch*
autism	*Autismus*
blindness	*Blindheit*
deaf	*gehörlos*
deafness	*Gehörlosigkeit*
dyslexia	*Legasthenie/Dyslexie*
dyslexic	*legasthenisch*
hearing impaired	*schwerhörig*
impairment	*Einschränkung*
isolated	*isoliert*
learning difficulties	*Lernschwierigkeiten*
limited mobility	*eingeschränkte Beweglichkeit*
outsider	*Außenseiter*
visually impaired	*sehschwach/ sehbehindert*
wheelchair user	*Rollstuhlfahrer/in*

Children and schools

to accept	*akzeptieren*
assessment	*Beurteilung/ Bewertung*
to be at ease	*entspannt sein*
to behave	*sich benehmen*
to belong	*zugehören*
creative	*kreativ*
to discriminate	*diskriminieren*
disruptive	*störend*
to fall behind	*in Rückstand geraten*
frustrating	*frustrierend*
to have access to	*zu etw Zugang haben*

10 Storytelling for the environment

SOCIAL TOPICS

We all love a good story. Many of the stories that we read, listen to on audiobooks or even watch in the form of films teach us something new, whether about ourselves or the world we live in. And because stories allow us to step back and observe how others face challenges, they can be used to address difficult or complex issues, such as coping with threats to the environment.

1 LOOKING AT THE TEXT

A Before you read the excerpt from the children's story below, read the title and look at the cover. What environmental issues shown below do you think the story might address?

air pollution

waste disposal

water pollution

endangered or extinct species

deforestation

global warming

B Now read the story. Were you right? What was different from what you had expected?

DINOSAURS AND ALL THAT RUBBISH

A man stood on a green, grassy hill and looked at a star. All he thought about and dreamed about was the star. The star was a thing of wonder and beauty to him, and he longed to visit it. He climbed to the top of a tall tree and reached out to the star. But he was nowhere near it.

As he sat on the tree, he heard birds singing. Soon the trees were filled with birds of all kinds and colours. Some of the birds flew up in the sky, nearer to the star. "That's it!" said the man. "I must fly! Now I know what I need. I must have a rocket to fly to my star."

The man owned some factories nearby. He ran to each one. "Build me a rocket," he ordered the people who worked there. "Cut down the trees, dig out the coal, burn whatever will burn, and keep the factories' furnaces going until you have built a rocket that can fly to a star." For weeks and months and years the rocket makers worked. The fires in the factories huffed and puffed. Smoke poured out, and rubbish piled up all over the grass and trees.

At last the rocket was ready – but now there was no place to launch it. Wherever the man looked, all he could see was rubbish and waste from the factories. The man took his rocket to the top of one of the biggest rubbish heaps and set off for the star.

When he landed on the star, the man looked about in surprise. There was nothing much to see. He walked and walked, but still he saw nothing beautiful on the whole star. There were no trees, no flowers; there was not even a blade of grass. He was very sad. The only thing of wonder the man saw was another star, far off in the dark sky. "I will go to that star," he said and away he went again in his rocket.

On Earth the piles of rubbish still smouldered and burned, and the mountains rumbled. Deep down inside the Earth the heat and noise woke up some dinosaurs and other ancient animals. They had been sleeping there, hidden away, for millions of years.

They heaved and stretched. The surface of the Earth cracked, and out came all sorts of creatures. A dinosaur held his nose as he looked around. "POOH!" he said. "If we are going to live here, we'll have to get busy and clean this place up." Some of the dinosaurs burned rubbish in volcanoes. Dancing dinosaurs broke up the roads.

As the rubbish was cleared, green shoots appeared bursting through cracks and climbing over old forgotten walls. Telephone poles and iron pylons were covered with trailing blossoms. A fresh new forest of flowers and trees spread like a smile around the world.

(The man returned to Earth but did not know it was Earth until a dinosaur told him.)

The man looked about him and saw that the dinosaur was right. "Please may I have a small part of it back?" he asked. "Please? Just a hill, or a tree or a flower?"

"No," said the dinosaur. "Not a part of it, but all of it. It is all yours, but it is also mine. Remember that. This time the Earth belongs to everyone, not parts of it to certain people but all of it to everyone, to be enjoyed and cared for." "Yes, EVERYONE!" sang the birds and the cats and the mice and the mammoths, the serpents, the dodos, and the apes. "EVERYONE!" came the chorus from all living creatures. "EVERYONE! EVERYONE!"

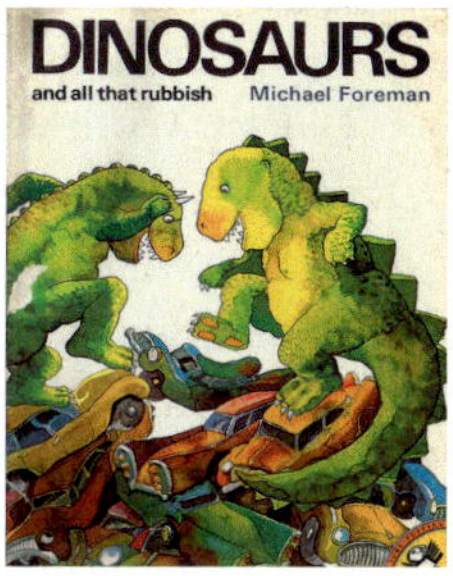

Abridged from: *Dinosaurs and all that Rubbish, by Michael Foreman*

C Work with a partner to complete the tasks below.

1. Think of a moral for the story. In one sentence, write the message you think children should learn.
2. Think of ways that you could integrate the story into other activities to teach children about the environment, e.g. acting out the story, grouping the words into good and bad aspects, etc. Share your ideas with the class.

2 WORKING WITH WORDS

A Copy the table and complete it with words from the story.

words that talk about nature	words that talk about things that damage nature
green, grassy hill	*rubbish*

B Look at these sentences about the environment and choose a word from the brackets to complete the gaps.

1. Our rivers used to be polluted, but the city cleaned ___ the water and now there are fish again. (about ▪ off ▪ up)
2. I often dream ___ living in a world with no pollution. (about ▪ for ▪ on)
3. When the dustmen were on strike, the rubbish piled ___ in the streets. (on ▪ through ▪ up)
4. The fields are covered ___ old plastic bags, tins and paper. (from ▪ up ▪ with)
5. It is important to teach our children to care ___ the world we live in. (after ▪ for ▪ over)
6. We should always think ___ [1] the consequences of our actions. Our world does not only belong ___ [2] us people but to all living creatures. (about ▪ for ▪ on) (by ▪ for ▪ to)

3 LISTENING: FILMS ABOUT THE ENVIRONMENT

→ Rezeption: Hörverstehen, S. 225

4/18 **Listen to three teachers who are talking about films that can be used to teach children about the environment. Copy this table and complete it with the information you hear.**

name of the film	environmental issues dealt with	suitable for young children?

4 BRAINSTORMING

Follow the steps below.

1 **Think.** Look at the photos on page 202 and think about the environmental issues shown there. For each picture, jot down some words that come to mind.

2 **Pair.** Work with a partner and choose an environmental issue (or issues) that would be suitable to discuss with young children. Then do some brainstorming on causes, effects and solutions. You might want to collect your ideas in a mind map.

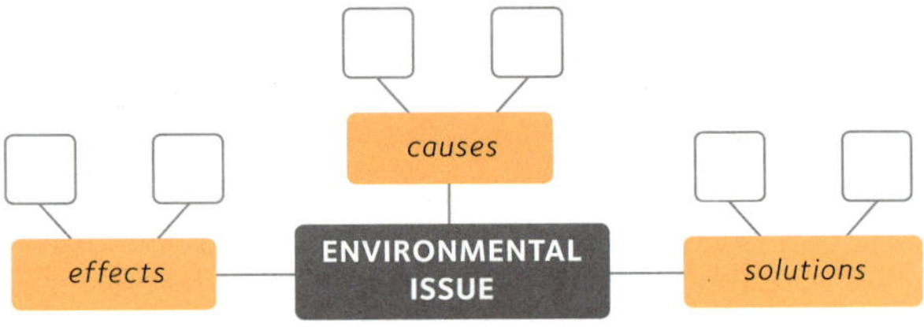

3 **Share.** Find another pair of students who have chosen the same issue(s). Work together to develop a lesson plan or a project. Present your ideas to the class.

5 WRITING ABOUT THE ENVIRONMENT

→ Produktion: Schreiben, S. 228

Do one of the tasks below.

1 You want to write a story about the environment that you could use with children. Write a short outline explaining the plot and the moral of the story. Think of your target group (how old the children are, what kind of class they are in), the type of story (picture book, short story, film), the main characters in the story (people or animals, or both), etc.

2 Think of a story or film you know that deals with the environment and write a short summary to explain the plot. Say whether you would recommend it, and if so, to whom.

Useful vocabulary for telling stories about the environment

Storytelling

to carry a moral message	*eine moralische Botschaft haben*
to engage sb's attention	*jds Aufmerksamkeit erregen*
fairy story / fairy tale	*Märchen*
main character	*Hauptfigur*
Once upon a time …	*Es war einmal …*
setting (of a story)	*Schauplatz*
to teach sb right and wrong	*jmd Recht und Unrecht beibringen*
to use one's imagination	*seine Fantasie benutzen*

Environment

biodegradable	*biologisch abbaubar*
chemical waste	*Chemiemüll*
to disrupt	*unterbrechen/stören*
ecosystem	*Ökosystem*
to emit	*ausstoßen*
food chain	*Nahrungskette*
greenhouse effect	*Treibhauseffekt*
landfill	*Deponie*
man-made	*vom Menschen verursacht*
nuclear waste	*radioaktiver Abfall*
sewage	*Abwasser*
to recycle/reuse	*wiederverwerten*

11 Programmes for feeding the poor

SOCIAL TOPICS

1 A SINGLE MAN TAKES THE INITIATIVE TO FEED THE POOR

By IOANNA FOTIADI

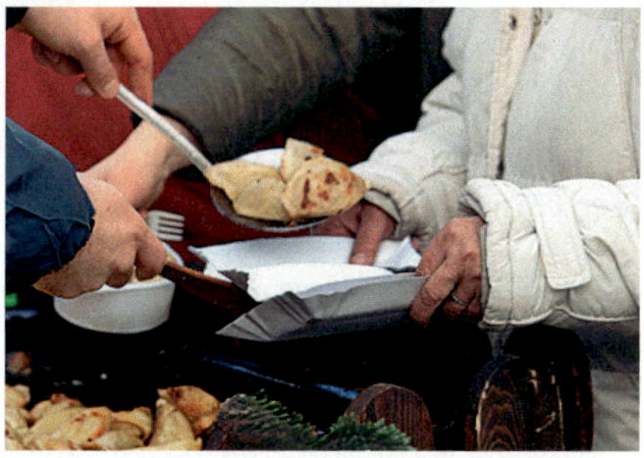

The life of 47-year-old Greek Constantinos Polychronopoulos was changed in a single day a few months ago when he saw two children fighting over a few rotten pieces of fruit at his local farmers' market. Polychronopoulos had already been unemployed for two years and admits that he felt like he had hit rock bottom. After seeing the children fighting over the fruit, however, Polychronopoulos decided to take action and help those who were worse off than himself, marshalling a few friends behind his idea and establishing a group called Allos Anthropos [The Other Person]. The members of the group get together and cook in a different neighbourhood every day, offering food to as many needy people as they can feed.

In Metaxourgeio, passers-by stop to look at what is going on as Polychronopoulos cooks up a massive pot of Neapolitan sauce for spaghetti. "I had hoped that I would never have to experience the kind of hunger we knew in the 40s," one elderly man says as he walks by, shaking his head sadly.

The aroma of cooking begins to draw a crowd of hungry people: elderly men and women, as well as entire families with small children. "Three months ago I felt completely disheartened," says Polychronopoulos. "But I was reborn here. I can communicate, I can share my thoughts and feelings." (219 words)

Abridged from: *www.ekathimerini.com*

2 OXFAM: THE POWER OF PEOPLE AGAINST POVERTY

The Oxford Committee for Famine Relief, now known as Oxfam, was founded in Oxford, England in 1942 by a group of people who wanted a more social state. Since then the organization has become involved in fighting the causes of famine and poverty.

Oxfam's goal is to help people to help themselves. Today in Britain, one in five lives in poverty.

It is not Oxfam's policy to hand out food, but they have recently been working with the Trussel Trust food bank organization to distribute cereal, tinned soup, and dried pasta to the disadvantaged. Why? Most people who come to food banks live off social benefits, and if there is a delay in receiving these benefits, they have no money, which often means they cannot buy food for themselves or their children. These include people who have low incomes, who are homeless or simply cannot afford to feed their children when they are at home during school holidays.

The number of people who are being forced to use food banks in order to feed their families has increased in the last few years, and the number of food bank parcels given to people has grown by 54 per cent in the last year. On 19 November 2014, Rachael Orr, head of Oxfam's UK poverty programme, was quoted as saying: "Food banks are both a lifeline for people at a time of crisis and a symptom of fundamental failure in our society." (239 words)

3 MISEREOR: COMMITTED TO FIGHTING POVERTY

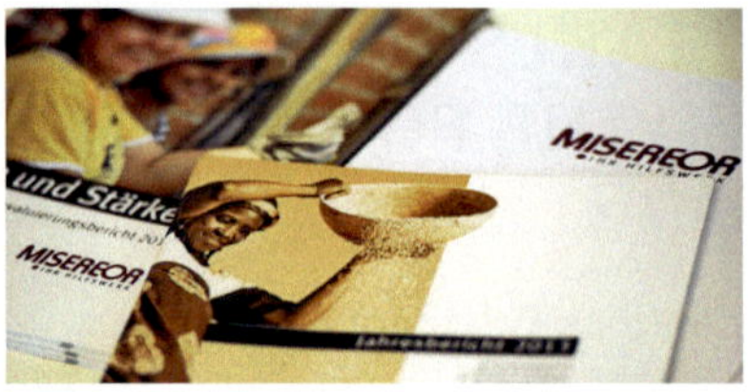

MISEREOR is the German Catholic Bishops' Organisation for Development Cooperation. For over 50 years MISEREOR has been committed to fighting poverty in Africa, Asia and Latin America. MISEREOR's support is available to any human being in need – regardless of their religion, ethnicity or gender.

MISEREOR supports the weakest members of society: the poor, the sick, the hungry and the disadvantaged. It is of no importance whether those in need of help are men or women, what religious beliefs they hold or where they come from.

The development projects supported by MISEREOR are as diverse as the causes and faces of poverty. They all have one thing in common, though. They all focus on the whole human person. As well as satisfying basic needs such as food security, they also help ensure that human rights are upheld and the way is paved for the people concerned to live in dignity. (149 words)

Abridged from: *www.misereor.org/about-us.html*

4 Vesperkirche – together at one table

The German winter is long. The generosity that comes with Christmas is slowly disappearing, and for the next few weeks a church in central Stuttgart, the Vesperkirche, becomes a second home for many people. Today Germany is classed as a rich country, but there are still many individuals and families who do not have the basic necessities such as enough food, health care and social integration.

This first Vesperkirche project was started in Stuttgart in 1995. Now there are over 20 such projects throughout Baden-Württemberg that give poor or homeless people a place to get a warm meal costing just €1.20. Most visitors can afford that amount, but even those who cannot are never turned away.

However, this project offers more than just a warm meal. It also offers those who come to the Vesperkirche advice about employment possibilities, help in solving conflicts, medical care and assistance or just a safe play area for their children. It even provides a bicycle repair service!

When the Stuttgart Vesperkirche opened in January 1995, there were 70 visitors. Twenty years later, in January 2015, the number of visitors had increased to 850. (189 words)

1 LOOKING AT THE TEXTS

→ Rezeption: Leseverstehen, S. 214

Copy the table and complete it with information from texts 1–4.

Name of the organization	Why the organization was started	Who is helped by the organization	How the organization helps

2 WORKING WITH WORDS

A Odd one out. Find the word that does not fit in each of the groups 1–5 below. Explain why it does not fit.

1	famine	hungry	hunger	food
2	advice	support	failure	care
3	distribute	afford	give	donate
4	gender	poor	disadvantaged	homeless
5	poverty	rock bottom	needy	necessities

B Complete the sentences with words from above. Use a word from group 1 for sentence 1, a word from group 2 for sentence 2, etc.

1 The children at the farmers' market were so ▬ that they fought over some rotten fruit.
2 The charity operates a food bank and also gives people ▬ on where to get help.
3 The organization uses a van to ▬ food and clothing to poor families.
4 The women slept under a bridge at night as they were ▬ and had nowhere else to go.
5 The man thought about killing himself when he hit ▬, but the Vesperkirche helped him.

3 RESEARCH AND PRESENTATION

→ Präsentieren, S. 243

Work with a partner. Research other programmes for the poor that you know of here in Germany or abroad. Present your results to the class. You can design a poster, prepare a PowerPoint presentation or give a short talk.

4 DISCUSSION

→ Interaktion, S. 246

Form groups of three and think about what kind of organization you would like to support and how. Inform the class, giving reasons for your choice.

Useful vocabulary for talking about supporting people in need

Problems

to be in debt	*Schulden haben*
bereavement	*Verlust/Trauerfall*
breakdown	*Zusammenbruch*
crisis	*Krise*
desperation	*Verzweiflung*
to die of starvation	*verhungern*
isolation	*Vereinsamung*
loneliness	*Einsamkeit*
to make ends meet	*über die Runden kommen*
malnourished	*unterernährt*
marginalized	*ausgegrenzt*
natural disaster	*Naturkatastrophe*
overwhelmed	*überfordert*
social exclusion	*soziale Ausgrenzung*
unemployed	*arbeitslos*

Support

a listening ear	*ein offenes Ohr*
companionship	*Gemeinschaft/ Mitmenschlichkeit*
counselling	*Therapie*
foster care	*Pflegeunterbringung*
homeless shelter	*Obdachlosenheim*
to lend a hand	*jmd helfen*
medical check-up	*Vorsorgeuntersuchung*
mentoring	*Betreuung*
to reach out to sb	*auf jdn zugehen*
shelter	*Unterkunft*
soup kitchen	*Suppenküche*
sustainable	*tragfähig*
to take somebody in	*jmd aufnehmen*
voluntary work	*Freiwilligendienst*

12 Technology in social and health care

SOCIAL TOPICS

It seems that every month there is a new app or gadget that becomes the latest must-have item. The most talked about innovations tend to be in the area of entertainment and communications, but that does not mean that other sectors are not benefiting from new technology. The article below introduces some new companies and their innovative health care products.

Health tech companies changing the world

Here are four of today's tech start-ups that are changing health care and the world:

Telesofia

Only about half of patients properly understand some medication instructions, even when they are as simple as "take one pill every four hours". That's the startling fact that led a team of doctors and techies to found Telesofia, an Israeli start-up that enables doctors to provide personalized instructions to patients in easy-to-understand videos. The videos, which can be pushed to any device, use illustrations and everyday language to make sure that doctors' orders turn into action at home. They also filter out irrelevant information, so that a 65-year-old man doesn't get sidetracked by medication warnings intended for breastfeeding mothers.

TotallyPregnant

Pregnancy mobile apps have become a booming segment of the app market, with offerings that include week-by-week pregnancy trackers, diet managers and even belly selfie functions. A new entrant, TotallyPregnant, seems to have rolled all of its competitors' functionality into one, while adding powerful location-based technology and the first-ever 3D fetus animation videos. Functions include informational videos, expert advice forums, baby gear shopping and a weekly pregnancy tracker. The app is free but generates revenue with links to online stores and in-app purchases of classes like Lamaze and yoga for pregnancy.

iCouch

iCouch uses videoconferencing to connect mental health professionals to patients. The entire interaction – from booking to payment – occurs online, which means that mental health professionals can reach patients anywhere in the world. The ease of use, and the fact that you don't even have to get off your couch, eliminates obstacles that prevent some people from getting much needed treatment. These are welcome developments for a branch of medicine that suffers from a severe shortage of providers and a stigma that keeps away some people in need of help.

HelpAround

People living with diabetes usually have to carry around and use a toolkit of medical equipment every day. But what if you run out of glucose tabs or forget your test strips? HelpAround's mobile app connects users to others in the area who might be able to provide missing supplies or even help with a blood test or an injection. The app also serves as a community for advice and support. The next iterations of HelpAround will branch out from diabetes to create networks of helpers for people with other chronic diseases and food allergies. (374 words)

Abridged from: *www.forbes.com*

1 LOOKING AT THE TEXT

→ Rezeption: Leseverstehen, S. 214

A Decide which products mentioned in the text fit the descriptions.

This product …

1 helps mothers-to-be.
2 reduces the amount of information a patient has to understand.
3 helps you find another person who is suffering from the same illness as you.

4 replaces face-to-face consultation.
5 helps people to understand doctors' instructions.
6 encourages healthy eating.
7 allows you to get help without leaving home.

B Answer these questions.

1 How does Telesofia help older people with cognitive difficulties?
2 In what way is TotallyPregnant similar to the apps you use, for example that it is free of charge?
3 Although not directly mentioned, who is iCouch designed for?
4 How exactly does the networking feature of HelpAround work?
5 In your opinion, which of the four gadgets mentioned in the text is the most useful? Why?

2 WORKING WITH WORDS

Match words from A and B to make expressions that fit the definitions. All of the expressions are in the text.

1 qualified people who help patients with psychological problems
2 a procedure done to check somebody's medical condition
3 an illness that lasts a long time and is difficult to cure
4 tools and machines used in health care
5 information on how to use a particular medicine
6 an online chatroom where you can get help from professionals
7 a procedure that is essential for curing an illness or injury
8 a simple way of speaking that avoids technical words

A

blood ▪ chronic ▪ everyday ▪ expert advice ▪ medical ▪ medication ▪ mental health ▪ much needed

B

disease ▪ equipment ▪ forum ▪ instructions ▪ language ▪ professionals ▪ test ▪ treatment

3 LISTENING

→ Rezeption: Hörverstehen, S. 225

4/19 In this radio programme, host Jason Harman interviews two people whose everyday lives have been helped by technology.

A Listen and say which guest – Paul or Lydia – uses the devices or technologies below. Careful: two items in the list are used by neither person.

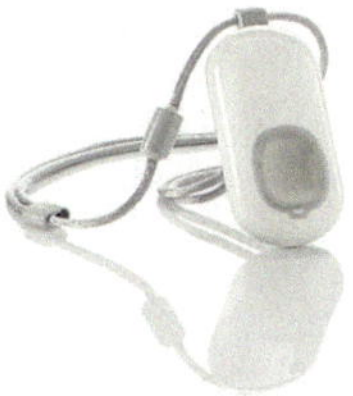

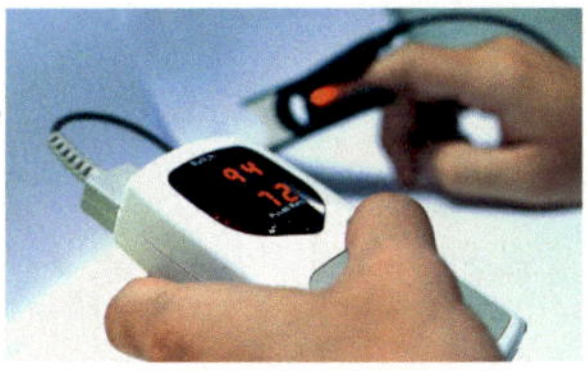

Bradley watch ▪
captioned telephone ▪
Lifeline pendant ▪
lung flute ▪
sensors ▪
talking computer ▪
talking microwave ▪
telehealth technology ▪
voice-controlled personal mobility assistant

B Listen again and takes notes in order to complete the following tasks.

coughing · epileptic fits · trouble breathing · blind · smoking · brain tumour · lung disease · fatigued · breathless · blood pressure · difficulty walking · operation

1. Describe what is wrong with Paul and Lydia and what caused their disability or illness. The words in the cloud will help you.
2. Explain the way technology has helped them manage their daily lives.
3. Comment on how their relationship to friends, family and other people has been influenced by the technology.

4 BRAINSTORMING

Working in a small group, follow the steps below and design a new gadget (or adapt an existing one) to help people in need.

1. First decide on the group or groups of people you would like to help. You can choose a target group from the list below or come up with your own ideas.

infants or small children ▪ people with cognitive problems ▪ people using wheelchairs ▪ people suffering from dementia or Alzheimer's ▪ people with hearing or visual impairments ▪ recovering alcoholics or drug addicts

2. Brainstorm gadgets or other technology that could improve the day-to-day life of the group you have chosen. It can be something simple like a device to help somebody to put on their socks, or more complicated, for example equipment to help somebody get out of the bath. You can research the internet for ideas.
3. Design a poster or a mini PowerPoint presentation describing the innovation, showing how it would work and who it would help. Then present your idea to the rest of the class.

5 WRITING

→ Produktion: Schreiben, S. 228

Write a comment about the role of technology in social or health care, addressing some or all of the following questions.

- In what areas of social and health care is technology very important and where does it play a less important role?
- What is the role of people vs. devices?
- Can there be such a thing as too much technology?

Useful vocabulary for talking about the role of technology in care

to administer	*verabreichen*	to interact with sth	*mit etw interagieren*
to alert	*alarmieren*	to keep track of	*etw im Auge behalten*
to analyze	*analysieren*	to monitor	*überwachen*
automatically	*automatisch*	practical advice	*praktische Ratschläge*
checkup	*medizinische Untersuchung*	to recuperate	*sich erholen/genesen*
emergency	*Notfall*	to remind	*erinnern*
emotional support	*emotionale Unterstützung*	report	*Bericht*
helpline	*Sorgentelefon*	to take sb's pulse	*den Puls von jmd messen*
hospital stay	*Krankenhausaufenthalt*	wearable technology	*tragbare Technologie*

APPENDIX

Unit 6, Text A, Exercise 4

→ Page 48

1 Fun tram tickets

Problem: Lots of people don't pay for tickets when they travel on public transport.
Current solution: Spend a lot of money on ticket inspectors who fine people without tickets.
Fun solution: Make it fun to buy a ticket: when you stamp it, you could win an instant lottery!

Old solution
Fun solution
Inspectors are fired – their salaries go into the jackpot !!
WIN

2 The speed camera lottery

Problem: People break the speed limit.
Current solution: Fine people who break the speed limit.
Fun solution: Reward people for keeping to the speed limit. Use the money from the fines.

3 Wiki traffic lights

Problem: Motorists jump red lights.
Current solution: Fine motorists who do this or take away their driving licence, or both.
Fun solution: Make it interesting to wait at traffic lights by answering general knowledge questions.

4 Pinball exercise machine

Problem: Neither young nor old people exercise enough.
Current solution: No solution.
Fun solution: Combine a step machine and a pinball machine to make exercising at the bus stop fun.

Unit 11, Text B, Exercise 5B

→ Page 107

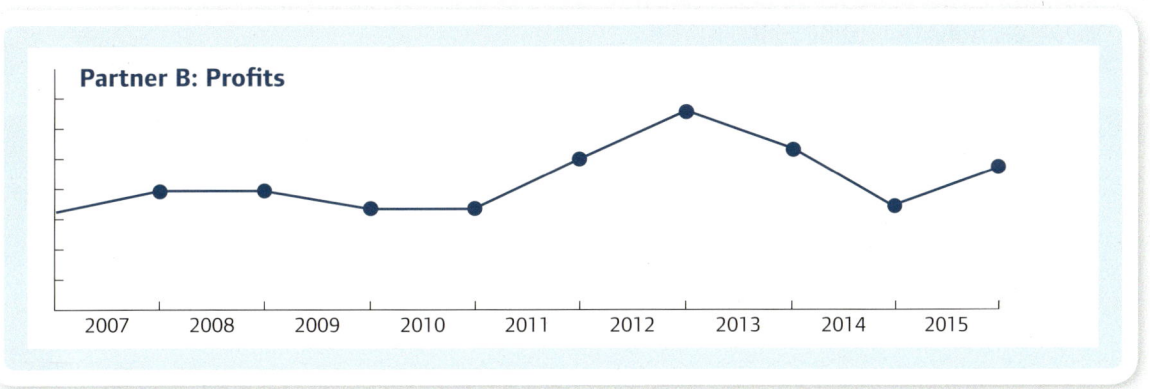

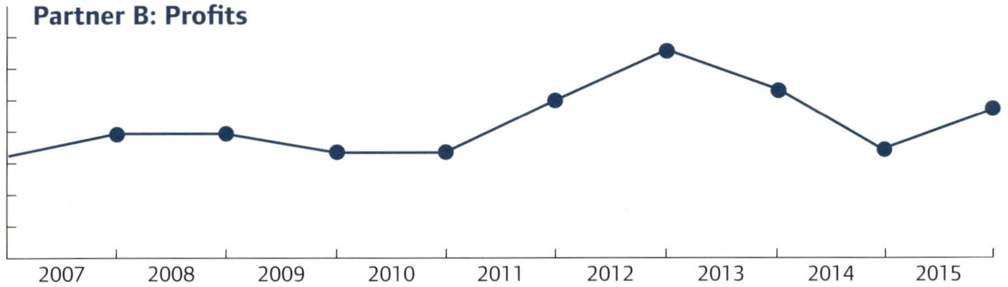

Skills files

Diese *Skills files* helfen Ihnen, Ihre Sprachfertigkeiten zu trainieren, damit Sie Erfolg in der Prüfung haben. Wenn Sie sich regelmäßig mit dem Lernprozess beschäftigen (mit den *Building skills boxes* und *Skills checklists* in den Units und den Materialien hier), fällt Ihnen der Umgang mit der englischen Sprache jeden Tag leichter. Hier gehen Sie Schritt für Schritt durch verschiedene Aufgabentypen und bekommen viele hilfreiche Tipps, wie Sie Ihre Fähigkeiten verbessern können. Um Ihre Kenntnisse zu festigen, gibt es auch Übungen zu den verschiedenen Strategien. Lösungen zu diesen Aufgaben finden Sie auf www.cornelsen.de/webcodes: Geben Sie einfach den Webcode FOSSKLO im Webcode-Suchfeld ein. Transkripte und Audio-Dateien finden Sie auch auf dieser Webseite durch Eingabe der Webcodes, die bei den entsprechenden Übungen stehen.

Lösungen → Webcode: FOSSKLO

1 REZEPTION: LESEVERSTEHEN

A Vorbereitung auf das Lesen (Vorhersage / *prediction*)

Eine Vorhersage bedeutet, dass Sie versuchen, den Inhalt des Textes zu erraten, bevor Sie ihn lesen. Wenn Sie sich hierzu Zeit nehmen, bevor Sie mit dem Lesen des Textes bzw. dem Beantworten der Fragen beginnen, können Sie den Text besser verstehen und Sie stellen sicher, die Aufgaben richtig zu lösen.

- Lesen Sie die Fragen und finden Sie heraus, was Sie tun sollen.
- Sehen Sie sich den Aufbau des Textes genau an und lesen Sie die Überschrift und Unterzeile bzw. die Einleitung, wenn es eine gibt. Das sollte Ihnen Hinweise liefern, worum es in dem Text geht.
- Sehen Sie sich die dazugehörigen Bilder bzw. Zeichnungen an und lesen Sie deren Unterschriften. Dies wird Ihnen helfen, sich vom Text „ein Bild zu machen".

B Grobverständnis (Sinn erfassen / *reading for gist / skimming*)

Lesen, um den Sinn zu erfassen oder einen Text überfliegen bedeutet, die wichtigsten Punkte schnell zu lesen. Nachdem Sie sich Gedanken dazu gemacht haben, wovon der Text handeln könnte (Vorhersage, s.o.):

- Lesen Sie den ersten Satz jeden Absatzes (und den letzten Satz, wenn der Absatz lang ist), denn dort können Sie häufig das Wesentliche des Textes entnehmen.
- Konzentrieren Sie sich auf die Schlüsselwörter, die Ihnen den Sinn des Textes vermitteln, z. B. Nomen, Verben und (häufig) die dazugehörigen Adjektive und Adverbien. Wörter, die unterstrichen bzw. fett gedruckt oder kursiv gestellt sind, sind i.d.R. wichtig.
- Überspringen Sie jene Wörter, die Sie nicht verstehen. Bleiben Sie ruhig! Meist wird die Bedeutung dieser Wörter aus dem Zusammenhang heraus klar, und manchmal taucht etwas später ein Synonym auf. Zum Schluss finden Sie wahrscheinlich heraus, dass Sie den Text verstehen, ohne diese Wörter zu kennen.
- Lesen Sie den ganzen letzten Absatz, da dieser häufig eine Zusammenfassung des Textes darstellt.

Üblicherweise folgen Prüfungstexte, die zum Überfliegen gedacht sind, einer klaren Struktur. Argumente und Beweise werden logisch präsentiert und wichtige Punkte werden häufig in der Zusammenfassung wiederholt.

Übung 1 (Fertigkeiten 1A und 1B)

A Bevor Sie die Fragen beantworten, sehen Sie sich den Textaufbau und das dazugehörige Foto genau an, und wählen Sie dann das beste Ende aus, um den folgenden Satz zu vervollständigen.

Prediction: The text is about …

a cycling versus walking as a free-time activity.
b accidents involving cyclists and walkers who are not paying attention.
c what happens when people walk on the road instead of on the pavement.

B Überfliegen Sie den Text und wählen Sie die passendste Antwort zu den folgenden Fragen aus.

1 What is the biggest danger for people cycling in the city?
- **a** busy traffic
- **b** listening to music while cycling
- **c** people listening to iPods while walking

2 What can happen as a result?
- **a** people get hurt
- **b** bicycles are destroyed
- **c** walkers and cyclists have arguments

C Beantworten Sie die restlichen Fragen zum Text in Ihren eigenen Worten.

1 When did the problem start?
2 What happened last year?
3 What do cyclists and pedestrians needs to do to change things?

Pedestrians are the great menace to cyclists

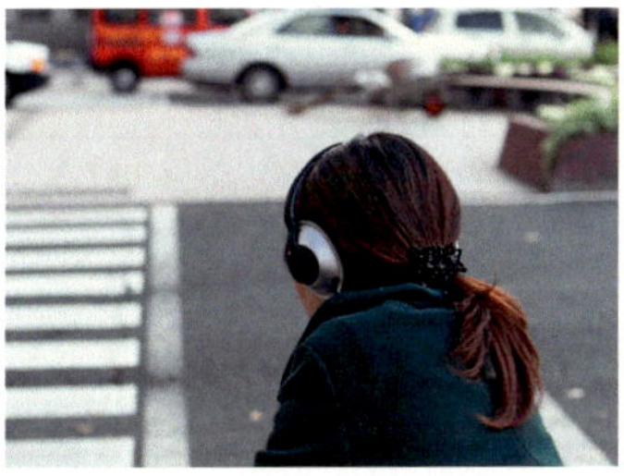

People wearing headphones do not take care when crossing roads

What do you think would be the greatest menace to cyclists riding around the roads of a busy city? Lorries, motorbikes, bendy buses, perhaps? Not in my experience. For me, arguably the biggest danger – and without doubt, the biggest irritation – are pedestrians, who, since the proliferation of the iPod, are more likely than any other moving object inadvertently to place themselves directly in my path while I'm cycling, forcing me either to brake suddenly or to swerve out into the traffic – both of which could end up in a nasty accident.

(…) Since the propagation of digital music players, an increasing number of people walk around in a complete daze – stepping into cycle lanes, walking out from behind stationary vehicles and crossing roads without so much as a turn of the head, to check if something is coming.

(…) Collisions between bikes and pedestrians can be fatal. Last year, for example, a teenager was killed in Buckingham when a cyclist crashed into her. By all accounts, the cyclist was at fault, and should certainly have slowed down, rather than simply shouting at the girl to get out of his way. Nevertheless, it shows the damage a bike can do in a collision with a pedestrian.

I understand that many cyclists are not very considerate on the roads, and that many pedestrians feel intimidated by cyclists who badger them off a crossing even when they've got a green man. My golden rule of the road is that everyone should give way to whoever has priority at the time.

(…) Pedestrians need to look where they're going and pay a little more respect to cyclists. I just hope it doesn't take more fatal collisions for this message to start getting through. (289 words)

Abridged from: *www.independent.co.uk*

C Mit unbekannten Wörtern umgehen

→ Vokabeln lernen, S. 220

Wenn Sie während des Lesens einem Wort begegnen, das Sie nicht kennen, sollten Sie sich fragen, ob es notwendig ist, das Wort zu verstehen, um den Text zu verstehen und die Fragen zu beantworten. Wenn Sie das Wort tatsächlich benötigen, versuchen Sie, bevor Sie nach dem Wörterbuch greifen (bzw. online nachschlagen), die Bedeutung des Wortes selbst herauszufinden. Manchmal verstehen Sie die Bedeutung eines Wortes, ohne es bewusst zu „kennen". Wenn dem nicht so ist, nutzen Sie folgende Strategien:

- Erarbeiten Sie es sich aus dem Zusammenhang heraus. Sehen Sie sich genau an, wie das Wort im Satz benutzt wird und wie es mit dem Inhalt dieser Textstelle zusammenhängt.
- Nutzen Sie Ihr Wissen über die deutsche Sprache. Viele englische Wörter haben ähnliche deutsche Entsprechungen bzw. stammen sie von derselben Wurzel ab, z. B.: *ten*/zehn, *light*/Licht, *night*/Nacht, *biology*/Biologie, *democracy*/Demokratie.
- Bringen Sie mehr über Wortbildung in Erfahrung (wie man Wörter aus anderen Wörtern bilden kann):

Vorsilben (*Prefixes*)

Vorsilben können die Bedeutung eines Wortes verändern.

anti-	'against'	clockwise → anticlockwise
co-	'together'	operate → co-operate
inter-	'between'	national → international
sub-	'under' / 'below'	standard → substandard
super-	'above' / 'over'	power → superpower
trans-	'across'	form → transform
dis-	'not' / 'opposite'	agree → disagree
in-		correct → incorrect
im-		possible → impossible
ir-		responsible → irresponsible
un-		friendly → unfriendly
mis-	'not correctly'	understand → misunderstand
re-	'again'	discover → rediscover

Nachsilben (*Suffixes*)

Nachsilben können die Wortart eines Wortes verändern.

Verbs → nouns

Verb	Suffix	Noun
organize	-ation	organization
express	-ion	expression
bake	-er	baker
begin	-ing	beginning
argue	-ment	argument

Nouns → adjectives

Noun	Suffix	Adjective
continent	-al	continental
beauty	-ful	beautiful
day	-ly	daily
hunger	-ry	hungry

Verbs → adjectives

Verb	Suffix	Adjective
advise	-able	advisable
rain	-y	rainy
care	-ing	caring

Adjectives → nouns

Adjective	Suffix	Noun
stupid	-ity	stupidity
happy	-ness	happiness

Adjectives → adverbs

Adjective	Suffix	Noun
awful	-ly	awfully
democratic	-ally	democratically

Übung 2 (Fertigkeit 1C)

Lesen Sie den ersten Absatz des Textes *Pedestrians are the great menace to cyclists* auf S. 215 noch einmal und suchen Sie die Wörter aus der u. s. Tabelle heraus. Schreiben Sie die Tabelle ab und notieren Sie, wie Sie die Wörter verstehen können, d. h. ähnliche Wörter auf Deutsch, Wortbildung, Zusammenhang. Drei der Wörter sind als Beispiele gegeben.

Words I can recognize without using my dictionary	How I know these words in this text	Word class in text	Definition	German
bendy (line 3)	word formation – verb "to bend" made into an adjective by adding -y	adjective	flexible	*biegsam*
pedestrians (line 5)				
cycling (line 7)	word formation – cycle → *gerund*	verb (present progressive form of *to cycle*)	to ride a bicycle	*Rad fahren*
brake (line 8)	from context: accident	verb	to make sth go slower	*bremsen*
swerve (line 8)				
nasty (line 9)				

D Ein Wörterbuch benutzen

→ Vokabeln lernen, S. 220

Ein Wörterbuch ist ein hilfreiches Werkzeug. Es hilft Ihnen, einen Text zu verstehen und Ihr Vokabular zu erweitern. Unabhängig von der Art des Wörterbuchs, das Sie nutzen – zwei- oder einsprachig –, ist Folgendes zu beachten:

- Stellen Sie sicher, dass Ihr Wörterbuch aktuell ist. Sprachen entwickeln sich sehr schnell, also sehen Sie im Impressum nach, ob es sich um eine „überarbeitete Auflage" (*updated version*) handelt.
- Lassen Sie bei Online-Wörterbüchern Vorsicht walten. Wörter haben in verschiedenen Zusammenhängen verschiedene Bedeutungen und Computer sind nicht schlau genug, um zu erfassen, welchen Zusammenhang Sie brauchen.
- Wählen Sie nicht die erstbeste Bedeutung aus, sondern lesen Sie alle Definitionen und überprüfen Sie sie ein zweites Mal, indem Sie die neu gefundenen Wörter nachschlagen.

- Stellen Sie sicher, dass Sie nach der richtigen Wortart suchen (Verb, Nomen, Adjektiv, Adverb).
- Vergewissern Sie sich, den Aufbau einer Seite eines Wörterbuchs verstanden zu haben. Ganz oben auf jeder Seite eines Wörterbuchs sehen Sie das erste Wort bzw. den ersten Satz sowie das letzte Wort bzw. den letzten Satz, das/der auf dieser Seite ausgeführt wird. Solange Sie das Alphabet beherrschen, werden Ihnen diese zwei Wörter helfen, das gesuchte Wort schnell zu finden.

Bevor Sie mit Ihrem Wörterbuch zu arbeiten beginnen:

- Lesen Sie die Inhaltsübersicht, um herauszufinden, was Ihr Wörterbuch neben Definitionen noch alles zu bieten hat. Lesen Sie die Nutzungshinweise sorgfältig durch – sie sind wichtig.
- Sehen Sie sich die Liste der Abkürzungen und Symbole sowie die Legende zur Verbbildung an und stellen Sie sicher, dass Sie deren Bedeutungen verstehen.
- Vergewissern Sie sich, dass Sie über Grundkenntnisse der Grammatiktermini verfügen. Wenn Sie die Bedeutung eines Adverbs nicht kennen, wird es Ihnen kaum helfen, ein Adverb nachzuschlagen.

Nutzen Sie ein Wörterbuch, um:

- **mit einem Text zu arbeiten.** Wenn Sie nach Anwendung aller Ihrer Fertigkeiten unbekannte Wörter immer noch nicht verstehen, schlagen Sie sie nach.
- **Ihr Vokabular zu erweitern.** Wenn Sie ein Ihnen unbekanntes Wort nachschlagen, nehmen Sie sich die Zeit, auch verwandte Wörter nachzuschlagen und eine Liste mit Wortfamilien anzulegen.
- ***Idioms*/Redensarten zu erlernen.** In einer Redensart wird ein Wort in einem feststehenden Satz verwendet und ist seiner eigentlichen Bedeutung nur entfernt ähnlich, z. B.: *„to get the wrong end of the stick“*. Wenn Sie wissen, was *„the wrong end“* und *„stick“* bedeuten, verstehen Sie möglicherweise immer noch nicht den vollständigen Satz (etwas in den falschen Hals bekommen).

Übung 3 (Fertigkeit 1D)

A Sie üben jetzt, Wörter in Ihrem zweisprachigen Wörterbuch zu finden.

1 You have been asked to mediate the following information to a tourist travelling in Germany. Use your bilingual dictionary to find the correct English expressions for the German word *Zug*.

> *Als Tourist in Deutschland reist man am bequemsten per Zug[1]. Im Zug[2] und in Bahnhöfen ist das Rauchen verboten. Falls Sie also Raucher sind, so denken Sie daran, dass schon ein einziger Zug[3] von einer Zigarette zu Problemen führen kann. Außerdem ist es ein typischer Zug[4] vieler Mitreisender, sich bei so etwas schnell zu beschweren. Und: Achten Sie darauf, im Zug[5] nicht in einem Zug[6] zu sitzen, sonst kriegen Sie einen steifen Hals!*

2 Now look up words in the text that you do not know and write them down. → Vokabeln lernen, S. 220

B Sie lernen nun Ihr einsprachiges Wörterbuch kennen und üben den Umgang mit ihm, indem Sie zwei Wörter des ersten Absatzes des Textes *Pedestrians are the great menace to cyclists*, S. 215, nachschlagen.

1 Read the dictionary entries and match the numbered sections to the definitions below.

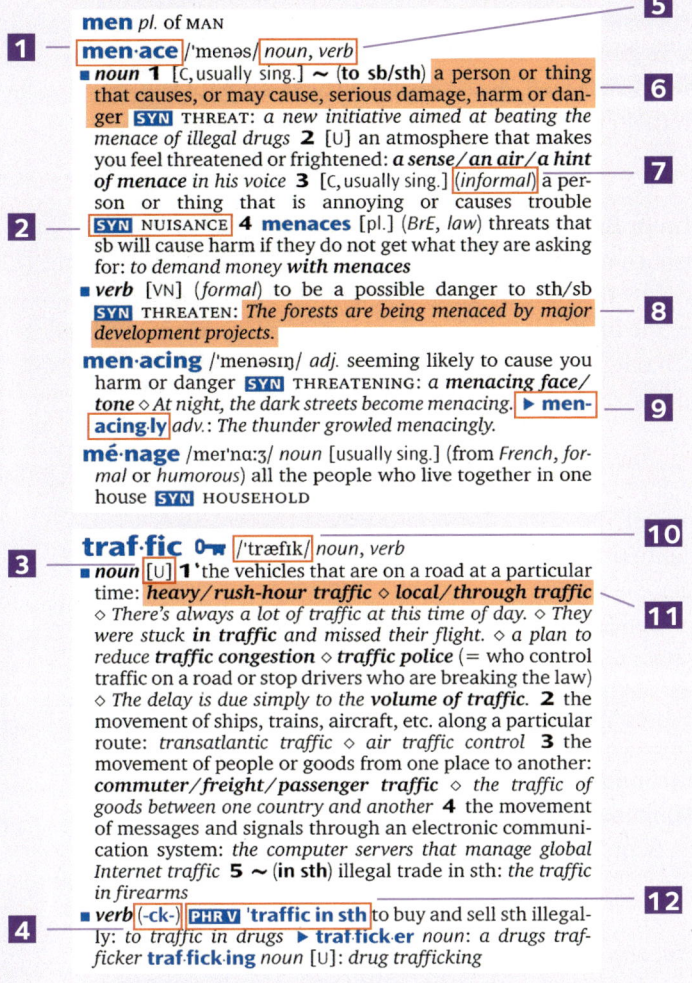

men *pl.* of MAN

1 **men·ace** /ˈmenəs/ *noun, verb* 5

■ *noun* **1** [C, usually sing.] **~ (to sb/sth)** a person or thing that causes, or may cause, serious damage, harm or danger SYN THREAT: *a new initiative aimed at beating the menace of illegal drugs* **2** [U] an atmosphere that makes you feel threatened or frightened: ***a sense/an air/a hint of menace*** *in his voice* **3** [C, usually sing.] (*informal*) a person or thing that is annoying or causes trouble SYN NUISANCE **4 menaces** [pl.] (*BrE, law*) threats that sb will cause harm if they do not get what they are asking for: *to demand money* ***with menaces*** 6 7

2

■ *verb* [VN] (*formal*) to be a possible danger to sth/sb SYN THREATEN: *The forests are being menaced by major development projects.* 8

men·acing /ˈmenəsɪŋ/ *adj.* seeming likely to cause you harm or danger SYN THREATENING: *a* ***menacing face/tone*** ◇ *At night, the dark streets become menacing.* ▶ **men·acing·ly** *adv.*: *The thunder growled menacingly.* 9

mé·nage /meɪˈnɑːʒ/ *noun* [usually sing.] (from *French, formal* or *humorous*) all the people who live together in one house SYN HOUSEHOLD

traf·fic 🗝 /ˈtræfɪk/ *noun, verb* 10

3 ■ *noun* [U] **1** the vehicles that are on a road at a particular time: ***heavy/rush-hour traffic*** ◇ ***local/through traffic*** ◇ *There's always a lot of traffic at this time of day.* ◇ *They were stuck* ***in traffic*** *and missed their flight.* ◇ *a plan to reduce* ***traffic congestion*** ◇ ***traffic police*** (= who control traffic on a road or stop drivers who are breaking the law) ◇ *The delay is due simply to the* ***volume of traffic***. **2** the movement of ships, trains, aircraft, etc. along a particular route: *transatlantic traffic* ◇ *air traffic control* **3** the movement of people or goods from one place to another: ***commuter/freight/passenger traffic*** ◇ *the traffic of goods between one country and another* **4** the movement of messages and signals through an electronic communication system: *the computer servers that manage global Internet traffic* **5 ~ (in sth)** illegal trade in sth: *the traffic in firearms* 11

4 ■ *verb* (-ck-) PHR V **ˈtraffic in sth** to buy and sell sth illegally: *to traffic in drugs* ▶ **traf·fick·er** *noun*: *a drugs trafficker* **traf·fick·ing** *noun* [U]: *drug trafficking* 12

A Collocations: words that are often used with the headword
B Definition: meaning of the word, usually with an example sentence
C Derivatives: words from the same word family
D Example sentence
E Forms: unusual plurals, participles or gerunds
F Grammatical information
G Headword: correct spelling and hyphenation (*Silbentrennung*)
H Phrasal verbs or idioms
I Pronunciation: sound of word (*Aussprache*); stress (*Betonung*)
J Register: formal, informal, slang, etc.
K Synonyms: words of similar meaning
L Word class: noun, verb, adjective, etc.

2 Answer these questions using the two dictionary entries.

1 What is a synonym for "menace" as it is used in the text?
2 Which three collocations are given for "menace"?
3 What is a synonym for the verb form of "menace"?
4 What are the adjective and adverb forms of "menace"?
5 Which two word classes (parts of speech) can "traffic" be?
6 How many collocations using the word "traffic" can you find in the dictionary entry? Here are three collocations to get you started: *heavy/rush-hour traffic; to be stuck in traffic*
7 What else can you use the noun "traffic" to talk about apart from road vehicles and the transport of people or goods?
8 List the nouns that go with the verb phrase "to traffic in sth".

3 Practise using a dictionary by looking up three words in the text that you still need to know.

E Vokabeln lernen

→ Ein Wörterbuch benutzen, S. 217

Das richtige Erlernen und Benutzen von Wörtern einer Fremdsprache macht Spaß, ist aber zeitaufwendig. Es gibt viele Arten, Vokabeln zu lernen. Sie können dies mithilfe von *Focus on Success* tun und diese Art des Lernens mit englischen Lese- und Hörverständnisübungen außerhalb des Unterrichts ergänzen. Es gibt natürlich auch eine Vielzahl von Onlineprogrammen und -spielen, um Vokabeln zu lernen, doch sie sind nicht so effektiv wie die Lernmethoden, die Sie sich selbst erarbeiten.

Listen und Zettel

- **Vokabellisten (nicht nur in einem Buch)**
  Vokabellisten, die in einem Notizbuch eingetragen werden, stellen einen leichten Weg dar, neue Wörter während des Unterrichts festzuhalten. Zuhause können Sie weitere Listen erstellen, z. B. von Lebensmitteln, die im Kühlschrank aufbewahrt werden, oder Sie schreiben Ihre Einkaufsliste auf Englisch oder Sie listen die Kleidungsstücke in Ihrem Kleiderschrank auf, nach Art, Farbe und Material sortiert.

- **Lernkarten**
  Schreiben Sie die Wörter, die Sie gern lernen möchten, auf Karteikarten. Schreiben Sie das englische Wort auf die eine Seite und die Übersetzung auf die andere. Fügen Sie eine Definition bzw. einen Beispielsatz auf Englisch unter die deutsche Übersetzung hinzu.

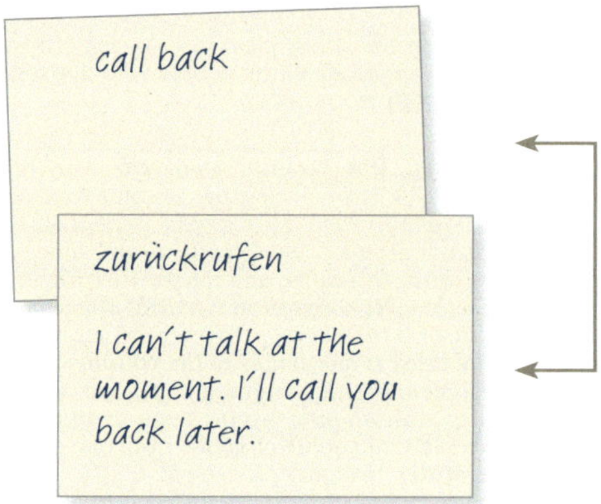

- **Klebezettel**
  Schreiben Sie die Bezeichnung eines Gegenstandes auf einen Notizzettel und kleben Sie ihn an den Gegenstand. Sie können nach Belieben Adjektive hinzufügen, z. B. *pretty picture, dirty laundry*.

Wortgitter und Wortgruppen

Während Ihrer Arbeit mit *Focus on Success* füllen Sie viele Wortgitter mit Wortfamilien aus. In den meisten Fällen werden Sie aufgefordert, ein Wortgitter mit unterschiedlichen Wortarten zu vervollständigen.

Noun	Verb	Adjective
enjoyment	enjoy	enjoyable
entertainment	entertain	entertaining

Wenn Sie sich auf eine Prüfung vorbereiten, können Sie Ihre Wortfamiliengitter um weitere Informationen verändern und ergänzen, z. B. indem Sie Sätze hinzufügen, in denen die Wörter im Kontext benutzt werden.

Word	Part of speech	Opposite	Synonym	Word in context
large	adjective	small	big	My mum comes from a large family. She has six sisters.
producer	noun	destroyer	manufacturer	Japan is a major producer of cars.

Verknüpfungen herstellen

- **Wortgabeln**
  Wortgabeln eignen sich gut zum Erlernen von Adjektiven und Verben.

delicious	
quick	
home-made	meal
lovely	
tasty	

find	
have	
make	friends
meet	
visit	

- **Mindmaps**
  Sie können Mindmaps zum Sammeln und Verknüpfen von Vokabeln wie auch von Ideen benutzen, um sich für eine Präsentation vorzubereiten oder einen Aufsatz und andere Schriftsätze zu planen. Der Vorteil von Mindmaps ist, dass Sie sie in jede beliebige Richtung ergänzen und erweitern können. Heben Sie bestimmte Aspekte farblich hervor. Wenn Sie eine Mindmap erstellen, vergleichen Sie Ihre mit der eines Mitstreiters / einer Mitstreiterin, der/die dasselbe Thema dargestellt hat. Es ist wahrscheinlich, dass Sie beide weitere Wörter zu Ihren Mindmaps hinzufügen können.

Gute Gewohnheiten entwickeln

- Lernen Sie Ihre Vokabeln regelmäßig und lernen Sie nie zu viel auf einmal. 20 Minuten jeden Tag sind besser als zwei Stunden pro Woche.
- Entscheiden Sie, wie häufig Sie wiederholen. Der Morgen vor der Prüfung ist nicht der effektivste Zeitpunkt. Wenn Sie Vokabeln regelmäßig das ganze Jahr hindurch wiederholen, brauchen Sie kurz vor der Prüfung nicht in Panik zu geraten.
- Ebenso wichtig ist, wo Sie lernen. Sie brauchen einen bequemen Ort mit ausreichend Licht. Es hilft auch, nicht von anderen Personen bzw. Lärm abgelenkt zu werden.
- Zu guter Letzt gehen Sie mit Ihren Lernhilfen sorgsam und ordentlich um.

F Scannen nach Einzelinformationen im Text (*reading for information / scanning*)

Beim Überfliegen eines Textes geht es um das schnelle Finden von bestimmten Informationen. In Texten wie Stellenanzeigen oder Infobroschüren müssen Sie bestimmte Informationen schnell herausfinden. Sie müssen den Text nicht in aller Tiefe lesen, doch Sie müssen sich den gesamten Text ansehen. Hierzu wenden Sie folgende Strategien an:

- Lesen Sie die Aufgaben und Fragen sorgfältig durch und stellen Sie sicher, dass Sie verstehen, was zu tun ist.
- Lesen Sie den Text schnell durch und halten Sie an, wenn Sie ein Schlüsselwort gefunden haben. Informationen zu Fragen zu Eigennamen, Zahlen, Ziffern und Geldbeträgen sollten relativ leicht zu finden sein. (Halten Sie nach Großbuchstaben, Prozentzeichen, Währungsangaben, usw. Ausschau.) Wenn Sie ein Schlüsselwort gefunden haben, lesen Sie um es herum, um die Frage zu beantworten.
- Wenn Sie ein Wort oder eine Redewendung nicht verstehen, halten Sie sich nicht damit auf. Überfliegen Sie den Text weiter, bis Sie am Ende angelangt sind. Sollte sich herausstellen, dass Sie das Wort benötigen, können Sie sich später noch darum kümmern.

Normalerweise werden die Fragen zum Text in der Reihenfolge gestellt, in der die Informationen im Text zu finden sind. In einer Prüfung können Sie den Text markieren bzw. sich die benötigten Details notieren, sobald Sie die Informationen finden, die Sie suchen.

Wenn Sie gefragt werden, Wh-Fragen zum Text zu beantworten, denken Sie daran, dass:

Who	nach Menschen fragt. Suchen Sie Informationen über die Hauptperson des Textes.
Where	nach einem Ort fragt.
When	nach einer Zeit fragt. Suchen Sie nach Wochentagen, Daten oder Uhrzeiten.
What	nach Objekten und Ereignissen fragt. Suchen Sie nach Informationen darüber oder Vorschlägen, warum etwas passiert (ist).
Why	nach einem Grund fragt. Suchen Sie nach Erklärungen, warum etwas passiert (ist).
How	nach einer Methode fragt. Suchen Sie Beschreibungen, wie etwas gemacht wird.

→ Fragen zum Text beantworten, S. 228

Übung 4 (Fertigkeit 1F)

Scannen Sie den Text *South Africa for families* unten und finden Sie die Antworten zu den Fragen heraus. Sagen Sie, wie Sie die Antworten so schnell gefunden haben.

1 What holiday destination is being advertised?
2 What is the best way to see the countryside?
3 How many lodges and how many guest houses can holidaymakers choose from?
4 How much does a holiday for a family of four cost?

South Africa for families

South Africa is the perfect destination for a family holiday. The time difference from the UK is only one to two hours so children quickly settle in after the flight.

Many national parks are malaria free so you needn't worry about going out to watch the wildlife. Our park lodges run children's programmes.

A hire car is perfect for getting around South Africa as you can come and go as you please so you can plan around your family's needs. Our guest house staff can give you lots of ideas about things to do so you can discover something new every day. You can choose from 8 lodges and 5 guest houses.

Cape Town, with its beautiful scenery and beaches

Here are just three of our many exciting activities:

- The Garden Route offers many adventurous excursions and places of interest.
- Enjoy whale watching on South Africa's Whale Coast.
- You can't travel to South Africa and not go on a safari and the game viewing possibilities in the Kruger National Park are amazing.

An 18-day trip for a family of four can cost as little as €2,000 per person.

We believe that once you have experienced our beautiful country, you will never want to go home. See you soon in South Africa! (206 words)

G Gründliches Lesen (*reading for detail / close reading*)

Gründliches Lesen bedeutet, einen Text Satz für Satz zu lesen. Hierzu gibt es folgende Strategien:

- Lesen Sie die Aufgabenstellung und die Fragen aufmerksam durch und stellen Sie sicher, dass Sie verstehen, was der Prüfer / die Prüferin von Ihnen will.
- Überfliegen Sie den Text, um einen Überblick über den Inhalt zu bekommen, und notieren Sie sich die wichtigsten Punkte. Lassen Sie diesen Schritt nicht aus. Er wird Ihnen später beim Beantworten der Fragen Zeit sparen.
- Suchen Sie Schlüsselwörter, die Ihnen helfen, die Frage(n) zu beantworten. Werden Sie z. B. nach der Meinung des Autors / der Autorin gefragt, suchen Sie nach Wörtern wie *think, believe, opinion,* usw.; das hilft Ihnen, dem Gedankengang des Autors / der Autorin zu folgen.
- Lesen Sie nun den Text Satz für Satz und beantworten Sie die Fragen.
- Wenn Sie fertig sind, lesen Sie sich Ihre Antworten durch und vergleichen Sie sie mit dem Text.

Übung 5 (Fertigkeit 1G)

Sagen Sie, ob die Aussagen unten in Bezug auf den Text *South Africa for families*, S. 222, richtig oder falsch sind.

Bitte notieren Sie sich jedes Mal den Grund für Ihre Wahl von richtig oder falsch. Die ersten zwei Aussagen sind für Sie bereits zugeordnet worden.

1 South Africa is a good place to take a family holiday. *true*
BEISPIEL *Headline: SA for familes; text: "a perfect destination for a family holiday"*
2 The time difference between South Africa and Britain is 5 hours. *false*
BEISPIEL *"time difference from the UK one to two hours"*
3 There is absolutely no risk of catching malaria in any of the national parks.
4 There are special activities for children who visit the parks.
5 You can get ideas for day trips at the tourist information office.
6 The highlight of the holiday is a safari.
7 The author of the text is sure that you will love his country.

H Sich während des Lesens Notizen machen

Sich während des Lesens Notizen zu machen ist sinnvoll. So können Sie sich die Informationen für später besser merken.

- Stellen Sie immer sicher, dass Sie den Text verstanden haben, bevor Sie sich Notizen machen. → Grobverständnis, S. 214
- Versehen Sie Ihren Notizzettel mit der Textüberschrift und der Quellenangabe. Die Quellenangabe ist wichtig, wenn Sie in Ihrem Aufsatz u.ä. zitieren wollen. Auch kann es vorkommen, dass Sie zu einem späteren Zeitpunkt auf den Originaltext zurückgreifen wollen.
- Sehen Sie sich den Text genau an und suchen Sie sich die wichtigsten Unterthemen heraus, die Sie als Überschriften benutzen können. Die Unterteilung des Textes in Absätze wird Ihnen dabei helfen. Verteilen Sie diese Überschriften großzügig über das Blatt und lassen Sie unter jeder Überschrift Platz für Notizen.
- Ihre Notizen bestehen aus Schlüsselwörtern, i.d.R. Nomen, Verben und Adjektiven. Konzentrieren Sie sich auf diese Wortarten.

- Halten Sie nach Signalen Ausschau, z. B. Wiederholungen, Wörter, die etwas unterstreichen, oder an die Leser direkt gestellte Fragen. Dies ist ein Anhaltspunkt, was der Autor / die Autorin als wichtig erachtet.
- Sind Sie hiermit fertig, überprüfen Sie, ob Sie alle Informationen haben, die Sie benötigen. Sie können durchaus über den gesamten Text verstreut sein.
- Denken Sie immer daran, sich nur Notizen zu machen. Verschwenden Sie keine Zeit mit dem Abschreiben ganzer Textabschnitte, lassen Sie unnötige Wörter wie Pronomen und Artikel weg und verwenden Sie Abkürzungen und Symbole.

Zeichen	
=	the same as
≠	not the same as
+,&	and

Abkürzungen	
e.g.	for example
km	kilometre
w., w/o	with, without
etc.	and so on

Wortverkürzungen	
govt	government
impt	important
kids	children

Übung 6 (Fertigkeit 1H)

Stellen Sie sich vor, Sie wurden gebeten, einen Kommentar über Paparazzi zu schreiben; Sie beziehen sich hierbei auf den Text *Paparazzi – not always the celebrity's best friend.* Lesen Sie den Text und stellen Sie sicher, dass Sie verstehen, worum es geht. Anschließend schreiben Sie sich die Notizen ab und vervollständigen sie mithilfe der o. g. Tipps.

Paparazzi – not always the celebrity's best friend
(Focus on Success, 2015)

benefits of paparazzi
- keep celebrities in the news
- fame and fortune for celebrities
- give the public information about stars

downsides of paparazzi
- invasion of privacy

PAPARAZZI – NOT ALWAYS THE CELEBRITY'S BEST FRIEND

A lot of people say that celebrities need the paparazzi to keep their faces in the news. You could say that is the only benefit of paparazzi. The downsides of the relationship between paparazzi and celebrities are many.

The paparazzi go to extremes to get their photos. Some of them earn thousands for a good shot of a star. If the star has problems, then the photo might bring a million.

Despite the laws about invasion of privacy, the paparazzi continually ignore them to get photos of celebrities. They stalk them while they are walking in a public place and they follow them with their cars. In some cases, the paparazzi put celebrities in danger. How often have we heard stories on the news about celebrities having car accidents as a result of being chased by paparazzi?

Film star Halle Berry was involved in a road accident involving the paparazzi a few years ago when a paparazzi followed her and drove into her car. The crash caused Halle Berry to hit a wall. The shock of the accident was bad enough but, at the time, the star was pregnant and she could have lost her baby. When she got out of her car, the paparazzi ran away. Halle Berry could have lost her baby, but they didn't stay to help or to check if everything was all right. Apart from the fact that the law says you have to stay around after you've caused an accident, don't these paparazzi have any feelings?

In another case involving a star, Tori Spelling, the American actress and author, was followed by paparazzi when she was driving her two children to school. Again, the car chase ended in an accident. This time, the paparazzi did not flee the scene. Instead, he stood beside the car and took photos.

Tori Spelling and her children survived the crash but some celebrities do not survive. The most famous paparazzi chase that ended in a crash was the one in which Princess Diana was killed. Although there was evidence that the driver of the car Diana was travelling in had been drinking, popular speculation is that the paparazzi caused the crash.

Whether they caused the crash or not, the behaviour of the paparazzi was typical – some left the scene while others took photos of the wrecked car. None of them tried to help the driver or any of the passengers. If that wasn't bad enough, three of the paparazzi took photographs of Diana as she was dying. How much of an invasion of privacy is it when someone takes a photo of you when you are dying?

An incident like this should never be repeated. Taking pictures after a crash in order to make money from them should result in the photographer being banned from taking photos for life.

What is to be done about the other problems? Would making invasion of privacy laws tougher discourage paparazzi from stalking celebrities? Should it be against the law to follow and take pictures of a parent taking children to school? Fame and fortune are fuelled by paparazzi photos.

As long as celebrities need and enjoy the attention, there will be paparazzi and as long as we, the public, are interested in what our favourite stars are doing, we need the paparazzi, too. (552 words)

2 REZEPTION: HÖRVERSTEHEN

A Vor dem Hören (Voraussage des Inhalts / Vorbereitung)

Sich auf die Hörübung vorzubereiten, verstärkt das Hörverständnis. Nutzen Sie hierzu alle Informationen, die sich auf der Seite befinden. Bevor Sie zuhören:

- Sehen Sie sich alle Fotos bzw. Illustrationen auf der Seite genau an. Sie liefern Ihnen Hinweise über den Ort der Aufzeichnung.
- Lesen Sie alle Ihnen zur Verfügung gestellten Hintergrundinformationen, z. B. eine Einleitung, die die Situation beschreibt und Auskunft darüber gibt, wie viele Personen Sie hören werden.
- Lesen Sie die Aufgabenstellung sorgfältig durch. Denken Sie daran, dass die Fragen, die Sie beantworten müssen, häufig der Reihenfolge entsprechen, in der die Informationen auf der Aufzeichnung vorkommen.
- Denken Sie nach, welche Wörter und Formulierungen Sie vielleicht hören werden und schreiben Sie sie auf.
- Schreiben Sie jede Ihnen vorgegebene Tabelle ab. Füllen Sie sie auf Englisch bereits vor der Hörübung soweit wie möglich aus und vervollständigen Sie sie während des Hörens.

B Während des ersten Hörens (Grobverständnis / *listening for gist*)

Ein Grobverständnis zu erhalten bedeutet, eine Ahnung zu bekommen, worum es in der Aufzeichnung geht. Während des ersten Hörens brauchen Sie nicht jedes Wort zu verstehen. Entwickeln Sie für das Hören möglichst folgende Fertigkeiten:

- Übergehen Sie Wörter, die Sie nicht verstehen.
- Konzentrieren Sie sich auf Schlüsselwörter.
- Machen Sie sich Notizen. Verwenden Sie Abkürzungen. Schreiben Sie so viel wie möglich auf, während Sie zuhören.

Ordnen Sie Ihre Notizen sofort nach dem Ende der Hörübung. Sie können sie später möglicherweise nicht mehr lesen.

Bemühen Sie sich, alle Fragen zu beantworten. Wenn Sie einen Teil der Informationen nicht verstanden haben, raten Sie, ausgehend von dem, was Sie verstanden haben.

Übung 1 (Fertigkeiten 2A und 2B)

10.30 Good morning, fans!

Gerry Davis interviews today's celebrities

In today's interview, Gerry talks to fitness celebrity Tina Michaelson while she takes a break from signing copies of her latest book for teenagers, **Do Sports and Learn Skills for Life!** in a London bookstore. During the interview, Tina explains how participating in sport teaches you skills that will help you your whole life long.

You read the announcement about the interview with Tina Michaelson and are interested in finding out more.

Listen to the interview and answer these questions in your own words.

1 What skill helps a team to win?
2 How does Gerry refer to this skill?
3 How can doing sport help you gain trust?
4 How long can sports relationships last?
5 What is the myth about students and sport?
6 What life skill can students use to prove that it is possible to be a good student and play sport?

A Sehen Sie sich das o.g. Beispiel einer Hörübung an. Sehen Sie sich das Foto genau an und lesen Sie die Programmanzeige. Lesen Sie sich die Aufgabenstellung und Fragen durch. Beantworten Sie die Fragen nicht. Dies tun Sie später. Wenn Sie sich sicher sind, alles verstanden zu haben, wählen Sie das beste Ende aus, um die folgenden Sätze zu vervollständigen.

1 The recording is of …
  a a private conversation.
  b a talk.
  c an interview.

2 The recording takes place …
  a at a celebrity fitness club.
  b in a bookstore.
  c on a school sports field.

3 The speakers are a
  a reporter and a fitness celebrity.
  b reporter and a fitness fan.
  c group of teenagers and a fitness celebrity.

4 The topic is …
  a skills to improve your sports perfomance.
  b developing useful skills through doing sport.
  c sports you can do all your life.

5 Three expressions I might hear are:
  a staying healthy, sport competitions, animal companions
  b life-long learning, learning to drive, nutrition
  c building relationships, team work, trusting others

B Schreiben Sie sich die zwei u.s. Sätze ab und vervollständigen Sie sie. Anschließend hören Sie die Aufzeichnung und überprüfen, ob Ihre Vorhersagen richtig waren.

I am going to listen to ▬ [1] with ▬ [2] about ▬ [3]
I expect to hear something about ▬ [4]

Hörtext → Webcode: FOSSKT1

C Während des zweiten Hörens (stichpunktartige Notizen machen)

Es ist schwierig, während des Zuhörens Notizen zu machen, weil die Aufzeichnung weiterläuft, während Sie schreiben. Daher verpassen Sie möglicherweise wichtige Informationen. Bleiben Sie ruhig! Sie haben sich bereits beim ersten Hören ein Grobverständnis angeeignet und notiert, was Sie verstehen konnten. Beim zweiten Hören versuchen Sie, sich so viel wie möglich an das zu erinnern, was Sie beim ersten Mal gehört haben. Wenn Sie es sich zur Gewohnheit machen, bei jedem Hören Stichpunkte aufzuschreiben, haben Sie bald den Bogen heraus.

Bevor Sie zuhören:

- Notieren Sie – wenn Sie die Zeit haben – Rubriken in Ihr Heft und schreiben Sie die Aufgabenstellung ganz oben auf Ihr Blatt. Wenn Sie die Anzahl der Sprecher/innen kennen, legen Sie eine Tabelle mit deren Namen an. Wenn Sie die Namen der Sprecher/innen nicht kennen, schreiben Sie ‚Sprecher/in 1', ‚Sprecher/in 2', usw.

Während Sie zuhören:

- Bleiben Sie bei der Aufgabenstellung und notieren Sie sich relevante Schlüsselwörter.
- Seien Sie aufmerksam und notieren Sie Ausdrücke, die die Gedanken strukturieren, z. B: *in my view, however, on the other hand*.
- Nutzen Sie Abkürzungen, um Zeit zu sparen.

→ Abkürzungen, S. 224

Nach dem Ende der Hörübung:

- Ordnen Sie Ihre Notizen frühestmöglich. Wenn Sie sich hierfür zu lang Zeit lassen, können Sie sie später möglicherweise nicht mehr deuten.

Wenn Sie in einer Prüfung Fragen zu einer Hörübung beantworten müssen:
- Formulieren Sie mithilfe Ihrer Stichpunkte die wichtigsten Punkte aus.
- Versuchen Sie, wenn Ihnen gewisse Details entgangen sind, die Antworten zu erraten, ausgehend von dem, was Sie verstanden haben.

Übung 2 (Fertigkeit 2C)

Sie hören die Aufnahme ein zweites Mal und erledigen die Aufgabe von S. 226. Hier sind die Fragen nochmal:

Hörtext → Webcode: FOSSKT1

1 What skill helps a team to win?
2 How does Gerry refer to this skill?
3 How can doing sport help you gain trust?
4 How long can sports relationships last?
5 What is the myth about students and sport?
6 What life skill can students use to prove that it is possible to be a good student and play sport?

1 **Übertragen Sie die Tabelle in Ihr Heft und füllen Sie sie während des Hörens aus.**

Questions	Tina	Gerry
1 *skill for winning teams*		
2 *another way to describe the skill*		
3 *gaining trust through sport*		
4 *sports relationship can last …*		
5 *myth – students and sport*		
6 *skill to prove can be good student and play sport*		

2 **Jetzt ordnen Sie Ihre Notizen und verwenden Sie sie zum Beantworten der Fragen.**

3 PRODUKTION: SCHREIBEN

A Fragen zum Text beantworten

Fragen zum Inhalt zu stellen ist eine beliebte Art herauszufinden, ob Sie einen Text verstanden haben. Bevor Sie zu schreiben beginnen:

- Stellen Sie sicher, dass Sie den Text verstehen. → Gründliches Lesen, S. 223
- Lesen Sie die Fragen sorgfältig durch.
- Fragen Sie sich: Was will der Lehrer / die Lehrerin bzw. der Prüfer / die Prüferin wissen?
- Schreiben Sie Ihre Stichpunkte auf Schmierpapier, wenn Sie Fragen aus Ihrem Buch beantworten. → Sich während des Lesens Notizen machen, S. 223
- Markieren Sie die wichtigen Textstellen während einer Prüfung bzw. einer Klassenarbeit in Ihrem Unterricht, indem Sie für verschiedene Fragen verschiedenfarbige Stifte verwenden.

Wh-Fragen beantworten

→ Scannen nach Einzelinformationen im Text, S. 221

Wenn Sie *Wh*-Fragen beantworten, denken Sie daran, dass:

- *Wh*-Fragen nicht einfach mit „ja“ oder „nein“ beantwortet werden können. Sie müssen diese Fragen jeweils kurz und sachlich beantworten.
- Wenn sich eine *Wh*-Frage auf eine bestimmte Handlung bezieht, Sie dasselbe Verb in Ihrer Antwort verwenden sollten.
  Where does Roger live? He lives in Berlin.

- Wenn in den Fragen allgemeine Verben wie *do* und *go* verwendet werden, Sie in Ihrer Antwort ein anderes, präzisierendes Verb wählen.
  Where did Mary go? She flew to New York.
  Why did she do it? She wanted to visit a friend who lives there.
- Antworten auf Fragen, die mit *why* beginnen, häufig *because* enthalten.
  Why is Mary working so hard? Because she needs to finish the project soon.
- Sie für *Why*-Fragen auch den Imperativ verwenden (*to* …) können. In diesem Fall wird vorausgesetzt, dass der Halbsatz mit *because* in der Antwort enthalten ist.
  Why does Roger go to the gym? To get in shape. = Because he wants to get in shape.

B Einen Text zusammenfassen

Einen Text zusammenzufassen bedeutet, ihn auf seine wesentlichen Informationen zu reduzieren. Sie werden möglicherweise gefragt, einen Text zusammenzufassen, um zu zeigen, dass Sie ihn verstanden haben. Bevor Sie beginnen:

- Stellen Sie sicher, dass Sie den Text verstehen. → Rezeption: Leseverstehen, S. 214
- Lesen Sie die Anweisungen aufmerksam durch und vergewissern Sie sich, dass Sie wissen, welche Informationen aus dem Text für den Leser / die Leserin wichtig sind. Sie können dies tun, indem Sie sich *Wh*-Fragen stellen. → Scannen nach Einzelinformationen im Text, S. 221
- Machen Sie sich auf Schmierpapier stichpunktartige Notizen. → Sich während des Lesens Notizen machen, S. 223

Nun beginnen Sie, Ihre Zusammenfassung zu schreiben.

- Beschreiben Sie in ein oder zwei einleitenden Sätzen, wovon der Text handelt.
- Lassen Sie alles Unnötige weg. Dies schließt Beispiele, ausführliche Listen, Namen, usw. ein.
- Verwenden Sie, soweit es geht, Ihre eigenen Worte. Verwenden Sie Synonyme für Wörter aus dem Text, z. B. *think – believe*, und formulieren Sie um, z. B. *recently – in recent years*.
- Versuchen Sie, Zitate in die indirekte Rede umzuwandeln, z. B. *The author states that …* → Grammar files: Indirect speech, S. 266
- Verlinken Sie Ideen und lassen Sie sie in der Reihenfolge, in der sie im Text erscheinen.
- Erinnern Sie sich! Sie sollten in einer Zusammenfassung eines Textes nicht Ihre eigene Meinung äußern.

Wenn Sie fertig sind, überprüfen Sie Ihre Rechtschreibung und Grammatik.

Übung 1 (Fertigkeiten 3A und 3B)

A Read the first paragraph of the text *Cyberbullying at Wiston* and answer the following questions.

1 Where did three teenagers from Wiston Vocational College have to appear yesterday?
2 Why were they there?
3 Who was their target?
4 How did they hurt her?
5 How did the police learn what had happened?
6 What were the consequences for the three teenagers?

B Summarize the complete text.

CYBERBULLYING AT WISTON

A group of three teenagers from Wiston Vocational College appeared at a juvenile court yesterday accused of using Face-book to be cruel to another student. The three teens, two boys and a girl, all aged 18, created a fake Facebook profile for another girl in their class and made it look like she wanted to live out her sexual fantasies on social media and in person. The girl's parents complained to the police and the three teenagers were quickly found. They were charged with causing their target emotional distress. All three were fined £1,000 and sentenced to do 30 days of voluntary work in a hospital. They were also banned from using Face-book, Twitter and other social media for six months.

According to the police, the group created a Facebook profile for Claire F, also 18-years old, three months ago. They manipulated real photos of Claire to make them look as if they were selfies which she herself had taken in a bedroom. The group also posted her mobile phone number.

Then they used the fake profile to pretend to be Claire and send sexual comments to other students. The mother of one of the pupils who received a sexual message reported the incident to the head of the college. She contacted Claire's parents. Before then, they knew nothing about the problem.

When they found out, Claire's parents were shocked. "Claire is a popular girl. She has always had a lot of friends and was involved in all kinds of after-school clubs," her father said. "Some weeks ago, though, she cut herself off from her social life and stopped going to her clubs," he went on. "She became isolated and my wife and I could see that she was unhappy. As we found out later, this change in Claire's behaviour started a few days after the fake Facebook account was set up," he said.

One of the accused waiting to return to court

The charges against the three teenagers state that they created the fake profile to cause trouble for Claire. Her lawyer said in court that Claire had not only suffered emotional distress, she had also wanted to do a work placement in a company who had rejected her application because of the fake profile.

The judge said: "Growing up is not always easy and many teenagers feel unhappy. Some are so unhappy and are therefore very cruel to other people. Sadly, cyber-bullying is on the rise," she went on. "I would like to see schools doing more to educate pupils and make it clear to them how much damage they can do to their peers by behaving in this way."

Claire's mother said, "I am glad that the court put such a high fine on the three kids. I think that is the only way you can discourage this. Make the bullies pay for the damage they have done." (472 words)

C Mindmaps zum Inhalt eines Aufsatzes erstellen

Wenn Sie einen Aufsatz schreiben sollen, ist es sinnvoll, Ihre Ideen in Form einer Mindmap festzuhalten und hierbei auf den Inhalt statt auf das Vokabular zu achten.

→ Vokabeln lernen, S. 220

Hier ist der Anfang einer Mindmap gemacht, passend zur u. s. Aufgabe. Sehen Sie, wie die drei Unterpunkte *benefits*, *dangers*, *questions* genutzt werden, um Argumente zu sammeln und Fragen aufzulisten, die im Aufsatz abgedeckt werden sollen.

TASK: **Describe / Comment on the benefits and the dangers of using social media.**

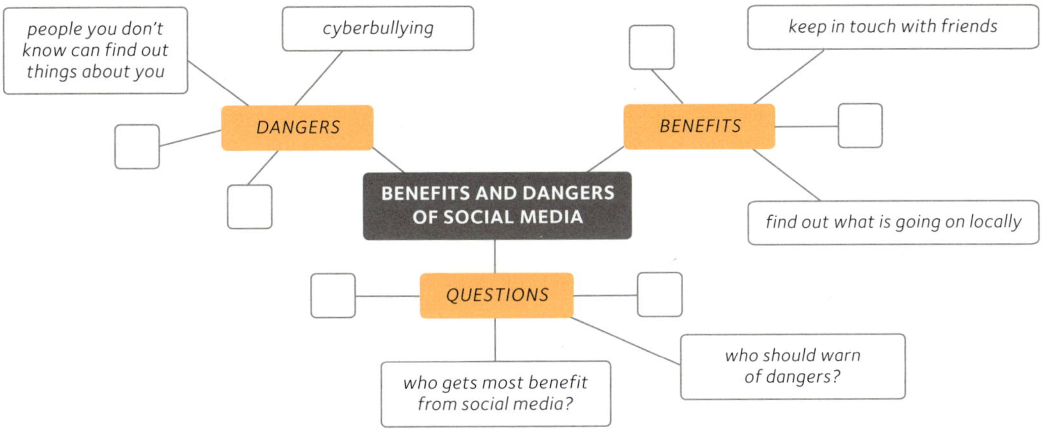

D Einen Text sinnvoll gliedern

→ *Language for writing*, hintere Umschlagsklappe

Wenn Sie etwas schriftlich verfassen, müssen Sie Ihren Text klar und logisch strukturieren, damit der Leser / die Leserin den roten Faden nicht verliert. Hierfür können Sie die Sprachelemente der hinteren Umschlagsklappe dieses Buches nutzen. Hier sind einige Beispiele, wie man mithilfe dieser Elemente einen Aufsatz strukturieren kann. Weitere finden Sie online mithilfe dieses Webcodes.

Phrases → Webcode: FOSSKP1

Argumente gliedern	*In the text, "Cyberbullying at Wiston", we saw how three pupils used social media to hurt another pupil.* ***First****, they …* ***Secondly/Then****, they …*
Eine Begründung anführen	***Due to / Because of / As a result of*** *this behaviour, Claire became isolated. She …*
Aspekte ergänzen	***In addition, / Moreover****, the girl didn't get a job she wanted.*
Einen Gegensatz ausdrücken	***Although/While*** *examples like these illustrate the dangers, social media has its benefits, too. Being active on social media can …*
Beispiele anführen	*Stephen Sutton,* ***for example****, who was diagnosed with terminal cancer aged 15, used social media …* → Using the internet to help others, S. 43
Ein Fazit ziehen	***To sum up / To conclude****, social media has its good and its bad sides.* ***On the one hand, … On the other hand, …***

Übung 2 (Fertigkeiten 3C und 3D)

A **Verwenden Sie die Informationen aus Ihrem Kursbuch und Ihre eigenen Ideen, um die Mindmap in der o.g. Erklärung der Fertigkeit 3C zu vervollständigen.**

B **Schreiben Sie die Überschriften des Abschnitts D ab und sammeln Sie Ideen für Sätze, die Sie verwenden können, um über die Vorteile und Gefahren von sozialen Medien zu schreiben.**

E Umgang mit Operatoren

Im Verlauf Ihrer Arbeit mit Ihrem Buch bzw. in einer Prüfung müssen Sie möglicherweise ein Schriftstück entsprechend besonderer Anweisungen (Operatoren) verfassen.

- Wenn Sie sich beim Schreiben auf den Text beziehen sollen, überfliegen Sie diesen, um sich einen Überblick über den Inhalt zu verschaffen. → Grobverständnis, S. 214
- Lesen Sie sich die Aufgabenstellung durch. Diese beinhaltet eine der Anweisungen aus der u. s. Tabellen. Es ist wichtig, dass Sie genau verstehen, was Sie tun sollen.
- Sammeln Sie Ideen, bevor Sie mit dem Schreiben beginnen. → Mindmaps erstellen, S. 231
- Stellen Sie sicher, dass Sie nicht dieselben Blickpunkte in unterschiedlichen Aufgaben wiederholen. Markieren Sie Textstellen für unterschiedliche Aufgaben mit unterschiedlichen Farben.
- Strukturieren Sie Ihre Antworten klar und logisch. → Einen Text sinnvoll gliedern, S. 231
- Verwenden Sie stets Ihre eigenen Worte, wenn Sie sich auf den Text beziehen. Suchen Sie Synonyme (z. B. *say* – *state*) sowie Möglichkeiten, Sätze in anderen Worten auszudrücken (z. B. *to a great extent* – *greatly*).

Übung 3 (Fertigkeit 3E)

Sehen Sie sich die Tabelle genau an und vergewissern Sie sich, dass Sie alle Anweisungen verstanden haben. Notieren Sie sich auf Deutsch:

1 wie viele Anweisungen aufgeführt sind.
2 zu welchen Überschriften die Anweisungen gehören.
3 wenn Sie Fakten, Gegenstände oder Zeichen finden sollen, die zeigen, dass etwas wahr ist.
4 wenn Sie objektiv von etwas die Vor- und Nachteile so darlegen sollen, wie sie im Text erscheinen.
5 wenn Sie Ihr eigenes Wissen einfließen lassen sollen, um die tiefere Bedeutung bzw. Botschaft eines Textes oder Witzes zu erklären.
6 wenn Sie beide Seiten einer Angelegenheit abwägen, und die Für und Wider anführen wollen.

Anweisungen, die sich auf den Inhalt beziehen

In den folgenden Anweisungen lenken Sie Ihre Aufmerksamkeit auf die Hauptgedanken des Autors / der Autorin.

Anweisung	Deutsch	Was Sie tun müssen
Summarize → Einen Text zusammenfassen, S. 229	*zusammenfassen*	Schreiben Sie die wichtigsten Textinhalte kurz und prägnant auf, und verwenden Sie hierzu Ihre eigenen Worte. Lassen Sie Ihre eigene Meinung in Form von Beispielen weg.

Outline	*darstellen*	Beschreiben Sie die wichtigsten Tatsachen und teilen Sie den Entwurf nach den wichtigsten Unterpunkten auf.
Point out	*aufzeigen*	Beziehen Sie sich auf bestimmte wesentliche Textinhalte, um deren Wichtigkeit aufzuzeigen.
Say what the text is about	*sagen, worum es im Text geht*	Skizzieren Sie in eigenen Worten kurz den Inhalt. Dies ist kürzer und weniger detailliert als eine Zusammenfassung.

Die folgenden Anweisungen werden häufig verwendet, um zu überprüfen, ob Sie den Text richtig verstanden haben.

Anweisung	Deutsch	Was Sie tun müssen
Describe	*beschreiben*	Geben Sie über eine Person oder Situation bzw. einen Gegenstand Details wieder. Sie sollten viele Adjektive benutzen.
Define	*bestimmen, umreißen, definieren*	Beschreiben Sie eine Situation, ein Problem, die Bedeutung eines Begriffs, usw. sehr genau.
Say / State / Explain why … or **State the reasons for …**	*angeben / sagen / erklären, warum* oder *die Gründe angeben für …*	Erklären Sie, warum jemand etwas tat bzw. warum etwas geschah.
Find evidence in the text to show …	*Belege im Text finden für …*	Suchen Sie nach Tatsachen, die zeigen, dass etwas wahr ist.

Anweisungen, um Standpunkte aus dem Text zu vergleichen und zu analysieren

→ Einen Aufsatz oder eine Stellungnahme schreiben, S. 234

Die folgenden, häufig benutzten Anweisungen müssen Sie sehr gründlich beantworten. Bevor Sie mit dem Schreiben beginnen, sollten Sie eine Tabelle mit zwei Spalten anlegen, um einzelne Aspekte zu vergleichen.

Anweisung	Deutsch	Was Sie tun müssen
Compare	*vergleichen*	Heben Sie die Unterschiede und Ähnlichkeiten zwischen zwei Sachen/Konzepten/usw. hervor.
Contrast	*gegenüberstellen*	Heben Sie die Unterschiede zwischen zwei Sachen/Konzepten/usw. hervor.
Point out	*beschreiben*	Stellen Sie objektiv die Vor- und Nachteile von etwas dar, wie sie im Text aufgeführt werden.

Entsprechend der folgenden Anweisungen erklären Sie die im Text ausgeführten Ansichten, lesen aber auch ‚zwischen den Zeilen' und erklären implizierte Bedeutungen. Stellen Sie sicher, dass Sie Ihre Antworten und die Struktur Ihres Aufsatzes gut planen.

Anweisung	Deutsch	Was Sie tun müssen
Analyse	*analysieren*	Beschreiben und erklären Sie bestimmte Aspekte detailliert.
Describe and explain	*beschreiben und erklären*	
Examine	*untersuchen*	

Anweisung, den Text zu interpretieren und eine Aussage zu kommentieren bzw. zu diskutieren

→ Einen Aufsatz oder eine Stellungnahme schreiben, S. 234

Entsprechend der folgenden Anweisung erklären und bewerten/evaluieren Sie sowohl die genannten als auch die implizierten Bedeutungen.

Anweisung	Deutsch	Was Sie tun müssen
Interpret	*interpretieren*	Erklären Sie die tiefere Bedeutung bzw. ‚Botschaft' einer Aussage bzw. eines Konzepts, usw. Verwenden Sie eigenes Hintergrundwissen und äußern Sie persönliche Ansichten.

Entsprechend der folgenden Anweisungen sollen Sie Ihre eigene Meinung darlegen. Wenn Sie schreiben, vertreten Sie Ihre Ansichten, doch erwähnen Sie auch Gegenargumente, um zu zeigen, dass Sie wissen, wovon Sie sprechen.

Anweisung	Deutsch	Was Sie tun müssen
Assess	*beurteilen*	Fällen Sie nach reiflicher Überlegung ein Urteil über etwas und liefern Sie Nachweise, die Ihre Meinung stützen.
Evaluate	*einschätzen, bewerten*	
Comment on	*Stellung nehmen zu*	

Entsprechend der folgenden Anweisungen sollen Sie objektiv sein. Denken Sie daran, Ihre Gedanken zunächst zu ordnen, und berücksichtigen Sie beide Seiten.

Anweisung	Deutsch	Was Sie tun müssen
Discuss	*erörtern*	Wägen Sie beide Seiten einer Sache ab und benennen Sie Für und Wider.

Übung 4 (Fertigkeit 3E)

Answer the questions about the text, *Cyberbullying at Wiston* on page 230, in your own words.

1 Describe what happened to Claire.
2 Find evidence in the text to show how Claire was affected by the bullying.

F Einen Aufsatz oder eine Stellungnahme schreiben

Einen längeren Text in einer Englischprüfung zu schreiben, stellt Ihr Sprachverständnis und Ihre Schaffenskraft auf die Probe. Wenn Sie aufgefordert sind, einen Aufsatz zu schreiben, müssen Sie eine objektive Haltung zu dem Thema einnehmen. Um dies zu erreichen, müssen Sie Argumente sammeln, die die in der Aufgabenstellung enthaltene These stützen und widerlegen. Wenn Sie „kommentieren" bzw. „diskutieren" sollen, wird erwartet, dass Sie Ihre Meinung zum Thema äußern. Hier ist es wichtig, dass Sie zur Untermauerung Ihrer Meinung Beispiele angeben.

→ Umgang mit Operatoren, S. 232

Bevor Sie mit dem Schreiben beginnen:

- Lesen Sie die Einleitung zu den Aufgaben mehrmals durch und stellen Sie sicher, dass Sie ganz genau verstehen, worüber Sie schreiben sollen.
- Achten Sie auf den genauen Wortlaut der Anweisungen. Suchen Sie nach Schlüsselwörtern in der Aufgabenstellung, die Ihnen sagt, was zu tun ist, z. B.: *identify*, *analyse*, *comment* usw.

Sobald Sie sicher sind, alles verstanden zu haben, nehmen Sie ein Blatt Schmierpapier und:

- Schreiben Sie eine Aussage auf, die sich auf die Frage bezieht, und arbeiten Sie die von Ihnen gewünschte Hauptaussage Ihres Texts heraus. Verwenden Sie für diese Aussage eine neutrale Ausdrucksweise. Schreiben Sie: *"Using social media can be beneficial or it can lead to problems."* Vermeiden Sie eine emotionale Schreibweise, wie z. B. diese: ~~*"Everybody knows that some people use social media to be nice and others use it to be nasty."*~~
- Notieren Sie Schlüsselwörter, Ausdrücke bzw. kurze Sätze, um Fakten zu veranschaulichen. Wenn Sie alles aufgeschrieben haben, lesen Sie sich Ihre Notizen durch und streichen Sie jene Ideen, die Ihre Hauptaussage nicht stützen.
- Arbeiten Sie die gemeinsamen Elemente Ihrer Stichpunkte heraus und listen Sie sie auf. Aus dieser Liste entsteht die Kernaussage des jeweiligen Absatzes im Hauptteil Ihres Aufsatzes.
- Ordnen Sie Ihre Punkte nach ihrer Wichtigkeit. Beginnen Sie mit dem unwichtigsten Punkt im ersten Absatz Ihres Hauptteils und schließen Sie mit dem stärksten Argument in Ihrem letzten Absatz des Hauptteils.

Zu guter Letzt verwenden Sie Ihre Notizen für einen Entwurf. Denken Sie daran, dass jedes längere Schriftstück eines Anfangs (Einleitung), eines Mittelteils (Hauptteil) und eines Endes (Abschluss) bedarf.

→ Mindmaps zum Inhalt eines Aufsatzes erstellen, S. 231
→ Einen Text sinnvoll gliedern, S. 231

Einleitung	Stellen Sie das Thema vor und legen Sie dar, wie Sie es angehen wollen.
Hauptteil	Verwenden Sie für jedes Argument einen Absatz. Sie können erst alle Argumente dafür und dann alle Argumente dagegen darlegen. Verwenden Sie Bindeglieder wie: *However, … That said, …* , um klarzustellen, dass Sie im folgenden Absatz eine gegenteilige Meinung darlegen. Verwenden Sie Ausdrücke wie: *In my opinion, My feeling is that …* , usw., wenn Sie Ihre Meinung äußern.
Abschluss	Wiederholen Sie Ihre Einleitung. Sagen Sie, ob Sie eine der zwei Seiten befürworten.

Das Schreiben Ihres Aufsatzes:

- Um den schwierigen Moment des Anfangs zu überwinden, können Sie als erste Tat den Wortlaut der Aufgabenstellung aufschreiben. Vergessen Sie nicht, nach Fertigstellung Ihres Aufsatzes diesen ersten Satz mit Ihren eigenen Worten umzuschreiben!
- Beginnen Sie für jedes neue Argument einen neuen Absatz und arbeiten Sie Ihre Argumentationslinie stets mithilfe von strukturschaffenden Ausdrücken klar heraus.

→ *Language for writing*, hintere Umschlagsklappe

- Bleiben Sie durchgehend fokussiert. Achten Sie darauf, dass jeder Absatz Ihres Aufsatzes zu Ihrer Hauptaussage passt.

Wenn Sie mit dem Schreiben fertig sind:

- Überprüfen Sie Ihre Rechtschreibung, Grammatik und Zeichensetzung sowie Ihren Satzbau.
- Lesen Sie sich das, was Sie geschrieben haben, genau durch und verbessern Sie den Aufsatz dort, wo es der Lesefluss erfordert.

Versuchen Sie in einer Prüfung, rechtzeitig mit dem Schreiben aufzuhören, um genau das tun zu können. Fünf bis zehn Minuten sollten hierfür ausreichend sein.

Übung 5 (Fertigkeit 3F)

A Read the following writing tasks and find key words which tell you what to cover in your text. Say which key words helped you decide. → Umgang mit Operatoren, S. 232

1. *Newspapers and magazines that publish paparazzi photos of celebrities can cause a lot of pain and misery. Describe the situation of celebrities, giving examples for and against this theory.*
2. *Reality shows that humiliate their candidates should be banned. Discuss this idea.*
3. *Groups of teenagers who are not intending to shop should be banned from shopping malls. Point out the main arguments for and against such a course of action.*

B Make notes on one of the tasks and produce an outline for your comment/essay.

4 PRODUKTION: BILDER UND CARTOONS BESCHREIBEN UND ANALYSIEREN

A Ein Bild beschreiben und deuten

Bevor Sie mit dem Schreiben beginnen, nehmen Sie Schmierpapier zur Hand, sehen sich das Bild genau an und machen sich Notizen zu den folgenden Fragen:

- Wer oder was spielt in dem Bild die Hauptrolle?
- Steht ein Element im Mittelpunkt? Warum?
- Schafft das Bild eine besondere Atmosphäre, z. B. von Gefahr, Glück?
- Was ist die „Botschaft" des Bildes?

Als Daumenregel sollte Ihre Antwort etwa zu ⅔ aus einer Bildbeschreibung und zu ⅓ aus einer Interpretation bestehen. Sagen Sie, welche Wirkung das Bild auf den Betrachter / die Betrachterin hat. Hilfreiche Redewendungen für eine Bildbeschreibung finden Sie mit Hilfe dieses Webcodes.

Phrases → **Webcode: FOSSKP2**

Übung 1 (Fertigkeit 4A)

Sehen Sie sich das Bild genau an und vervollständigen Sie die Notizen mit Wörtern aus dem Kasten.

clouds ▪ dangers ▪ having fun ▪ imagine ▪ no swimming ▪ sign ▪ unconcerned ▪ viewer

Main parts: three people ___[1] in the sea. Blue skies with a few ___[2] on the horizon. Sign shows that ___[3] is allowed here.
Focus: on the ___[4].
Atmosphere: relaxed, holiday atmosphere; no indication of any immediate ___[5].
Message: the people are ___[6] by the sign – they could have difficulties but the ___[7] can only ___[8] what these might be.

B Einen Cartoon beschreiben und deuten

Die o.g. Vorschläge zur Vorbereitung auf eine Bildbeschreibung eignen sich auch zur Vorbereitung auf die Beschreibung eines Cartoons. Denken Sie jedoch immer daran, dass ein/e Cartoonist/in auf etwas Besonderes hinweisen will. Die drei wichtigsten Techniken hierfür sind:

- Karikaturen, also ein oder mehrere körperliche Merkmale übertrieben darstellen.

- Symbole, d. h. ein bekanntes Bild verwenden, um eine Idee zu transportieren, z. B. die Freiheitsstatue, um die USA zu verkörpern.
- Bildunterschriften bzw. Sprechblasen, die die Botschaft in wenigen Worten zusammenfassen bzw. den Charakteren als Aussage zugedacht sind.

Bevor Sie über den Cartoon zu schreiben beginnen, stellen Sie sich folgende Fragen:

- Wie sind die Sachen/Personen/Charaktere gezeichnet? Sind die Personen als Karikaturen dargestellt? Stellen sie einen bestimmten „Personentyp" dar?
- Sind Symbole vorhanden? Wenn ja, was repräsentieren sie?
- Sind in der Zeichnung Nummern, Daten oder leicht erkennbare Orte zu sehen? Wenn ja, welche Funktion erfüllen sie? Was teilen sie uns mit?
- Was ist der Standpunkt des Cartoonisten / der Cartoonistin zum ausgewählten Thema?
- Welche Botschaft transportiert der Cartoon? Wie wird diese Botschaft vermittelt?

Sehen Sie sich alles auf dem Cartoon genau an und beschreiben Sie ihn ausführlich; verwenden Sie hier die Verlaufsform der Gegenwart, um auszudrücken, was die Personen tun. Denken Sie daran, dass Sie, wenn Sie die Botschaft des Cartoons nicht verstehen, sagen können, dass es *unclear* oder *ambiguous* ist. Hilfreiche Redewendungen für eine Bildbeschreibung finden Sie mit Hilfe dieses Webcodes.

Phrases → Webcode: FOSSKP2

C Ein Bild bzw. Cartoon mit einem Text vergleichen

Wenn Sie ein Bild bzw. Cartoon mit einem Text vergleichen sollen, lesen Sie den Text sorgfältig durch und sagen Sie, ob er die Botschaft der betreffenden Abbildung aufgreift oder nicht. Begründen Sie Ihre Antwort, z. B. *The image supports the text in the following way: first, … , then, … . Although the picture/cartoon shows … the text says that … .*

Übung 2 (Fertigkeiten 4B und 4C)

A Sehen Sie sich den Cartoon genau an und wählen Sie die richtige Antwort aus, um die Beschreibung zu vervollständigen.

The cartoon shows a group of middle-aged people who could be (*business people / parents*)[1]. They are sitting at a round table in a (*school / meeting room*).[2] A sign on the table indicates that the people are talking about how to persuade people to (*eat/shop*)[3] more. The man with the glasses appears to be (*making a point to / disagreeing with*)[4] his two companions. It is likely that he is the person saying the words (*above/under*)[5] the cartoon. According to these words, the man believes that kids are (*less/more*)[6] likely to believe advertising messages than adults. The message of the cartoon is (*ambiguous/ clear*)[7]. The cartoonist believes that people who work in the advertising industry are (*cynical/concerned*)[8] about consumers.

"It won't bother us if we're not allowed to aim our ads at the kids. The adults are easier to fool anyway."

B Lesen Sie den u. s. Text und wählen Sie das beste Satzende aus, um den Vergleich zwischen dem Text und der Cartoonbotschaft zu vervollständigen.

According to a recent study, advertising aimed at young people is an important factor in deciding how kids spend their money. Young people between the ages of 13 and 17 appear to be most influenced by advertising. The study discovered that this age group is more influenced by advertising messages than adults are. As an indication that this may be true, the study discovered that requests by kids and young people for advertised products decrease as they get older.
A spokesperson for the study said: "Consumers tend to become more critical about their purchases and less susceptible to advertising as they grow up."

1 Both the cartoon and the text describe how
   - **a** all age groups react to advertising.
   - **b** to persuade people to buy goods.
   - **c** young people compare to adults when it comes to viewing advertising.

2 The speaker in the cartoon appears to believe that, when it comes to advertising,
   - **a** adults have better judgement than kids.
   - **b** everyone is convinced by the messages the industry puts out.
   - **c** kids are more critical than adults.

3 The text,
   - **a** however, gives a completely different view of the subject.
   - **b** on the one hand, agrees with the cartoon.
   - **c** on the other hand, suggests that no-one is convinced by advertising.

4 According to the text, as kids grow up, they
   - **a** are less accepting of advertising messages.
   - **b** ask their parents for more.
   - **c** spend more money on consumer goods.

5 If we are to believe the text, the advertising executive portrayed in the cartoon is
   - **a** analysing his target groups correctly.
   - **b** incorrect in his analysis of his target groups.
   - **c** taking a risk by not advertising to kids.

5 PRODUKTION: SCHAUBILDER UND STATISTIKEN BESCHREIBEN UND ANALYSIEREN

Diagramme und Kurvenbilder werden verwendet, um Informationen visuell darzustellen.

TYPES OF DIAGRAMS

Table

	Germany	UK
2010	568	261
2015	822	98

Bar chart

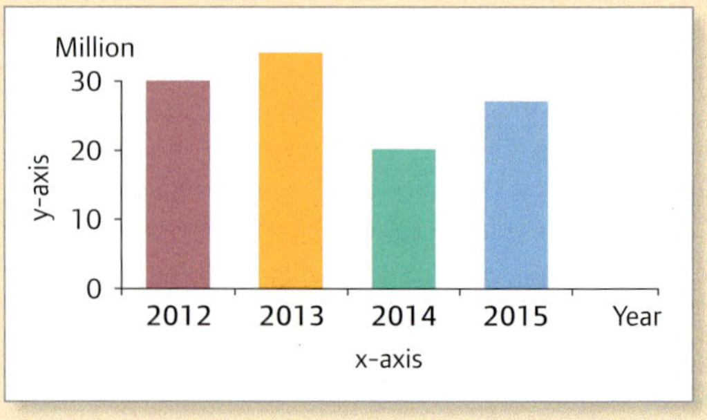

Pie chart

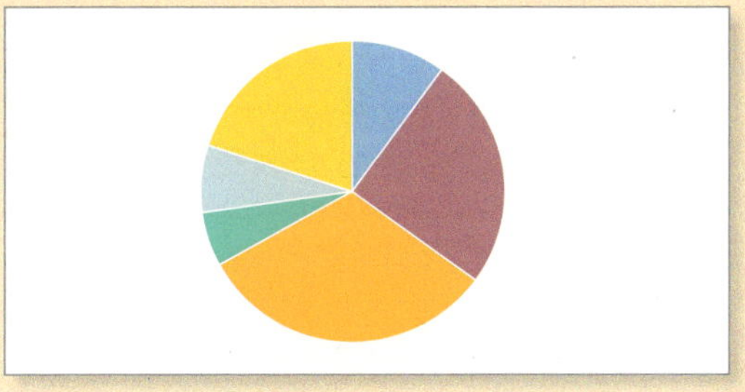

Graph, line graph

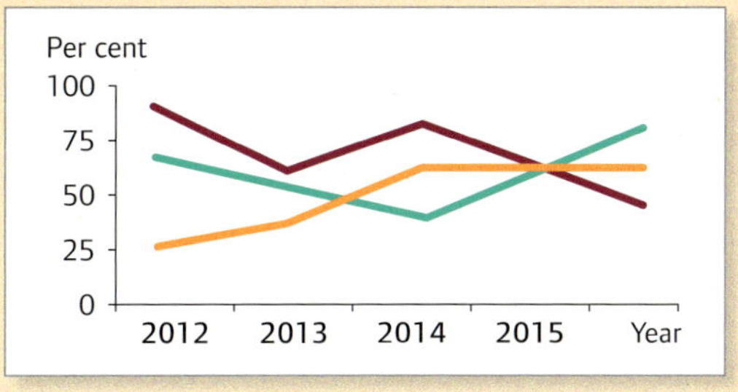

Bevor Sie mit dem Schreiben beginnen, nehmen Sie Schmierpapier zur Hand, sehen sich die Abbildung genau an und machen sich zu folgenden Fragen Notizen:

- Was sagt die Überschrift aus? Welche Beschriftung liegt vor?
- Welche Zahlen und Einheiten werden verwendet, um die Daten darzustellen?
- Wenn ein Balkendiagramm / eine Kurve vorliegt, wofür steht die x-Achse? Wofür die y-Achse?
- Welche Muster können Sie in den Daten erkennen?
- Welche Schlüsse können Sie aus diesen Mustern ziehen?
- Wie verhält sich die Abbildung zu Dingen, die Sie bereits wissen, z. B. zu einem Text, den Sie kürzlich gelesen haben, oder zu Informationen aus der Einleitung zur Aufgabenstellung?

Um Ihre Beschreibung und Analyse der Abbildung zu ordnen, nutzen Sie Ihre Notizen folgendermaßen:

▪ eine Einleitung zum Diagramm bzw. Kurvenbild (Überschrift)	*The diagram / graph shows / refers to …*
▪ ein Überblick dessen, was es darstellt	*The figures in the table show …* *The x-axis shows … , the y-axis shows*
▪ eine ausführliche Beschreibung der Informationen	*The graph shows a huge increase …*
▪ die Beziehung zwischen den Kategorien	*Car X has twice as much … as Car Y.*
▪ eine Auswertung des Diagramms bzw. Kurvenbilds	*The figures indicate that …*

Hilfreiche Redewendungen, Schaubilder zu beschreiben, finden Sie mit Hilfe dieses Webcodes.

Phrases → Webcode: FOSSKP3

Übung 1 (Fertigkeit 5)

Vervollständigen Sie die Beschreibung und Analyse des Diagramms auf Seite 240 mit Wörtern aus dem Kasten.

compared to ▪ constant increase ▪ fluctuate ▪ huge increase ▪
remained more or less constant ▪ rise ▪ shows ▪ small dip ▪
the number of devices in millions ▪ the year

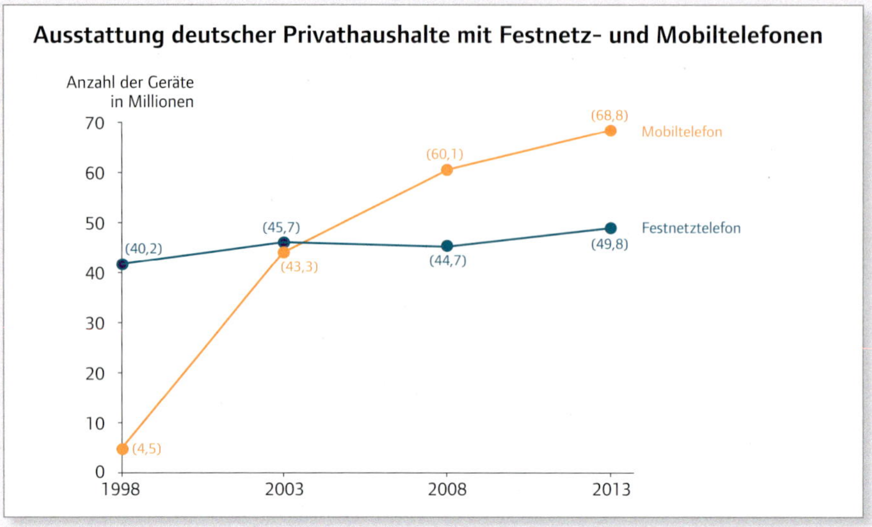

The line graph ___[1] the development in the numbers of landlines and mobile phones in German private households from 1998 to 2013. The x-axis shows ___[2] and the y-axis shows ___[3]. In 1998, there were only 4.5 million mobiles in German households ___[4] 40.2 million landlines. During the next 15 years, the numbers of landlines ___[5] (all in all an increase of less than 20%), whereas the number of mobile phones showed a ___[6]. By 2013, there were just 49.8 million landlines compared to 68.8 million mobiles. In the case of mobile phones, we see ___[7] in numbers over the years, whereas the numbers of landlines ___[8], showing a rise in total numbers during the years 1998 to 2003. This is followed by a ___[9] in total numbers between 2003 and 2008 and a further ___[10] to 49.8 million in 2013.

6 SCHRIFTLICHE MEDIATION

Mediation ist das Übertragen wesentlicher Textelemente von einer Sprache in eine andere. Mediation ist nicht mit dem Wort „Übersetzung" austauschbar. Sie sollen nur den Sinn des Textes übertragen und bestimmte Informationen wiedergeben.

A Vorbereitung

- Lesen Sie sich die Anweisungen sorgfältig durch. Vergewissern Sie sich, dass Sie wissen:
  - warum die Informationen in einer anderen Sprache wiedergegeben werden, z. B. weil Ihr Kollegium über Entwicklungen Ihres Tätigkeitsfeldes informiert werden sollen.
  - für wen die Mediation gedacht ist, z. B. für andere Schüler/innen, Ihr/e Chef/in.
  - welches Medium Sie nutzen sollen, z. B. eine E-Mail, eine Informationsbroschüre.
- Lesen Sie den Text zügig, um den groben Sinn zu erfassen. Verschwenden Sie keine Zeit mit einzelnen Wörtern bzw. Wörtern, die Sie nicht verstehen. → Grobverständnis, S. 214
- Lesen Sie die Anweisungen noch einmal, dann gehen Sie den Text ein weiteres Mal durch und suchen nach Textpassagen, die jene Informationen enthalten, die Sie zur Lösung der Aufgabe benötigen. In einer Prüfung können Sie die betreffenden Stellen unterstreichen oder farblich hervorheben. Folgende Textstellen können als unwesentlich betrachtet werden: Wiederholungen (oft eingeleitet durch *in other words, to put it another way*) und Anekdoten und Exkurse (*by the way, incidentally*).

B Einen Mediationstext schreiben

Schreiben Sie die wichtigsten Punkte des Textes in klarem, einfachem Deutsch auf. Halten Sie sich an das, was im Originaltext gesagt wurde. Wenn Sie damit fertig sind:

- Lesen Sie Ihren Text Korrektur, d. h. überprüfen Sie die Rechtschreibung und Grammatik.
- Lesen Sie sich Ihren Text durch und stellen Sie sicher, dass der Inhalt des Originals klar und verständlich übertragen wurde.
- Überprüfen Sie, dass Sie nur solche Informationen übernommen haben, die für die Aufgabe relevant sind.
- Überprüfen Sie, dass Sie für die Zielgruppe Ihres Textes angemessen formuliert haben.
- Überprüfen Sie, dass Sie die Mediation in dem nötigen Medium übermittelt haben.

Übung (Fertigkeit 6)

A Lesen Sie sich die Anweisungen sorgfältig durch und machen sich Notizen zur Situation und der Aufgabenstellung.

Situation: Sie machen ein Praktikum in einem Jugendzentrum vor Ort. Das Zentrum bietet für seine freiwilligen Helfer/innen regelmäßig Weiterbildungen an. Die nächste Weiterbildung befasst sich mit der wachsenden Anzahl von Kindern in Europa, die in Patchwork-Familien aufwachsen. Diese Weiterbildung wird auch die finanzielle Lage der Familien beleuchten.

Aufgabe: Ihr Chef / Ihre Chefin lässt Sie den Text *Changing face of the British family* lesen und die Situation im Vereinigten Königreich beschreiben. Er/Sie möchte, dass Sie ein Flugblatt erstellen, welches die wichtigsten Informationen darüber enthält, warum Stieffamilien in ihrer Anzahl zunehmen; dieses Flugblatt möchte er/sie während der Weiterbildung verteilen.

B Lesen Sie nun den Text und machen sich auf Englisch zu den Punkten Notizen, die Sie für Ihre Mediation benötigen.

C Jetzt können Sie Ihren Text verfassen. Vermitteln Sie die wesentlichen Punkte auf Deutsch und behalten hierbei die Zielgruppe im Auge, die Ihre Mediation lesen wird. Berücksichtigen Sie auch das Medium, das Sie benutzen sollen.

Changing face of the British family: One in three now has a step-child Nearly two million children live in a two-parent family, study reveals

Parents increasingly regard serial relationships as normal behaviour

Nearly a third of all couples bringing up children have a child from an earlier relationship in their family, a report said yesterday.

The rapidly growing number of step-families means that nearly two million children live in a two-parent family – but with one parent who is not their own.

The army of step-children has appeared as their parents increasingly come to regard serial relationships, not one committed marriage, as normal behaviour.

A report said that the majority of parents have had at least one partnership in the past that they regarded as long-term. New details of how the shape of families has been twisted by the decline of lifelong marriage and the rise of temporary cohabitation were revealed in a study of 20,000 people carried out for an insurance company.

The findings of the Family Finances report produced for Aviva were released in advance of the latest national divorce figures, published by the Office for National Statistics today.

These are expected to show that couples who do marry rather than just live together are increasingly likely to stay together. Sarah Poulter of Aviva said: 'This research shows that there is no "normal" family any more. What was seen as the traditional model is becoming more and more diverse.
'It is now quite usual for a child to have three parents, and to live in a family that includes step-parents, half-brothers and half-sisters.'
The polling found that almost half of all adults who live with a spouse or partner or with children – 49 per cent – have had at least one past relationship which they regarded as committed, either a marriage or a cohabitation. One in six have had two past relationships they thought were permanent, and one in 20 has had three or more. The result is that 30 per cent of present two-parent families include a child from a former relationship.
The report said only one in three of these step-families gets any sort of financial help from the parent of the step-child. A third of these get only occasional payments – while only a quarter of parents whose children live with other families provide regular payments.
The analysis suggests a third of step-families that do get financial help actually rely on the payments to get by.
It also found that one in eight adults who have been through a separation postponed the break-up because they could not afford to find anywhere else to live.
Latest official figures say that there are around 5.7 million families with children under the age of 16, or under 18 and still in school. In just over two thirds of these – around four million – the parents are married. (442 words)

From: *www.dailymail.co.uk*

7 ÜBERSETZEN

Einen Text zu übersetzen verlangt Sorgfalt und Geduld. Im Gegensatz zur Mediation ist für eine Übersetzung jedes Wort des Originaltextes wichtig. Ihre Aufgabe als Übersetzer/in ist es, den Sinn des Textes mit deutschen Entsprechungen zu reproduzieren.

Merken Sie sich folgende Regeln:

- Übersetzer/innen haben keine eigene „Stimme". Selbst wenn Sie mit der Aussage nicht einverstanden sind, dürfen Sie weder den Text an sich noch den Ton verändern.
- Von Ihnen werden weder Bewertungen noch Meinungsäußerungen erwartet.
- Streben Sie keine wortgetreue Übersetzung an, denn das ist unmöglich. Stattdessen konzentrieren Sie sich beim Lesen auf Informationsblöcke, die Sie dann als Ganzes übersetzen.

Bevor Sie mit dem Schreiben beginnen:

- Lesen Sie die Überschrift sowie den gesamten Text, um einen Überblick zu bekommen.
  → Grobverständnis, S. 214
- Lesen Sie den Text noch einmal, doch dieses Mal achten Sie auf Einzelheiten. Machen Sie sich beim Lesen Notizen.
  → Gründliches Lesen, S. 223
  → Sich während des Lesens Notizen machen, S. 223
- Schreiben Sie sich Wörter und Strukturen auf, die Sie nicht verstehen.
- Wenden Sie Ihre Fertigkeiten zur Worterkennung an, um sich die Bedeutung von unbekannten Wörtern und Satzstrukturen zu erarbeiten. Verwenden Sie Ihr Wörterbuch nur, wenn es nicht anders geht.
  → Mit unbekannten Wörtern umgehen, S. 216
  → Ein Wörterbuch benutzen, S. 217

Ihre Übersetzung verfassen

Wenn Sie den Text verstanden haben, können Sie mit dem Erstellen Ihrer deutschen Fassung beginnen. Schreiben Sie Ihren ersten Entwurf ‚doppelzeilig' – so haben Sie Platz für Korrekturen.

Wenn Sie mit Ihrer Übersetzung fertig sind:

- Vergleichen Sie Ihren Text und das Original Satz für Satz, um sicherzustellen, dass Sie nichts ausgelassen haben.
- Lesen Sie Ihren Text durch und vergewissern Sie sich, dass er klar und verständlich ist.
- Überprüfen Sie Ihre Rechtschreibung und Grammatik. Lassen Sie insbesondere bei den Verben und den nachfolgend genannten Problembereichen Vorsicht walten.

Tipps – Grammatik, Stil und Vokabular

Jeder Text enthält unterschiedlich knifflige Aspekte, über die Sie nachdenken müssen. Seien Sie bei den folgenden Bereichen besonders sorgfältig.

- **Knifflige grammatische Strukturen**
  - Partizipialkonstruktionen → S. 268
  - Konstruktionen mit Gerundium → S. 262
  - Passivkonstruktionen → S. 261
  - Relativsätze ohne Relativpronomen → S. 269
  - Adverbien → S. 270
  - Komparative und Superlative → S. 271
  - Verben in der Verlaufsform → S. 249–254

- **Wortstellung**
  - Verwenden Sie im Englischen stets die Reihenfolge S–V–O (*subject – verb – object*).
  - Denken Sie daran: Wenn ein deutscher Satz z. B. mit einem Adverb beginnt, wird das Verb versetzt, auf Englisch jedoch bleibt die Reihenfolge S–V–O erhalten.

- **Die Form eines Wortes ändern**

  BEISPIELE: *There is a need to …* → Es ist notwendig, zu …
  (englisch: Nomen → deutsch: Adjektiv)
  She used to work in France. → Früher arbeitete sie in Frankreich.
  (englisch: Verbkonstruktion → deutsch: Adverb)

- **Partikeln und Ausdrücke**

  BEISPIEL: *since* = seit (*He has been working since 6 am.*)
  = da, weil (*Since he didn't have his phone with him, he couldn't call her.*)

- **Falsche Freunde**

  BEISPIEL: *actual* = tatsächlich / *topical, current* = aktuell

- **Häufig verwechselte Wörter**

  BEISPIEL: *advice/advise*
  He gave me some advice. Rat(schlag)
  He advised me to see a doctor. beraten

8 PRÄSENTIEREN

Im Verlauf Ihres Schuljahres könnten Sie aufgefordert werden, eine Präsentation vorzubereiten und zu geben. Die Fertigkeit des Präsentierens können Sie in der Schule üben; das gibt Ihnen jene Sicherheit, die Sie brauchen, um eine Präsentation auf der Arbeit zu geben. An der Schule fallen Präsentationen im Allgemeinen in eine von zwei Kategorien: eine informative, objektive

Präsentation, die auf Tatsachen beruht, und eine subjektive Präsentation, in der Sie Ihre eigene Meinung zu einem strittigen Thema vertreten.

A Vorbereitung

- Sammeln Sie möglichst viele Informationen und Ideen zu dem Thema, indem Sie im Internet und in Büchern recherchieren, mit Experten/Expertinnen sprechen, ein Brainstorming machen, usw.
- Wählen Sie jene Ideen aus, die Ihr Thema am sinnvollsten widerspiegeln, und machen Sie sich Notizen.
- Verwenden Sie Ihre Notizen, um Ihre Ideen in logische Einheiten einzuteilen.
- Ordnen Sie diese Einheiten so, dass ein roter Faden klar erkennbar ist.
- Stellen Sie Ihre Präsentation zusammen und benutzen Sie hierzu eine der u. s. Gliederungen.

Um eine informative Präsentation zu planen, z. B. *Local opportunities for work experience*.
- **Einleitung:** Das Benennen Ihres Themas und eine kurze Erläuterung über den Aufbau Ihrer Präsentation (ca. 15 % Ihrer Präsentation)
- **Entwicklung:** Beweise, die Ihre Vorstellungen belegen (ca. 75 %)
- **Schluss:** Wiederholung Ihrer Ideen und eine knappe Zusammenfassung der wichtigsten Fakten und Zahlen (ca. 10 %)

Um eine Präsentation zu einem umstrittenen Thema zu planen, z. B. *Hash should be legalized*
- **Einleitung:** Objektiver Lösungsvorschlag zu einem strittigen Problem. Äußern Sie Ihre eigene Meinung noch nicht. (ca. 10 % Ihrer Präsentation)
- **Entwicklung 1:** Argumente für den Vorschlag (*pros*) (ca. 40 %)
- **Entwicklung 2:** Argumente gegen den Vorschlag (*cons*) (ca. 40 %)
(Wie auch immer Sie persönlich zu dem Vorschlag stehen, streben Sie ein ausgewogenes Verhältnis zwischen Ihren *pros* und *cons* an.)
- **Schluss:** Ihre Meinung mit einer kurzen Angabe von Gründen. (ca. 10 %)

- Wenn Sie das geschrieben haben, was Sie sagen wollten, lesen Sie Ihre Präsentation durch. Suchen Sie nach Stellen, wo Sie etwas kürzen oder löschen können. Fragen Sie sich immer wieder: Kann ich das noch kürzer, präziser ausdrücken?
- Erstellen Sie sich nun Stichwortkarten als Erinnerungshilfe für die wichtigsten Informationen. Schreiben Sie auf Karteikarten; schreiben Sie deutlich und in Großbuchstaben und niemals ganze Sätze – Sie benötigen nur Stichwörter.
- Es hilft, Ihre Präsentation als Trockenübung zu geben, besonders vor einem Publikum.

Übung 1 (Fertigkeit 8A)

A Entscheiden Sie, welche der folgenden Themen Sie zu einer Meinungsäußerung veranlassen, weil sie für Sie strittig sind.

1 Fitness studios in our area: numbers, prices and facilities
2 The state – not the children – should look after the elderly
3 The rise of global warming from the early 1960s to the present day
4 Using animals in medical research helps people

B **Wählen Sie eines der strittigen Themen aus. Sammeln Sie fünf Argumente für und gegen den Vorschlag.**

C **Halten Sie Ihre Meinung zu dem von Ihnen ausgewählten Vorschlag schriftlich fest. Fassen Sie Ihre Gründe kurz zusammen.**

B Das Verwenden von Folien und Handouts während einer Präsentation

Folien können bei Schaubildern sinnvoll, aber als Teil Ihrer Präsentation auch hinderlich sein. Aus diesem Grund fragen Sie sich bitte vor dem Erstellen von Folien, ob sie notwendig sind. Wenn ja:

- Beschränken Sie die Textmenge auf ein Minimum und stellen Sie sicher, dass die Rechtschreibung stimmt.
- Vergewissern Sie sich, dass Kurvenbilder und andere Abbildungen groß genug sind, um von den Zuhörern/Zuhörerinnen erkannt zu werden.

Handouts sind Unterlagen, die Ihre Präsentation unterstützen. Ein Teil dieser Unterlagen enthält ggf. die von Ihnen verwendeten Folien; andere Handouts ergänzen bzw. erweitern die Informationen, die Sie präsentiert haben. Sie sollten prägnante Informationen oder/und Illustrationen enthalten und ordentlich getippt bzw. gedruckt sein. Sie sollten nicht Ihre Präsentation in einer Kurzfassung enthalten.

C Eine Präsentation halten

- Beginnen Sie mit einer Begrüßung Ihrer Zuhörer/Zuhörerinnen und stellen Sie anschließend sich und Ihr Thema vor. Versuchen Sie, das Interesse und die Aufmerksamkeit Ihrer Zuhörerschaft von Anfang an zu wecken. Sagen Sie, wie lang Sie über etwas reden werden, z. B.: *"In the next 10 minutes, I will share my ideas about …"*
- Teilen Sie Ihrem Hörerkreis mit, wie Sie Ihre Präsentation unterteilt haben bzw. wie viele Punkte Sie abdecken wollen, z. B.: *"I've divided my talk into three sections: first … second …"*
- Setzen Sie für Ihre Zuhörer/Zuhörerinnen während der Präsentation Signale, damit diese wissen, was als Nächstes kommt. So helfen Sie ihnen, Ihrer Kernaussage leichter zu folgen. Sie sollten auch klar vermitteln, wie ein Teil Ihrer Präsentation mit dem nächsten zusammenhängt; dies tun Sie mittels Hinweisen. Lassen Sie sie wissen, wo Sie sind. Nützliche Redewendungen finden Sie online mit diesem Webcode.

  Phrases → **Webcode: FOSSKP4**
- Nachdem Sie das Ende Ihrer Präsentation eingeläutet haben, fassen Sie sich kurz und kommen Sie zum Ende. Ermutigen Sie Ihre Zuhörer/Zuhörerinnen, Fragen zu stellen.

Übung 2 (Fertigkeit 8C)

Hören Sie zu, wie jemand eine Präsentation beginnt und beendet. Machen Sie sich Notizen und nehmen Sie hierzu die u. s. Überschriften zu Hilfe.

Hörtext → Webcode: FOSSKT2

Das Publikum begrüßen	Sich selbst vorstellen	Den Aufbau der Präsentation beschreiben	Über Fragen und Handouts informieren	Die Präsentation beenden

D Körpersprache

- Nehmen Sie Augenkontakt auf.
- Sehen Sie in die Zuhörerschaft und lächeln Sie.
- Stehen Sie nicht steif da und verschränken Sie Ihre Arme nicht vor Ihrem Körper.
- Lesen Sie Ihre Präsentation nicht vor. Schreiben Sie nieder, was Sie sagen wollen, dann lernen Sie es, und dann sagen Sie es.

Übung 3 (Fertigkeiten 8 A bis D)

Choose one of the topics below and follow the instructions. If you have the chance, ask your teacher if you can give the presentation in class as extra practice.

- Wählen Sie ein Thema aus und nutzen Sie die Informationen aus dieser Lektion, um sich inhaltlich vorzubereiten.
  Topic 1: How to give a good presentation
  Topic 2: The theory and practice of skills as described in Focus on Success
- Erstellen Sie Folien und Handreichungen, wenn Sie sicher sind, dass Sie sie benötigen.
- Wenn Sie die Möglichkeit haben, bitten Sie Ihren Lehrer/Ihre Lehrerin, die Präsentation als zusätzliche Übung vor der Klasse halten zu dürfen und bitten Sie ihn/sie oder Ihre Mitschüler/innen (*peer correction*) um Rückmeldungen.

9 INTERAKTION

Sie werden möglicherweise im Unterricht bzw. als Teil einer Prüfung aufgefordert, an einer Diskussion bzw. einem Rollenspiel mitzuwirken. Beide dieser Aufgaben schließen einen Austausch mit anderen Menschen ein. Folgen Sie den u.s. allgemeinen Tipps.

Tipps für einen guten Austausch

- Verinnerlichen Sie die Ausdrücke auf der hinteren Umschlaginnenseite und verwenden Sie sie im Unterricht, sooft Sie können. → *Language for discussion*, hintere Umschlagsklappe
- Halten Sie sich an das Thema.
- Bleiben Sie locker und denken Sie, bevor Sie sprechen.
- Bleiben Sie immer höflich und geben Sie anderen die Möglichkeit zu reden. Hören Sie aktiv zu und gehen Sie auf die anderen Teilnehmer/innen ein. Nehmen Sie Augenkontakt auf und zeigen Sie Interesse, Überraschung, usw. Stellen Sie Fragen.
- Hören Sie aufmerksam zu, was die anderen sagen.
- Werten Sie andere niemals ab. Wenn ein/e andere/r Teilnehmer/in Probleme zu haben scheint, helfen Sie ihm/ihr, indem Sie in Worte fassen, was (Sie glauben, was) er/sie ausdrücken möchte, z. B.:
  So, you mean that … I think I understand what you're getting at. It's as if …

An Diskussionen teilnehmen

In einer Diskussion sollten Sie Ihre Meinung zum Ausdruck bringen.

- Lesen Sie die Anweisungen sorgfältig durch und entscheiden Sie, was Sie sagen möchten.
- Machen Sie sich Notizen und schreiben Sie einige Schlüsselwörter bzw. -ausdrücke auf Englisch auf.

- Versuchen Sie vorauszusehen, was die anderen Teilnehmer/innen sagen könnten. Überlegen Sie sich, wie Sie hierzu reagieren würden, und fügen Sie Ihren Notizen englische Ausdrücke der Zustimmung bzw. Widerrede hinzu.

Ein Rollenspiel gestalten

Ein Rollenspiel gibt die Situation und Rollen vor, die Sie spielen und erkunden.

- Lesen Sie Ihre Rollenkarte sorgfältig durch. Ihre Rollenkarte sagt Ihnen, wer Sie sind und was Sie sagen sollen. Selbst wenn Sie nicht mit dem einverstanden sind, was Ihre Figur sagt bzw. wie sie sich benimmt, „denken" Sie sich in diese Rolle hinein.
- Machen Sie sich Notizen zu den Argumenten, die Ihre Figur sagen könnte, um ihren Standpunkt zu vertreten.

Übung 1 (Fertigkeit 9)

Role play

Situation: You are going to play the role of one of four people involved in a podium discussion about free apps which are used by electronic companies to advertise and persuade teenagers to buy other apps and online games.

A Arbeiten Sie in Vierergruppen und entscheiden Sie, wer welche Rolle übernimmt. Machen Sie sich Notizen zu dem, was Sie sagen möchten, und beginnen Sie dann das Rollenspiel.

Ray Dawson: advertising analyst
You know what you are talking about and are used to people listening to you.
You believe that these apps will help companies make money.
Nobody is being forced to play these games.

Jane Jones: online marketing manager for an electronic company
You are keen to promote your company's games and think people will have a lot of fun with them.
The company is not marketing the apps as educational games; they are marketed solely as games for fun.

Michael/a Griffin: a teenager
You have a lot of experience with online games.
Your older brother plays online games, too.
You used to spend a lot of time playing them, but you play less now as you have to concentrate on your school subjects.
You know some pupils who are addicted to games, but most of your friends are sensible and don't spend all day online.

Sam Dawson: the parent of two teenagers, aged 12 and 13
You are concerned about the effect these free apps will have on young people. You would like to see this type of advertising banned.
Your children have smart phones and electronic equipment like all their friends.
You worry that your children's school work will suffer if they spend too much time playing games.

B Wenn Sie fertig sind, bleiben Sie in Ihren Gruppen und sprechen Sie über die Übung. Tauschen Sie sich über folgende Punkte aus:

- Konnte jede/r Teilnehmer/in seine/ihre Ansichten klar vermitteln?
- Waren alle höflich?
- Hörten alle einander zu?

10 PRÜFUNGSSTRATEGIEN

Alles, was Sie während Ihres Schuljahres gelernt haben, wird Ihnen zu guten Prüfungsergebnissen verhelfen. Seit dem Beginn Ihres Englischkurses haben Sie dieselbe Art von Aufgaben gelöst, die Sie in der Prüfung bekommen, einschließlich Lesen, Schreiben und sich beim Reden abwechseln. Das Durcharbeiten der *Building skills boxes* der jeweiligen Units sowie dieses *Skills*-Anhangs hat Ihnen die Strategien vermittelt, die Sie für einen Test bzw. eine Prüfung benötigen.

Die folgenden Tipps helfen Ihnen, in jedem Test bzw. in jeder Prüfung Ihr Bestes zu geben:

A Die schriftliche Prüfung

- Lesen Sie sich alle Fragen sorgfältig durch und stellen Sie sicher, dass Sie wissen, was zu tun ist.
- Entscheiden Sie, bei welchen Aufgaben Sie sich besonders sicher sind, dass Sie sie lösen können, und welche die meisten Punkte bringen. Gehen Sie diese Aufgaben zuerst an.
- In Bezug auf textbezogene Fragen fragen Sie sich: Welche Textstelle/n benötige ich zur Beantwortung der Frage?
- In Bezug auf Fragen zum Hörverständnis fragen Sie sich: Worauf muss ich achten?
- In Bezug auf schriftliche Aufgaben fragen Sie sich: Welche Art von Text muss ich schreiben? Dann machen Sie sich Notizen und ordnen Sie Ihren Text, bevor Sie die Endfassung schreiben. Zum Schluss überprüfen Sie Rechtschreibung und Grammatik.
- Wenn Sie mit den Prüfungsaufgaben fertig sind und bevor Sie Ihre Aufgaben abgeben, überprüfen Sie, dass Sie alle Anweisungen und jede Aufgabe ordentlich erfüllt haben. Vergewissern Sie sich, keine Frage ausgelassen zu haben.

B Die mündliche Prüfung

- Lesen Sie die Aufgabenstellung durch und legen Sie Ihre Argumentationslinie fest.
- Sofern es erlaubt ist, machen Sie sich Notizen zu dem, was Sie sagen möchten, und zwar bevor Sie zu reden beginnen (Stichpunkte reichen aus).
- Denken Sie an die idiomatischen Ausdrücke, die Sie gelernt haben, sowie die Strategie, sich abzuwechseln.
- Versuchen Sie, die Argumente vorauszuahnen, die der andere Teilnehmer / die anderen Teilnehmerinnen verwenden könnte. Versuchen Sie, Ihre Reaktion auf diese Argumente vorauszuahnen, und verwenden Sie hierfür Ausdrücke der Zustimmung, Widerrede, usw.
- Wenn Sie plötzlich einen Gedächtnisausfall haben und sich an kein einziges Wort erinnern können, umschreiben Sie, was Sie sagen möchten. Reden Sie weiter!

Wenden Sie diese Tipps bei nächster Gelegenheit an, z. B. bei einem Klassentest oder einer gestellten Prüfung. Die Rückmeldungen, die Sie auf Ihre Darbietung von Ihrer Klasse bekommen, zeigt Ihnen, in welchen Bereichen Sie sich noch verbessern können.

Diese *Grammar files* führen Sie durch die wichtigsten Elemente der englischen Grammatik und erklären die Formen und den Gebrauch der Strukturen. Sie können die hier angebotenen Übungen nutzen, um zu üben und Ihre Kenntnisse zu vertiefen. Die Lösungen dazu finden Sie auf www.cornelsen.de/webcodes. Geben Sie einfach den Webcode FOSGRLO im Webcode-Suchfeld ein.

Lösungen → Webcode: FOSGRLO

SIMPLE PRESENT ▪ PRESENT PROGRESSIVE

Form

	Simple present	Present progressive
Aussage	I/you/we/they **play** he/she/it **plays**	I **am playing** you/we/they **are playing** he/she/it **is playing**
Verneinung	I/you/we/they **don't play** he/she/it **doesn't play**	**I'm not playing** you/we/they **aren't playing** he/she/it **isn't playing**
Frage + Kurzantwort	Do I/you/we/they **play**? ▪ Yes, I/you/we/they **do**. ▪ No, I/you/we/they **don't**. Does he/she/it **play**? ▪ Yes, he/she/it **does**. ▪ No, he/she/it **doesn't**.	**Am** I **playing?** ▪ Yes, I **am**. ▪ No, **I'm not**. **Are** you/we/they **playing**? ▪ Yes, you/we/they **are**. ▪ No, you/we/they **aren't**. **Is** he/she/it **playing**? ▪ Yes, he/she/it **is**. ▪ No, he/she/it **isn't**.

Simple present

- In der dritten Person Singular (z. B. nach *he, Sandra, the coffee*) hängt man *s* an das Verb an bzw. *es*, wenn das Verb auf einen Zischlaut (z. B. *ch*) endet.
- Frage und Verneinung bildet man mit *do/don't* und *does/doesn't*. In Sätzen mit *does/doesn't* hat das Verb kein *(e)s*.

Present progressive

- Wenn das Verb auf *e* endet, fällt das *e* vor *ing* weg: *hope – hoping*.
- Bei einem einsilbigen Verb, das auf einen einzelnen Vokal + einzelnen Konsonanten endet, verdoppelt man den Konsonanten: *stop – sto**pp**ing, plan – pla**nn**ing*.

Gebrauch

Simple present	Present progressive
I **come** from Germany.	Wait for me! **I'm coming**.
I **don't eat** much chocolate.	It's hot today and **I'm eating** an ice-cream.
This train **doesn't stop** in Hexford.	Why **is** the train **stopping** on the bridge today?
Germany sometimes **plays** against England.	Today Germany **is playing** against Ireland.
Moni is a designer. She **designs** clothes.	At the moment she **is designing** a new style of jeans.

- Mit dem **simple present** beschreibt man einen Normalzustand und was eigentlich immer so ist – regelmäßige Vorgänge, Gewohnheiten und was zum Tagesablauf gehört, was man beruflich und in der Freizeit macht.
- Mit dem **present progressive** beschreibt man ein momentanes Geschehen, einen Einzelvorgang, der gerade im Verlauf begriffen ist.
- Das **present progressive** verwendet man auch für eine vorübergehende Tätigkeit, die mit Unterbrechungen über eine gewisse Zeit ausgeübt wird, eine vorübergehende Situation im Leben: *This week **I'm helping** my friend to repair his moped.*
- Das **simple present** und das **present progressive** verwendet man häufig mit den folgenden typischen Zeitangaben:

Simple present	Present progressive
▪ always, often, usually, sometimes, never ▪ every morning/day/year ▪ at … o'clock, in the morning, at lunchtime, after school ▪ on Monday(s), at the weekend, in June, in the summer	▪ now, at the moment, just ▪ today, this week, this month, this summer

Was sonst noch wichtig ist

- Das **simple present** verwendet man auch, um etwas zu erzählen – eine Filmhandlung, eine Story, einen Witz oder den Inhalt einer Sendung oder eines Textes:
  *The film tells the story of Julian Timbo and how he **becomes** a great star.*
  *In today's programme Kelly Green **talks** about her career.*
- **!** Bestimmte Verben kann man nur im **simple present** verwenden.

have, need, want, like, love, hate, prefer, know, think, remember, understand, believe, realize, seem, mean, belong to

- Wenn *have* aber eine Tätigkeit beschreibt, kann es auch im **present progressive** stehen.

have = „haben, besitzen"	*have* beschreibt eine Tätigkeit
Sorry, I **have** no time.	I**'m having** lunch / a cup of tea.
Stars **have** a lot of money.	We**'re having** a great time/party.

- Das **present progressive** verwendet man auch für zukünftige Vorhaben, wenn Vorkehrungen oder Abmachungen bereits getroffen wurden oder jemand eine bestimmte Zeiteinteilung für sich vorgenommen hat:
  *I**'m** meeting Sam this evening. We**'re going** to the cinema.*
  *Susan **is flying** to London next week.*

1 Complete the sentences with simple present forms of the verbs in brackets.

EXAMPLES: **A** (you/know) ▬ [1] Emma Gordon? → **A** Do you know Emma Gordon?
B No, ▬ [2]. I (not know) ▬ [3] her. → **B** No, I don't. I don't know her.

1 **A** (you/speak) ▬ [1] English?
B Yes, ▬ [2]. But I (not use) ▬ [3] it very often.

2 **A** (your friend Mike / have) ___[1] a car?
B No, ___[2]. But he (have) ___[3] a motorbike.
3 **A** (English people / watch) ___[1] German films?
B No, ___[2]. They (not watch) ___[3] many non-British or non-American films.
4 **A** (your coffee / taste) ___[1] good?
B Yes, ___[2]. It (taste) ___[3] bitter, I like that.

2 Complete the sentences with present progressive forms of the verbs in brackets.

1 **A** What (you/do) ___[1] at the moment? (you/work) ___[2]?
B No, ___[3]. I (check) ___[4] my Facebook page.
2 **A** What language (that woman / speak) ___[1]? (she/speak) ___[2] Spanish?
B No, ___[3]. She (speak) ___[4] Portuguese.
3 **A** Sorry, (I/phone) ___[1] in the middle of your meal?
B No, ___[2]. We (not eat) ___[3] at the moment.
4 **A** (Dennis/come) ___[1] with us to the Swimarena this afternoon?
B Yes, ___[2]. He (come) ___[3] on his moped.

3 Complete the sentences with the correct simple present or present progressive forms of the verbs in brackets.

1 I (try out) ___[1] a new provider. I (think) ___[2] it's better than my old one.
2 Where (you/come) ___ from? Are you Canadian?
3 What (Manuela/do) ___ ? Is she a radio journalist too?
4 What (Manuela/do) ___[1] today? (she/interview) ___[2] Kelly Green?
5 Tunisia is a hot country. It (not rain) ___ much.
6 Oh no! It (rain) ___ . We can forget our barbecue.

SIMPLE PAST ▪ PAST PROGRESSIVE

Form

	Simple past	Past progressive
Aussage	I/you/he/she/it/we/they **played**	I/he/she/it **was playing** you/we/they **were playing**
Verneinung	I/you/he/she/it/we/they **didn't play**	I/he/she/it **wasn't playing** you/we/they **weren't playing**
Frage + Kurzantwort	**Did** I/you/he/she/it/we/they **play**? ▪ Yes, I / … **did**. / ▪ No, I / … **didn't.**	**Was** I/he/she/it **playing**? ▪ Yes, I/he/she/it **was**. ▪ No, I/he/she/it **wasn't**. **Were** you/we/they **playing**? ▪ Yes, you/we/they **were**. ▪ No, you/we/they **weren't**.

Simple past

- Wenn ein regelmäßiges Verb auf *e* endet, hängt man nur *d* an (*hope – hoped*).
- Bei einem einsilbigen Verb, das auf einen einzelnen Vokal + einzelnen Konsonanten endet, verdoppelt man den Konsonanten: *stop – sto**pp**ed*, *plan – pla**nn**ed*.
- **!** Unregelmäßige Verben haben eigene Formen – s. Liste auf S. 349.

- Frage und Verneinung bildet man in allen Personen mit *did/didn't*. Das Verb steht dann in der Grundform und hat keine *(e)d* -Endung.

Gebrauch

Simple past	Past progressive
Last year I **was** in London on my birthday.	I **was staying** with an English family.
I **didn't see** my boyfriend last week.	He **was doing** a work placement project.
Why **did** the computer **crash**?	Nobody **was using** it.

- Mit dem **simple past** beschreibt man etwas, das in der Vergangenheit zu einem bestimmten Zeitpunkt oder in einem bestimmten Zeitraum geschehen ist.
- Mit dem **past progressive** beschreibt man etwas, das in der Vergangenheit zu einem bestimmten Zeitpunkt gerade im Gange war. Das kann auch eine vorübergehende Tätigkeit sein, die mit Unterbrechungen über eine gewisse Zeit ausgeübt wurde.

Was sonst noch wichtig ist

- Mit dem **past progressive** beschreibt man einen länger andauernden Vorgang, der durch ein Ereignis von kurzer Dauer unterbrochen wird. Dieses kurze Ereignis steht im **simple past.**
  I ***was checking*** *my newsfeed when an SMS from Julie* ***arrived****.*
  We ***were walking*** *home when Martina* ***passed*** *us on her moped.*

- ! Bestimmte Verben kann man nicht im **past progressive**, sondern nur im **simple past** verwenden.

need, want, like, love, hate, prefer, know, think, remember, understand, believe, realize, seem, mean, belong to

1 Complete the sentences with simple past forms of the verbs in brackets.

1 **A** (you/make) ___[1] a pizza at the weekend?
B No,I (not do) ___[2]. I (buy) ___[3] one.
2 **A** When (you/speak) ___[1] to your friend in England last?
B I (skype) ___[2] with her last weekend.
3 **A** (your brother/go) ___[1] to Zurich by plane?
B No, he (not do) ___[2]. He (not fly) ___[3]. He (go) ___[4] by car. He (drive) ___[5] there.
4 **A** Why (you/not come) ___[1] to Amy's party last weekend?
B I (not feel) ___[2] good. I (spend) ___[3] the whole day in bed.

2 Complete the sentences with past progressive forms of the verbs in brackets.

1 **A** You were on the phone. Who (you/speak) ___[1] to? (you/talk) ___[2] to that Susie again?
B No, I (not talk) ___[3] to another girl. I (check) ___[4] something with my mum.
2 **A** Where (you/sit) ___[1] at the concert?
B I (not sit) ___[2]. I (stand) ___[3] because there weren't any seats left.
3 **A** What (Mark/do) ___[1] out in the cold?
B He (wait) ___[2] for his brother.
4 **A** (you/ have) ___[1] a good time when I saw you?
B No, I was really bored. Nothing (happen) ___[2].

3 In each sentence there is one simple past and one past progressive form. Complete the sentences with the correct forms of the verbs in brackets.

1 I (answer) ___[1] the last question in the test when the teacher (tell) ___[2] us to stop.
2 Where (you/go) ___[1] when I (see) ___[2] you yesterday?
3 At 8.30 yesterday evening? I (be) ___[1] at home, I (play) ___[2] a computer game.
4 My friends and I (just leave) ___[1] when it (start) ___[2] to rain.
5 It (not rain) ___[1] when I (get) ___[2] on the bus.
6 It was a cold day. Samira (not want) ___[1] a cold drink so she (drink) ___[2] coffee.

PRESENT PERFECT ▪ PRESENT PERFECT PROGRESSIVE

Form

	Present perfect	Present perfect progressive
Aussage	I/you/we/they **have played** he/she/it **has played**	I/you/we/they **have been playing** he/she/it **has been playing**
Verneinung	I/you/we/they **haven't played** he/she/it **hasn't played**	I/you/we/they **haven't been playing** he/she/it **hasn't been playing**
Frage + Kurzantwort	**Have** I/you/we/they **played**? ▪ Yes, I/you/we/they **have**. ▪ No, I/you/we/they **haven't**. **Has** he/she/it **played**? ▪ Yes, he/she/it **has**. ▪ No, he/she/it **hasn't**.	**Have** I/you/we/they **been playing**? ▪ Yes, I/you/we/they **have**. ▪ No, I/you/we/they **haven't**. **Has** he/she/it **been playing**? ▪ Yes, he/she/it **has**. ▪ No, he/she/it **hasn't**.

Present perfect

- Bei regelmäßigen Verben hat das Partizip die gleiche Form wie im **simple past**. Es gelten die gleichen Schreibbesonderheiten (s. S. 251).
- **!** Das Partizip unregelmäßiger Verben hat eine eigene Form – s. Liste auf S. 349. Es ist manchmal identisch mit dem **simple past**, manchmal aber nicht.

Gebrauch

Present perfect	Present perfect progressive
We**'ve finished** the test.	We**'ve been working** non-stop.
I **haven't had** this phone long.	I**'ve been using** my friend's phone.
Has the rain **stopped**?	How long **has** it **been raining**?

- Mit dem **present perfect** sagt man, dass etwas geschehen ist.
- Mit dem **present perfect progressive** sagt man, dass etwas eine Zeit lang bis jetzt angedauert hat.
- Beim **present perfect** steht oft ein Ergebnis im Vordergrund, während beim **present perfect progressive** das Andauern betont wird.
- **!** Bestimmte Verben kann man nicht im **progressive** verwenden.

need, want, like, love, hate, prefer, know, think, remember, understand, believe, realize, seem, mean, belong to

Was sonst noch wichtig ist

- **!** Wenn etwas in der Vergangenheit angefangen hat und bis jetzt andauert, verwendet man das **present perfect (progressive)** – nicht, wie im Deutschen, eine Gegenwartsform.
  *I'**ve lived** / I'**ve been living** here **for** five years. (I ~~live~~ here for …)*
  *We'**ve sat** / We'**ve been sitting** here **since** half past one / **since** it started to rain.*
  (We ~~sit~~ here since …)

- *For* + Zeitraum (*five years, a few days*) – Antwort auf die Frage „wie lange?"
  Since + Zeitpunkt (*2012, Sunday*) – Antwort auf die Frage „seit wann?"
  *I haven't seen Jenny **for** a few days. Is she ill?*
  *I haven't seen her **since** Sunday / **since** we played tennis together.*

1 Complete the sentences with present perfect forms of the verbs in brackets.

1 I (see) ▬[1] the new movie. (you/see) ▬[2] it?
2 Susanne (make) ▬ copies for everyone.
3 My visa (not arrive) ▬[1]. (yours/arrive) ▬[2]?
4 We (not meet) ▬[1] before. But I (hear) ▬[2] a lot about you.
5 (you/have) ▬[1] lunch? I (not eat) ▬[2].

2 Complete the sentences with present perfect progressive forms of the verbs in brackets.

1 I (wait) ▬[1] a long time. I (play) ▬[2] a computer game to help pass the time.
2 They (talk) ▬[1] all evening. They (discuss) ▬[2] the new project.
3 How long (you/work) ▬ on your presentation?
4 How long (it/snow) ▬ ?
5 We (not chat) ▬[1], we (work) ▬[2] hard!

3 Decide whether you should use *for* or *since* with the following expressions.

1 eighteen months
2 a year and a half
3 Tuesday morning
4 last January
5 two seconds
6 ages
7 2009
8 Christmas

4 Correct these sentences. Use the present perfect.

1 ~~I live here for six years.~~
2 ~~We know each other for a long time.~~
3 ~~Marina is ill all this week.~~
4 ~~We have this computer for years.~~
5 ~~How long are you a member of this club?~~

SIMPLE PAST ▪ PRESENT PERFECT

Gebrauch

Present perfect	Simple past
I **have been** to London.	I **went** there *last year*.
We'**ve had** rain today. We'**ve** *just* **had** a shower.	*Yesterday* it **rained** all afternoon.
Have you **seen** this film *before*?	I **saw** it *last month* with Jack.
Has Mark **phoned** *yet*? – Yes, he **has**.	*When* **did** he **phone**? – He **called** *half an hour ago*.

- Mit dem **present perfect** sagt man, dass etwas – irgendwann – in der Zeit bis jetzt geschehen ist, wann ist entweder unwichtig oder unbekannt. Man stellt nur fest, **dass** etwas geschehen ist. Wird der Zeitpunkt genannt, darf man das **present perfect nicht** verwenden.
- Das **simple past** wird verwendet, wenn etwas in der Vergangenheit zu einem bestimmten Zeitpunkt oder in einem bestimmten Zeitraum geschehen ist und dieser Zeitpunkt/Zeitraum genannt wird.

Was sonst noch wichtig ist

- Das **present perfect** und **simple past** verwendet man mit typischen Zeitangaben.

Present perfect	Simple past
ein unbestimmter Zeitpunkt in der ganzen Zeit bis jetzt	ein bestimmter Zeitpunkt oder Zeitraum der abgeschlossenen Vergangenheit
already, (not) yet, before, so far, ever, never, just	yesterday, last week/month/year, … ago, when? what time? in 2013, on 13 October, in February

- Vor allem im amerikanischen Englisch werden *already, (not) yet, ever, never* und *just* auch mit dem **simple past** verwendet.
- Wenn man etwas erzählt, verwendet man manchmal beide Zeitformen im gleichen Zusammenhang. Zuerst berichtet man mit dem **present perfect** die „nackte" Neuigkeit, anschließend nennt man weitere Einzelheiten (einschl. des Zeitpunkts) mit dem **simple past**.
  *Ron **has broken** his leg. He **had** an accident on his moped **yesterday on his way home**.*
  *I**'ve heard** from Maria. She **sent** me an SMS **10 minutes ago**.*
- Auch wenn kein Zeitpunkt genannt wird, muss man das **simple past** verwenden, wenn etwas zu einem ganz bestimmten Zeitpunkt geschehen sein muss.
  *The team **didn't win** any medals at the London Olympics.*
  [Die Olympiade in London fand zu einem bestimmten Zeitpunkt der Vergangenheit statt.]
- Das **present perfect** verwendet man oft, wenn etwas Auswirkungen auf die Gegenwart hat.
  *I**'ve been** to London. (= Ich kenne London.)*
  *They**'ve put** the prices up 20%. (= Es ist zu teuer geworden. Diese Preise will ich nicht zahlen.)*

1 Make dialogues as in the example.

EXAMPLES:
A (you/ever/watch) ▬[1] an international football match live?
B Yes, I ▬[2] . I (see) ▬[3] Germany against Denmark last year.
A Have you ever watched an international football match live?
B Yes, I have. I saw Germany against Denmark last year.

1 **A** (you/ever/meet) ▬[1] a celebrity?
B No,I ▬[2]. But I (see) ▬[3] a B-list celebrity in Berlin last month.
2 **A** (you/make) ▬[1] notes for the summary task yet?
B No, I ▬[2]. But I (read) ▬[3] the text again last night.
3 **A** (you/ever/have) ▬[1] an accident?
B No, I ▬[2]. But my brother (break) ▬[3] his leg on a skiing trip in January.
4 **A** (you/buy) ▬[1] your new bike yet?
B Yes, I ▬[2]. I (find) ▬[3] a great offer on the internet.

2 Complete the sentences with the correct verb form: present perfect or simple past.

1 Last year I (take) ▬ a trip to Ireland.
2 I (be) ▬ there twice now.
3 I (make) ▬ good friends when I was there. We chat nearly every week.
4 Last time I (fly) ▬ with a new airline.
5 Flying (become) ▬ very cheap over the years.
6 The first time I (go) ▬[1] to Ireland it (cost) ▬[2] a lot of money.

PAST PERFECT ▪ SIMPLE PAST

Form des past perfect

Aussage	I/you/we/they/he/she/it **had played**
Verneinung	I/you/we/they/he/she/it **hadn't played**
Frage + Kurzantwort	**Had** I/you/we/they/he/she/it **played**? ▪ Yes, I/you/we/they/he/she/it **had**. ▪ No, I/you/we/they/he/she/it **hadn't**.

- Das **past perfect** bildet man in allen Personen gleich, mit *had* + Partizip Perfekt.

Gebrauch des past perfect

I got to the station two minutes late and the train **had** already **left**.
At four o'clock in the afternoon I still **hadn't eaten** anything.

- Mit dem **past perfect** sagt man, dass etwas zu einem Zeitpunkt in der Vergangenheit bereits geschehen und abgeschlossen war.

Unterschied zum simple past

- Wenn man z. B. eine Geschichte erzählt und es zwei oder mehr Geschehnisse gab, die miteinander in einem Zusammenhang standen, verwendet man das **simple past**.
  *The plane **landed**, we **got off**, **collected** our bags and **went** to the car park.*
- Wenn es wichtig ist, auszudrücken, dass sich ein Geschehen vor einem anderen ereignet hatte, verwendet man für das zeitlich erste Geschehen das **past perfect**.
  *I **wanted** to phone my girlfriend, but **couldn't** find my phone. **I'd left** it on the plane!*
- Nach *after*, *before*, *until* und *as soon as* kann entweder das **simple past** oder das **past perfect** stehen.
  *After I **arrived / had arrived** home, I called the airline.*
- ! *'d* kann für *had*, aber auch für *would* stehen.
  *At my grandma's 70th birthday there was loads to eat. After two platefuls I**'d (I had)** eaten enough but my boyfriend said, "I**'d (I would)** like some more, please."*

1 Which happened first, A or B?

	A	B
1	We went out	after it had stopped raining.
2	I was short of cash	because I had spent so much on presents.
3	Jack had already arrived	when I got there.
4	The policewoman explained to me	what had happened.
5	There I was at the bank	and I had left my wallet at home.

2 In each sentence there is one verb in the simple past and one in the past perfect. Complete the sentences with the correct forms.

1 The road (be) ▬[1] blocked. There (be) ▬[2] an accident.
2 We (not drive) ▬[1] far, when a warning light (come) ▬[2] on.
3 I (run) ▬[1], but the flight (close) ▬[2].
4 I (not remember) ▬[1] the man, although I (meet) ▬[2] him the year before.
5 Meg (invite) ▬[1] Tony to her party, but he (already make) ▬[2] other plans.

WILL FUTURE ▪ *GOING TO* FUTURE

Form

	will	*going to*
Aussage	I/you/we/they/he/she/it **will play**	I **am going to play** you/we/they **are going to play** he/she/it **is going to play**
Verneinung	I/you/we/they/he/she/it **won't play**	I**'m not going to play** you/we/they **aren't going to play** he/she/it **isn't going to play**
Frage + Kurzantwort	**Will** I/you/we/they/he/she/it **play**? ▪ Yes, I/you/we/they/he/she/it **will**. ▪ No I/you/we/they/he/she/it **won't**.	**Am/Are/Is … going to play?** ▪ Yes, … **am/are/is**. ▪ No, … am **not/aren't/isn't**.

- Die Verneinung von *will* heißt *won't*. *Won't* ist die Kurzform von *will not*. Die Kurzform von *will* ist *'ll*.

Gebrauch

will	*going to*
We **will know** the result of the casting show soon.	I've decided. I'm never **going to take part** in a casting show.
I**'ll** perhaps/probably **be** late home tonight.	All the class **is going to meet** up at Jogi's.
I think / am sure you**'ll get** the job.	Who **is going to drive** you to the interview?

- Es gibt keine wirklich feste Regel, wann *will* und wann *going to* verwendet wird. In manchen Kontexten sind sie austauschbar. Als Faustregel gilt:
  – wenn man eine Vorhersage ausdrückt, verwendet man *will;*
  – wenn man eine Absicht, einen Plan oder ein Vorhaben ausdrückt, verwendet man *going to*.
- Nach Ausdrücken wie *I think*, *I promise*, *I hope*, *I'm sure*, *I expect* wird häufig *will* verwendet. *Going to* ist aber oft auch möglich.

Was sonst noch wichtig ist

- Um einen spontanen Entschluss (oft ein Angebot) auszudrücken, verwendet man *will*. Eine Gegenwartsform ist nicht möglich:
  *That bag looks heavy. Let me help you. I'**ll carry** it for you.* [Nicht: ~~*I carry it for you.*~~]
  *Tea or coffee for you? – Oh I **won't have** anything to drink, thanks.* [Nicht: ~~*I don't have …*~~]
- Beachten Sie den Unterschied zwischen einem spontanen und einem vorüberlegten Entschluss:
  *Someone is at the door. – OK, I'**ll see** who it is.* [spontan]
  *Susie has bought cinema tickets for this evening. We'**re going to see** a new movie.* [vorüberlegt]
- *Going to* verwendet man auch für Vorhersagen, wenn man aufgrund von eindeutigen Vorzeichen sagen kann, dass etwas mit Bestimmtheit eintreten wird:
  *Look at that car! It's far too fast. Oh no! It'**s going to crash**. There'**s going to be** an accident.*
- Mit *going to* macht man auch Vorhersagen aufgrund von persönlichen Annahmen. Man ist überzeugt, dass etwas mit Bestimmtheit eintreten wird:
  *Oil **is going to become** more and more expensive.*
  *When the exam results come out, some of us **are going to be** disappointed.*
- Man kann auch das **present progressive** für zukünftige Vorhaben verwenden, wenn Vorkehrungen oder Abmachungen bereits getroffen wurden oder jemand eine bestimmte Zeiteinteilung für sich vorgenommen hat:
  *I'**m meeting** Sam this evening. We'**re going** to the cinema.*
  *Susan **is flying** to London next week.*

1 Complete the sentences with *will/won't*.

1 Holidays on the moon (not happen) ▬ in my lifetime.
2 Sorry, but there (not be) ▬ enough time for a visit to Disneyland.
3 Why (there / not be) ▬ enough time?
4 When (we / find out) ▬ what the cost is going to be?
5 Next year is our anniversary. This school (be) ▬ 25 years old.

2 Complete the sentences with *going to*.

1 We've got so many interesting things planned. The project week (be) ▬ a big success.
2 I (ask) ▬ Tom if he can help me with this maths homework.
3 (the police officer / arrest) ▬ that man?
4 We don't need a hotel. We (stay) ▬ with friends.
5 This is a really difficult task. It (not be) ▬ easy.

3 Complete the translation.

1	Du musst uns nicht fahren. Wir nehmen ein Taxi.	You don't have to drive us. We ▬ a taxi.
2	Ich helfe Ihnen mit Ihrer Tasche.	I ▬ you with your bag.
3	Ich hole dir ein Pflaster.	I ▬ you a plaster.
4	Wir nehmen eine große Pizza und zwei Cola bitte.	We ▬ a pizza and two colas, please.
5	Lass mal, ich bezahle.	Leave it to me, I ▬ .

MODAL VERBS

Verben und ihre Bedeutung

can	Keith **can** come any time.	*können*
may	I'm not sure, but we **may** be late.	*werden/können (vielleicht)*
might	Don **might** have €50 he can lend us.	*könnte(n) (vielleicht)*
must	We **must** warn Mark.	*müssen*
should	They **should** be more careful.	*sollte(n)*
ought to	I **ought to** phone my mum.	*sollte(n)*
be allowed to	**Are** we **allowed to** take photos?	*dürfen*

can, could, was/were able to

Gegenwart	I **can** see you.
Vergangenheit ▪ generelle Fähigkeit ▪ bestimmte Einzelsituation	 I **could** swim at the age of six. I **was able to** catch the last bus.

- Nur *was/were able to* ist möglich, wenn man sagt, was jemandem in einer Einzelsituation in der Vergangenheit gelang. In Fragen und verneinten Sätzen kann man aber auch *could(n't)* verwenden:
  ***Were you able to** see / **Could** you see who was driving?*
  *There were so many people in the room. I **wasn't able to** move / **couldn't** move.*
- Nur Formen von *be able to* sind im **present perfect** möglich:
  *I **haven't been able to** contact Martina yet.*
- Man kann entweder *can* oder *will be able to* verwenden, wenn man über die Zukunft spricht.
  *Shaun **can** come / **will be able to** come this evening.*
  *I haven't got the money with me now, but I **can** pay / **will be able to** pay you tomorrow.*

must, mustn't, needn't, don't/doesn't have to, had to

Gegenwart ▪ Aussage ▪ Verneinung ▪ Frage	 We **must** meet more often. I **mustn't** forget Julia's birthday. You **don't have to** wait for me. You **needn't** wait for me. How many tests **do** you **have to** do?	 *wir müssen* *ich darf nicht* *du musst nicht* *du musst/brauchst nicht* *müssen Sie?*
Vergangenheit ▪ Aussage ▪ Verneinung ▪ Frage	 I **had to** work late yesterday evening. Nina **didn't have to** read her text aloud. How much extra **did** you **have to** pay?	 *ich musste* *Nina musste nicht* *musstet ihr?*

- **!** *mustn't* ist ein Verbot und entspricht „nicht dürfen“. „nicht müssen“ drückt man mit *don't/doesn't have to* aus.
- Fragen und verneinte Sätze mit *have to* bildet man mit dem Hilfsverb *do*.

Was sonst noch wichtig ist

- *can* drückt aus, dass etwas generell möglich ist:
  *It **can** be very wet in November.*
- *can* kann man nicht verwenden, wenn man ausdrücken will, dass etwas möglicherweise der Fall ist:
  *We **may** / **might** / **could** be late. It depends on the traffic.* [Nicht: ~~*We can be late.*~~]
- *can't* und *couldn't* kann man nicht verwenden, wenn man ausdrücken will, dass etwas möglicherweise nicht der Fall ist:
  *The weather's awful. The flight **may** / **might not** go today.* [Nicht: ~~*The flight can't / couldn't go.*~~]

1 Decide if the underlined verb is correct. Correct the incorrect sentences.

1 I'm sorry, I can't help you today.
2 I can forgive him now. But a couple of months ago I couldn't.
3 I had to hurry, but I could get the train.
4 It was foggy and the plane couldn't land.
5 I could speak to the teacher before the test.
6 I haven't been able to reach him. Perhaps he is on holiday.

2 Decide if A or B is right.

1 I **A** mustn't / **B** don't have to forget to pay for the concert tickets.
2 You **A** mustn't / **B** don't have to come if you don't want to.
3 When was your flight? **A** Must you / **B** Did you have to get up very early?
4 You **A** mustn't / **B** needn't forget your passport.
5 We **A** needn't / **B** mustn't check in till 40 minutes before the flight.
6 He **A** mustn't / **B** needn't park there. That's the teachers' car park.

3 Decide which of the sentences are not correct.

1 **A** The problem may have something to do with the battery.
B The problem might have something to do with the battery.
C The problem could have something to do with the battery.

2 **A** The train may be late this morning.
B The train can be late this morning.
C The train might be late this morning.

3 **A** Sue could be trying to skype me. I'll switch the computer on.
B Sue can be trying to skype me. I'll switch the computer on.
C Sue might be trying to skype me. I'll switch the computer on.

4 **A** Ask Jerry. He can know.
B Ask Jerry. He could know.
C Ask Jerry. He might know.

THE PASSIVE

Form

	Aktiv	Passiv
Simple present	I **stop** you/we/they **stop** he/she/it **stops**	I **am stopped** you/we/they **are stopped** he/she/it **is stopped**
Simple past	I/he/she/it **stopped** you/we/they **stopped**	I/he/she/it **was stopped** you/we/they **were stopped**
Present perfect	I/you/we/they **have stopped** he/she/it **has stopped**	I/you/we/they **have been stopped** he/she/it **has been stopped**
Past perfect	I/you/we/they/he/she/it **had stopped**	I/you/we/they/he/she/it **had been stopped**
Futur mit *will*	I/you/we/they/he/she/it **will stop**	I/you/we/they/he/she/it **will be stopped**

- *be* + Partizip (z. B. *be stopped*) ist der Passivinfinitiv. Diese Form verwendet man nach *will* und *going to* und auch nach Modalverben wie *can, must, might, could*:
  *This law **must be stopped**.*

Gebrauch

Aktiv	Passiv
People **speak** English in South Africa.	English **is spoken** in South Africa.
Someone **stole** my phone.	My phone **was stolen**.
My mum **drove** us to the airport.	We **were driven** to the airport **by** my mum.
Police **fired** shots to control the protesters.	Shots **were fired**.

- In einem Aktivsatz sagen wir, was jemand aktiv tut. In einem Passivsatz sagen wir, was getan wird.
- Das Passiv wird verwendet, wenn es unwichtig/unbekannt ist, von wem etwas getan wird.
- In den meisten Passivsätzen wird die Person nicht genannt. Wenn sie doch genannt wird, fügt man sie mit *by* an (nicht *from!*):
  *In the film the policeman was played **by** Tom Hanks.* [Nicht: ~~*from Tom Hanks*~~]
- Das Passiv wird viel in Medienberichten und technischen Beschreibungen verwendet, weil es neutraler klingt:
  *The President **will be welcomed** to Britain by the Prime Minister.*
  *The machine **can be operated** in energy-saving mode.*
- Manchmal verwenden Politiker/innen, Journalist/innen und Autor/innen bewusst das Passiv, um sich von dem zu distanzieren, was sie erzählen, um „offizieller" zu wirken:
  *Hard-working families in this country tell me that too much **is being paid** to the unemployed.*

Was sonst noch wichtig ist

- Die Passivform von den **progressive tenses** wird mit *being* + Partizip gebildet:
  *A new hotel **is being built**.*
  *At the flea market all sorts of things **were being bought** and **sold**.*

- In einem Passivsatz wird das Objekt eines Aktivsatzes zum Subjekt:

Subjekt	Verb	Objekt
People in Italy	*eat*	***more fruit.***
More fruit	*is eaten.*	

- Im Gegensatz zum Deutschen kann im Englischen auch ein indirektes Objekt zum Subjekt eines Passivsatzes werden:

Subjekt	Verb	indirektes Objekt	direktes Objekt
Journalists	*asked*	***the President***	*a lot of questions.*
The President	*was asked*		*a lot of questions.*

Zu den Verben, bei denen dieses Satzmuster möglich ist, zählen:

ask, buy, give, offer, pay, promise, sell, send, show, tell

1 Complete the sentences with passive forms of the verbs in brackets. Be careful of the tenses.

1 When we got to the house, it was clear that we (not expect) ■■ .
2 The hotel (sell) ■■ to a Russian company last January.
3 Whenever someone enters the building at night, the alarm (activate) ■■ by the CCTV system.
4 The windows (not clean) ■■ very often. The window cleaner comes twice a year.
5 Mr Thomas's talk will last 20 minutes. Questions (can ask) ■■ at the end.
6 All windows (must close) ■■ at the end of the day.
7 I warn you: if anything like this happens again, the police (inform) ■■ .
8 The text is perfect now. All the mistakes (correct) ■■ .

2 Say the same thing in the passive.

EXAMPLES:	They quickly introduced new technology.	New technology was quickly introduced.
	Nobody gave me an invitation.	I wasn't given an invitation.
1	Someone has stolen my mobile phone!	My mobile phone ■■ !
2	They paid him €500.	He ■■ .
3	Make sure that someone writes all this down.	Make sure that all this ■■ .
4	Has anyone asked you to help?	■■ you ■■ to help?
5	Somebody showed me how to operate the new system.	I ■■ how to operate the new system.
6	They've offered Tony the position.	Tony ■■ .

VERB + INFINITIVE ▪ VERB + GERUND

Gebrauch

Verb + Infinitiv	Verb + Gerundium (*ing*-Form)
I **wanted to** meet up with Mike and **managed to** organise it.	I **suggest** going by train.
We **can't afford** to wait much longer.	Sandra **avoided** talking to Matthew at the party.

Viele Verben, u. a. folgende:	
afford (*sich leisten*)	hope (*hoffen*)
choose (*wählen*)	learn (*lernen*)
decide (*sich entscheiden*)	manage (*es schaffen*)
demand (*verlangen*)	offer (*anbieten*)
encourage (*ermuntern*)	plan (*planen*)
expect (*erwarten*)	promise (*versprechen*)
hesitate (*zögern*)	refuse (*sich weigern*)
	seem (*scheinen*)
	threaten (*drohen*)

Wenige Verben, v. a. folgende:	
avoid (*vermeiden*)	(not) mind (*etwas/nichts dagegen haben*)
dislike (*ungern tun*)	miss (*vermissen*)
enjoy (*gern tun*)	practise (*üben*)
finish (*zu Ende bringen*)	recommend (*empfehlen*)
give up (*aufgeben*)	risk (*riskieren*)
imagine (*sich vorstellen*)	suggest (*vorschlagen*)
involve (*mit sich bringen*)	

Was sonst noch wichtig ist

- Auf bestimmte Verben kann ohne Bedeutungsunterschied ein Infinitiv oder eine *ing*-Form folgen: *like, love, hate, prefer, continue.*

- Einige Verben haben aber unterschiedliche Bedeutungen, je nachdem ob ein Gerundium oder ein Infinitiv folgt:
  z. B. *remember to do sth* = daran denken, etwas zu tun
  (*Please remember to learn your vocabulary.*)
  remember doing sth = sich erinnern, etwas getan zu haben
  (*I remember learning about gerunds at school.*)
  stop to do sth = anhalten, um etw (Anderes) zu tun
  (*Shall we stop to buy some food at this supermarket?*)
  stop doing sth = aufhören, etwas zu tun
  (*I've stopped eating chocolate because it's unhealthy.*)

- ! Beachten Sie: *like* + Infinitiv oder *ing*-Form, *dislike* nur + *ing*-Form, ***would*** *like/love/hate/prefer* nur + Infinitiv.

- Verben, die auf eine Präposition folgen, stehen als Gerundium.
  Jane is responsible ***for sending*** *all our letters.*
  I decided ***against going*** *to the party.*

- Eine *ing*-Form kann auch Subjekt in einem Satz sein:
  *Travell****ing*** *can be hard.*

- Die *ing*-Form kann auch ein eigenes Objekt haben:
  *Travell****ing*** *long distances can be hard.*

1 Complete the sentences with the infinitive or gerund of the verb in brackets.

1. After half an hour I gave up (wait) ▬ .
2. I refuse (give) ▬ this matter anymore of my time!
3. I don't mind (show) ▬ you around.
4. They threatened (call) ▬ the police.
5. We must avoid (make) ▬ the same mistake again.
6. I'd like (stay) ▬ at home.
7. Why did you give up (walk) ▬ to school?
8. Rachel seems (need) ▬ some help.

IF SENTENCES

Einleitung

In einem *if*-Satz wird gesagt, was unter bestimmten Voraussetzungen geschehen wird, geschehen würde oder geschehen wäre. Solche Sätze bestehen aus zwei Teilen. Der *if*-Teil nennt die Bedingung, der andere Teil nennt die Folge:

Bedingung	Folge
If the police find out, *Wenn die Polizei es herausbekommt,*	he'll be in trouble. *wird er Ärger bekommen.* [Das wird geschehen]
If I won a lot of money, *Wenn ich viel Geld gewinnen würde,*	I would buy a fast car. *würde ich mir ein schnelles Auto kaufen.* [Das würde geschehen]
If you had asked me, *Wenn du mich gefragt hättest,*	I would have helped you. *hätte ich dir geholfen.* [Das wäre geschehen]

Form

	If-Teil	Hauptsatz
Typ 1	**Simple present** If you **work** hard,	***will* future** you**'ll earn** a lot of money.
Typ 2	**Simple past** If I **wanted** an easy life,	***would* + Infinitive** **I'd marry** someone rich.
Typ 3	**Past perfect** If we **had taken** a taxi,	***would* + *have* + Past participle** we **wouldn't have missed** the flight.

- Anstelle von *will* kann auch ein Modalverb wie *can*, *might* oder *should* im Hauptsatz stehen.
  *If you work hard, you **can** earn a lot of money.*
  Anstelle von *would* kann ein Modalverb wie *could*, *might* oder *should* stehen.
  *If I wanted to earn more money, I **could** find a second job.*
- **!** *would* steht nie im *if*-Teil!
- *would* kann zu *'d* verkürzt werden. *'d* ist aber auch die Kurzform von *had*:
  *I**'d** have left (= I **would** have left) home earlier if I**'d** checked (= **had** checked) the times.*
- Wenn der *if*-Teil am Satzanfang steht, wird er meist mit einem Komma vom Hauptsatz getrennt. Der Hauptsatz kann auch zuerst stehen. Dann verwendet man meist kein Komma.
  If it rains today, I'll go shopping. ABER *I'll go shopping if it rains today.*
- Die Unterschiede zwischen den drei Typen hängen davon ab, wie wahrscheinlich es ist, dass die Bedingung erfüllt wird.

Gebrauch

Typ 1	Es ist gut möglich oder wahrscheinlich, dass die Bedingung erfüllt wird. *If it rains, we'll get wet.*
Typ 2	Es ist unmöglich oder unwahrscheinlich, dass die Bedingung erfüllt wird. *If I was five years old, I'd be in kindergarten.* [Ich bin aber nicht fünf Jahre alt, also ist die Bedingung unmöglich.] *If I became famous, I'd have a lot of money.* [Es ist aber unwahrscheinlich, dass ich berühmt werde.]

Typ 3	Es ist völlig unmöglich und absolut ausgeschlossen, dass die Bedingung erfüllt wird. *If Brad Pitt had been born a girl, would he have become famous?* [Er ist aber nicht als Mädchen geboren worden. Die Bedingung war nie Wirklichkeit und kann niemals erfüllt werden.]

- Sowohl mit Typ 2 als auch mit Typ 3 wird über etwas spekuliert:

Typ 2: was wäre, wenn …	Typ 3: was wäre gewesen, wenn …

- In Typ 2 steht das **simple past**. Es wird aber nicht über die Vergangenheit gesprochen.
- In Typ 3 wird über die Vergangenheit gesprochen.

1 In each sentence one verb is in the simple present, one verb in the future with *will*. Complete the sentences with the correct forms of the verbs in brackets.

1. If the packet (arrive) ___[1] by Friday, that (be) ___[2] OK.
2. If Manni (say) ___[1] that again, I (explode) ___[2]!
3. She (not understand) ___[1] you if you (not speak) ___[2] more slowly.
4. What (you/do) ___[1] if they (not offer) ___[2] you the job?
5. If we (not take) ___[1] a break soon, I (die) ___[2] of hunger.
6. If they (invite) ___[1] you, (you/go) ___[2]?

2 Complete the translation. All the sentences are type 2 conditional sentences.

1. Wenn ich Zeit hätte, würde ich Ihnen helfen.
   If I ___[1] time, I ___[2] you.
2. Wenn ich Max besser kennen würde, wüsste ich, wie ich ihm helfen könnte.
   If I ___[1] Max better, I ___[2] how to help him.
3. Wenn du Francesca fragen würdest, was würde sie sagen?
   If you ___[1] Francesca, what ___[2]?
4. Was würde passieren, wenn wir einfach nichts tun würden?
   What ___[1] if we simply ___[2] nothing?
5. Es wäre besser, wenn Sie später noch einmal anrufen könnten.
   It ___[1] better if you ___[2] again later.
6. Was tätest du, wenn die andere Firma mehr Geld bieten würde?
   What ___[1] if the other firm ___[2] more money?

3 Say the same thing with a conditional sentence type 3.

EXAMPLE: I didn't know about the meeting so I didn't come.
If I had known about the meeting, I would have come.

1. Jenny didn't hear about the job so she didn't apply. — If Jenny ___
2. They didn't have enough money so they didn't buy any souvenirs. — If they ___
3. I didn't have my mobile with me so I didn't call you. — If I ___

EXAMPLE: Jack had to work on Saturday. That's why he didn't come swimming with us.
If Jack hadn't had to work on Saturday, he would have come swimming with us.

4. I had my mobile with me. That's why I took photos. — If I ___
5. I stopped to talk to Martin. That's why I was late. — If I ___
6. They drove too fast. That's why they had an accident. — If they ___

INDIRECT SPEECH

Zeitverschiebung

Direkte Rede: Gegenwartsform von Vollverb oder Hilfsverb	Indirekte Rede: Vergangenheitsform von Vollverb oder Hilfsverb
▪ **Simple present:** *"I **know**."* *"Mark **doesn't** know."*	▪ **Simple past:** *She said (that) she **knew**.* *She said (that) Mark **didn't** know.*
▪ **Present progressive:** *"Ann **is** working."*	▪ **Past progressive:** *He said (that) Ann **was** working.*
▪ **Present perfect:** *"We **have** eaten."*	▪ **Past perfect:** *They said (that) they **had** eaten.*

- Wenn wir wörtliche Rede indirekt wiedergeben, gibt es eine Zeitverschiebung beim Verb. Im Englischen heißt diese Zeitverschiebung *backshifting*. Die Verbform wird um eine Stufe „nach hinten verschoben". Diese Verschiebung hat nichts mit der Zeit an sich zu tun, sondern drückt einen Perspektivenwechsel aus.
- Vergangenheitsformen von Voll- oder Hilfsverben bleiben in der indirekten Rede unverändert. Sie sind ja bereits „verschoben":
  "I met Tom in town." → *Susie said she met Tom in town.*
  "We had already eaten." → *They said they had already eaten.*
  Eine **simple past**-Form kann aber wahlweise in eine **past perfect**-Form „verschoben" werden.
- *can* und *will* werden zu *could* und *would* „verschoben"; *could*, *might* und *should* bleiben unverändert:
  *"I **can** come."* → *I said I **could** come.*
  *"You **will** soon find out."* → *I said they **would** soon find out.*

Fragen, Bitten und Befehle

Fragen	
"Is it raining?" "Do you speak French?" "Where is Tom?"	She asked **if/whether** it is/was raining. They asked me **if/whether** I speak/spoke French. They wanted to know where Tom is/was.
Bitten	
"Can you help me, please?" "Please don't tell my dad."	He **asked** me **to** help. She **asked** me **not to** tell her dad.
Befehle	
"Sit down." "Don't talk."	She **told** me **to** sit down. He **told** us **not to** talk.

- Wenn man eine wörtliche Frage umformuliert, in der *do/does/did* stand, erscheint *do/does/did* in der indirekten Rede nicht:
  *"**Does** Tom know?"* → *Susie wanted to know if/whether Tom **knows/knew**.*
  *"**Did** you win?"* → *He asked me if/whether we **won**.*

Was sonst noch wichtig ist

- Wenn mit einem Verb im **simple present** berichtet wird (hier unterstrichen), bleibt die Zeitform der direkten Rede grundsätzlich erhalten:

Direkte Rede	Indirekte Rede
"I **buy** a lot online."	Martina says (that) she **buys** a lot online.
"What **is** your address?"	They want to know what our address **is**.

- Auch wenn mit einem Verb im **simple past** berichtet wird, ist eine Zeitverschiebung nicht immer zwingend. Entscheidend ist, ob der Zeitraum vorbei ist, in dem die Aussage ursprünglich Gültigkeit hatte:
  Vor einem Fußballspiel sagt ein Trainer: *"We **will** win."*
  Nach Beendigung des Spiels wird berichtet: *The trainer **said** his team would win.*

  Wenn das Berichtete immer oder immer noch gültig ist, muss keine Zeitverschiebung erfolgen:
  Eine Physiklehrerin erzählt: *"Water **freezes** at zero."*
  Es wird später berichtet: *She told us that water **freezes** at zero.*

  Ann verspricht: *"When I meet Martin, I **will** ask him."*
  Solange Ann Martin nicht getroffen hat, kann berichtet werden: *Ann said she **will** ask Martin.*

- Weil Zeitverschiebung mit Perspektivenwechsel zu tun hat, wird sie oft bewusst gewählt, wenn man sich von dem, was man berichtet, distanzieren und zeigen will, dass man dessen Wahrheitsgehalt nicht garantiert:
  Ein Minister verspricht: *"We **won't** increase taxes."*
  Eine Zeitung berichtet: *The minister said the government **wouldn't** increase taxes.*

1 Complete the second sentence as in the example. Use backshifting.

EXAMPLE: "They won't agree." (They will accept the offer.)
→ But you said they would accept the offer.

1 "We can't get into the system." (We have the password.) — But you said ___
2 "I'm afraid I don't have time." (I'll discuss this with you today.) — But you said ___ with me ___
3 "I'm not going to the class meeting." (I don't want to miss it.) — But you said ___
4 "I'm too tired." (I'll go to the gym with you.) — But you said ___ with me.
5 "I don't know where to go." (I know the way.) — But you said you ___
6 "I believe Michael." (He is lying.) — But you said ___

2 Complete the second sentence as in the example. Use backshifting.

EXAMPLE: "Did anyone call while I was away?"
→ Tony wanted to know if anyone had called while he was away.

1 "Do you know the address?" → Penny asked me if I ___
2 "Please don't park there." → They asked me ___
3 "Who drives that red car?" → Someone wanted to know ___
4 "What did you do with all those spare copies?" → He wanted to know ___
5 "Who used the room last?" → He demanded to know ___
6 "Please wait outside." → They asked ___

PARTICIPLES

Form und Gebrauch

	Present participle (+*ing*)	Past participle (+ *ed*)
Nach *when, while, after, before*	**When/While/After/Before** surf**ing** the internet, I found some useful addresses.	
Anstelle eines Satzglieds mit *and* + Verb	The man helped us **and showed** us where to go. → The man helped us **showing** us where to go.	
Anstelle eines Relativsatzes mit Verb	Verb in der Gegenwart: Hydroponic farming is a new method **which is getting** a lot of attention. → Hydroponic farming is a new method **getting** a lot of attention.	Verb in der Vergangenheit oder im Passiv: Morton was the man **who people saw / who was seen** near the building. → Morton was the man **seen** near the building.

Was sonst noch wichtig ist

- Sätze mit Partizipien werden vor allem in der Schriftsprache verwendet. Mündlich sind sie auch möglich, klingen aber zeitweise gestelzt. In der gesprochenen Sprache verwendet man vorzugsweise Sätze mit Subjekt und Verb.

PRONOUNS AND POSSESSIVE ADJECTIVES

Form und Gebrauch

Subject pronouns		Object pronouns	Possessive adjectives
Wer?		*Wen? Wem?*	*Wessen?*
ich	I	me	my
du, Sie	you	you	your
er/sie/es	he/she/it	him/her/it	his/her/its
wir	we	us	our
ihr, Sie	you	you	your
sie	they	them	their

- Zwischen ‚mich' und ‚mir', ‚ihn' und ‚ihm', usw. macht man im Englischen keinen Unterschied. Es gibt jeweils nur eine Form.
- Die besitzanzeigenden Begleiter (*my, your, usw.*) verändern ihre Form nicht.

1 Which is the right word?

Mo and Jo are in a holiday hotel.

Mo *She / They*[1] is by the pool again.
Jo Who?
Mo Lil Martin, that sports celebrity. Can't you see *her / she*[2]?

Jo Is *she* / *they*[3] with *he* / *him*[4]? *Her* / *Their*[5] playboy.
Mo He isn't *her* / *their*[6] playboy. He's *her* / *she*[7] trainer. *They* / *Them*[8] are in *her* / *their*[9] usual place. *He's* / *His*[10] nice.
Jo I'm not interested in *they* / *them*[11]. Celebrities! Stop looking. This is *our* / *us*[12] holiday.
Mo I think *they're* / *their*[13] cool. Not like you. *Your* / *You're*[14] not cool. Why are *we* / *us*[15] still together? Look at *we* / *us*[16]. The non-cool pair of the year.

2 Complete the sentences with the correct translation of *sie/Sie*.

1. *Wer ist sie? Ist sie unsere neue Lehrerin?* — Who is ■ ? Is ■ our new teacher?
2. *Deine Schwester ist nett. Ich mag sie.* — Your sister is nice. I like ■ .
3. *Sind Sie Kanadier?* — Are ■ Canadian?
4. *Toni und Wally sind aus Memphis, sie sind Jazzmusiker.* — Toni and Wally are from Memphis, ■ are jazz musicians.
5. *Schön, Sie wiederzusehen.* — Nice to see ■ again.
6. *Meine Freundin lebt in London, ich besuche sie oft dort.* — My girlfriend lives in London, I often visit ■ there.

RELATIVE CLAUSES

Form und Gebrauch

A 'grade A' student is someone **who/that** is very good.

Stress is something **which/that** can affect people of all ages.

- Mit einem Relativsatz bestimmt man Personen oder Sachen näher.
- Relativsätze, die Personen genauer bestimmen, werden durch *who* oder *that* eingeleitet.
- Relativsätze, die Sachen genauer bestimmen, werden durch *which* oder *that* eingeleitet.

Was sonst noch wichtig ist

- In den Beispielsätzen oben ist das Relativpronomen *who/which/that* Subjekt des Relativsatzes. Danach folgt direkt das Verb.
- Ein Relativpronomen kann auch Objekt sein. Dann steht zwischen dem Relativpronomen und dem Verb ein anderes Pronomen oder ein Ausdruck mit einem Nomen (hier unterstrichen). Dieses Pronomen bzw. dieser Ausdruck ist Subjekt des Relativsatzes:
  *Sue is online a lot. Mike is a guy (**who/that**) she met online.*
  *Teen Times is a magazine (**which/that**) my friend Duke buys.*

  Wenn *who/which/that* Objekt ist, kann man es weglassen.
- *Who/which/that* kann Objekt eines Verbs sein, wie in den Beispielen eben, oder Objekt einer Präposition (z. B. *to*, *with*, *about*, *for*, *of*). Auch hier kann das Relativpronomen weggelassen werden. Die Präposition steht dabei meist am Satzende:
  *Mrs Waters was the name of the teacher (**who/that**) Carrie spoke to.*
  *Here's the web address (**which/that**) I was talking about.*

1 Decide if you can leave out the relative pronoun.

1. The person who wrote this handbook has done a very good job.
2. The youth hostel that we stayed in was not in the centre of the city.
3. The computer which I like best is too expensive.
4. I think there's someone over there who I've met before.
5. Anyone who wants to come with me, please let me know by Thursday afternoon.
6. What am I going to do now with all the copies that I made?

2 Correct the sentences – if there is a mistake.

EXAMPLES: *The text who you looked at yesterday has been changed. The text which/that …*
I know someone who knows the manager. [The sentence is correct.]

1. Who is the person who can best help me?
2. I know someone has a lot of experience.
3. The hotel we stayed in was called The Angler.
4. I've just had an email from the people who we met at that concert.
5. The person that signs the letter may not be the person wrote it.
6. What's the address of that firm that built that new hotel?

ADJECTIVES ▪ ADVERBS OF MANNER

Form und Gebrauch

Adjektiv	Adverb der Art und Weise
1. Ann is a **careful** driver. *Ann ist eine vorsichtige Autofahrerin.*	3. She drives **carefully**. *Sie fährt vorsichtig.*
2. Ann/She is **careful**. *Ann ist vorsichtig.*	4. She is **especially** careful in fog. *Sie ist besonders vorsichtig bei Nebel.*
	5. She doesn't drive **very** fast. *Sie fährt nicht besonders schnell.*
	6. She's **really** disciplined. *Sie ist wirklich diszipliniert.*

- Das fett gedruckte Wort ist ein Adjektiv oder Adverb. Das unterstrichene Wort ist das Bezugswort – das, worüber das Adjektiv/Adverb etwas aussagt.
- Ein Adjektiv beschreibt, wie jemand oder etwas ist. Es bezieht sich auf ein Nomen (z. B. *Ann*) oder Pronomen (z. B. *she*). Es steht vor einem Nomen (Satz 1) oder nach dem Verb *be* (Satz 2).
- Ein Adverb beschreibt oft, wie jemand etwas tut (z. B. *carefully*), und bezieht sich auf ein Verb (Satz 3).
- Ein Adverb kann aber auch ein anderes Wort verstärken oder abschwächen (z. B. *extremely, very, really*). Es bezieht sich dann auf ein Adjektiv (Satz 4), auf ein anderes Adverb (Satz 5) oder ein Partizip (Satz 6).

Was sonst noch wichtig ist

- Mit Adverbien der Art und Weise sagt man, wie etwas geschieht oder getan wird. Meist werden sie gebildet, indem man *ly* an das entsprechende Adjektiv anhängt:
*Mark is **quick**. He works **quickly**.*

- Beachten Sie diese Schreibbesonderheiten bei der Endung *ly*:

Adjektiv auf Konsonant + *y*: *y* wird zu *i*	The test is easy. I can do it eas**ily**.
Adjektiv auf *le*: *le* fällt weg	The weather is terrible. It's terrib**ly** cold.
Adjektiv auf *ic*: *al* wird eingefügt	It's automatic. It changes automati**cally**.

- ! Das zu *good* gehörige Adverb heißt *well*:
Tanja is a good tennis player. She plays ***well****.* [Nicht: ~~*She plays good.*~~]
- ! Einige wenige Adverbien der Art und Weise haben die gleiche Form wie das Adjektiv:
early, *late*, *fast*, *hard*.
- Nach bestimmten Verben verwendet man kein Adverb der Art und Weise, sondern ein Adjektiv.

Verben, die einen Zustand beschreiben	*seem, become, remain*
Verben, die eine Eigenschaft von etwas beschreiben. Man kann die Eigenschaft mit einem der fünf Sinne wahrnehmen.	*look* (nur in der Bedeutung „aussehen"), *sound* (sich anhören), *feel* (sich fühlen, sich anfühlen), *taste* (schmecken), *smell* (riechen)

1 Complete the dialogues with the adjective or adverb form of the words in brackets.

1 Please be ▬ . (careful)
2 Drive ▬ . (careful)
3 I like the idea. It sounds ▬ . (good)
4 You look ▬ . (nervous)
5 Why are you ▬ ? (nervous)
6 You play the piano very ▬ . (good)
7 My boss answered ▬ , 'I have no time for that now.' (angry)
8 Everything was so ▬ organized. (beautiful)

2 Say the same with the word in brackets.

EXAMPLE: She has a soft voice. (speak) → *She speaks softly.*

1 His question was not very polite. (ask) → He didn't ask ▬
2 Your German is very good. (speak German) → You ▬
3 She had a happy smile. (smile) → She ▬
4 It was a strange feeling. (feel) → I ▬
5 Maureen is a fast runner. (run) → Maureen ▬
6 We don't have regular meetings. (meet) → We ▬
7 Our guests were unexpected. (come) → Our guests ▬
8 Stuntmen and women have a dangerous life. (live) → They ▬

COMPARISON OF ADJECTIVES AND ADVERBS

Form

	Komparativ (1. Steigerungsstufe)	Superlativ (2. Steigerungsstufe)
Einsilbige Adjektive: *er/est* anhängen	Which brand is **cheaper**?	Which is **cheapest**?
Zweisilbige Adjektive auf Konsonanten + *y*: *y* wird zu *i*, *er/est* anhängen	Question 2 is **easier**.	Which is the **easiest** question?

Mehrsilbige Adjektive: *more/most* voranstellen	My job is **more interesting**.	Who has the **most interesting** job?
Adverbien formgleich mit Adjektiv: *er/est* anhängen	John drives **faster**.	Who drives **fastest**?
Adverbien auf *ly*: *more/most* voranstellen	Who works **most carefully**?	Who works **most carefully**?

- Wichtige Adjektive und Adverbien haben Sonderformen:

good/well	*better*	*best*
bad(ly)	*worse*	*worst*

- Zu den Adverbien, die mit dem entsprechenden Adjektiv formgleich sind, zählen: *early, late, fast, hard, long*
- Schreibbesonderheiten:
  - Adjektiv auf *e*: nur *r/st* anhängen (*nice – nicer – nicest*)
  - Adjektiv auf Einzelvokal + Einzelkonsonanten: Konsonanten verdoppeln (*big – bi**gg**er – bi**gg**est*).

Gebrauch

Gleichsetzung: *as … as*	I'm **as old as** Jenny. („*so alt wie*")
	I work **as hard as** everybody else. („*so hart wie*")
Ungleichsetzung: *er/more … than*	I'm **older than** Martina. („*älter als*")
	I work **more carefully than** Thomas. („*sorgfältiger als*")

- Nicht *as*, sondern *than* entspricht dem deutschen „als":
  „Ich bin älter **als** du" = *I am older* ***than*** *you.* (Nicht: ~~*I am older as you.*~~)

Was sonst noch wichtig ist

- Nach *as* und *than* steht ein Pronomen in der Objektform:
  Jürgen is as old as ***me****. Tanja's younger brother is taller than* ***her****.*

1 Make comparisons with the words in brackets.

EXAMPLE: In the summer I have a (long) longer working day than in the winter.

1 This is one of the (complicated) ___[1] systems I have ever had to use.
2 In a foreign language, reading is normally (easy) ___[1] ___[2] listening.
3 The old handbook was much (thin) ___[1] ___[2] this one.
4 I feel (bad) ___[1] ___[2] yesterday.
5 The tickets aren't (cheap) ___[1] ___[2] last year. They're (expensive) ___[3].

2 Complete the sentences with the comparative or superlative form of the adverb.

1 You have to work (hard) ___ .
2 The new member of the team is doing (good) ___ now that he's had some training.
3 Four companies suggested solutions, but the German company solved the problem (efficient) ___ .
4 My club is playing (bad) ___ than at any time this season.
5 The changes are happening (gradual) ___ than we expected.

POSITION OF ADVERBS OF TIME

Einleitung

- Wir unterscheiden zwischen Adverbien (ein Wort) und adverbialen Bestimmungen (mehr als ein Wort).
  *Ron **always** works hard.* [Adverb]
  *He works (1) **every day** (2) **from nine to six**.* [zwei adverbiale Bestimmungen]

- Grundsätzlich gibt es drei mögliche Stellungen für Adverbien und adverbiale Bestimmungen in einem englischen Satz.

Satzanfang	**Usually** I don't work on a Sunday.
Satzmitte	I don't **usually** work on a Sunday.
Satzende	I don't work on a Sunday **usually**.

- Viele Adverbien und adverbiale Bestimmungen können am Satzanfang oder -ende stehen. Dieser Sprachgebrauch unterscheidet sich wenig vom deutschen. Wichtige Unterschiede gibt es bei der Stellung in der Satzmitte.
- In der Satzmitte stehen Adverbien der Häufigkeit (*always, usually, normally, regularly, often, sometimes, never*) sowie kurze Adverbien wie *ever, just, now, soon, still, already*.
- Nicht in der Satzmitte, sondern am Satzende stehen *yesterday, today, again* sowie adverbiale Bestimmungen. Dazu gehören z. B. Bestimmungen mit *every, last, ago*, Uhr- und Tageszeiten:
  *I went swimming **today**.* [Nicht: ~~*I went today swimming.*~~]
  *They flew to Canada **last year**.* [Nicht: ~~*They flew last year to Canada.*~~]

Gebrauch

Stellung in der Satzmitte	
Vor einem Verb im **simple present** oder **simple past**	*I **never** smoke. He **quickly** said goodbye.*
Hinter einem Hilfsverb	*We don't **normally** drive. She has **never** asked.*
Hinter einer Form des Verbs *be*	*Anna is **always** happy. You weren't **often** here.*

- In den Beispielen ist das Adverb **fett** gedruckt, das Verb/Hilfsverb unterstrichen.

Was sonst noch wichtig ist

- **!** Ein Adverb oder eine adverbiale Bestimmung kann nicht zwischen einem Verb und seinem Objekt stehen!
  *We **always** take the bus.* [Nicht: ~~*We take always the bus.*~~]
  *Stan watches TV **in the evening**.* [Nicht: ~~*Stan watches in the evening TV.*~~]

Which position is right for the adverb / adverbial: A or B?

1. We **A** are **B** well prepared. (always)
2. I don't **A** drink **B** tea. (often)
3. We **A** make **B** mistakes. (never)
4. We **A** have **B** made a mistake. (never)
5. I've **A** seen this film **B**. (several times)
6. We've been **A** to San Francisco **B**. (once before)
7. This **A** happens to me **B**. (always)
8. The test doesn't **A** take **B** long. (usually)

COUNTABLE AND UNCOUNTABLE NOUNS

Einleitung

Nicht zählbare Nomen haben keine Mehrzahlform und man kann weder *a/an* noch eine Zahl davorsetzen:

zählbar *one book, two books, three books, etc.*

nicht zählbar *weather, money, traffic, etc.* [Nicht: ~~*a weather, two moneys, three traffics*~~]

Gebrauch

- Bestimmte Nomen sind im Deutschen zählbar, im Englischen aber nicht.

advice	*Rat, Ratschlag, Ratschläge*	housework	*Hausarbeit, Hausarbeiten*
bread	*Brot*	information	*Information, Informationen*
damage	*Schaden, Schäden*	knowledge	*Wissen, Kenntnisse*
equipment	*Ausrüstung, Geräte*	paper	*Papier, Zettel*
furniture	*Möbel*	progress	*Fortschritt, Fortschritte*
hair	*Haar, Haare*	proof	*Beweis, Beweise*
help	*Hilfe, Hilfen, Hilfestellungen*	toast	*Toast*
homework	*Hausaufgabe, Hausaufgaben*	work	*Arbeit, Arbeiten*

- Nicht zählbare Nomen verwendet man mit *this/that* und *much*. Das Verb nach einem nicht zählbaren Nomen steht immer im Singular:
  ***This information** is interesting.* (Diese Information ist / Diese Informationen sind interessant.)
  *How **much homework** is there today?* (Wie viele Hausaufgaben sind heute auf?)

- Mit Ausdrücken wie *a piece of* oder *a bit of* kann man Ersatzsingular- und Pluralformen bilden:
  *Can I have **a piece of paper**, please?* (einen Zettel)
  *They gave me **two** useful **bits of information**.* (zwei nützliche Informationen)

QUANTIFIERS

Gebrauch von *some* und *any*

Aussage	I need **some** more time. Show me **some** photos.
Verneinung	I do**n't** want **any** tea, thanks. There were**n't any** interesting films.
Frage	Is there **any** butter? Does their letter give **any** details?
Bitte oder Angebot	Can I have **some** ketchup, please? Would you like **some** help?

Gebrauch von *much, many, little, a little, few, a few*

Nicht zählbar	Plural
I don't have **much** money.	Are there **many** good shops?
There is **little** time. *(wenig)*	There were **few** tourists. *(wenige)*
I need **a little** help. *(etwas, ein wenig)*	Can you give me **a few** tips? *(ein paar, einige)*

Diese Liste enthält ca. 1100 Wörter und Ausdrücke, die in **Focus on Success – 5th edition: Ausgabe Soziales** als bekannt vorausgesetzt werden. Nicht aufgeführt, jedoch vorausgesetzt, sind einige elementare Wörter wie einfache Strukturwörter, Präpositionen, Zahlen, Farben, Wochentage usw. sowie internationale Wörter wie *email, hotel, cowboy* usw.
Die folgende Liste ist nach Themenbereiche angelegt. Auch innerhalb der Themenbereiche sind die Vokabeln nach sinnvollen Wortfeldern angeordnet. Dadurch eignet sich die Liste nicht nur zum Nachschlagen, sondern auch zum Lernen.

PEOPLE *(Menschen)*

people *Personen*
population *Bevölkerung, Einwohner*
nationality *Staatsangehörigkeit*
race *Rasse*
racist *rassistisch; Rassist/in*
society *Gesellschaft*
social *gesellschaftlich, sozial*
human *menschlich, Mensch*
adult *Erwachsene/r*
child *Kind*
teenager *Teenager/in*
sex *Geschlecht*
lady *Dame*
man *Mann, Mensch*
men *Männer, Menschen*
woman *Frau*
women *Frauen*
male *männlich*
female *weiblich, Frauen-*
boy *Junge*
girl *Mädchen*
couple *Paar*
married *verheiratet*
to **get married** *heiraten*
Mr *Herr*
Mrs, Ms *Frau*
boyfriend *Freund*
girlfriend *Freundin*
age *Alter*
born *geboren*
life *Leben*
death *Tod, Todesfall*
anybody *jemand, jede/r/s*
anyone *jemand, jede/r/s*
nobody *niemand*
some *einige, etwas*
somebody *jemand*
someone *jemand*
everybody *jede/r/s*
everyone *jede/r/s, alle*
no-one *niemand, keiner*
guest *Gast*
host *Gastgeber/in*
leader *Leiter/in, Führer/in*
loser *Verlierer/in*
member *Mitglied*
group *Gruppe*
crowd *(Menschen-)Menge*

FAMILY *(Familie)*

family *Familie*
parents *Eltern*
parent *Elternteil*
father *Vater*
mother *Mutter*
dad *Papa*
mum, mom *Mama, Mutter*
stepfather *Stiefvater*
stepmother *Stiefmutter*
husband *(Ehe-)Mann*
wife *(Ehe-)Frau*
children *Kinder*
son *Sohn*
daughter *Tochter*
brother *Bruder*
sister *Schwester*
brothers and sisters *Geschwister*
cousin *Cousin/e*
grandparents *Großeltern*
grandfather *Großvater*
grandmother *Großmutter*
grandchildren *Enkel(kinder)*
aunt *Tante*
uncle *Onkel*

EMOTIONS *(Gefühle)*

to **feel** *(sich) fühlen*
feeling, emotion *Gefühl*
happy *glücklich, froh, zufrieden*
joy *Freude*
pleased *zufrieden*
(to) **surprise** *Überraschung; überraschen*
mad *verrückt, toll*
unhappy *unglücklich, unzufrieden, traurig*
sad *traurig*
to **cry** *schreien, weinen*
angry (with sb) *wütend, böse (auf jdn), zornig*
crazy *verrückt*
to **be afraid (of)** *(sich) fürchten (vor)*
to **be frightened of** *Angst haben vor, sich fürchten vor*
tired *müde*

BODY AND CLOTHING *(Körper und Kleidung)*

body *Körper*
physical *physisch, körperlich*
leg *Bein*
arm *Arm*
hand *Hand*
shoulder *Schulter*
hair *Haar(e)*
to **touch** *anfassen, berühren*
head *Kopf*
face *Gesicht*
eye *Auge*
to **look** *(aus)sehen, blicken*
nose *Nase*
to **smell** *riechen*
mouth *Mund*
voice *Stimme*
to **smile** *lächeln*
to **speak** *sprechen, reden*
ear *Ohr*
to **listen** *zuhören*
to **hear** *hören*
to **sound** *klingen*
tooth *Zahn*
heart *Herz*
blood *Blut*
skin *Haut*
health *Gesundheit*
healthy *gesund*
well *gesund, gut*
able *fähig, in der Lage*
flexible *flexibel*
illness *Krankheit*
ill *krank*
sick *krank*
painful *schmerzhaft*
fat *dick*
thin *dünn*
short *kurz, klein*
small *klein*
tall *groß, hochgewachsen*
big *groß, kräftig*
weak *schwach*
strong *stark, kräftig*
old *alt*
young *jung*
clothing *Bekleidung*
clothes *Kleidung, Kleider*
fashion *Mode*
(to) **dress** *Kleid; sich kleiden*

to **wear** *tragen, anhaben*
to **cover** *(be)decken*
to **wash** *waschen, spülen*
to **spray** *(be)sprühen*
comfortable *bequem*
uncomfortable *unbequem*
elegant *elegant*
coat *Mantel*
shirt *Hemd*
shoes *Schuhe*
trainers *Turnschuhe*
boot *Stiefel*
bag *Tasche*
uniform *Uniform*

JOBS AND WORK (Beruf und Arbeit)

to **work** *arbeiten, funktionieren*
worker *Arbeiter/in*
job *Arbeit, Stelle*
factory *Fabrik*
business *Geschäft, Firma*
company *Gesellschaft, Firma, Unternehmen*
firm *Firma*
office *Büro, Amt*
assistant *Assistent/in, Verkäufer/in*
director *Direktor/in, Geschäftsführer/in, Vorstand*
boss *Chef/in*
customer *Kunde, Kundin*
meeting *Konferenz, Besprechung*
model *Modell, Vorbild*
project *Projekt*
programme *Programm*
expert *Fachmann/frau*
doctor *Arzt, Ärztin*
police *Polizei*
politician *Politiker/in*
farmer *Bauer/Bäuerin, Landwirt/in*

SCHOOL (Schule)

education *Erziehung, Schulbildung, Ausbildung*
school *Schule*
to **learn** *lernen, erfahren*
college *Fachhochschule*
to **train** *trainieren, ausbilden, schulen, eine Ausbildung machen*
training *Ausbildung, Schulung, Training*
university *Universität*
(to) **study** *Lernen, Studium; lernen, studieren*
course *Kurs, Lehrgang*
class *Klasse, Kurs*
desk *(Schreib-)Tisch*
seat *Sitz, Platz*
teacher *Lehrer/in*
to **teach** *unterrichten, lehren*
pupil *Schüler/in*
student *Student/in, Lernende/r*
subject *(Schul-)Fach, Thema*
English *englisch*
German *deutsch*
history *Geschichte*
topic *Thema*
question *Frage*
exercise *Übung*
task *Aufgabe*
exam *Prüfung*
homework *Hausaufgaben*
notes *Notizen*
rule *Vorschrift, Regel*
to **match** *zuordnen, (zusammen) passen*
correct *richtig*
true *richtig, wahr*
false *falsch*

HOUSES AND HOMES (Haus und Einrichtung)

house *Haus*
home *Zuhause, Heim, Heimat; nach Hause*
flat *Wohnung*
to **live** *wohnen, leben*
address *Adresse*
door *Tür*
key *Schlüssel, Schlüssel-, Haupt-*
roof *Dach*
window *Fenster*
stairs *Treppe*
upstairs *(nach) oben*
downstairs *(nach) unten*
room *Zimmer, Raum*
bedroom *Schlafzimmer*
(to) **clean** *sauber; reinigen, säubern*
household *Haushalt*
furniture *Möbel*
bed *Bett*
table *Tisch*
chair *Stuhl, Sessel*
bath *Bad*
shower *Dusche*
kitchen *Küche*
floor *Etage, (Fuß-)Boden*
alarm *Alarm(anlage)*

HOBBIES AND SPORT (Hobbys und Sport)

to **like** *mögen, gern tun*
to **interest** *interessieren*
to **enjoy** *genießen, gefallen*
(to) **love** *Liebe; lieben, sehr gern mögen*
favourite *Lieblings-*
fun *Spaß, amüsant, lustig*
exercise *Bewegung, körperliche Betätigung, Sport*
prize *Preis, Gewinn, Auszeichnung*
active *aktiv, tätig, aktiviert*
to **play** *spielen*
match *Spiel, Wettkampf*
game *Spiel*
ball *Ball, Kugel*
to **kick** *treten*
score *Ergebnis, Punkt(estand)*
to **win** *gewinnen, siegen*
winner *Gewinner/in, Sieger/in*
to **swim** *schwimmen*
to **fish** *angeln*
bicycle *Fahrrad*
cycling *Radfahren*
bike *Rad*
to **ride** *reiten, (Rad) fahren*
(to) **dance** *Tanz; tanzen*
dancer *Tänzer/in*
concert *Konzert*
television *Fernsehen, Fernseher*
viewer *Zuschauer/in*
radio/TV programme *Radio-/Fernsehsendung*
to **smoke** *rauchen*

SOCIETY AND SOCIAL PROBLEMS (Gesellschaft und soziale Probleme)

religion *Religion*
politics *Politik*
political *politisch*
right *Recht*
(to) **vote** *Stimme, Abstimmung, Wahl; stimmen, abstimmen, wählen*
to **allow** *erlauben, (zu)lassen*
(to) **control** *Kontrolle, Regelung, Steuerung; kontrollieren, regeln, steuern*
poor *arm, schlecht, mangelhaft*
rich *reich, wohlhabend*
protest *Protest*
crime *Verbrechen, Kriminalität*
conflict *Konflikt, Auseinandersetzung*
problem *Problem*
crisis, crises *Krise, Krisen*
danger *Gefahr*
dangerous *gefährlich*
serious *ernst, schwer*
wrong *falsch*
to **hurt** *verletzen*
to **hit** *(auf)schlagen, (auf)treffen*
to **break** *brechen*
to **burn** *(ver)brennen*
to **fight** *(be)kämpfen*
to **die** *sterben*
dead *tot*
to **kill** *töten*
gun *Schusswaffe, Pistole*
to **protect** *(be)schützen*
to **hide** *verstecken, verbergen*
drug *Droge*
risk *Risiko*
mistake *Fehler, Irrtum*
to **forbid** *verbieten*
to **forget** *vergessen*
to **ignore** *ignorieren*
to **steal** *stehlen*

personal *persönlich*
chance *Gelegenheit, Chance, Zufall*
responsible *verantwortlich*
law *Gesetz, Recht*
case *Fall*

INTERACTING WITH PEOPLE (*Umgehen mit Menschen*)

to **communicate** *sich verständigen, mitteilen, kommunizieren*
to **talk** *sprechen, reden*
to **say** *sagen*
to **tell** *sagen, erzählen, erkennen*
truth *Wahrheit*
to **ask** *fragen, bitten*
(to) **answer** *Antwort; (be)antworten*
(to) **reply** *Antwort, Erwiderung; antworten, erwidern*
to **realize** *bemerken, erkennen, verstehen, klar werden*
to **understand** *verstehen, begreifen*
to **translate** *übersetzen, übertragen*
to **explain** *erklären*
to **repeat** *wiederholen*
to **agree** *zustimmen, vereinbaren, sich einigen*
to **express** *ausdrücken, äußern*
to **be sorry** *leidtun*
to **discuss** *diskutieren (über), besprechen*
to **argue** *argumentieren, (sich) streiten*
argument *Argument; Streit*
to **shout** *schreien, brüllen*
to **order** *befehlen, bestellen, ordnen*
to **direct** *leiten*
to **shock** *erschüttern, schockieren*
reaction *Reaktion*
to **warn** *warnen, hinweisen*
to **disappoint** *enttäuschen*
(to) **promise** *Versprechen; versprechen*
to **help** *helfen*
to **share** *(sich) teilen, gemeinsam (be) nutzen, mitteilen*
together *zusammen*
to **show** *zeigen*
to **connect** *verbinden*
(to) **call** *Anruf; (an)rufen, nennen*
to **ring** *läuten, anrufen*
(to) **phone** *Telephon; anrufen*
mobile phone *Handy, Mobiltelefon*
to **chat** *sich unterhalten, plaudern, chatten (mit)*
dialogue *Dialog*
conversation *Unterhaltung*
to **introduce** *(sich) vorstellen, einführen*
to **meet** *(zusammen)treffen, begegnen*
to **greet** *(be)grüßen*
(to) **kiss** *Kuss; küssen*
to **laugh** *lachen*
(to) **joke** *Witz; scherzen, Witze machen*
(to) **offer** *Angebot; (an)bieten*
to **invite** *einladen*
party *Party, Partei*

to **arrange** *arrangieren, vereinbaren*
to **inform** *informieren*
(to) **report** *Bericht; berichten, melden*
to **notice** *bemerken*
to **guess** *raten, schätzen*

READING AND WRITING (*Lesen und Schreiben*)

to **read** *lesen*
reader *Leser/in*
story *Erzählung, Geschichte*
mail *Post*
letter *Brief, Buchstabe*
to **send** *senden, schicken*
document *Dokument, Schriftstück, Papier*
briefcase *Aktentasche*
key *Taste*
table *Tabelle*
diagram *Diagramm, Grafik*
content *Inhalt*
to **write** *schreiben*
paper *Papier, Zeitung*
pencil *Bleistift*
point *Punkt; Sinn*
word *Wort*
phrase *Wendung, Formulierung*
sentence *Satz*
line *Zeile*
message *Mitteilung, Nachricht, Botschaft*
slogan *Werbespruch*
form *Form, Formular*
summary *Zusammenfassung*
introduction *Einleitung, Einführung*
page *Seite*
title *Titel*
information *Auskunft, Information(en)*
dictionary *Wörterbuch*
to **mean** *bedeuten, meinen, heißen*
meaning *Bedeutung*
emphasis *Hervorhebung*
(to) **copy** *Kopie; kopieren, abschreiben*
(to) **list** *Liste, Aufzählung; aufzählen, aufführen, auflisten*
to **note** *beachten, notieren*
to **note down** *aufschreiben, notieren*
(to) **complete** *vollständig; vervollständigen, abschließen*
(to) **comment** *Kommentar, Bemerkung; kommentieren*
to **describe** *beschreiben*
description *Beschreibung, Schilderung*
detail *Detail*
stereotype *Klischee*
example *Beispiel*
language *Sprache*
grammar *Grammatik*
vocabulary *Wortschatz*
style *Stil*
clear *klar, deutlich*
formal *formell, förmlich*
dear *liebe/r*

BELIEFS AND ATTITUDES (*Glaube und Einstellungen*)

to **believe (in sb/sth)** *(an jdn/etw) glauben*
to **consider** *nachdenken über, halten für, in Betracht ziehen*
to **think** *denken, meinen, finden, glauben*
view *Ansicht, Meinung, Aussicht*
opinion *Meinung, Einschätzung*
positive *positiv, bejahend*
opposite *Gegenteil; entgegengesetzt, gegenüber(liegend)*
to **dislike** *nicht mögen*
to **hate** *hassen, nicht mögen*
option *Option, Wahl, Alternative*
idea *Idee, Gedanke, Ahnung*
(to) **hope** *Hoffnung; hoffen*
(to) **dream** *Traum; träumen*
to **want** *wollen*
to **wish** *wünschen*
to **remember** *sich erinnern, daran denken*
to **suppose** *vermuten, annehmen*
to **imagine** *sich vorstellen*
to **seem** *(er)scheinen*
to **prove** *beweisen*
real *echt, wirklich*
to **worry** *sich Sorgen machen, bekümmern*
to **know** *kennen, wissen*
reason *Vernunft, Grund*
to **need** *brauchen, benötigen*
necessary *nötig, erforderlich*

MOVEMENT (*Bewegung*)

to **move** *(sich) bewegen, umziehen*
fast *schnell*
slow *langsam*
to **go** *gehen, fahren*
to **walk** *(zu Fuß) gehen*
step *Schritt*
to **run** *laufen*
to **jump** *springen*
to **climb** *klettern, steigen*
to **fall** *fallen, stürzen, abstürzen*
to **sit** *sitzen, sich setzen*
to **stand** *stehen, aushalten*
to **rise** *steigen*
to **turn** *(sich) drehen, (sich) wenden*
to **arrive** *ankommen*
to **come** *kommen*
to **enter** *betreten, eintreten, eingeben*
to **leave** *(ver)lassen*
to **bring** *bringen, holen*
to **carry** *tragen*
to **put** *setzen, stellen, legen*
to **press** *drücken*
to **push** *drücken, schieben*
to **pull** *ziehen*
to **lead** *führen*
to **follow** *(be)folgen*

to **pass** *vorbeigehen, vergehen; bestehen*
(to) **hurry** *Eile; sich beeilen*
to **rush** *sich beeilen*
to **reach** *greifen, erreichen*
to **catch** *fangen, nehmen, erwischen*
to **disappear** *verschwinden*

TOWNS AND BUILDINGS (*Städte und Gebäude*)

city *(Groß-)Stadt*
town *Stadt*
village *Dorf*
neighbourhood *Nachbarschaft*
street *Straße*
path *(Fuß-)Weg, Pfad*
road *(Land-)Straße*
sign *Zeichen, Schild*
corner *Ecke*
map *Karte*
local *örtlich, lokal*
building *Gebäude*
church *Kirche*
tower *Turm*
hospital *Krankenhaus*
supermarket *Supermarkt*
market *Markt*
entrance *Eingang, Einfahrt*
bridge *Brücke*
farm *Bauernhof*

TRAFFIC, TRAVEL AND HOLIDAYS (*Verkehr, Reisen und Urlaub*)

holiday *Ferien, Urlaub, Feiertag*
abroad *im/ins Ausland*
foreign *fremd*
national *national, staatlich, Landes-*
country *Land, Staat*
European *europäisch*
American *amerikanisch*
tour *Tour, Rundgang*
trip *Ausflug, Reise, Besuch*
visitor *Besucher/in, Gast*
ticket *Eintrrittskarte, Fahrkarte*
to **travel** *reisen, fahren*
to **visit** *besuchen, besichtigen*
to **plan** *planen*
transport *Beförderung, Verkehr(smittel), Transport*
boat *Boot, Schiff*
ship *Schiff*
bus *(Linien-)Bus*
truck *Laster, Lkw*
car *Auto*
vehicle *Fahrzeug, Wagen*
to **drive** *(Auto) fahren*
to **deliver** *liefern*
driver *Fahrer/in*
plane *Flugzeug*
helicopter *Hubschrauber*
flight *Flug*
to **fly** *fliegen*
airport *Flughafen*
train *Zug*
underground *unterirdisch; U-Bahn*
station *Bahnhof*
ticket *Fahrkarte, Eintrittskarte*
to **miss** *verpassen, vermissen*
(to) **return** *Rückkehr, Rückreise; zurückkehren, zurückgehen*
beach *Strand*
to **relax** *sich erholen, sich ausruhen, sich entspannen*
photo *Foto*

MONEY AND SHOPPING (*Geld und Einkaufen*)

money *Geld*
to **earn** *verdienen*
to **afford** *es sich leisten können*
to **spend** *(Geld) ausgeben, (Zeit) verbringen*
to **buy** *kaufen*
to **pay** *(be)zahlen*
to **sell** *(sich) verkaufen*
to **charge** *berechnen, verlangen, (auf)laden*
(to) **cost** *Kosten; kosten*
price *(Kauf-)Preis*
worth *wert*
bill *Rechnung*
present *Geschenk*
prize *Preis*
free *kostenlos, frei*
cheap *billig, günstig*
expensive *teuer*
luxury *Luxus*
card *Karte*
cash *Bargeld, Geld*
to **change** *(aus)wechseln, (sich) ändern*
to **borrow** *borgen, (aus)leihen*
to **belong** *gehören zu, angehören*
to **own** *besitzen*
to **prefer** *vorziehen, bevorzugen, lieber mögen*
to **choose** *(aus)wählen*
available *verfügbar, erhältlich*
product *Produkt, Erzeugnis*
to **produce** *produzieren, herstellen*
shop *Laden, Geschäft*
shopping *Einkaufen*
sale *Verkauf*
success *Erfolg*
to **open** *öffnen*
to **close** *schließen*
open *offen*
closed *geschlossen*

EATING AND DRINKING (*Essen und Trinken*)

to **eat** *essen*
food *Essen, Nahrung*
to **cook** *kochen*
to **prepare** *(sich) vorbereiten*
meal *Essen, Mahlzeit*
breakfast *Frühstück*
lunch *Mittagessen*
dinner *(Abend-)Essen*
to **taste** *schmecken*
hunger *Hunger*
hungry *hungrig*
thirst *Durst*
thirsty *durstig*
meat *Fleisch*
beef *Rindfleisch*
vegetable *Gemüse*
potato *Kartoffel*
carrot *Karotte, Möhre*
fruit *Obst, Frucht, Früchte*
fresh *frisch*
salt *Salz*
sugar *Zucker*
chicken *Huhn, Hähnchen*
egg *Ei*
cheese *Käse*
chocolate *Schokolade, Praline*
cake *Kuchen, Torte*
bread *Brot*
sweet *süß; Süßigkeit*
to **drink** *trinken*
mineral water *Mineralwasser*
tea *Tee*
juice *Saft*
alcohol *Alkohol*
wine *Wein*
beer *Bier*
cup *Tasse*
glass *Glas*
bottle *Flasche*
knife *Messer*
fork *Gabel*
spoon *Löffel*
plate *Platte, Teller*
bowl *Schüssel*
box *Kiste, Kästchen, Schachtel*
packet *Schachtel, Packung, Tüte*

NATURE AND WEATHER (*Natur und Wetter*)

nature *Natur, Art*
natural *natürlich*
planet *Planet*
world *Welt*
continent *Erdteil, Kontinent*
environment *Umwelt, Umfeld*
earth *Erde*
air *Luft*
water *Wasser*
wood *Holz, Wald*
ice *Eis*
fire *Feuer*
sky *Himmel*
mountain *(größerer) Berg*
river *Fluss*
wind *Wind*
rain *Regen*
sun *Sonne*
storm *Sturm*

heat *Hitze, Wärme*
hot *heiß, warm*
warm *warm*
cold *kalt*
to **dry** *trocknen*
wet *nass*
light *Licht; hell, leicht*
to **shine** *scheinen*
dark *dunkel*
animal *Tier*
dog *Hund*
cat *Katze*
bird *Vogel*
fish *Fisch*
flower *Blume*
plant *Pflanze*
tree *Baum*
to **recycle** *wiederverwerten*
(to) **waste** *Verschwendung, Vergeudung; verschwenden, vergeuden*

SCIENCE AND TECHNOLOGY (*Wissenschaft und Technik*)

science *Wissenschaft*
technology *Technik, Technologie*
scientist *Wissenschaftler/in*
chemical *chemisch, Chemie-; Chemikalie*
technical *technisch*
to **build** *(auf)bauen*
tool *Werkzeug*
device *Gerät, Apparat*
machine *Gerät, Maschine*
data *Daten*
image *Bild*
to **switch on** *anschalten, einschalten*
to **switch off** *abschalten, ausschalten*
to **click** *klicken, anklicken*
to **print** *drucken*
electric *elektrisch, Strom-*
electricity *Elektrizität, Strom*
power *Kraft, Strom*
method *Methode, Verfahren*
to **repair** *reparieren*
new *neu*
safe *sicher*
automatic *automatisch*

ART AND CULTURE (*Kunst und Kultur*)

art *Kunst*
picture *Bild*
symbol *Symbol, Zeichen*
scene *Szene*
culture *Kultur*
to **act** *handeln*
movie *Film*
cinema *Kino*
theatre *Theater*
book *Buch*
author *Verfasser/in, Autor/in*
article *Artikel*
illustration *Abbildung, Illustration*
newspaper *Zeitung*
magazine *Zeitschrift*
news *Neuigkeit(en), Nachricht(en)*
media *Medien*
song *Lied*
singer *Sänger/in*
music *Musik*
band *Kapelle, Band*
guitar *Gitarre*
piano *Klavier*

QUALITIES AND CHARACTERISTICS (*Eigenschaften und Besonderheiten*)

character *Charakter*
kind *Art, Sorte*
similar *ähnlich*
different *anders, verschieden*
difference *Unterschied*
advantage *Vorteil*
disadvantage *Nachteil*
to **be** *sein*
to **become** *werden*
to **include** *einschließen, umfassen, aufnehmen, einbeziehen*

DESCRIBING PEOPLE AND SITUATIONS (*Menschen und Situationen beschreiben*)

private *privat, zurückgezogen*
friendly *freund(schaft)lich*
kind *nett, lieb*
interesting *interessant*
individual *individuell, einzeln, Einzel-*
typical *typisch*
boring *langweilig*
funny *komisch, lustig, merkwürdig*
busy *beschäftigt, belebt, hektisch; besetzt*
lazy *faul*
helpful *hilfreich, nützlich, hilfsbereit*
careful *vorsichtig, sorgfältig, aufmerksam*
creative *schöpferisch, kreativ*
romantic *romantisch*
smart *schick, clever*
stupid *dumm, albern, doof*
silly *albern*
nice *schön, nett*
tough *zäh, stark*
strict *streng, strikt*
polite *höflich*
rude *unhöflich, rüde*
pretty *hübsch*
beautiful *schön*
ugly *hässlich*
positive *positiv*
negative *negativ, verneinend*
strange *fremd, seltsam*
normal *normal*
perfect *vollkommen, perfekt*
special *besondere*
well-known *sehr bekannt, berühmt*
famous *berühmt*
popular *beliebt, populär*
unknown *unbekannt*
good *gut*
better *besser*
best *beste/r/s, am besten*
great *groß(artig)*
amazing *erstaunlich, verblüffend, toll*
excellent *ausgezeichnet, hervorragend*
wonderful *wunderbar, großartig*
fantastic *fantastisch, wunderbar*
bad *schlecht, schlimm*
worse *schlechter, schlimmer*
worst *schlechteste/r/s, schlimmste/r/s*
horrible, awful, terrible *furchtbar, schrecklich*
easy *leicht, einfach*
basic *elementar*
simple *einfach*
hard *schwer, schwierig, hart*
difficult *schwer, schwierig*
important *wichtig*
successful *erfolgreich*
exciting *aufregend, spannend*
useful *nützlich*
fair *fair, gerecht*
unfair *unfair, ungerecht*
poor *arm*
wealthy *reich*
loud *laut*
quiet, silent *ruhig, still*
wet *nass*
dry *trocken*
slow *langsam*
quick *schnell, rasch*

DESCRIBING OBJECTS (*Gegenstände beschreiben*)

type *Art, Typ*
object *Gegenstand, Ding, Objekt*
thing *Sache, Ding, Gegenstand*
piece *Stück, Teil*
unit *Einheit, Stück, Lektion*
colour *Farbe*
this *dies, diese/r/s*
that *das*
these *diese*
those *jene*
their *ihr/e/r/s*

Size – Shape – Weight (*Größe – Form – Gewicht*)

shape *Form, Gestalt*
line *Linie*
circle *Kreis*
hole *Loch*
size *Größe*
little *klein, wenig*
to **grow** *wachsen, (an)steigen*

big *groß*
large *groß, umfangreich*
weight *Gewicht*
heavy *stark, schwer*
light *leicht*
to **fill** *füllen, ausfüllen*
full *voll, vollständig*
empty *leer*
wide *breit, weit, groß*
narrow *eng*
long *lang*
short *kurz*
hard *fest*
soft *weich*

ACTIONS AND PROCESSES (*Handlungen und Prozesse*)

action *Aktion, Handlung, Tat*
activity *Tätigkeit*
result *Ergebnis, Folge*
to **do** *tun, machen*
to **happen** *passieren, geschehen*
to **start** *anfangen, starten, beginnen*
to **continue** *fortsetzen, weitermachen*
to **finish** *beenden, erledigen*
to **stop** *(an)halten, aufhören (mit)*
to **result from** *folgen aus*
to **let** *erlauben, (zu)lassen*

Necessity, Probability, Possibility (*Notwendigkeit, Wahrscheinlichkeit, Möglichkeit*)

condition *Bedingung*
may *dürfen, können, mögen*
maybe *vielleicht*
possible *möglich, denkbar*
impossible *unmöglich*
probably *wahrscheinlich*
can *können, dürfen*
could *konnte/n, könnte/n*
would *würde/n*
might *können, könnte/n*
will *werde(n), wollen*
should *sollen, sollte/n*
must *müssen*
to **have to** *müssen*

Everyday actions (*Alltagshandlungen*)

to **take** *nehmen, bringen, dauern*
to **decide** *(sich) entscheiden, beschließen*
decision *Entscheidung*
to **make** *machen*
to **fix** *festlegen, reparieren*
to **check** *(über)prüfen*
to **organize** *organisieren*
to **get** *holen, bekommen, werden, gelangen*
to **give** *geben*
to **receive** *erhalten, bekommen, empfangen*
to **hold** *abhalten, veranstalten*
to **keep** *(be)halten, bleiben*
to **spare** *übrig haben*
to **set** *setzen*
(to) **mix** *Mischung; mischen*
to **remove** *entfernen*
to **avoid** *vermeiden*
to **wait** *warten*
to **watch** *beobachten*
to **see** *sehen*
to **search** *(durch)suchen*
to **find** *finden, suchen*
to **use** *benutzen, verwenden*
to **try** *versuchen, (aus)probieren*
(to) **experience** *Erfahrung, Erlebnis; erfahren, erleben*
to **open** *öffnen, beginnen*
to **develop** *entwickeln*
to **save** *retten, sichern*
to **recover** *sich erholen*
to **sleep** *schlafen*
to **wake up** *aufwachen, aufwecken*

TIME (*Zeit*)

period *Periode, Zeitraum*
date *Datum, Termin*
beginning *Anfang*
to **begin** *anfangen, beginnen*
(to) **end** *Ende, Schluss; (be)enden*
final *letzte/r/s, End-*
first *erste/r/s, zuerst*
last *letzte/r/s, zuletzt*
time *Zeit, Mal*

Days, months, ... (*Tage, Monate, ...*)

second *Sekunde*
minute *Minute*
hour *Stunde*
o'clock *... Uhr*
day *Tag*
morning *Morgen*
afternoon *Nachmittag*
evening *Abend*
night *Nacht*
tonight *heute Abend/Nacht*
today *heute*
yesterday *gestern*
tomorrow *morgen*
week *Woche*
weekend *Wochenende*
month *Monat*
year *Jahr*
season *Saison, Jahreszeit*
spring *Frühling*
summer *Sommer*
autumn *Herbst*
winter *Winter*
Christmas *Weihnachten*
Easter *Ostern*
birthday *Geburtstag*
age *Zeitalter*

Frequency (*Häufigkeit*)

sometimes *manchmal*
often *oft, häufig*
usual *gewöhnlich, normal*
usually *normalerweise, gewöhnlich, meistens*
regular *regelmäßig, regulär, normal*
daily *täglich*
always *immer*
never *nie(mals)*

Other words for talking about time (*andere Zeitangaben*)

early *früh*
late *spät*
later *später*
until *bis*
now *nun, jetzt*
then *dann*
ago *vor*
as *wie, als, da*
yet *schon, bereits*
not yet *noch nicht*
before *vor(her)*
after *nach*
past *vorbei, nach; Vergangenheit*
present *Gegenwart; gegenwärtig, aktuell*
future *Zukunft; (zu)künftig*
soon *bald*
suddenly *plötzlich*
only *nur, einzig*
once *einmal, einst*
twice *zweimal*
again *wieder*
next *nächste/r/s; danach*
already *schon, bereits*
recent *neueste/r/s, letzte/r/s, aktuell*
recently *neulich, in letzter Zeit*
while *während*
at the moment *momentan, augenblicklich*
nowadays *heutzutage*
forever *für immer*
ever *je(mals)*
ready *fertig, bereit*

PLACE AND DIRECTION (*Orts- und Richtungsangaben*)

space *(Zwischen-)Raum, Ort, Platz, Abstand, Weltall*
place *Stelle, Platz*
situation *Situation, Lage*
outside *außer(halb) (von)*
outdoors *draußen, im Freien*
inside *innerhalb (von), drinnen*
indoors *drinnen*
far *weit (entfernt)*
near *bei, nahe*
around *herum*
away *weg, entfernt*
back *zurück*
forward *vorwärts, nach vorn*

Prepositions (*Präpositionen*)

across *(quer) über, in ganz*
along *entlang*
over *(vor)über*
under *unter*
between *zwischen*
through *durch*
behind *hinter, hinten*
against *gegen*
about *über, etwa*

Other words for describing places (*andere Ortsangaben*)

direct *direkt*
state *Zustand, Staat*
to **stay** *bleiben, übernachten*
here *hier*
there *da, dort(hin)*
anywhere *irgendwo(hin)*
somewhere *irgendwo(hin)*
nowhere *nirgends*
front *Vorderseite*
side *Seite, Rand*
top *Spitze, Gipfel; Spitzen-*
bottom *Boden, Unterseite*
high *hoch*
low *tief, niedrig*
distance *Entfernung, Abstand, Strecke*
mile *Meile*
north *Norden, Nord-*
east *Osten*
south *Süden, Süd-*
west *Westen*
middle *Mitte*
left *linke/r/s, links*
right *rechts*
up *nach oben*
down *nach unten*
above *oben, über*
below *unten, unter*

QUANTITY (*Menge*)

number *Nummer, Zahl*
to **count** *zählen*
to **add** *zusammenzählen, hinzufügen*
plus *plus*
limit *Grenze*
all *alle(s)*
whole *ganz, Ganzes*
almost *fast, beinahe*
nearly *beinahe, fast*
very *sehr*
really *wirklich, eigentlich, tatsächlich*
a lot *viel, sehr*
lots of *viel, viele*
many *viele*
most *meist*
much *viel*
more *mehr*
extra *zusätzlich*
double *doppelt*
both *beide*
pair *Paar*
enough *ausreichend, genug*
half *Hälfte; halb*
part *Teil*
quite *ziemlich, ganz*
less *weniger, abzüglich*
few *ein paar, wenig/e/r/s*
a little *ein wenig, etwas*
alone *allein(e)*
minimum *Minimum; minimal*
none *kein/e/r/s*
nothing *nichts*
neither *auch nicht, keine/r/s*
any *irgendetwas, welche/r/s, jede/r/s*
anything *etwas, alles*
another *noch eine*
other *andere/r/s*
each *jede/r/s*
every *jede/r/s*
everything *alles*
exactly *exakt, genau*
certain *bestimmt*
specific *bestimmt, spezifisch*
general *allgemein*
just *einfach, nur, genau, gerade*

CONNECTORS (*Strukturwörter*)

because *weil*
so *also, damit, deshalb, so (dass)*
simply *einfach*
certainly *sicherlich, bestimmt*
for example *zum Beispiel*
such as *wie zum Beispiel*
(in this) way *Weg, Methode, auf diese Art (und Weise)*
but *aber, sondern*
however *doch, jedoch*
except *außer*
else *andere/r/s*
than *als*
whether *ob*
if *wenn, falls, ob*
or *oder*
same *gleiche/r/s, der-, die-, dasselbe*
also *auch, außerdem*
too *zu, auch*
with *mit, bei*
without *ohne*
in case *falls*
perhaps *vielleicht, eventuell*
even *sogar (noch)*
anyway *jedenfalls, sowieso*

USEFUL WORDS AND PHRASES
(*Nützliche Wörter und Wendungen*)

(to) **welcome** *willkommen; willkommen heißen, begrüßen*
excuse me *Entschuldigung*
please *bitte*
of course *natürlich, selbstverständlich*
sure *freilich, sicher(lich)*
thanks *Dank; danke*
unfortunately *leider*
basically *eigentlich, im Grunde*
total *(End-)Summe; völlig, (ins)gesamt, Gesamt-*
main *hauptsächlich, wichtigste/r/s, Haupt-*
something *etwas*
fact *Tatsache, Fakt*
tip *Vorschlag, Hinweis, Tipp*
pros and cons *Für und Wider*

QUESTION WORDS
(*Fragewörter*)

what? *was?, welche/r/s?*
where? *wo(hin)?*
when? *wenn?, wann?*
who? *wer?, welche(r/s)?*
which? *welche/r/s?*
why? *warum?*
how? *wie?*

Unit word list

Dieses Wörterverzeichnis enthält alle Wörter in **Focus on Success – 5th edition: Ausgabe Soziales** in der Reihenfolge ihres Erscheinens. Nicht aufgeführt sind die Wörter aus der *Basic word list* sowie internationale Wörter wie *hotel*, *email* usw.
Die Wörter der *Social Options*-Seiten werden in den darauf folgenden Units nicht vorausgesetzt.
Wörter, die in den Hörverständnistexten vorkommen, sind mit einem CD-Symbol gekennzeichnet.
Wörter, die in den *Files* vorkommen, sind mit einem türkisfarbenen Balken gekennzeichnet.

AE = American English
BE = British English
pl = plural
sb = somebody
sth = something
etw = etwas
jd = jemand
jdm = jemandem
jdn = jemanden
jds = jemandes

UNIT 1

page 6

cult [kʌlt]	Kult
celebrity [sə'lebrəti]	Prominente/r, Prominenz
neighbour ['neɪbə]	Nachbar/in
to **sort** [sɔːt]	sortieren, einordnen
to **rank sb/sth** [ræŋk]	jdn/etw einstufen, jdn/etw (ein-)ordnen
order ['ɔːdə]	Reihenfolge
popularity [ˌpɒpju'lærəti]	Beliebtheit, Popularität
to **deserve** [dɪ'zɜːv]	verdienen
status ['steɪtəs]	Status, Stellung
to **define** [dɪ'faɪn]	definieren
to **study sth** ['stʌdi]	etw genau betrachten
headline ['hedlaɪn]	Schlagzeile, Überschrift
to **make sth up** [ˌmeɪk 'ʌp]	etw erfinden, sich etw ausdenken
store [stɔː]	Geschäft, Laden
midnight ['mɪdnaɪt]	Mitternacht
shopper ['ʃɒpə]	Käufer/in, Kunde/Kundin
legend ['ledʒənd]	Legende
face-lift ['feɪslɪft]	Facelifting, Gesichtsstraffung
jewellery ['dʒuːəlri]	Schmuck

page 7

to **get sth right** [ˌget 'raɪt]	etw richtig machen, etw gut hinbekommen
statement ['steɪtmənt]	Aussage, Feststellung, Behauptung
gig [gɪg]	(Rock-, Pop-, Jazz-)Konzert
to **queue** [kjuː]	sich (in einer Warteschlange) anstellen
charity ['tʃærəti]	Benefiz-, Wohltätigkeit(s-)
to **tour** [tʊə]	auf Tour gehen
bracket ['brækɪt]	Klammer
to **appear** [ə'pɪə]	auftreten, erscheinen
to **break sth up** [ˌbreɪk 'ʌp]	etw zertrümmern, etw demolieren
to **hit the headlines** [ˌhɪt ðə 'hedlaɪnz]	in die Schlagzeilen kommen, Schlagzeilen machen
to **collect** [kə'lekt]	sammeln
fortune ['fɔːtʃuːn]	Vermögen
autograph ['ɔːtəgrɑːf]	Autogramm
formula ['fɔːmjələ]	Formel
race [reɪs]	Rennen
event [ɪ'vent]	Veranstaltung, Ereignis

page 8

skill [skɪl]	Fähigkeit, Fertigkeit
to **predict** [prɪ'dɪkt]	voraussagen, vorhersagen
use [juːs]	Gebrauch, Nutzen
to **make use of sth** [ˌmeɪk 'juːs əv]	von etw Gebrauch machen, etw nutzen
clue [kluː]	Hinweis, Anhaltspunkt
to **go with sth** ['gəʊ wɪð]	zu etw gehören
caption ['kæpʃn]	Bildunterschrift
further ['fɜːðə]	weitere/r/s
like [laɪk]	wie
idol ['aɪdl]	Idol
good looking [ˌgʊd 'lʊkɪŋ]	gutaussehend, attraktiv
talented ['tæləntɪd]	begabt, talentiert
to **be scared** [bi 'skeəd]	Angst haben
onto ['ɒntə]	auf
stage [steɪdʒ]	Bühne
huge [hjuːdʒ]	riesig, Riesen-
audience ['ɔːdiəns]	Publikum
member of the audience [ˌmembər əv ði 'ɔːdiəns]	Zuschauer/in
to **feel uncomfortable** [ˌfiːl ʌn'kʌmftəbl]	sich unbehaglich fühlen
judge [dʒʌdʒ]	Richter/in, Juror/in
spot [spɒt]	Platz, Stelle
change [tʃeɪndʒ]	Wandel, Verwandlung
to **take place** [ˌteɪk 'pleɪs]	stattfinden
to **perform** [pə'fɔːm]	singen, spielen, auftreten
to **wave sth** [weɪv]	etw schwenken, mit etw wedeln
magical ['mædʒɪkl]	magisch, traumhaft
cheers *pl* [tʃɪəz]	Jubel, Applaus
to **wash over sb/sth** ['wɒʃ əʊvə]	jdn überkommen, etw überschwemmen
life-changing ['laɪf tʃeɪndʒɪŋ]	lebensverändernd
to **hold sb back** [ˌhəʊld 'bæk]	jdn bremsen
to **move on** [ˌmuːv 'ɒn]	weiterkommen, weitergehen
level ['levl]	Stufe, Niveau, Ebene
competition [ˌkɒmpə'tɪʃn]	Wettbewerb, Wettkampf
to **finish second** [ˌfɪnɪʃ 'sekənd]	Zweite/r werden
to **sign** [saɪn]	unterschreiben
contract ['kɒntrækt]	Vertrag
record company ['rekɔːd kʌmpəni]	Plattenfirma
to **release** [rɪ'liːs]	veröffentlichen
follow-up ['fɒləʊ ʌp]	Folge-, Nachfolger
career [kə'rɪə]	Karriere, Laufbahn

page 9

to **compare** [kəm'peə]	vergleichen
nervous ['nɜːvəs]	aufgeregt, nervös

to **shake** [ʃeɪk]	zittern
dirty ['dɜːti]	schmutzig
to **criticize** ['krɪtɪsaɪz]	kritisieren
show [ʃəʊ]	(TV-, Radio-)Sendung
to **take part in sth** [ˌteɪk 'pɑːt ɪn]	an etw teilnehmen
to **make sb up** [ˌmeɪk 'ʌp]	jdn schminken
script [skrɪpt]	Drehbuch
to **practise** ['præktɪs]	üben, trainieren
to **look forward to sth** [ˌlʊk 'fɔːwəd tə]	sich auf etw freuen

page 10

on one's own [ɒn wʌnz 'əʊn]	allein
background ['bækgraʊnd]	Hintergrund
to **be related to sth** [bi rɪ'leɪtɪd tə]	mit etw in Zusammenhang stehen
fame [feɪm]	Ruhm
childhood sweetheart [ˌtʃaɪldhʊd 'swiːthɑːt]	Jugendliebe
to **split (up)** [splɪt]	*(Paar:)* sich trennen
current ['kʌrənt]	aktuell
achievement [ə'tʃiːvmənt]	Errungenschaft, Leistung
to **inspire** [ɪn'spaɪə]	inspirieren, anregen
challenge ['tʃælɪndʒ]	Herausforderung, (große) Aufgabe
relationship [rɪ'leɪʃnʃɪp]	Beziehung, Verhältnis
lover ['lʌvə]	Geliebte/r, Liebhaber/in
tabloid press ['tæblɔɪd pres]	Boulevardpresse

page 11

expression [ɪk'spreʃn]	Ausdruck
to **cry one's eyes out** [ˌkraɪ wʌnz 'aɪz aʊt]	wie ein Schlosshund heulen
close [kləʊs]	nah, dicht, eng
to **fulfil** [fʊl'fɪl]	erfüllen
pleasure ['pleʒə]	Vergnügen
My pleasure. [ˌmaɪ 'pleʒə]	Gern geschehen.
to **prove** [pruːv]	beweisen
fashion designer ['fæʃn dɪzaɪnə]	Modeschöpfer/in
to **design** [dɪ'zaɪn]	entwerfen, gestalten
scene [siːn]	Szene
ordinary ['ɔːdnri]	normal, gewöhnlich
pretty ['prɪti]	ziemlich
attention [ə'tenʃn]	Aufmerksamkeit, Beachtung
on the other hand [ɒn ði 'ʌðə hænd]	andererseits
public ['pʌblɪk]	öffentlich
platform ['plætfɔːm]	Podium
to **talk sth over** [ˌtɔːk 'əʊvə]	etw besprechen
to **accept** [ək'sept]	akzeptieren, gutheißen
to **concentrate on sth** ['kɒnsntreɪt ɒn]	sich auf etw konzentrieren
to **support** [sə'pɔːt]	unterstützen
openness ['əʊpənnəs]	Offenheit
step [step]	Schritt
collection [kə'lekʃn]	Kollektion
label ['leɪbl]	(Mode-)Firma, Marke
to **admire** [əd'maɪə]	bewundern
to **focus on sth** ['fəʊkəs ɒn]	sich auf etw konzentrieren
role-play ['rəʊl pleɪ]	Rollenspiel
to **role-play** ['rəʊl pleɪ]	mit verteilten Rollen spielen
area ['eəriə]	Gebiet, Bereich, Feld
to **thank** [θæŋk]	danken
charts *pl* [tʃɑːts]	Hitparade
footballer ['fʊtbɔːlə]	Fußballer/in
to **congratulate sb on sth** [kən'grætʃuleɪt]	jdm zu etw gratulieren
support [sə'pɔːt]	Unterstützung, Hilfe
to **face sth** [feɪs]	sich einer Sache stellen
to **train** [treɪn]	trainieren
match [mætʃ]	Spiel, Partie, Match

UNIT 2

page 12

participant [pɑː'tɪsɪpənt]	Teilnehmer/in
spectator [spek'teɪtə]	Zuschauer/in
survey ['sɜːveɪ]	Umfrage
according to [ə'kɔːdɪŋ tə]	entsprechend, nach, gemäß
keep-fit [ˌkiːp'fɪt]	Fitness(-)
aerobics [eə'rəʊbɪks]	Aerobic
to **be keen on sth** [bi 'kiːn ɒn]	auf etw versessen sein

page 13

to **ring the doorbell** [ˌrɪŋ ðə 'dɔːbel]	(an der Tür) klingeln, läuten
stadium ['steɪdiəm]	Stadion
chess [tʃes]	Schach
chess set ['tʃes set]	Schachspiel *(Figuren + Brett)*
swimming pool ['swɪmɪŋ puːl]	Schwimmbad
racing car ['reɪsɪŋ kɑː]	Rennwagen
rules *pl* **of the game** [ˌruːlz əv ðə 'geɪm]	Spielregeln
since [sɪns]	seit
gym [dʒɪm]	Fitness-Studio
changing room ['tʃeɪndʒɪŋ ruːm]	Umkleidekabine, Umkleide
cold [kəʊld]	Erkältung
World Cup [ˌwɜːld 'kʌp]	Weltpokal
national team [ˌnæʃnəl 'tiːm]	Nationalmannschaft
personality [ˌpɜːsə'næləti]	Persönlichkeit
involved in sth [ɪn'vɒlvd ɪn]	an etw beteiligt, bei etw engagiert
to **lose** [luːz]	verlieren
interest (in sth) ['ɪntrəst]	Interesse (an etw)
to **look up to sb** [ˌlʊk 'ʌp tə]	zu jdm aufsehen, jdn bewundern
champion ['tʃæmpiən]	Meister/in
hero ['hɪərəʊ]	Held
to **overcome** [ˌəʊvə'kʌm]	überwinden
disability [ˌdɪsə'bɪləti]	Behinderung
swimmer ['swɪmə]	Schwimmer/in
medal ['medl]	Medaille

page 14

ending ['endɪŋ]	Schluss, Ende
illegal [ɪ'liːgl]	verboten, illegal
substance ['sʌbstəns]	Substanz, Stoff
to **improve** [ɪm'pruːv]	(sich) verbessern, (sich) steigern
performance [pə'fɔːməns]	Leistung, Abschneiden
injury ['ɪndʒəri]	Verletzung
to **occur** [ə'kɜː]	vorfallen, geschehen
paragraph ['pærəgrɑːf]	*(Text:)* Absatz
professional [prə'feʃənl]	professionell, Profi-
to **record** [rɪ'kɔːd]	aufzeichnen
decade ['dekeɪd]	Jahrzehnt
throughout the decades [θruːˌaʊt ðə 'dekeɪdz]	durch/über die Jahrzehnte
improvement in sth [ɪm'pruːvmənt ɪn]	Verbesserung bei etw

material [mə'tɪəriəl]	Material, Werkstoff
to **come fourth** [ˌkʌm 'fɔːθ]	Vierte/r werden
to **compete** [kəm'piːt]	(bei einem Wettbewerb) antreten
junior ['dʒuːniə]	Junioren-
national ['næʃnəl]	Landes-, national
triathlon [traɪ'æθlən]	Triathlon
cyclist ['saɪklɪst]	Radfahrer/in
racing cyclist ['reɪsɪŋ saɪklɪst]	Radrennfahrer/in
to **announce** [ə'naʊns]	verkünden, ankündigen
retirement [rɪ'taɪəmənt]	Rücktritt, Rückzug
competitive [kəm'petətɪv]	wettkampfmäßig
agency ['eɪdʒənsi]	Agentur
sample ['sɑːmpl]	Probe
to **charge sb with sth** [tʃɑːdʒ]	jdn einer Sache beschuldigen, jdn einer Sache anklagen
organization [ˌɔːgənaɪ'zeɪʃn]	Organisation
according to [ə'kɔːdɪŋ tə]	laut, zufolge
Olympic [ə'lɪmpɪk]	olympisch
committee [kə'mɪti]	Komitee
study ['stʌdi]	Untersuchung, Studie
historical [hɪ'stɒrɪkl]	historisch
evolution [ˌiːvə'luːʃn]	Entwicklung
phenomenon [fə'nɒmɪnən]	Phänomen, Erscheinung
century ['sentʃəri]	Jahrhundert
to **refer to sb/sth** [rɪ'fɜː tə]	jdn/etw erwähnen, sich auf jdn/etw beziehen
mixture ['mɪkstʃə]	Mischung
cocaine [kəʊ'keɪn]	Kokain
caffeine ['kæfiːn]	Koffein
strychnine ['strɪkniːn]	Strychnin
nitroglycerine [ˌnaɪtrəʊ'glɪsəriːn]	Nitroglycerin
to **stimulate** ['stɪmjuleɪt]	anregen, stimulieren
breathing ['briːðɪŋ]	Atmung
to **suffer sth** ['sʌfə]	an etw leiden, etw erleiden
hallucination [həˌluːsɪ'neɪʃn]	Halluzination, Wahnvorstellung
to **refuse** [rɪ'fjuːz]	sich weigern
to **chase sb** [tʃeɪs]	jdn verfolgen, jdn jagen
to **bat an eyelid** [ˌbæt ən 'aɪlɪd]	mit der Wimper zucken
to **dope** [dəʊp]	dopen
to **enter a competition** [ˌentər ə kɒmpə'tɪʃn]	an einem Wettkampf/ Wettbewerb teilnehmen
guy [gaɪ]	Typ, Kerl
corrupt [kə'rʌpt]	korrupt
to **cycle on** [ˌsaɪkl 'ɒn]	weiterradeln

page 15

to **summarize** ['sʌməraɪz]	zusammenfassen
notebook ['nəʊtbʊk]	Heft, Notizbuch
heading ['hedɪŋ]	Rubrik, Überschrift
reference (to sth) ['refərəns]	Verweis (auf etw)
aspect ['æspekt]	Gesichtspunkt, Aspekt
sub-heading [ˌsʌb 'hedɪŋ]	Teilrubrik, Zwischenüberschrift
to **scan** [skæn]	*(Text)* überfliegen
repetition [ˌrepə'tɪʃn]	Wiederholung
connection [kə'nekʃn]	Verbindung
legal ['liːgl]	erlaubt, legal
to **structure** ['strʌktʃə]	strukturieren
to **appear** [ə'pɪə]	scheinen
in general [ɪn 'dʒenrəl]	im Allgemeinen, generell
to **sum up** [ˌsʌm 'ʌp]	zusammenfassen
to sum up [tə ˌsʌm 'ʌp]	zusammenfassend

page 16

to **highlight** ['haɪlaɪt]	hervorheben
to **join** [dʒɔɪn]	beitreten, eintreten, mitmachen
at all [ət 'ɔːl]	überhaupt
beside [bɪ'saɪd]	neben
to **replace** [rɪ'pleɪs]	ersetzen, austauschen
instructor [ɪn'strʌktə]	Lehrer/in
to **trip** [trɪp]	stolpern
to **fit** [fɪt]	passen
muscle ['mʌsl]	Muskel
to **ache** [eɪk]	schmerzen, wehtun
energy ['enədʒi]	Energie
session ['seʃn]	Sitzung
to **suggest** [sə'dʒest]	vorschlagen
to **take sb along** [ˌteɪk ə'lɒŋ]	jdn mitnehmen
craze [kreɪz]	Modewelle, Trend
workout ['wɜːkaʊt]	(Fitness-)Training
called [kɔːld]	namens
tape [teɪp]	(Ton-)Band
instead of [ɪn'sted əv]	anstatt
to **cancel** ['kænsl]	absagen, stornieren
traditional [trə'dɪʃənl]	traditionell
to **improvise** ['ɪmprəvaɪz]	improvisieren
to **name** [neɪm]	nennen, benennen
it wasn't long before … [ɪt wɒznt ˌlɒŋ bɪ'fɔː]	es dauerte nicht lange, bis …
worldwide ['wɜːldwaɪd]	weltweit

page 17

overweight [ˌəʊvə'weɪt]	übergewichtig
slim [slɪm]	schlank
cardiovascular [ˌkɑːdiəʊ'væskjələ]	Herz-Kreislauf-
metabolism [mə'tæbəlɪzəm]	Stoffwechsel
calorie ['kæləri]	Kalorie
to **measure** ['meʒə]	messen
blood vessel ['blʌd vesl]	Blutgefäß
joy [dʒɔɪ]	Freude
excitement [ɪk'saɪtmənt]	Begeisterung
musical ['mjuːzɪkl]	musikalisch, Musik-
process ['prəʊses]	Ablauf, Vorgang, Prozess
to **change sth into sth** ['tʃeɪndʒ ɪntə]	etw in etw umwandeln
growth [grəʊθ]	Wachstum
attractive [ə'træktɪv]	attraktiv, anziehend
speaker ['spiːkə]	Sprecher/in
to **panic** ['pænɪk]	in Panik geraten
to **get the hang of it** [ˌget ðə 'hæŋ əv ɪt]	den richtigen Dreh finden
relevant ['reləvənt]	relevant, wichtig
mainly ['meɪnli]	hauptsächlich
atmosphere ['ætməsfɪə]	Stimmung, Atmosphäre
to **join in** [ˌdʒɔɪn 'ɪn]	mitmachen
to **stand up** [ˌstænd 'ʌp]	aufstehen, sich hinstellen
school leaving party ['skuːl liːvɪŋ pɑːti]	Schulabgangsfeier
benefit ['benɪfɪt]	Nutzen, Vorteil, Pluspunkt
to **strengthen** ['streŋθn]	kräftigen, stärken
lung [lʌŋ]	Lunge
to **increase sth** [ɪn'kriːs]	etw steigern
to **reduce** [rɪ'djuːs]	senken, reduzieren, verringern
stress [stres]	Belastung, Stress
to **boost** [buːst]	ankurbeln
to **burn** [bɜːn]	(sich) verbrennen
to **lose weight** [ˌluːz 'weɪt]	abnehmen

last but not least [ˌlɑːst bʌt nɒt ˈliːst]	zu guter Letzt, nicht zuletzt
to **feel low** [ˌfiːl ˈləʊ]	schlecht gelaunt sein, deprimiert sein
stressed [strest]	angestrengt, gestresst
worried [ˈwʌrid]	besorgt, beunruhigt
care [keə]	Sorge
to **talk sb through sth** [ˈtɔːk θruː]	jdm etw der Reihe nach erklären
warm-up [ˈwɔːm ʌp]	Aufwärmen
cool down [ˌkuːl ˈdaʊn]	Abkühlen
dance routine [ˈdɑːns ruːtiːn]	Tanzschritte
move [muːv]	Schritt, Bewegung
to **shake sth** [ʃeɪk]	etw schütteln, mit etw wackeln
hip [hɪp]	Hüfte
touch [tʌtʃ]	Berührung
to **get sb hooked** [ˌget ˈhʊkt]	jdn anfixen
to **give sth a try** [ˌɡɪv ə ˈtraɪ]	etw ausprobieren
unhealthy [ʌnˈhelθi]	nicht gesund
first name [ˈfɜːst neɪm]	Vorname
All the best, [ˌɔːl ðə ˈbest]	Mit besten Grüßen, Alles Gute

UNIT 3

page 18

brand [brænd]	Marke
power [ˈpaʊə]	Macht, Stärke, Kraft
to **write down** [ˌraɪt ˈdaʊn]	aufschreiben
to **shop** [ʃɒp]	einkaufen
fashionable [ˈfæʃnəbl]	modisch
gap [ɡæp]	Lücke
to **come down to sth** [ˌkʌm ˈdaʊn tə]	auf etw hinauslaufen, auf etw ankommen
quality [ˈkwɒləti]	Qualität
emotional [ɪˈməʊʃənl]	gefühlsmäßig, emotional
thinking [ˈθɪŋkɪŋ]	Denken
to **go for sth** [ˈɡəʊ fə]	etw nehmen, etw gut finden

page 19

consumer [kənˈsjuːmə]	Verbraucher/in, Konsument/in
choice [tʃɔɪs]	Wahl, Entscheidung
availability [əˌveɪləˈbɪləti]	Verfügbarkeit
affordable [əˈfɔːdəbl]	erschwinglich
though [ðəʊ]	aber, dagegen, allerdings
packaging [ˈpækɪdʒɪŋ]	Verpackung
to **affect** [əˈfekt]	beeinflussen, sich auswirken auf
background [ˈbækɡraʊnd]	Herkunft
sportswear [ˈspɔːtsweə]	Sportkleidung
to **advertise sth** [ˈædvətaɪz]	etw bewerben, für etw werben
goods *pl* [ɡʊdz]	Waren, Güter
to **suggest** [səˈdʒest]	unterstellen, suggerieren
athlete [ˈæθliːt]	Sportler/in, Athlet/in
over-achiever [ˌəʊvərəˈtʃiːvə]	Überflieger
to **look for sb/sth** [ˈlʊk fə]	jdn/etw suchen
to **achieve sth** [əˈtʃiːv]	etw erreichen, etw leisten
to **display** [dɪˈspleɪ]	zeigen
value [ˈvæljuː]	Wert
belief [bɪˈliːf]	Überzeugung
depending on [dɪˈpendɪŋ ɒn]	je nach(dem)
to **persuade** [pəˈsweɪd]	überzeugen, überreden
including [ɪnˈkluːdɪŋ]	einschließlich
to **pack** [pæk]	verpacken
to **identify with sb/sth** [aɪˈdentɪfaɪ wɪð]	sich mit jdm/etw identifizieren
to **grow up** [ˌɡrəʊ ˈʌp]	aufwachsen

page 20

sold out [ˌsəʊld ˈaʊt]	ausverkauft
to **rewrite** [ˌriːˈraɪt]	umformulieren, neu schreiben
position [pəˈzɪʃn]	Stelle, Stellung, Position
allowance [əˈlaʊəns]	Taschengeld
actually [ˈæktʃuəli]	in der Tat, eigentlich, wirklich
similarity [ˌsɪməˈlærəti]	Ähnlichkeit
discount [ˈdɪskaʊnt]	Rabatt, Nachlass
discount label [ˈdɪskaʊnt leɪbl]	Billigmarke
sweater [ˈswetə]	Pullover
preference [ˈprefrəns]	Vorliebe
to **celebrate** [ˈselɪbreɪt]	feiern
athletic [æθˈletɪk]	sportlich, athletisch
challenging [ˈtʃælɪndʒɪŋ]	anspruchsvoll, fordernd

page 21

comparison [kəmˈpærɪsn]	Steigerung *(von Adjektiven)*
crowded [ˈkraʊdɪd]	voll (mit Leuten), überfüllt
tasty [ˈteɪsti]	schmackhaft, lecker
to **download** [ˌdaʊnˈləʊd]	herunterladen
competitive [kəmˈpetətɪv]	konkurrenzfähig, *(Preise:)* günstig
to **collect sth** [kəˈlekt]	etw abholen
to **sponsor** [ˈspɒnsə]	(finanziell) unterstützen, sponsern
run [rʌn]	Lauf
it's not long before [ɪts nɒt ˌlɒŋ ˈbɪfɔː]	es dauert nicht lange, bis
to **pick sb/sth up** [ˌpɪk ˈʌp]	jdn/etw abholen
stripe [straɪp]	Streifen
(it's a) pity [ˈpɪti]	schade
you guys [ˌju ˈɡaɪz]	ihr
gear [ɡɪə]	Ausrüstung, Kleidung
Thank goodness! [ˌθæŋk ˈɡʊdnəs]	Gott sei Dank!
lovely [ˈlʌvli]	schön, nett, hübsch
What's up? [ˌwɒts ˈʌp]	Was gibt's? Was ist los?
fee [fiː]	Gebühr
entrance fee [ˈentrəns fiː]	Teilnahmegebühr
still [stɪl]	(immer) noch, dennoch
to **matter** [ˈmætə]	wichtig sein, darauf ankommen
to **feel comfortable** [ˌfiːl ˈkʌmftəbl]	sich wohlfühlen
affordability [əˌfɔːdəˈbɪləti]	Erschwinglichkeit, Bezahlbarkeit
to **interrupt** [ˌɪntəˈrʌpt]	unterbrechen, ins Wort fallen
to **pretend** [prɪˈtend]	vorgeben; so tun, als ob
sweatshop [ˈswetʃɒp]	Ausbeutungsbetrieb
What's going on? [ˌwɒts ɡəʊɪŋ ˈɒn]	Was ist los?
amateur [ˈæmətə]	Amateur(-), Hobby-
professional [prəˈfeʃənl]	Profi
to **meet up** [ˌmiːt ˈʌp]	sich treffen
to **cheer for sb** [ˈtʃɪə fə]	jdn anfeuern, jdm zujubeln
even though [ˈiːvn ðəʊ]	selbst wenn, obwohl
sports gear [ˈspɔːts ɡɪə]	Sportkleidung, Sportausrüstung

page 22

flap [flæp]	Umschlagklappe
cover ['kʌvə]	(Buch-)Umschlag, Einband
logical(ly) ['lɒdʒɪkl]	logisch
debate [dɪ'beɪt]	Diskussion, Debatte
to **make sure** [ˌmeɪk 'ʃʊə]	sicherstellen; dafür sorgen, dass
whenever [wen'evə]	jedes Mal, wenn; wann (auch) immer
to **pay attention to sth** [ˌpeɪ ə'tenʃn tə]	auf etw achten
to **give an opinion** [ˌgɪv ən ə'pɪniən]	eine Meinung äußern
to **give a reason** [ˌgɪv ə 'ri:zn]	eine Begründung anführen
to **disagree with sth** [ˌdɪsə'gri: wɪð]	einer Sache nicht zustimmen, gegen etw sein, etw ablehnen
to **keep sth safe** [ˌki:p 'seɪf]	etw aufbewahren
on the one hand [ɒn ðə 'wʌn hænd]	einerseits
in fact [ɪn 'fækt]	um genau zu sein, eigentlich
to **take sth into account** [ˌteɪk ɪntu ə'kaʊnt]	etw in Betracht ziehen, etw berücksichtigen
on the whole [ɒn ðə 'həʊl]	im Großen und Ganzen

page 23

victim ['vɪktɪm]	Opfer
either … or [ˌaɪðə 'ɔ:]	entweder … oder
(the) latest ['leɪtɪst]	der/die/das allerneueste/n
to **suit sb** [su:t]	*(Kleidung:)* jdm stehen
to **walk along sth** [wɔ:k]	etw *(Straße etc.)* entlanggehen
high street ['haɪ stri:t]	Hauptgeschäftsstraße, Einkaufsstraße
glossy ['glɒsi]	Hochglanz-
toned [təʊnd]	straff, durchtrainiert
to **photo-shop** ['fəʊtəʊ ʃɒp]	mit Photoshop bearbeiten
cover ['kʌvə]	Titelseite
fingernail ['fɪŋgəneɪl]	Fingernagel
to **squeeze oneself into sth** ['skwi:z ɪntə]	sich in etw hineinzwängen
skinny ['skɪni]	hauteng
copy ['kɒpi]	Nachahmung, Imitat
watch [wɒtʃ]	Armbanduhr
up to ['ʌp tə]	bis
to **admit** [əd'mɪt]	zugeben, (ein)gestehen
stuff [stʌf]	Zeug, Sache(n)
to **bet** [bet]	wetten
for what it's worth [fə wɒt ɪts 'wɜ:θ]	meiner (bescheidenen) Meinung nach
to **stick to sth** ['stɪk tə]	bei etw bleiben, sich an etw halten
item (of clothing) ['aɪtəm]	Kleidungsstück
to **suit sb/sth** [su:t]	zu jdm/etw passen
no matter … [ˌnəʊ 'mætə]	ganz egal, …
to **draw attention to sb/sth** [ˌdrɔ: ə'tenʃn tə]	Aufmerksamkeit auf jdn/etw ziehen
acne ['ækni]	Akne
Yuck! [jʌk]	Igitt! Bäh!
as far as I'm concerned [əz ˌfɑ:r əz ˌaɪm kən'sɜ:nd]	was mich betrifft
a bit [ə 'bɪt]	ein bisschen
tight [taɪt]	knapp, eng
to **stare at sb** ['steər ət]	jdn anstarren
matter ['mætə]	Angelegenheit, Sache
unique [ju'ni:k]	einzigartig
to **copy** ['kɒpi]	nachahmen, imitieren
to **experiment** [ɪk'sperɪmənt]	experimentieren
particular [pə'tɪkjələ]	bestimmt, speziell
secret ['si:krɪt]	Geheimnis
to **overdo it** [ˌəʊvə'du: ɪt]	es übertreiben
all at once [ˌɔ:l ət 'wʌns]	auf einmal
I'm afraid [aɪm ə'freɪd]	leider
criticism (of sb/sth) ['krɪtɪsɪzəm]	Kritik (an jdm/etw)
fake [feɪk]	Fälschung, Imitation
collection [kə'lekʃn]	Sammlung

page 24

bullet point ['bʊlɪt pɔɪnt]	Stichpunkt
preparation (for sth) [ˌprepə'reɪʃn]	Vorbereitung (auf etw)
waste of time [ˌweɪst əf 'taɪm]	Zeitverschwendung
to **keep up with sb/sth** [ˌki:p 'ʌp wɪð]	mit jdm/etw Schritt halten
to **influence** ['ɪnfluəns]	beeinflussen

UNIT 4

page 25

leisure ['leʒə]	Freizeit, Muße
to **surf the internet** [ˌsɜ:f ði 'ɪntənet]	im Internet surfen
to **mind sth** [maɪnd]	etw gegen etw haben
to **hang out** [ˌhæŋ 'aʊt]	rumhängen, sich rumtreiben
lack [læk]	Mangel
area ['eəriə]	Gegend, Region
riding ['raɪdɪŋ]	Reiten
lesson ['lesn]	(Unterrichts-)Stunde
photography [fə'tɒgrəfi]	Fotografie, Foto-
to **save up** [ˌseɪv 'ʌp]	sparen

page 26

instead [ɪn'sted]	stattdessen
to **interpret** [ɪn'tɜ:prɪt]	interpretieren
cartoon [kɑ:'tu:n]	Karikatur
to **analyse** ['ænəlaɪz]	analysieren
instructions *pl* [ɪn'strʌkʃnz]	Anleitung, Anweisung(en)
drawing ['drɔ:ɪŋ]	Zeichnung
speech bubble ['spi:tʃ bʌbl]	Sprechblase
to **relate to sth** [rɪ'leɪt tə]	sich auf etw beziehen
to **get sth** [get]	etw verstehen, etw kapieren
joke [dʒəʊk]	Witz
to **study sth** ['stʌdi]	sich etw genau ansehen
cartoonist [kɑ:'tu:nɪst]	Karikaturist/in
to **draw** [drɔ:]	zeichnen
to **make a point** [ˌmeɪk ə 'pɔɪnt]	ein Argument vortragen, etw sagen wollen
human being [ˌhju:mən 'bi:ɪŋ]	Mensch, menschliches Wesen

page 27

among [ə'mʌŋ]	unter, inmitten, zwischen
shopping mall ['ʃɒpɪŋ mɔ:l]	Einkaufspassage, Einkaufszentrum
curfew ['kɜ:fju:]	Sperrstunde
unless [ən'les]	es sei denn, außer wenn
to **put an end to sth** [ˌpʊt ən 'end tə]	mit etw Schluss machen, einen Schlussstrich unter etw ziehen
at least [ət 'li:st]	zumindest, mindestens
to **accompany** [ə'kʌmpəni]	begleiten
legal guardian [ˌli:gl 'gɑ:diən]	Vormund, Erziehungsberechtigte/r
to **approach sb** [ə'prəʊtʃ]	an jdn herantreten

to **provide** [prə'vaɪd]	zur Verfügung stellen
ID [ˌaɪ 'diː]	Personalausweis
although [ɔːl'ðəʊ]	obwohl
to **object to sth** [əb'dʒekt tə]	etw ablehnen, gegen etw Einwände haben
spokesman ['spəʊksmən]	Sprecher
to **argue** ['ɑːgjuː]	argumentieren, geltend machen
retailer ['riːteɪlə]	Einzelhändler/in
to **back** [bæk]	unterstützen
to **respect** [rɪ'spekt]	respektieren
incident ['ɪnsɪdənt]	Vorfall, Zwischenfall
complaint [kəm'pleɪnt]	Beschwerde, Klage, Reklamation
bid [bɪd]	Versuch
to **maintain sth** [meɪn'teɪn]	etw aufrecht erhalten
to **estimate** ['estɪmeɪt]	schätzen
to **state** [steɪt]	darlegen, festlegen
appropriate(ly) [ə'prəʊpriət]	angemessen, passend
...-oriented ['ɔːriəntɪd]	...orientiert
adequate(ly) ['ædɪkwət]	ausreichend, angemessen
to **cover** ['kʌvə]	bedecken
visible ['vɪzəbl]	sichtbar
undergarments *pl* ['ʌndəgɑːmənts]	Unterwäsche
permitted [pə'mɪtɪd]	erlaubt, gestattet
measure ['meʒə]	Maßnahme
to **divide** [dɪ'vaɪd]	teilen
intent [ɪn'tent]	Absicht
to **loiter** ['lɔɪtə]	herumlungern
initiative [ɪ'nɪʃətɪv]	Aktion, Initiative
to **escort sb** [ɪ'skɔːt]	jdn begleiten, jdn eskortieren
exemption [ɪg'zempʃn]	Ausnahme, Befreiung
to **boast sth** [bəʊst]	etw aufweisen (können)
to **abridge** [ə'brɪdʒ]	*(Text)* kürzen
to **adapt** [ə'dæpt]	*(Text)* bearbeiten

page 28

mediation [ˌmiːdi'eɪʃn]	Vermittlung
written ['rɪtn]	schriftlich
sense [sens]	Sinn
to **be aimed at sb** [bi 'eɪmd ət]	sich an jdn richten
to **paraphrase** ['pærəfreɪz]	umschreiben, paraphrasieren
sort [sɔːt]	Art, Sorte
to **re-read** [ˌriː 'riːd]	erneut lesen
colleague ['kɒliːg]	Kollege/-in
translation [træns'leɪʃn]	Übersetzung
to **mess around** [ˌmes ə'raʊnd]	herumalbern, herumgammeln
to **cause** [kɔːz]	verursachen
to **be on sale** [bi ɒn 'seɪl]	angeboten werden, zum Verkauf stehen
to **move house** [ˌmuːv 'haʊs]	umziehen
to **lift** [lɪft]	heben
to **complain** [kəm'pleɪn]	sich beschweren, sich beklagen

page 29

social skills *pl* [ˌsəʊʃl 'skɪlz]	Sozialkompetenz
to **exchange** [ɪks'tʃeɪndʒ]	austauschen
moans *pl* [məʊnz]	Gejammer, Genörgel
sex [seks]	Geschlecht
the opposite sex [ði ˌɒpəzɪt 'seks]	das andere Geschlecht
to **text** [tekst]	eine SMS schicken, simsen
to **post** [pəʊst]	*(im Internet)* posten
peer [pɪə]	Gleichaltrige/r, Altersgenosse
to **interact** [ˌɪntər'ækt]	interagieren, aufeinander eingehen
network ['netwɜːk]	Netz, Netzwerk
site [saɪt]	Website
to **get together** [ˌget tə'geðə]	sich treffen
apart from [ə'pɑːt frəm]	abgesehen von, außer
to **look after sb** [lʊk 'ɑːftə]	sich um jdn kümmern
siblings *pl* ['sɪblɪŋz]	Geschwister
nearby ['nɪəbaɪ]	in der Nähe
opportunity [ˌɒpə'tjuːnəti]	Gelegenheit, Möglichkeit, Chance
to **socialize** ['səʊʃəlaɪz]	sich treffen, unter Leute gehen
to **be pleased** [bi 'pliːzd]	sich freuen
to **keep in touch** [ˌkiːp ɪn 'tʌtʃ]	in Verbindung bleiben
face to face [ˌfeɪs tə 'feɪs]	persönlich
contact ['kɒntækt]	Kontakt, Verbindung
ability [ə'bɪləti]	Fähigkeit, Befähigung
especially [ɪ'speʃəli]	besonders, insbesondere

page 30

to **come round** [ˌkʌm 'raʊnd]	vorbeikommen
till [tɪl]	bis
all right by me [ɔːl ˌraɪt baɪ 'miː]	in Ordnung für mich
there's little point in doing sth [ðeəz ˌlɪtl pɔɪnt ɪn 'duːɪŋ]	es hat wenig Sinn, etw zu tun

JOB SKILLS 1

page 31

vocational college [vəʊˌkeɪʃənl 'kɒlɪdʒ]	Fachoberschule, Berufskolleg
work experience ['wɜːk ɪkspɪəriəns]	Praktikum
writer ['raɪtə]	Verfasser/in
suggestion [sə'dʒestʃən]	Vorschlag
to **apply for a job** [əˌplaɪ fər ə 'dʒɒb]	sich auf eine Stelle bewerben
trainee [treɪ'niː]	Auszubildende/r
native language [ˌneɪtɪv 'læŋgwɪdʒ]	Muttersprache
secretary ['sekrətri]	Sekretär/in
backpacker ['bækpækə]	Rucksacktourist/in
hostel ['hɒstl]	Herberge, Wohnheim
sometime ['sʌmtaɪm]	irgendwann
Cheers! [tʃɪəz]	Tschüs! Mach's gut! Danke!
insight ['ɪnsaɪt]	Einblick
to **run** [rʌn]	*(Unternehmen)* führen, betreiben
at first hand [ət ˌfɜːst 'hænd]	aus erster Hand, hautnah
contact details *pl* ['kɒntækt diːteɪlz]	Kontaktdaten
to **mention** ['menʃn]	erwähnen
to **attach sth** [ə'tætʃ]	*(E-Mail:)* etw beifügen, etw anhängen
job advertisement ['dʒɒb ədvɜːtɪsmənt]	Stellenanzeige, -ausschreibung
to **let sb know sth** [ˌlet 'nəʊ]	jdm etw mitteilen
at the latest [ət ðə 'leɪtɪst]	spätestens
Yours sincerely [ˌjɔːz sɪn'sɪəli]	*(Brief:)* Mit freundlichen Grüßen

page 32

to **contrast** [kən'trɑːst]	gegenüberstellen, vergleichen
abbreviation [əˌbriːvi'eɪʃn]	Abkürzung
chatty ['tʃæti]	mitteilsam, geschwätzig
etiquette ['etɪket]	Etikette, Regeln
subject line ['sʌbdʒɪkt laɪn]	*(Brief:)* Betreffzeile
to **get into the habit of doing sth** [ˌget ɪntə ðə 'hæbɪt əv]	sich angewöhnen, etw zu tun
to **type sth in** [ˌtaɪp 'ɪn]	etw eintippen
capital letter [ˌkæpɪtl 'letə]	Großbuchstabe
spelling ['spelɪŋ]	Rechtschreibung
application [ˌæplɪ'keɪʃn]	Bewerbung
to **submit** [səb'mɪt]	einreichen, vorlegen, zusenden
to **take sth further** [ˌteɪk 'fɜːðə]	etw (weiter) verfolgen
to **confirm** [kən'fɜːm]	bestätigen
to **be available** [bi ə'veɪləbl]	*(Telefon:)* zu sprechen sein
set-up ['setʌp]	Aufbau

page 33

to **separate** ['sepəreɪt]	trennen, loslösen
to **soften** ['sɒfn]	mildern, abmildern
surname ['sɜːneɪm]	Nachname
proper name [ˌprɒpə 'neɪm]	Eigenname
line [laɪn]	Leitung
digit ['dɪdʒɪt]	Ziffer
separately ['seprətli]	einzeln
e.g. [ˌiː 'dʒiː]	z. B.
to **spell** [spel]	buchstabieren
to **put sb through** [ˌpʊt 'θruː]	*(Telefon:)* jdn durchstellen, jdn verbinden
to **leave a message** [ˌliːv ə 'mesɪdʒ]	eine Nachricht hinterlassen

page 34

as things turn out [əz ˌθɪŋz tɜːn 'aʊt]	wie sich herausstellt
appointment [ə'pɔɪntmənt]	Termin, Verabredung
to **bother sb** ['bɒðə]	jdn belästigen, jdn stören
luck [lʌk]	Glück
to **be unavailable** [bi ˌʌnə'veɪləbl]	*(Telefon:)* nicht zu sprechen sein
to **have a chat** [həv a 'tʃæt]	sich unterhalten, miteinander plaudern
leaflet ['liːflət]	Broschüre, Merkblatt
attachment [ə'tætʃmənt]	*(E-Mail:)* Anhang
definitely ['defɪnətli]	absolut, ganz sicher
to **hold the line** [ˌhəʊld ðə 'laɪn]	am Apparat bleiben
likely ['laɪkli]	wahrscheinlich
caller ['kɔːlə]	Anrufer/in
to **carry out** [ˌkæri 'aʊt]	durchführen, ausführen
to **respond to sth** [rɪ'spɒnd tə]	auf etw reagieren, auf etw antworten
to **take a message** [ˌteɪk ə 'mesɪdʒ]	etw ausrichten, eine Nachricht notieren
to **read sth back** [ˌriːd 'bæk]	etw (zur Kontrolle) vorlesen
to **enquire about sth** [ɪn'kwaɪər əbaʊt]	sich nach etw erkundigen
department [dɪ'pɑːtmənt]	Abteilung
accounts [ə'kaʊnts]	Buchhaltung
to **hold on** [ˌhəʊld 'ɒn]	warten
engaged [ɪn'geɪdʒd]	*(Telefon:)* besetzt

UNIT 5

page 35

virtual ['vɜːtʃuəl]	virtuell
role [rəʊl]	Rolle
poster ['pəʊstə]	Plakat
gallery ['gæləri]	Galerie
gallery walk ['gæləri wɔːk]	Galerierundgang
to **put sth up** [ˌpʊt 'ʌp]	etw *(Bild etc.)* aufhängen
per [pə]	pro

page 36

to **skim** [skɪm]	*(Text)* überfliegen
to **underline** [ˌʌndə'laɪn]	unterstreichen
bold [bəʊld]	fett(gedruckt)
type [taɪp]	Schrift, Type
italics *pl* [ɪ'tælɪks]	Kursivschrift
lonely ['ləʊnli]	einsam
habit ['hæbɪt]	Gewohnheit
Briton ['brɪtn]	Brite/Britin
average ['ævərɪdʒ]	Durchschnitt
poll [pəʊl]	Umfrage
to **suggest** [sə'dʒest]	darauf hindeuten, nahelegen
third [θɜːd]	Drittel
user ['juːzə]	Benutzer/in
quarter ['kwɔːtə]	Viertel
usage ['juːsɪdʒ]	Nutzung
to **exceed** [ɪk'siːd]	übersteigen
to **base on sth** ['beɪs ɒn]	auf etw basieren
to **carry out** [ˌkæri 'aʊt]	durchführen, ausführen
primary ['praɪməri]	Haupt-, hauptsächlich
reader ['riːdə]	Dozent/in
psychology [saɪ'kɒlədʒi]	Psychologie
to **tend to do sth** ['tend tə]	dazu neigen, etw zu tun
largely ['lɑːdʒli]	weitgehend, überwiegend
dependent on sth [dɪ'pendənt ɒn]	von etw abhängig
all the time [ˌɔːl ðə 'taɪm]	ständig, die ganze Zeit
to **cut sb off from sth** [ˌkʌt 'ɒf frəm]	jdn von etw abschneiden
several ['sevrəl]	mehrere
left out of sth [ˌleft 'aʊt əv]	von etw ausgeschlossen
to **isolate** ['aɪsəleɪt]	absondern, isolieren

page 37

at the expense of sth [ət ði ɪk'spens əv]	auf Kosten von etw
regardless of sth [rɪ'gɑːdləs əv]	ungeachtet einer Sache
update ['ʌpdeɪt]	Aktualisierung
to **engage with sb** [ɪn'geɪdʒ wɪð]	auf jdn zugehen
channel ['tʃænl]	Kanal
to **listen in** [ˌlɪsn 'ɪn]	mithören
presence ['prezns]	Anwesenheit, Präsenz
amount [ə'maʊnt]	Betrag
sum [sʌm]	Summe
representative [ˌreprɪ'zentətɪv]	repräsentativ
to **get involved with sb** [ˌget ɪn'vɒlvd wɪð]	mit jdm zu tun haben
account [ə'kaʊnt]	Konto
to **be called** [bi 'kɔːld]	heißen
unfit [ʌn'fɪt]	nicht fit
to **spell** [spel]	buchstabieren, (richtig) schreiben
handwriting ['hændraɪtɪŋ]	Handschrift
thumb [θʌm]	Daumen

childhood ['tʃaɪldhʊd]	Kindheit
to **hand sth in** [ˌhænd 'ɪn]	etw abgeben
suggestion [sə'dʒestʃən]	Vorschlag
to **take a vote** [ˌteɪk ə 'vəʊt]	abstimmen

page 38

entry ['entri]	*(Blog:)* Beitrag, Meldung
importance [ɪm'pɔːtns]	Bedeutung, Wichtigkeit
anecdote ['ænɪkdəʊt]	Anekdote
call for help [ˌkɔːl fə 'help]	Hilferuf
wall [wɔːl]	Wand, Pinnwand
conclusion [kən'kluːʒn]	Schlussfolgerung, Schluss
helpline ['helplaɪn]	Hotline, Sorgentelefon
to **suffer from sth** ['sʌfə frəm]	unter etw leiden
solution [sə'luːʃn]	Lösung
counsellor ['kaʊnsələ]	Berater/in
to **take a call** [ˌteɪk ə 'kɔːl]	einen Anruf entgegennehmen, ans Telefon gehen
to **go viral** [ˌgəʊ 'vaɪrəl]	sich (im Internet) rasend schnell verbreiten
to **laugh at sb** ['lɑːf ət]	über jdn lachen, jdn auslachen
to **point at sb/sth** ['pɔɪnt ət]	auf jdn/etw zeigen
desperate ['despərət]	verzweifelt
fully ['fʊli]	vollkommen, völlig
cruel [kruːəl]	grausam, gemein
to **trust** [trʌst]	vertrauen
appointment [ə'pɔɪntmənt]	Termin
talk [tɔːk]	Gerede
advice [əd'vaɪs]	(guter) Rat, Ratschläge
to **see sb** [siː]	zu jdm gehen
practical ['præktɪkl]	zweckmäßig, praktisch (umsetzbar)
to **delete** [dɪ'liːt]	löschen, tilgen
to **advise sb** [əd'vaɪz]	jdn beraten, jdm etw raten
to **contact sb** ['kɒntækt]	sich mit jdm in Verbindung setzen

page 39

to **block** [blɒk]	sperren
to **deactivate** [ˌdiː'æktɪveɪt]	stilllegen, deaktivieren
legal action [ˌliːgl 'ækʃn]	rechtliche Schritte
to **take legal action** [teɪk ˌliːgl 'ækʃn]	rechtliche Schritte unternehmen
setting ['setɪŋ]	Einstellung
to **bother sb** ['bɒðə]	jdn belästigen
right-hand ['raɪt hænd]	rechte/r/s, auf der rechten Seite
screen [skriːn]	Bildschirm
to **reactivate** [ˌrɪ'æktɪveɪt]	wieder in Betrieb nehmen, reaktivieren
at any time [ət ˌeni 'taɪm]	jederzeit
to **log in** [ˌlɒg 'ɪn]	sich einloggen
to **log out** [ˌlɒg 'aʊt]	sich ausloggen
deletion [dɪ'liːʃn]	Löschung, Tilgung
epitaph ['epɪtɑːf]	Grabinschrift
e.g. [ˌiː 'dʒiː]	z. B.
to **hire sb** ['haɪə]	jdn beauftragen, jdn engagieren
lawyer ['lɔːjə]	Anwalt/Anwältin
specialist lawyer [ˌspeʃəlɪst 'lɔːjə]	Fachanwalt/-anwältin
service ['sɜːvɪs]	Dienst, Dienstleistung
provider [prə'vaɪdə]	Anbieter
thousand ['θaʊznd]	tausend, Tausend

page 40

unwanted [ˌʌn'wɒntɪd]	unerwünscht
schoolboy ['skuːlbɔɪ]	Schuljunge
drunken ['drʌŋkən]	betrunken
crasher ['kræʃə]	ungeladener Gast
to **trash sth** [træʃ]	etw demolieren
pound [paʊnd]	Pfund
reveller ['revələ]	Feiernde/r
to **gatecrash** ['geɪtkræʃ]	uneingeladen erscheinen
damage ['dæmɪdʒ]	Schaden
vomit ['vɒmɪt]	Erbrochenes
terraced *BE* ['terəst]	Reihenhaus-
property ['prɒpəti]	Immobilie(n), Anwesen
riot ['raɪət]	Aufstand, Aufruhr
riot police ['raɪət pəliːs]	Bereitschaftspolizei
to **break up** [ˌbreɪk 'ʌp]	*(Menschenmenge)* zerstreuen
trouble ['trʌbl]	Ärger, Problem(e)
danger ['deɪndʒə]	Gefahr
details *pl* ['diːteɪlz]	Angaben
to **realise** ['rɪəlaɪz]	wissen, erkennen, klar sein
invitation [ˌɪnvɪ'teɪʃn]	Einladung
to **throw** [θrəʊ]	werfen
to **throw a party** [ˌθrəʊ ə 'pɑːti]	eine Party geben/schmeißen
privacy ['prɪvəsi]	Privatsphäre
absolutely ['æbsəluːtli]	absolut
essential [ɪ'senʃl]	wesentlich, unerlässlich
to **make sb aware of sth** [ˌmeɪk ə'weər əv]	jdn über etw informieren, jdn auf etw hinweisen
poisoning ['pɔɪzənɪŋ]	Vergiftung
laughing gas ['lɑːfɪŋ gæs]	Lachgas
canister ['kænɪstə]	Dose, Büchse
to **toss** [tɒs]	werfen
living room ['lɪvɪŋ ruːm]	Wohnzimmer
carpet ['kɑːpɪt]	Teppich(boden)
to **clean up** [ˌkliːn 'ʌp]	aufräumen, saubermachen
to **damage** ['dæmɪdʒ]	beschädigen
skylight ['skaɪlaɪt]	Oberlicht, Dachfenster
bouncer ['baʊnsə]	Türsteher/in
in advance [ɪn əd'vɑːns]	im Voraus
unable [ʌn'eɪbl]	nicht in der Lage, unfähig
to **cope (with sth)** ['kəʊp wɪð]	etw bewältigen, mit etw klarkommen, mit etw fertig werden
to **turn up** [ˌtɜːn 'ʌp]	auftauchen
shocked [ʃɒkt]	schockiert
to **drop sb off** [ˌdrɒp 'ɒf]	jdn (wohin)bringen
aged [eɪdʒd]	im Alter von
to **wreck** [rek]	demolieren
chaos ['keɪɒs]	Chaos
to **do sb harm** [du 'hɑːm]	jdm etwas (an)tun
apparently [ə'pærəntli]	anscheinend
reputation [ˌrepju'teɪʃn]	Ansehen, Ruf
to **shoot up** [ˌʃuːt 'ʌp]	rasant ansteigen

page 41

immediately [ɪ'miːdiətli]	unverzüglich, unmittelbar, sofort
to **get drunk** [ˌget 'drʌŋk]	sich betrinken
to **deal with sth** ['diːl wɪð]	mit etw zurechtkommen, mit etw umgehen
to **look sth up** [ˌlʊk 'ʌp]	etw *(Vokabel etc.)* nachschlagen
context ['kɒntekst]	Zusammenhang, Kontext
uninvited [ˌʌnɪn'vaɪtɪd]	un(ein)geladen
noise [nɔɪz]	Lärm
next door [ˌnekst 'dɔː]	nebenan
to **end up** [ˌend 'ʌp]	landen

page 42

text message	['tekst mesɪdʒ]	SMS
to **upload**	[ˌʌp'ləʊd]	hochladen

page 43

mess	[mes]	Chaos
to **expand**	[ɪk'spænd]	erweitern
to **act out**	[ˌækt 'aʊt]	spielen, vorspielen
horrified	['hɒrɪfaɪd]	entsetzt
invite	['ɪnvaɪt]	Einladung
to **wash**	[wɒʃ]	abwaschen, abwischen
to **apologize**	[ə'pɒlədʒaɪz]	sich entschuldigen
behaviour	[bɪ'heɪvjə]	Benehmen, Verhalten
cancer	['kænsə]	Krebs *(Krankheit)*
fundraiser	['fʌndreɪzə]	Spendensammler/in
to **raise money**	[ˌreɪz 'mʌni]	Geld beschaffen
charity	['tʃærəti]	Wohltätigkeit, wohltätige Zwecke
plight	[plaɪt]	Notlage
to **spread**	[spred]	sich verbreiten
to **diagnose sb with sth**	['daɪəgnəʊz wɪð]	etw *(Krankheit)* bei jdm feststellen/diagnostizieren
terminal	['tɜːmɪnl]	im Endstadium, tödlich
rather than	['rɑːðə ðən]	anstatt
to **dwell on sth**	['dwel ɒn]	sich mit etw aufhalten
misfortune	[ˌmɪs'fɔːtʃuːn]	Unglück, Missgeschick
to **draw up**	[ˌdrɔː 'ʌp]	*(Text)* verfassen, abfassen
bucket	['bʌkɪt]	Eimer
bucket list	['bʌkɪt lɪst]	*Dinge, die man getan haben sollte, bevor man stirbt*
skydive	['skaɪdaɪv]	Fallschirmsprung
drums *pl*	[drʌmz]	Schlagzeug
final	['faɪnl]	Finale
initially	[ɪ'nɪʃəli]	anfangs, anfänglich
to **set out to do sth**	[ˌset 'aʊt tə]	sich vornehmen, etw tun
fundraising	['fʌndreɪzɪŋ]	Spendensammeln, Geldbeschaffung
campaign	[kæm'peɪn]	Aktion, Kampagne
to **attract**	[ə'trækt]	anlocken, anziehen
to **attract attention**	[əˌtrækt ə'tenʃn]	Aufmerksamkeit erregen
inspirational	[ˌɪnspɪ'reɪʃnəl]	anregend, inspirierend
to **benefit**	['benɪfɪt]	nutzen, Nutzen bringen, profitieren
to **research sth**	[rɪ'sɜːtʃ]	etw recherchieren, Nachforschungen über etw anstellen
findings *pl*	['faɪndɪŋz]	Ergebnisse

page 44

to **think twice**	[θɪŋk 'twaɪs]	gründlich überlegen
per cent	[pə 'sent]	Prozent
common	['kɒmən]	verbreitet, üblich
appearance	[ə'pɪərəns]	Aussehen, Äußeres, (äußere) Erscheinung
to **spiral out of control**	['spaɪrəl]	außer Kontrolle geraten
in particular	[ɪn pə'tɪkjələ]	insbesondere
lovable	['lʌvəbl]	liebenswert
worthwhile	[ˌwɜːθ'waɪl]	lohnend
to **value**	['væljuː]	wertschätzen, schätzen
to **reveal**	[rɪ'viːl]	enthüllen, verraten
to **create**	[kri'eɪt]	erstellen, kreieren
nail	[neɪl]	Fingernagel
embarrassing	[ɪm'bærəsɪŋ]	peinlich
solid	['sɒlɪd]	fest, solide
dependable	[dɪ'pendəbl]	zuverlässig, verlässlich
employer	[ɪm'plɔɪə]	Arbeitgeber/in
to **look for**	['lʊk fə]	suchen
to **remind sb (of sth)**	[rɪ'maɪnd]	jdn (an etw) erinnern
suit	[suːt]	Anzug

UNIT 6

page 45

advertising	['ædvətaɪzɪŋ]	Werbung
billboard	['bɪlbɔːd]	Reklametafel, Plakatwand
digital signage	[ˌdɪdʒɪtl 'saɪnɪdʒ]	digitale Außenwerbung
ad, advert, advertisment	[æd, 'ædvɜːt, əd'vɜːtɪsmənt]	Anzeige, Werbung
viral ad	[ˌvaɪrəl 'æd]	Internet-Werbespot
element	['elɪmənt]	Baustein, Element
ambition	[æm'bɪʃn]	Ziel, Ehrgeiz
emotion	[ɪ'məʊʃn]	Gefühl, Emotion
entertainment	[ˌentə'teɪnmənt]	Unterhaltung
excitement	[ɪk'saɪtmənt]	Spannung, Aufregung
fascination	[ˌfæsɪ'neɪʃn]	Faszination
horror	['hɒrə]	Schrecken
tragedy	['trædʒədi]	Tragödie
humour	['hjuːmə]	Humor
mystery	['mɪstri]	Rätsel, Rätselhaftigkeit
provocation	[ˌprɒvə'keɪʃn]	Provokation
reward	[rɪ'wɔːd]	Belohnung, Lohn
to **contain**	[kən'teɪn]	enthalten

page 46

theory	['θɪəri]	Theorie
giant	['dʒaɪənt]	riesig, riesenhaft
note	[nəʊt]	Ton, Note
likely	['laɪkli]	wahrscheinlich
to **be likely to do sth**	[bi 'laɪkli tə]	etw wahrscheinlich tun (werden)
to **skip sth**	[skɪp]	etw auslassen, etw überspringen
escalator	['eskəleɪtə]	Rolltreppe
in favor of doing sth *AE*	[ɪn 'feɪvər əv]	um (stattdessen) etw zu tun
to **compose**	[kəm'pəʊz]	komponieren
subway *AE*	['sʌbweɪ]	U-Bahn
to **view sth**	[vjuː]	(sich) etw ansehen
concept	['kɒnsept]	Idee, Gedanke, Konzept
to **create**	[kri'eɪt]	(er)schaffen, entwerfen, kreieren
ad(vertising) agency	['æd eɪdʒənsi]	Werbeagentur
goal	[gəʊl]	Ziel, Absicht
do-good	['duː gʊd]	weltverbessernd
to **promote sth**	[prə'məʊt]	für etw werben, etw bewerben
environmentally friendly	[ɪnˌvaɪrənˌmentəli 'frendli]	umweltfreundlich
increasingly	[ɪn'kriːsɪŋli]	zunehmend
competitive	[kəm'petətɪv]	umkämpft, wettbewerbsintensiv
eco-	['iːkəʊ]	Öko-
traditional	[trə'dɪʃənl]	herkömmlich
effective	[ɪ'fektɪv]	wirksam, effektiv
competition	[ˌkɒmpə'tɪʃn]	Konkurrenz, Konkurrenzkampf
environmental(ly)	[ɪnˌvaɪrən'mentl]	umweltmäßig, Umwelt-
sound	[saʊnd]	solide, untadelig

fierce [fɪəs]	heftig, erbittert
innovative ['ɪnəveɪtɪv]	innovativ
approach [ə'prəʊtʃ]	Ansatz, Herangehensweise
deputy manager [ˌdepjəti 'mænɪdʒə]	stellvertretende/r Geschäftsführer/in
commuter [kə'mjuːtə]	Pendler/in
to **choose sth over sth** ['tʃuːz əʊvə]	etw einer anderen Sache vorziehen
to **increase** [ɪn'kriːs]	steigen, zunehmen
phase [feɪz]	Phase
release [rɪ'liːs]	Veröffentlichung
to **enter sth** ['entə]	an etw teilnehmen
contest ['kɒntest]	Wettbewerb
to **submit sth** [səb'mɪt]	etw einreichen, etw einsenden
once [wʌns]	sobald
submission [səb'mɪʃn]	Einsendung
thoughtful ['θɔːtfl]	wohlüberlegt, gut durchdacht
game machine ['ɡeɪm məʃiːn]	Videospielgerät, Spielautomat
to **turn sb/sth into sb/sth** ['tɜːn ɪntə]	jdn/etw zu jdm/etw machen
can [kæn]	Dose
to **encourage sb to do sth** [ɪn'kʌrɪdʒ]	jdn ermuntern, etw zu tun
to **invent** [ɪn'vent]	erfinden
bottle bank ['bɒtl bæŋk]	Glascontainer
arcade [ɑː'keɪd]	Spielautomat
amusement arcade [ə'mjuːzmənt ɑːkeɪd]	Spielhalle
noise [nɔɪz]	Geräusch
passer-by ['pɑːsə baɪ]	Passant/in
display [dɪ'spleɪ]	Bildschirm, Anzeige, Display
conventional [kən'venʃənl]	konventionell, herkömmlich

page 47

deep [diːp]	tief
rubbish ['rʌbɪʃ]	Müll, Abfall
rubbish bin ['rʌbɪʃ bɪn]	Mülltonne
crash [kræʃ]	Schlag, Krach
to **step** [step]	treten
to **be fun** [bi 'fʌn]	Spaß machen
to **protect** [prə'tekt]	schützen
metal ['metl]	Metall
government ['ɡʌvənmənt]	Regierung, öffentliche Verwaltung
clever ['klevə]	intelligent, klug, schlau, clever
ground [ɡraʊnd]	(Erd-)Boden
effect [ɪ'fekt]	Wirkung, Effekt

page 48

in addition [ɪn ə'dɪʃn]	außerdem, darüber hinaus
for this reason [fə ðɪs 'riːzn]	aus diesem Grund
presentation [ˌprezn'teɪʃn]	Vortrag, Referat, Präsentation
to **give a presentation** [ɡɪv ə ˌprezn'teɪʃn]	ein Referat halten
slide [slaɪd]	Dia, (Overhead-)Folie
to **take turns** [ˌteɪk 'tɜːnz]	sich abwechseln
spelling ['spelɪŋ]	Rechtschreibung
to **number** ['nʌmbə]	nummerieren
hand-held ['hænd held]	in der Hand gehalten
quick reference [ˌkwɪk 'refərəns]	schnelles Nachschlagen
presenter [prɪ'zentə]	Vortragende/r
to **form** [fɔːm]	bilden
to **present** [prɪ'zent]	vorstellen, präsentieren
invention [ɪn'venʃn]	Erfindung
tram [træm]	Straßenbahn, Tram
public transport [ˌpʌblɪk 'trænspɔːt]	öffentliche Verkehrsmittel
ticket inspector ['tɪkɪt ɪnspektə]	Fahrkartenkontrolleur/in
to **fine sb** [faɪn]	jdn mit einer Geldbuße belegen
to **stamp** [stæmp]	stempeln, abstempeln
lottery ['lɒtəri]	Lotterie, Verlosung
instant(ly) ['ɪnstənt]	sofortig, augenblicklich
salary ['sæləri]	Gehalt
speed [spiːd]	Geschwindigkeit
speed camera ['spiːd kæmərə]	Geschwindigkeitsüberwachungskamera, Radarfalle
speed limit ['spiːd lɪmɪt]	Geschwindigkeitsbegrenzung
to **reward** [rɪ'wɔːd]	belohnen
fine [faɪn]	Geldbuße
traffic lights *pl* ['træfɪk laɪts]	Ampel
motorist *BE* ['məʊtərɪst]	Autofahrer/in
to **jump red lights** [ˌdʒʌmp red 'laɪts]	bei Rot über eine Ampel fahren
driving licence ['draɪvɪŋ laɪsns]	Führerschein
knowledge ['nɒlɪdʒ]	Wissen, Kenntnis(se)
visuals *pl* ['vɪʒuəlz]	visuelle Hilfsmittel
OHP transparency [ˌəʊ eɪtʃ 'piː trænspærənsi]	Overheadfolie
introductions *pl* [ˌɪntrə'dʌkʃnz]	Vorstellen
to **hand over** [ˌhænd 'əʊvə]	übergeben
in conclusion [ɪn kən'kluːʒn]	abschließend, zum Schluss
to **be pleased to do sth** [bi 'pliːzd tə]	etw gern tun

page 49

giant ['dʒaɪənt]	Riese
to **make the difference** [ˌmeɪk ðə 'dɪfrəns]	entscheidend sein, den entscheidenden Unterschied ausmachen
to **start out** [ˌstɑːt 'aʊt]	(zunächst) anfangen
office clerk ['ɒfɪs klɑːk]	Büroangestellte/r
soap [səʊp]	Seife
dope [dəʊp]	Depp
managing director [ˌmænɪdʒɪŋ də'rektə]	Geschäftsführer/in
in-tray ['ɪn treɪ]	Posteingang(skorb)
to **fire sb** ['faɪə]	jdn feuern
to **hire sb** ['haɪə]	jdn einstellen
I've never looked back. [aɪv ˌnevə lʊkt 'bæk]	Ich habe es nie bereut.
to **set up** [ˌset 'ʌp]	*(Unternehmen)* gründen
manufacturer [ˌmænju'fæktʃərə]	Hersteller/in, Produzent/in
to **know sth inside out** [nəʊ ˌɪnsaɪd 'aʊt]	etw in- und auswendig kennen
to **stand out** [ˌstænd 'aʊt]	auffallen, herausstechen
research [rɪ'sɜːtʃ]	Recherche, Nachforschungen, Untersuchungen
to **colour** ['kʌlə]	färben
hair care ['heəkeə]	Haarpflege
secret ['siːkrɪt]	heimlich, geheim
fascinating ['fæsɪneɪtɪŋ]	faszinierend
caller ['kɔːlə]	Anrufer/in
line [laɪn]	Leitung
to **legalize** ['liːɡəlaɪz]	legalisieren

lying ['laɪɪŋ]	Lügen
seriously ['sɪəriəsli]	im Ernst
to **cook a meal** [ˌkʊk ə 'miːl]	eine Mahlzeit zubereiten, ein Essen kochen
to **paint** [peɪnt]	malen
trash [træʃ]	Müll
beetle ['biːtl]	Käfer
bare [beə]	kahl, nackt
college ['kɒlɪdʒ]	Fachhochschule
promotion [prə'məʊʃn]	Werbung
broke [brəʊk]	kaputt
niche [nɪtʃ]	Nische
targeted ['tɑːgɪtɪd]	gezielt
blanket ['blæŋkɪt]	pauschal, umfassend
to **be designed to do sth** [bi dɪ'zaɪnd tə]	dazu gedacht sein, etw zu tun; darauf ausgelegt sein, etw zu tun
maximum ['mæksɪməm]	maximal, Höchst-
to **be supposed to do sth** [bi sə'pəʊzd tə]	etw tun sollen
to **ship** [ʃɪp]	verschicken
to **bottle** ['bɒtl]	in Flaschen abfüllen
vending machine ['vendɪŋ məʃiːn]	(Verkaufs-)Automat
to **donate** [dəʊ'neɪt]	spenden
vacation *AE* [və'keɪʃn]	Urlaub
to **join** [dʒɔɪn]	mitmachen, *(Radio etc.:)* in einer Sendung sein, *(Telefon:)* (mit jdm) sprechen
washing powder ['wɒʃɪŋ paʊdə]	Waschpulver
sales *pl* [seɪlz]	Verkauf, Verkäufe, Absatz, Vertrieb
factor ['fæktə]	Faktor
life-cycle ['laɪf saɪkl]	Lebensdauer, Lebenszyklus
maximum ['mæksɪməm]	Höchstwert
car wash ['kɑː wɒʃ]	Autowaschanlage
hairdressing salon ['heədresɪŋ sælɒn]	Friseursalon
electrician [ɪˌlek'trɪʃn]	Elektriker/in
perfume ['pɜːfjuːm]	Parfüm
sports car ['spɔːts kɑː]	Sportwagen

page 50

to **intend** [ɪn'tend]	beabsichtigen
arrangement [ə'reɪndʒmənt]	Abmachung, Vereinbarung, Vorbereitung, Regelung
salesman ['seɪlzmən]	Verkäufer, Vertreter
deal [diːl]	Geschäft, Abschluss
profit ['prɒfɪt]	Gewinn, Profit
Head Office [ˌhed 'ɒfɪs]	Zentrale, Direktion, Hauptverwaltung
Human Resources (HR) [ˌhjuːmən rɪ'sɔːsɪz]	Personal(abteilung)
luck [lʌk]	Glück
Good luck! [ˌgʊd 'lʌk]	Viel Glück!
limited ['lɪmɪtɪd]	begrenzt, beschränkt
publisher ['pʌblɪʃə]	Verleger/in
straight [streɪt]	direkt, gleich
to **phone in** [ˌfəʊn 'ɪn]	(in einer Sendung) anrufen
to **get bored** [ˌget 'bɔːd]	sich langweilen
to **launch** [lɔːntʃ]	*(Produkt)* auf den Markt bringen, einführen

page 51

commercial [kə'mɜːʃl]	(Werbe-)Spot
to **pick sth out** [ˌpɪk 'aʊt]	etw heraussuchen
to **read sth closely** [ˌriːd 'kləʊsli]	etw genau (durch)lesen
capital letter [ˌkæpɪtl 'letə]	Großbuchstabe
to **come across sth** [ˌkʌm ə'krɒs]	auf etw stoßen
visionary ['vɪʒənri]	Visionär/in
genius ['dʒiːniəs]	Genie
to **brand a product** [ˌbrænd ə 'prɒdʌkt]	ein Markenprodukt schaffen
household name ['haʊshəʊld neɪm]	bekannter Name, Begriff
sunny ['sʌni]	sonnig
threatening ['θretnɪŋ]	bedrohlich
scary ['skeəri]	unheimlich, beängstigend
to **come up with sth** [ˌkʌm 'ʌp wɪð]	sich etw ausdenken, sich etw einfallen lassen
likeable ['laɪkəbl]	sympathisch
to **be about to do sth** [bi ə'baʊt tə]	im Begriff sein, etw zu tun; gerade dabei sein, etw zu tun
to **target sb** ['tɑːgɪt]	jdn ins Visier nehmen, auf jdn abzielen
strategy ['strætədʒi]	Strategie
high-end [ˌhaɪ 'end]	hochklassig, hochwertig
everyday ['evrideɪ]	alltäglich, Alltags-
constant ['kɒnstənt]	ständig, andauernd
to **discover** [dɪ'skʌvə]	entdecken
function ['fʌŋkʃn]	Funktion
powerful ['paʊəfl]	stark, mächtig, kräftig
manual ['mænjuəl]	Bedienungsanleitung
jargon ['dʒɑːgən]	Fachsprache, Jargon
entrepreneur [ˌɒntrəprə'nɜː]	Unternehmer/in
accessible [ək'sesəbl]	zugänglich, erreichbar, offen
to **feel sth** [fiːl]	etw anfassen, etw ertasten
mouse [maʊs]	Maus
to **survive** [sə'vaɪv]	überleben
to **rebuild** [ˌriː'bɪld]	umbauen, erneuern
series ['sɪəriːz]	Reihe, Serie

page 52

to **continue to do sth** [kən'tɪnjuː tə]	etw weiterhin tun
graph [grɑːf]	Diagramm, Kurve
chart [tʃɑːt]	Diagramm, Tabelle
bar chart ['bɑː tʃɑːt]	Säulendiagramm
figure ['fɪgə]	Zahl, Ziffer
statistics [stə'tɪstɪks]	Statistik(en)
visual ['vɪʒuəl]	visuell
change [tʃeɪndʒ]	Veränderung
spending ['spendɪŋ]	Ausgaben, Aufwendungen
billion ['bɪliən]	Milliarde
per cent [pə'sent]	Prozent
note [nəʊt]	Hinweis
directory [də'rektəri]	Telefonbuch
source [sɔːs]	Quelle

page 53

axis ['æksɪs]	Achse
line chart ['laɪn tʃɑːt]	Liniendiagramm
upwards ['ʌpwədz]	steigend
downwards ['daʊnwədz]	fallend
percentage [pə'sentɪdʒ]	Prozentsatz, Anteil
point [pɔɪnt]	Komma
target group ['tɑːgɪt gruːp]	Zielgruppe
branded goods *pl* [ˌbrændɪd 'gʊdz]	Markenware, Markenartikel
writer ['raɪtə]	Autor/in, Schriftsteller/in

page 54

ethical ['eθɪkl]	ethisch, (moralisch) verantwortlich

drinking water ['drɪŋkɪŋ wɔːtə] Trinkwasser
maker ['meɪkə] Hersteller *(Firma)*
to **market** ['mɑːkɪt] vermarkten
candy bar *US* ['kændi bɑː] Schokoriegel
rectangular [rek'tæŋgjələ] rechteckig
chocolate bar ['tʃɒklət bɑː] Schokoriegel
the in thing [ðiː 'ɪn θɪŋ] der letzte Schrei
toothpaste ['tuːθpeɪst] Zahnpasta, Zahncreme
smile ['lʌvəbl] Lächeln
morals *pl* ['mɒrəlz] Moralvorstellungen
if …, that is. [ðæt 'ɪz] wenn … überhaupt / auch wirklich …

environmental protection [ɪn,vaɪrən'mentl prə'tekʃn] Umweltschutz
brewery ['bruːəri] Brauerei
trend [trend] Trend, Tendenz
purity ['pjʊərəti] Reinheit
regulations *pl* [,regju'leɪʃnz] Vorschriften, Bestimmungen
drinker ['drɪŋkə] Trinker/in
conscience ['kɒnʃəns] Gewissen
to **launch an ad campaign** [,lɔːntʃ ən 'æd kæmpeɪn] eine Werbekampagne starten
square metre ['skweə miːtə] Quadratmeter
rainforest ['reɪn fɒrɪst] Regenwald
to **drop** [drɒp] fallen
jump [dʒʌmp] Sprung
to **recognize** ['rekəgnaɪz] (wieder)erkennen
in need [ɪn 'niːd] bedürftig, in Not
candy maker *US* ['kændi meɪkə] Süßwarenhersteller
previously ['priːviəsli] zuvor, vorher
therapy ['θerəpi] Therapie
to **illustrate** ['ɪləstrəɪt] zeigen, veranschaulichen
to **mention** ['menʃn] erwähnen, nennen
honest ['ɒnɪst] ehrlich, anständig

UNIT 7

page 55

beyond [bɪ'jɒnd] darüber hinaus
Hinduism ['hɪnduːɪzəm] Hinduismus
Catholicism [kə'θɒləsɪzəm] Katholizismus, der katholische Glaube

Judaism ['dʒuːdeɪɪzəm] Judaismus, Judentum
extended [ɪk'stendɪd] erweitert
extended family [ɪk,stendɪd 'fæməli] Großfamilie
immediate [ɪ'miːdiət] unmittelbar
peer group ['pɪə gruːp] Altersgruppe, Bezugsgruppe, Umfeld

role model ['rəʊl mɒdl] Vorbild
chore [tʃɔː] (lästige Routine-)Aufgabe

page 56

safely ['seɪfli] mit Gewissheit
twin [twɪn] Zwilling
to **spoil** [spɔɪl] *(Kind)* verwöhnen
to **turn to sb** ['tɜːn tə] sich an jdn wenden
day-to-day [,deɪ tə 'deɪ] tagtäglich
chat [tʃæt] Unterhaltung, Schwätzchen

to **go under** [,gəʊ 'ʌndə] Pleite gehen
financial [faɪ'nænʃl] finanziell, Finanz-
to **get sb through** [,get 'θruː] jdn durchbringen; jdm helfen, etw zu überstehen

these days [ðiːz 'deɪz] zur Zeit
freedom ['friːdəm] Freiheit
root [ruːt] Wurzel
what's more [wɒts 'mɔː] zudem
to **set an example** [,set ən ɪg'zɑːmpl] ein Beispiel setzen, mit gutem Beispiel vorangehen

to **have a hard time** [həv ə ,hɑːd 'taɪm] es schwer haben
to **be caught** [bi 'kɔːt] festsitzen, in der Klemme sitzen

page 57

to **gossip** ['gɒsɪp] tratschen, schwatzen
to **borrow sth** ['bɒrəʊ] sich etw ausleihen
noisy ['nɔɪzi] laut, lärmend
nuclear ['njuːkliə] Kern-
various ['veəriəs] verschieden, mehrere, allerlei

to **be involved in sth** [bi ɪn'vɒlvd ɪn] sich an etw beteiligen, bei etw mitmachen
drama ['drɑːmə] Schauspiel
whatever [wɒt'evə] was auch immer
at the end of the day [ət ði end əv ðə 'deɪ] letzten Endes, unterm Strich
cheerful ['tʃɪəfl] fröhlich
tea *BE* [tiː] *Zwischenmahlzeit am Nachmittag, Abendessen*

to **be a pain (in the neck)** [bi ə 'peɪn] jdm auf die Nerven gehen
to **mind one's own business** [,maɪnd wʌnz əʊn 'bɪznəs] sich um seinen eigenen Kram kümmern
tension ['tenʃn] Spannung
laugh [lɑːf] Lachen, Gelächter
hill [hɪl] Berg, Anhöhe, Hügel
grass [grɑːs] Rasen, Gras
independent [,ɪndɪ'pendənt] unabhängig
unnecessary [ʌn'nesəsəri] überflüssig, unnötig
abbreviation [ə,briːvi'eɪʃn] Abkürzung
needs *pl* [niːdz] Bedürfnisse, Bedarf

page 58

lifestyle ['laɪfstaɪl] Lebensweise, Lebensführung

to **tidy up** [,taɪdi 'ʌp] aufräumen
housework ['haʊswɜːk] Hausarbeit
to **do (the/some) ironing** [duː 'aɪənɪŋ] bügeln
paperwork ['peɪpəwɜːk] Büroarbeit, Schreibarbeit
feature ['fiːtʃə] Hintergrundbericht, Reportage

talent ['tælənt] Begabung, Talent

page 59

drama club ['drɑːmə klʌb] Schauspiel-AG
to **feel embarrassed** [,fiːl ɪm'bærəst] sich genieren, sich schämen
to **raise sth** [reɪz] etw *(Thema etc.)* ansprechen

to **respond (to sth)** [rɪ'spɒnd] (auf etw) reagieren, (auf etw) antworten
sympathetic(ally) [,sɪmpə'θetɪk] einfühlsam
to **point sth out** [,pɔɪnt 'aʊt] auf etw hinweisen
informal [ɪn'fɔːml] informell, locker
contracted [kən'træktɪd] zusammengezogen
shy [ʃaɪ] schüchtern
saying ['seɪɪŋ] Sprichwort, Redensart

page 60

grade *AE* [greɪd]		Note
grade A student [ˌgreɪd ˈeɪ stjuːdnt]		Einserschüler/in
ridiculous(ly) [rɪˈdɪkjələs]		lächerlich, unglaublich
to make it [ˈmeɪk ɪt]		es schaffen
to start on sb [stɑːt]		jdn angreifen, jdn kritisieren
to hoover [ˈhuːvə]		staubsaugen
load [ləʊd]		Ladung
washing [ˈwɒʃɪŋ]		Wäsche
plus [plʌs]		außerdem
nosey [ˈnəʊzi]		(auf unangenehme Weise) neugierig
receipt [rɪˈsiːt]		Quittung
by the way [baɪ ðə ˈweɪ]		übrigens, nebenbei erwähnt
part-time [ˌpɑːtˈtaɪm]		Teilzeit-
to ban sb from doing sth [ˈbæn frəm]		jdm verbieten, etw zu tun
to feel left out [fiːl ˌleft ˈaʊt]		sich ausgeschlossen fühlen
to turn into sth [ˈtɜːn ɪntə]		zu etw werden
to take sth [teɪk]		etw ertragen
to drive sb away [ˌdraɪv əˈweɪ]		jdn vertreiben
to cut a long story short [tə kʌt ə lɒŋ ˌstɔːri ˈʃɔːt]		lange Rede, kurzer Sinn
benefits *pl* [ˈbenɪfɪts]		Sozialleistungen
Department for Work and Pensions [dɪˌpɑːtmənt fə ˌwɜːk ən ˈpenʃnz]		*brit.* Arbeits- und Sozialministerium
to manage [ˈmænɪdʒ]		verwalten, regeln
welfare [ˈwelfeə]		Sozialfürsorge, Sozialhilfe
benefits office [ˈbenɪfɪts ɒfɪs]		Sozialamt
to drop [drɒp]		fallen, *(Noten:)* schlechter werden
properly [ˈprɒpəli]		richtig, ordentlich, korrekt
in order to [ɪn ˈɔːdə tə]		um … zu
to find sb sth [faɪnd]		jdm etw besorgen
brief(ly) [briːf]		kurz, knapp
grade *AE* [greɪd]		Note

page 61

idiomatic [ˌɪdiəˈmætɪk]		idiomatisch, redensartlich
weekday [ˈwiːkdeɪ]		Werktag, Wochentag
suitable [ˈsuːtəbl]		passend
as necessary [əz ˈnesəsəri]		nötigenfalls
to get on [ˌget ˈɒn]		vorwärtskommen, zurechtkommen
to get over sth [ˌget ˈəʊvə]		über etw hinwegkommen, etw verkraften
tiny [ˈtaɪni]		winzig
stage [steɪdʒ]		Phase, Abschnitt
move [muːv]		Schritt, Umzug

page 62

mind [maɪnd]		Gedanken
to go from bad to worse [gəʊ frəm ˌbæd tə ˈwɜːs]		immer schlimmer werden
ahead [əˈhed]		voraus, vorausliegend
to step off [ˌstep ˈɒf]		aussteigen
to blow [bləʊ]		wehen, blasen
steadily [ˈstedɪli]		ununterbrochen
to pull sth tight [ˌpʊl ˈtaɪt]		etw straff ziehen
lane [leɪn]		Weg, Gasse
towards sth [təˈwɔːdz]		zu etw hin, auf etw zu
to return to sth [rɪˈtɜːn tə]		sich wieder einer Sache zuwenden
youth [juːθ]		Jugend

to fall behind [ˌfɔːl bɪˈhaɪnd]		zurückfallen, in Rückstand geraten
false start [ˌfɔːls ˈstɑːt]		Fehlstart
respect [rɪˈspekt]		Achtung, Respekt
experienced [ɪkˈspɪəriənst]		erfahren
efficient(ly) [ɪˈfɪʃnt]		effizient
first of all [ˌfɜːst əv ˈɔːl]		zuallererst
I suppose [aɪ səˈpəʊz]		wohl
shared house [ˌʃeəd ˈhaʊs]		Wohngemeinschaft
to check sth out [ˌtʃek ˈaʊt]		sich etw ansehen
comfortable [ˈkʌmftəbl]		angenehm
to get sth wrong [ˌget ˈrɒŋ]		bei etw einen Fehler machen, etw falsch machen
monthly [ˈmʌnθli]		monatlich
budget [ˈbʌdʒɪt]		Etat, Haushalt, Budget
heating [ˈhiːtɪŋ]		Heizung
bill [bɪl]		Rechnung
on time [ɒn ˈtaɪm]		pünktlich
credit rating [ˈkredɪt reɪtɪŋ]		(Bewertung/Einstufung der) Bonität, Kreditwürdigkeit
disaster [dɪˈzɑːstə]		Katastrophe
to lend sb sth [lend]		jdm etw leihen
it doesn't matter [ɪt dʌznt ˈmætə]		es ist egal
by oneself [baɪ wʌnˈself]		allein
strong advice [ˌstrɒŋ ədˈvaɪs]		dringender Rat
washing up [ˌwɒʃɪŋ ˈʌp]		Geschirrspülen
and so on [ənd ˈsəʊ ɒn]		und so weiter
(French) fries *pl AE* [fraɪz]		Pommes frites
to go wrong [ˌgəʊ ˈrɒŋ]		schieflaufen
to get angry [ˌget ˈæŋgri]		sich ärgern
to get upset [ˌget ʌpˈset]		sich aufregen
thought [θɔːt]		Gedanke
boomerang [ˈbuːməræŋ]		Bumerang
to rescue [ˈreskjuː]		retten, bergen

page 63

usefulness [ˈjuːsfəlnəs]		Nutzen, Zweckmäßigkeit
to sniff sth [snɪf]		an etw riechen
duvet cover [ˈduːveɪ kʌvə]		Bettdeckenbezug
raw [rɔː]		roh
chips *pl BE* [tʃɪps]		Pommes frites
nutrient [ˈnjuːtriənt]		Nährstoff
to be up to sth [bi ˈʌp tə]		etw vorhaben
on a need-to-know basis [ɒn ə ˌniːd tə ˈnəʊ beɪsɪs]		im (unumgänglichen) Bedarfsfall
alive [əˈlaɪv]		lebendig, am Leben
sink [sɪŋk]		Spüle

page 64

repercussion [ˌriːpəˈkʌʃn]		Auswirkung, Konsequenz
only child [ˌəʊnli ˈtʃaɪld]		Einzelkind
that [ðæt]		so
researcher [rɪˈsɜːtʃə]		Forscher/in, Wissenschaftler/in
policy [ˈpɒləsi]		Politik, Vorgehensweise
to introduce *(a law)* [ˌɪntrəˈdjuːs]		*(ein Gesetz)* einbringen
toy [tɔɪ]		Spielzeug
gracefully [ˈgreɪsfəli]		würdevoll
pocket money [ˈpɒkɪt mʌni]		Taschengeld
pressure [ˈpreʃə]		Druck
to leave sb sth [liːv]		jdm etw hinterlassen
to conduct sth [kənˈdʌkt]		etw durchführen

ignored [ɪɡ'nɔːd]	unbeachtet
scared [skeəd]	verängstigt
ideally [aɪ'diːəli]	idealerweise

UNIT 8

page 65

realistic [ˌriːə'lɪstɪk]	realistisch
doer ['duə]	Macher/in
investigative [ɪn'vestɪɡətɪv]	erforschend, Untersuchungs-
thinker ['θɪŋkə]	Denker/in
organizer ['ɔːɡənaɪzə]	Organisator/in
artistic [ɑː'tɪstɪk]	künstlerisch
creator [kri'eɪtə]	Schöpfer/in
enterprising ['entəpraɪzɪŋ]	geschäftstüchtig, risikofreudig
persuader [pə'sweɪdə]	*jd, der andere überzeugt und mitreißt*
helper ['helpə]	Helfer/in
mechanical [mɪ'kænɪkl]	mechanisch
mechanic [mɪ'kænɪk]	Mechaniker/in
carpenter ['kɑːpəntə]	Zimmerer/in, Schreiner/in
engineer [ˌendʒɪ'nɪə]	Ingenieur/in
police officer [pə'liːs ɒfɪsə]	Polizist/in
to **observe** [əb'zɜːv]	beobachten
to **investigate** [ɪn'vestɪɡeɪt]	ermitteln, untersuchen
to **evaluate** [ɪ'væljueɪt]	bewerten, beurteilen
to **solve** [sɒlv]	lösen
psychologist [saɪ'kɒlədʒɪst]	Psychologe/-in
management consultant [ˌmænɪdʒmənt kən'sʌltənt]	Unternehmensberater/in
programmer ['prəʊɡræmə]	Programmierer/in
clerical ['klerɪkl]	Büro-
numerical [njuː'merɪkl]	Zahl-, zahlenmäßig
instruction [ɪn'strʌkʃn]	Anweisung
accountant [ə'kaʊntənt]	Buchhalter/in
administrator [əd'mɪnɪstreɪtə]	Verwalter/in
intuitional [ˌɪntju'ɪʃnəl]	intuitiv
unstructured [ʌn'strʌktʃəd]	unstrukturiert
imagination [ɪˌmædʒɪ'neɪʃn]	Phantasie, Vorstellungskraft
creativity [ˌkriːeɪ'tɪvəti]	schöpferische Begabung, Kreativität
journalist ['dʒɜːnəlɪst]	Journalist/in
architect ['ɑːkɪtekt]	Architekt/in
designer [dɪ'zaɪnə]	Gestalter/in, Designer/in, Konstrukteur/in
dancer ['dɑːnsə]	Tänzer/in
organizational [ˌɔːɡənaɪ'zeɪʃənl]	organisatorisch
economic [ˌiːkə'nɒmɪk]	wirtschaftlich
gain [ɡeɪn]	Gewinn, Vorteil
politician [ˌpɒlə'tɪʃn]	Politiker/in
to **enlighten** [ɪn'laɪtn]	aufklären
caring ['keərɪŋ]	fürsorglich
to **be skilled with sth** [bi 'skɪld wɪð]	mit etw gut umgehen können
social worker ['səʊʃl wɜːkə]	Sozialarbeiter/in
nurse [nɜːs]	Krankenpfleger/-schwester
priest [priːst]	Priester/in, Geistliche/r
company car ['kʌmpəni kɑː]	Firmenwagen
flexible ['fleksəbl]	flexibel
working hours *pl* [ˌwɜːkɪŋ 'aʊəz]	Arbeitszeiten
pay [peɪ]	Bezahlung, Lohn
promotion [prə'məʊʃn]	Beförderung, (beruflicher) Aufstieg
promotion prospects *pl* [prə'məʊʃn prɒspekts]	Aufstiegschancen
working conditions *pl* [ˌwɜːkɪŋ kən'dɪʃnz]	Arbeitsbedingungen
job security [ˌdʒɒb sɪ'kjʊərəti]	sicherer Arbeitsplatz
insurance [ɪn'ʃʊərəns]	Versicherung
medical insurance [ˌmedɪkl ɪn'ʃʊərəns]	Krankenversicherung
category ['kætəɡəri]	Kategorie
involved [ɪn'vɒlvd]	dazugehörig
to **involve** [ɪn'vɒlv]	mit sich bringen, umfassen
to **design** [dɪ'zaɪn]	konstruieren, planen
construction worker [kən'strʌkʃn wɜːkə]	Bauarbeiter/in
ideal [aɪ'diːəl]	ideal
baker ['beɪkə]	Bäcker/in
satisfying ['sætɪsfaɪɪŋ]	befriedigend
rewarding [rɪ'wɔːdɪŋ]	lohnend, erfüllend

page 66

job advertisement [ˌdʒɒb əd'vɜːtɪsmənt]	Stellenanzeige, -ausschreibung
work experience ['wɜːk ɪkspɪəriəns]	Praktikum
temporary ['temprəri]	vorübergehend, befristet
recruitment [rɪ'kruːtmənt]	Personalbeschaffung
job title ['dʒɒb taɪtl]	Stellenbezeichnung
full-time [ˌfʊl 'taɪm]	Vollzeit-
requirement [rɪ'kwaɪəmənt]	Voraussetzung, Bedingung, Anforderung
board and lodging [ˌbɔːd ənd 'lɒdʒɪŋ]	Kost und Logis
return airfare [rɪˌtɜːn 'eəfeə]	Kosten für Hin- und Rückflug
maximum (max.) ['mæksɪməm]	höchstens, maximal
to **apply (for a job)** [ə'plaɪ]	sich (um/auf eine Stelle) bewerben
to **email sb** ['iːmeɪl]	jdm eine E-Mail schicken
CV (curriculum vitae) [ˌsiː 'viː, kəˌrɪkjələm 'viːtaɪ]	Lebenslauf
cover letter ['kʌvə letə]	Anschreiben, Begleitschreiben
internship ['ɪntɜːnʃɪp]	Praktikum
charity ['tʃærəti]	Wohltätigkeitsorganisation
to **set sth up** [ˌset 'ʌp]	etw einrichten
community [kə'mjuːnəti]	Gemeinde, Gemeinschaft
to **staff** [stɑːf]	(mit Personal) besetzen
highly motivated [ˌhaɪli 'məʊtɪveɪtɪd]	hochmotiviert
intern ['ɪntɜːn]	Praktikant/in
to **volunteer to do sth** [ˌvɒlən'tɪə tə]	sich bereit erklären, etw zu tun
management ['mænɪdʒmənt]	Führung, Management
administration [ədˌmɪnɪ'streɪʃn]	Verwaltung
fully ['fʊli]	vollständig
fully equipped [ˌfʊli ɪ'kwɪpt]	vollausgestattet
location [ləʊ'keɪʃn]	Standort, Ort
to **insure** [ɪn'ʃʊə]	versichern
accommodation [əˌkɒmə'deɪʃn]	Unterkunft
homestay accommodation ['həʊmsteɪ əkɒmədeɪʃn]	Unterbringung bei Gasteltern

travel expenses *pl* ['trævl ɪkspensɪz]	Reisekosten, Fahrtkosten
registered ['redʒɪstəd]	eintragen, (staatlich) anerkannt
post [pəʊst]	Stelle, Posten
to **advertise a job** [ˌædvətaɪz ə 'dʒɒb]	eine Stelle ausschreiben
technician [tek'nɪʃn]	Techniker/in
allowance [ə'laʊəns]	Aufwandsentschädigung
asap (as soon as possible) [ˌeɪ es eɪ 'piː]	baldmöglichst
duration [dju'reɪʃn]	Dauer
to **be responsible for sth** [bi rɪ'spɒnsəbl fə]	für etw zuständig/verantwortlich sein
set [set]	Kulisse
lighting ['laɪtɪŋ]	Beleuchtung, Licht
prop [prɒp]	Requisite
maintenance ['meɪntənəns]	Wartung, Instandhaltung
equipment [ɪ'kwɪpmənt]	Ausrüstung, Geräte
candidate ['kændɪdət]	Bewerber/in
electrical [ɪ'lektrɪkl]	elektrisch, Elektro-
DIY (do-it-yourself) [ˌdiː aɪ 'waɪ]	Heimwerker-, Heimwerken
shift [ʃɪft]	Schicht
equal opportunities *pl* [ˌiːkwəl ɒpə'tjuːnətiz]	Chancengleichheit
employer [ɪm'plɔɪə]	Arbeitgeber/in

page 67

equivalent [ɪ'kwɪvələnt]	Entsprechung
to **administer** [əd'mɪnɪstə]	verwalten
to **accommodate** [ə'kɒmədeɪt]	unterbringen
to **maintain** [meɪn'teɪn]	warten, instand halten
equality [ɪ'kwɒləti]	Gleichheit
volunteer [ˌvɒlən'tɪə]	(freiwilliger) Helfer/in
voluntary ['vɒləntri]	freiwillig
administrative [əd'mɪnɪstrətɪv]	Verwaltungs-
technological [ˌteknə'lɒdʒɪkl]	technologisch
terms *pl* [tɜːmz]	Bedingungen, Konditionen
owner ['əʊnə]	Besitzer/in
medical ['medɪkl]	medizinisch
secretary ['sekrətri]	Sekretär/in
bank clerk ['bæŋk klɑːk]	Bankangestellte/r
elsewhere [ˌels'weə]	woanders, anderswo
to **supply** [sə'plaɪ]	liefern, bieten
sustainable [sə'steɪnəbl]	nachhaltig
treatment ['triːtmənt]	Behandlung

page 68

qualification [ˌkwɒlɪfɪ'keɪʃn]	Abschluss, Qualifikation
typing ['taɪpɪŋ]	Schreibmaschinenschreiben
standard ['stændəd]	Niveau
surgery ['sɜːdʒəri]	(Arzt-)Praxis
pleasant ['pleznt]	angenehm
as regards ... [əz rɪ'gɑːdz]	was ... betrifft
band [bænd]	Gehaltsstufe, Gehaltsklasse
pay scale ['peɪ skeɪl]	Lohntarif, Lohntabelle
secure [sɪ'kjuə]	sicher
shortage ['ʃɔːtɪdʒ]	Mangel
staff [stɑːf]	Personal, Belegschaft, Mitarbeiter/innen
satisfaction [ˌsætɪs'fækʃn]	Zufriedenheit
profession [prə'feʃn]	Beruf
caring profession ['keərɪŋ prəfeʃn]	Pflegeberuf
maths [mæθs]	Mathe(matik) *(Schulfach)*
trainee [treɪ'niː]	Auszubildende/r
cashier [kæ'ʃɪə]	Kassierer/in
to **cash a cheque** [ˌkæʃ ə 'tʃek]	einen Scheck einlösen
payment ['peɪmənt]	Zahlung
microwave ['maɪkrəweɪv]	Mikrowelle
entry level pay [ˌentri levl 'peɪ]	Einstiegsgehalt, Anfangsgehalt
customer services advisor [ˌkʌstəmə 'sɜːvɪsɪz ədvaɪzə]	Kundenberater/in
apprenticeship [ə'prentɪʃɪp]	Ausbildung, Lehre
qualified ['kwɒlɪfaɪd]	mit Abschluss, qualifiziert
crisis ['kraɪsɪs]	Krise
careers advisor [kə'rɪəz ədvaɪzə]	Berufsberater/in
entry level ['entri levl]	Einstieg, Anfang
a word of warning [ə ˌwɜːd əv 'wɔːnɪŋ]	Hinweis, Warnung
ambitious [æm'bɪʃəs]	ehrgeizig
plate [pleɪt]	Teller
to **offer sb sth on a plate** [ˌɒfər ɒn ə 'pleɪt]	jdm etw auf dem Silbertablett servieren
yearly ['jɪəli]	jährlich, Jahres-
income ['ɪnkʌm]	Einkommen
irregular [ɪ'regjələ]	unregelmäßig
salesperson ['seɪlzpɜːsn]	Vertreter/in, Verkäufer/in
to **work hard** [ˌwɜːk 'hɑːd]	hart arbeiten, fleißig sein

page 69

workplace ['wɜːkpleɪs]	Arbeitsplatz
to **mind sth** [maɪnd]	auf etw achten
to **grab sth** [græb]	sich etw schnappen
wheely ['wiːli]	auf Rollen
filing cabinet ['faɪlɪŋ kæbɪnət]	Aktenschrank
to **make for sth** ['meɪk fə]	sich auf den Weg nach etw machen
to **be on the increase** [bi ɒn ði 'ɪŋkriːs]	auf dem Vormarsch sein, zunehmen
driving force [ˌdraɪvɪŋ 'fɔːs]	treibende Kraft
ever-improving [ˌevər ɪm'pruːvɪŋ]	stetig besser werdend
electronics *pl* [ˌɪlek'trɒnɪks]	Elektronik
employee [ɪm'plɔɪiː]	Angestellte/r, Beschäftigte/r
workforce ['wɜːkfɔːs]	Belegschaft
increase ['ɪŋkriːs]	Zunahme, Steigerung
to **cause sb to do sth** [kɔːz]	jdn dazu veranlassen, etw zu tun
to **rethink** ['riːθɪŋk]	überdenken
corporate ['kɔːpərət]	Unternehmens-, von Unternehmen
infrastructure ['ɪnfrəstrʌktʃə]	Infrastruktur
manufacturing [ˌmænju'fæktʃərɪŋ]	Fertigung
to **require** [rɪ'kwaɪə]	erfordern, benötigen
mobile ['məʊbaɪl]	mobil
pad [pæd]	(Notiz-)Block; Bude
minimum ['mɪnɪməm]	Mindestmaß, -menge, Minimum
by default [baɪ dɪ'fɔːlt]	automatisch
therefore ['ðeəfɔː]	daher, deshalb, demzufolge
meeting room ['miːtɪŋ ruːm]	Sitzungsraum, Besprechungsraum
to **plug in(to)** [ˌplʌg 'ɪn]	anschließen, einstecken

to **counteract sth** [ˌkaʊntərˈækt]	einer Sache entgegenwirken
loneliness [ˈləʊnlinəs]	Einsamkeit
homing [ˈhəʊmɪŋ]	Heimfindeverhalten *(z. B. von Brieftauben)*
instinct [ˈɪnstɪŋkt]	Instinkt
to **acknowledge** [əkˈnɒlɪdʒ]	anerkennen, zugeben
allotted [əˈlɒtɪd]	zugewiesen
car park [ˈkɑː pɑːk]	Parkplatz, -haus, -garage
to **tend to do sth** [ˈtend tə]	dazu neigen, etw zu tun
spot [spɒt]	Platz, Ort, Fleck, Punkt
gradual [ˈɡrædʒuəl]	schrittweise, allmählich
development [dɪˈveləpmənt]	Entwicklung
to **address** [əˈdres]	*(Problem etc.)* ansprechen, angehen, thematisieren
concern [kənˈsɜːn]	Sorge, Befürchtung
wide-ranging [ˈwaɪd reɪndʒɪŋ]	breit gefächert
cultural [ˈkʌltʃərəl]	kulturell, kulturbezogen
practice [ˈpræktɪs]	Praxis, Ausübung, Verfahren, Ablauf, Praktik
informality [ˌɪnfɔːˈmæləti]	Formlosigkeit, Ungezwungenheit
norm [nɔːm]	Norm
senior [ˈsiːniə]	leitend
department [dɪˈpɑːtmənt]	Abteilung
legal department [ˌliːɡl dɪˈpɑːtmənt]	juristische Abteilung
finance [ˈfaɪnæns]	Finanz(-)
majority [məˈdʒɒrəti]	Mehrheit
to **be territorial** [bi ˌterəˈtɔːriəl]	sein Revier verteidigen
open-plan office [ˌəʊpən plæn ˈɒfɪs]	Großraumbüro
to **personalise** [ˈpɜːsnəlaɪz]	individuell gestalten
barrier [ˈbæriə]	Hürde
to **cross** [krɒs]	überqueren, überwinden
to **judge** [dʒʌdʒ]	beurteilen
in time [ɪn ˈtaɪm]	rechtzeitig

page 70

to **drop in** [ˌdrɒp ˈɪn]	vorbeikommen, hereinschauen
to **gravitate to sth** [ˈɡrævɪteɪt tə]	von etw angezogen werden
continuity [ˌkɒntɪˈjuːəti]	Kontinuität, Fortdauer
belonging [bɪˈlɒŋɪŋ]	Zugehörigkeit
to **shake sth off** [ˌʃeɪk ˈɒf]	etw abschütteln
totally [ˈtəʊtəli]	voll und ganz
suit [suːt]	Anzug
tie [taɪ]	Krawatte
to **dress down** [ˌdres ˈdaʊn]	sich leger kleiden
sector [ˈsektə]	Sektor, Bereich
global(ly) [ˈɡləʊbl]	weltweit, global
to **downsize** [ˈdaʊnsaɪz]	verkleinern, gesundschrumpfen
prestigious [preˈstɪdʒəs]	repräsentativ, prestigeträchtig
rapid(ly) [ˈræpɪd]	rasch, schnell
centrally heated [ˌsentrəli ˈhiːtɪd]	zentralbeheizt
moveable [ˈmuːvəbl]	beweglich, mobil
fixed [fɪkst]	fest, festgelegt, fest installiert
routine [ruːˈtiːn]	(fester) Ablauf, Routine

page 71

to **store** [stɔː]	aufbewahren, lagern
file [faɪl]	Akte, Ordner
office block [ˈɒfɪs blɒk]	Bürogebäude
sudden [ˈsʌdn]	plötzlich
to **employ sb** [ɪmˈplɔɪ]	jdn beschäftigen, jdn einstellen
casual [ˈkæʒuəl]	leger, zwanglos
to **mediate** [ˈmiːdieɪt]	vermitteln
technique [tekˈniːk]	Methode, Technik
gist [dʒɪst]	das Wesentliche
to **take a seat** [ˌteɪk ə ˈsiːt]	Platz nehmen
premises *pl* [ˈpremɪsɪz]	Geschäftsräume
permanent [ˈpɜːmənənt]	dauerhaft
Must rush. [ˌmʌst ˈrʌʃ]	Ich muss weg.
to **get back to sb** [ˌɡet ˈbæk tə]	sich bei jdm (zurück)melden

page 72

finance director [ˌfaɪnæns dəˈrektə]	kaufmännische/r Leiter/in
chain [tʃeɪn]	Kette
market share [ˌmɑːkɪt ˈʃeə]	Marktanteil
competitor [kəmˈpetɪtə]	Konkurrent/in, Konkurrenz
to **break down** [ˌbreɪk ˈdaʊn]	zusammenbrechen
strike [straɪk]	Streik
to **go on strike** [ˌɡəʊ ɒn ˈstraɪk]	streiken
receptionist [rɪˈsepʃənɪst]	Empfangsmitarbeiter/in
job rotation [ˈdʒɒb rəʊteɪʃn]	Arbeitsplatzrotation, (innerbetrieblicher) Arbeitsplatzwechsel
to **stand in for sb** [ˌstænd ˈɪn fə]	jdn vertreten
to **retrain** [ˌriːˈtreɪn]	umschulen

page 73

to **draw** [drɔː]	ziehen
to **split** [splɪt]	(sich) aufteilen
separate [ˈseprət]	getrennt, separat
to **conduct sth** [kənˈdʌkt]	etw durchführen
to **ensure** [ɪnˈʃʊə]	sicherstellen; dafür sorgen, dass
to **conclude** [kənˈkluːd]	schließen, beenden

page 74

to **balance** [ˈbæləns]	im Gleichgewicht halten
single mom [ˌsɪŋɡl ˈmɒm]	Alleinerziehende
widowed [ˈwɪdəʊd]	verwitwet
sb is diagnosed with … [ˈdaɪəɡnəʊzd]	bei jdm wird … festgestellt, diagnostiziert
to **cope** [kəʊp]	zurechtkommen
upset [ˌʌpˈset]	verstimmt, verärgert
so-called [ˌsəʊ ˈkɔːld]	sogenannt
generation [ˌdʒenəˈreɪʃn]	Generation
to **take care of sb** [teɪk ˈkeə əv]	sich um jdn kümmern
to **age** [eɪdʒ]	altern
balance [ˈbæləns]	Gleichgewicht, Balance
to **manage** [ˈmænɪdʒ]	(es) schaffen
assistance [əˈsɪstəns]	Hilfe, Unterstützung
emergency plan [ɪˈmɜːdʒənsi plæn]	Notfallplan
caregiver [ˈkeəɡɪvə]	pflegende/r Angehörige/r, Betreuer/in
to **take time off** [teɪk ˌtaɪm ˈɒf]	sich frei nehmen

... **could be a lifesaver** ['laɪfseɪvə]	... könnte lebensrettend sein
perks *pl* [pɜːks]	freiwillige Sonder-/Sozialleistungen
voucher ['vaʊtʃə]	Gutschein
nursery ['nɜːsəri]	Kinderhort

JOB SKILLS 2

page 75

office assistant [ˌɒfɪs əˈsɪstənt]	Bürokaufmann/-frau
duty ['djuːti]	Aufgabe, Pflicht, Arbeit
located in [ləʊ'keɪtɪd ɪn]	in (... gelegen)
accurate ['ækjərət]	genau
to **be willing to do sth** [bi 'wɪlɪŋ tə]	bereit sein, etw zu tun
a must [ə 'mʌst]	ein Muss
plc [ˌpiː el 'siː]	AG
business studies ['bɪznəs stʌdiz]	Betriebswirtschaft
to **seek** [siːk]	suchen
to **update** [ˌʌp'deɪt]	aktualisieren
spreadsheet ['spredʃiːt]	Tabellenkalkulation
to **be equivalent to sth** [bi ɪ'kwɪvələnt tə]	einer Sache entsprechen
native speaker [ˌneɪtɪv 'spiːkə]	Muttersprachler/in
fluent ['fluːənt]	*(Sprache:)* fließend
oral ['ɔːrəl]	mündlich
intermediate [ˌɪntə'miːdiət]	mittlere/r/s *(Niveau)*
pressure ['preʃə]	Druck
reference ['refərəns]	Referenz, Zeugnis
referee [ˌrefə'riː]	Referenzgeber
on request [ɒn rɪ'kwest]	auf Wunsch, auf Verlangen

page 76

body ['bɒdi]	*(Brief:)* Hauptteil
complimentary close [ˌkɒmplɪˌmentri 'kləʊz]	*(Brief:)* Schlussformel
enclosure (encl.) [ɪn'kləʊʒə]	*(Brief:)* Anlage
inside address [ˌɪnsaɪd ə'dres]	Empfängeranschrift
salutation [ˌsælju'teɪʃn]	*(Brief:)* Anrede
signature ['sɪgnətʃə]	Unterschrift
writer's address [ˌraɪtəz ə'dres]	Absenderanschrift
attn. (= attention) [ə'tenʃn]	*(Brief:)* zu Händen
ref. (= reference) ['refərəns]	*(Brief:)* Zeichen
copy ['kɒpi]	Ausgabe
currently ['kʌrəntli]	zur Zeit
to **be keen to do sth** [bɪ 'kiːn tə]	etw unbedingt tun wollen
English-speaking ['ɪŋglɪʃ spiːkɪŋ]	englischsprachig
in addition to sth [ɪn ə'dɪʃn tə]	zusätzlich zu etw
to **be an asset to sb** [bi ən 'æset tə]	für jdn eine Bereicherung sein
to **appreciate** [ə'priːʃieɪt]	zu schätzen wissen, schätzen
to **grant sb sth** [grɑːnt]	jdm etw gewähren
interview ['ɪntəvjuː]	Vorstellungsgespräch

page 77

section ['sekʃn]	Abschnitt
applicant ['æplɪkənt]	Bewerber/in
to **compile** [kəm'paɪl]	erstellen, zusammenstellen
educational [ˌedʒu'keɪʃənl]	schulisch, Bildungs-
item ['aɪtəm]	Punkt, Gegenstand
correction [kə'rekʃn]	Korrekturlesen, Korrektur
to **pin** [pɪn]	(mit einer Nadel) befestigen, anbringen

page 78

to **interview sb** ['ɪntəvjuː]	mit jdm ein Vorstellungsgespräch führen
strength [streŋθ]	Stärke
weakness ['wiːknəs]	Schwäche
to **report to sb** [rɪ'pɔːt tə]	jdm unterstellt sein
surprised [sə'praɪzd]	erstaunt, überrascht
superior [suː'pɪəriə]	Vorgesetzte/r
to **invite sb to do sth** [ɪn'vaɪt tə]	jdn auffordern, etw zu tun
Speaking. ['spiːkɪŋ]	*(Telefon:)* Am Apparat.
to **go backpacking** [ˌgəʊ 'bækpækɪŋ]	auf Rucksacktour gehen
to **gain** [geɪn]	erwerben
to **take responsibility** [teɪk rɪˌspɒnsə'bɪləti]	Verantwortung übernehmen
right away [ˌraɪt ə'weɪ]	sofort
careless ['keələs]	nachlässig
as far as I'm concerned [əz ˌfɑːr əz ˌaɪm kən'sɜːnd]	von mir aus, was mich betrifft
to **attend sth** [ə'tend]	an etw teilnehmen
reservation [ˌrezə'veɪʃn]	Reservierung
assessment [ə'sesmənt]	Beurteilung, Einstufung
to **send sth out** [ˌsend 'aʊt]	etw verschicken
interviewer ['ɪntəvjuːə]	*Person, die ein Vorstellungsgespräch führt*
responsibility [rɪˌspɒnsə'bɪləti]	Aufgabe, Zuständigkeit

UNIT 9

page 79

multiculturalism [ˌmʌlti'kʌltʃərəlɪzm]	Multikulturalität, Multikulturismus, kulturelle Vielfalt
festival ['festɪvl]	Fest, Festtag, Festival
to **light** [laɪt]	*(Kerze etc.)* anzünden
to **march** [mɑːtʃ]	marschieren
candle ['kændl]	Kerze
dragon ['drægən]	Drachen
lantern ['læntən]	Laterne
pipe band ['paɪp bænd]	Dudelsackkapelle
New Year [ˌnjuː 'jɪə]	Neujahr
lion ['laɪən]	Löwe
display [dɪ'spleɪ]	Vorführung
parade [pə'reɪd]	Parade
march [mɑːtʃ]	Marsch
ceilidh ['keɪlɪ]	*geselliges Beisammensein mit Musik und Tanz (schottischer Brauch)*
midsummer [ˌmɪd'sʌmə]	Mittsommer, Sommersonnenwende
cuisine [kwɪ'ziːn]	Küche, Kochkunst
craft [krɑːft]	Handwerk

page 80

refugee [ˌrefju'dʒiː]	Flüchtling
coast [kəʊst]	Küste
to **separate** ['sepəreɪt]	trennen, abspalten
violent ['vaɪələnt]	heftig
given name ['gɪvn neɪm]	Vorname
soldier ['səʊldʒə]	Soldat/in
to **kick sth down** [ˌkɪk 'daʊn]	etw eintreten

to **wave sth around** [ˌweɪv əˈraʊnd]	mit etw herumfuchteln
rifle [ˈraɪfl]	Gewehr
to **drag** [dræg]	zerren
to **force** [fɔːs]	zwingen
facing sth [ˈfeɪsɪŋ]	gegen etw, mit dem Gesicht zu etw
to **be in command** [bi ˌɪn kəˈmɑːnd]	das Kommando führen, die Befehle geben, das Sagen haben
inch [ɪntʃ]	Zoll *(= 2,54 cm)*
to **shudder** [ˈʃʌdə]	erschaudern, zittern
fear [fɪə]	Angst
to **tremble** [ˈtrembl]	beben, zittern
to **look on** [ˌlʊk ˈɒn]	zusehen
terrified [ˈterɪfaɪd]	entsetzt
to **shoot** [ʃuːt]	schießen
bullet [ˈbʊlɪt]	(Gewehr-)Kugel
to **scream** [skriːm]	schreien
peace [piːs]	Frieden
to **raise sth** [reɪz]	etw anheben, etw hochheben
to **point sth at sb** [ˈpɔɪnt ət]	etw auf jdn richten, mit etw auf jdn zielen
traitor [ˈtreɪtə]	Verräter/in
enemy [ˈenəmi]	Feind/in
forehead [ˈfɔːhed]	Stirn
mongrel [ˈmɒŋgrəl]	Mischling, Bastard
to **drop one's voice** [ˌdrɒp wʌnz ˈvɔɪs]	die Stimme senken
equally [ˈiːkwəli]	gleichermaßen, genauso
safety [ˈseɪfti]	Sicherheit
authority [ɔːˈθɒrəti]	Behörde
welcoming [ˈwelkəmɪŋ]	gastfreundlich

page 81

evil [ˈiːvl]	böse, schlecht
border [ˈbɔːdə]	Grenze
body [ˈbɒdi]	Leichnam
law [lɔː]	Justiz
kind [kaɪnd]	freundlich, gütig, nett
to **arrest** [əˈrest]	verhaften
detention centre [dɪˈtenʃn sentə]	Auffanglager, Haftanstalt
homeless [ˈhəʊmləs]	obdachlos
unpleasant [ʌnˈpleznt]	unangenehm, unschön
court [kɔːt]	Gericht(shof)
basket [ˈbɑːskɪt]	Korb
amount [əˈmaʊnt]	Menge
tinned [tɪnd]	in Dosen, Dosen-
checkout [ˈtʃekaʊt]	Kasse
counter [ˈkaʊntə]	Schalter, Theke
to **drop one's eyes** [ˌdrɒp wʌnz ˈaɪz]	den Blick senken
deal [diːl]	Abmachung, Geschäft
wallet [ˈwɒlɪt]	Brieftasche, (Herren-)Portemonnaie
voucher [ˈvaʊtʃə]	Gutschein
asylum seeker [əˈsaɪləm siːkə]	Asylbewerber/in
change [tʃeɪndʒ]	Wechselgeld
queue [kjuː]	Warteschlange
courtroom [ˈkɔːtruːm]	Gerichtssaal
to **humiliate** [hjuːˈmɪlieɪt]	demütigen, erniedrigen
meanwhile [ˈmiːnwaɪl]	inzwischen, unterdessen
to **file** [faɪl]	feilen
nail [neɪl]	Nagel
to **comb** [kəʊm]	kämmen
exhibition [ˌeksɪˈbɪʃn]	Ausstellung
humiliation [hjuːˌmɪliˈeɪʃn]	Demütigung, Erniedrigung
proud [praʊd]	stolz
penny [ˈpeni]	Pfennig, Penny
to **reduce sb to sth** [rɪˈdjuːs]	jdn zu etw bringen
to **amount to sth** [əˈmaʊnt tə]	auf etw hinauslaufen
to **live off aid** [lɪv ˌɒf ˈeɪd]	von Sozialhilfe leben
to **wonder** [ˈwʌndə]	sich fragen
mathematician [ˌmæθəməˈtɪʃn]	Mathematiker/in
promising [ˈprɒmɪsɪŋ]	vielversprechend
airline [ˈeəlaɪn]	Fluglinie
silent(ly) [ˈsaɪlənt]	still, schweigend
to **shake one's head** [ˌʃeɪk wʌnz ˈhed]	den Kopf schütteln
in disgust [ɪn dɪsˈgʌst]	angewidert
to **shuffle** [ˈʃʌfl]	schlurfen
line [laɪn]	Reihe
down the line [ˌdaʊn ðə ˈlaɪn]	weiter
death [deθ]	Tod

page 82

understanding [ˌʌndəˈstændɪŋ]	Verständnis
to **make a point to sb** [ˌmeɪk ə ˈpɔɪnt tə]	jdm etw zu verstehen geben
to **recognize** [ˈrekəgnaɪz]	(wieder)erkennen
to **jump the queue** [ˌdʒʌmp ðə ˈkjuː]	sich vordrängeln
to **wait for one's turn** [ˌweɪt fə wʌnz ˈtɜːn]	warten, bis man an der Reihe ist
to **face sb** [feɪs]	jdn konfrontieren
goal [gəʊl]	*(Ballspiel:)* Tor
to **behave** [bɪˈheɪv]	sich benehmen, sich verhalten

page 83

earnings *pl* [ˈɜːnɪŋz]	Einkünfte, Verdienst
reduction [rɪˈdʌkʃn]	Verringerung, Senkung
pride [praɪd]	Stolz
on top of [ɒn ˈtɒp əv]	auf
cupboard [ˈkʌbəd]	Schrank
health and safety [ˌhelθ ənd ˈseɪfti]	Arbeitsschutz
cure [kjʊə]	Heilung, Therapie
cost of living [ˌkɒst əv ˈlɪvɪŋ]	Lebenshaltungskosten
great-grandfather [ˌgreɪt ˈgrænfɑːðə]	Urgroßvater
to **take pride in sth** [ˌteɪk ˈpraɪd ɪn]	auf etw Wert legen, sich mit etw Mühe geben
excellent [ˈeksələnt]	ausgezeichnet, hervorragend
to **land** [lænd]	landen

page 84

purpose [ˈpɜːpəs]	Absicht, Zweck
What now for …? [ˌwɒt ˈnaʊ fə]	Wie steht es um …?
policy [ˈpɒləsi]	Politik, Kurs, Konzept
harmony [ˈhɑːməni]	Harmonie
to **have the guts to do sth** [həv ðe ˈgʌts tə]	den Mumm haben, etw zu tun
law [lɔː]	Gesetz
to **pass a law** [ˌpɑːs ə ˈlɔː]	ein Gesetz verabschieden
to **reject** [rɪˈdʒekt]	ablehnen, zurückweisen
to **deport** [dɪˈpɔːt]	abschieben

violent ['vaɪələnt]	gewalttätig
gang [gæŋ]	Bande
Muslim ['mʊzlɪm]	muslimisch, Moslem
to **take over** [ˌteɪk 'əʊvə]	die Macht übernehmen
to **save oneself sth** [seɪv]	sich etw ersparen
to **calm down** [ˌkɑːm 'daʊn]	sich beruhigen
not … either [nɒt 'aɪðə]	auch nicht
minority [maɪ'nɒrəti]	Minderheit
moderate ['mɒdərət]	gemäßigt, maßvoll
MP (Member of Parliament) [ˌem 'piː]	Parlamentsabgeordnete/r
wave [weɪv]	Welle
descendant [dɪ'sendənt]	Nachfahre, Nachkomme
contribution [ˌkɒntrɪ'bjuːʃn]	Beitrag
to **make a contribution** [ˌmeɪk ə ˌkɒntrɪ'bjuːʃn]	einen Beitrag leisten
to **be a two-way street** [bi ə ˌtuː weɪ 'striːt]	auf Gegenseitigkeit beruhen
vibrant ['vaɪbrənt]	dynamisch, voller Leben
peaceful ['piːsfl]	friedlich
varied ['veərid]	vielfältig, abwechslungsreich
to **hide (away)** [haɪd]	sich verstecken, sich verbergen
to **put sth down to sth** [ˌpʊt 'daʊn tə]	etw einer Sache zuschreiben
ethnic ['eθnɪk]	ethnisch, Volks-
to **integrate** ['ɪntɪgreɪt]	(sich) integrieren
He has a (good) point. [hiː ˌhæz ə 'pɔɪnt]	Da ist etwas dran. Da hat er recht.
migrant ['maɪgrənt]	Migrant/in
racial ['reɪʃl]	rassisch, Rassen-

page 85

lively ['laɪvli]	lebendig, lebhaft, rege
population [ˌpɒpju'leɪʃn]	Bevölkerung
struggle ['strʌgl]	Kampf
engine ['endʒɪn]	Motor

page 86

shipyard ['ʃɪpjɑːd]	Werft
to **fall in love with sb/sth** [ˌfɔːl ɪn 'lʌv wɪð]	sich in jdn/etw verlieben
to **emigrate** ['emɪgreɪt]	auswandern
to **build sth up** [ˌbɪld 'ʌp]	etw aufbauen
deportation [dɪpɔː'teɪʃn]	Abschiebung
to **escape from sth** [ɪ'skeɪp frəm]	einer Sache entkommen
port [pɔːt]	Hafen, Hafenstadt
parliament ['pɑːləmənt]	Parlament
to **retire** [rɪ'taɪə]	in den Ruhestand gehen, in Rente gehen
unemployment [ˌʌnɪm'plɔɪmənt]	Arbeitslosigkeit
to **claim unemployment benefits** [ˌkleɪm ʌnɪm'plɔɪmənt benɪfɪts]	Arbeitslosengeld beziehen
housing ['haʊzɪŋ]	Wohnungsbau, Wohnungen
approximately (approx.) [ə'prɒksɪmətli]	zirka (ca.)
presenter [prɪ'zentə]	Moderator/in
agricultural [ˌægrɪ'kʌltʃərəl]	landwirtschaftlich, Landwirtschafts-
free movement [ˌfriː 'muːvmənt]	Freizügigkeit
rural ['rʊərəl]	ländlich
uncontrolled [ˌʌnkən'trəʊld]	ungeregelt, unkontrolliert
incomer ['ɪnkʌmə]	Zuzügler, Ankömmling
issue ['ɪʃuː]	Streitpunkt, Frage, Problem, Thema
the other way round [ði ˌʌðə weɪ 'raʊnd]	umgekehrt
economy [ɪ'kɒnəmi]	Wirtschaft
war [wɔː]	Krieg
replacement [rɪ'pleɪsmənt]	Ersatz, Ersetzung, Austausch
unemployment rate [ˌʌnɪm'plɔɪmənt reɪt]	Arbeitslosenquote
pressure ['preʃə]	Druck

page 87

course of action [ˌkɔːs əv 'ækʃn]	Vorgehen, Maßnahmen
sir [sɜː]	mein Herr
jacket ['dʒækɪt]	Jacke, Jackett
to **deal with sth** ['diːl wɪð]	mit etw zu tun haben
label ['leɪbl]	Beschriftung, Bezeichnung
explanation [ˌeksplə'neɪʃn]	Erläuterung, Erklärung
to **select** [sɪ'lekt]	auswählen
to **contrast** [kən'trɑːst]	gegenüberstellen, vergleichen
to **take sb in** [ˌteɪk 'ɪn]	jdn aufnehmen
host [həʊst]	Gastgeber
approximate [ə'prɒksɪmət]	ungefähr, angenähert
similarly ['sɪmələli]	in ähnlicher Weise, genauso, ebenso

page 88

sensitive ['sensətɪv]	einfühlsam, feinfühlig
care [keə]	Versorgung, Fürsorge
nursing ['nɜːsɪŋ]	Pflege, Krankenpflege
eager ['iːgə]	bestrebt, darauf aus
to **make sure** [ˌmeɪk 'ʃʊə]	sicherstellen
patient ['peɪʃnt]	Patient/in
male [meɪl]	Mann, männliche Person
in regards to [ɪn rɪ'gɑːdz tə]	bezüglich
modesty ['mɒdəsti]	Bescheidenheit, Anstand, Sittsamkeit
to **hold** [həʊld]	halten, innehaben
vice versa [ˌvaɪs 'vɜːsə]	umgekehrt
intimate ['ɪntɪmət]	intim, eng, persönlich
to **meet sb's needs** [miːt 'niːdz]	jds Bedürfnisse erfüllen
respectful [rɪ'spektfl]	respektvoll
still [stɪl]	dennoch
gay [geɪ]	schwul, lesbisch
gender ['dʒendə]	Geschlecht
grateful ['greɪtfl]	dankbar
to **assist** [ə'sɪst]	assistieren, helfen
to **appreciate** [ə'priːʃieɪt]	schätzen, zu schätzen wissen
health care provider [ˌhelθkeə prə'vaɪdə]	Gesundheitsdienstleister
paramedic [ˌpærə'medɪk]	Sanitäter/in
to **give birth** [gɪv 'bɜːθ]	gebären, entbinden
setting ['setɪŋ]	Umgebung
to **make a fuss** [fʌs]	sich anstellen, Umstände machen
rather ['rɑːðə]	lieber, eher
since [sɪns]	weil, da
modest ['mɒdɪst]	bescheiden, sittsam
to **be aware of sth** [bi ə'weər əv]	sich einer Sache bewusst sein, etw kennen
expectation [ˌekspek'teɪʃn]	Erwartung
to **take care of sb** [teɪk 'keə əv]	sich um jdn kümmern
perspective [pə'spektɪv]	Perspektive, Blickwinkel

UNIT 10

page 89

clothing bank ['kləʊðɪŋ bæŋk]	Altkleidersammelbehälter
beggar ['begə]	Bettler/in
to **beg for sth** ['beg fə]	um etw betteln
donation [dəʊ'neɪʃn]	Spende

page 90

blockbuster ['blɒkbʌstə]	Straßenfeger
poverty ['pɒvəti]	Armut
producer [prə'dju:sə]	Produzent/in
Not on our watch. [nɒt ɒn 'aʊə wɒtʃ]	Nicht mit uns!
mission ['mɪʃn]	Auftrag, Mission
atrocities *pl* [ə'trɒsətiz]	Gräueltaten
to **invite sb to do sth** [ɪn'vaɪt]	jdn auffordern, etw zu tun
to **lobby sb** ['lɒbi]	auf jdn Einfluss nehmen
donor ['dəʊnə]	Spender/in
schooling ['sku:lɪŋ]	Schulbesuch, Schulbildung
benefactor ['benɪfæktə]	Wohltäter/in
sponsorship ['spɒnsəʃɪp]	Förderung
accountancy [ə'kaʊntənsi]	Buchhaltung, Rechnungswesen
tear [tɪə]	Träne
loan [ləʊn]	Darlehen, Kredit
foundation [faʊn'deɪʃn]	Stiftung
to **feed** [fi:d]	ernähren, mit Nahrung versorgen
life saving ['laɪf seɪvɪŋ]	lebensrettend
medicine ['medsn]	Arznei(mittel), Medizin
handout ['hændaʊt]	Almosen
ongoing ['ɒngəʊɪŋ]	laufend
to **empower sb to do sth** [ɪm'paʊə]	jdn befähigen, etw zu tun
self-sustainable [ˌself sə'steɪnəbl]	selbsttragend, lebensfähig
to **enable** [ɪ'neɪbl]	befähigen
to **make a difference** [ˌmeɪk ə 'dɪfrəns]	etw bewirken
valuable ['væljuəbl]	wertvoll
along the way [əˌlɒŋ ðə 'weɪ]	dabei, währenddessen
to **value** ['vælju:]	wertschätzen, schätzen
from all walks of life [frəm ˌɔ:l wɔ:ks əv 'laɪf]	aus allen Gesellschaftsschichten, aus allen Lebensbereichen
currently ['kʌrəntli]	zur Zeit
to **trouble sb** ['trʌbl]	jdn bekümmern, jdm Schwierigkeiten bereiten
Salvation Army [sælˌveɪʃn 'ɑ:mi]	Heilsarmee
toddler ['tɒdlə]	Kleinkind
disadvantaged [ˌdɪsəd'vɑ:ntɪdʒd]	benachteiligt
day centre ['deɪ sentə]	Tagesstätte
companionship [kəm'pæniənʃɪp]	Gemeinschaft, Gesellschaft

page 91

homelessness ['həʊmləsnəs]	Obdachlosigkeit
psychological [ˌsaɪkə'lɒdʒɪkl]	psychologisch
armed [ɑ:md]	bewaffnet
home country [ˌhəʊm 'kʌntri]	Heimatland
in the long term [ɪn ðə 'lɒŋ tɜ:m]	langfristig
in the short term [ɪn ðə ˌʃɔ:t 'tɜ:m]	kurzfristig
horrific [hə'rɪfɪk]	schrecklich, entsetzlich
act [ækt]	Handlung, Tat
to **finance** ['faɪnæns]	finanzieren
(the) good [gʊd]	Wohl

page 92

giving ['gɪvɪŋ]	Spenden
level ['levl]	Grad, Höhe
gross domestic product (GDP) [ˌgrəʊs dəˌmestɪk 'prɒdʌkt]	Bruttosozialprodukt
tax [tæks]	Steuer
to **give to charity** [ˌgɪv tə 'tʃærəti]	(für wohltätige Zwecke) spenden
good cause [gʊd 'kɔ:z]	guter Zweck
disabled [dɪs'eɪbld]	behindert
surgery ['sɜ:dʒəri]	Operation
in need [ɪn 'ni:d]	bedürftig, in Not
regardless of sth [rɪ'gɑ:dləs əv]	ungeachtet einer Sache
religious [rɪ'lɪdʒəs]	religiös
funding ['fʌndɪŋ]	Finanzierung, Geldmittel
to **feel sorry for sb** [ˌfi:l 'sɒri fə]	jd tut einem leid
responsibility [rɪˌspɒnsə'bɪləti]	Verantwortung, Zuständigkeit
to **fund** [fʌnd]	finanzieren
charitable ['tʃærətəbl]	wohltätig, gemeinnützig
line graph ['laɪn grɑ:f]	Liniendiagramm
striking ['straɪkɪŋ]	auffallend, auffällig, hervorstechend
progression [prə'greʃn]	Entwicklung, Steigerung
to **rank sixth** [ræŋk 'sɪksθ]	den sechsten Platz einnehmen
times [taɪmz]	mal

page 93

attitude ['ætɪtju:d]	Einstellung, Haltung
walk [wɔ:k]	Spaziergang, Rundgang
gardening ['gɑ:dnɪŋ]	Gartenarbeit
target ['tɑ:gɪt]	Ziel
feedback ['fi:dbæk]	Reaktion(en), Rückmeldung(en)
English-speaking ['ɪŋglɪʃ spi:kɪŋ]	englischsprachig
pen friend ['pen frend]	Brieffreund/in

page 94

orphan ['ɔ:fn]	Waise
orphanage ['ɔ:fənɪdʒ]	Waisenhaus
Boxing Day ['bɒksɪŋ deɪ]	2. Weihnachtstag
to **strike** [straɪk]	treffen
fishing village ['fɪʃɪŋ vɪlɪdʒ]	Fischerdorf
to **be asleep** [bi ə'sli:p]	schlafen
scream [skri:m]	Schrei
to **smash** [smæʃ]	zertrümmern, zerstören
to **sweep away** [ˌswi:p ə'weɪ]	fortschwemmen, erfassen, wegreißen
whilst [waɪlst]	während
despite [dɪ'spaɪt]	trotz
blow [bləʊ]	Schlag
to **escape sth narrowly** [ɪˌskeɪp 'nærəʊli]	einer Sache knapp entkommen
to **hitch-hike** ['hɪtʃ haɪk]	per Anhalter fahren, trampen

embassy ['embəsi]	Botschaft
to **rejoin sb** [rɪ'dʒɔɪn]	jdn wieder treffen
to **adopt sb** [ə'dɒpt]	jdn adoptieren
ultimately ['ʌltɪmətli]	letztlich, letztendlich
strength [streŋθ]	Stärke, Kraft
humanitarian [hjuːˌmænɪ'tæriən]	humanitär
a great deal [ə ˌgreɪt 'diːl]	eine erhebliche Menge
to **hand sth out** [ˌhænd 'aʊt]	etw verteilen, etw ausgeben
confidence ['kɒnfɪdəns]	Selbstvertrauen, Zuversicht
to **knock sb off sth** [ˌnɒk 'ɒf]	jdn von etw herunterstoßen, von etw herunterfallen
to **be worse off** [bi ˌwɜːs 'ɒf]	schlechter dran sein
independence [ˌɪndɪ'pendəns]	Unabhängigkeit
movement ['muːvmənt]	Bewegung
enterprise ['entəpraɪz]	Unternehmen
to **found** [faʊnd]	gründen
commitment to sth [kə'mɪtmənt tə]	Engagement für etw, Einsatz für etw
portion ['pɔːʃn]	Teil
sole [səʊl]	alleinig
essentials *pl* [ɪ'senʃlz]	lebensnotwendige Güter
shelter ['ʃeltə]	Unterkunft
nutrition [nju'trɪʃn]	Nahrung, Ernährung
medication [ˌmedɪ'keɪʃn]	Arzneimittel
to **make an impact** [ˌmeɪk ən 'ɪmpækt]	etw bewirken, etw verändern
opening ['əʊpnɪŋ]	Eröffnung
memory of sb ['meməri]	Gedenken an jdn
to **mark** [mɑːk]	*(Jahrestag etc.)* begehen
anniversary [ˌænɪ'vɜːsəri]	Jahrestag

page 95

to **destroy** [dɪ'strɔɪ]	zerstören
force [fɔːs]	Gewalt, Kraft
ride [raɪd]	Fahrt
unpaid [ˌʌn'peɪd]	unbezahlt
intention [ɪn'tenʃn]	Absicht
hurricane ['hʌrɪkən]	Wirbelsturm
flood [flʌd]	Überschwemmung
fatality [fə'tæləti]	Todesfall, Todesopfer
NGO (non-governmental organization) [ˌen dʒiː 'əʊ]	Nichtregierungsorganisation
citizen ['sɪtɪzn]	Bürger/in
to **put in work** [pʊt ˌɪn 'wɜːk]	Arbeit leisten

page 96

occupation [ˌɒkju'peɪʃn]	Beruf, Tätigkeit, Beschäftigung
contribution [ˌkɒntrɪ'bjuːʃn]	(finanzielle) Zuwendung, Spende
madam ['mædəm]	gnädige Frau
banker ['bæŋkə]	Bankkaufmann/-frau
earthquake ['ɜːθkweɪk]	Erdbeben
to **have spare cash** [həv ˌspeə 'kæʃ]	Geld übrig haben
to **run** [rʌn]	*(Unternehmen etc.)* führen, betreiben
to **transfer** [træns'fɜː]	*(Geld)* überweisen
so far [ˌsəʊ 'fɑː]	bislang
medical student [ˌmedɪkl 'stjuːdnt]	Medizinstudent/in
walk-in medical centre [ˌwɔːk ɪn 'medɪkl sentə]	Ambulanz

page 97

saleswoman ['seɪlzwʊmən]	Verkäuferin
myth [mɪθ]	Mythos, Märchen
aid [eɪd]	Hilfe
disease [dɪ'ziːz]	Krankheit
common ['kɒmən]	verbreitet, üblich
misunderstanding [ˌmɪsʌndə'stændɪŋ]	Missverständnis
developing country [dɪˌveləpɪŋ 'kʌntri]	Entwicklungsland
to **treat** [triːt]	behandeln
corrupt [kə'rʌpt]	korrupt, bestechlich
official [ə'fɪʃl]	Beamte/r, Funktionär/in
concrete ['kɒŋkriːt]	konkret
mosquito net [məs'kiːtəʊ net]	Moskitonetz
farming ['fɑːmɪŋ]	Landwirtschaft
health care ['helθ keə]	Gesundheitswesen, medizinische Versorgung
preventable [prɪ'ventəbl]	vermeidbar
proverb ['prɒvɜːb]	Sprichwort
for a lifetime [fər ə 'laɪftaɪm]	ein Leben lang

page 98

at the same time [ət ðə ˌseɪm 'taɪm]	gleichzeitig
runner ['rʌnə]	Läufer/in
to **raise (money)** [reɪz 'mʌni]	(Geld) sammeln, einbringen
hospice ['hɒspɪs]	Hospiz, Sterbeklinik

UNIT 11

page 99

reach [riːtʃ]	Reichweite
bread roll ['bred rəʊl]	Brötchen
cardboard ['kɑːdbɔːd]	Pappe
supply chain [sə'plaɪ tʃeɪn]	Lieferkette
item ['aɪtəm]	Artikel, Gegenstand
to **manufacture** [ˌmænju'fæktʃə]	fertigen, herstellen
raw product [ˌrɔː 'prɒdʌkt]	Ausgangsprodukt, Roherzeugnis
to **originate from** [ə'rɪdʒɪneɪt frəm]	kommen aus
within [wɪ'ðɪn]	innerhalb, binnen
to **grow** [grəʊ]	*(Pflanze)* anbauen
to **import** [ɪm'pɔːt]	importieren, einführen
wheat [wiːt]	Weizen
lettuce ['letɪs]	Kopfsalat

page 100

globalization [ˌgləʊbəlaɪ'zeɪʃn]	Globalisierung
case study ['keɪs stʌdi]	Fallstudie
growth [grəʊθ]	Wachstum, Zunahme
trade [treɪd]	Handel
influence ['ɪnfluəns]	Einfluss
to **spread** [spred]	sich ausbreiten, sich verbreiten
trader ['treɪdə]	Händler/in
trading ['treɪdɪŋ]	Handel
cooperative [kəʊ'ɒpərətɪv]	Genossenschaft
to **transform** [træns'fɔːm]	(völlig) verändern
to **raise sth** [reɪz]	etw steigern, etw erhöhen
to **switch to sth** ['swɪtʃ tə]	auf etw umstellen
organic [ɔː'gænɪk]	biologisch, Bio-

buyer ['baɪə]	Einkäufer/in
facilities *pl* [fə'sɪlətiz]	Anlage(n), Einrichtungen
to **process** [prəʊ'ses]	verarbeiten
finished product [ˌfɪnɪʃt 'prɒdʌkt]	Endprodukt
clinic ['klɪnɪk]	Klinik
secondary school ['sekəndri sku:l]	weiterführende Schule
textile ['tekstaɪl]	Textil-
back [bæk]	Rücken
to **care about sth** ['keər əbaʊt]	sich um etw kümmern
to **injure** ['ɪndʒə]	verletzen
to **collapse** [kə'læps]	einstürzen
deadline ['dedlaɪn]	Frist, Termin
order ['ɔ:də]	Auftrag, Bestellung
to **fill an order** [ˌfɪl ən 'ɔ:də]	einen Auftrag ausführen
union ['ju:niən]	Gewerkschaft
to **take action** [ˌteɪk 'ækʃn]	handeln
offshore [ˌɒf'ʃɔ:]	im/ins Ausland
folks *pl* [fəʊks]	Leute
carpentry ['kɑ:pəntri]	Schreinerei
depressed [dɪ'prest]	*(Wirtschaft:)* flau, am Boden
to **re-skill** [ˌri: 'skɪl]	umschulen
computer-aided [kəm'pju:tər eɪdɪd]	computergestützt
automated ['ɔ:təmeɪtɪd]	automatisiert
to **expand** [ɪk'spænd]	expandieren, ausweiten
electronic [ˌɪlek'trɒnɪk]	elektronisch, Elektronik-
component [kəm'pəʊnənt]	Bauteil
export ['ekspɔ:t]	Ausfuhr, Export
to **turn out** [ˌtɜ:n 'aʊt]	sich herausstellen
co-worker ['kəʊwɜ:kə]	Kollege/-in
to **go inland** [gəʊ 'ɪnlænd]	ins Landesinnere gehen
employment [ɪm'plɔɪmənt]	Anstellung, Arbeit
people ['pi:pl]	Volk

page 101

to **mention** ['menʃn]	erwähnen, nennen
to **change for the better** [ˌtʃeɪndʒ fə ðə 'betə]	sich zum Besseren verändern
point of view [ˌpɔɪnt əv 'vju:]	Perspektive, Blickwinkel, Standpunkt
to **farm** [fɑ:m]	*(Land)* bewirtschaften
to **govern** ['gʌvn]	regieren, verwalten, führen
agreement [ə'gri:mənt]	Vereinbarung, Absprache
to **construct** [kən'strʌkt]	bauen, errichten, konstruieren
transformation [ˌtrænzfə'meɪʃn]	(grundlegende) Veränderung, Umwandlung
expansion [ɪk'spænʃn]	Ausweitung, Expansion
to **look a mess** [ˌlʊk ə 'mes]	fürchterlich aussehen
democracy [dɪ'mɒkrəsi]	Demokratie

page 102

petrol ['petrəl]	Benzin
petrol-driven ['petrəl drɪvn]	benzingetrieben
mass production [ˌmæs prə'dʌkʃn]	Massenproduktion
personal transport [ˌpɜ:sənl 'trænspɔ:t]	Individualverkehr
to **export** [ɪk'spɔ:t]	ausführen, exportieren
complex ['kɒmpleks]	komplex
link [lɪŋk]	Verbindung, Verknüpfung, Beziehung
plant [plɑ:nt]	Fabrik, Werk, Anlage
to **link** [lɪŋk]	verbinden, verknüpfen
aircraft ['eəkrɑ:ft]	Flugzeug
maker ['meɪkə]	Hersteller, -bauer
shared [ʃeəd]	gemeinsam
to **test** [test]	erproben, testen
even so ['i:vn səʊ]	dennoch, allerdings

page 103

order ['ɔ:də]	Bestellung
straight away [streɪt ə'weɪ]	sofort
particularly [pə'tɪkjələli]	besonders
related [rɪ'leɪtɪd]	zugehörig
to **consist of sth** [kən'sɪst əv]	aus etw bestehen
ironic [aɪ'rɒnɪk]	ironisch
to **remind sb (of sth)** [rɪ'maɪnd]	jdn (an etw) erinnern
secondly ['sekəndli]	zweitens
collapse [kə'læps]	Einsturz
sharp [ʃɑ:p]	scharf
attack [ə'tæk]	Attacke, Angriff
care [keə]	Sorge, Fürsorge, Sorgfalt

page 104

to **re-shore** [ˌri: 'ʃɔ:]	*(Industrie)* wieder im Inland ansiedeln, wieder ins Inland verlagern
head [hed]	Leiter/in, Chef/in
industrialized [ɪn'dʌstriəlaɪzd]	industrialisiert
low-cost [ˌləʊ'kɒst]	billig, kostengünstig
to **undercut** [ˌʌndə'kʌt]	unterbieten
section ['sekʃn]	Bereich, Teil
industrial [ɪn'dʌstriəl]	Industrie-
wasteland ['weɪstlənd]	Brachland
wage [weɪdʒ]	Lohn
floor care ['flɔ: keə]	Bodenpflege
slight [slaɪt]	leicht, gering
overheads *pl* ['əʊvəhedz]	Fixkosten, Betriebskosten
rent [rent]	Miete
labour ['leɪbə]	Arbeit

page 105

demand [dɪ'mɑ:nd]	Nachfrage
to **meet a demand** [ˌmi:t ə dɪ'mɑ:nd]	eine Nachfrage befriedigen
delay [dɪ'leɪ]	Verzögerung
stock [stɒk]	(Lager-)Bestand, Vorrat
breakage ['breɪkɪdʒ]	Bruchschaden
faulty ['fɔ:lti]	defekt, fehlerhaft
balance ['bæləns]	Bilanz, Saldo
water heater ['wɔ:tə hi:tə]	Warmwasserbereiter, Boiler
cash machine ['kæʃ məʃi:n]	Geldautomat
rate [reɪt]	Tempo, Quote, Rate, Anteil
loss [lɒs]	Verlust
to **slow** [sləʊ]	sich verlangsamen, sich abschwächen
to **balance** ['bæləns]	ausgleichen
roughly ['rʌfli]	ungefähr

page 106

development [dɪ'veləpmənt]	*(Immobilie:)* Erschließung, Bau
to **hyphenate** ['haɪfəneɪt]	mit einem Bindestrich schreiben
to **decrease** [dɪ'kri:s]	abnehmen, zurückgehen
to **decline** [dɪ'klaɪn]	zurückgehen, fallen, sinken
sharp(ly) [ʃɑ:p]	stark
steady ['stedi]	kontinuierlich, stabil
slightly ['slaɪtli]	geringfügig, leicht
climb [klaɪm]	Anstieg
fall [fɔ:l]	Absturz, Rückgang

decrease ['diːkriːs]	Abnahme, Rückgang
decline [dɪ'klaɪn]	Rückgang
to **remain** [rɪ'meɪn]	bleiben

page 107

sales *pl* [seɪlz]	Umsatz
sales director ['seɪlz dərektə]	Verkaufsleiter/in, Vertriebsleiter/in
to **identify** [aɪ'dentɪfaɪ]	erkennen, bestimmen, identifizieren
recession [rɪ'seʃn]	Rezession
flat [flæt]	*(Umsatz etc.:)* konstant, unverändert
to **face sth** [feɪs]	mit etw konfrontiert werden, sich einer Sache gegenüber sehen
to **fight back** [ˌfaɪt 'bæk]	sich wehren, sich zurückkämpfen
optimistic [ˌɒptɪ'mɪstɪk]	optimistisch
running ['rʌnɪŋ]	in Folge
to **cut costs** [kʌt 'kɒsts]	Kosten senken
to **go out of business** [gəʊ ˌaʊt əv 'bɪznəs]	das Geschäft aufgeben, Pleite gehen
partly ['pɑːtli]	teils, teilweise
operation [ˌɒpə'reɪʃn]	Betrieb, Geschäftstätigkeit
bottom line [ˌbɒtəm 'laɪn]	das, worauf es (unterm Strich) ankommt
to **last** [lɑːst]	dauern, andauern, so bleiben

page 108

pandemic [pæn'demɪk]	Pandemie
deadly ['dedli]	tödlich
on record [ɒn 'rekɔːd]	aktenkundig, dokumentiert
influenza [ˌɪnflu'enzə]	Grippe
infection [ɪn'fekʃn]	Infektion
living quarters *pl* ['lɪvɪŋ kwɔːtəz]	Wohnbereich
troop [truːp]	Truppe
flu [fluː]	Grippe
virus, *pl* **viruses** ['vaɪrəs]	Virus
globe [gləʊb]	Globus
overseas [ˌəʊvə'siːz]	nach/in Übersee
severe [sɪ'vɪə]	ernst, schwer
extremely [ɪk'striːmli]	äußerst, außerordentlich
infectious disease [ɪnˌfekʃəs dɪ'ziːz]	Infektionskrankheit
swine flu ['swaɪn fluː]	Schweinegrippe
progress ['prəʊgres]	Fortschritt(e)
to **be faced with** [bi 'feɪst wɪð]	konfrontiert werden mit
to **recommend** [ˌrekə'mend]	empfehlen
to **screen** [skriːn]	untersuchen, überprüfen
to **exit** ['eksɪt]	verlassen
traveller ['trævələ]	Reisende/r
temperature ['temprətʃə]	Temperatur
fever ['fiːvə]	Fieber
symptom ['sɪmptəm]	Symptom, Anzeichen
to **contract (a disease)** [kən'trækt]	sich (mit einer Krankheit) infizieren/anstecken
affected [ə'fektɪd]	betroffen
health care worker ['helθkeə wɜːkə]	Bedienstete/r im Gesundheitswesen
to **undergo** [ˌʌndə'gəʊ]	sich unterziehen
quarantine ['kwɒrəntiːn]	Quarantäne
mask [mɑːsk]	Maske
stomach pain ['stʌmək peɪn]	Bauchschmerzen
outbreak ['aʊtbreɪk]	Ausbruch *(Krankheit)*
diarrhoea [ˌdaɪə'rɪə]	Durchfall
vaccine ['væksiːn]	Impfstoff
hygiene ['haɪdʒiːn]	Hygiene
to **prevent** [prɪ'vent]	verhindern, vorbeugen

UNIT 12

page 109

changing ['tʃeɪndʒɪŋ]	im Wandel
jobless ['dʒɒbləs]	arbeitslos
elderly ['eldəli]	älter; Senioren
pension ['penʃn]	Rente, Pension
burden ['bɜːdn]	Last, Belastung, Bürde
pensioner ['penʃənə]	Rentner/in
to **recover** [rɪ'kʌvə]	sich erholen
joblessness ['dʒɒbləsnəs]	Arbeitslosigkeit
millennial [mɪ'leniəl]	Jahrtausend-
to **campaign** [kæm'peɪn]	kämpfen
her native Pakistan [hə ˌneɪtɪv pækɪ'stɑːn]	ihr Geburtsland Pakistan
to **shoot sb** [ʃuːt]	jdn erschießen
to **be left for dead** [bi ˌleft fə 'ded]	als tot zurückgelassen werden
emergency [ɪ'mɜːdʒənsi]	Notfall, Not-
to **recover fully** [rɪˌkʌvə 'fʊli]	wieder völlig gesund werden

page 110

to **make room** [meɪk 'ruːm]	Platz machen
to **address sb** [ə'dres]	jdn ansprechen
to **pass sth on** [ˌpɑːs 'ɒn]	etw weitergeben, etw weiterreichen
degree [dɪ'griː]	Abschluss
to **juggle** ['dʒʌgl]	miteinander vereinbaren, jonglieren
casual job [ˌkæʒuəl 'dʒɒb]	Nebenjob
to **self-fund** [ˌself 'fʌnd]	selbst finanzieren
congressman ['kɒŋgresmən]	Kongressabgeordneter
retail ['riːteɪl]	Einzelhandel(s-)
to **make sb redundant** [ˌmeɪk rɪ'dʌndənt]	jdn (betriebsbedingt) entlassen
previous ['priːviəs]	vorherig, früher
to **land sth** [lænd]	etw an Land ziehen
middle management [ˌmɪdl 'mænɪdʒmənt]	mittlere Führungsebene
skilled [skɪld]	qualifiziert, erfahren
to **be sick of sth** [bi 'sɪk əv]	von etw die Nase voll haben
rather ['rɑːðə]	eher, lieber
endless ['endləs]	endlos, fortwährend
to **terminate** ['tɜːmɪneɪt]	beenden
full-time [ˌfʊl 'taɪm]	Vollzeit-
nannying ['næniɪŋ]	Kinderbetreuung
out-of-state [ˌaʊt əf 'steɪt]	in einem anderen Bundesstaat
application [ˌæplɪ'keɪʃn]	Bewerbung
applicant ['æplɪkənt]	Bewerber/in
pay packet ['peɪ pækɪt]	Lohntüte, Gehalt
minimum wage [ˌmɪnɪməm 'weɪdʒ]	Mindestlohn
editor ['edɪtə]	Herausgeber/in
to **take a chance on sb** [ˌteɪk ə 'tʃɑːns ɒn]	es mit jdm versuchen, jdm eine Chance geben
to **state** [steɪt]	erklären, feststellen
ought to ['ɔːt tə]	sollen
contributor [kən'trɪbjuːtə]	Autor/in *(von Zeitschriftenartikeln)*
entry-level ['entri levl]	Einstiegs-

to **be rigged against sb** [bi 'rɪgd əgenst]	jdn (systematisch) benachteiligen, gegen jdn arbeiten
graduate ['grædʒuət]	Absolvent/in
stream [stri:m]	Strom
to **be unique to sth** [bi ju'ni:k tə]	etw ausschließlich betreffen
lazy ['leɪzi]	faul
to **mooch off sth** [ˌmu:tʃ 'ɒf]	von etw schmarotzen
hopeless ['həʊpləs]	hoffnungslos

page 111

dole [dəʊl]	Arbeitslosengeld
dole bludger ['dəʊl blʌdʒə]	Sozialschmarotzer
useless ['ju:sləs]	nutzlos
unexpected(ly) [ˌʌnɪk'spektɪd]	unerwartet
afterwards ['ɑ:ftəwədz]	danach, darauf
publication [ˌpʌblɪ'keɪʃn]	Veröffentlichung
edition [ɪ'dɪʃn]	Ausgabe
to **outline** ['aʊtlaɪn]	skizzieren, grob beschreiben

page 112

journalism ['dʒɜ:nəlɪzəm]	Journalismus
assistance [ə'sɪstəns]	Hilfe, Unterstützung
graduation [ˌgrædʒu'eɪʃn]	(Schul-/Universitäts-) Abschluss
interview ['ɪntəvju:]	Vorstellungsgespräch
interviewer ['ɪntəvju:ə]	*Person, die ein Vorstellungsgespräch führt*
interviewee [ˌɪntəvju:'i:]	*Person, mit der ein Vorstellungsgespräch geführt wird*
shipbuilding ['ʃɪpbɪldɪŋ]	Schiffbau
to **interview sb** ['ɪntəvju:]	mit jdm ein Vorstellungsgespräch führen
to **meet a deadline** [ˌmi:t ə 'dedlaɪn]	eine Frist / einen Termin einhalten

page 113

to **play the piano** [ˌpleɪ ðə pi'ænəʊ]	Klavier spielen
harbour ['hɑ:bə]	Hafen
to **read sth back** [ˌri:d 'bæk]	etw (zur Kontrolle) vorlesen
to **edit** ['edɪt]	*(Text)* redigieren, bearbeiten
original material [əˌrɪdʒənl mə'tɪəriəl]	eigene Beiträge
to **confirm** [kən'fɜ:m]	bestätigen

page 114

retirement [rɪ'taɪəmənt]	Ruhestand, Rente
to **age** [eɪdʒ]	altern
founder ['faʊndə]	Gründer/in
resource [rɪ'sɔ:s]	Ressource
senior citizen [ˌsi:niə 'sɪtɪzn]	Senior/in, ältere/r Mitbürger/in
to **be still going strong** [bi ˌstɪl gəʊɪŋ 'strɒŋ]	gut dabei sein, immer noch in Form sein
startling ['stɑ:tlɪŋ]	alarmierend, erschreckend, erstaunlich
scrapheap ['skræhi:p]	Schrotthaufen
to **retire sb** [rɪ'taɪə]	jdn in den Ruhestand versetzen
social engineering [ˌsəʊʃl ˌendʒɪ'nɪərɪŋ]	Änderung gesellschaftlicher Strukturen, angewandte Sozialwissenschaft
to **be past it** [bi 'pɑ:st ɪt]	die besten Jahre hinter sich haben, jenseits von Gut und Böse sein
mental(ly) ['mentl]	geistig
to **ignore** [ɪg'nɔ:]	nicht beachten, ignorieren
reliability [rɪˌlaɪə'bɪləti]	Zuverlässigkeit, Verlässlichkeit
wish [wɪʃ]	Wunsch
to **act as sth** ['ækt əz]	als etw fungieren
adviser [əd'vaɪzə]	Berater/in
lifetime ['laɪftaɪm]	(ganzes) Leben
to **guide** [gaɪd]	führen
heart-warming ['hɑ:t wɔ:mɪŋ]	herzerwärmend
to **team up with sb** [ˌti:m 'ʌp wɪð]	mit jdm zusammenarbeiten, sich mit jdm zusammentun
home for the elderly [ˌhəʊm fə ði 'eldəli]	Altenheim
native speaker [ˌneɪtɪv 'spi:kə]	Muttersprachler/in
retirement home [rɪ'taɪəmənt həʊm]	Altersheim

page 115

ancient ['eɪnʃənt]	alt, historisch, antik
gay [geɪ]	schwul, lesbisch
equal society [ˌi:kwəl sə'saɪəti]	gerechte Gesellschaft

page 116

to **work sth out** [ˌwɜ:k 'aʊt]	etw herausfinden
closely related [ˌkləʊsli rɪ'leɪtɪd]	eng verwandt
to **make sense** [ˌmeɪk 'sens]	Sinn ergeben, sinnvoll sein
characteristic [ˌkærəktə'rɪstɪk]	Merkmal, charakteristische Eigenschaft
wedding ['wedɪŋ]	Hochzeit
affluent ['æfluənt]	wohlhabend
construction company [kən'strʌkʃn kʌmpəni]	Baufirma
to **stop sb from doing sth** [stɒp]	jdn daran hindern, etw zu tun
to **carry on** [ˌkæri 'ɒn]	weitermachen
tiring ['taɪərɪŋ]	anstrengend
warehouse ['weəhaʊs]	Lager
forklift (truck) ['fɔ:klɪft]	Gabelstapler

page 117

fuel ['fju:əl]	Brennstoff, Treibstoff
sadly ['sædli]	leider
there's no escape from the fact that [ðeəz nəʊ ɪˌskeɪp frəm ðə 'fækt ðət]	man kann nicht außer Acht lassen, dass; man muss der Tatsache ins Auge sehen, dass
allowance [ə'laʊəns]	Zuschuss
per annum [pər 'ænəm]	pro Jahr
to **support** [sə'pɔ:t]	*(Argument)* untermauern, stützen
moreover [mɔ:r'əʊvə]	überdies
furthermore [ˌfɜ:ðə'mɔ:]	darüber hinaus
for instance [fə'rɪnstəns]	zum Beispiel

page 118

childcare ['tʃaɪld keə]	Kinderbetreuung
to **echo** ['ekəʊ]	(wider)hallen, nachklingen
grandfather clock [ˌgrænfɑ:ðə 'klɒk]	Standuhr
melancholy ['melənkəli]	melancholisch, wehmütig
squeal [skwi:l]	Kreischen
delight [dɪ'laɪt]	Vergnügen, Freude
nursery ['nɜ:səri]	Kinderhort
sitting room ['sɪtɪŋ ru:m]	Wohnzimmer
literally ['lɪtərəli]	buchstäblich

centre ['sentə] Zentrum
reserved [rɪ'zɜːvd] reserviert, vorbehalten
rarely ['reəli] selten
to **rent** [rent] mieten
granny ['græni] Oma
to **relieve** [rɪ'liːv] erleichtern, *(Druck)* verringern, lindern

exhausted [ɪg'zɔːstɪd] erschöpft
in return [ɪn rɪ'tɜːn] im Gegenzug, als Ausgleich
dementia [dɪ'menʃə] Demenz
to **prompt** [prɒmpt] auffordern
at ease [ət 'iːz] zwanglos, unverkrampft
patient ['peɪʃnt] Patient/in
care worker ['keə wɜːkə] Pfleger/in
nursing home ['nɜːsɪŋ həʊm] Pflegeheim
to **urge** [ɜːdʒ] drängen
to **adopt sth** [ə'dɒpt] etw übernehmen
to **cope** [kəʊp] zurechtkommen
to **expect** [ɪk'spekt] erwarten, annehmen
to **examine** [ɪg'zæmɪn] untersuchen, prüfen

JOB SKILLS 3

page 119

to **give directions** [ˌgɪv də'rekʃnz] den Weg beschreiben
booking ['bʊkɪŋ] Buchung
reservation [ˌrezə'veɪʃn] Reservierung
to **be located in** [bi ləʊ'keɪtɪd ɪn] sich in … befinden, in … liegen
directions *pl* [də'rekʃnz] Wegbeschreibung
to **turn right/left** [ˌtɜːn 'raɪt, 'left] rechts/links abbiegen
café ['kæfeɪ] Café
within walking distance [wɪðɪn 'wɔːkɪŋ dɪstəns] in Laufweite
straight ahead [ˌstreɪt ə'hed] geradeaus
to **keep to the right/left** [ˌkiːp tə 'raɪt, 'left] sich rechts/links halten

page 120

accounts [ə'kaʊnts] Buchhaltung
storeroom ['stɔːruːm] Lagerraum
marvellous ['mɑːvələs] toll, phantastisch
corridor ['kɒrɪdɔː] Flur, Gang
next to ['nekst tə] neben
impressed [ɪm'prest] beeindruckt
to **find one's way around** [faɪn wʌnz ˌweɪ ə'raʊnd] sich zurechtfinden
photocopier ['fəʊtəʊkɒpiə] Fotokopiergerät
office supplies *pl* ['ɒfɪs səplaɪz] Büromaterial
Research and Development (R&D) [rɪˌsɜːtʃ ən dɪ'veləpmənt] Forschung(s-) und Entwicklung(sabteilung)
quality control ['kwɒləti kəntrəʊl] Qualitätskontrolle
reception [rɪ'sepʃn] Empfang
remaining [rɪ'meɪnɪŋ] übrig, verbleibend
blank [blæŋk] leer, frei
memory ['meməri] Gedächtnis
emergency exit [i'mɜːdʒənsi eksɪt] Notausgang, Fluchtweg
emergency exit plan [iˌmɜːdʒənsi 'eksɪt plæn] Fluchtwegplan
to **exhibit** [ɪg'zɪbɪt] ausstellen
trade fair ['treɪd feə] Handelsmesse, Fachmesse

non-smoking [ˌnɒn'sməʊkɪŋ] Nichtraucher-
as requested [əz rɪ'kwestɪd] wie gewünscht
Best wishes [ˌbest 'wɪʃɪz] *(Brief:)* Mit den besten Wünschen

page 121

to **be due** [bi 'djuː] *(Flugzeug etc.:)* planmäßig ankommen

confirmation [ˌkɒnfə'meɪʃn] Bestätigung
to **let sb know sth** [ˌlet 'nəʊ] jdm etw mitteilen, jdm etw sagen
(business) contact ['kɒntækt] Ansprechpartner/in, Geschäftspartner/in
Regards [rɪ'gɑːdz] *(Brief:)* Viele Grüße
to **reserve** [rɪ'zɜːv] reservieren
ranking ['ræŋkɪŋ] Rangfolge
seating ['siːtɪŋ] Bestuhlung
wheelchair ['wiːltʃeə] Rollstuhl
projector [prə'dʒektə] Beamer
screen [skriːn] Leinwand
selection [sɪ'lekʃn] Auswahl
non-alcoholic [ˌnɒn ælkə'hɒlɪk] alkoholfrei
vegetarian [ˌvedʒə'teəriən] vegetarisch
to **exceed** [ɪk'siːd] überschreiten

page 122

wheelchair access ['wiːltʃeər ækses] behindertengerechter Zugang
throughout [θruː'aʊt] überall, in ganz …
disabled facilities *pl* [dɪsˌeɪbld fə'sɪlətiz] behindertengerechte Toiletten
equipped with [ɪ'kwɪpt wɪð] ausgestattet mit
stationery ['steɪʃənri] Schreibpapier, Schreibwaren
dietary ['daɪətri] Ernährungs
to **cater for sth** ['keɪtə fə] auf etw eingehen
to **stay overnight** [ˌsteɪ əʊvə'naɪt] übernachten
reasonable ['riːznəbl] vernünftig
to **mix and match** [ˌmɪks ən 'mætʃ] individuell zusammenstellen
marker ['mɑːkə] Filzstift
to **cater** ['keɪtə] Speisen und Getränke liefern
buffet lunch ['bʊfeɪ lʌntʃ] Lunchbuffet
rental price ['rentl praɪs] Mietpreis

UNIT 13

page 123

priority [praɪ'ɒrəti] Priorität, Vorrang
data protection [ˌdeɪtə prə'tekʃn] Datenschutz
waste [weɪst] Müll
dependence [dɪ'pendəns] Abhängigkeit
extremism [ɪk'striːmɪzm] Extremismus
identity [aɪ'dentəti] Identität
theft [θeft] Diebstahl
radicalization [ˌrædɪklaɪ'zeɪʃn] Radikalisierung
surveillance [sɜː'veɪləns] Überwachung
terrorist ['terərɪst] Terrorist/in, Terror-
attack [ə'tæk] Anschlag, Attentat

page 124

finishing line ['fɪnɪʃɪŋ laɪn] Ziellinie
pressure cooker ['preʃə kʊkə] Schnellkochtopf
bomb [bɒm] Bombe
to **explode** [ɪk'spləʊd] explodieren

suspect ['sʌspekt]	Verdächtige/r
firefight ['faɪəfaɪt]	Schusswechsel
manhunt ['mænhʌnt]	Verbrecherjagd
to **shut down** [ˌʃʌt 'daʊn]	schließen
resident ['rezɪdənt]	Anwohner/in, Bewohner/in
urban ['ɜːbən]	städtisch, Stadt-
desert ['dezət]	Wüste
back yard [ˌbæk 'jɑːd]	Hinterhof
to **state** [steɪt]	aussagen
to **bomb sth** [bɒm]	einen Bombenanschlag auf etw verüben
to **claim** [kleɪm]	behaupten
to **radicalize** ['rædɪklaɪz]	radikalisieren
to **engage in sth** [ɪn'geɪdʒ ɪn]	aktiv werden
violence ['vaɪələns]	Gewalt
multiple ['mʌltɪpl]	mehrere, vielfach
to **dominate** ['dɒmɪneɪt]	beherrschen, dominieren
battlefield ['bætlfiːld]	Schlachtfeld
century ['sentʃəri]	Jahrhundert
commander [kə'mɑːndə]	Kommandant/in, Anführer/in
modernity [mə'dɜːnəti]	Moderne
impact ['ɪmpækt]	Einfluss, Auswirkung
mobility [məʊ'bɪləti]	Mobilität
to **originate from sth** [ə'rɪdʒɪneɪt frəm]	von etw ausgehen, aus etw kommen
weapon ['wepən]	Waffe
access to sth ['ækses tə]	Zugriff auf etw, Zugang zu etw
destructive [dɪ'strʌktɪv]	zerstörerisch
to **plague** [pleɪg]	plagen, heimsuchen
tactic ['tæktɪk]	Taktik
essentially [ɪ'senʃəli]	im Wesentlichen
law enforcement ['lɔː ɪnfɔːsmənt]	Gesetzesvollzug, Innere Sicherheit, Exekutive
criminal justice [ˌkrɪmɪnl 'dʒʌstɪs]	Strafjustiz
arsenal ['ɑːsnəl]	Instrumentarium, Waffenlager
law enforcement agency ['lɔː ɪnfɔːsmənt eɪdʒənsi]	Strafverfolgungsbehörde, Exekutivorgan
extension [ɪk'stenʃn]	Erweiterung, Ausbau
to **root sth out** [ˌruːt 'aʊt]	etw beseitigen, etw ausmerzen
mass media *pl* [ˌmæs 'miːdiə]	Massenmedien
cable news ['keɪbl njuːz]	TV-Nachrichtensender
responsible [rɪ'spɒnsəbl]	verantwortungsvoll
breathless(ly) ['breθləs]	atemlos
to **await** [ə'weɪt]	erwarten, abwarten

page 125

bomber ['bɒmə]	Bombenattentäter/in
explosive device [ɪkˌspləʊsɪv dɪ'vaɪs]	Sprengsatz
to **sensationalize sth** [sen'seɪʃənlaɪz]	reißerisch über etw berichten
suicide ['suːɪsaɪd]	Selbstmord
suicide bomber [ˌsuːɪsaɪd 'bɒmə]	Selbstmordattentäter/in
devastating ['devəsteɪtɪŋ]	verheerend
attacker [ə'tækə]	Attentäter/in
explosive [ɪk'spləʊsɪv]	Sprengstoff
innocent ['ɪnəsnt]	unschuldig
cross [krɒs]	Kreuz
guilty ['gɪlti]	schuldig
police station [pə'liːs steɪʃn]	Polizeiwache

page 126

to **have one's say** [həv wʌnz 'seɪ]	seine Meinung äußern, zu Wort kommen
threat [θret]	Bedrohung
to **be under threat** [bi ˌʌndə 'θret]	bedroht werden
Christian ['krɪstʃən]	christlich, Christ/in
army [ɑːmi]	Armee
officer ['ɒfɪsə]	Offizier/in
to **get you nowhere** [ˌget jə 'nəʊweə]	zu nichts führen, nichts bringen
conflict zone ['kɒnflɪkt zəʊn]	Krisenregion, Konfliktzone
host [həʊst]	(Radio-/TV-)Moderator/in
law and order [ˌlɔː ənd 'ɔːdə]	Recht und Ordnung
security forces *pl* [sɪ'kjʊərəti fɔːsɪz]	Sicherheitskräfte
armed forces *pl* [ˌɑːmd 'fɔːsɪz]	Streitkräfte
massive(ly) ['mæsɪv]	massiv
to **border with sth** ['bɔːdə wɪð]	an etw grenzen
to **supply sb with sth** [sə'plaɪ]	jdn mit etw versorgen, jdm mit etw beliefern
westerner ['westənə]	Mensch aus der westlichen Welt
to **arm sb** [ɑːm]	jdn bewaffnen
pacifist ['pæsɪfɪst]	Pazifist/in
to **be in favour of sth** [bi ɪn 'feɪvər əv]	für etw sein
man of the cloth [ˌmæn əv ðə 'klɒθ]	Geistlicher
prayer [preə]	Gebet
prayer vigil ['preə vɪdʒɪl]	Gebetswache
to **pray** [preɪ]	beten
to **join together** [ˌdʒɔɪn tə'geðə]	sich zusammenschließen

page 127

to **prevent** [prɪ'vent]	verhindern, verhüten
thorough(ly) ['θʌrə]	gründlich, sorgfältig
entirely [ɪn'taɪəli]	völlig, ganz
to **put** [pʊt]	formulieren, sagen, in Worte fassen
security service [sɪ'kjʊərəti sɜːvɪs]	Geheimdienst
sensitive ['sensətɪv]	sensibel, *(Information:)* vertraulich
internal [ɪn'tɜːnl]	inländisch, Inlands-
to **post** [pəʊst]	*(Brief:)* einwerfen, schicken
anonymous(ly) [ə'nɒnɪməs]	anonym
police force [pə'liːs fɔːs]	Polizei
precaution [prɪ'kɔːʃn]	Vorkehrung, Sicherheitsmaßnahme
to **be willing to do sth** [bi 'wɪlɪŋ tə]	bereit sein, etw zu tun

page 128

to **defend** [dɪ'fend]	verteidigen
to **let oneself in for sth** [ˌlet wʌnself 'ɪn fə]	sich auf etw einlassen
to **harm sb** [hɑːm]	jdm schaden
self-defence [ˌself dɪ'fens]	Selbstverteidigung
specialist ['speʃəlɪst]	Spezial-, Fach-
request [rɪ'kwest]	Bitte, Wunsch, Anfrage
to **instruct sb to do sth** [ɪn'strʌkt]	jdn beauftragen, etw zu tun
to **install** [ɪn'stɔːl]	installieren

undetectable [ˌʌndɪ'tektəbl]	nicht erkennbar, nicht nachweisbar
spyware ['spaɪweə]	Spionagesoftware
to **transmit** [træns'mɪt]	übertragen, übermitteln, senden
to **track sb** [træk]	jds Spur verfolgen
to **log** [lɒg]	aufzeichnen, protokollieren
school-age ['sku:l eɪdʒ]	im Schulalter
to **intercept** [ˌɪntə'sept]	abfangen, abhören
to **be mistaken** [bi mɪ'steɪkən]	sich irren
keystroke ['ki:strəʊk]	Tastenanschlag, Herunterdrücken einer Taste
handy ['hændi]	praktisch
to **input** ['ɪnpʊt]	eingeben
access code ['ækses kəʊd]	Zugangscode

page 129

silent ['saɪlənt]	stumm
microphone ['maɪkrəfəʊn]	Mikrofon
to **go unnoticed** [ˌgəʊ ʌn'nəʊtɪst]	unbemerkt bleiben
to **switch to sth** ['swɪtʃ tə]	auf etw umschalten
delivery [dɪ'lɪvəri]	Lieferung
van [væn]	Lieferwagen
lawnmower ['lɔ:nməʊə]	Rasenmäher
to **refuse sth** [rɪ'fju:z]	etw verweigern
to **knock sth off** [ˌnɒk 'ɒf]	etw abschlagen
mirror ['mɪrə]	Spiegel
to **stick sth on** [ˌstɪk 'ɒn]	etw befestigen
washing machine ['wɒʃɪŋ məʃi:n]	Waschmaschine
to **be priced at …** [bi 'praɪst ət]	… kosten
purchase ['pɜ:tʃəs]	Kauf
to **advise** [əd'vaɪz]	(jdm etw) raten
to **save** [seɪv]	*(Daten)* sichern
embarrassing [ɪm'bærəsɪŋ]	peinlich, unangenehm
to **prompt sb to do sth** [prɒmpt]	jdn veranlassen, etw zu tun
to **withdraw** [wɪð'drɔ:]	*(Geld)* abheben
untraceable [ˌʌn'treɪsəbl]	nicht ausfindig zu machen
to **be sick and tired of sth** [bi ˌsɪk ən 'taɪəd əv]	die Nase von etw gestrichen voll haben
straightaway [ˌstreɪtə'weɪ]	sofort, sogleich
nasty ['nɑ:sti]	gemein, hässlich, böse
to **beg sb to do sth** [beg]	jdn anflehen, etw zu tun
to **concede** [kən'si:d]	eingestehen, einräumen
utter ['ʌtə]	völlig, vollkommen
defeat [dɪ'fi:t]	Niederlage
obtainable [əb'teɪnəbl]	erhältlich
suspicious [sə'spɪʃəs]	misstrauisch
spouse [spaʊz]	Ehegatte
to **spy on sb** ['spaɪ ɒn]	jdn ausspionieren
the small print [ðə 'smɔ:l prɪnt]	das Kleingedruckte
tormentor [tɔ:'mentə]	Peiniger
encrypted [ɪn'krɪptɪd]	verschlüsselt
in person [ɪn 'pɜ:sn]	persönlich

page 130

means of transport [ˌmi:nz əf 'trænspɔ:t]	Verkehrsmittel
to **obtain sth** [əb'teɪn]	etw erhalten, an etw gelangen
to **launch an attack** [ˌlɔ:ntʃ ən ə'tæk]	einen Angriff starten
consequence ['kɒnsɪkwəns]	Folge, Konsequenz
to **cancel** ['kænsl]	abbrechen, abblasen
cybercrime ['saɪbəkraɪm]	Cyberkriminalität
bank robbery ['bæŋk rɒbəri]	Banküberfall, Bankraub
to **rob a bank** [ˌrɒb ə 'bæŋk]	eine Bank überfallen, eine Bank ausrauben
to **hijack** ['haɪdʒæk]	kapern

page 131

extract ['ekstrækt]	Auszug, Ausschnitt
novel ['nɒvl]	Roman
to **associate** [ə'səʊʃieɪt]	in Verbindung bringen, assoziieren
term [tɜ:m]	Begriff
to **publish** ['pʌblɪʃ]	veröffentlichen
fictional ['fɪkʃənl]	fiktiv
totalitarian [ˌtəʊtælɪ'tæriən]	totalitär
to **gaze** [geɪz]	starren, blicken
to **contrive** [kən'traɪv]	bewerkstelligen
beneath [bɪ'ni:θ]	unterhalb, unter
telescreen ['telɪskri:n]	Televisor
whisper ['wɪspə]	Flüstern
field of vision [ˌfi:ld əv 'vɪʒn]	Sichtfeld
plaque [plɑ:k]	Platte, Tafel
to **command** [kə'mɑ:nd]	beherrschen
to **plug in on sth** [ˌplʌg 'ɪn ɒn]	sich in etw einschalten
wire ['waɪə]	Draht
guesswork ['geswɜ:k]	Mutmaßung, Spekulation
at any rate [ət eni 'reɪt]	auf jeden Fall
assumption [ə'sʌmpʃn]	Annahme
to **overhear** [ˌəʊvə'hɪə]	belauschen, aufschnappen
darkness ['dɑ:knəs]	Dunkelheit
movement ['mu:vmənt]	Bewegung
to **scrutinize** ['skru:tənaɪz]	genau ansehen, überprüfen
parallel ['pærəlel]	Parallele

page 132

CCTV (closed-circuit television) [ˌsi: si: ti: 'vi:]	Videoüberwachung
CCTV camera [ˌsi: si: ti: 'vi: kæmərə]	Überwachungskamera
to **be located** [bi ləʊ'keɪtɪd]	sich befinden
to **disclose** [dɪs'kləʊz]	offenlegen
campaigner [kæm'peɪnə]	Aktivist/in
care home ['keə həʊm]	Pflegeheim
scheme [ski:m]	Plan, Programm
invaluable [ɪn'væljuəbl]	unschätzbar, unbezahlbar
crime detection ['kraɪm dɪtekʃn]	Aufdecken von Straftaten
evidence ['evɪdəns]	Beweise, Beweismittel
murder ['mɜ:də]	Mord
footage ['fʊtɪdʒ]	Film-/Bildmaterial
to **be a stark reminder** [bi ə ˌstɑ:k rɪ'maɪndə]	etw jäh vor Augen führen, etw überdeutlich machen
potential(ly) [pə'tenʃl]	potenziell
to **monitor** ['mɒnɪtə]	überwachen
to **recognise** ['rekəgnaɪz]	anerkennen, begreifen
democratic [ˌdemə'krætɪk]	demokratisch
to **threaten** ['θretn]	bedrohen

page 134

scarce [skeəs]	knapp, rar
federal ['fedərəl]	Bundes-, auf Bundesebene geltend
to **source sth** [sɔ:s]	etw beziehen, beschaffen
personnel [ˌpɜ:sə'nel]	Personal
to **meet** [mi:t]	*(Bedarf)* decken

level of requirement [ˌlevl əv rɪ'kwaɪəmənt] Bedarfsniveau
carer ['keərə] Betreuer/in, Pfleger/in
reportedly [rɪ'pɔːtɪdli] Berichten zufolge
unfilled [ʌn'fɪld] unbesetzt
nursing ['nɜːsɪŋ] Pflege, Krankenpflege
association [əˌsəʊʃi'eɪʃn] Verband, Vereinigung
health care professional [ˌhelθkeə prə'feʃnl] Gesundheitsfachkraft
to **miss** [mɪs] fehlen
to **recruit sb** [rɪ'kruːt] jdn anwerben, jdn neu einstellen

placement ['pleɪsmənt] Stellenvermittlung
to **manage** ['mænɪdʒ] (es) schaffen
... is due to do sth [djuː] ... soll/wird etw tun
pilot project ['paɪlət prɒdʒekt] Pilotprojekt
to **declare** [dɪ'kleə] verkünden
spokesperson ['spəʊkspɜːsn] Sprecher/in
social prestige [ˌsəʊʃl pre'stiːʒ] soziale Anerkennung
seldom ['seldəm] selten
to **apply** [ə'plaɪ] anwenden, ausüben
aggressive [ə'gresɪv] aggressiv
recruiter [rɪ'kruːtə] Personalvermittler/in, Anwerber/in
profitable ['prɒfɪtəbl] Gewinn bringend, einträglich
compensation [ˌkɒmpən'seɪʃn] (finanzieller) Ausgleich

UNIT 14

page 135

solar ['səʊlə] Sonnen-, Solar-
biomass ['baɪəʊmæs] Biomasse
fossil fuel ['fɒsl fjuːəl] fossiler Brennstoff
geothermal power [dʒiːəʊˌθɜːml 'paʊə] Erdwärme
hydro-electric power [ˌhaɪdrəʊ ɪˌlektrɪk 'paʊə] Wasserkraft
methane ['miːθeɪn] Methan
nuclear power [ˌnjuːkliə 'paʊə] Kernkraft
solar power [ˌsəʊlə 'paʊə] Sonnenenergie
tidal power [ˌtaɪdl 'paʊə] Gezeitenkraft
wind power ['wɪnd paʊə] Windkraft
renewable [rɪ'njuːəbl] erneuerbar
breakdown ['breɪkdaʊn] Zusammenbruch
to **make sth up** [ˌmeɪk 'ʌp] etw ausmachen

page 136

climate ['klaɪmət] Klima
climate change ['klaɪmət tʃeɪndʒ] Klimawandel
angry ['æŋgri] aufgebracht, ungehalten
man-made ['mæn meɪd] künstlich, menschlichen Ursprungs
cause [kɔːz] Ursache
global warming [ˌgləʊbl 'wɔːmɪŋ] Erderwärmung
advocate ['ædvəkət] Befürworter/in
scientist ['saɪəntɪst] (Natur-)Wissenschaftler/in
denier [dɪ'naɪə] Leugner/in
carbon dioxide [ˌkɑːbən daɪ'ɒksaɪd] Kohlendioxid
carbon dioxide level [ˌkɑːbən daɪ'ɒksaɪd levl] Kohlendioxidkonzentration, -gehalt

previously ['priːviəsli] zuvor, vorher
variability [ˌveəriə'bɪləti] Schwankung, Unbeständigkeit
degree [dɪ'griː] Grad
CEO (Chief Executive Officer) [ˌsiː iː 'əʊ] Vorstandsvorsitzende/r
to **try sb** [traɪ] jdn vor Gericht stellen
high crime [ˌhaɪ 'kraɪm] Schwerverbrechen
humanity [hjuː'mænəti] Menschheit, Menschlichkeit
coal [kəʊl] Kohle
coal-fired ['kəʊl faɪəd] kohlegetrieben
power plant ['paʊə plɑːnt] Kraftwerk
to **be to blame** [bi tə 'bleɪm] Schuld sein
to **quote** [kwəʊt] zitieren
news anchor ['njuːz æŋkə] Nachrichtensprecher/in
large-scale ['lɑːdʒ skeɪl] in großem Umfang/Ausmaß
greenhouse gas [ˌgriːnhaʊs 'gæs] Treibhausgas
to **reflect** [rɪ'flekt] reflektieren
to **escape** [ɪ'skeɪp] entweichen
termperature ['temprətʃə] Temperatur

page 137

atmospheric [ˌætməs'ferɪk] atmosphärisch, in der Atmosphäre
to **pass** [pɑːs] überschreiten
beyond [bɪ'jɒnd] jenseits, über
major ['meɪdʒə] bedeutend, wichtig, groß
disastrous [dɪ'zɑːstrəs] katastrophal, verheerend
unstoppable [ˌʌn'stɒpəbl] unaufhaltsam
cyclone ['saɪkləʊn] Wirbelsturm, Zyklon, Sturmtief
to **warm** [wɔːm] sich erwärmen
ocean ['əʊʃn] Ozean, Weltmeer
ice sheet ['aɪs ʃiːt] Eisdecke
to **melt** [melt] schmelzen, abschmelzen
sea level ['siː levl] Meeresspiegel
island ['aɪlənd] Insel
coastal ['kəʊstl] Küsten-
to **drown** [draʊn] ertrinken, im Meer versinken
worrying ['wʌriɪŋ] besorgniserregend
emission [ɪ'mɪʃn] Ausstoß, Emission
panel ['pænl] Gremium, Ausschuss
to **prepare** [prɪ'peə] *(Bericht etc.)* erstellen, verfassen
as long as [əz 'lɒŋ əz] solange
co-author [ˌkəʊ 'ɔːθə] Mitautor/in, Mitverfasser/in
economics [ˌiːkə'nɒmɪks] Ökonomie, Wirtschaft(swissenschaft)
urgently ['ɜːdʒəntli] dringend, nachdrücklich
carbon ['kɑːbən] Kohlenstoff
investment [ɪn'vestmənt] Investition
existing [ɪg'zɪstɪŋ] bestehend, vorhanden
to **commute** [kə'mjuːt] (zur Arbeit) pendeln
to **pollute** [pə'luːt] (die Umwelt) verschmutzen
in turn [ɪn 'tɜːn] wiederum
quality of life [ˌkwɒləti əv 'laɪf] Lebensqualität
to **limit** ['lɪmɪt] begrenzen, einschränken
at the same time [ət ðə ˌseɪm 'taɪm] gleichzeitig
to **encourage** [ɪn'kʌrɪdʒ] fördern
largely ['lɑːdʒli] größtenteils, überwiegend
sceptic ['skeptɪk] Skeptiker/in
flooding ['flʌdɪŋ] Überschwemmung
to **call for sth** ['kɔːl fə] zu etw aufrufen

Unit word list

page 138

oil [ɔɪl]	Öl
natural gas [ˌnætʃrəl 'gæs]	Erdgas
to **power** ['paʊə]	antreiben, mit Energie versorgen
by contrast [baɪ 'kɒntrɑːst]	im Gegensatz dazu, dagegen
to **flood** [flʌd]	überschwemmen

page 139

Head of Science [ˌhed əf 'saɪəns]	Fachbereichsleiter/in Naturwissenschaft
sixth-form college ['sɪksθ fɔːm kɒlɪdʒ]	Oberstufenzentrum, Studienkolleg
grateful ['greɪtfl]	dankbar
to **specialize in sth** ['speʃəlaɪz ɪn]	sich auf etw spezialisieren
research [rɪ'sɜːtʃ]	Forschung
plain [pleɪn]	schlicht
freely ['friːli]	ungehindert, nach Belieben
unlike [ˌʌn'laɪk]	anders als
power station ['paʊə steɪʃn]	Kraftwerk, Elektrizitätswerk
ton [tʌn]	Tonne
to **provide sth** [prə'vaɪd]	für etw sorgen
pollution [pə'luːʃn]	Umweltverschmutzung

page 140

conference ['kɒnfərəns]	Konferenz
journey ['dʒɜːni]	Reise, Fahrt
sb's take on sth ['teɪk ɒn]	jds Einschätzung von etw
controversial [ˌkɒntrə'vɜːʃl]	umstritten
hydraulic [haɪ'drɔːlɪk]	hydraulisch
to **fracture** ['fræktʃə]	brechen, aufbrechen
shale [ʃeɪl]	Schiefer
rock [rɒk]	Fels, Gestein
to **inquire** [ɪn'kwaɪə]	nachfragen, sich erkundigen
to **drill** [drɪl]	bohren
to **pump** [pʌmp]	pumpen
crack [kræk]	Spalte
surface ['sɜːfɪs]	Oberfläche
well [wel]	Bohrloch
enthusiastic(ally) [ɪnˌθjuːzi'æstɪk]	begeistert
requirement [rɪ'kwaɪəmənt]	Bedarf
to **rely on sth** [rɪ'laɪ ɒn]	sich auf etw verlassen, auf etw angewiesen sein
to **light up** [ˌlaɪt 'ʌp]	leuchten, aufleuchten
one by one [ˌwʌn baɪ 'wʌn]	der Reihe nach
tunnel ['tʌnl]	Tunnel
nuclear power station [ˌnjuːkliə 'paʊə steɪʃn]	Kernkraftwerk
nuclear plant [ˌnjuːkliə 'plɑːnt]	Kernkraftwerk
to **close down** [ˌkləʊz 'daʊn]	stilllegen
working life [ˌwɜːkɪŋ 'laɪf]	Betriebsdauer
barrage ['bærɑːʒ]	Staumauer

page 141

subsidy ['sʌbsədi]	Subvention
corrosion [kə'rəʊʒn]	Korrosion, Zersetzung
cost-effective [ˌkɒst ɪ'fektɪv]	rentabel
close to ['kləʊs tə]	nahe bei, in der Nähe von
onshore [ˌɒn'ʃɔː]	an Land
to **become annoyed** [ˌbɪkʌm ə'nɔɪd]	sich ärgern, sich aufregen
wind farm ['wɪnd fɑːm]	Windpark
offshore [ˌɒf'ʃɔː]	auf See
to **invest** [ɪn'vest]	investieren
to **pick** [pɪk]	wählen, aussuchen
by chance [baɪ 'tʃɑːns]	zufällig

page 142

to **opt for sth** ['ɒpt fə]	sich für etw entscheiden
to **corrode** [kə'rəʊd]	korrodieren, zersetzen
vehicle ['viːəkl]	Fahrzeug
to **turn sth on** [ˌtɜːn 'ɒn]	etw an-/einschalten
structure ['strʌktʃə]	Bauwerk, Konstruktion
press conference ['pres kɒnfərəns]	Pressekonferenz
editor ['edɪtə]	Redakteur/in
commercial [kə'mɜːʃl]	gewerblich, kommerziell
planning permission ['plænɪŋ pəmɪʃn]	Baugenehmigung

page 143

electricity bill [ɪˌlek'trɪsəti bɪl]	Stromrechnung
to **beg** [beg]	flehen, eindringlich bitten
council ['kaʊnsl]	(Stadt-, Gemeinde-)Rat
application [ˌæplɪ'keɪʃn]	Antrag
farmland ['fɑːmlænd]	Ackerland, landwirtschaftliche Nutzfläche
drilling ['drɪlɪŋ]	Bohrung(en)
drilling rig ['drɪlɪŋ rɪg]	Bohrturm
waste water [ˌweɪst 'wɔːtə]	Abwasser
worries *pl* ['wʌriz]	Bedenken
councillor ['kaʊnsələ]	Ratsmitglied
to **leak** [liːk]	sickern, entweichen
groundwater ['graʊndwɔːtə]	Grundwasser
supplies *pl* [sə'plaɪz]	Vorräte, Vorkommen
tap [tæp]	Wasserhahn
on fire [ɒn 'faɪə]	in Flammen
concrete ['kɒŋkriːt]	Beton
steel [stiːl]	Stahl
well casing ['wel keɪsɪŋ]	Bohrlochverrohrung, Bohrlochwandung
regulation [ˌregju'leɪʃn]	Vorschrift
in return [ɪn rɪ'tɜːn]	im Gegenzug, als Ausgleich
to **be required to do sth** [bi rɪ'kwaɪəd tə]	etw tun müssen; verpflichtet sein, etw zu tun
community benefits *pl* [kə'mjuːnəti benɪfɪts]	Zahlungen an die Gemeinde
earnings *pl* ['ɜːnɪŋz]	Einnahmen, Gewinn
golf course ['gɒlf kɔːs]	Golfplatz
to **treat** [triːt]	*(Abwasser)* klären
to **weigh** [weɪ]	abwägen
to **calm** [kɑːm]	beruhigen
in principle [ɪn 'prɪnsəpl]	prinzipiell, grundsätzlich

page 144

appliance [ə'plaɪəns]	Haushaltsgerät
scrap [skræp]	Schrott
proportion [prə'pɔːʃn]	Anteil
broken ['brəʊkən]	kaputt, defekt
to **fit sth with sth** [fɪt]	etw mit etw ausstatten
tracking device ['trækɪŋ dɪvaɪs]	Ortungsgerät
trace [treɪs]	Spur
estimate ['estɪmət]	Schätzung
loudspeaker [ˌlaʊd'spiːkə]	Lautsprecher
fridge [frɪdʒ]	Kühlschrank

poisonous ['pɔɪzənəs]	giftig
arsenic ['ɑːsnɪk]	Arsen
lead [led]	Blei
mercury ['mɜːkjəri]	Quecksilber
to **forbid** [fə'bɪd]	verbieten, untersagen
to **dump** [dʌmp]	*(Müll)* (wild) abladen
toxic ['tɒksɪk]	giftig, Gift-
nationwide ['neɪʃnwaɪd]	landesweit
remaining [rɪ'meɪnɪŋ]	übrig, verbleibend
to **ship** [ʃɪp]	versenden, verschiffen
to **profit** ['prɒfɪt]	profitieren
battery pack ['bætəri pæk]	Akku
interval ['ɪntəvl]	(zeitlicher) Abstand
to **unload** [ˌʌn'ləʊd]	entladen
alarm [ə'lɑːm]	Alarmsignal
collection [kə'lekʃn]	Abholung
to **shine light on sth** [ˌʃaɪn 'laɪt ɒn]	Licht auf etw werfen
shadowy ['ʃædəʊi]	zwielichtig
customs *pl* ['kʌstəmz]	Zoll
powerless ['paʊələs]	machtlos, unfähig
stop [stɒp]	Station
dubious ['djuːbiəs]	zweifelhaft
dealer ['diːlə]	Händler/in
exporter [ɪk'spɔːtə]	Exporteur/in
wait [weɪt]	Warten, Wartezeit
capital ['kæpɪtl]	Hauptstadt
out in the open [ˌaʊt ɪn ði 'əʊpən]	im Freien
to **pile** [paɪl]	stapeln
mud [mʌd]	Schlamm
umbrella [ʌm'brelə]	Regenschirm
clearance sale ['klɪərəns seɪl]	Räumungsverkauf
farther ['fɑːðə]	weiter
mark [mɑːk]	Markierung, Zeichen
to **shake sth** [ʃeɪk]	an etw rütteln
to **activate** ['æktɪveɪt]	aktivieren
dump [dʌmp]	Müllhalde

page 145

hub [hʌb]	Drehkreuz, (Verkehrs-) Knoten
forwarding agency ['fɔːwədɪŋ eɪdʒənsi]	Spedition
shipping company ['ʃɪpɪŋ kʌmpəni]	Transportunternehmen, Spediteur, Reederei
middleman ['mɪdlmən]	Zwischenhändler
value chain ['væljuː tʃeɪn]	Wertschöpfungskette
to **break sth apart** [ˌbreɪk ə'pɑːt]	etw auseinandernehmen
to **set fire to sth** [ˌset 'faɪə tə]	etw anzünden
insulating foam ['ɪnsjuleɪtɪŋ fəʊm]	Isolierschaum
cable ['keɪbl]	Kabel
coating ['kəʊtɪŋ]	Ummantelung, (Kabel-) Mantel
copper ['kɒpə]	Kupfer
district ['dɪstrɪkt]	Bezirk
breeding ground ['briːdɪŋ graʊnd]	Brutplatz
migratory bird [ˌmaɪgrətri 'bɜːd]	Zugvogel
graveyard ['greɪvjɑːd]	Friedhof
to **poison** ['pɔɪzn]	vergiften
to **gut** [gʌt]	ausweiden, ausschlachten
worthless (to sb) ['wɜːθləs]	wertlos (für jdn)
scrapyard ['skræpjɑːd]	Schrottplatz
mystery ['mɪstri]	Rätsel, Geheimnis
to **get rid of sth** [ˌget 'rɪd əv]	etw loswerden

page 146

radical ['rædɪkl]	radikal
forest ['fɒrɪst]	Wald
chilly ['tʃɪli]	frostig
dozen ['dʌzn]	Dutzend
fare [feə]	Kost
log [lɒg]	Baumstumpf, Holzklotz
campfire ['kæmpfaɪə]	Lagerfeuer
overseas [ˌəʊvə'siːz]	nach/in Übersee
continental [ˌkɒntɪ'nentl]	kontinental, zum (europäischen) Festland gehörig
fledgling ['fledʒlɪŋ]	in den Kinderschuhen steckend, neu erwacht
thermometer [θə'mɒmɪtə]	Thermometer
to **be edging above freezing** [ˌedʒɪŋ əˌbʌv 'friːzɪŋ]	knapp über dem Gefrierpunkt anzeigen
to **bite** [baɪt]	beißen
easterly ['iːstəli]	Ost-, östlich
zero ['zɪərəʊ]	Null
welfare ['welfeə]	Wohl, Wohlergehen
foot, *pl* **feet (ft)** [fʊt, fiːt]	Fuß *(Längenmaß, entspricht 30,5 cm)*
snow [snəʊ]	Schnee
onion ['ʌnjən]	Zwiebel
wrapped up [ˌræpt 'ʌp]	eingepackt
layer ['leɪə]	Schicht
occasional [ə'keɪʒənl]	gelegentlich
accident ['æksɪdənt]	Unfall
indoor ['ɪndɔː]	im Haus, Innen-
leaves *pl* [liːvz]	Laub
to **toughen up** [ˌtʌfn 'ʌp]	abhärten
flu [fluː]	Grippe
to **contract (a disease)** [kən'trækt]	sich (mit einer Krankheit) infizieren/anstecken
tick [tɪk]	Zecke
bite [baɪt]	Biss, (Insekten-)Stich
to **outweigh sth** [ˌaʊt'weɪ]	schwerer als etw wiegen
massive ['mæsɪv]	massiv, gewaltig
mental ['mentl]	geistig, psychisch, seelisch
to **attend** [ə'tend]	besuchen
confident ['kɒnfɪdənt]	(selbst)sicher
outgoing ['aʊtgəʊɪŋ]	kontaktfreudig
handful ['hændfʊl]	Handvoll
to **enroll** [ɪn'rəʊl]	*(an einer Schule o. ä.)* anmelden
obsession [əb'seʃn]	Besessenheit, Wahn, Zwang
adoption [ə'dɒpʃn]	Übernahme, Aneignung
to **prove** [pruːv]	sich erweisen
red tape bureaucracy [ˌred 'teɪp bjʊərɒkrəsi]	übertriebene Bürokratie
environmental [ɪnˌvaɪrən'mentl]	Umwelt-
prompt [prɒmpt]	Stichwort, Vorgabe
allergy ['ælədʒi]	Allergie
toy [tɔɪ]	Spielzeug
dirt [dɜːt]	Schmutz, Dreck
germ [dʒɜːm]	Keim, Bakterie
wild [waɪld]	wild

UNIT 15

page 147

cactus ['kæktəs]	Kaktus
drought [draʊt]	Dürre
exploitation [ˌeksplɔɪ'teɪʃn]	Ausbeutung, Abbau *(von Rohstoffen)*
over-exploitation [ˌəʊvər eksplɔɪ'teɪʃn]	Raubbau, übermäßiger Abbau
stork [stɔːk]	Storch
famine ['fæmɪn]	Hungersnot

page 148

to **be equivalent to sth** [bi ɪ'kwɪvələnt tə]	einer Sache entsprechen
crop [krɒp]	Nutzpflanze, Feldfrucht
pastureland ['pɑːstʃəlænd]	Weideland
to **hit** [hɪt]	erreichen
crop production ['krɒp prədʌkʃn]	Pflanzenproduktion, pflanzliche Erzeugung
to **demand** [dɪ'mɑːnd]	nachfragen, verlangen
rich [rɪtʃ]	*(Nahrung)* gehaltvoll, reichhaltig
to **succeed** [sək'siːd]	erfolgreich sein, Erfolg haben
diet ['daɪət]	Ernährung, Kost
vital ['vaɪtl]	lebensnotwendig, unerlässlich
to **clear** [klɪə]	räumen, roden
prairie ['preəri]	Prärie
forest ['fɒrɪst]	Wald
ecosystem ['iːkəʊsɪstəm]	Ökosystem
ice-free ['aɪs friː]	eisfrei
agriculture ['ægrɪkʌltʃə]	Landwirtschaft
species ['spiːʃiːz]	*(Biologie:)* Art
to **store** [stɔː]	speichern
catastrophe [kə'tæstrəfi]	Katastrophe
square mile ['skweə maɪl]	Quadratmeile
ice-covered ['aɪs kʌvəd]	eisbedeckt
undeveloped [ˌʌndɪ'veləpt]	*(Land:)* unbebaut
cropland ['krɒplænd]	Ackerland
to **plant** [plɑːnt]	pflanzen, anpflanzen

page 149

share [ʃeə]	Anteil
fresh water [ˌfreʃ 'wɔːtə]	Süßwasser
lake [leɪk]	(Binnen-)See
wetland ['wetlənd]	Feuchtgebiet, Sumpfgebiet
acre ['eɪkə]	Morgen *(ca. 4047 qm)*
variety [və'raɪəti]	(Pflanzen-)Sorte
greatly ['greɪtli]	erheblich
farm chemicals *pl* ['fɑːm kemɪklz]	Landwirtschaftschemikalien
polluting [pə'luːtɪŋ]	umweltschädlich
fertilizer ['fɜːtəlaɪzə]	Dünger, Düngemittel
precious ['preʃəs]	kostbar
irrigation [ˌɪrɪ'geɪʃn]	Bewässerung
biofuel [ˌbaɪəʊ'fjuːəl]	Biokraftstoff
grain [greɪn]	Getreide
consumption [kən'sʌmpʃn]	Verbrauch, Konsum
to **consume** [kən'sjuːm]	verbrauchen, konsumieren
to **cut** [kʌt]	reduzieren, einschränken
use-by date ['juːs baɪ deɪt]	Haltbarkeitsdatum
cooperation [kəʊˌɒpə'reɪʃn]	Zusammenarbeit, Zusammenwirken

page 150

destruction [dɪ'strʌkʃn]	Zerstörung
equals ['iːkwəlz]	gleich
midday [ˌmɪd'deɪ]	Mittag
to **multiply** ['mʌltɪplaɪ]	multiplizieren
junior ['dʒuːniə]	Jung-, Nachwuchs-
dawn [dɔːn]	Morgendämmerung
garment ['gɑːmənt]	Kleidungsstück

page 151

graphic ['græfɪk]	Grafik
to **join sth** [dʒɔɪn]	etw (miteinander) verbinden
divorce [dɪ'vɔːs]	Scheidung
to **work sth out** [ˌwɜːk 'aʊt]	etw ausrechnen
utility bills *pl* [juː'tɪləti bɪlz]	Rechnungen für Versorgungsleistungen
food pantry *AE* ['fuːd pæntri]	Tafel, karitative Essensausgabe
parcel ['pɑːsl]	Paket
to **take the point** [ˌteɪk ðə 'pɔɪnt]	den Standpunkt verstehen

page 152

GM (genetically modified) [ˌdʒiː 'em]	genmanipuliert
to **fear** [fɪə]	fürchten
selection [sɪ'lekʃn]	Auslese, Selektion
to **adapt (to sth)** [ə'dæpt]	sich (an etw) anpassen
adaptation [ˌædæp'teɪʃn]	Anpassung, Anpassungsleistung
gene [dʒiːn]	Gen
to **pass sth to sb** ['pɑːs tə]	jdm etw weiterreichen
to **reproduce** [ˌriːprə'djuːs]	sich fortpflanzen
to **become extinct** [bɪˌkʌm ɪk'stɪŋkt]	aussterben
to **breed** [briːd]	züchten
livestock ['laɪvstɒk]	Vieh
pre-historic [ˌpriː hɪ'stɒrɪk]	prähistorisch
selective [sɪ'lektɪv]	selektiv
breeding ['briːdɪŋ]	Zucht, Züchtung
feature ['fiːtʃə]	Merkmal, Eigenschaft
to **aim at sth** ['eɪm ət]	etw anstreben
wool [wʊl]	Wolle
sheep [ʃiːp]	Schaf
resistance [rɪ'zɪstəns]	Widerstandsfähigkeit, Resistenz
herd [hɜːd]	Herde
crop [krɒp]	Ernte
productive [prə'dʌktɪv]	produktiv
to **modify** ['mɒdɪfaɪ]	modifizieren
genetic [dʒə'netɪk]	genetisch
seed [siːd]	Samen, Saatgut
laboratory [lə'bɒrətri]	Labor
by laboratory design [baɪ ləˌbɒrətri dɪ'zaɪn]	im Labor geplant
herbicide ['hɜːbɪsaɪd]	Unkrautvernichtungsmittel
spray [spreɪ]	Spritzmittel
weed [wiːd]	Unkraut
pollen ['pɒlən]	Blütenstaub, Pollen
to **fertilize** ['fɜːtəlaɪz]	befruchten
in no time [ɪn 'nəʊ taɪm]	im Nu
resistant to sth [rɪ'zɪstənt tə]	resistent gegen etw
chemical control (of pests) [ˌkemɪkl kən'trəʊl]	Schädlingsbekämpfung(smittel)
downside ['daʊnsaɪd]	Nachteil
hydroponics [ˌhaɪdrəʊ'pɒnɪks]	Hydrokultur

page 153

hydroponic [ˌhaɪdrəʊ'pɒnɪk]	Hydrokultur-
soil [sɔɪl]	Erde, Boden, Erdreich
thick [θɪk]	dick, stark
to **absorb** [əb'sɔːb]	aufnehmen, absorbieren
flow [fləʊ]	Strom, Fluss
to **take off** [ˌteɪk 'ɒf]	*(Flugzeug:)* abheben, starten
passenger ['pæsɪndʒə]	Passagier
to **take off** [ˌteɪk 'ɒf]	*(Produkt:)* gut anlaufen, gut ankommen
to **take up space** [ˌteɪk ʌp 'speɪs]	Platz einnehmen
vertical(ly) ['vɜːtɪkl]	senkrecht, vertikal
to **float** [fləʊt]	(auf dem Wasser) treiben
productivity [ˌprɒdʌk'tɪvəti]	Produktivität

page 154

to **trick sb into doing sth** [trɪk]	jdn (mit einer List) dazu bringen, etw zu tun
to **take sth on** [ˌteɪk 'ɒn]	*(Aufgabe)* übernehmen
to **take sb on** [ˌteɪk 'ɒn]	es mit jdm aufnehmen, gegen jdn antreten
to **hunt** [hʌnt]	jagen
protein ['prəʊtiːn]	Eiweiß, Protein
fishing ['fɪʃɪŋ]	Fischerei, Befischung
to **maintain stocks** [meɪnˌteɪn 'stɒks]	den Bestand erhalten
population [ˌpɒpju'leɪʃn]	*(Biologie:)* Population
to **crash** [kræʃ]	abstürzen, zusammenbrechen
severe [sɪ'vɪə]	ernst, schwer
diamond-shaped ['daɪəmənd ʃeɪpt]	rautenförmig
cage [keɪdʒ]	Käfig
unpolluted [ˌʌnpə'luːtɪd]	unverschmutzt

page 155

dome [dəʊm]	Kuppel
to **harvest** ['hɑːvɪst]	ernten
horizontal(ly) [ˌhɒrɪ'zɒntl]	waagrecht, horizontal
turn [tɜːn]	Runde, Umdrehung
running cost ['rʌnɪŋ kɒst]	Betriebskosten
frame [freɪm]	Rahmen
container [kən'teɪnə]	Behälter
shelf, shelves [ʃelf, ʃelfvz]	Regal, Regale
surprisingly [sə'praɪzɪŋli]	erstaunlicherweise
light bulb ['laɪt bʌlb]	Glühbirne
hectare ['hekteə]	Hektar
to **fail** [feɪl]	ausfallen
starvation [stɑː'veɪʃn]	Hunger
food security ['fuːd sɪkjʊərəti]	Ernährungssicherung
proposal [prə'pəʊzl]	Vorschlag
to **seek** [siːk]	suchen
redevelopment [ˌriːdɪ'veləpmənt]	Sanierung
splendid ['splendɪd]	prächtig
turbine ['tɜːbaɪn]	Turbine
hall [hɔːl]	Saal, Halle
Grade 1 building [ˌgreɪd 'wʌn bɪldɪŋ]	denkmalgeschütztes Gebäude
to **pull down** [ˌpʊl 'daʊn]	*(Gebäude)* abreißen
to **redevelop** [ˌriːdɪ'veləp]	sanieren
committee [kə'mɪti]	Ausschuss, Kommission, Komitee
chairperson ['tʃeəpɜːsn]	Vorsitzende/r

page 156

scale [skeɪl]	Ausmaß, Umfang
to **depend on sth** [dɪ'pend ɒn]	von etw abhängen, auf etw angewiesen sein
cassava [kə'sɑːvə]	Maniok, Kassava
pest [pest]	Schädling
diversity [daɪ'vɜːsəti]	Vielfalt
to **deter** [dɪ'tɜː]	abschrecken, abhalten
to **certify** ['sɜːtɪfaɪ]	zertifizieren
credit ['kredɪt]	Verdienst
undergraduate [ˌʌndə'grædʒuət]	Student/in *(vor dem ersten akad. Grad)*
non-profit [ˌnɒn'prɒfɪt]	gemeinnützig
to **lurch** [lɜːtʃ]	schlingern, taumeln
steep [stiːp]	steil
rutted ['rʌtɪd]	zerfurcht, ausgefahren
pickup ['pɪkʌp]	Pritschenwagen
to **green** [griːn]	begrünen
to **drift** [drɪft]	wehen
slope [sləʊp]	Hang
forested ['fɒrɪstɪd]	bewaldet
brick [brɪk]	Ziegel
partially ['pɑːʃəli]	teilweise
to **plaster** ['plɑːstə]	verputzen
corrugated metal [ˌkɒrəgeɪtɪd 'metl]	Wellblech
short-sleeved [ˌʃɔːt 'sliːvd]	kurzärmlig
blouse [blaʊz]	Bluse
wraparound skirt [ˌræpəraʊnd 'skɜːt]	Wickelrock
porch [pɔːtʃ]	Veranda
to **raise** [reɪz]	*(Pflanzen)* anbauen
passion fruit ['pæʃn fruːt]	Passionsfrucht
spinach ['spɪnɪtʃ]	Spinat
leafy vegetable [ˌliːfi 'vedʒtəbl]	Blattgemüse
backup ['bækʌp]	Ersatz, Reserve
strategic(ally) [strə'tiːdʒɪk]	strategisch
row [rəʊ]	Reihe
sunflower ['sʌnflaʊə]	Sonnenblume
whitefly ['waɪtflaɪ]	Mottenschildlaus
compost ['kɒmpɒst]	Kompost
runoff ['rʌnɒf]	Abfluss, abfließendes Wasser
to **contaminate** [kən'tæmɪneɪt]	verunreinigen, kontaminieren
stream [striːm]	Bach, Fließgewässer
life-altering ['laɪf ɔːltərɪŋ]	lebensverändernd
liberation [lɪbə'reɪʃn]	Befreiung
debt [det]	Schulden
crippling ['krɪplɪŋ]	lähmend, mörderisch
expense [ɪk'spens]	Kosten, Aufwand
annual ['ænjuəl]	jährlich
per capita income [pə ˌkæpɪtə 'ɪnkʌm]	Pro-Kopf-Einkommen

page 157

skeptical *AE* ['skeptɪkl]	skeptisch
to **be aware of sth** [bi ə'weər əv]	sich einer Sache bewusst sein, etw kennen
sweeping views *pl* [ˌswiːpɪŋ 'vjuːz]	atemberaubende Ausblicke, umwerfende Sicht
to **cultivate** ['kʌltɪveɪt]	bewirtschaften
terraced ['terəst]	terrassiert
scarred [skɑːd]	vernarbt, gezeichnet
to **erode** [ɪ'rəʊd]	erodieren
terrace ['terəs]	Terrasse
to **retain** [rɪ'teɪn]	zurückhalten, behalten, bewahren

page 158

senior *AE* ['si:niə] Schüler/in der Abschlussklasse *(US High School)*
during ['djʊərɪŋ] während
academic [ˌækə'demɪk] Schul-, akademisch
to **collect sth** [kə'lekt] etw (ab)holen
not even [nɒt 'i:vn] nicht einmal
puddle ['pʌdl] Pfütze, Tümpel
unsanitary [ʌn'sænətri] unhygienisch
to **result in** [rɪ'zʌlt ɪn] führen zu
to **suffer from sth** ['sʌfə frəm] an etw leiden
diarrhoea [ˌdaɪə'rɪə] Durchfall
access ['ækses] Zugang
enrolling the help of ... [ɪn'rəʊlɪŋ] mithilfe von ...
well [wel] Quelle, Brunnen
catchment tank ['kætʃmənt tæŋk] Auffangbehälter
hygiene ['haɪdʒi:n] Hygiene
morale [mɒrəl] Moral, geistig-seelische Verfassung
happiness ['hæpinəs] Glück, Zufriedenheit
sanitation [ˌsænɪ'teɪʃn] Hygiene
textbook ['tekstbʊk] Lehrbuch

UNIT 16

page 159

compass ['kʌmpəs] Kompass
contraceptive [ˌkɒntrə'septɪv] Verhütungsmittel
internal combustion engine [ɪnˌtɜ:nl kəm'bʌstʃən endʒɪn] Verbrennungsmotor
printing press ['prɪntɪŋ pres] Druckerpresse
refrigeration [rɪˌfrɪdʒə'reɪʃn] Kühlung, Kälteerzeugung
wheel [wi:l] Rad

page 160

spread [spred] Verbreitung, Ausbreitung
to **type in** [ˌtaɪp 'ɪn] eintippen
café ['kæfeɪ] Café
to **hit** [hɪt] *(Taste)* drücken
transaction [træn'zækʃn] (Geschäfts-)Vorgang, Transaktion
additional [ə'dɪʃənl] zusätzlich
to **fail** [feɪl] versagen
dramatic(ally) [drə'mætɪk] dramatisch
colonial power [kəˌləʊniəl 'paʊə] Kolonialmacht
to **lay cables** [ˌleɪ 'keɪblz] Kabel verlegen
landline ['lændlaɪn] Festnetz(-)
highway *AE* ['haɪweɪ] Autobahn
textbook ['tekstbʊk] Lehrbuch
(radio/TV) station ['steɪʃn] (Radio-/Fernseh-)Sender
jungle ['dʒʌŋgl] Dschungel
savannah [sə'vænə] Savanne
button ['bʌtn] Knopf, Button
merchant ['mɜ:tʃənt] Händler/in
to **access sth** ['ækses] auf etw zugreifen
harvest ['hɑ:vɪst] Ernte
veterinarian [ˌvetərɪ'neəriən] Tierarzt/-ärztin, Veterinär/in
to **function** ['fʌŋkʃn] fungieren, funktionieren
substitute ['sʌbstɪtju:t] Ersatz
to **keep watch over sb** [ˌki:p 'wɒtʃ əʊvə] über jdn wachen, jdn beobachten
to **be in power** [bi ɪn 'paʊə] an der Macht sein
cutting-edge [ˌkʌtɪŋ 'edʒ] Spitzen-, auf dem neusten Stand
limitation [ˌlɪmɪ'teɪʃn] Einschränkung
obstacle ['ɒbstəkl] Hindernis
enabled [ɪ'neɪbld] fähig
to **coax sth out of sth** [kəʊks] etw aus etw herausholen
trajectory [trə'dʒektəri] Flugbahn, Weg
breed [bri:d] Rasse
calving ['kɑ:vɪŋ] Kalben
feed [fi:d] Futter
fertility cycle [fə'tɪləti saɪkl] Fruchtbarkeitszyklus
illiterate [ɪ'lɪtərət] Analphabet/in
to **practise** ['præktɪs] praktizieren
remote [rɪ'məʊt] entlegen
diagnosis, diagnoses [ˌdaɪəg'nəʊsɪs, ˌdaɪəg'nəʊsi:s] Diagnose, Diagnosen

page 161

epidemic [ˌepɪ'demɪk] Epidemie, Seuche
influential [ˌɪnflu'enʃl] einflussreich
consulting firm [kən'sʌltɪŋ fɜ:m] Beratungsfirma
satisfied ['sætɪsfaɪd] zufrieden(gestellt)
ranking ['ræŋkɪŋ] Rangliste
governance ['gʌvnəns] Regierungshandeln
leadership ['li:dəʃɪp] Führung
to **award sth to sb** [ə'wɔ:d] jdm etw verleihen, jdm etw zuerkennen
commendable [kə'mendəbl] vorbildlich
in a row [ɪn ə 'rəʊ] nacheinander
worthy of sth ['wɜ:ði əv] einer Sache würdig
primarily [praɪ'merəli] vorrangig, hauptsächlich
civil society [ˌsɪvl sə'saɪəti] Bürgergesellschaft
border customs officer [ˌbɔ:də 'kʌstəmz ɒfɪsə] (Grenz-)Zollbeamte/r
to **extort** [ɪk'stɔ:t] erpressen, abnötigen
to **pressure** ['preʃə] unter Druck setzen
election [ɪ'lekʃn] Wahl
tribe [traɪb] Stamm
to **overcome** [ˌəʊvə'kʌm] bewältigen, überwinden
isolated ['aɪsəleɪtɪd] abgeschottet, abgeschieden, isoliert
to **sow** [səʊ] säen
discord ['dɪskɔ:d] Zwietracht
commerce ['kɒmɜ:s] Handel
mid-century [ˌmɪd 'sentʃəri] Jahrhundertmitte
IT developer [ˌaɪ 'ti:] IT-Entwickler/in

page 162

addition [ə'dɪʃn] Hinzufügung
convention [kən'venʃn] Übereinkunft, Gepflogenheit, Konvention
to **speak up** [ˌspi:k 'ʌp] lauter sprechen
to **answer the phone** [ˌɑ:nsə ðə 'fəʊn] ans Telefon gehen

page 163

case [keɪs] Koffer
trainers *pl* ['treɪnəz] Turnschuhe
for ages [fər 'eɪdʒɪz] ewig, eine Ewigkeit
library ['laɪbrəri] Bibliothek, Bücherei
at one time [ət ˌwʌn 'taɪm] gleichzeitig
comprehensive school [kɒmprɪ'hensɪv sku:l] Gesamtschule
to **confiscate** ['kɒnfɪskeɪt] beschlagnahmen, konfiszieren

page 164

artificial intelligence [ɑːtɪˌfɪʃl ɪnˈtelɪdʒəns]	künstliche Intelligenz
aim [eɪm]	Absicht, Ziel, Zweck
scary [ˈskeəri]	gruselig, schaurig
tempting [ˈtemptɪŋ]	verlockend
to **dismiss sth as sth** [dɪsˈmɪs]	etw als etw abtun
notion [ˈnəʊʃn]	Vorstellung, Auffassung
to **point to sth** [ˈpɔɪnt tə]	auf etw hindeuten
progress [ˈprəʊgres]	Fortschritt(e)
driverless [ˈdraɪvələs]	führerlos
civilization [ˌsɪvəlaɪˈzeɪʃn]	Zivilisation
to **magnify** [ˈmægnɪfaɪ]	vergrößern, verstärken
eradication [ɪˌrædɪˈkeɪʃn]	Ausrottung
military [ˈmɪlətri]	Militär
autonomous [ɔːˈtɒnəməs]	autonom
superhuman [ˌsuːpəˈhjuːmən]	übermenschlich
to **outsmart** [ˌaʊtˈsmɑːt]	überlisten, austricksen
to **manipulate** [məˈnɪpjuleɪt]	manipulieren
institute [ˈɪnstɪtjuːt]	Institut
vastness [ˈvɑːstnəs]	unermessliche Weite
universe [ˈjuːnɪvɜːs]	Universum
The best is yet to come. [ðe ˌbest ɪs jet tə ˈkʌm]	Das Beste kommt noch. Die besten Zeiten stehen uns noch bevor.
meaningful [ˈmiːnɪŋfl]	wichtig, bedeutend, sinnstiftend
to **gather** [ˈgæðə]	sammeln, zusammentragen
completion [kəmˈpliːʃn]	Ausführung, Erledigung *(einer Aufgabe)*
course [kɔːs]	Weg, Vorgehensweise
either [ˈaɪðə]	eine/r/s *(von beiden)*
extinction [ɪkˈstɪŋkʃn]	Vernichtung, Ausrottung, Aussterben
crossroads [ˈkrɒsrəʊdz]	Scheideweg

page 165

outcome [ˈaʊtkʌm]	Ergebnis, Resultat
superior [suːˈpɪəriə]	überlegen
alien [ˈeɪliən]	außerirdisch
to **devote** [dɪˈvəʊt]	widmen
industrialist [ɪnˈdʌstriəlɪst]	Industrielle/r
general [ˈdʒenrəl]	General
to **reap the benefits** [ˌriːp ðə ˈbenɪfɪts]	die Früchte ernten, die Vorteile nutzen

page 166

to **enjoy oneself** [ɪnˈdʒɔɪ wʌnself]	sich (gut) amüsieren
vase [vɑːz]	Vase
missing [ˈmɪsɪŋ]	vermisst
test drive [ˈtest draɪv]	Testfahrt
road testing [ˈrəʊd testɪŋ]	Fahrversuche, Fahrerprobung, Straßentests
test track [ˈtest træk]	Teststrecke
to **perform** [pəˈfɔːm]	(leistungsmäßig) abschneiden
failure [ˈfeɪljə]	Ausfall, Defekt
(car) crash [kræʃ]	Autounfall
accident [ˈæksɪdənt]	Unfall
human error [ˌhjuːmən ˈerə]	menschliches Versagen
property damage [ˈprɒpəti dæmɪdʒ]	Sachschaden, Sachschäden
association [əˌsəʊsiˈeɪʃn]	Verband, Vereinigung
freeway *AE* [ˈfriːweɪ]	Autobahn
smooth(ly) [smuːð]	reibungslos
to **speed up** [ˌspiːd ˈʌp]	beschleunigen
to **slow down** [ˌsləʊ ˈdaʊn]	bremsen
tailback [ˈteɪlbæk]	Rückstau
gallon [ˈgælən]	Gallone *(= 3,78 l in den USA)*
service station [ˈsɜːvɪs steɪʃn]	Tankstelle

page 167

to **suffer from sth** [ˈsʌfə frəm]	unter etw zu leiden haben
in-car entertainment [ˌɪn kɑːr entəˈteɪnmənt]	Unterhaltungselektronik im Auto
operator [ˈɒpəreɪtə]	Betreiber/in
city planner [ˈsɪti plænə]	Stadtplaner/in
emergency service [ɪˈmɜːdʒənsi sɜːvɪs]	Notfalldienst
accident and emergency department (A&E) [ˌæksɪdənt ənd ɪˈmɜːdʒənsi dɪpɑːtmənt]	Notaufnahme
legislature [ˈledʒɪsleɪtʃə]	Gesetzgebung
special committee [ˌspeʃl kəˈmɪti]	Sonderausschuss
representative [ˌreprɪˈzentətɪv]	Repräsentant/in, Abgeordnete/r
pressures *pl* [ˈpreʃəz]	Belastungen
robot [ˈrəʊbɒt]	Roboter
domestic [dəˈmestɪk]	heimisch, Inlands-
to **declare** [dɪˈkleə]	verkünden

page 168

robotics [rəʊˈbɒtɪks]	Robotertechnik
dishwasher [ˈdɪʃwɒʃə]	Spülmaschine
to **load the dishwasher** [ˌləʊd ðə ˈdɪʃwɒʃə]	die Spülmaschine einräumen
to **unveil** [ˌʌnˈveɪl]	enthüllen, vorstellen
to **manipulate** [məˈnɪpjuleɪt]	handhaben, bedienen
unfamiliar [ˌʌnfəˈmɪliə]	unbekannt, ungewohnt
humanlike [ˈhjuːmənlaɪk]	menschenähnlich
grasp [grɑːsp]	Griff
outing [ˈaʊtɪŋ]	Ausflug, Ausfahrt
depth [depθ]	(räumliche) Tiefe
wrist [rɪst]	Handgelenk
to **calculate** [ˈkælkjuleɪt]	berechnen
to **grasp** [grɑːsp]	greifen, ergreifen
novel [ˈnɒvl]	neu, neuartig
robotic [rəʊˈbɒtɪk]	Roboter-
obstruction [əbˈstrʌkʃn]	Hindernis
to **go for sth** [ˈgəʊ fə]	etw wählen, etw wagen
collaborator [kəˈlæbəreɪtə]	Mitarbeiter/in
ambitious [æmˈbɪʃəs]	ehrgeizig
a bunch of [ə ˈbʌntʃ əv]	eine Menge
to **scatter** [ˈskætə]	verteilen, verstreuen
set [set]	Menge
to **figure out** [ˌfɪgər ˈaʊt]	herausfinden
to **assign sb sth** [əˈsaɪn]	jdm etw zuweisen, jdn mit etw beauftragen
duty [ˈdjuːti]	Aufgabe, Pflicht
necessity [nəˈsesəti]	Notwendigkeit
manipulative [məˈnɪpjələtɪv]	manipulativ
faculty [ˈfæklti]	Fähigkeit
cutlery [ˈkʌtləri]	Besteck
fiddly [ˈfɪdli]	knifflig, fummelig
symmetrical [sɪˈmetrɪkl]	symmetrisch
to **represent** [ˌreprɪˈzent]	vertreten, repräsentieren
airborne drone [ˌeəbɔːn ˈdrəʊn]	Flugdrohne

novelty ['nɒvlti]	Neues, Neuartiges
to **perform sth** [pə'fɔːm]	etw ausführen, etw durchführen
alongside [əˌlɒŋ'saɪd]	neben
uncertainty [ʌn'sɜːtnti]	Ungewissheit

page 169

unstructured [ʌn'strʌktʃəd]	unstrukturiert
discipline ['dɪsəplɪn]	Disziplin
mechanical engineering [mɪˌkænɪkl ˌendʒɪ'nɪərɪŋ]	Maschinenbau
electrical engineering [ɪˌlektrɪkl ˌendʒɪ'nɪərɪŋ]	Elektrotechnik
unexpected [ˌʌnɪk'spektɪd]	unerwartet
setback ['setbæk]	Rückschlag
to **complicate** ['kɒmplɪkeɪt]	komplizieren
pinkie ['pɪŋki]	kleiner Finger
to **approach sth** [ə'prəʊtʃ]	sich einer Sache nähern
to **be keen to do sth** [bi 'kiːn tə]	etw unbedingt tun wollen
to **transfer** [træns'fɜː]	übergeben, weitergeben
bi-manual [ˌbaɪ 'mænjuəl]	beidhändig
to **lack sth** [læk]	etw nicht haben
sense of touch [ˌsens əf 'tʌtʃ]	Tastsinn
tactile sensing [ˌtæktaɪl 'sensɪŋ]	Tastempfinden
sufficient [sə'fɪʃnt]	ausreichend, hinreichend
to **operate** ['ɒpəreɪt]	tätig sein
enthusiastic about sth [ɪnˌθjuːzi'æstɪk əbaʊt]	von etw begeistert
acronym ['ækrənɪm]	Akronym, Abkürzung
homage ['hɒmɪdʒ]	Reverenz
flaxen-haired [ˌflæksn 'heəd]	strohblond, flachsblond
to **chuckle** ['tʃʌkl]	kichern, schmunzeln
unpredictable [ˌʌnprɪ'dɪktəbl]	launenhaft, unkalkulierbar

page 170

belt [belt]	Gurt, Gürtel
bracelet ['breɪslət]	Armband, Armreifen
to **attach sth to sth** [ə'tætʃ]	etw an etw befestigen
length [leŋθ]	Länge, Dauer
intensity [ɪn'tensəti]	Intensität
overview ['əʊvəvjuː]	Überblick, Übersicht
to **track** [træk]	verfolgen, tracken
motivator ['məʊtɪveɪtə]	Motivator, Antreiber
sport medicine practitioner [ˌspɔːt medsn præk'tɪʃənə]	Sportmediziner/in
intense [ɪn'tens]	intensiv
push-up ['pʊʃ ʌp]	Liegestütze
crunch [krʌntʃ]	Sit-up
squat [skwɒt]	Kniebeuge
set [set]	Satz, Zusammenstellung
to **unlock** [ˌʌn'lɒk]	freischalten, entsperren
random ['rændəm]	zufällig, beliebig
gadget ['gædʒɪt]	Gerät, technischer Krimskrams
peer pressure [ˌpɪə 'preʃə]	Gruppendruck, Einfluss der Clique
motivational tool [məʊtɪˌveɪʃənl 'tuːl]	Motivierungshilfe, motivationsförderndes Werkzeug

JOB SKILLS 4

page 171

email exchange ['iːmeɪl ɪkstʃeɪndʒ]	E-Mail-Korrespondenz
initial [ɪ'nɪʃl]	erste/r/s
to **attend sth** [ə'tend]	an etw teilnehmen
member of staff [ˌmembər əf 'stɑːf]	Mitarbeiter/in
to **get to know sb** [ˌget tə 'nəʊ]	jdn kennen lernen
in good time [ɪn ˌgʊd 'taɪm]	rechtzeitig

page 172

seating ['siːtɪŋ]	Bestuhlung
projector [prə'dʒektə]	Beamer
reception [rɪ'sepʃn]	Empfang
handout ['hændaʊt]	Arbeitsblatt
refreshment [rɪ'freʃmənt]	Erfrischung
name tag ['neɪm tæg]	Namensschild
place card ['pleɪs kɑːd]	Platzkarte, Tischkarte
to **leak** [liːk]	auslaufen
to **dry out** [ˌdraɪ 'aʊt]	austrocknen
pad [pæd]	Notizblock
to **type sth up** [ˌtaɪp 'ʌp]	etw (am Computer) formulieren, etw ausarbeiten
agenda [ə'dʒendə]	Tagesordnung
on sb's behalf [ɒn bɪ'hɑːf]	in jds Namen
item ['aɪtəm]	Tagesordnungspunkt

page 173

break [breɪk]	Pause
cloud [klaʊd]	Wolke
gossip ['gɒsɪp]	Klatsch, Tratsch
taboo [tə'buː]	Tabu
to **convince** [kən'vɪns]	überzeugen
chilly ['tʃɪli]	kühl
Research and Development (R&D) [rɪˌsɜːtʃ ən dɪ'veləpmənt]	Forschung(s-) und Entwicklung(sabteilung)
section ['sekʃn]	Abteilung
to **get down to business** [get ˌdaʊn tə 'bɪznəs]	zur Sache kommen

page 174

millennium [mɪ'leniəm]	Jahrtausend
talk [tɔːk]	Vortrag
to **customize** ['kʌstəmaɪz]	auf den Kundenbedarf zuschneiden
to **near** [nɪə]	sich nähern
to **get down to business** [ˌget 'daʊn tə 'bɪznəs]	zur Sache kommen
focus ['fəʊkəs]	Schwerpunkt
to **distribute** [dɪ'strɪbjuːt]	verteilen, austeilen
to **conclude** [tə kən'kluːd]	abschließend
bit [bɪt]	Teil

SOCIAL TOPIC 1

page 175

to **put up**	[ˌpʊt ˈʌp]	aufstellen
pub	[pʌb]	Kneipe
individual	[ˌɪndɪˈvɪdʒuəl]	Einzelne/r, Individuum
at first	[ət ˈfɜːst]	zuerst, zunächst, anfangs
to **pour**	[pɔː]	gießen, schütten
momentum	[məˈmentəm]	Schwung, Fahrt
to **freeze**	[friːz]	einfrieren
brain	[breɪn]	Gehirn
awareness	[əˈweənəs]	Bewusstsein
need to do sth	[niːd]	etw tun müssen
soaked	[səʊkt]	durchnässt
combination	[ˌkɒmbɪˈneɪʃn]	Kombination, Verbindung
besides	[bɪˈsaɪdz]	außer, neben
critic	[ˈkrɪtɪk]	Kritiker/in
wildfire	[ˈwaɪldfaɪə]	Lauffeuer, Flächenbrand
breast cancer	[ˈbrest kænsə]	Brustkrebs
to **nominate**	[ˈnɒmɪneɪt]	nominieren
thrilled	[θrɪld]	begeistert
critical	[ˈkrɪtɪkl]	kritisch
finally	[ˈfaɪnəli]	schließlich, zum Schluss
brave	[breɪv]	tapfer, mutig

page 176

they used to do sth	[ˈjuːs tə]	sie machten früher *(üblicherweise)* etwas
to **make an effort**	[ˌmeɪk ən ˈefət]	sich Mühe geben

page 177

to **motivate**	[ˈməʊtɪveɪt]	motivieren

SOCIAL TOPIC 2

page 178

to **bombard**	[bɒmˈbɑːd]	bombardieren
sugary	[ˈʃʊgəri]	zuckerhaltig, zuckersüß
to **leave sb alone**	[ˌliːv əˈləʊn]	jdn in Ruhe lassen
ban (on)	[bæn]	Verbot (von)
care assistant	[ˈkeə əsɪstənt]	Erzieher/in *(Kindergarten)*
medic	[ˈmedɪk]	Arzt/Ärztin
childminder	[ˈtʃaɪldmaɪndə]	Babysitter/in, Tagesmutter
to **vet**	[vet]	gründlich prüfen
to **have sb's best interests at heart**	[best ɪntrəsts ət ˈhɑːt]	jds Bestes wollen, das Beste für jdn wollen
to **serve**	[sɜːv]	(be)dienen
shareholder	[ˈʃeəhəʊldə]	Aktionär/in, Teilhaber/in, Gesellschafter/in
well-being	[ˈwel biːɪŋ]	Wohl(befinden)
of no concern	[əv nəʊ kənˈsɜːn]	ohne Relevanz; nicht von Interesse
sophisticated	[səˈfɪstɪkeɪtɪd]	raffiniert, anspruchsvoll
insecurity	[ˌɪnsɪˈkjʊərəti]	Unsicherheit
need	[niːd]	Bedürfnis
to **handle sth**	[ˈhændl]	mit etw umgehen
commercial pressures *pl*	[kəˌmɜːʃl ˈpreʃəz]	wirtschaftliche Zwänge

page 179

commercial channel	[kəˌmɜːʃl ˈtʃænl]	privater Fernsehsender
lie	[laɪ]	Lüge
obvious	[ˈɒbviəs]	offensichtlich, klar
broadcaster	[ˈbrɔːdkɑːstə]	Sender
to **be lucky**	[bi ˈlʌki]	Glück haben
preschooler	[ˈpriːskuːlə]	Vorschulkind

page 180

knock-on effect	[ˌnɒkˈɒn ɪfekt]	Folgewirkung
obesity	[əʊˈbiːsəti]	Fettleibigkeit

SOCIAL TOPIC 3

page 181

bright	[braɪt]	freundlich *(Wetter)*, hell, strahlend
term	[tɜːm]	Schul-/Studienzeit *(im Gegensatz zu Ferien)*; Trimester
job	[dʒɒb]	Aufgabe
chaotic	[keɪˈɒtɪk]	chaotisch
alarm clock	[əˈlɑːm klɒk]	Wecker
porridge	[ˈpɒrɪdʒ]	Haferbrei
honey	[ˈhʌni]	Honig
with a grin	[grɪn]	grinsend
attendance	[əˈtendəns]	Anwesenheit
concentration	[ˌkɒnsnˈtreɪʃn]	Konzentration

page 182

to **get up**	[ˌget ˈʌp]	aufstehen
to **get dressed**	[get ˈdrest]	sich anziehen
maple syrup	[ˌmeɪpl ˈsɪrəp]	Ahornsirup
confused	[kənˈfjuːzd]	verwirrt
unorganized	[ʌnˈɔːgənaɪzd]	unorganisiert

page 183

nation	[ˈneɪʃn]	Staat, Nation
relative	[ˈrelətɪv]	relativ
plenty (of)	[ˈplenti]	reichlich, viel
rest	[ˈrest]	Rest
day care facility	[ˌdeɪkeə fəˈsɪləti]	Tageseinrichtung
to **set aside**	[ˌset əˈsaɪd]	vorsehen *(Mittel)*
all-day school	[ˌɔːl deɪ ˈskuːl]	Ganztagsschule
latchkey kid	[ˈlætʃkiː kɪd]	Schlüsselkind
listener	[ˈlɪsnə]	Zuhörer/in
fearful	[ˈfɪəfl]	ängstlich
soup	[suːp]	Suppe
to **concentrate**	[ˈkɒnsntreɪt]	sich konzentrieren
circumstances *pl*	[ˈsɜːkəmstənsɪz]	Umstände
immigrant	[ˈɪmɪgrənt]	Einwanderer/in
intensive	[ɪnˈtensɪv]	intensiv
curriculum	[kəˈrɪkjələm]	Lehrplan
to **extend**	[ɪkˈstend]	erweitern, ausdehnen
extra-curricular	[ˌekstrə kəˈrɪkjulə]	außerschulisch
self-reliant	[ˌself rɪˈlaɪənt]	selbstständig
supportive	[səˈpɔːtɪv]	(unter)stützend

SOCIAL TOPIC 4

page 184

to **start out**	[ˌstɑːt ˈaʊt]	beginnen, am Anfang stehen
to **refer to sb as**	[rɪˈfɜː]	jdn bezeichnen als
stepping stone	[ˈstepɪŋ stəʊn]	Sprungbrett
hairdresser	[ˈheədresə]	Friseur/in

to **react (to)** [ri'ækt]	reagieren (auf)
to **nurture** ['nɜːtʃə]	entwickeln, pflegen, fördern
child abuse ['tʃaɪld əbjuːs]	Kindesmissbrauch, -misshandlung
to **assume** [ə'sjuːm]	annehmen, davon ausgehen

page 185

towards [tə'wɔːdz]	auf … zu, in Richtung auf
demanding [dɪ'mɑːndɪŋ]	anstrengend, anspruchsvoll
residence ['rezɪdəns]	*(Alten-, Pflege-)* Heim
long-term [ˌlɒŋ 'tɜːm]	langfristig, Langzeit-
crèche [kreʃ]	Krippe
substance misuse [ˌsʌbstəns ˌmɪs'juːs]	Drogenmissbrauch
outreach worker ['aʊtriːtʃ wɜːkə]	Straßensozialarbeiter/in
alcoholic [ˌælkə'hɒlɪk]	Alkoholiker/in
addict ['ædɪkt]	Abhängige/r

page 186

school leaver ['skuːl liːvə]	Schulabgänger/in
interested (in) ['ɪntrəstɪd]	interessiert (an)
client ['klaɪənt]	Kunde/Kundin
sexist ['seksɪst]	sexistisch
pregnant ['pregnənt]	schwanger
to **employ** [ɪm'plɔɪ]	beschäftigen, einstellen *(Personal)*

SOCIAL TOPIC 5

page 187

to **settle in** [ˌsetl 'ɪn]	sich einleben
one-to-one [ˌwʌn tə 'wʌn]	Einzel-
input ['ɪnpʊt]	Eingabe, Beitrag, Input
schoolmate ['skuːlmeɪt]	Mitschüler/in
discussion [dɪ'skʌʃn]	Diskussion, Besprechung
recording [rɪ'kɔːdɪŋ]	Aufnahme, Aufzeichnung
column ['kɒləm]	Spalte
country of origin [ˌkʌntri əv 'ɒrɪdʒɪn]	Ursprungsland, Herkunftsland
switchboard ['swɪtʃbɔːd]	Schalttafel

page 188

to **pledge** [pledʒ]	sich verpflichten
to **chatter away** [ˌtʃætər ə'weɪ]	losplaudern
makeshift ['meɪkʃɪft]	provisorisch
food stall ['fuːd stɔːl]	Imbissstand
local ['ləʊkl]	Einheimische/r
paraphernalia [ˌpærəfə'neɪliə]	Zubehör, Ausrüstung
to **flock** [flɒk]	strömen
solidarity [ˌsɒlɪ'dærəti]	Solidarität
mentorship program ['mentəʃɪp prəʊgræm]	Mentorenprogramm
to **co-found** ['kəʊfaʊnd]	mitbegründen
mentoring ['mentərɪŋ]	Patenschaft, Mentoring
offside [ˌɒf'saɪd]	Abseits
to **invoke** [ɪn'vəʊk]	zitieren, anführen
metaphor ['metəfə]	Metapher
to **stray** [streɪ]	abweichen, sich verirren
margin ['mɑːdʒɪn]	Rand
outsider [ˌaʊt'saɪdə]	Außenseiter/in
to **belong** [bɪ'lɒŋ]	dazugehören

page 189

interpreter [ɪn'tɜːprɪtə]	Dolmetscher/in
to **grant** [grɑːnt]	gewähren, einräumen
permit ['pɜːmɪt]	Bewilligung
fascist ['fæʃɪst]	faschistisch
regime [reɪ'ʒiːm]	Regime
fence [fens]	Zaun
tradition [trə'dɪʃn]	Tradition, Brauch

SOCIAL TOPIC 6

page 190

to **combine** [kəm'baɪn]	verbinden, kombinieren
gap year ['gæp jɪə]	*das Jahr zwischen Schulabgang und Studienbeginn*
keen [kiːn]	begeistert
desire [dɪ'zaɪə]	Wunsch, Verlangen
livelihood ['laɪvlihʊd]	Existenzgrundlage, Lebensunterhalt
workforce ['wɜːkfɔːs]	Erwerbstätige, Erwerbsbevölkerung
agrochemical [ˌægrəʊ'kemɪkl]	Agrochemikalie
conjunction [kən'dʒʌŋkʃn]	Verbindung
grower ['grəʊə]	Anbauer/in
greenhouse ['griːnhaʊs]	Treibhaus
insect ['ɪnsekt]	Insekt
continuous [kən'tɪnjuəs]	kontinuierlich, anhaltend
consistent [kən'sɪstənt]	gleichbleibend
yield [jiːld]	Ertrag
corn [kɔːn]	Getreide, *(AE)* Mais
duck [dʌk]	Ente
goat [gəʊt]	Ziege
pig [pɪg]	Schwein
ginger ['dʒɪndʒə]	Ingwer
palm nut ['pɑːm nʌt]	Palmkern

page 191

based in ['beɪst ɪn]	ansässig in

page 192

to **come along** [ˌkʌm ə'lɒŋ]	vorbeikommen

SOCIAL TOPIC 7

page 193

caring professional [ˌkeərɪŋ prə'feʃənl]	in einem Sozialberuf Tätige/r
coffee ['kɒfi]	Kaffee
sweatshop ['swetʃɒp]	Ausbeutungsbetrieb
uproar ['ʌprɔː]	Aufruhr
to **inspect** [ɪn'spekt]	inspizieren, kontrollieren
day off [ˌdeɪ 'ɒf]	freier Tag, Urlaubstag
committed (to) [kə'mɪtɪd]	engagiert (für)
to **discriminate against** [dɪ'skrɪmɪneɪt əgenst]	diskriminieren
marital status [ˌmærɪtl 'steɪtəs]	Familienstand
weekly ['wiːkli]	wöchentlich
institution [ˌɪnstɪ'tjuːʃn]	Institution
to **make a stand** [ˌmeɪk ə 'stænd]	Farbe bekennen, ein Zeichen setzen
coffee bean ['kɒfi biːn]	Kaffeebohne
food miles *pl* ['fuːd maɪlz]	Transportwege der Nahrungsmittel
day out [ˌdeɪ 'aʊt]	Tagesausflug

page 194

petrol-guzzling ['petrəl gʌzlɪŋ]	spritfressend
to **taxi around** [ˌtæksi ə'raʊnd]	herumkutschieren

energy-saving light bulb [ˌenədʒi seɪvɪŋ 'laɪt bʌlb]	Energiesparlampe
to **insist** [ɪn'sɪst]	darauf bestehen
label ['leɪbl]	Kennzeichnung, Etikett, Schild(chen)
terrible ['terəbl]	schrecklich, furchtbar
developing country [dɪˌveləpɪŋ 'kʌntri]	Entwicklungsland

page 195

global issue [ˌgləʊbl 'ɪʃuː]	globales Problem
response [rɪ'spɒns]	Antwort, Stellungnahme

SOCIAL TOPIC 8

page 196

obese [əʊ'biːs]	fettleibig
to **double** ['dʌbl]	(sich) verdoppeln
years to come [ˌjɪəz tə 'kʌm]	die kommenden Jahre
entire [ɪn'taɪə]	ganz, vollständig
shift [ʃɪft]	Verschiebung, Verlagerung, Wandel
to **bring up** [ˌbrɪŋ 'ʌp]	erziehen, aufziehen
economist [ɪ'kɒnəmɪst]	Wirtschaftswissen-schaftler/in
to **gain weight** [ˌgeɪn 'weɪt]	zunehmen
kindergartener ['kɪndəgɑːtnə]	Kindergartenkind
percentile [pə'sentaɪl]	Perzentile
to **rocket** ['rɒkɪt]	in die Höhe schnellen
classified ['klæsɪfaɪd]	klassifiziert
to **accelerate** [ək'seləreɪt]	beschleunigen
to **soar** [sɔː]	steigen
couch potato [ˌkaʊtʃ pə'teɪtəʊ]	Stubenhocker/in, Dauer-glotzer/in
to **contribute** [kən'trɪbjuːt]	beitragen
weighty ['weɪti]	gewichtig, Gewichts-

page 197

soft drink ['sɒft drɪŋk]	alkoholfreies Getränk
intake ['ɪnteɪk]	Zufuhr, Aufnahme
playground ['pleɪgraʊnd]	Spielplatz
crisps *pl, BE* [krɪsps]	Kartoffelchips
single parent ['sɪŋgl peərənt]	alleinerziehend
cereal ['sɪəriəl]	Getreideflocken, Müsli, Cerealien
to **diet** ['daɪət]	Diät halten
depression [dɪ'preʃn]	Depression(en)
self-esteem [ˌself ɪ'stiːm]	Selbstachtung, Selbstwert-gefühl
to **snack** [snæk]	eine Kleinigkeit zu sich nehmen, etwas zwischen-durch essen
comfort ['kʌmfət]	Komfort, Trost, Hilfe
processed food ['prəʊsest]	verarbeitete Lebensmittel
sugared ['ʃʊgəd]	gezuckert
to **overeat** [ˌəʊvər'iːt]	zu viel essen
to **brainstorm** ['breɪnstɔːm]	Ideen (ungeordnet) sammeln

SOCIAL TOPIC 9

page 199

inclusion [ɪn'kluːʒn]	Einbeziehung, Einbindung, *Inklusion*
keyword ['kiːwɜːd]	Schlagwort, Schlüsselwort
ambassador [æm'bæsədə]	Botschafter/in
significance [sɪg'nɪfɪkəns]	Bedeutung, Stellenwert
Down's syndrome ['daʊnz sɪndrəʊm]	Down-Syndrom
perception [pə'sepʃn]	Wahrnehmung
to **break new ground** [ˌbreɪk njuː 'graʊnd]	(sich) Neuland erschließen
actor ['æktə]	Schauspieler/in
to **make history** [ˌmeɪk 'hɪstəri]	Geschichte schreiben
learning disability ['lɜːnɪŋ dɪsəbɪləti]	Lernbehinderung, Lernschwäche
high-profile [ˌhaɪ 'prəʊfaɪl]	prominent, mit hohem Bekanntheitsgrad

page 200

to **stress** [stres]	betonen, hervorheben
to **struggle** ['strʌgl]	kämpfen, sich abmühen
signal ['sɪgnəl]	Signal, Zeichen
to **afford sb sth** [ə'fɔːd]	jdm etw ermöglichen
inclusive [ɪn'kluːsɪv]	offen, (frei) zugänglich
to **overlook** [ˌəʊvə'lʊk]	übersehen
trait [treɪt]	Wesenszug, Eigenschaft
honesty ['ɒnəstɪ]	Ehrlichkeit
accuracy ['ækjərəsi]	Genauigkeit
prevalent ['prevələnt]	(weit) verbreitet, vorherrschend
to **recall** [rɪ'kɔːl]	sich erinnern
to **strive** [straɪv]	streben, bemüht sein
classroom ['klɑːsruːm]	Klassenzimmer, Klassenraum
law of the land [ˌlɔː əv ðə 'lænd]	geltendes Recht
principal ['prɪnsəpl]	Direktor/in, Schulleiter/in
behavioural problem [bɪˌeɪvjərəl 'prɒbləm]	Verhaltensstörung
special needs class [ˌspeʃl 'niːdz klɑːs]	Förderklasse
specialized training [ˌspeʃəlaɪzd 'treɪnɪŋ]	Spezialausbildung, Fach-ausbildung

page 201

to **place** [pleɪs]	setzen, platzieren
disorder [dɪs'ɔːdə]	(Funktions-)Störung *(Krankheit)*

SOCIAL TOPIC 10

page 202

storytelling ['stɔːritelɪŋ]	Geschichtenerzählen
audiobook ['ɔːdiəʊbʊk]	Hörbuch
excerpt ['eksɜːpt]	Auszug, Ausschnitt
disposal [dɪ'spəʊzl]	Entsorgung
deforestation [diːˌfɒrɪ'steɪʃn]	Waldzerstörung
dinosaur ['daɪnəsɔː]	Dinosaurier
grassy ['grɑːsi]	grasbewachsen
star [stɑː]	Stern
beauty ['bjuːti]	Schönheit
to **long** [lɒŋ]	sich sehnen, verlangen
to **reach out to sb/sth** [ˌriːtʃ 'aʊt]	die Hand nach jdm/etw ausstrecken
nowhere near ['nəʊweə nɪə]	bei weitem nicht, nicht annähernd
furnace ['fɜːnɪs]	(Industrie-)Ofen, Hochofen
to **huff and puff** *(ugs)* [ˌhʌf ənd 'pʌf]	schnaufen und keuchen
smoke [sməʊk]	Rauch
to **pour out** [ˌpɔːr 'aʊt]	herausströmen

to **pile up** [ˌpaɪl 'ʌp]	sich häufen, sich auftürmen
wherever [weər'evə]	wo (auch) immer
heap [hiːp]	Halde
to **set off** [ˌset 'ɒf]	aufbrechen

page 203

to **look about** [ˌlʊk ə'baʊt]	sich umschauen
blade of grass [ˌbleɪd əv 'grɑːs]	Grashalm
pile [paɪl]	Haufen
to **smoulder** ['sməʊldə]	schwelen
to **rumble** ['rʌmbl]	rumpeln, grollen
to **heave** [hiːv]	(sich) (er-)heben, hieven
to **stretch** [stretʃ]	sich strecken
to **crack** [kræk]	aufbrechen, bersten
creature ['kriːtʃə]	Geschöpf, (Lebe-)Wesen
to **hold one's nose** [həʊld]	sich die Nase zuhalten
volcano [vɒl'keɪnəʊ]	Vulkan
shoot [ʃuːt]	Trieb *(einer Pflanze)*, Spross
to **burst** [bɜːst]	(aus)brechen
wall [wɔːl]	Mauer
pole [pəʊl]	Mast
iron ['aɪən]	eisern
pylon ['paɪlən]	Mast, Pfeiler
trailing ['treɪlɪŋ]	rankend
blossom ['blɒsəm]	Blüte
mammoth ['mæməθ]	Mammut
serpent ['sɜːpənt]	(Riesen-)Schlange
dodo ['dəʊdəʊ]	Dodo *(ausgestorbene Vogelart)*
ape [eɪp]	Menschenaffe
chorus ['kɔːrəs]	Chor, Refrain
moral ['mɒrəl]	Moral
to **fall asleep** [ˌfɔːl ə'sliːp]	einschlafen
dustman *BE* ['dʌstmən]	Müllwerker/in, Müllmann/-frau
plastic bag [ˌplæstɪk 'bæg]	Plastiktüte
tin [tɪn]	Dose, Büchse

page 204

used up [ˌjuːzd 'ʌp]	aufgebraucht, verbraucht
lush [lʌʃ]	üppig
hyphen ['haɪfn]	Bindestrich, Trennstrich
cute [kjuːt]	süß
penguin ['peŋgwɪn]	Pinguin
overfishing [ˌəʊvə'fɪʃɪŋ]	Überfischung
niece [niːs]	Nichte
ice age ['aɪs eɪdʒ]	Eiszeit
icy ['aɪsi]	vereist
habitat ['hæbɪtæt]	natürlicher Lebensraum
documentary [ˌdɒkju'mentri]	Dokumentarfilm, Dokumentarsendung
walrus ['wɔːlrəs]	Walross
polar bear ['pəʊlə beə]	Eisbär
underneath [ˌʌndə'niːθ]	(dar)unter
arctic ['ɑːktɪk]	arktisch
tale [teɪl]	Erzählung
to **happen to do sth** ['hæpən]	etw zufällig tun
channel hopping ['tʃænl hɒpɪŋ]	Zappen
copy ['kɒpi]	Exemplar
to **jot down** [ˌdʒɒt 'daʊn]	notieren
plot [plɒt]	Handlung(sverlauf)

SOCIAL TOPIC 11

page 205

poor [pʊə]	die Armen
single ['sɪŋgl]	einzelne/r/s
rotten ['rɒtn]	faul, verdorben
unemployed [ˌʌnɪm'plɔɪd]	arbeitslos
to **hit rock bottom** [hɪt ˌrɒk 'bɒtm]	den Tiefpunkt erreichen
to **marshal** ['mɑːʃl]	sammeln, zusammenstellen
to **establish** [ɪ'stæblɪʃ]	etablieren, aufbauen, festigen
needy ['niːdi]	bedürftig
passer-by [ˌpɑːsə 'baɪ]	Passant/in
pot [pɒt]	Kanne, Topf, Becher
sauce [sɔːs]	Soße
aroma [ə'rəʊmə]	Duft
disheartened [dɪs'hɑːtnd]	entmutigt, niedergeschlagen
reborn [ˌriː'bɔːn]	wiedergeboren
relief [rɪ'liːf]	Erleichterung, Entlastung, Linderung
food bank ['fuːd bæŋk]	Tafel
lifeline ['laɪflaɪn]	Rettungsanker
fundamental [ˌfʌndə'mentl]	wesentlich, grundsätzlich
failure ['feɪljə]	Versagen, Ausfall, Zusammenbruch

page 206

Catholic ['kæθəlɪk]	katholisch
bishop ['bɪʃəp]	Bischof
ethnicity [eθ'nɪsəti]	Ethnizität, Volkszugehörigkeit
diverse [daɪ'vɜːs]	unterschiedlich, vielfältig
human rights [ˌhjuːmən 'raɪts]	Menschenrechte
to **uphold** [ʌp'həʊld]	bewahren, schützen
to **pave** [peɪv]	pflastern
dignity ['dɪgnəti]	Würde
generosity [ˌdʒenə'rɒsəti]	Großzügigkeit
central ['sentrəl]	zentral
classed [klɑːst]	eingestuft
integration [ˌɪntɪ'greɪʃn]	Integration
to **turn away** [ˌtɜːn ə'weɪ]	abweisen

SOCIAL TOPIC 12

page 208

innovation [ˌɪnə'veɪʃn]	Innovation, Neuerung
communication [kəˌmjuːnɪ'keɪʃn]	Verständigung, Kommunikation
pill [pɪl]	Pille
techie ['teki]	Technikfreak
to **personalize** ['pɜːsənəlaɪz]	persönlich/individuell gestalten
order ['ɔːdə]	Verordnung
to **filter out** [ˌfɪltə 'aʊt]	ausfiltern
irrelevant [ɪ'reləvənt]	irrelevant
to **sidetrack** ['saɪdtræk]	ablenken
intended [ɪn'tendɪd]	gedacht, vorgesehen
to **breastfeed** ['brestfiːd]	stillen
pregnancy ['pregnənsi]	Schwangerschaft
to **boom** [buːm]	blühen, boomen
segment ['segmənt]	Abschnitt, Teilstück, Segment
offering ['ɒfərɪŋ]	Angebot
belly ['beli]	Bauch
new entrant [njuː 'entrənt]	Neueinsteiger

rolled into one [rəʊld ɪntə 'wʌn]	in einem
functionality [ˌfʌŋkʃə'næləti]	Funktionalität
fetus *AE* (*BE* **foetus**) ['fiːtəs]	Fötus
animation [ˌænɪ'meɪʃn]	Animation
informational [ˌɪnfə'meɪʃənl]	informatorisch
to **generate** ['dʒenəreɪt]	erzeugen, generieren
revenue ['revənjuː]	Einkünfte, Einnahmen
interaction [ˌɪntər'ækʃn]	Interaktion
to **eliminate** [ɪ'lɪmɪneɪt]	eliminieren, beseitigen
branch [brɑːntʃ]	Zweig
stigma ['stɪgmə]	Stigma, Makel
glucose tab ['gluːkəʊs tæb]	Traubenzuckertablette
test strip ['test strɪp]	Teststreifen
injection [ɪn'dʒekʃn]	Spritze, Injektion
iteration [ˌɪtə'reɪʃn]	Iteration, Wiederholung
to **branch out** [ˌbrɑːntʃ 'aʊt]	verzweigen
chronic ['krɒnɪk]	chronisch
food allergy ['fuːd ælədʒi]	Lebensmittelallergie

page 209

face-to-face [ˌfeɪs tə 'feɪs]	im persönlichen Gespräch
consultation [ˌkɒnsl'teɪʃn]	Arztbesuch, Beratung
cognitive ['kɒgnətɪv]	kognitiv
procedure [prə'siːdʒə]	Vorgang, Verfahren
to **cure** [kjʊə]	heilen
painter ['peɪntə]	Maler/in
decorator ['dekəreɪtə]	Dekorateur/in, Raumausstatter/in
headache ['hedeɪk]	Kopfschmerzen
examination [ɪgˌzæmɪ'neɪʃn]	Untersuchung
brain tumour ['brein tjuːmə]	Hirntumor
operation [ˌɒpə'reɪʃn]	Operation
blind [blaɪnd]	blind
epileptic fit [ˌepɪˌleptɪk 'fɪt]	epileptischer Anfall
to **regain** [rɪ'geɪn]	wiedererlangen
Paralympian [ˌpærə'lɪmpiən]	paralympisch
gold medallist [ˌgəʊld 'medəlɪst]	Goldmedaillengewinner/in
sight [saɪt]	Sehkraft
hand [hænd]	Zeiger
ball bearing [ball 'beərɪŋ]	Kugellagerkugel
guide dog ['gaɪd dɒg]	Blindenhund
voice-controlled [ˌvɔɪs kən'trəʊld]	sprachgesteuert
locator [ləʊ'keɪtə]	Ortungsgerät
route [ruːt]	Route, Strecke
command [kə'mɑːnd]	Befehl, Kommando
sensor ['sensə]	Sensor
to **raise an alarm** [ˌreɪz ən ə'lɑːm]	Alarm auslösen
lifeline pendant [ˌlaɪflaɪn 'pendənt]	Hausnotrufsender *(als Halsband)*
pendant ['pendənt]	Anhänger
neck [nek]	Hals
no longer [nəʊ 'lɒŋgə]	nicht mehr
breathless ['breθləs]	außer Atem
fatigued [fə'tiːgd]	erschöpft, ermüdet
to **cough** [kʌf]	husten
frightening ['fraɪtnɪŋ]	beängstigend
to **breathe** [briːð]	atmen
ambulance ['æmbjələns]	Krankenwagen
COPD [siː əʊ piː 'diː]	chronisch obstruktive Lungenerkrankung
cigarette [ˌsɪgə'ret]	Zigarette
to **refer sb to sb/sth** [rɪ'fɜː]	jdn zu jdm überweisen, jdn an etw verweisen
telehealth ['telihelθ]	Telemedizin
complicated ['kɒmplɪkeɪtɪd]	kompliziert
oxygen ['ɒksɪdʒən]	Sauerstoff
automatically [ˌɔːtə'mætɪkli]	automatisch
to **be put off** [ˌpʊt 'ɒf]	sich abschrecken lassen
peace of mind [ˌpiːs əv 'maɪnd]	Sicherheit, innere Ruhe
captioned telephone [ˌkæpʃnd 'telifəʊn]	*Telefon mit Textanzeige für Menschen mit Hörschädigung*
lung flute ['lʌŋ fluːt]	*Atemphysiotherapiegerät zur Verbesserung der Lungenfunktion bei COPD*

page 210

infant ['ɪnfənt]	Kleinkind
impairment [ɪm'peəmənt]	Beeinträchtigung
sock [sɒk]	Socke

A–Z word list

Dieses Wörterverzeichnis enthält alle Wörter in **Focus on Success – 5th edition: Ausgabe Soziales** in alphabetischer Reihenfolge. Nicht aufgeführt sind die Wörter aus der *Basic word list* sowie internationale Wörter wie *hotel*, *email* usw.
Wörter, die in den Hörverständnistexten vorkommen, sind mit einem *T* hinter der Seitenzahl gekennzeichnet. Wörter, die in den *Files* vorkommen, sind mit einem *F* hinter der Seitenzahl gekennzeichnet.

A

abbreviation *32* Abkürzung
ability *29* Fähigkeit, Befähigung
about, to **be ~ to do sth** *51* im Begriff sein, etw zu tun; gerade dabei sein, etw zu tun
to **abridge** *27* *(Text)* kürzen
absolutely *40* absolut
to **absorb** *153* aufnehmen, absorbieren
abuse, child ~ *184* Kindesmissbrauch, -misshandlung
academic *158* Schul-, akademisch
to **accelerate** *196* beschleunigen
to **accept** *11T* akzeptieren, gutheißen
access *158* Zugang; to **~ sth** *160* auf etw zugreifen; **~ code** *128* Zugangscode; **~ to sth** *124* Zugriff auf etw, Zugang zu etw; **wheelchair ~** *122* behindertengerechter Zugang
accessible *51* zugänglich, erreichbar, offen
accident *146* Unfall; **~ and emergency department (A&E)** *167* Notaufnahme
to **accommodate** *67* unterbringen
accommodation *66* Unterkunft; **homestay ~** *66* Unterbringung bei Gasteltern
to **accompany** *27* begleiten
according to *12* entsprechend, nach, gemäß; *14* laut, zufolge
account *37* Konto; to **take sth into ~** *23* etw in Betracht ziehen, etw berücksichtigen
accountancy *90* Buchhaltung, Rechnungswesen
accountant *65* Buchhalter/in
accounts *34* Buchhaltung
accuracy *200* Genauigkeit
accurate *75* genau
to **ache** *16* schmerzen, wehtun
to **achieve sth** *19* etw erreichen, etw leisten
achievement *10* Errungenschaft, Leistung
to **acknowledge** *69* anerkennen, zugeben
acne *24* Akne
acre *149* Morgen *(ca. 4047qm)*
acronym *169* Akronym, Abkürzung
act *91* Handlung, Tat; to **~ as sth** *114* als etw fungieren; to **~ out** *43* spielen, vorspielen
action, course of ~ *87* Vorgehen, Maßnahmen; **legal ~** *39* rechtliche Schritte; to **take ~** *100* handeln; to **take legal ~** *39* rechtliche Schritte unternehmen
to **activate** *144* aktivieren
actor *199* Schauspieler/in
actually *20* in der Tat, eigentlich, wirklich
ad *45* Anzeige, Werbung; **viral ~** *45* Internet-Werbespot
ad(vertising) agency *46* Werbeagentur
to **adapt** *27* *(Text)* bearbeiten; *152* sich anpassen
adaptation *152* Anpassung, Anpassungsleistung
addict *185* Abhängige/r
addition *162* Hinzufügung; **in ~** *48* außerdem, darüber hinaus; **in ~ to sth** *76* zusätzlich zu etw
additional *160* zusätzlich
to **address** *69* *(Problem etc.)* ansprechen, angehen, thematisieren; **~ sb** *110* jdn ansprechen
address, writer's ~ *76* Absenderanschrift
adequate(ly) *27* ausreichend, angemessen
to **administer** *67* verwalten
administration *66* Verwaltung
administrative *67* Verwaltungs-
administrator *65* Verwalter/in
to **admire** *11* bewundern
to **admit** *24* zugeben, (ein)gestehen
adopt, to **~ sb** *94* jdn adoptieren; to **~ sth** *118* etw übernehmen
adoption *146* Übernahme, Aneignung
advance, in ~ *40* im Voraus
advert *45* Anzeige, Werbung
advertise, to **~ a job** *66* eine Stelle ausschreiben; to **~ sth** *19* etw bewerben, für etw werben
advertisement *45* Anzeige, Werbung; **job ~** *31* Stellenanzeige, -ausschreibung
advertising *45* Werbung; **ad(vertising) agency** *46* Werbeagentur
advice *38T* (guter) Rat, Ratschläge; **strong ~** *62T* dringender Rat
to **advise** *129* (jdm etw) raten; **~ sb** *38* jdn beraten, jdm etw raten
adviser *114* Berater/in
advisor, careers ~ *68* Berufsberater/in; **customer services ~** *68T* Kundenberater/in
advocate *136* Befürworter/in
aerobics *12* Aerobic
to **affect** *19* beeinflussen, sich auswirken auf
affected *108* betroffen
affluent *116* wohlhabend
to **afford sb sth** *200* jdm etw ermöglichen
affordability *22* Erschwinglichkeit, Bezahlbarkeit
affordable *19* erschwinglich
afraid, I'm ~ *24* leider
afterwards *111* danach, darauf
to **age** *74* altern
age, for ~s *163* ewig, eine Ewigkeit
aged *40* im Alter von
agency *14* Agentur; **ad(vertising) ~** *46* Werbeagentur; **forwarding ~** *145* Spedition; **law enforcement ~** *124* Strafverfolgungsbehörde, Exekutivorgan
agenda *172* Tagesordnung
aggressive *134* aggressiv
agreement *101* Vereinbarung, Absprache
agricultural *86T* landwirtschaftlich, Landwirtschafts-
agriculture *148* Landwirtschaft
agrochemical *190* Agrochemikalie
ahead *62* voraus, vorausliegend
aid *97* Hilfe; to **live off ~** *81* von Sozialhilfe leben
aim *164* Absicht, Ziel, Zweck; to **~ at sth** *152* etw anstreben
aimed, to **be ~ at sb** *28* sich an jdn richten
airborne drone *168* Flugdrohne
aircraft *102* Flugzeug
airfare, return ~ *66* Kosten für Hin- und Rückflug
airline *81* Fluglinie
alarm *144* Alarmsignal; **~ clock** *181* Wecker; to **raise an ~** *209T* Alarm auslösen
alcoholic *185* Alkoholiker/in
alien *165* außerirdisch
alive *63* lebendig, am Leben
all, ~ at once *24* auf einmal; **~ right by me** *30* in Ordnung für mich; **~ the time** *36* ständig, die ganze Zeit; **at ~** *16* überhaupt; **first of ~** *62T* zuallererst
all-day school *183T* Ganztagsschule
allergy *146* Allergie; **food ~** *208* Lebensmittelallergie
allotted *69* zugewiesen

allowance *20* Taschengeld; *66* Aufwandsentschädigung; *117T* Zuschuss
alone, to **leave sb ~** *178* jdn in Ruhe lassen
along, ~ the way *90* dabei, währenddessen; to **take sb ~** *16* jdn mitnehmen
alongside *168* neben
although *27* obwohl
amateur *22* Amateur(-), Hobby-
ambassador *199* Botschafter/in
ambition *45* Ziel, Ehrgeiz
ambitious *68* ehrgeizig
ambulance *209T* Krankenwagen
among *27* unter, inmitten, zwischen
amount *37* Betrag; *81* Menge; to **~ to sth** *81* auf etw hinauslaufen
amusement arcade *46* Spielhalle
to **analyse** *26* analysieren
anchor, news ~ *136* Nachrichtensprecher/in
ancient *115* alt, historisch, antik
and so on *62T* und so weiter
anecdote *38* Anekdote
angry *136* aufgebracht, ungehalten; to **get ~** *62T* sich ärgern
animation *208* Animation
anniversary *94* Jahrestag
to **announce** *14* verkünden, ankündigen
annoyed, to **become ~** *141* sich ärgern, sich aufregen
annual *156* jährlich
annum, per ~ *117T* pro Jahr
anonymous(ly) *127* anonym
to **answer the phone** *162* ans Telefon gehen
any, at ~ rate *131* auf jeden Fall; **at ~ time** *39* jederzeit
apart, ~ from *29* abgesehen von, außer; to **break sth ~** *145* etw auseinandernehmen
ape *203* Menschenaffe
to **apologize** *43* sich entschuldigen
apparently *40* anscheinend
to **appear** *7* auftreten, erscheinen; *15* scheinen
appearance *44* Aussehen, Äußeres, (äußere) Erscheinung
appliance *144* Haushaltsgerät
applicant *77* Bewerber/in
application *32* Bewerbung; *143T* Antrag
to **apply** *134* anwenden, ausüben; **~ (for a job)** *31* sich (um/auf eine Stelle) bewerben
appointment *34* Termin, Verabredung; *38T* Termin
to **appreciate** *76* schätzen, zu schätzen wissen
apprenticeship *68T* Ausbildung, Lehre
approach *46* Ansatz, Herangehensweise; to **~ sb** *27* an jdn herantreten; to **~ sth** *169* sich einer Sache nähern
appropriate(ly) *27* angemessen, passend
approximate *87* ungefähr, angenähert
approximately (approx.) *86* zirka (ca.)
arcade *46* Spielautomat; **amusement ~** *46* Spielhalle
architect *65* Architekt/in
arctic *204T* arktisch
area *11* Gebiet, Bereich, Feld; *25* Gegend, Region
to **argue** *27* argumentieren, geltend machen
to **arm sb** *126T* jdn bewaffnen
armed *91* bewaffnet; **~ forces** *pl* *126T* Streitkräfte
army *126* Armee; **Salvation A~** *90* Heilsarmee
aroma *205* Duft
arrangement *50* Abmachung, Vereinbarung, Vorbereitung, Regelung
to **arrest** *81* verhaften
arsenal *124* Instrumentarium, Waffenlager
arsenic *144* Arsen
artificial intelligence *164* künstliche Intelligenz
artistic *65* künstlerisch
as, ~ long ~ *137* solange; **~ regards …** *68T* was … betrifft; **~ things turn out** *34* wie sich herausstellt
asap (as soon as possible) *66* baldmöglichst
aside, to **set ~** *183T* vorsehen *(Mittel)*
asleep, to **be ~** *94* schlafen; to **fall ~** *203* einschlafen
aspect *15* Gesichtspunkt, Aspekt
assessment *78* Beurteilung, Einstufung
asset, to **be an ~ to sb** *76* für jdn eine Bereicherung sein
to **assign sb sth** *168* jdm etw zuweisen, jdn mit etw beauftragen
to **assist** *88* assistieren, helfen
assistance *74* Hilfe, Unterstützung
assistant, care ~ *178* Erzieher/in *(Kindergarten)*; **office ~** *75* Bürokaufmann/-frau
to **associate** *131* in Verbindung bringen, assoziieren
association *134* Verband, Vereinigung
to **assume** *184* annehmen, davon ausgehen
assumption *131* Annahme
asylum seeker *81* Asylbewerber/in
at first *175* zuerst, zunächst, anfangs
athlete *19* Sportler/in, Athlet/in
athletic *21* sportlich, athletisch
atmosphere *17T* Stimmung, Atmosphäre
atmospheric *137* atmosphärisch, in der Atmosphäre
atrocities *pl* *90* Gräueltaten
attach, to **~ sth** *31* *(E-Mail:)* etw beifügen, etw anhängen; to **~ sth to sth** *170* etw an etw befestigen
attachment *34* *(E-Mail:)* Anhang
attack *103* Attacke, Angriff; *123* Anschlag, Attentat; to **launch an ~** *130* einen Angriff starten
attacker *125* Attentäter/in
to **attend** *146* besuchen; to **~ sth** *78* an etw teilnehmen
attendance *181* Anwesenheit
attention *11T* Aufmerksamkeit, Beachtung; to **attract ~** *43* Aufmerksamkeit erregen; to **draw ~ to sb/sth** *24* Aufmerksamkeit auf jdn/etw ziehen; to **pay ~ to sth** *23* auf etw achten
attitude *93* Einstellung, Haltung
attn. (= attention) *76* *(Brief:)* zu Händen
to **attract** *43* anlocken, anziehen; **~ attention** *43* Aufmerksamkeit erregen
attractive *17* attraktiv, anziehend
audience *8* Publikum; **member of the ~** *8* Zuschauer/in
audiobook *202* Hörbuch
authority *80* Behörde
autograph *7* Autogramm
automated *100* automatisiert
automatically *209T* automatisch
autonomous *164* autonom
availability *19* Verfügbarkeit
available, to **be ~** *32* *(Telefon:)* zu sprechen sein
average *36* Durchschnitt
to **await** *124* erwarten, abwarten
to **award sth to sb** *161* jdm etw verleihen, jdm etw zuerkennen
aware, to **be ~ of sth** *88* sich einer Sache bewusst sein, etw kennen; to **make sb ~ of sth** *40* jdn über etw informieren, jdn auf etw hinweisen
awareness *175* Bewusstsein
away, right ~ *78* sofort
axis *53* Achse

B

back *100* Rücken; to **~** *27* unterstützen; **~ yard** *124* Hinterhof; to **get ~ to sb** *71T* sich bei jdm (zurück) melden
background *10* Hintergrund; *19* Herkunft
backpacker *31* Rucksacktourist/in
backpacking, to **go ~** *78* auf Rucksacktour gehen
backup *156* Ersatz, Reserve
baker *65* Bäcker/in
balance *74* Gleichgewicht, Balance; *105* Bilanz, Saldo; to **~** *74* im Gleichgewicht halten; *105* ausgleichen
ball bearing *209T* Kugellagerkugel
to **ban sb from doing sth** *60* jdm verbieten, etw zu tun
ban (on) *178* Verbot (von)
band *68T* Gehaltsstufe, Gehaltsklasse
bank, ~ clerk *67* Bankangestellte/r; **~ robbery** *130* Banküberfall, Bankraub; **bottle ~** *46* Glascontainer; **clothing ~** *89* Altkleidersammelbehälter; **food ~** *205* Tafel; to **rob a ~** *130* eine Bank überfallen, eine Bank ausrauben
banker *96T* Bankkaufmann/-frau
bar, ~ chart *52* Säulendiagramm; **candy ~** *AE* *54* Schokoriegel; **chocolate ~** *54* Schokoriegel

bare *49T* kahl, nackt
barrage *140* Staumauer
barrier *69* Hürde
to **base on sth** *36* auf etw basieren
based in *191* ansässig in
basis, on a need-to-know ~ *63* im (unumgänglichen) Bedarfsfall
basket *81* Korb
to **bat an eyelid** *14* mit der Wimper zucken
battery pack *144* Akku
battlefield *124* Schlachtfeld
to **be put off** *209T* sich abschrecken lassen
bean, coffee ~ *193* Kaffeebohne
beauty *202* Schönheit
beetle *49T* Käfer
to **beg** *143* flehen, eindringlich bitten; **~ for sth** *89* um etw betteln; **~ sb to do sth** *129* jdn anflehen, etw zu tun
beggar *89* Bettler/in
behalf, on sb's ~ *172* in jds Namen
to **behave** *82* sich benehmen, sich verhalten
behaviour *43* Benehmen, Verhalten
behavioural problem *200* Verhaltensstörung
being, human ~ *26* Mensch, menschliches Wesen
belief *19* Überzeugung
belly *208* Bauch
to **belong** *188* dazugehören
belonging *70* Zugehörigkeit
belt *170* Gurt, Gürtel
beneath *131* unterhalb, unter
benefactor *90* Wohltäter/in
benefit *17T* Nutzen, Vorteil, Pluspunkt; to **~** *43* nutzen, Nutzen bringen, profitieren
benefits *pl 60* Sozialleistungen; **~ office** *60* Sozialamt; **community ~** *pl 143T* Zahlungen an die Gemeinde; to **reap the ~** *165* die Früchte ernten, die Vorteile nutzen
beside *16* neben
besides *175* außer, neben
best, All the ~ *17* Mit besten Grüßen, Alles Gute
to **bet** *24* wetten
beyond *55* darüber hinaus; *137* jenseits, über
bid *27* Versuch
bill *62T* Rechnung; **electricity ~** *143* Stromrechnung; **utility ~s** *pl 151* Rechnungen für Versorgungsleistungen
billboard *45* Reklametafel, Plakatwand
billion *52* Milliarde
bi-manual *169* beidhändig
bin, rubbish ~ *47* Mülltonne
biofuel *149* Biokraftstoff
biomass *135* Biomasse
birth, to **give ~** *88* gebären, entbinden
bishop *206* Bischof
bit *174* Teil; **a ~** *24* ein bisschen
bite *146* Biss, (Insekten-)Stich; to **~** *146* beißen
blade of grass *203* Grashalm
blame, to **be to ~** *136* Schuld sein
blank *120* leer, frei
blanket *49T* pauschal, umfassend
blind *209T* blind
to **block** *39* sperren
block, office ~ *71* Bürogebäude
blockbuster *90* Straßenfeger
blood vessel *17* Blutgefäß
blossom *203* Blüte
blouse *156* Bluse
blow *94* Schlag; to **~** *62* wehen, blasen
bludger, dole ~ *111* Sozialschmarotzer
board and lodging *66* Kost und Logis
to **boast sth** *27* etw aufweisen (können)
body *76 (Brief:)* Hauptteil; *81* Leichnam
bold *36* fett(gedruckt)
bomb *124* Bombe; to **~ sth** *124* einen Bombenanschlag auf etw verüben
to **bombard** *178* bombardieren
bomber *125* Bombenattentäter/in; **suicide ~** *125* Selbstmordattentäter/in
booking *119* Buchung
to **boom** *208* blühen, boomen
boomerang *62T* Bumerang
to **boost** *17T* ankurbeln
border *81* Grenze; to **~ with sth** *126T* an etw grenzen; **~ customs officer** *161* (Grenz-)Zollbeamte/r
bored, to **get ~** *50* sich langweilen
to **borrow sth** *57* sich etw ausleihen
bother, to **~ sb** *34* jdn belästigen, jdn stören
to **bottle** *49T* in Flaschen abfüllen
bottle bank *46* Glascontainer
bottom line *107T* das, worauf es (unterm Strich) ankommt
bouncer *40* Türsteher/in
Boxing Day *94* 2. Weihnachtstag
bracelet *170* Armband, Armreifen
bracket *7* Klammer
brain *175* Gehirn; **~ tumour** *209T* Hirntumor
to **brainstorm** *197* Ideen (ungeordnet) sammeln
branch *208* Zweig; to **~ out** *208* verzweigen
brand *18* Marke; to **~ a product** *51* ein Markenprodukt schaffen
branded goods *pl 53* Markenware, Markenartikel
brave *175* tapfer, mutig
bread roll *99* Brötchen
break *173* Pause; to **~ down** *72* zusammenbrechen; to **~ new ground** *199* (sich) Neuland erschließen; to **~ sth apart** *145* etw auseinandernehmen; to **~ sth up** *7* etw zertrümmern, etw demolieren; to **~ up** *40 (Menschenmenge)* zerstreuen
breakage *105* Bruchschaden
breakdown *135* Zusammenbruch
breast cancer *175* Brustkrebs
to **breastfeed** *208* stillen
to **breathe** *209T* atmen
breathing *14* Atmung
breathless *209T* außer Atem
breathlessly *124* atemlos
breed *160* Rasse; to **~** *152* züchten
breeding *152* Zucht, Züchtung; **~ ground** *145* Brutplatz
brewery *54* Brauerei
brick *156* Ziegel
brief(ly) *60* kurz, knapp
bright *181* freundlich *(Wetter)*, hell, strahlend
to **bring up** *196* erziehen, aufziehen
Briton *36* Brite/Britin
broadcaster *179* Sender
broke *49T* kaputt
broken *144* kaputt, defekt
bubble, speech ~ *26* Sprechblase
bucket *43* Eimer; **~ list** *43* Dinge, die man getan haben sollte, bevor man stirbt
budget *62T* Etat, Haushalt, Budget
buffet lunch *122* Lunchbuffet
to **build sth up** *86* etw aufbauen
bulb, energy-saving light ~ *194* Energiesparlampe; **light ~** *155T* Glühbirne
bullet *80* (Gewehr-)Kugel; **~ point** *24* Stichpunkt
bunch, a ~ of *168* eine Menge
burden *109* Last, Belastung, Bürde
to **burn** *17T* (sich) verbrennen
to **burst** *203* (aus)brechen
business, ~ studies *75* Betriebswirtschaft; to **get down to ~** *174* zur Sache kommen; to **go out of ~** *107T* das Geschäft aufgeben, Pleite gehen; to **mind one's own ~** *57* sich um seinen eigenen Kram kümmern
button *160* Knopf, Button
buyer *100* Einkäufer/in
by, ~ oneself *62T* allein; **~ the way** *60* übrigens, nebenbei erwähnt; **one ~ one** *140* der Reihe nach

C

cabinet, filing ~ *69* Aktenschrank
cable *145* Kabel; **~ news** *124* TV-Nachrichtensender
cactus *147* Kaktus
café *119* Café
caffeine *14* Koffein
cage *154* Käfig
to **calculate** *168* berechnen
call, to **~ for sth** *137* zu etw aufrufen; **~ for help** *38* Hilferuf; to **take a ~** *38T* einen Anruf entgegennehmen, ans Telefon gehen
called *16* namens; to **be ~** *37* heißen
caller *34* Anrufer/in
to **calm** *143* beruhigen; **~ down** *84* sich beruhigen
calorie *17* Kalorie
calving *160* Kalben
camera, speed ~ *48F* Geschwindigkeitsüberwachungskamera, Radarfalle
campaign *43* Aktion, Kampagne; to **~** *109* kämpfen; to **launch an ad ~** *54* eine Werbekampagne starten
campaigner *132* Aktivist/in
campfire *146* Lagerfeuer

can *46* Dose
to **cancel** *16* absagen, stornieren; *130* abbrechen, abblasen
cancer *43* Krebs *(Krankheit, Sternzeichen)*; **breast** ~ *175* Brustkrebs
candidate *66* Bewerber/in
candle *79* Kerze
candy, ~ **bar** *AE 54* Schokoriegel; ~ **maker** *AE 54* Süßwarenhersteller
canister *40* Dose, Büchse
capita, per ~ **income** *156* Pro-Kopf-Einkommen
capital *144* Hauptstadt; ~ **letter** *32* Großbuchstabe
caption *8* Bildunterschrift
captioned telephone *209 Telefon mit Textanzeige für Menschen mit Hörschädigung*
car, ~ **park** *69* Parkplatz, -haus, -garage; ~ **wash** *49* Autowaschanlage; **company** ~ *65* Firmenwagen; **racing** ~ *13* Rennwagen; **sports** ~ *49* Sportwagen
carbon *137* Kohlenstoff; ~ **dioxide** *136* Kohlendioxid; ~ **dioxide level** *136* Kohlendioxidkonzentration, -gehalt
card, place ~ *172* Platzkarte, Tischkarte
cardboard *99* Pappe
cardiovascular *17* Herz-Kreislauf-
care *17T* Sorge; *88* Versorgung, Fürsorge; *103* Sorgfalt; to ~ **about sth** *100* sich um etw kümmern; ~ **assistant** *178* Erzieher/in *(Kindergarten)*; ~ **home** *132* Pflegeheim; ~ **worker** *118* Pfleger/in; **floor** ~ *104* Bodenpflege; **hair** ~ *49T* Haarpflege; **health** ~ *97* Gesundheitswesen, medizinische Versorgung; to **take** ~ **of sb** *74* sich um jdn kümmern
career *8* Karriere, Laufbahn
careers advisor *68* Berufsberater/in
caregiver *74* pflegende/r Angehörige/r, Betreuer/in
careless *78* nachlässig
carer *134* Betreuer/in, Pfleger/in
caring *65* fürsorglich; ~ **profession** *68T* Pflegeberuf; ~ **professional** *193* in einem Sozialberuf Tätige/r
carpenter *65* Zimmerer/in, Schreiner/in
carpentry *100* Schreinerei
carpet *40* Teppich(boden)
carry, to ~ **on** *116* weitermachen; to ~ **out** *34* durchführen, ausführen
cartoon *26* Karikatur
cartoonist *26* Karikaturist/in
case *163* Koffer; ~ **study** *100* Fallstudie
cash, to ~ **a cheque** *68T* einen Scheck einlösen; ~ **machine** *105* Geldautomat; to **have spare** ~ *96T* Geld übrig haben
cashier *68T* Kassierer/in
casing, well ~ *143T* Bohrlochverrohrung, Bohrlochwandung
cassava *156* Maniok, Kassava
casual *71* leger, zwanglos; ~ **job** *110* Nebenjob
catastrophe *148* Katastrophe
catchment tank *158* Auffangbehälter
category *65* Kategorie
to **cater** *122* Speisen und Getränke liefern; ~ **for sth** *122* auf etw eingehen
Catholic *206* katholisch
Catholicism *55* Katholizismus, der katholische Glaube
caught, to **be** ~ *56* festsitzen, in der Klemme sitzen
cause *136* Ursache; to ~ *28* verursachen; to ~ **sb to do sth** *69* jdn dazu veranlassen, etw zu tun; **good** ~ *92* guter Zweck
CCTV, ~ **(closed-circuit television)** *132* Videoüberwachung; ~ **camera** *132* Überwachungskamera
ceilidh *79* geselliges Beisammensein mit Musik und Tanz *(schottischer Brauch)*
to **celebrate** *21* feiern
celebrity *6* Prominente/r, Prominenz
cent, per ~ *44* Prozent
central *206* zentral
centrally heated *70* zentralbeheizt
centre *118* Zentrum
century *14* Jahrhundert
CEO (Chief Executive Officer) *136* Vorstandsvorsitzende/r
cereal *197* Getreideflocken, Müsli, Cerealien
to **certify** *156* zertifizieren
chain *72* Kette; **supply** ~ *99* Lieferkette; **value** ~ *145* Wertschöpfungskette
chairperson *155* Vorsitzende/r
challenge *10* Herausforderung, (große) Aufgabe
challenging *21* anspruchsvoll, fordernd
champion *13* Meister/in
chance, by ~ *141* zufällig; to **take a** ~ **on sb** *110* es mit jdm versuchen, jdm eine Chance geben
change *8* Wandel, Verwandlung; *52* Veränderung; *81* Wechselgeld; to ~ **for the better** *101* sich zum Besseren verändern; to ~ **sth into sth** *17* etw in etw umwandeln
changing *109* im Wandel; ~ **room** *13* Umkleidekabine, Umkleide
channel *37* Kanal; ~ **hopping** *204T* Zappen; **commercial** ~ *179* privater Fernsehsender
chaos *40* Chaos
chaotic *181* chaotisch
characteristic *116* Merkmal, charakteristische Eigenschaft
to **charge sb with sth** *14* jdn einer Sache beschuldigen, jdn einer Sache anklagen
charitable *92* wohltätig, gemeinnützig
charity *7* Benefiz-, Wohltätigkeit(s-); *43* Wohltätigkeit, wohltätige Zwecke; *66* Wohltätigkeitsorganisation; to **give to** ~ *92* (für wohltätige Zwecke) spenden
chart *52* Diagramm, Tabelle; **bar** ~ *52* Säulendiagramm; **line** ~ *53* Liniendiagramm
charts *pl 11* Hitparade
to **chase sb** *14* jdn verfolgen, jdn jagen
chat *56* Unterhaltung, Schwätzchen; to **have a** ~ *34* sich unterhalten, miteinander plaudern
to **chatter away** *188* losplaudern
chatty *32* mitteilsam, geschwätzig
to **check sth out** *62T* sich etw ansehen
checkout *81* Kasse
to **cheer for sb** *22* jdn anfeuern, jdm zujubeln
cheerful *57* fröhlich
cheers *pl 8* Jubel, Applaus
Cheers! *31* Tschüs! Mach's gut! Danke!
chemical control (of pests) *152* Schädlingsbekämpfung(smittel)
chemicals, farm ~ *pl 149* Landwirtschaftschemikalien
chess *13* Schach; ~ **set** *13* Schachspiel *(Figuren + Brett)*
child, ~ **abuse** *184* Kindesmissbrauch, -misshandlung; **only** ~ *64* Einzelkind
childcare *118* Kinderbetreuung
childhood *37* Kindheit; ~ **sweetheart** *10* Jugendliebe
childminder *178* Babysitter/in, Tagesmutter
chilly *146* frostig; *173* kühl
chips *pl BE 63* Pommes frites
chocolate bar *54* Schokoriegel
choice *19* Wahl, Entscheidung
to **choose sth over sth** *46* etw einer anderen Sache vorziehen
chore *55* (lästige Routine-)Aufgabe
chorus *203* Chor, Refrain
Christian *126* christlich, Christ/in
chronic *208* chronisch
to **chuckle** *169* kichern, schmunzeln
cigarette *209T* Zigarette
circumstances *pl 183* Umstände
citizen *95* Bürger/in; **senior** ~ *114* Senior/in, ältere/r Mitbürger/in
city planner *167* Stadtplaner/in
civil society *161* Bürgergesellschaft
civilization *164* Zivilisation
to **claim** *124* behaupten; to ~ **unemployment benefits** *86* Arbeitslosengeld beziehen
classed *206* eingestuft
classified *196* klassifiziert
classroom *200* Klassenzimmer, Klassenraum
to **clean up** *40* aufräumen, saubermachen
to **clear** *148* räumen, roden
clearance sale *144* Räumungsverkauf
clerical *65* Büro-
clerk, bank ~ *67* Bankangestellte/r; **office** ~ *49T* Büroangestellte/r
clever *47* intelligent, klug, schlau, clever

client *186* Kunde/Kundin
climate *136* Klima; ~ **change** *136* Klimawandel
climb *106* Anstieg
clinic *100* Klinik
clock, alarm ~ *181* Wecker; **grandfather ~** *118* Standuhr
close *11* nah, dicht, eng; to ~ **down** *140* stilllegen; ~ **to** *141* nahe bei, in der Nähe von; **complimentary ~** *76 (Brief:)* Schlussformel
closely related *116* eng verwandt
cloth, man of the ~ *126T* Geistlicher
clothing bank *89* Altkleidersammelbehälter
cloud *173* Wolke
club, drama ~ *59* Schauspiel-AG
clue *8* Hinweis, Anhaltspunkt
coal *136* Kohle; **~-fired** *136* kohlegetrieben
coast *80* Küste
coastal *137* Küsten-
coating *145* Ummantelung, (Kabel-)Mantel
co-author *137* Mitautor/in, Mitverfasser/in
to **coax sth out of sth** *160* etw aus etw herausholen
cocaine *14* Kokain
coffee *193* Kaffee; ~ **bean** *193* Kaffeebohne
to **co-found** *188* mitbegründen
cognitive *209* kognitiv
cold *13* Erkältung
collaborator *168* Mitarbeiter/in
collapse *103* Einsturz; to ~ *100* einstürzen
colleague *28* Kollege/-in
to **collect** *7* sammeln; ~ **sth** *22* etw (ab)holen
collection *11T* Kollektion; *24* Sammlung; *144* Abholung
college *49T* Fachhochschule; **vocational ~** *31* Fachoberschule, Berufskolleg
colonial power *160* Kolonialmacht
to **colour** *49T* färben
column *187* Spalte
to **comb** *81* kämmen
combination *175* Kombination, Verbindung
to **combine** *190* verbinden, kombinieren
combustion, internal ~ engine *159* Verbrennungsmotor
to **come,** ~ **across sth** *51* auf etw stoßen; ~ **along** *192T* vorbeikommen; ~ **down to sth** *18* auf etw hinauslaufen, auf etw ankommen; ~ **fourth** *14* Vierte/r werden; ~ **round** *30* vorbeikommen; ~ **up with sth** *51* sich etw ausdenken, sich etw einfallen lassen
comfort *197* Komfort, Trost, Hilfe
comfortable *62T* angenehm; to **feel ~** *22* sich wohlfühlen
command *209T* Befehl, Kommando; to ~ *131* beherrschen; to **be in ~** *80* das Kommando führen, die Befehle geben, das Sagen haben
commander *124* Kommandant/in, Anführer/in
commendable *161* vorbildlich
commerce *161* Handel
commercial *51* (Werbe-)Spot; *142* gewerblich, kommerziell; ~ **channel** *179* privater Fernsehsender; ~ **pressures** *pl* *178* wirtschaftliche Zwänge
commitment to sth *94* Engagement für etw, Einsatz für etw
committed (to) *193* engagiert (für)
committee *14* Komitee; *155* Ausschuss, Kommission, Komitee; **special ~** *167* Sonderausschuss
common *44* verbreitet, üblich
communication *208* Verständigung, Kommunikation
community *66* Gemeinde, Gemeinschaft; ~ **benefits** *pl* *143T* Zahlungen an die Gemeinde
to **commute** *137 (zur Arbeit)* pendeln
commuter *46* Pendler/in
companionship *90* Gemeinschaft, Gesellschaft
company, ~ **car** *65* Firmenwagen; **record ~** *8* Plattenfirma
to **compare** *9* vergleichen
comparison *21* Steigerung *(von Adjektiven)*
compass *159* Kompass
compensation *134* (finanzieller) Ausgleich
to **compete** *14 (bei einem Wettbewerb)* antreten
competition *8* Wettbewerb, Wettkampf; *46* Konkurrenz, Konkurrenzkampf
competitive *14* wettkampfmäßig; *21* konkurrenzfähig, *(Preise:)* günstig; *46* umkämpft, wettbewerbsintensiv
competitor *72* Konkurrent/in, Konkurrenz
to **compile** *77* erstellen, zusammenstellen
to **complain** *28* sich beschweren, sich beklagen
complaint *27* Beschwerde, Klage, Reklamation
completion *164* Ausführung, Erledigung (einer Aufgabe)
complex *102* komplex
to **complicate** *169* komplizieren
complicated *209T* kompliziert
complimentary close *76 (Brief:)* Schlussformel
component *100* Bauteil
to **compose** *46* komponieren
compost *156* Kompost
comprehensive school *163* Gesamtschule
computer-aided *100* computergestützt
to **concede** *129* eingestehen, einräumen
to **concentrate** *183* sich konzentrieren; ~ **on sth** *11T* sich auf etw konzentrieren
concentration *181* Konzentration
concept *46* Idee, Gedanke, Konzept
concern *69* Sorge, Befürchtung; **as far as I'm ~ed** *24* was mich betrifft; *78* von mir aus
to **conclude** *73* schließen, beenden; *174* abschließend
conclusion *38* Schlussfolgerung, Schluss; **in ~** *48* abschließend, zum Schluss
concrete *97* konkret; *143T* Beton
conditions, working ~ *pl* *65* Arbeitsbedingungen
conduct, to ~ **sth** *64* etw durchführen
conference *140* Konferenz; **press ~** *142* Pressekonferenz
confidence *94* Selbstvertrauen, Zuversicht
confident *146* (selbst)sicher
to **confirm** *32* bestätigen
confirmation *121* Bestätigung
to **confiscate** *163* beschlagnahmen, konfiszieren
conflict zone *126* Krisenregion, Konfliktzone
confused *182* verwirrt
to **congratulate sb on sth** *11* jdm zu etw gratulieren
congressman *110* Kongressabgeordneter
conjunction *190* Verbindung
connection *15* Verbindung
conscience *54* Gewissen
consequence *130* Folge, Konsequenz
to **consist of sth** *103* aus etw bestehen
consistent *190* gleichbleibend
constant *51* ständig, andauernd
to **construct** *101* bauen, errichten, konstruieren
construction, ~ **company** *116* Baufirma; ~ **worker** *65* Bauarbeiter/in
consultant, management ~ *65* Unternehmensberater/in
consultation *209* Arztbesuch, Beratung
consulting firm *161* Beratungsfirma
to **consume** *149* verbrauchen, konsumieren
consumer *19* Verbraucher/in, Konsument/in
consumption *149* Verbrauch, Konsum
contact *29* Kontakt, Verbindung; to ~ **sb** *38* sich mit jdm in Verbindung setzen; **(business) ~** *121* Ansprechpartner/in, Geschäftspartner/in; ~ **details** *pl* *31* Kontaktdaten
to **contain** *45* enthalten
container *155T* Behälter
to **contaminate** *156* verunreinigen, kontaminieren
contest *46* Wettbewerb
context *41* Zusammenhang, Kontext
continental *146* kontinental, zum (europäischen) Festland gehörig

to **continue to do sth** *52* etw weiterhin tun
continuity *70* Kontinuität, Fortdauer
continuous *190* kontinuierlich, anhaltend
contraceptive *159* Verhütungsmittel
contract *8* Vertrag; to ~ **(a disease)** *108* sich (mit einer Krankheit) anstecken/infizieren
contracted *59* zusammengezogen
to **contrast** *32* gegenüberstellen, vergleichen; **by** ~ *138* im Gegensatz dazu, dagegen
to **contribute** *196* beitragen
contribution *84* Beitrag; *96* (finanzielle) Zuwendung, Spende; to **make a** ~ *84* einen Beitrag leisten
contributor *110* Autor/in *(von Zeitschriftenartikeln)*
to **contrive** *131* bewerkstelligen
control, chemical ~ **(of pests)** *152* Schädlingsbekämpfung(smittel); **quality** ~ *120* Qualitätskontrolle; to **spiral out of** ~ *44* außer Kontrolle geraten
controversial *140* umstritten
convention *162* Übereinkunft, Gepflogenheit, Konvention
conventional *46* konventionell, herkömmlich
to **convince** *173* überzeugen
to **cook a meal** *49T* eine Mahlzeit zubereiten, ein Essen kochen
cooker, pressure ~ *124* Schnellkochtopf
cool down *17T* Abkühlen
cooperation *149* Zusammenarbeit, Zusammenwirken
cooperative *100* Genossenschaft
COPD *209T* chronisch obstruktive Lungenerkrankung
to **cope** *74* zurechtkommen; ~ **with sth** *40* etw bewältigen, mit etw klarkommen, mit etw fertig werden
copper *145* Kupfer
copy *24* Nachahmung, Imitat; *76* Ausgabe; *204T* Exemplar; to ~ *24* nachahmen, imitieren
corn *190* Getreide, *(AE)* Mais
corporate *69* Unternehmens-, von Unternehmen
correction *77* Korrekturlesen, Korrektur
corridor *120* Flur, Gang
to **corrode** *142* korrodieren, zersetzen
corrosion *141* Korrosion, Zersetzung
corrugated metal *156* Wellblech
corrupt *14* korrupt; *97* korrupt, bestechlich
cost, ~ **of living** *83* Lebenshaltungskosten; ~**-effective** *141* rentabel; **running** ~ *155* Betriebskosten
couch potato *196* Stubenhocker/in, Dauerglotzer/in
to **cough** *209T* husten
council *143T* (Stadt-, Gemeinde-)Rat
councillor *143T* Ratsmitglied
counsellor *38T* Berater/in
counter *81* Schalter, Theke
to **counteract sth** *69* einer Sache entgegenwirken
country, ~ **of origin** *187* Ursprungsland, Herkunftsland; **developing** ~ *194* Entwicklungsland
course *164* Weg, Vorgehensweise; ~ **of action** *87* Vorgehen, Maßnahmen; **golf** ~ *143T* Golfplatz
court *81* Gericht(shof)
courtroom *81* Gerichtssaal
cover *23* (Buch-)Umschlag, Einband; *24* Titelseite; to ~ *27* bedecken; ~ **letter** *66* Anschreiben, Begleitschreiben; **duvet** ~ *63* Bettdeckenbezug
co-worker *100* Kollege/-in
crack *140* Spalte; to ~ *203* aufbrechen, bersten
craft *79* Handwerk
crash *47* Schlag, Krach; to ~ *154* abstürzen, zusammenbrechen; **(car)** ~ *166T* Autounfall
crasher *40* ungeladener Gast
craze *16* Modewelle, Trend
to **create** *44* erstellen; *46* (er)schaffen, entwerfen, kreieren
creativity *65* schöpferische Begabung, Kreativität
creator *65* Schöpfer/in
creature *203* Geschöpf, (Lebe-)Wesen
crèche *185* Krippe
credit *156* Verdienst; ~ **rating** *62T* (Bewertung/Einstufung der) Bonität, Kreditwürdigkeit
crime, ~ **detection** *132* Aufdecken von Straftaten; **high** ~ *136* Schwerverbrechen
criminal justice *124* Strafjustiz
crippling *156* lähmend, mörderisch
crisis *68T* Krise
crisps *pl BE* *197* Kartoffelchips
critic *175* Kritiker/in
critical *175* kritisch
criticism (of sb/sth) *24* Kritik (an jdm/etw)
to **criticize** *9* kritisieren
crop *152* Ernte; *148* Nutzpflanze, Feldfrucht; ~ **production** *148* Pflanzenproduktion, pflanzliche Erzeugung
cropland *148* Ackerland
cross *125* Kreuz; to ~ *69* überqueren, überwinden
crossroads *164* Scheideweg
crowded *21* voll *(mit Leuten)*, überfüllt
cruel *38T* grausam, gemein
crunch *170* Sit-up
to **cry one's eyes out** *11* wie ein Schlosshund heulen
cuisine *79* Küche, Kochkunst
cult *6* Kult
to **cultivate** *157* bewirtschaften
cultural *69* kulturell, kulturbezogen
Cup, World ~ *13* Weltpokal
cupboard *83* Schrank
cure *83* Heilung, Therapie; to ~ *209* heilen
curfew *27* Sperrstunde
current *10* aktuell
currently *76* zur Zeit
curriculum *183* Lehrplan
customer services advisor *68T* Kundenberater/in
to **customize** *174* auf den Kundenbedarf zuschneiden
customs *pl* *144* Zoll; **border** ~ **officer** *161* (Grenz-)Zollbeamte/r
to **cut** *149* reduzieren, einschränken; ~ **costs** *107T* Kosten senken; ~ **sb off from sth** *36* jdn von etw abschneiden; ~ **a long story short** *60* lange Rede, kurzer Sinn
cute *204T* süß
cutlery *168* Besteck
cutting-edge *160* Spitzen-, auf dem neusten Stand
CV (curriculum vitae) *66* Lebenslauf
cybercrime *130* Cyberkriminalität
cycle, to ~ **on** *14* weiterradeln; **fertility** ~ *160* Fruchtbarkeitszyklus
cyclist *14* Radfahrer/in; **racing** ~ *14* Radrennfahrer/in
cyclone *137* Wirbelsturm, Zyklon, Sturmtief

D

damage *40* Schaden; to ~ *40* beschädigen; **property** ~ *166T* Sachschaden, Sachschäden
dance routine *17T* Tanzschritte
dancer *65* Tänzer/in
danger *40* Gefahr
darkness *131* Dunkelheit
data protection *123* Datenschutz
dawn *150* Morgendämmerung
day, at the end of the ~ *57* letzten Endes, unterm Strich; ~ **centre** *90* Tagesstätte; ~ **off** *193* freier Tag, Urlaubstag; ~ **out** *193* Tagesausflug; ~**-to-**~ *56* tagtäglich; **these** ~**s** *56* zur Zeit
day care facility *183T* Tageseinrichtung
to **deactivate** *39* stilllegen, deaktivieren
dead, to **be left for** ~ *109* als tot zurückgelassen werden
deadline *100* Frist, Termin; to **meet a** ~ *112* eine Frist / einen Termin einhalten
deadly *108* tödlich
deal *50* Geschäft, Abschluss; *81* Abmachung; to ~ **with sth** *41* mit etw zurechtkommen, mit etw umgehen; *87* mit etw zu tun haben; **a great** ~ *94* eine erhebliche Menge
dealer *144* Händler/in
death *81* Tod
debate *23* Diskussion, Debatte
debt *156* Schulden
decade *14* Jahrzehnt; **throughout the** ~**s** *14* durch/über die Jahrzehnte
to **declare** *134* verkünden
decline *106* Rückgang; to ~ *106* zurückgehen, fallen, sinken
decorator *209T* Dekorateur/in, Raumausstatter/in

decrease *106* Abnahme, Rückgang; to ~ *106* abnehmen, zurückgehen
deep *47* tief
default, by ~ *69* automatisch
defeat *129* Niederlage
to **defend** *128* verteidigen
to **define** *6* definieren
definitely *34* absolut, ganz sicher
deforestation *202* Waldzerstörung
degree *110* Abschluss; *136* Grad
delay *105* Verzögerung
to **delete** *38T* löschen, tilgen
deletion *39* Löschung, Tilgung
delight *118* Vergnügen, Freude
delivery *129* Lieferung
demand *105* Nachfrage; to ~ *148* nachfragen, verlangen; to **meet a ~** *105* eine Nachfrage befriedigen
demanding *185* anstrengend, anspruchsvoll
dementia *118* Demenz
democracy *101* Demokratie
democratic *132* demokratisch
denier *136* Leugner/in
department *34* Abteilung; **D~ for Work and Pensions** *60* brit. Arbeits- und Sozialministerium; **legal ~** *69* juristische Abteilung
to **depend on sth** *156* von etw abhängen, auf etw angewiesen sein
dependable *44* zuverlässig, verlässlich
dependence *123* Abhängigkeit
dependent on sth *36* von etw abhängig
depending on *20* je nach(dem)
to **deport** *84* abschieben
deportation *86* Abschiebung
depressed *100* *(Wirtschaft:)* flau, am Boden
depression *197* Depression(en)
depth *168* *(räumliche)* Tiefe
deputy manager *46* stellvertretende/r Geschäftsführer/in
descendant *84* Nachfahre, Nachkomme
desert *124* Wüste
to **deserve** *6* verdienen
design, to ~ *11T* entwerfen, gestalten; *65* konstruieren, planen; **by laboratory ~** *152* im Labor geplant
designed, to **be ~ to do sth** *49T* dazu gedacht sein, etw zu tun; darauf ausgelegt sein, etw zu tun
designer *65* Gestalter/in, Designer/in, Konstrukteur/in; **fashion ~** *11T* Modeschöpfer/in
desire *190* Wunsch, Verlangen
desperate *38T* verzweifelt
despite *94* trotz
to **destroy** *95* zerstören
destruction *150* Zerstörung
destructive *124* zerstörerisch
details *pl* *40* Angaben; **contact ~** *pl* *31* Kontaktdaten
detection, crime ~ *132* Aufdecken von Straftaten
detention centre *81* Auffanglager, Haftanstalt

to **deter** *156* abschrecken, abhalten
devastating *125* verheerend
developer, IT ~ *161* IT-Entwickler/in
developing country *194* Entwicklungsland
development *69* Entwicklung; *106* *(Immobilie:)* Erschließung, Bau; **Research and D~ (R&D)** *120* Forschung(s-) und Entwicklung (sabteilung)
device, explosive ~ *125* Sprengsatz; **tracking ~** *144* Ortungsgerät
to **devote** *165* widmen
to **diagnose sb with sth** *43* etw *(Krankheit)* bei jdm feststellen/ diagnostizieren
diagnosed, sb is ~ with ... *74* bei jdm wird ... festgestellt, diagnostiziert
diagnosis, *pl* **diagnoses** *160* Diagnose, Diagnosen
diamond-shaped *154* rautenförmig
diarrhoea *108* Durchfall
diet *148* Ernährung, Kost; to ~ *197* Diät halten
dietary *122* Ernährungs-
difference, to **make a ~** *90* etw bewirken; to **make the ~** *49T* entscheidend sein, den entscheidenden Unterschied ausmachen
digit *33* Ziffer
digital signage *45* digitale Außenwerbung
dignity *206* Würde
dinosaur *202* Dinosaurier
dioxide, carbon ~ *136* Kohlendioxid; **carbon ~ level** *136* Kohlendioxidkonzentration, -gehalt
directions *pl* *119* Wegbeschreibung; to **give ~** *119* den Weg beschreiben
director, finance ~ *72* kaufmännische/r Leiter/in
directory *52* Telefonbuch
dirt *146* Schmutz, Dreck
dirty *9* schmutzig
disability *13* Behinderung
disabled *92* behindert; **~ facilities** *pl* *122* behindertengerechte Toiletten
disadvantaged *90* benachteiligt
to **disagree with sth** *23* einer Sache nicht zustimmen, gegen etw sein, etw ablehnen
disaster *62T* Katastrophe
disastrous *137* katastrophal, verheerend
discipline *169* Disziplin
to **disclose** *132* offenlegen
discord *161* Zwietracht
discount *21* Rabatt, Nachlass; **~ label** *21* Billigmarke
to **discover** *51* entdecken
to **discriminate against** *193* diskriminieren
discussion *187T* Diskussion, Besprechung
disease *97* Krankheit; **infectious ~** *108* Infektionskrankheit
disgust, in ~ *81* angewidert

disheartened *205* entmutigt, niedergeschlagen
dishwasher *168* Spülmaschine; to **load the ~** *168* die Spülmaschine einräumen
to **dismiss sth as sth** *164* etw als etw abtun
disorder *201T* (Funktions-)Störung *(Krankheit)*
display *46* Bildschirm, Anzeige, Display; *79* Vorführung; to ~ *19* zeigen
disposal *202* Entsorgung
to **distribute** *174* verteilen, austeilen
district *145* Bezirk
diverse *206* unterschiedlich, vielfältig
diversity *156* Vielfalt
to **divide** *27* teilen
divorce *151* Scheidung
DIY (do-it-yourself) *66* Heimwerker-, Heimwerken
documentary *204T* Dokumentarfilm, Dokumentarsendung
dodo *203* Dodo *(ausgestorbene Vogelart)*
doer *65* Macher/in
do-good *46* weltverbessernd
dole *111* Arbeitslosengeld; **~ bludger** *111* Sozialschmarotzer
dome *155* Kuppel
domestic *167* heimisch, Inlands-; **gross ~ product (GDP)** *92* Bruttosozialprodukt
to **dominate** *124* beherrschen, dominieren
to **donate** *49T* spenden
donation *89* Spende
donor *90* Spender/in
door, next ~ *41* nebenan
doorbell, to **ring the ~** *13* *(an der Tür)* klingeln, läuten
dope *49T* Depp; to ~ *14* dopen
to **double** *196* (sich) verdoppeln
down, ~ the line *81* weiter; to **get ~ to business** *174* zur Sache kommen
to **download** *21* herunterladen
Down's syndrome *199* Down-Syndrom
downside *152* Nachteil
to **downsize** *70* verkleinern, gesundschrumpfen
downwards *53* fallend
dozen *146* Dutzend
to **drag** *80* zerren
dragon *79* Drachen
drama *57* Schauspiel; **~ club** *59* Schauspiel-AG
dramatic(ally) *160* dramatisch
to **draw** *26* zeichnen; *73* ziehen; **~ attention to sb/sth** *24* Aufmerksamkeit auf jdn/etw ziehen; **~ up** *43* *(Text)* verfassen, abfassen
drawing *26* Zeichnung
to **dress down** *70* sich leger kleiden
dressed, to **get ~** *182* sich anziehen
to **drift** *156* wehen
to **drill** *140* bohren
drilling *143T* Bohrung(en); **~ rig** *143T* Bohrturm
drinker *54* Trinker/in

drinking water *54* Trinkwasser
to **drive sb away** *60* jdn vertreiben
driverless *164* führerlos
driving, ~ force *69* treibende Kraft; **~ licence** *48F* Führerschein
drone, airborne ~ *168* Flugdrohne
to **drop** *54* fallen; *60* schlechter werden *(Noten)*; **~ in** *70* vorbeikommen, hereinschauen; **~ one's eyes** *81* den Blick senken; **~ one's voice** *80* die Stimme senken; **~ sb off** *40* jdn (wohin)bringen
drought *147* Dürre
to **drown** *137* ertrinken, im Meer versinken
drums *pl* *43* Schlagzeug
drunk, to **get ~** *41* sich betrinken
drunken *40* betrunken
to **dry out** *172* austrocknen
dubious *144* zweifelhaft
duck *190* Ente
due, … is ~ to do sth *134* … soll/wird etw tun; to **be ~** *121 (Flugzeug etc.:)* planmäßig ankommen
dump *145* Müllhalde; to **~** *144 (Müll)* (wild) abladen
duration *66* Dauer
during *158* während
dustman *BE* *203* Müllwerker/in, Müllmann/-frau
duty *75* Aufgabe, Pflicht, Arbeit; *168* Aufgabe, Pflicht
duvet cover *63* Bettdeckenbezug
to **dwell on sth** *43* sich mit etw aufhalten

E

e.g. *33* z. B.
eager *88* bestrebt, darauf aus
earnings *pl* *83* Einkünfte, Verdienst; *143T* Einnahmen, Gewinn
earthquake *96T* Erdbeben
ease, at ~ *118* zwanglos, unverkrampft
easterly *146* Ost-, östlich
to **echo** *118* (wider)hallen, nachklingen
eco- *46* Öko-
economic *65* wirtschaftlich
economics *137* Ökonomie, Wirtschaft(swissenschaft)
economist *196* Wirtschaftswissenschaftler/in
economy *86T* Wirtschaft
ecosystem *148* Ökosystem
to **edge,** to **be edging above freezing** *146* knapp über dem Gefrierpunkt anzeigen
to **edit** *113 (Text)* redigieren, bearbeiten
edition *111* Ausgabe
editor *110* Herausgeber/in; *142* Redakteur/in
educational *77* schulisch, Bildungs-
effect *47* Wirkung, Effekt
effective *46* wirksam, effektiv
efficient(ly) *62T* effizient
effort, to **make an ~** *176* sich Mühe geben

either *164* eine/r/s (von beiden); **~ … or** *24* entweder … oder; **not … ~** *84* auch nicht
elderly *109* älter; Senioren; **home for the ~** *114* Altenheim
election *161* Wahl
electrical *66* elektrisch, Elektro-; **~ engineering** *169* Elektrotechnik
electrician *49* Elektriker/in
electricity bill *143* Stromrechnung
electronic *100* elektronisch, Elektronik-
electronics *pl* *69* Elektronik
element *45* Baustein, Element
to **eliminate** *208* eliminieren, beseitigen
elsewhere *67* woanders, anderswo
email, to **~ sb** *66* jdm eine E-Mail schicken; **~ exchange** *171* E-Mail-Korrespondenz
embarrassed, to **feel ~** *59* sich genieren, sich schämen
embarrassing *44* peinlich; *129* peinlich, unangenehm
embassy *94* Botschaft
emergency *109* Notfall, Not-; **accident and ~ department (A&E)** *167* Notaufnahme; **~ exit** *120* Notausgang, Fluchtweg; **~ exit plan** *120* Fluchtwegplan; **~ plan** *74* Notfallplan; **~ service** *167* Notfalldienst
to **emigrate** *86* auswandern
emission *137* Ausstoß, Emission
emotion *45* Gefühl, Emotion
emotional *18* gefühlsmäßig, emotional
to **employ** *186* beschäftigen, einstellen *(Personal)*; **~ sb** *71* jdn beschäftigen, jdn einstellen
employee *69* Angestellte/r, Beschäftigte/r
employer *44* Arbeitgeber/in; *66* Arbeitgeber
employment *100* Anstellung, Arbeit
to **empower sb to do sth** *90* jdn befähigen, etw zu tun
to **enable** *90* befähigen
enabled *160* fähig
enclosure (encl.) *76 (Brief:)* Anlage
to **encourage** *137* fördern; **~ sb to do sth** *46* jdn ermuntern, etw zu tun
encrypted *129* verschlüsselt
end, to **~ up** *41* landen; **at the ~ of the day** *57* letzten Endes, unterm Strich; to **put an ~ to sth** *27* mit etw Schluss machen, einen Schlussstrich unter etw ziehen
ending *14* Schluss, Ende
endless *110* endlos, fortwährend
enemy *80* Feind/in
energy *16* Energie; **~-saving light bulb** *194* Energiesparlampe
enforcement, law ~ *124* Gesetzesvollzug, Innere Sicherheit, Exekutive; **law ~ agency** *124* Strafverfolgungsbehörde, Exekutivorgan
engage, to **~ in sth** *124* für etw aktiv werden; to **~ with sb** *37* auf jdn zugehen

engaged *34 (Telefon:)* besetzt
engine *85* Motor
engineer *65* Ingenieur/in
engineering, electrical ~ *169* Elektrotechnik; **mechanical ~** *169* Maschinenbau; **social ~** *114* Änderung gesellschaftlicher Strukturen, angewandte Sozialwissenschaft
English-speaking *76* englischsprachig
to **enjoy oneself** *166* sich (gut) amüsieren
to **enlighten** *65* aufklären
to **enquire about sth** *34* sich nach etw erkundigen
to **enroll** *146 (an einer Schule o.ä.)* anmelden; **~ing the help of …** *158* mithilfe von …
to **ensure** *73* sicherstellen; dafür sorgen, dass
to **enter, ~ a competition** *14* an einem Wettkampf/Wettbewerb teilnehmen; **~ sth** *46* an etw teilnehmen
enterprise *94* Unternehmen
enterprising *65* geschäftstüchtig, risikofreudig
entertainment *45* Unterhaltung; **in-car ~** *167* Unterhaltungselektronik im Auto
enthusiastic about sth *169* von etw begeistert
enthusiastically *140* begeistert
entire *196* ganz, vollständig
entirely *127* völlig, ganz
entrance fee *22* Teilnahmegebühr
entrepreneur *51* Unternehmer/in
entry *38 (Blog:)* Beitrag, Meldung; **~ level** *68* Einstieg, Anfang; **~-level** *110* Einstiegs-; **~ level pay** *68T* Einstiegsgehalt, Anfangsgehalt
environmental *46* umweltmäßig, Umwelt-; **~ protection** *54* Umweltschutz
environmentally friendly *46* umweltfreundlich
epidemic *161* Epidemie, Seuche
epileptic fit *209T* epileptischer Anfall
epitaph *39* Grabinschrift
equal, ~ opportunities *pl* *66* Chancengleichheit; **~ society** *115* gerechte Gesellschaft
equality *67* Gleichheit
equally *80* gleichermaßen, genauso
equals *150* gleich
equipment *66* Ausrüstung, Geräte
equipped, ~ with *122* ausgestattet mit; **fully ~** *66* vollausgestattet
equivalent *67* Entsprechung; to **be ~ to sth** *75* einer Sache entsprechen
eradication *164* Ausrottung
to **erode** *157* erodieren
error, human ~ *166T* menschliches Versagen
escalator *46* Rolltreppe
escape, to **~** *136* entweichen; to **~ from sth** *86* einer Sache entkommen; to **~ sth narrowly** *94* einer Sache knapp entkommen; **there's no ~ from the fact that** *117T* man kann nicht außer

Acht lassen, dass; man muss der Tatsache ins Auge sehen, dass
to **escort sb** *27* jdn begleiten, jdn eskortieren
especially *29* besonders, insbesondere
essential *40* wesentlich, unerlässlich
essentially *124* im Wesentlichen
essentials *pl 94* lebensnotwendige Güter
to **establish** *205* etablieren, aufbauen, festigen
estimate *144* Schätzung; to ~ *27* schätzen
ethical *54* ethisch, (moralisch) verantwortlich
ethnic *84* ethnisch, Volks-
ethnicity *206* Ethnizität, Volkszugehörigkeit
etiquette *32* Etikette, Regeln
to **evaluate** *65* bewerten, beurteilen
even, ~ so *102* dennoch, allerdings; **~ though** *22* selbst wenn, obwohl; **not ~** *158* nicht einmal
event *7* Veranstaltung, Ereignis
ever-improving *69* stetig besser werdend
everyday *51* alltäglich, Alltags-
evidence *132* Beweise, Beweismittel
evil *81* böse, schlecht
evolution *14* Entwicklung
examination *209T* Untersuchung
to **examine** *118* untersuchen, prüfen
example, to **set an ~** *56* ein Beispiel setzen, mit gutem Beispiel vorangehen
to **exceed** *36* übersteigen; *121* überschreiten
excellent *83* ausgezeichnet, hervorragend
excerpt *202* Auszug, Ausschnitt
exchange, to **~** *29* austauschen; **email ~** *171* E-Mail-Korrespondenz
excitement *17* Begeisterung; *45* Spannung, Aufregung
exemption *27* Ausnahme, Befreiung
exhausted *118* erschöpft
to **exhibit** *120* ausstellen
exhibition *81* Ausstellung
existing *137* bestehend, vorhanden
exit, to **~** *108* verlassen; **emergency ~** *120* Notausgang, Fluchtweg; **emergency ~ plan** *120* Fluchtwegplan
to **expand** *43* erweitern; *100* expandieren, ausweiten
expansion *101* Ausweitung, Expansion
to **expect** *118* erwarten, annehmen
expectation *88* Erwartung
expense *156* Kosten, Aufwand; **at the ~ of sth** *37* auf Kosten von etw
expenses, travel ~ *pl 66* Reisekosten, Fahrtkosten
experience, work ~ *31* Praktikum
experienced *62T* erfahren
to **experiment** *24* experimentieren
explanation *87* Erläuterung, Erklärung
to **explode** *124* explodieren
exploitation *147* Ausbeutung, Abbau *(von Rohstoffen)*
explosive *125* Sprengstoff; **~ device** *125* Sprengsatz
export *100* Ausfuhr, Export; to ~ *102* ausführen, exportieren
exporter *144* Exporteur/in
expression *11* Ausdruck
to **extend** *183* erweitern, ausdehnen
extended *55* erweitert; **~ family** *55* Großfamilie
extension *124* Erweiterung, Ausbau
extinct, to **become ~** *152* aussterben
extinction *164* Vernichtung, Ausrottung, Aussterben
to **extort** *161* erpressen, abnötigen
extract *131* Auszug, Ausschnitt
extra-curricular *183* außerschulisch
extremely *108* äußerst, außerordentlich
extremism *123* Extremismus
eyelid, to **bat an ~** *14* mit der Wimper zucken

F

face, to **~ sb** *82* jdn konfrontieren; to **~ sth** *11* sich einer Sache stellen; *107T* mit etw konfrontiert werden, sich einer Sache gegenüber sehen; **~-lift** *6* Facelifting, Gesichtsstraffung
faced, to **be ~ with** *108* konfrontiert werden mit
face-to-face *29* persönlich; *209* im persönlichen Gespräch
facilities *pl 100* Anlage(n), Einrichtungen; **disabled ~** *pl 122* behindertengerechte Toiletten
facing sth *80* gegen etw, mit dem Gesicht zu etw
fact, in ~ *23* um genau zu sein, eigentlich; **there's no escape from the ~ that** *117T* man kann nicht außer Acht lassen, dass; man muss der Tatsache ins Auge sehen, dass
factor *49* Faktor
faculty *168* Fähigkeit
to **fail** *155T* ausfallen; *160* versagen
failure *166T* Ausfall, Defekt; *205* Versagen, Ausfall, Zusammenbruch
fair, trade ~ *120* Handelsmesse, Fachmesse
fake *24* Fälschung, Imitation
fall *106* Absturz, Rückgang; to **~ behind** *62* zurückfallen, in Rückstand geraten; to **~ in love with sb/sth** *86* sich in jdn/etw verlieben
false start *62* Fehlstart
fame *10* Ruhm
family, extended ~ *55* Großfamilie
famine *147* Hungersnot
far, as ~ as I'm concerned *24* was mich betrifft; *78* von mir aus; **so ~** *96T* bislang
fare *146* Kost
to **farm** *101* *(Land)* bewirtschaften
farm, ~ chemicals *pl 149* Landwirtschaftschemikalien; **wind ~** *141* Windpark
farming *97* Landwirtschaft
farmland *143T* Ackerland, landwirtschaftliche Nutzfläche
farther *144* weiter
fascinating *49T* faszinierend
fascination *45* Faszination
fascist *189* faschistisch
fashion designer *11T* Modeschöpfer/in
fashionable *18* modisch
fatality *95* Todesfall, Todesopfer
fatigued *209T* erschöpft, ermüdet
faulty *105* defekt, fehlerhaft
favor, in ~ of doing sth *AE 46* um (stattdessen) etw zu tun
favour, to **be in ~ of sth** *126T* für etw sein
fear *80* Angst; to ~ *152* fürchten
fearful *183T* ängstlich
feature *58* Hintergrundbericht, Reportage; *152* Merkmal, Eigenschaft
federal *134* Bundes-, auf Bundesebene geltend
fee *22* Gebühr; **entrance ~** *22* Teilnahmegebühr
feed *160* Futter; to ~ *90* ernähren, mit Nahrung versorgen
feedback *93* Reaktion(en), Rückmeldung(en)
to **feel, ~ comfortable** *22* sich wohlfühlen; **~ embarrassed** *59* sich genieren, sich schämen; **~ left out** *60* sich ausgeschlossen fühlen; **~ low** *17T* schlecht gelaunt sein, deprimiert sein; **~ sorry for sb** *92* jd tut einem leid; **~ sth** *51* etw anfassen, etw ertasten; **~ uncomfortable** *8* sich unbehaglich fühlen
fence *189* Zaun
fertility cycle *160* Fruchtbarkeitszyklus
to **fertilize** *152* befruchten
fertilizer *149* Dünger, Düngemittel
festival *79* Fest, Festtag, Festival
fetus *AE* (*BE* **foetus)** *208* Fötus
fever *108* Fieber
fictional *131* fiktiv
fiddly *168* knifflig, fummelig
field of vision *131* Sichtfeld
fierce *46* heftig, erbittert
to **fight back** *107T* sich wehren, sich zurückkämpfen
figure *52* Zahl, Ziffer
to **figure out** *168* herausfinden
file *71* Akte, Ordner; to ~ *81* feilen
filing cabinet *69* Aktenschrank
to **fill an order** *100* einen Auftrag ausführen
to **filter out** *208* ausfiltern
final *43* Finale
finally *175* schließlich, zum Schluss
finance *69* Finanz(-); to ~ *91* finanzieren; **~ director** *72* kaufmännische/r Leiter/in
financial *56* finanziell, Finanz-
to **find, ~ one's way around** *120* sich zurechtfinden; **~ sb sth** *60* jdm etw besorgen

findings *pl 43* Ergebnisse
fine *48F* Geldbuße; to **~ sb** *48F* jdn mit einer Geldbuße belegen
fingernail *24* Fingernagel
to **finish second** *8* Zweite/r werden
finished product *100* Endprodukt
finishing line *124* Ziellinie
fire, to **~ sb** *49T* jdn feuern; **on ~** *143T* in Flammen; to **set ~ to sth** *145* etw anzünden
firefight *124* Schusswechsel
first, at ~ hand *31* aus erster Hand, hautnah; **~ name** *17* Vorname; **~ of all** *62T* zuallererst
fishing *154* Fischerei, Befischung; **~ village** *94* Fischerdorf
fit, to **~** *16* passen; to **~ sth with sth** *144* etw mit etw ausstatten; **epileptic ~** *209T* epileptischer Anfall
fixed *70* fest, festgelegt, fest installiert
flap *23* Umschlagklappe
flat *107T (Umsatz etc.:)* konstant, unverändert
flaxen-haired *169* strohblond, flachsblond
fledgling *146* in den Kinderschuhen steckend, neu erwacht
flexible *65* flexibel
to **float** *153 (auf dem Wasser)* treiben
to **flock** *188* strömen
flood *95* Überschwemmung; to **~** *138* überschwemmen
flooding *137* Überschwemmung
floor care *104* Bodenpflege
flow *153* Strom, Fluss
flu *108* Grippe; **swine ~** *108* Schweinegrippe
fluent *75 (Sprache:)* fließend
flute, lung ~ *209 Atemphysiotherapiegerät zur Verbesserung der Lungenfunktion bei COPD*
foam, insulating ~ *145* Isolierschaum
focus *174* Schwerpunkt; to **~ on sth** *11* sich auf etw konzentrieren
folks *pl 100* Leute
follow-up *8* Folge-, Nachfolger
food, ~ allergy *208* Lebensmittelallergie; **~ bank** *205* Tafel; **~ miles** *pl 193* Transportwege der Nahrungsmittel; **~ pantry** *AE 151* Tafel, karitative Essensausgabe; **~ security** *155T* Ernährungssicherung; **~ stall** *188* Imbissstand; **processed ~** *197* verarbeitete Lebensmittel
foot, *pl* **feet (ft)** *146* Fuß *(Längenmaß, entspricht 30,5 cm)*
footage *132* Film-/Bildmaterial
footballer *11* Fußballer/in
to **forbid** *144* verbieten, untersagen
force *95* Gewalt, Kraft; to **~** *80* zwingen; **driving ~** *69* treibende Kraft; **police ~** *127* Polizei
forces, armed ~ *pl 126T* Streitkräfte; **security ~** *pl 126T* Sicherheitskräfte
forehead *80* Stirn
forest *146* Wald
forested *156* bewaldet

forklift (truck) *116* Gabelstapler
to **form** *48* bilden
formula *7* Formel
fortune *7* Vermögen
forward, to **look ~ to sth** *9* sich auf etw freuen
forwarding agency *145* Spedition
fossil fuel *135* fossiler Brennstoff
to **found** *94* gründen
foundation *90* Stiftung
founder *114* Gründer/in
to **fracture** *140* brechen, aufbrechen
frame *155* Rahmen
freedom *56* Freiheit
freely *139* ungehindert, nach Belieben
freeway *AE 166T* Autobahn
to **freeze** *175* einfrieren
freezing, to **be edging above ~** *146* knapp über dem Gefrierpunkt anzeigen
fresh water *149* Süßwasser
fridge *144* Kühlschrank
fries, (French) ~ *pl AE 62T* Pommes frites
frightening *209T* beängstigend
fuel *117* Brennstoff; **fossil ~** *135* fossiler Brennstoff
to **fulfil** *11* erfüllen
full-time *66* Vollzeit-
fully *38T* vollkommen, völlig; *66* vollständig; **~ equipped** *66* vollausgestattet
fun, to **be ~** *47* Spaß machen
function *51* Funktion; to **~** *160* fungieren, funktionieren
functionality *208* Funktionalität
to **fund** *92* finanzieren
fundamental *205* wesentlich, grundsätzlich
funding *92* Finanzierung, Geldmittel
fundraiser *43* Spendensammler/in
fundraising *43* Spendensammeln, Geldbeschaffung
furnace *202* (Industrie-)Ofen, Hochofen
further *8* weitere/r/s; to **take sth ~** *32* etw (weiter) verfolgen
furthermore *117* darüber hinaus
fuss, to **make a ~** *88* sich anstellen, Umstände machen

G

gadget *170* Gerät, technischer Krimskrams
gain *65* Gewinn, Vorteil; to **~** *78* erwerben; to **~ weight** *196* zunehmen
gallery *35* Galerie; **~ walk** *35* Galerierundgang
gallon *166T* Gallone *(= 3,78 l in den USA)*
game, ~ machine *46* Videospielgerät, Spielautomat; **rules** *pl* **of the game** *13* Spielregeln
gang *84* Bande
gap *18* Lücke; **~ year** *190 das Jahr zwischen Schulabgang und Studienbeginn*
gardening *93* Gartenarbeit

garment *150* Kleidungsstück
gas, laughing ~ *40* Lachgas; **natural ~** *138* Erdgas
to **gatecrash** *40* uneingeladen erscheinen
to **gather** *164* sammeln, zusammentragen
gay *88* schwul, lesbisch
to **gaze** *131* starren, blicken
gear *22* Ausrüstung, Kleidung; **sports ~** *22* Sportkleidung, Sportausrüstung
gender *88* Geschlecht
gene *152* Gen
general *165* General; **in ~** *15* im Allgemeinen, generell
to **generate** *208* erzeugen, generieren
generation *74* Generation
generosity *206* Großzügigkeit
genetic *152* genetisch
genius *51* Genie
geothermal power *135* Erdwärme
germ *146* Keim, Bakterie
to **get, ~ on** *61* vorwärtskommen, zurechtkommen; **~ over sth** *61* über etw hinwegkommen, etw verkraften; **~ sth** *26* etw verstehen, etw kapieren; **~ up** *182* aufstehen
giant *49T* Riese; *46* riesig, riesenhaft
gig *7 (Rock-, Pop-, Jazz-)*Konzert
ginger *190* Ingwer
gist *71* das Wesentliche
to **give, ~ a presentation** *48* ein Referat halten; **~ a reason** *23* eine Begründung anführen; **~ an opinion** *23* eine Meinung äußern; **~ birth** *88* gebären, entbinden; **~ sth a try** *17T* etw ausprobieren; **~ to charity** *92* (für wohltätige Zwecke) spenden
given name *80* Vorname
giving *92* Spenden
global *70* weltweit, global; **~ issue** *195* globales Problem; **~ warming** *136* Erderwärmung
globalization *100* Globalisierung
globe *108* Globus
glossy *24* Hochglanz-
glucose tab *208* Traubenzuckertablette
GM (genetically modified) *152* genmanipuliert
go, to **~ for sth** *18* etw nehmen, etw gut finden; *168* etw wählen, etw wagen; to **~ under** *56* Pleite gehen; to **~ with sth** *8* zu etw gehören; **What's ~ing on?** *22* Was ist los?
goal *46* Ziel, Absicht; *82 (Ballspiel:)* Tor
goat *190* Ziege
gold medallist *209T* Goldmedaillengewinner/in
golf course *143T* Golfplatz
good, (the) ~ *91* Wohl; **~ looking** *8* gutaussehend, attraktiv
Thank goodness! *22* Gott sei Dank!
goods *pl 19* Waren, Güter; **branded ~** *pl 53* Markenware, Markenartikel
gossip *173* Klatsch, Tratsch; to **~** *57* tratschen, schwatzen

to **govern** *101* regieren, verwalten, führen
governance *161* Regierungshandeln
government *47* Regierung, öffentliche Verwaltung
to **grab sth** *69* sich etw schnappen
gracefully *64* würdevoll
grade *AE* *60* Note; **G~ 1 building** *155* denkmalgeschütztes Gebäude; **A student** *60* Einserschüler/in
gradual *69* schrittweise, allmählich
graduate *110* Absolvent/in
graduation *112* (Schul-/Universitäts-) Abschluss
grain *149* Getreide
grandfather clock *118* Standuhr
granny *118* Oma
to **grant** *189* gewähren, einräumen; **~ sb sth** *76* jdm etw gewähren
graph *52* Diagramm, Kurve; **line ~** *92* Liniendiagramm
graphic *151* Grafik
grasp *168* Griff; to **~** *168* greifen, ergreifen
grass *57* Rasen, Gras
grassy *202* grasbewachsen
grateful *88* dankbar
graveyard *145* Friedhof
to **gravitate to sth** *70* von etw angezogen werden
great-grandfather *83* Urgroßvater
greatly *149* erheblich
to **green** *156* begrünen
greenhouse *190* Treibhaus
greenhouse gas *136* Treibhausgas
grin, with a ~ *181* grinsend
gross domestic product (GDP) *92* Bruttosozialprodukt
ground *47* (Erd-)Boden; **breeding ~** *145* Brutplatz; to **break new ~** *199* (sich) Neuland erschließen
groundwater *143T* Grundwasser
group, peer ~ *55* Altersgruppe, Bezugsgruppe, Umfeld; **target ~** *53* Zielgruppe
to **grow** *99* *(Pflanze)* anbauen; **~ up** *20* aufwachsen
grower *190* Anbauer/in
growth *17* Wachstum; *100* Wachstum, Zunahme
guardian, legal ~ *27* Vormund, Erziehungsberechtigte/r
guesswork *131* Mutmaßung, Spekulation
to **guide** *114* führen
guide dog *209T* Blindenhund
guilty *125* schuldig
to **gut** *145* ausweiden, ausschlachten
guts, to **have the ~ to do sth** *84* den Mumm haben, etw zu tun
guy *14* Typ, Kerl
guys, you ~ *22* ihr
gym *13* Fitness-Studio

H

habit *36* Gewohnheit; to **get into the ~ of doing sth** *32* sich angewöhnen, etw zu tun
habitat *204T* natürlicher Lebensraum
hair care *49T* Haarpflege
hairdresser *184* Friseur/in
hairdressing salon *49* Friseursalon
hall *155* Saal, Halle
hallucination *14* Halluzination, Wahnvorstellung
hand *209T* Zeiger; to **~ over** *48* übergeben; to **~ sth in** *37* etw abgeben; to **~ sth out** *94* etw verteilen, etw ausgeben; **at first ~** *31* aus erster Hand, hautnah; **on the one ~** *23* einerseits
handful *146* Handvoll
hand-held *48* in der Hand gehalten
to **handle sth** *178* mit etw umgehen
handout *90* Almosen; *172* Arbeitsblatt
handwriting *37* Handschrift
handy *128* praktisch
hang, to **~ out** *25* rumhängen, sich rumtreiben; to **get the ~ of it** *17* den richtigen Dreh finden
to **happen to do sth** *204T* etw zufällig tun
happiness *158* Glück, Zufriedenheit
harbour *113* Hafen
hard, to **have a ~ time** *56* es schwer haben
harm, to **~ sb** *128* jdm schaden; to **do sb ~** *40* jdm etwas (an)tun
harmony *84* Harmonie
harvest *160* Ernte; to **~** *155* ernten
head *104* Leiter/in, Chef/in; **H~ of Science** *139* Fachbereichsleiter/in Naturwissenschaft; **H~ Office** *50* Zentrale, Direktion, Hauptverwaltung; to **shake one's ~** *81* den Kopf schütteln
headache *209T* Kopfschmerzen
heading *15* Rubrik, Überschrift
headline *6* Schlagzeile, Überschrift; to **hit the ~s** *7* in die Schlagzeilen kommen, Schlagzeilen machen
health, ~ and safety *83* Arbeitsschutz; **~ care** *97* Gesundheitswesen, medizinische Versorgung; **~ care, professional** *134* Gesundheitsfachkraft; **~ care provider** *88* Gesundheitsdienstleister; **~ care worker** *108* Bedienstete/r im Gesundheitswesen
heap *202* Halde
heart, to **have sb's best interests at ~** *178* jds Bestes wollen, das Beste für jdn wollen
heart-warming *114* herzerwärmend
heater, water ~ *105* Warmwasserbereiter, Boiler
heating *62T* Heizung
to **heave** *203* (sich) (er-)heben, hieven
hectare *155T* Hektar
helper *65* Helfer/in
helpline *38* Hotline, Sorgentelefon
herbicide *152* Unkrautvernichtungsmittel
herd *152* Herde
hero *13* Held
to **hide (away)** *84* sich verstecken, sich verbergen
high, ~ crime *136* Schwerverbrechen; **~ street** *24* Hauptgeschäftsstraße, Einkaufsstraße
high-end *51* hochklassig, hochwertig
to **highlight** *16* hervorheben
high-profile *199* prominent, mit hohem Bekanntheitsgrad
highway *AE* *160* Autobahn
to **hijack** *130* kapern
hill *57* Berg, Anhöhe, Hügel
Hinduism *55* Hinduismus
hip *17T* Hüfte
hire, to **~ sb** *39* jdn beauftragen, jdn engagieren; *49T* jdn einstellen
historical *14* historisch
history, to **make ~** *199* Geschichte schreiben
to **hit** *148* erreichen; *160* *(Taste)* drücken; **~ rock bottom** *205* den Tiefpunkt erreichen; **~ the headlines** *7* in die Schlagzeilen kommen, Schlagzeilen machen
to **hitch-hike** *94* per Anhalter fahren, trampen
to **hold** *88* halten, innehaben; **~ on** *34* warten; **~ one's nose** *203* sich die Nase zuhalten; **~ sb back** *8* jdn bremsen; **~ the line** *34* am Apparat bleiben
homage *169* Reverenz
home, ~ country *91* Heimatland; **~ for the elderly** *114* Altenheim
homeless *81* obdachlos
homelessness *91* Obdachlosigkeit
homestay accommodation *66* Unterbringung bei Gasteltern
homing *69* Heimfindeverhalten *(z. B. von Brieftauben)*
honest *54* ehrlich, anständig
honesty *200* Ehrlichkeit
honey *181* Honig
hooked, to **get sb ~** *17T* jdn anfixen
to **hoover** *60* staubsaugen
hopeless *110* hoffnungslos
hopping, channel ~ *204T* Zappen
horizontal *155* waagrecht, horizontal
horrific *91* schrecklich, entsetzlich
horrified *43* entsetzt
horror *45* Schrecken
hospice *98* Hospiz, Sterbeklinik
host *87* Gastgeber; *126T* (Radio-/TV-) Moderator/in
hostel *31* Herberge, Wohnheim
hours, working ~ *pl* *65* Arbeitszeiten
house, shared ~ *62T* Wohngemeinschaft; to **move ~** *28* umziehen
household name *51* bekannter Name, Begriff
housework *58* Hausarbeit
housing *86* Wohnungsbau, Wohnungen
hub *145* Drehkreuz, (Verkehrs-)Knoten

to **huff and puff** *(ugs) 202* schnaufen und keuchen
huge *8* riesig, Riesen-
human, ~ being *26* Mensch, menschliches Wesen; **~ error** *166T* menschliches Versagen; **Human Resources (HR)** *50* Personal(abteilung)
human rights *206* Menschenrechte
humanitarian *94* humanitär
humanity *136* Menschheit, Menschlichkeit
humanlike *168* menschenähnlich
to **humiliate** *81* demütigen, erniedrigen
humiliation *81* Demütigung, Erniedrigung
humour *45* Humor
to **hunt** *154* jagen
hurricane *95* Wirbelsturm
hydraulic *140* hydraulisch
hydro-electric power *135* Wasserkraft
hydroponic *153* Hydrokultur-
hydroponics *152* Hydrokultur
hygiene *108* Hygiene
hyphen *204T* Bindestrich, Trennstrich
to **hyphenate** *106* mit einem Bindestrich schreiben

I

ice sheet *137* Eisdecke
ice age *204T* Eiszeit
ice-covered *148* eisbedeckt
ice-free *148* eisfrei
icy *204T* vereist
ID *27* Personalausweis
ideal *65* ideal
ideally *64* idealerweise
to **identify** *107* erkennen, bestimmen, identifizieren; **~ with sb/sth** *20* sich mit jdm/etw identifizieren
identity *123* Identität
idiomatic *61* idiomatisch, redensartlich
idol *8* Idol
to **ignore** *114* nicht beachten
ignored *64* unbeachtet
illegal *14* verboten, illegal
illiterate *160* Analphabet/in
to **illustrate** *54* zeigen, veranschaulichen
imagination *65* Phantasie, Vorstellungskraft
immediate *55* unmittelbar
immediately *41* unverzüglich, unmittelbar, sofort
immigrant *183* Einwanderer/-in
impact *124* Einfluss, Auswirkung; to **make an ~** *94* etw bewirken, etw verändern
impairment *210* Beeinträchtigung
to **import** *99* importieren, einführen
importance *38* Bedeutung, Wichtigkeit
impressed *120* beeindruckt
to **improve** *14* (sich) verbessern, (sich) steigern
improvement in sth *14* Verbesserung bei etw
to **improvise** *16* improvisieren
in, the ~ thing *54* der letzte Schrei
in-car entertainment *167* Unterhaltungselektronik im Auto
inch *80* Zoll *(= 2,54 cm)*
incident *27* Vorfall, Zwischenfall
including *20* einschließlich
inclusion *199* Einbeziehung, Einbindung, *Inklusion*
inclusive *200* offen, (frei) zugänglich
income *68* Einkommen; **per capita ~** *156* Pro-Kopf-Einkommen
incomer *86T* Zuzügler, Ankömmling
increase *69* Zunahme, Steigerung; to **~** *46* steigen, zunehmen; to **~ sth** *17T* etw steigern; to **be on the ~** *69* auf dem Vormarsch sein, zunehmen
increasingly *46* zunehmend
independence *94* Unabhängigkeit
independent *57* unabhängig
individual *175* Einzelne/r, Individuum
indoor *146* im Haus, Innen-
industrial *104* Industrie-
industrialist *165* Industrielle/r
industrialized *104* industrialisiert
infant *210* Kleinkind
infection *108* Infektion
infectious disease *108* Infektionskrankheit
influence *100* Einfluss; to **~** *24* beeinflussen
influential *161* einflussreich
influenza *108* Grippe
informal *59* informell, locker
informality *69* Formlosigkeit, Ungezwungenheit
informational *208* informatorisch
infrastructure *69* Infrastruktur
initial *171* erste/r/s
initially *43* anfangs, anfänglich
initiative *27* Aktion, Initiative
injection *208* Spritze, Injektion
to **injure** *100* verletzen
injury *14* Verletzung
inland, to **go ~** *100* ins Landesinnere gehen
innocent *125* unschuldig
innovation *208* Innovation, Neuerung
innovative *46* innovativ
input *187T* Eingabe, Beitrag, Input; to **~** *128* eingeben
to **inquire** *140* nachfragen, sich erkundigen
insect *190* Insekt
insecurity *178* Unsicherheit
inside address *76* Empfängeranschrift
insight *31* Einblick
to **insist** *194* darauf bestehen
to **inspect** *193* inspizieren, kontrollieren
inspector, ticket ~ *48F* Fahrkartenkontrolleur/in
inspirational *43* anregend, inspirierend
to **inspire** *10* inspirieren, anregen
to **install** *128* installieren
instance, for **~** *117* zum Beispiel
instant *48F* sofortig, augenblicklich
instead *26* stattdessen; **~ of** *16* anstatt
instinct *69* Instinkt
institute *164* Institut
institution *193* Institution
to **instruct sb to do sth** *128* jdn beauftragen, etw zu tun
instruction *65* Anweisung
instructions *pl 26* Anleitung, Anweisung(en)
instructor *16* Lehrer/in
insulating foam *145* Isolierschaum
insurance *65* Versicherung; **medical ~** *65* Krankenversicherung
to **insure** *66* versichern
intake *197* Zufuhr, Aufnahme
to **integrate** *84* (sich) integrieren
integration *206* Integration
to **intend** *50* beabsichtigen
intended *208* gedacht, vorgesehen
intense *170* intensiv
intensity *170* Intensität
intensive *183* intensiv
intent *27* Absicht
intention *95* Absicht
to **interact** *29* interagieren, aufeinander eingehen
interaction *208* Interaktion
to **intercept** *128* abfangen, abhören
interest (in) *12* Interesse (an)
interested (in) *186* interessiert (an)
intermediate *75* mittlere/r/s (Niveau)
intern *66* Praktikant/in
internal *127* inländisch, Inlands-; **~ combustion engine** *159* Verbrennungsmotor
internship *66* Praktikum
to **interpret** *26* interpretieren
interpreter *189* Dolmetscher/in
to **interrupt** *22* unterbrechen, ins Wort fallen
interval *144* (zeitlicher) Abstand
interview *76* Vorstellungsgespräch; to **~ sb** *78* mit jdm ein Vorstellungsgespräch führen
interviewee *112* Person, mit der ein Vorstellungsgespräch geführt wird
interviewer *78* Person, die ein Vorstellungsgespräch führt
intimate *88* intim, eng, persönlich
in-tray *49T* Posteingang(skorb)
to **introduce** *(a law) 64 (ein Gesetz)* einbringen
introductions *pl 48* Vorstellen
intuitional *65* intuitiv
invaluable *132* unschätzbar, unbezahlbar
to **invent** *46* erfinden
invention *48* Erfindung
to **invest** *141* investieren
to **investigate** *65* ermitteln, untersuchen
investigative *65* erforschend, Untersuchungs-
investment *137* Investition
invitation *40* Einladung
invite *43* Einladung; to **~ sb to do sth** *78* jdn auffordern, etw zu tun
to **invoke** *188* zitieren, anführen

to **involve** *65* mit sich bringen, umfassen
involved *65* dazugehörig; ~ **in sth** *13* an etw beteiligt, bei etw engagiert; to **be ~ in sth** *57* sich an etw beteiligen, bei etw mitmachen; to **get ~ with sb** *37* mit jdm zu tun haben
iron *203* eisern
ironic *103* ironisch
ironing, to **do (the/some) ~** *58* bügeln
irregular *68* unregelmäßig
irrelevant *208* irrelevant
irrigation *149* Bewässerung
island *137* Insel
to **isolate** *36* absondern, isolieren
isolated *161* abgeschottet, abgeschieden, isoliert
issue *86T* Streitpunkt, Frage, Problem, Thema; **global ~** *195* globales Problem
IT developer *161* IT-Entwickler/in
italics *pl 36* Kursivschrift
item *77* Punkt; *99* Artikel, Gegenstand; *172* Tagesordnungspunkt; **~ (of clothing)** *24* Kleidungsstück
iteration *208* Iteration, Wiederholung

J

jacket *87T* Jacke, Jackett
jargon *51* Fachsprache, Jargon
jewellery *6* Schmuck
job *181* Aufgabe; **casual ~** *110* Nebenjob; **~ advertisement** *31* Stellenanzeige, -ausschreibung; **~ rotation** *72* Arbeitsplatzrotation, (innerbetrieblicher) Arbeitsplatzwechsel; **~ security** *65* sicherer Arbeitsplatz; **~ title** *66* Stellenbezeichnung
jobless *109* arbeitslos
joblessness *109* Arbeitslosigkeit
to **join** *16* beitreten, eintreten, mitmachen; *49T* mitmachen, *(Radio etc.:)* in einer Sendung sein, *(Telefon:)* (mit jdm) sprechen; **~ in** *17T* mitmachen; **~ sth** *151* etw (miteinander) verbinden; **~ together** *126T* sich zusammenschließen
joke *26* Witz
to **jot down** *204* notieren
journalism *112* Journalismus
journalist *65* Journalist/in
journey *140* Reise, Fahrt
joy *17* Freude
Judaism *55* Judaismus, Judentum
judge *8* Richter/in, Juror/in; to **~** *69* beurteilen
to **juggle** *110* miteinander vereinbaren, jonglieren
jump *54* Sprung; to **~ red lights** *48F* bei Rot über eine Ampel fahren; to **~ the queue** *82* sich vordrängeln
jungle *160* Dschungel
junior *14* Junioren-; *150* Jung-, Nachwuchs-
justice, criminal ~ *124* Strafjustiz

K

keen *190* begeistert; to **be ~ on sth** *12* auf etw versessen sein; to **be ~ to do sth** *76* etw unbedingt tun wollen
to **keep, ~ in touch** *29* in Verbindung bleiben; **~ sth safe** *23* etw aufbewahren; **~ to the right/left** *119* sich rechts/links halten; **~ up with sb/sth** *24* mit jdm/etw Schritt halten; **~ watch over sb** *160* über jdn wachen, jdn beobachten
keep-fit *12* Fitness(-)
keystroke *128* Tastenanschlag, Herunterdrücken einer Taste
keyword *199* Schlagwort, Schlüsselwort
to **kick sth down** *80* etw eintreten
kind *81* freundlich, gütig, nett
kindergartener *196* Kindergartenkind
to **knock, ~ sb off sth** *94* jdn von etw herunterstoßen, von etw herunterfallen; **~ sth off** *129* etw abschlagen
knock-on effect *180* Folgewirkung
know, to **~ sth inside out** *49T* etw in- und auswendig kennen; to **get to ~ sb** *171* jdn kennen lernen; to **let sb ~ sth** *31* jdm etw mitteilen, jdm etw sagen
knowledge *48F* Wissen, Kenntnis(se)

L

label *11* (Mode-)Firma, Marke; *87* Beschriftung, Bezeichnung; *194* Kennzeichnung, Etikett, Schild(chen); **discount ~** *21* Billigmarke
laboratory *152* Labor; **by ~ design** *152* im Labor geplant
labour *104* Arbeit
lack *25* Mangel; to **~ sth** *169* etw nicht haben
lake *149* (Binnen-)See
land, to **~** *83* landen; to **~ sth** *110* etw an Land ziehen; **law of the ~** *200* geltendes Recht
landline *160* Festnetz(-)
lane *62* Weg, Gasse
language, native ~ *31* Muttersprache
lantern *79* Laterne
largely *36* weitgehend, überwiegend; *137* größtenteils, überwiegend
large-scale *136* in großem Umfang/Ausmaß
last, to **~** *107T* dauern, andauern, so bleiben; **~ but not least** *17T* zu guter Letzt, nicht zuletzt
latchkey kid *183T* Schlüsselkind
latest, (the) ~ *24* der/die/das allerneueste/n; **at the ~** *31* spätestens
laugh *57* Lachen, Gelächter; to **~ at sb** *38T* über jdn lachen, jdn auslachen
laughing gas *40* Lachgas
to **launch** *50* *(Produkt)* auf den Markt bringen, einführen; **~ an ad campaign** *54* eine Werbekampagne starten; **~ an attack** *130* einen Angriff starten

law *84* Gesetz; *81* Justiz; **~ and order** *126T* Recht und Ordnung; **~ enforcement** *124* Gesetzesvollzug, Innere Sicherheit, Exekutive; **~ enforcement agency** *124* Strafverfolgungsbehörde, Exekutivorgan; **~ of the land** *200* geltendes Recht; to **pass a ~** *84* ein Gesetz verabschieden
lawnmower *129* Rasenmäher
lawyer *39* Anwalt/Anwältin; **specialist ~** *39* Fachanwalt/-anwältin
to **lay cables** *160* Kabel verlegen
layer *146* Schicht
lazy *110* faul
lead *144* Blei
leadership *161* Führung
leaflet *34* Broschüre, Merkblatt
leafy vegetable *156* Blattgemüse
to **leak** *143T* sickern, entweichen; *172* auslaufen
learning disability *199* Lernbehinderung, Lernschwäche
least, at ~ *27* zumindest, mindestens; **last but not ~** *17T* zu guter Letzt, nicht zuletzt
to **leave, ~ a message** *33* eine Nachricht hinterlassen; **~ sb alone** *178* jdn in Ruhe lassen; **~ sb sth** *64* jdm etw hinterlassen
leaves *pl 146* Laub
left, ~ out of sth *36* von etw ausgeschlossen; to **be ~ for dead** *109* als tot zurückgelassen werden; to **feel ~ out** *60* sich ausgeschlossen fühlen
legal *15* erlaubt, legal; **~ action** *39* rechtliche Schritte; **~ department** *69* juristische Abteilung; **~ guardian** *27* Vormund, Erziehungsberechtigte/r; to **take ~ action** *39* rechtliche Schritte unternehmen
to **legalize** *49T* legalisieren
legend *6* Legende
legislature *167* Gesetzgebung
leisure *25* Freizeit, Muße
to **lend sb sth** *62T* jdm etw leihen
length *170* Länge, Dauer
lesson *25* (Unterrichts-)Stunde; Lektion
to **let, ~ oneself in for sth** *128* sich auf etw einlassen; **~ sb know sth** *31* jdm etw mitteilen, jdm etw sagen
letter, capital ~ *32* Großbuchstabe; **cover ~** *66* Anschreiben, Begleitschreiben
lettuce *99* Kopfsalat
level *8* Stufe, Niveau, Ebene; *92* Grad, Höhe; **carbon dioxide ~** *136* Kohlendioxidkonzentration, -gehalt; **entry ~** *68* Einstieg, Anfang; **entry ~ pay** *68T* Einstiegsgehalt, Anfangsgehalt; **~ of requirement** *134* Bedarfsniveau; **sea ~** *137* Meeresspiegel
liberation *156* Befreiung
library *163* Bibliothek, Bücherei
licence, driving ~ *48F* Führerschein
lie *179* Lüge
life, quality of ~ *137* Lebensqualität

life saving 90 lebensrettend
life-altering 156 lebensverändernd
life-changing 8 lebensverändernd
life-cycle 49 Lebensdauer, Lebenszyklus
lifeline 205 Rettungsanker
lifeline pendant 209T Hausnotrufsender *(als Halsband)*
lifesaver, ... could be a ~ 74 ... könnte lebensrettend sein
lifestyle 58 Lebensweise, Lebensführung
lifetime 114 (ganzes) Leben; **for a ~** 97 ein Leben lang
to **lift** 28 heben
light, to ~ 79 *(Kerze etc.)* anzünden; to **~ up** 140 leuchten, aufleuchten; **energy-saving ~ bulb** 194 Energiesparlampe; **~ bulb** 155T Glühbirne
lighting 66 Beleuchtung, Licht
lights, traffic ~ *pl* 48F Ampel
like 8 wie
likeable 51 sympathisch
likely 34 wahrscheinlich; to **be ~ to do sth** 46 etw wahrscheinlich tun (werden)
limit, to ~ 137 begrenzen, einschränken; **speed ~** 48F Geschwindigkeitsbegrenzung
limitation 160 Einschränkung
limited 50 begrenzt, beschränkt
line 33 Leitung; 81 Reihe; **down the ~** 81 weiter; **~ chart** 53 Liniendiagramm; **subject ~** 32 *(Brief:)* Betreffzeile; to **hold the ~** 34 am Apparat bleiben
link 102 Verbindung, Verknüpfung, Beziehung; to ~ 102 verbinden, verknüpfen
lion 79 Löwe
to **listen in** 37 mithören
listener 183T Zuhörer/in
literally 118 buchstäblich
little, there's ~ point in doing sth 30 es hat wenig Sinn, etw zu tun
to **live off aid** 81 von Sozialhilfe leben
livelihood 190 Existenzgrundlage, Lebensunterhalt
lively 85 lebendig, lebhaft, rege
livestock 152 Vieh
living, cost of ~ 83 Lebenshaltungskosten; **~ room** 40 Wohnzimmer
load 60 Ladung; to **~ the dishwasher** 168 die Spülmaschine einräumen
loan 90 Darlehen, Kredit
to **lobby sb** 90 auf jdn Einfluss nehmen
local 188 Einheimische/r
located, ~ in 75 in (... gelegen); to **be ~ in** 119 sich in ... befinden, in ... liegen
location 66 Standort, Ort
locator 209T Ortungsgerät
lodging, board and ~ 66 Kost und Logis
log 146 Baumstumpf, Holzklotz; to ~ 128 aufzeichnen, protokollieren; to **~ in** 39 sich einloggen; to **~ out** 39 sich ausloggen
logical(ly) 23 logisch
to **loiter** 27 herumlungern
loneliness 69 Einsamkeit
lonely 36 einsam
long, to ~ 202 sich sehnen, verlangen; **as ~ as** 137 solange; **it wasn't ~ before ...** 16 es dauerte nicht lange, bis ...; **it's not ~ before** 22 es dauert nicht lange, bis
longer, no ~ 209T nicht mehr
long-term 185 langfristig, Langzeit-
to **look, ~ about** 203 sich umschauen; **~ after sb** 29 sich um jdn kümmern; **~ for** 44 suchen; **~ for sb/sth** 19 jdn/etw suchen; **~ forward to sth** 9 sich auf etw freuen; **~ on** 80 zusehen; **~ sth up** 41 etw *(Vokabel etc.)* nachschlagen; **~ up to sb** 13 zu jdm aufsehen, jdn bewundern; **I've never ~ed back.** 49T Ich habe es nie bereut.
looking, good ~ 8 gutaussehend, attraktiv
to **lose** 13 verlieren; **~ weight** 17T abnehmen
loss 105 Verlust
lottery 48F Lotterie, Verlosung
loudspeaker 144 Lautsprecher
lovable 44 liebenswert
love, to **fall in ~ with sb/sth** 86 sich in jdn/etw verlieben
lovely 22 schön, nett, hübsch
lover 10 Geliebte/r, Liebhaber/in
low-cost 104 billig, kostengünstig
luck 34 Glück; **Good ~!** 50 Viel Glück!
lucky, to **be ~** 179 Glück haben
lunch, buffet ~ 122 Lunchbuffet
lung 17T Lunge; **~ flute** 209 *Atemphysiotherapiegerät zur Verbesserung der Lungenfunktion bei COPD*
to **lurch** 156 schlingern, taumeln
lush 204T üppig
lying 49T Lügen

M

machine, game ~ 46 Videospielgerät, Spielautomat
madam 96T gnädige Frau
magical 8 magisch, traumhaft
to **magnify** 164 vergrößern, verstärken
mainly 17T hauptsächlich
to **maintain** 67 warten, instand halten; **~ sth** 27 etw aufrecht erhalten; **~ stocks** 154 den Bestand erhalten
maintenance 66 Wartung, Instandhaltung
major 137 bedeutend, wichtig, groß
majority 69 Mehrheit
to **make, ~ a point** 26 ein Argument vortragen, etw sagen wollen; **~ a stand** 193 Farbe bekennen, ein Zeichen setzen; **~ an effort** 176 sich Mühe geben; **~ for sth** 69 sich auf den Weg nach etw machen; **~ history** 199 Geschichte schreiben; **~ it** 60 es schaffen; **~ sb up** 9 jdn schminken; **~ sth up** 6 etw erfinden, sich etw ausdenken; 135 etw ausmachen; **~ sure** 23 sicherstellen; dafür sorgen, dass; 88 sicherstellen; **~ use of sth** 8 von etw Gebrauch machen, etw nutzen
maker 54 Hersteller, -bauer; **candy ~** *AE* 54 Süßwarenhersteller
makeshift 188 provisorisch
male 88 Mann, männliche Person
mall, shopping ~ 27 Einkaufspassage, Einkaufszentrum
mammoth 203 Mammut
to **manage** 60 verwalten, regeln; 74 (es) schaffen
management 66 Führung, Management; **~ consultant** 65 Unternehmensberater/in; **middle ~** 110 mittlere Führungsebene
managing director 49T Geschäftsführer/in
manhunt 124 Verbrecherjagd
to **manipulate** 164 manipulieren; 168 handhaben, bedienen
manipulative 168 manipulativ
man-made 136 künstlich, menschlichen Ursprungs
manual 51 Bedienungsanleitung; **bi-~** 169 beidhändig
to **manufacture** 99 fertigen, herstellen
manufacturer 49T Hersteller/in, Produzent/in
manufacturing 69 Fertigung
maple syrup 182 Ahornsirup
march 79 Marsch; to ~ 79 marschieren
margin 188 Rand
marital status 193 Familienstand
mark 144 Markierung, Zeichen; to ~ 94 *(Jahrestag etc.)* begehen
marker 122 Filzstift
market, to ~ 54 vermarkten; **~ share** 72 Marktanteil
to **marshal** 205 sammeln, zusammenstellen
marvellous 120 toll, phantastisch
mask 108 Maske
mass, ~ media *pl* 124 Massenmedien; **~ production** 102 Massenproduktion
massive 146 massiv, gewaltig
massive(ly) 126T massiv
match 11 Spiel, Partie, Match
material 14 Material, Werkstoff; **original ~** 113 eigene Beiträge
mathematician 81 Mathematiker/in
maths 68T Mathe(matik) *(Schulfach)*
matter 24 Angelegenheit, Sache; to ~ 22 wichtig sein, darauf ankommen; **it doesn't ~** 62T es ist egal; **no ~ ...** 24 ganz egal, ...
maximum 49T maximal, Höchst-; 49 Höchstwert
maximum (max.) 66 höchstens, maximal
meaningful 164 wichtig, bedeutend, sinnstiftend
means of transport 130 Verkehrsmittel
meanwhile 81 inzwischen, unterdessen

measure *27* Maßnahme; to ~ *17* messen
mechanic *65* Mechaniker/in
mechanical *65* mechanisch; ~ **engineering** *169* Maschinenbau
medal *13* Medaille
media, mass ~ *pl* *124* Massenmedien
to **mediate** *71* vermitteln
mediation *28* Vermittlung
medic *178* Arzt/Ärztin
medical *67* medizinisch; ~ **insurance** *65* Krankenversicherung; ~ **student** *96T* Medizinstudent/in; **walk-in ~ centre** *96T* Ambulanz
medication *94* Arzneimittel
medicine *90* Arznei(mittel), Medizin
to **meet** *134* *(Bedarf)* decken; ~ **a deadline** *112* eine Frist / einen Termin einhalten; ~ **a demand** *105* eine Nachfrage befriedigen; ~ **sb's needs** *88* jds Bedürfnisse erfüllen; ~ **up** *22* sich treffen
meeting room *69* Sitzungsraum, Besprechungsraum
melancholy *118* melancholisch, wehmütig
to **melt** *137* schmelzen, abschmelzen
member, ~ **of staff** *171* Mitarbeiter/in; ~ **of the audience** *8* Zuschauer/in
memory *120* Gedächtnis; ~ **of sb** *94* Gedenken an jdn
mental *146* geistig, psychisch, seelisch; **~(ly)** *114* geistig
to **mention** *31* erwähnen, nennen
mentoring *188* Patenschaft, Mentoring
mentorship program *188* Mentorenprogramm
merchant *160* Händler/in
mercury *144* Quecksilber
mess *43* Chaos; to **look a** ~ *101* fürchterlich aussehen
to **mess around** *28* herumalbern, herumgammeln
message, text ~ *42* SMS; to **take a** ~ *34* etw ausrichten, eine Nachricht notieren
metabolism *17* Stoffwechsel
metal *47* Metall; **corrugated** ~ *156* Wellblech
metaphor *188* Metapher
methane *135* Methan
microphone *129* Mikrofon
microwave *68T* Mikrowelle
mid-century *161* Jahrhundertmitte
midday *150* Mittag
middle management *110* mittlere Führungsebene
middleman *145* Zwischenhändler
midnight *6* Mitternacht
midsummer *79* Mittsommer, Sommersonnenwende
migrant *84* Migrant/in
migratory bird *145* Zugvogel
miles, food ~ *pl* *193* Transportwege der Nahrungsmittel
military *164* Militär
millennial *109* Jahrtausend-
millennium *174* Jahrtausend
mind *62* Gedanken; to ~ **one's own business** *57* sich um seinen eigenen Kram kümmern; to ~ **sth** *25* etw gegen etw haben; *69* auf etw achten; **peace of** ~ *209T* Sicherheit, innere Ruhe
minimum *69* Mindestmaß, -menge, Minimum; ~ **wage** *110* Mindestlohn
minority *84* Minderheit
mirror *129* Spiegel
misfortune *43* Unglück, Missgeschick
to **miss** *134* fehlen
missing *166* vermisst
mission *90* Auftrag, Mission
mistaken, to be ~ *128* sich irren
misunderstanding *97* Missverständnis
to **mix and match** *122* individuell zusammenstellen
mixture *14* Mischung
moans *pl* *29* Gejammer, Genörgel
mobile *69* mobil
mobility *124* Mobilität
model, role ~ *55* Vorbild
moderate *84* gemäßigt, maßvoll
modernity *124* Moderne
modest *88* bescheiden, sittsam
modesty *88* Bescheidenheit, Anstand, Sittsamkeit
to **modify** *152* modifizieren
mom, single ~ *74* Alleinerziehende
momentum *175* Schwung, Fahrt
money, pocket ~ *64* Taschengeld; to **raise** ~ *43* Geld beschaffen
mongrel *80* Mischling, Bastard
to **monitor** *132* überwachen
monthly *62T* monatlich
to **mooch off sth** *110* von etw schmarotzen
moral *203* Moral
morale *158* Moral, geistig-seelische Verfassung
morals *pl* *54* Moralvorstellungen
more, what's ~ *56* zudem
moreover *117* überdies
mosquito net *97* Moskitonetz
to **motivate** *177* motivieren; **highly ~d** *66* hochmotiviert
motivational tool *170* Motivierungshilfe, motivationsförderndes Werkzeug
motivator *170* Motivator, Antreiber
motorist *BE* *48F* Autofahrer/in
mouse *51* Maus
move *17T* Schritt, Bewegung; *61* Schritt, Umzug; to ~ **house** *28* umziehen; to ~ **on** *8* weiterkommen, weitergehen
moveable *70* beweglich, mobil
movement *94* Bewegung; **free** ~ *86T* Freizügigkeit
MP (Member of Parliament) *84* Parlamentsabgeordnete/r
mud *144* Schlamm
multiculturalism *79* Multikulturalität, Multikulturismus, kulturelle Vielfalt
multiple *124* mehrere, vielfach
to **multiply** *150* multiplizieren
murder *132* Mord
muscle *16* Muskel
musical *17* musikalisch, Musik-
Muslim *84* muslimisch, Moslem
must, a ~ *75* ein Muss; **M~ rush.** *71T* Ich muss weg.
mystery *45* Rätsel, Rätselhaftigkeit; *145* Rätsel, Geheimnis
myth *97* Mythos, Märchen

N

nail *44* Fingernagel; *81* Nagel
name, to ~ *16* nennen, benennen; **first** ~ *17* Vorname; **given** ~ *80* Vorname; **household** ~ *51* bekannter Name, Begriff; **proper** ~ *33* Eigenname
nannying *110* Kinderbetreuung
nasty *129* gemein, hässlich, böse
nation *183* Staat, Nation
national *14* Landes-, national; ~ **team** *13* Nationalmannschaft
nationwide *144* landesweit
native, her ~ **Pakistan** *109* ihr Geburtsland Pakistan; ~ **language** *31* Muttersprache; ~ **speaker** *75* Muttersprachler/in
natural gas *138* Erdgas
near, to ~ *174* sich nähern; **nowhere** ~ *202* bei weitem nicht, nicht annähernd
nearby *29* in der Nähe
necessary, as ~ *61* nötigenfalls
necessity *168* Notwendigkeit
neck *209T* Hals
need *178* Bedürfnis; **in** ~ *54* bedürftig, in Not; to ~ **to do sth** *175* etw tun müssen
needs *pl* *57* Bedürfnisse, Bedarf; to **meet sb's** ~ *88* jds Bedürfnisse erfüllen
need-to-know, on a ~ **basis** *63* im (unumgänglichen) Bedarfsfall
needy *205* bedürftig
neighbour *6* Nachbar/in
nervous *9* aufgeregt, nervös
net, mosquito ~ *97* Moskitonetz
network *29* Netz, Netzwerk
new entrant *208* Neueinsteiger
New Year *79* Neujahr
news, cable ~ *124* TV-Nachrichtensender; ~ **anchor** *136* Nachrichtensprecher/in
next, ~ **door** *41* nebenan; ~ **to** *120* neben
NGO (non-governmental organization) *95* Nichtregierungsorganisation
niche *49T* Nische
niece *204T* Nichte
nitroglycerine *14* Nitroglycerin
no longer *209T* nicht mehr
noise *41* Lärm; *46* Geräusch
noisy *57* laut, lärmend
to **nominate** *175* nominieren
non-alcoholic *121* alkoholfrei
non-profit *156* gemeinnützig
non-smoking *120* Nichtraucher-
norm *69* Norm
nosey *60* *(auf unangenehme Weise)* neugierig

note *52* Hinweis; *46* Ton, Note
notebook *15* Heft, Notizbuch
notion *164* Vorstellung, Auffassung
novel *131* Roman; *168* neu, neuartig
novelty *168* Neues, Neuartiges
now, What ~ for ...? *84* Wie steht es um ...?
nowhere, ~ near *202* bei weitem nicht, nicht annähernd; to **get you ~** *126* zu nichts führen, nichts bringen
nuclear *57* Kern-; **~ plant** *140* Kernkraftwerk; **~ power** *135* Kernkraft; **~ power station** *140* Kernkraftwerk
to **number** *48* nummerieren
numerical *65* Zahl-, zahlenmäßig
nurse *65* Krankenpfleger/-schwester
nursery *74* Kinderhort
nursing *88* Pflege, Krankenpflege; **~ home** *118* Pflegeheim
to **nurture** *184* entwickeln, pflegen, fördern
nutrient *63* Nährstoff
nutrition *94* Nahrung, Ernährung

O

obese *196* fettleibig
obesity *180* Fettleibigkeit
to **object to sth** *27* etw ablehnen, gegen etw Einwände haben
to **observe** *65* beobachten
obsession *146* Besessenheit, Wahn, Zwang
obstacle *160* Hindernis
obstruction *168* Hindernis
to **obtain sth** *130* etw erhalten, an etw gelangen
obtainable *129* erhältlich
obvious *179* offensichtlich, klar
occasional *146* gelegentlich
occupation *96* Beruf, Tätigkeit, Beschäftigung
to **occur** *14* vorfallen, geschehen
ocean *137* Ozean, Weltmeer
of no concern *178* ohne Relevanz; nicht von Interesse
to **offer sb sth on a plate** *68* jdm etw auf dem Silbertablett servieren
offering *208* Angebot
office, ~ assistant *75* Bürokaufmann/-frau; **~ block** *71* Bürogebäude; **~ clerk** *49T* Büroangestellte/r
officer *126* Offizier/in
official *97* Beamte/r, Funktionär/in
offshore *100* im/ins Ausland; *141* auf See
offside *188* Abseits
OHP transparency *48* Overheadfolie
oil *138* Öl
Olympic *14* olympisch
on, and so ~ *62T* und so weiter
once *46* sobald; **all at ~** *24* auf einmal
one, ~-to-~ *187T* Einzel-
ongoing *90* laufend
onion *146* Zwiebel
only child *64* Einzelkind
onshore *141* an Land
onto *8* auf
open, out in the ~ *144* im Freien
opening *94* Eröffnung
openness *11T* Offenheit
open-plan office *69* Großraumbüro
to **operate** *169* tätig sein
operation *107T* Betrieb, Geschäftstätigkeit; *209T* Operation
operator *167* Betreiber/in
opinion, to **give an ~** *23* eine Meinung äußern
opportunities, equal ~ *pl 66* Chancengleichheit
opportunity *29* Gelegenheit, Möglichkeit, Chance
opposite, the ~ sex *29* das andere Geschlecht
to **opt for sth** *142* sich für etw entscheiden
optimistic *107T* optimistisch
oral *75* mündlich
order *6* Reihenfolge; *103* Bestellung; *100* Auftrag, Bestellung; *208* Verordnung; **in ~ to** *60* um ... zu; **law and ~** *126T* Recht und Ordnung
ordinary *11T* normal, gewöhnlich
organic *100* biologisch, Bio-
organization *14* Organisation
organizational *65* organisatorisch
organizer *65* Organisator/in
oriented, ...-~ *27* ...orientiert
origin, country of ~ *187* Ursprungsland, Herkunftsland
original material *113* eigene Beiträge
to **originate, ~ from** *99* kommen aus; **~ from sth** *124* von etw ausgehen, aus etw kommen
orphan *94* Waise
orphanage *94* Waisenhaus
other, on the ~ hand *11T* andererseits; **the ~ way round** *86T* umgekehrt
ought to *110* sollen
outbreak *108* Ausbruch *(Krankheit)*
outcome *165* Ergebnis, Resultat
outgoing *146* kontaktfreudig
outing *168* Ausflug, Ausfahrt
to **outline** *111* skizzieren, grob beschreiben
out-of-state *110* in einem anderen Bundesstaat
outreach worker *185* Straßensozialarbeiter/in
outsider *188* Außenseiter/in
to **outsmart** *164* überlisten, austricksen
to **outweigh sth** *146* schwerer als etw wiegen
over-achiever *19* Überflieger
to **overcome** *13* überwinden; *161* bewältigen
to **overdo it** *24* es übertreiben
to **overeat** *197* zu viel essen
over-exploitation *147* Raubbau, übermäßiger Abbau
overfishing *204T* Überfischung
overheads *pl 104* Fixkosten, Betriebskosten
to **overhear** *131* belauschen, aufschnappen
to **overlook** *200* übersehen
overnight, to **stay ~** *122* übernachten
overseas *108* nach/in Übersee
overview *170* Überblick, Übersicht
overweight *17* übergewichtig
own, on one's ~ *10* allein; to **mind one's ~ business** *57* sich um seinen eigenen Kram kümmern
owner *67* Besitzer/in
oxygen *209T* Sauerstoff

P

pacifist *126T* Pazifist/in
to **pack** *20* verpacken; **battery ~** *144* Akku
packaging *19* Verpackung
packet, pay ~ *110* Lohntüte, Gehalt
pad *69* (Notiz-)Block; Bude; *172* Notizblock
pain, stomach ~ *108* Bauchschmerzen; to **be a ~ (in the neck)** *57* jdm auf die Nerven gehen
to **paint** *49T* malen
painter *209T* Maler/in
palm nut *190* Palmkern
pandemic *108* Pandemie
panel *137* Gremium, Ausschuss
to **panic** *17* in Panik geraten
pantry, food ~ *AE 151* Tafel, karitative Essensausgabe
paperwork *58* Büroarbeit, Schreibarbeit
parade *79* Parade
paragraph *14 (Text:)* Absatz
parallel *131* Parallele
Paralympian *209T* paralympisch
paramedic *88* Sanitäter/in
paraphernalia *188* Zubehör, Ausrüstung
to **paraphrase** *28* umschreiben, paraphrasieren
parcel *151* Paket
parent, single ~ *197* alleinerziehend
park, car ~ *69* Parkplatz, -haus, -garage
parliament *86* Parlament
part, to **take ~ in sth** *9* an etw teilnehmen
partially *156* teilweise
participant *12* Teilnehmer/in
particular *24* bestimmt, speziell; **in ~** *44* insbesondere
particularly *103* besonders
partly *107T* teils, teilweise
part-time *60* Teilzeit-
party, school leaving ~ *17T* Schulabgangsfeier; to **throw a ~** *40* eine Party geben/schmeißen
to **pass** *137* überschreiten; **~ a law** *84* ein Gesetz verabschieden; **~ sth on** *110* etw weitergeben, etw weiterreichen; **~ sth to sb** *152* jdm etw weiterreichen
passenger *153* Passagier

passer-by *46* Passant/in
passion fruit *156* Passionsfrucht
past, to **be ~ it** *114* die besten Jahre hinter sich haben, jenseits von Gut und Böse sein
pastureland *148* Weideland
patient *88* Patient/in
to **pave** *206* pflastern
pay *65* Bezahlung, Lohn; to **~ attention to sth** *23* auf etw achten; **entry level ~** *68T* Einstiegsgehalt, Anfangsgehalt; **~ packet** *110* Lohntüte, Gehalt; **~ scale** *68T* Lohntarif, Lohntabelle
payment *68T* Zahlung
peace *80* Frieden; **~ of mind** *209T* Sicherheit, innere Ruhe
peaceful *84* friedlich
peer *29* Gleichaltrige/r, Altersgenosse; **~ group** *55* Altersgruppe, Bezugsgruppe, Umfeld; **~ pressure** *170* Gruppendruck, Einfluss der Clique
pen friend *93* Brieffreund/in
pendant *209T* Anhänger
penguin *204T* Pinguin
penny *81* Pfennig, Penny
pension *109* Rente, Pension
pensioner *109* Rentner/in
people *100* Volk
per *35* pro; **~ annum** *117T* pro Jahr; **~ capita income** *156* Pro-Kopf-Einkommen; **~ cent** *44, 52* Prozent
percentage *53* Prozentsatz, Anteil
percentile *196* Perzentile
perception *199* Wahrnehmung
to **perform** *8* singen, spielen, auftreten; *166T* (leistungsmäßig) abschneiden; **~ sth** *168* etw ausführen, etw durchführen
performance *14* Leistung; Abschneiden
perfume *49* Parfüm
perks *pl* *74* freiwillige Sonder-/Sozialleistungen
permanent *71T* dauerhaft
permission, planning ~ *142* Baugenehmigung
permit *189* Bewilligung
permitted *27* erlaubt, gestattet
person, in ~ *129* persönlich
personal transport *102* Individualverkehr
to **personalise** *69* individuell gestalten
personality *13* Persönlichkeit
to **personalize** *208* persönlich/individuell gestalten
personnel *134* Personal
perspective *88* Perspektive, Blickwinkel
to **persuade** *20* überzeugen, überreden
persuader *65* jd, der andere überzeugt und mitreißt
pest *156* Schädling
petrol *102* Benzin
petrol-driven *102* benzingetrieben
petrol-guzzling *194* spritfressend
phase *46* Phase
phenomenon *14* Phänomen, Erscheinung
to **phone in** *50* *(in einer Sendung)* anrufen
photocopier *120* Fotokopiergerät
photography *25* Fotografie, Foto-
to **photo-shop** *24* mit Photoshop bearbeiten
piano, to **play the ~** *113* Klavier spielen
to **pick** *141* wählen, aussuchen; **~ sb/sth up** *22* jdn/etw abholen; **~ sth out** *51* etw heraussuchen
pickup *156* Pritschenwagen
pig *190* Schwein
pile *203* Haufen; to **~** *144* stapeln; to **~ up** *202* sich häufen, sich auftürmen
pill *208* Pille
pilot project *134* Pilotprojekt
to **pin** *77* (mit einer Nadel) befestigen, anbringen
pinkie *169* kleiner Finger
pipe band *79* Dudelsackkapelle
pity, (it's a) ~ *22* schade
place, to **~** *201T* setzen, platzieren; **~ card** *172* Platzkarte, Tischkarte; to **take ~** *8* stattfinden
placement *134* Stellenvermittlung
to **plague** *124* plagen, heimsuchen
plain *139* schlicht
plan, emergency ~ *74* Notfallplan
planner, city ~ *167* Stadtplaner/in
planning permission *142* Baugenehmigung
plant *102* Fabrik, Werk, Anlage; to **~** *148* pflanzen, anpflanzen; **nuclear ~** *140* Kernkraftwerk; **power ~** *136* Kraftwerk
plaque *131* Platte, Tafel
to **plaster** *156* verputzen
plastic bag *203* Plastiktüte
plate *68* Teller; to **offer sb sth on a ~** *68* jdm etw auf dem Silbertablett servieren
platform *11T* Podium
to **play the piano** *113* Klavier spielen
playground *197* Spielplatz
plc *75* AG
pleasant *68T* angenehm
pleased, to **be ~** *29* sich freuen; to **be ~ to do sth** *48* etw gern tun
pleasure *11T* Vergnügen; **My ~.** *11T* Gern geschehen.
to **pledge** *188* sich verpflichten
plenty (of) *183T* reichlich, viel
plight *43* Notlage
plot *204* Handlung(sverlauf)
to **plug, ~ in on sth** *131* sich in etw einschalten; **~ in(to)** *69* anschließen, einstecken
plus *60* außerdem
pocket money *64* Taschengeld
point *53* Komma; to **~ at sb/sth** *38T* auf jdn/etw zeigen; to **~ sth at sb** *80* etw auf jdn richten, mit etw auf jdn zielen; to **~ sth out** *59* auf etw hinweisen; to **~ to sth** *164* auf etw hindeuten; **bullet ~** *24* Stichpunkt; **He has a (good) ~.** *84* Da ist etwas dran. Da hat er recht.; **~ of view** *101* Perspektive, Blickwinkel, Standpunkt; **there's little ~ in doing sth** *30* es hat wenig Sinn, etw zu tun; to **make a ~** *26* ein Argument vortragen, etw sagen wollen; to **make a ~ to sb** *82* jdm etw zu verstehen geben; to **take the ~** *151* den Standpunkt verstehen
to **poison** *145* vergiften
poisoning *40* Vergiftung
poisonous *144* giftig
polar bear *204T* Eisbär
pole *203* Mast
police, ~ force *127* Polizei; **~ officer** *65* Polizist/in; **~ station** *125* Polizeiwache; **riot ~** *40* Bereitschaftspolizei
policy *64* Politik, Vorgehensweise; *84* Politik, Kurs, Konzept
politician *65* Politiker/in
poll *36* Umfrage
pollen *152* Blütenstaub, Pollen
to **pollute** *137* *(die Umwelt)* verschmutzen
polluting *149* umweltschädlich
pollution *139* Umweltverschmutzung
pool, swimming ~ *13* Schwimmbad
poor *205* die Armen
popularity *6* Beliebtheit, Popularität
population *85* Bevölkerung; *154* *(Biologie:)* Population
porch *156* Veranda
porridge *181* Haferbrei
port *86* Hafen, Hafenstadt
portion *94* Teil
position *20* Stelle, Stellung, Position
post *66* Stelle, Posten; to **~** *29* *(im Internet)* posten; *127* *(Brief:)* einwerfen, schicken
poster *35* Plakat
pot *205* Kanne, Topf, Becher
potato, couch ~ *196* Stubenhocker/in, Dauerglotzer/in
potential(ly) *132* potenziell
pound *40* Pfund
to **pour** *175* gießen, schütten
to **pour out** *202* herausströmen
poverty *90* Armut
powder, washing ~ *49* Waschpulver
power *18* Macht, Stärke, Kraft; to **~** *138* antreiben, mit Energie versorgen; **geothermal ~** *135* Erdwärme; **hydroelectric ~** *135* Wasserkraft; **nuclear ~** *135* Kernkraft; **nuclear ~ station** *140* Kernkraftwerk; **~ plant** *136* Kraftwerk; **~ station** *139* Kraftwerk, Elektrizitätswerk; **solar ~** *135* Sonnenenergie; **tidal ~** *135* Gezeitenkraft; **wind ~** *135* Windkraft; to **be in ~** *160* an der Macht sein
powerful *51* stark, mächtig, kräftig
powerless *144* machtlos, unfähig
practical *38T* zweckmäßig, praktisch (umsetzbar)
practice *69* Praxis, Ausübung, Verfahren, Ablauf, Praktik

to **practise** *9* üben, trainieren; *160* praktizieren
practitioner, sport medicine ~ *170* Sportmediziner/in
prairie *148* Prärie
to **pray** *126T* beten
prayer *126T* Gebet; ~ **vigil** *126T* Gebetswache
precaution *127* Vorkehrung, Sicherheitsmaßnahme
precious *149* kostbar
to **predict** *8* voraussagen, vorhersagen
preference *21* Vorliebe
pregnancy *208* Schwangerschaft
pregnant *186* schwanger
pre-historic *152* prähistorisch
premises *pl 71T* Geschäftsräume
preparation (for sth) *24* Vorbereitung (auf etw)
to **prepare** *137 (Bericht etc.)* erstellen, verfassen
preschooler *179* Vorschulkind
presence *37* Anwesenheit, Präsenz
to **present** *48* vorstellen, präsentieren
presentation *48* Vortrag, Referat, Präsentation; to **give a ~** *48* ein Referat halten
presenter *48* Vortragende/r; *86T* Moderator/in
press, ~ conference *142* Pressekonferenz; **printing ~** *159* Druckerpresse; **tabloid ~** *10* Boulevardpresse
pressure *64* Druck; to ~ *161* unter Druck setzen; **peer ~** *170* Gruppendruck, Einfluss der Clique; ~ **cooker** *124* Schnellkochtopf
pressures *pl 167* Belastungen; **commercial ~** *pl 178* wirtschaftliche Zwänge
prestige, social ~ *134* soziale Anerkennung
prestigious *70* repräsentativ, prestigeträchtig
to **pretend** *22* vorgeben; so tun, als ob
pretty *11T* ziemlich
prevalent *200* (weit) verbreitet, vorherrschend
to **prevent** *108* verhindern, vorbeugen; *127* verhindern, verhüten
preventable *97* vermeidbar
previous *110* vorherig, früher
previously *54* zuvor, vorher
price, rental ~ *122* Mietpreis
priced, to **be ~ at ...** *129* ... kosten
pride *83* Stolz; to **take ~ in sth** *83* auf etw Wert legen, sich mit etw Mühe geben
priest *65* Priester/in, Geistliche/r
primarily *161* vorrangig, hauptsächlich
primary *36* Haupt-, hauptsächlich
principal *200* Direktor/in, Schulleiter/in
principle, in ~ *143* prinzipiell, grundsätzlich
print, the small ~ *129* das Kleingedruckte
printing press *159* Druckerpresse
priority *123* Priorität, Vorrang
privacy *40* Privatsphäre
procedure *209* Vorgang, Verfahren
process *17* Ablauf, Vorgang, Prozess; to ~ *100* verarbeiten
processed food *197* verarbeitete Lebensmittel
producer *90* Produzent/in
productive *152* produktiv
productivity *153* Produktivität
profession *68T* Beruf; **caring ~** *68T* Pflegeberuf
professional *14* professionell, Profi-; *22* Profi; **caring ~** *193* in einem Sozialberuf Tätige/r
profit *50* Gewinn, Profit; to ~ *144* profitieren
profitable *134* Gewinn bringend, einträglich
programmer *65* Programmierer/in
progress *108* Fortschritt(e)
progression *92* Entwicklung, Steigerung
projector *121* Beamer
promising *81* vielversprechend
to **promote sth** *46* für etw werben, etw bewerben
promotion *49T* Werbung; *65* Beförderung, (beruflicher) Aufstieg; ~ **prospects** *pl 65* Aufstiegschancen
prompt *146* Stichwort, Vorgabe; to ~ *118* auffordern; to ~ **sb to do sth** *129* jdn veranlassen, etw zu tun
prop *66* Requisite
proper name *33* Eigenname
properly *60* richtig, ordentlich, korrekt
property *40* Immobilie(n), Anwesen; ~ **damage** *166T* Sachschaden, Sachschäden
proportion *144* Anteil
proposal *155* Vorschlag
prospects, promotion ~ *pl 65* Aufstiegschancen
to **protect** *47* schützen
protection, data ~ *123* Datenschutz
protein *154* Eiweiß, Protein
proud *81* stolz
to **prove** *11T* beweisen; *146* sich erweisen
proverb *97* Sprichwort
to **provide** *27* zur Verfügung stellen; to ~ **sth** *139* für etw sorgen
provider *39* Anbieter; **health care ~** *88* Gesundheitsdienstleister
provocation *45* Provokation
psychological *91* psychologisch
psychologist *65* Psychologe/-in
psychology *36* Psychologie
pub *175* Kneipe
public *11T* öffentlich; ~ **transport** *48F* öffentliche Verkehrsmittel
publication *111* Veröffentlichung
to **publish** *131* veröffentlichen
publisher *50* Verleger/in
puddle *158* Pfütze, Tümpel
puff, to **huff and ~** *(ugs) 202* schnaufen und keuchen
to **pull, ~ down** *155* (Gebäude) abreißen; ~ **sth tight** *62* etw straff ziehen
to **pump** *140* pumpen
purchase *129* Kauf
purity *54* Reinheit
purpose *84* Absicht, Zweck
push-up *170* Liegestütze
to **put** *127* formulieren, sagen, in Worte fassen; ~ **an end to sth** *27* mit etw Schluss machen, einen Schlussstrich unter etw ziehen; ~ **in work** *95* Arbeit leisten; ~ **sb through** *33 (Telefon:)* jdn durchstellen, jdn verbinden; ~ **sth down to sth** *84* etw einer Sache zuschreiben; ~ **sth up** *35* etw *(Bild etc.)* aufhängen; ~ **up** *175* aufstellen
pylon *203* Mast, Pfeiler

Q

qualification *68* Abschluss, Qualifikation
qualified *68T* mit Abschluss, qualifiziert
quality *18* Qualität; ~ **control** *120* Qualitätskontrolle; ~ **of life** *137* Lebensqualität
quarantine *108* Quarantäne
quarter *36* Viertel; **living ~s** *pl 108* Wohnbereich
queue *81* Warteschlange; to ~ *7* sich *(in einer Warteschlage)* anstellen; to **jump the ~** *82* sich vordrängeln
quick reference *48* schnelles Nachschlagen
to **quote** *136* zitieren

R

race *7* Rennen
racial *84* rassisch, Rassen-
racing, ~ car *13* Rennwagen; ~ **cyclist** *14* Radrennfahrer/in
radical *146* radikal
radicalization *123* Radikalisierung
to **radicalize** *124* radikalisieren
rainforest *54* Regenwald
to **raise** *156 (Pflanzen)* anbauen; ~ **(money)** *98* (Geld) sammeln, einbringen; ~ **an alarm** *209T* Alarm auslösen; ~ **sth** *59* etw *(Thema etc.)* ansprechen; *80* etw anheben, etw hochheben; *100* etw steigern, etw erhöhen
random *170* zufällig, beliebig
to **rank, ~ sb/sth** *6* jdn/etw einstufen, jdn/etw (ein-)ordnen; ~ **sixth** *92* den sechsten Platz einnehmen
ranking *121* Rangfolge; *161* Rangliste
rapid(ly) *70* rasch, schnell
rarely *118* selten
rate *105* Tempo, Quote, Rate, Anteil; **at any ~** *131* auf jeden Fall; **unemployment ~** *86T* Arbeitslosenquote

rather *88* lieber, eher; ~ **than** *43* anstatt
rating, credit ~ *62T* (Bewertung/Einstufung der) Bonität, Kreditwürdigkeit
raw *63* roh; ~ **product** *99* Ausgangsprodukt, Roherzeugnis
reach *99* Reichweite
to **reach out to sb/sth** *202* die Hand nach jdm/etw ausstrecken
to **react (to)** *184* reagieren (auf)
to **reactivate** *39* wieder in Betrieb nehmen, reaktivieren
to **read,** ~ **sth back** *34* etw *(zur Kontrolle)* vorlesen; ~ **sth closely** *51* etw genau (durch)lesen
reader *36* Dozent/in
to **realise** *40* wissen, erkennen, klar sein
realistic *65* realistisch
to **reap the benefits** *165* die Früchte ernten, die Vorteile nutzen
reason, for this ~ *48* aus diesem Grund; to **give a ~** *23* eine Begründung anführen
reasonable *122* vernünftig
reborn *205* wiedergeboren
to **rebuild** *51* umbauen, erneuern
to **recall** *200* sich erinnern
receipt *60* Quittung
reception *120* Empfang
receptionist *72* Empfangsmitarbeiter/in
recession *107T* Rezession
to **recognize** *54* (wieder)erkennen; *132* anerkennen, begreifen
to **recommend** *108* empfehlen
record, to ~ *14* aufzeichnen; **on ~** *108* aktenkundig, dokumentiert; ~ **company** *8* Plattenfirma
recording *187* Aufnahme, Aufzeichnung
to **recover** *109* sich erholen; ~ **fully** *109* wieder völlig gesund werden
to **recruit sb** *134* jdn anwerben, jdn neu einstellen
recruiter *134* Personalvermittler/in, Anwerber/in
recruitment *66* Personalbeschaffung
rectangular *54* rechteckig
red lights, to **jump ~** *48F* bei Rot über eine Ampel fahren
red tape bureaucracy *146* übertriebene Bürokratie
to **redevelop** *155* sanieren
redevelopment *155* Sanierung
to **reduce** *17T* senken, reduzieren, verringern; ~ **sb to sth** *81* jdn zu etw bringen
reduction *83* Verringerung, Senkung
redundant, to **make sb ~** *110* jdn (betriebsbedingt) entlassen
ref. (= reference) *76* *(Brief:)* Zeichen
to **refer,** ~ **to sb as** *184* jdn bezeichnen als; ~ **to sb/sth** *14* jdn/etw erwähnen, sich auf jdn/etw beziehen; ~ **sb to sb/sth** *209T* jdn zu jdm überweisen, jdn an etw verweisen
referee *75* Referenzgeber
reference *75* Referenz, Zeugnis; **quick ~** *48* schnelles Nachschlagen; ~ **(to sth)** *15* Verweis (auf etw)
to **reflect** *136* reflektieren
refreshment *172* Erfrischung
refrigeration *159* Kühlung, Kälteerzeugung
refugee *80* Flüchtling
to **refuse** *14* sich weigern; ~ **sth** *129* etw verweigern
to **regain** *209T* wiedererlangen
regardless, ~ **of sth** *37* ungeachtet einer Sache
regards, R~ *121* *(Brief:)* Viele Grüße; **as ~ …** *68T* was … betrifft; **in ~ to** *88* bezüglich
regime *189* Regime
registered *66* eintragen, (staatlich) anerkannt
regulation *143T* Vorschrift
regulations *pl 54* Vorschriften, Bestimmungen
to **reject** *84* ablehnen, zurückweisen
to **rejoin sb** *94* jdn wieder treffen
to **relate to sth** *26* sich auf etw beziehen
related *103* zugehörig; **closely ~** *116* eng verwandt; to **be ~ to sth** *10* mit etw in Zusammenhang stehen
relationship *10* Beziehung, Verhältnis
relative *183* relativ
release *46* Veröffentlichung; to ~ *8* veröffentlichen
relevant *17* relevant, wichtig
reliability *114* Zuverlässigkeit, Verlässlichkeit
relief *205* Erleichterung, Entlastung, Linderung
to **relieve** *118* erleichtern, *(Druck)* verringern, lindern
religious *92* religiös
to **rely on sth** *140* sich auf etw verlassen, auf etw angewiesen sein
to **remain** *106* bleiben
remaining *120* übrig, verbleibend
remind, to ~ **sb (of sth)** *44* jdn (an etw) erinnern
reminder, to **be a stark ~** *132* etw jäh vor Augen führen, etw überdeutlich machen
remote *160* entlegen
renewable *135* erneuerbar
rent *104* Miete; to ~ *118* mieten
rental price *122* Mietpreis
repercussion *64* Auswirkung, Konsequenz
repetition *15* Wiederholung
to **replace** *16* ersetzen, austauschen
replacement *86T* Ersatz, Ersetzung, Austausch
to **report to sb** *78* jdm unterstellt sein
reportedly *134* Berichten zufolge
to **represent** *168* vertreten, repräsentieren
representative *37* repräsentativ; *167* Repräsentant/in, Abgeordnete/r
to **reproduce** *152* sich fortpflanzen
reputation *40* Ansehen, Ruf
request *128* Bitte, Wunsch, Anfrage; **on ~** *75* auf Wunsch, auf Verlangen
requested, as ~ *120* wie gewünscht
to **require** *69* erfordern, benötigen
required, to **be ~ to do sth** *143T* etw tun müssen; verpflichtet sein, etw zu tun
requirement *66* Voraussetzung, Bedingung, Anforderung; *140* Bedarf; **level of ~** *134* Bedarfsniveau
to **re-read** *28* erneut lesen
to **rescue** *62T* retten, bergen
research *49T* Recherche, Nachforschungen, Untersuchungen; *139* Forschung; to ~ **sth** *43* etw recherchieren, Nachforschungen über etw anstellen; **R~ and Development (R&D)** *120* Forschung(s-) und Entwicklung (sabteilung)
researcher *64* Forscher/in, Wissenschaftler/in
reservation *78* Reservierung
to **reserve** *121* reservieren
reserved *118* reserviert, vorbehalten
to **re-shore** *104* *(Industrie)* wieder im Inland ansiedeln, wieder ins Inland verlagern
residence *185* *(Alten-, Pflege-)* Heim
resident *124* Anwohner/in, Bewohner/in
resistance *152* Widerstandsfähigkeit, Resistenz
resistant to sth *152* resistent gegen etw
to **re-skill** *100* umschulen
resource *114* Ressource
resources, Human R~ (HR) *50* Personal(abteilung)
respect *62* Achtung, Respekt; to ~ *27* respektieren
respectful *88* respektvoll
to **respond** *34* antworten, reagieren
response *195* Antwort, Stellungnahme
responsibility *78* Aufgabe, Zuständigkeit; *92* Verantwortung, Zuständigkeit; to **take ~** *78* Verantwortung übernehmen
responsible *124* verantwortungsvoll; to **be ~ for sth** *66* für etw zuständig/verantwortlich sein
rest *183T* Rest
to **result in** *158* führen zu
retail *110* Einzelhandel(s-)
retailer *27* Einzelhändler/in
to **retain** *157* zurückhalten, behalten, bewahren
to **rethink** *69* überdenken
to **retire** *86* in den Ruhestand gehen, in Rente gehen; ~ **sb** *114* jdn in den Ruhestand versetzen
retirement *14* Rücktritt, Rückzug; *114* Ruhestand, Rente; ~ **home** *114* Altersheim
to **retrain** *72* umschulen

return, to ~ **to sth** *62* sich wieder einer Sache zuwenden; **in** ~ *118* im Gegenzug, als Ausgleich; ~ **airfare** *66* Kosten für Hin- und Rückflug
to **reveal** *44* enthüllen, verraten
reveller *40* Feiernde/r
revenue *208* Einkünfte, Einnahmen
reward *45* Belohnung, Lohn; to ~ *48F* belohnen
rewarding *65* lohnend, erfüllend
to **rewrite** *20* umformulieren, neu schreiben
rich *148 (Nahrung)* gehaltvoll, reichhaltig
rid, to **get** ~ **of sth** *145* etw loswerden
ride *95* Fahrt
ridiculous(ly) *60* lächerlich, unglaublich
riding *25* Reiten
rifle *80* Gewehr
rig, drilling ~ *143T* Bohrturm
rigged, to **be** ~ **against sb** *110* jdn (systematisch) benachteiligen, gegen jdn arbeiten
right, all ~ **by me** *30* in Ordnung für mich; ~ **away** *78* sofort; to **get sth** ~ *7* etw richtig machen, etw gut hinbekommen
right-hand *39* rechte/r/s, auf der rechten Seite
to **ring the doorbell** *13 (an der Tür)* klingeln, läuten
riot *40* Aufstand, Aufruhr; ~ **police** *40* Bereitschaftspolizei
road testing *166T* Fahrversuche, Fahrerprobung, Straßentests
to **rob a bank** *130* eine Bank überfallen, eine Bank ausrauben
robbery, bank ~ *130* Banküberfall, Bankraub
robot *167* Roboter
robotic *168* Roboter-
robotics *168* Robotertechnik
rock *140* Fels, Gestein
rock bottom, to **hit** ~ *205* den Tiefpunkt erreichen
to **rocket** *196* in die Höhe schnellen
role *35* Rolle; ~ **model** *55* Vorbild
role-play *11* Rollenspiel; to ~ *11* mit verteilten Rollen spielen
roll, bread ~ *99* Brötchen
rolled into one *208* in einem
room, changing ~ *13* Umkleidekabine, Umkleide; to **make** ~ *110* Platz machen
root *56* Wurzel; to ~ **sth out** *124* etw beseitigen, etw ausmerzen
rotation, job ~ *72* Arbeitsplatzrotation, (innerbetrieblicher) Arbeitsplatzwechsel
rotten *205* faul, verdorben
roughly *105* ungefähr
round, the other way ~ *86T* umgekehrt
route *209T* Route, Strecke
routine *70* (fester) Ablauf, Routine; **dance** ~ *17T* Tanzschritte
row *156* Reihe; **in a** ~ *161* nacheinander
rubbish *47* Müll, Abfall; ~ **bin** *47* Mülltonne
rules *pl* **of the game** *13* Spielregeln
to **rumble** *203* rumpeln, grollen
run *22* Lauf; to ~ *31 (Unternehmen)* führen, betreiben; *96T (Unternehmen etc.)* führen, betreiben
runner *98* Läufer/in
running *107T* in Folge; ~ **cost** *155* Betriebskosten
runoff *156* Abfluss, abfließendes Wasser
rural *86T* ländlich
rush, Must ~. *71T* Ich muss weg.
rutted *156* zerfurcht, ausgefahren

S

sadly *117T* leider
safe, to **keep sth** ~ *23* etw aufbewahren
safely *56* mit Gewissheit
safety *80* Sicherheit; **health and** ~ *83* Arbeitsschutz
salary *48F* Gehalt
sale, clearance ~ *144* Räumungsverkauf; to **be on** ~ *28* angeboten werden, zum Verkauf stehen
sales *pl* *49* Verkauf, Verkäufe, Absatz, Vertrieb; *107* Umsatz; ~ **director** *107* Verkaufsleiter/in, Vertriebsleiter/in
salesman *50* Verkäufer, Vertreter
salesperson *68* Vertreter/in, Verkäufer/in
saleswoman *97* Verkäuferin
salon, hairdressing ~ *49* Friseursalon
salutation *76 (Brief:)* Anrede
Salvation Army *90* Heilsarmee
same, at the ~ **time** *98* gleichzeitig
sample *14* Probe
sanitation *158* Hygiene
satisfaction *68T* Zufriedenheit
satisfied *161* zufrieden(gestellt)
satisfying *65* befriedigend
sauce *205* Soße
savannah *160* Savanne
to **save** *129 (Daten)* sichern; ~ **oneself sth** *84* sich etw ersparen; ~ **up** *25* sparen
say, to **have one's** ~ *126* seine Meinung äußern, zu Wort kommen
saying *59* Sprichwort, Redensart
scale *156* Ausmaß, Umfang; **pay** ~ *68T* Lohntarif, Lohntabelle
to **scan** *15 (Text)* überfliegen
scarce *134* knapp, rar
scared *64* verängstigt; to **be** ~ *8* Angst haben
scarred *157* vernarbt, gezeichnet
scary *51* unheimlich, beängstigend; *164* gruselig, schaurig
to **scatter** *168* verteilen, verstreuen
scene *11T* Szene
sceptic *137* Skeptiker/in
scheme *132* Plan, Programm
school, ~ **leaving party** *17T* Schulabgangsfeier; **secondary** ~ *100* weiterführende Schule
school leaver *186* Schulabgänger/in
school-age *128* im Schulalter
schoolboy *40* Schuljunge
schooling *90* Schulbesuch, Schulbildung
schoolmate *187T* Mitschüler/in
science, Head of S~ *139* Fachbereichsleiter/in Naturwissenschaft
scientist *136* (Natur-)Wissenschaftler/in
scrap *144* Schrott
scrapheap *114* Schrotthaufen
scrapyard *145* Schrottplatz
scream *94* Schrei; to ~ *80* schreien
screen *39* Bildschirm; *121* Leinwand; to ~ *108* untersuchen, überprüfen
script *9* Drehbuch
to **scrutinize** *131* genau ansehen, überprüfen
sea level *137* Meeresspiegel
seat, to **take a** ~ *71T* Platz nehmen
seating *121* Bestuhlung
secondary school *100* weiterführende Schule
secondly *103* zweitens
secret *24* Geheimnis; *49T* heimlich, geheim
secretary *31* Sekretär/in
section *77* Abschnitt; *104* Bereich, Teil; *173* Abteilung
sector *70* Sektor, Bereich
secure *68T* sicher
security, food ~ *155T* Ernährungssicherung; **job** ~ *65* sicherer Arbeitsplatz; ~ **forces** *pl* *126T* Sicherheitskräfte; ~ **service** *127* Geheimdienst
to **see sb** *38T* zu jdm gehen
seed *152* Samen, Saatgut
to **seek** *75* suchen
seeker, asylum ~ *81* Asylbewerber/in
segment *208* Abschnitt, Teilstück, Segment
seldom *134* selten
to **select** *87* auswählen
selection *121* Auswahl; *152* Auslese, Selektion
selective *152* selektiv
self-defence *128* Selbstverteidigung
self-esteem *197* Selbstachtung, Selbstwertgefühl
to **self-fund** *110* selbst finanzieren
self-reliant *183* selbstständig
self-sustainable *90* selbsttragend, lebensfähig
sell, sold out *20* ausverkauft
to **send sth out** *78* etw verschicken
senior *AE* *158* Schüler/in der Abschlussklasse *(US High School)*; *69* leitend; ~ **citizen** *114* Senior/in, ältere/r Mitbürger/in
to **sensationalize sth** *125* reißerisch über etw berichten
sense *28* Sinn; ~ **of touch** *169* Tastsinn; to **make** ~ *116* Sinn ergeben, sinnvoll sein

sensing, tactile ~ *169* Tastempfinden
sensitive *88* einfühlsam, feinfühlig; *127* sensibel, *(Information:)* vertraulich
sensor *209T* Sensor
separate *73* getrennt, separat; to ~ *33* trennen, loslösen; *80* trennen, abspalten
separately *33* einzeln
series *51* Reihe, Serie
seriously *49T* im Ernst
serpent *203* (Riesen-)Schlange
to **serve** *178* (be)dienen
service *39* Dienst, Dienstleistung; **security ~** *127* Geheimdienst; **~ station** *166T* Tankstelle
services, customer ~ advisor *68T* Kundenberater/in
session *16* Sitzung
set *66* Kulisse; *170* Satz, Zusammenstellung; *168* Menge; to ~ **an example** *56* ein Beispiel setzen, mit gutem Beispiel vorangehen; to ~ **fire to sth** *145* etw anzünden; to ~ **out to do sth** *43* sich vornehmen, etw tun; to ~ **sth up** *66* etw einrichten; to ~ **up** *49T* *(Unternehmen)* gründen; **chess ~** *13* Schachspiel *(Figuren + Brett)*
to **set off** *202* aufbrechen
setback *169* Rückschlag
setting *39* Einstellung; *88* Umgebung
to **settle in** *187T* sich einleben
set-up *32* Aufbau
several *36* mehrere
severe *108* ernst, schwer
sex *29* Geschlecht; **the opposite ~** *29* das andere Geschlecht
sexist *186* sexistisch
shadowy *144* zwielichtig
to **shake** *9* zittern; **~ one's head** *81* den Kopf schütteln; **~ sth** *17T* etw schütteln, mit etw wackeln; *144* an etw rütteln; **~ sth off** *70* etw abschütteln
shale *140* Schiefer
share *149* Anteil; **market ~** *72* Marktanteil
shared *102* gemeinsam; **~ house** *62T* Wohngemeinschaft
shareholder *178* Aktionär/in, Teilhaber/in, Gesellschafter/in
sharp *106* stark; *103* scharf
sheep *152* Schaf
sheet, ice ~ *137* Eisdecke
shelf, *pl* **shelves** *155T* Regal
shelter *94* Unterkunft
shift *66* Schicht; *196* Verschiebung, Verlagerung, Wandel
to **shine light on sth** *144* Licht auf etw werfen
to **ship** *49T* verschicken; *144* versenden, verschiffen
shipbuilding *112* Schiffbau
shipping company *145* Transportunternehmen, Spediteur, Reederei
shipyard *86* Werft
shocked *40* schockiert
shoot *203* Trieb *(einer Pflanze)*, Spross; to ~ *80* schießen; to **~ sb** *109* jdn erschießen; to ~ **up** *40* rasant ansteigen
to **shop** *18* einkaufen
shopper *6* Käufer/in, Kunde/Kundin
shopping mall *27* Einkaufspassage, Einkaufszentrum
short, to cut a long story ~ *60* lange Rede, kurzer Sinn
shortage *68T* Mangel
short-sleeved *156* kurzärmlig
show *9* *(TV-, Radio-)*Sendung
to **shudder** *80* erschaudern, zittern
to **shuffle** *81* schlurfen
to **shut down** *124* schließen
shy *59* schüchtern
siblings *pl* *29* Geschwister
sick, to **be ~ and tired of sth** *129* die Nase von etw gestrichen voll haben; to **be ~ of sth** *110* von etw die Nase voll haben
to **sidetrack** *208* ablenken
sight *209T* Sehkraft
to **sign** *8* unterschreiben
signage, digital ~ *45* digitale Außenwerbung
signal *200* Signal, Zeichen
signature *76* Unterschrift
significance *199* Bedeutung, Stellenwert
silent *129* stumm
silent(ly) *81* still, schweigend
similarity *21* Ähnlichkeit
similarly *87* in ähnlicher Weise, genauso, ebenso
since *13* seit; *88* weil, da
sincerely, Yours ~ *31* *(Brief:)* Mit freundlichen Grüßen
single *205* einzelne/r/s; **~ mom** *74* Alleinerziehende; **~ parent** *197* alleinerziehend
sink *63* Spüle
sir *87T* mein Herr
site *29* Website
sitting room *118* Wohnzimmer
sixth-form college *139* Oberstufenzentrum, Studienkolleg
skeptical *AE* *157* skeptisch
skill *8* Fähigkeit, Fertigkeit
skilled *110* qualifiziert, erfahren; to **be ~ with sth** *65* mit etw gut umgehen können
skills, social ~ *pl* *29* Sozialkompetenz
to **skim** *36* *(Text)* überfliegen
skinny *24* hauteng
to **skip sth** *46* etw auslassen, etw überspringen
skirt, wraparound ~ *156* Wickelrock
skydive *43* Fallschirmsprung
skylight *40* Oberlicht, Dachfenster
slide *48* Dia, (Overhead-)Folie
slight(ly) *104* leicht, gering(fügig)
slim *17* schlank
slope *156* Hang
to **slow** *105* (sich) verlangsamen, hemmen; **~ down** *166T* bremsen
small, the ~ print *129* das Kleingedruckte
to **smash** *94* zertrümmern, zerstören
smile *54* Lächeln
smoke *202* Rauch
smooth(ly) *166T* reibungslos
to **smoulder** *203* schwelen
to **snack** *197* eine Kleinigkeit zu sich nehmen, etwas zwischendurch essen
to **sniff sth** *63* an etw riechen
snow *146* Schnee
so far *96T* bislang
soaked *175* durchnässt
soap *49T* Seife
to **soar** *196* steigen
so-called *74* sogenannt
social, ~ engineering *114* Änderung gesellschaftlicher Strukturen, angewandte Sozialwissenschaft; **~ prestige** *134* soziale Anerkennung; **~ skills** *pl* *29* Sozialkompetenz; **~ worker** *65* Sozialarbeiter/in
to **socialize** *29* sich treffen, unter Leute gehen
society, civil ~ *161* Bürgergesellschaft; **equal ~** *115* gerechte Gesellschaft
sock *210* Socke
soft drink *197* alkoholfreies Getränk
to **soften** *33* mildern, abmildern
soil *153* Erde, Boden
solar *135* Sonnen-, Solar-; **~ power** *135* Sonnenenergie
sold out *20* ausverkauft
soldier *80* Soldat/in
sole *94* alleinig
solid *44* fest, solide
solidarity *188* Solidarität
solution *38T* Lösung
to **solve** *65* lösen
sometime *31* irgendwann
sophisticated *178* raffiniert, anspruchsvoll
sorry, to **feel ~ for sb** *92* jd tut einem leid
sort *28* Art, Sorte; to ~ *6* sortieren, einordnen
sound *46* solide, untadelig
soup *183T* Suppe
source *52* Quelle; to **~ sth** *134* etw beziehen, beschaffen
to **sow** *161* säen
space, to **take up ~** *153* Platz einnehmen
spare, to **have ~ cash** *96T* Geld übrig haben
to **speak up** *162* lauter sprechen
speaker *17* Sprecher/in; **native ~** *75* Muttersprachler/in
Speaking. *78* *(Telefon:)* Am Apparat.
special committee *167* Sonderausschuss
special needs class *200* Förderklasse
specialist *128* Spezial-, Fach-; **~ lawyer** *39* Fachanwalt/-anwältin
to **specialize in sth** *139* sich auf etw spezialisieren
specialized training *200* Spezialausbildung, Fachausbildung

species 148 *(Biologie:)* Art
spectator 12 Zuschauer/in
speech bubble 26 Sprechblase
speed 48F Geschwindigkeit; to ~ **up** 166T beschleunigen; ~ **camera** 48F Geschwindigkeitsüberwachungskamera, Radarfalle; ~ **limit** 48F Geschwindigkeitsbegrenzung
to **spell** 33 buchstabieren; 37 buchstabieren, (richtig) schreiben
spelling 32 Rechtschreibung
spending 52 Ausgaben, Aufwendungen
spinach 156 Spinat
to **spiral out of control** 44 außer Kontrolle geraten
splendid 155 prächtig
to **split** 73 (sich) aufteilen; ~ **(up)** 10 *(Paar:)* sich trennen
to **spoil** 56 *(Kind)* verwöhnen
spokesman 27 Sprecher
spokesperson 134 Sprecher/in
to **sponsor** 22 *(finanziell)* unterstützen, sponsern
sponsorship 90 Förderung
sport medicine practitioner 170 Sportmediziner/in
sports, ~ **car** 49 Sportwagen; ~ **gear** 22 Sportkleidung, Sportausrüstung
sportswear 19 Sportkleidung
spot 8 Platz, Stelle; 69 Platz, Ort, Fleck, Punkt
spouse 129 Ehegatte
spray 152 Spritzmittel
spread 160 Verbreitung, Ausbreitung; to ~ 43 sich verbreiten; 100 sich ausbreiten, sich verbreiten
spreadsheet 75 Tabellenkalkulation
to **spy on sb** 129 jdn ausspionieren
spyware 128 Spionagesoftware
square, ~ **metre** 54 Quadratmeter; ~ **mile** 148 Quadratmeile
squat 170 Kniebeuge
squeal 118 Kreischen
to **squeeze oneself into sth** 24 sich in etw hineinzwängen
stadium 13 Stadion
staff 68T Personal, Belegschaft, Mitarbeiter; to ~ 66 *(mit Personal)* besetzen; **member of** ~ 171 Mitarbeiter/in
stage 8 Bühne; 61 Phase, Abschnitt
stall, food ~ 188 Imbissstand
to **stamp** 48F stempeln, abstempeln
stand, to ~ **in for sb** 72 jdn vertreten; to ~ **out** 49T auffallen, herausstechen; to ~ **up** 17T aufstehen, sich hinstellen; to **make a** ~ 193 Farbe bekennen, ein Zeichen setzen
standard 68T Niveau
star 202 Stern
to **stare at sb** 24 jdn anstarren
stark, to **be a** ~ **reminder** 132 etw jäh vor Augen führen, etw überdeutlich machen
to **start,** ~ **on sb** 60 jdn angreifen, jdn kritisieren; ~ **out** 49T (zunächst) anfangen; 184 beginnen, am Anfang stehen
startling 114 alarmierend, erschreckend, erstaunlich
starvation 155T Hunger
to **state** 27 darlegen, festlegen; 110 erklären, feststellen; 124 aussagen
statement 7 Aussage, Feststellung, Behauptung
station, (radio/TV) ~ 160 (Radio-/Fernseh-)Sender; **nuclear power** ~ 140 Kernkraftwerk; **police** ~ 125 Polizeiwache; **power** ~ 139 Kraftwerk, Elektrizitätswerk
stationery 122 Schreibpapier, Schreibwaren
statistics 52 Statistik(en)
status 6 Status, Stellung
to **stay overnight** 122 übernachten
steadily 62 ununterbrochen
steady 106 kontinuierlich, stabil
steel 143T Stahl
steep 156 steil
step 11T Schritt; to ~ 47 treten; to ~ **off** 62 aussteigen
stepping stone 184 Sprungbrett
to **stick,** ~ **sth on** 129 etw befestigen; ~ **to sth** 24 bei etw bleiben, sich an etw halten
stigma 208 Stigma, Makel
still 22 (immer) noch; dennoch; 88 dennoch; to **be** ~ **going strong** 114 gut dabei sein, immer noch in Form sein
to **stimulate** 14 anregen, stimulieren
stock 105 (Lager-)Bestand, Vorrat
stocks, to **maintain** ~ 154 den Bestand erhalten
stomach pain 108 Bauchschmerzen
stone, stepping ~ 184 Sprungbrett
stop 144 Station; to ~ **sb from doing sth** 116 jdn daran hindern, etw zu tun
store 6 Geschäft, Laden; to ~ 71 aufbewahren, lagern; 148 speichern
storeroom 120 Lagerraum
stork 147 Storch
story, to cut a long ~ **short** 60 lange Rede, kurzer Sinn
storytelling 202 Geschichtenerzählen
straight 50 direkt, gleich; ~ **ahead** 119 geradeaus; ~ **away** 103 sofort
straightaway 129 sofort, sogleich
strategic(ally) 156 strategisch
strategy 51 Strategie
to **stray** 188 abweichen, sich verirren
stream 110 Strom; 156 Bach, Fließgewässer
street, high ~ 24 Hauptgeschäftsstraße, Einkaufsstraße
strength 78 Stärke; 94 Stärke, Kraft
to **strengthen** 17T kräftigen, stärken
stress 17T Belastung, Stress; to ~ 200 betonen, hervorheben
stressed 17T angestrengt, gestresst
to **stretch** 203 sich strecken
strike 72 Streik; to ~ 94 treffen; to **go on** ~ 72 streiken
striking 92 auffallend, auffällig, hervorstechend
stripe 22 Streifen
to **strive** 200 streben, bemüht sein
strong, ~ **advice** 62T dringender Rat; to **be still going** ~ 114 gut dabei sein, immer noch in Form sein
structure 142 Bauwerk, Konstruktion; to ~ 15 strukturieren
struggle 85 Kampf; to ~ 200 kämpfen, sich abmühen
strychnine 14 Strychnin
studies, business ~ 75 Betriebswirtschaft
study 14 Untersuchung, Studie; to ~ **sth** 6 etw genau betrachten; 26 sich etw genau ansehen
stuff 24 Zeug, Sache(n)
sub-heading 15 Teilrubrik, Zwischenüberschrift
subject line 32 *(Brief:)* Betreffzeile
submission 46 Einsendung
to **submit** 32 einreichen, vorlegen, zusenden; to ~ **sth** 46 etw einreichen, etw einsenden
subsidy 141 Subvention
substance 14 Substanz, Stoff
substance misuse 185 Drogenmissbrauch
substitute 160 Ersatz
subway *AE* 46 U-Bahn
to **succeed** 148 erfolgreich sein, Erfolg haben
sudden 71 plötzlich
suffer, to ~ **from sth** 38 unter etw leiden; 158 an etw leiden; 167 unter etw zu leiden haben; to ~ **sth** 14 an etw leiden, etw erleiden
sufficient 169 ausreichend, hinreichend
sugared 197 gezuckert
sugary 178 zuckerhaltig, zuckersüß
to **suggest** 16 vorschlagen; 19 unterstellen, suggerieren; 36 darauf hindeuten, nahelegen
suggestion 31 Vorschlag
suicide 125 Selbstmord; ~ **bomber** 125 Selbstmordattentäter/in
suit 44 Anzug; to ~ **sb** 24 *(Kleidung:)* jdm stehen; to ~ **sb/sth** 24 zu jdm/etw passen
suitable 61 passend
sum 37 Summe; to ~ **up** 15 zusammenfassen; **To** ~ **up, …** 15 Zusammenfassend …
to **summarize** 15 zusammenfassen
sunflower 156 Sonnenblume
sunny 51 sonnig
superhuman 164 übermenschlich
superior 78 Vorgesetzte/r; 165 überlegen
supplies *pl* 143T Vorräte, Vorkommen; **office** ~ *pl* 120 Büromaterial
to **supply** 67 liefern, bieten; to ~ **sb with sth** 126T jdn mit etw versorgen, jdm mit etw beliefern; ~ **chain** 99 Lieferkette

support *11* Unterstützung, Hilfe; to ~ *11T* unterstützen; *117 (Argument)* untermauern, stützen
supportive *183* (unter)stützend
suppose, I ~ *62T* wohl
supposed, to **be ~ to do sth** *49T* etw tun sollen
sure, to **make** ~ *23* sicherstellen; dafür sorgen, dass; *88* sicherstellen
to **surf the internet** *25* im Internet surfen
surface *140* Oberfläche
surgery *68T* (Arzt-)Praxis; *92* Operation
surname *33* Nachname
surprised *78* erstaunt, überrascht
surprisingly *155T* erstaunlicherweise
surveillance *123* Überwachung
survey *12* Umfrage
to **survive** *51* überleben
suspect *124* Verdächtige/r
suspicious *129* misstrauisch
sustainable *67* nachhaltig
sweater *21* Pullover
sweatshop *22* Ausbeutungsbetrieb
sweep, to ~ **away** *94* fortschwemmen, erfassen, wegreißen; **~ing views** *pl 157* atemberaubende Ausblicke, umwerfende Sicht
sweetheart, childhood ~ *10* Jugendliebe
swimmer *13* Schwimmer/in
swimming pool *13* Schwimmbad
swine flu *108* Schweinegrippe
to **switch, ~ to sth** *100* auf etw umstellen; *129* auf etw umschalten
switchboard *187* Schalttafel
symmetrical *168* symmetrisch
sympathetic(ally) *59* einfühlsam
symptom *108* Symptom, Anzeichen

T

tabloid press *10* Boulevardpresse
taboo *173* Tabu
tactic *124* Taktik
tactile sensing *169* Tastempfinden
tag, name ~ *172* Namensschild
tailback *166T* Rückstau
take, to ~ **action** *100* handeln; to ~ **care of sb** *74* sich um jdn kümmern; to ~ **legal action** *39* rechtliche Schritte unternehmen; to ~ **off** *153 (Flugzeug:)* abheben, starten; *153 (Produkt:)* gut anlaufen, gut ankommen; to ~ **over** *84* die Macht übernehmen; to ~ **part in sth** *9* an etw teilnehmen; to ~ **place** *8* stattfinden; to ~ **sb along** *16* jdn mitnehmen; to ~ **sb in** *87* jdn aufnehmen; to ~ **sb on** *154* es mit jdm aufnehmen, gegen jdn antreten; to ~ **sth** *60* etw ertragen; to ~ **sth further** *32* etw (weiter) verfolgen; to ~ **sth into account** *23* etw in Betracht ziehen, etw berücksichtigen; to ~ **sth on** *154* etw *(Aufgabe)* übernehmen; to ~ **the point** *151* den Standpunkt verstehen; to ~ **time off** *74* sich frei nehmen; to ~ **turns** *48* sich abwechseln; to ~ **up space** *153* Platz einnehmen; **sb's ~ on sth** *140* jds Einschätzung von etw
tale *204T* Erzählung
talent *58* Begabung, Talent
talented *8* begabt, talentiert
talk *38T* Gerede; *174* Vortrag; to ~ **sb through sth** *17T* jdm etw der Reihe nach erklären; to ~ **sth over** *11T* etw besprechen
tank, catchment ~ *158* Auffangbehälter
tap *143T* Wasserhahn
tape *16* (Ton-)Band
target *93* Ziel; to ~ **sb** *51* jdn ins Visier nehmen, auf jdn abzielen; ~ **group** *53* Zielgruppe
targeted *49T* gezielt
tasty *21* schmackhaft, lecker
tax *92* Steuer
to **taxi around** *194* herumkutschieren
tea *BE 57* Zwischenmahlzeit am Nachmittag, Abendessen
team, to ~ **up with sb** *114* mit jdm zusammenarbeiten, sich mit jdm zusammentun; **national** ~ *13* Nationalmannschaft
tear *90* Träne
techie *208* Technikfreak
technician *66* Techniker/in
technique *71* Methode, Technik
technological *67* technologisch
telehealth *209T* Telemedizin
telescreen *131* Televisor
temperature *108* Temperatur
temporary *66* vorübergehend, befristet
tempting *164* verlockend
to **tend to do sth** *36* dazu neigen, etw zu tun
tension *57* Spannung
term *131* Begriff; *181* Schul-/Studienzeit *(im Gegensatz zu Ferien)*; Trimester; **in the long** ~ *91* langfristig; **in the short** ~ *91* kurzfristig
terminal *43* im Endstadium, tödlich
to **terminate** *110* beenden
terms *pl 67* Bedingungen, Konditionen
terrace *157* Terrasse
terraced *BE 40* Reihenhaus-; ~ *157* terrassiert
terrible *194* schrecklich, furchtbar
terrified *80* entsetzt
territorial, to **be** ~ *69* sein Revier verteidigen
terrorist *123* Terrorist/in, Terror-
to **test** *102* erproben, testen
test drive *166T* Testfahrt
test strip *208* Teststreifen
text, to ~ *29* eine SMS schicken, simsen; ~ **message** *42* SMS
textbook *158* Lehrbuch
textile *100* Textil-
thank, to ~ *11* danken, sich bedanken; **T~ goodness!** *22* Gott sei Dank!; ~ **you** *39* danke(schön)
that *64* so; **if …, ~ is.** *54* wenn … überhaupt / auch wirklich …
theft *123* Diebstahl
theory *46* Theorie
therapy *54* Therapie
therefore *69* daher, deshalb, demzufolge
thermometer *146* Thermometer
these days *56* zur Zeit
thick *153* dick, stark
things, as ~ turn out *34* wie sich herausstellt
to **think twice** *44* gründlich überlegen
thinker *65* Denker/in
thinking *18* Denken
third *36* Drittel
thorough(ly) *127* gründlich, sorgfältig
though *19* aber, dagegen, allerdings; **even** ~ *22* selbst wenn, obwohl
thought *62T* Gedanke
thoughtful *46* wohlüberlegt, gut durchdacht
thousand *39* tausend, Tausend
threat *126* Bedrohung; to **be under** ~ *126* bedroht werden
to **threaten** *132* bedrohen
threatening *51* bedrohlich
thrilled *175* begeistert
through, to **get sb** ~ *56* jdn durchbringen; jdm helfen, etw zu überstehen; to **put sb** ~ *33 (Telefon:)* jdn durchstellen, jdn verbinden
throughout *122* überall, in ganz …; ~ **the decades** *14* durch/über die Jahrzehnte
to **throw** *40* werfen; to ~ **a party** *40* eine Party geben/schmeißen
thumb *37* Daumen
tick *146* Zecke
ticket inspector *48F* Fahrkartenkontrolleur/in
tidal power *135* Gezeitenkraft
to **tidy up** *58* aufräumen
tie *70* Krawatte
tight *24* knapp, eng
till *30* bis
time, all the ~ *36* ständig, die ganze Zeit; **at any** ~ *39* jederzeit; **at one** ~ *163* gleichzeitig; **at the same** ~ *98* gleichzeitig; **in good** ~ *171* rechtzeitig; **in no** ~ *152* im Nu; **in** ~ *69* rechtzeitig; **on** ~ *62T* pünktlich; **waste of** ~ *24* Zeitverschwendung; to **take ~ off** *74* sich frei nehmen
times *92* mal
tin *203* Dose, Büchse
tinned *81* in Dosen, Dosen-
tiny *61* winzig
tired, to **be sick and ~ of sth** *129* die Nase von etw gestrichen voll haben
tiring *116* anstrengend
title, job ~ *66* Stellenbezeichnung
toddler *90* Kleinkind
together, to **get** ~ *29* sich treffen
ton *139* Tonne
toned *24* straff, durchtrainiert
tool, motivational ~ *170* Motivierungshilfe, motivationsförderndes Werkzeug

toothpaste *54* Zahnpasta, Zahncreme
top, on ~ of *83* auf
tormentor *129* Peiniger
to **toss** *40* werfen
totalitarian *131* totalitär
totally *70* voll und ganz
touch *17T* Berührung; **sense of ~** *169* Tastsinn; to **keep in ~** *29* in Verbindung bleiben
to **toughen up** *146* abhärten
to **tour** *7* auf Tour gehen
towards *185* auf … zu, in Richtung auf; **~ sth** *62* zu etw hin, auf etw zu
toxic *144* giftig, Gift-
toy *64* Spielzeug
trace *144* Spur
track, to **~** *170* verfolgen, tracken; to **~ sb** *128* jds Spur verfolgen; **test ~** *166T* Teststrecke
tracking device *144* Ortungsgerät
trade *100* Handel; **~ fair** *120* Handelsmesse, Fachmesse
trader *100* Händler/in
trading *100* Handel
tradition *189* Tradition, Brauch
traditional *16* traditionell; *46* herkömmlich
traffic lights *pl 48F* Ampel
tragedy *45* Tragödie
trailing *203* rankend
to **train** *11* trainieren
trainee *31* Auszubildende/r
trainers *pl 163* Turnschuhe
trait *200* Wesenszug, Eigenschaft
traitor *80* Verräter/in
trajectory *160* Flugbahn, Weg
tram *48F* Straßenbahn, Tram
transaction *160* (Geschäfts-)Vorgang, Transaktion
to **transfer** *96T (Geld)* überweisen; *169* übergeben, weitergeben
to **transform** *100* (völlig) verändern
transformation *101* (grundlegende) Veränderung, Umwandlung
translation *28* Übersetzung
to **transmit** *128* übertragen, übermitteln, senden
transparency, OHP ~ *48* Overheadfolie
transport, means of ~ *130* Verkehrsmittel; **personal ~** *102* Individualverkehr; **public ~** *48F* öffentliche Verkehrsmittel
trash *49T* Müll; to **~ sth** *40* etw demolieren
travel expenses *pl 66* Reisekosten, Fahrtkosten
traveller *108* Reisende/r
to **treat** *97* behandeln; *143T (Abwasser)* klären
treatment *67* Behandlung
to **tremble** *80* beben, zittern
trend *54* Trend, Tendenz
triathlon *14* Triathlon
tribe *161* Stamm
to **trick sb into doing sth** *154* jdn *(mit einer List)* dazu bringen, etw zu tun
to **trip** *16* stolpern
troop *108* Truppe
trouble *40* Ärger, Problem(e); to **~ sb** *90* jdn bekümmern, jdm Schwierigkeiten bereiten
to **trust** *38T* vertrauen
try, to **~ sb** *136* jdn vor Gericht stellen; to **give sth a ~** *17T* etw ausprobieren
tumour, brain ~ *209T* Hirntumor
tunnel *140* Tunnel
turbine *155* Turbine
turn *155* Runde, Umdrehung; to **~ away** *206* abweisen; to **~ into sth** *60* zu etw werden; to **~ out** *100* sich herausstellen; to **~ right/left** *119* rechts/links abbiegen; to **~ sb/sth into sb/sth** *46* jdn/etw zu jdm/etw machen; to **~ sth on** *142* etw an-/einschalten; to **~ to sb** *56* sich an jdn wenden; to **~ up** *40* auftauchen; **as things ~ out** *34* wie sich herausstellt; **in ~** *137* wiederum; to **take ~s** *48* sich abwechseln; to **wait for one's ~** *82* warten, bis man an der Reihe ist
twice, to **think ~** *44* gründlich überlegen
twin *56* Zwilling
type *36* Schrift, Type; to **~ sth in** *32* etw eintippen; to **~ sth up** *172* etw *(am Computer)* formulieren, etw ausarbeiten
typing *68T* Schreibmaschinenschreiben

U

ultimately *94* letztlich, letztendlich
umbrella *144* Regenschirm
unable *40* nicht in der Lage, unfähig
unavailable, to **be ~** *34 (Telefon:)* nicht zu sprechen sein
uncertainty *168* Ungewissheit
uncomfortable, to **feel ~** *8* sich unbehaglich fühlen
uncontrolled *86T* ungeregelt, unkontrolliert
to **undercut** *104* unterbieten
undergarments *pl 27* Unterwäsche
to **undergo** *108* sich unterziehen
undergraduate *156* Student/in *(vor dem ersten akad. Grad)*
to **underline** *36* unterstreichen
underneath *204T* (dar)unter
understanding *82* Verständnis
undetectable *128* nicht erkennbar, nicht nachweisbar
undeveloped *148 (Land:)* unbebaut
unemployed *205* arbeitslos
unemployment *86* Arbeitslosigkeit; **~ rate** *86T* Arbeitslosenquote
unexpected *169* unerwartet
unexpected(ly) *111* unerwartet
unfamiliar *168* unbekannt, ungewohnt
unfilled *134* unbesetzt
unfit *37* nicht fit
unhealthy *17* nicht gesund
uninvited *41* un(ein)geladen
union *100* Gewerkschaft
unique *24* einzigartig; to **be ~ to sth** *110* etw ausschließlich betreffen
universe *164* Universum
unless *27* es sei denn, außer wenn
unlike *139* anders als
to **unload** *144* entladen
to **unlock** *170* freischalten, entsperren
unnecessary *57* überflüssig, unnötig
unnoticed, to **go ~** *129* unbemerkt bleiben
unorganized *182* unorganisiert
unpaid *95* unbezahlt
unpleasant *81* unangenehm, unschön
unpolluted *154* unverschmutzt
unpredictable *169* launenhaft, unkalkulierbar
unsanitary *158* unhygienisch
unstoppable *137* unaufhaltsam
unstructured *65* unstrukturiert
untraceable *129* nicht ausfindig zu machen
to **unveil** *168* enthüllen, vorstellen
unwanted *40* unerwünscht
up, ~ to *24* bis; **What's ~?** *22* Was gibt's? Was ist los?; to **be ~ to sth** *63* etw vorhaben
update *37* Aktualisierung; to **~** *75* aktualisieren
to **uphold** *206* bewahren, schützen
to **upload** *42* hochladen
uproar *193* Aufruhr
upset *74* verstimmt, verärgert; to **get ~** *62T* sich aufregen
upwards *53* steigend
urban *124* städtisch, Stadt-
to **urge** *118* drängen
urgently *137* dringend, nachdrücklich
usage *36* Nutzung
use *8* Gebrauch, Nutzen; to **make ~ of sth** *8* von etw Gebrauch machen, etw nutzen
use-by date *149* Haltbarkeitsdatum
used to, they ~ do sth *176* sie machten früher *(üblicherweise)* etwas
used up *204T* aufgebraucht, verbraucht
usefulness *63* Nutzen, Zweckmäßigkeit
useless *111* nutzlos
user *36* Benutzer/in
utility bills *pl 151* Rechnungen für Versorgungsleistungen
utter *129* völlig, vollkommen

V

vacation *AE 49T* Urlaub
vaccine *108* Impfstoff
valuable *90* wertvoll
value *19* Wert; to **~** *44* wertschätzen, schätzen; **~ chain** *145* Wertschöpfungskette
van *129* Lieferwagen
variability *136* Schwankung, Unbeständigkeit
varied *84* vielfältig, abwechslungsreich
variety *149* (Pflanzen-)Sorte
various *57* verschieden, mehrere, allerlei
vase *166* Vase
vastness *164* unermessliche Weite
vegetable, leafy ~ *156* Blattgemüse

vegetarian *121* vegetarisch
vehicle *142* Fahrzeug
vending machine *49T* (Verkaufs-) Automat
vertical *153* senkrecht, vertikal
vessel, blood ~ *17* Blutgefäß
to **vet** *178* gründlich prüfen
veterinarian *160* Tierarzt/-ärztin, Veterinär/in
vibrant *84* dynamisch, voller Leben
vice versa *88* umgekehrt
victim *24* Opfer
view, to **~ sth** *46* (sich) etw ansehen; **point of ~** *101* Perspektive, Blickwinkel, Standpunkt
vigil, prayer ~ *126T* Gebetswache
village, fishing ~ *94* Fischerdorf
violence *124* Gewalt
violent *80* heftig; *84* gewalttätig
viral, ~ ad *45* Internet-Werbespot; to **go ~** *38T* sich *(im Internet)* rasend schnell verbreiten
virtual *35* virtuell
virus, *pl* **viruses** *108* Virus
visible *27* sichtbar
vision, field of ~ *131* Sichtfeld
visionary *51* Visionär/in
visual *52* visuell
visuals *pl* *48* visuelle Hilfsmittel
vital *148* lebensnotwendig, unerlässlich
vocational college *31* Fachoberschule, Berufskolleg
voice, to **drop one's ~** *80* die Stimme senken
voice-controlled *209T* sprachgesteuert
volcano *203* Vulkan
voluntary *67* freiwillig
volunteer *67* (freiwilliger) Helfer/in; to **~ to do sth** *66* sich bereit erklären, etw zu tun
vomit *40* Erbrochenes
vote, to **take a ~** *37* abstimmen
voucher *74* Gutschein

W

wage *104* Lohn; **minimum ~** *110* Mindestlohn
wait *144* Warten, Wartezeit; to **~ for one's turn** *82* warten, bis man an der Reihe ist
walk *93* Spaziergang, Rundgang; to **~ along sth** *24* etw *(Straße etc.)* entlanggehen; **from all ~s of life** *90* aus allen Gesellschaftsschichten, aus allen Lebensbereichen; **gallery ~** *35* Galerierundgang
walk-in medical centre *96T* Ambulanz
walking, within ~ distance *119* zu Fuß erreichbar
wall *38* Wand, Pinnwand; *203* Mauer
wallet *81* Brieftasche, (Herren-) Portemonnaie
walrus *204T* Walross
war *86T* Krieg
warehouse *116* Lager
to **warm** *137* sich erwärmen
warming, global ~ *136* Erderwärmung
warm-up *17T* Aufwärmen
warning, a word of ~ *68* Hinweis, Warnung
wash, to **~** *43* abwaschen, abwischen; to **~ over sb/sth** *8* jdn überkommen, etw überschwemmen; **car ~** *49* Autowaschanlage
washing *60* Wäsche; **~ machine** *129* Waschmaschine; **~ powder** *49* Waschpulver; **~ up** *62T* Geschirrspülen
waste *123* Müll; **~ of time** *24* Zeitverschwendung; **~ water** *143T* Abwasser
wasteland *104* Brachland
watch *24* Armbanduhr; **Not on our ~.** *90* Nicht mit uns!; to **keep ~ over sb** *160* über jdn wachen, jdn beobachten
water heater *105* Warmwasserbereiter, Boiler
wave *84* Welle; to **~ sth** *8* etw schwenken, mit etw wedeln; to **~ sth around** *80* mit etw herumfuchteln
way, along the ~ *90* dabei, währenddessen; **by the ~** *60* übrigens, nebenbei erwähnt; **the other ~ round** *86T* umgekehrt; to **be a two-~ street** *84* auf Gegenseitigkeit beruhen
weakness *78* Schwäche
weapon *124* Waffe
wedding *116* Hochzeit
weed *152* Unkraut
weekday *61* Werktag, Wochentag
weekly *193* wöchentlich
to **weigh** *143T* abwägen
weight, to **gain ~** *196* zunehmen; to **lose ~** *17T* abnehmen
weighty *196* gewichtig, Gewichts-
welcoming *80* gastfreundlich
welfare *60* Sozialfürsorge, Sozialhilfe; *146* Wohl, Wohlergehen
well *140* Bohrloch; *158* Quelle, Brunnen; **~ casing** *143T* Bohrlochverrohrung, Bohrlochwandung
well-being *178* Wohl(befinden)
westerner *126T* Mensch aus der westlichen Welt
wetland *149* Feuchtgebiet, Sumpfgebiet
whatever *57* was auch immer
wheat *99* Weizen
wheel *159* Rad
wheelchair *121* Rollstuhl; **~ access** *122* behindertengerechter Zugang
wheely *69* auf Rollen
whenever *23* jedes Mal, wenn; wann (auch) immer
wherever *202* wo (auch) immer
whilst *94* während
whisper *131* Flüstern
whitefly *156* Mottenschildlaus
whole, on the ~ *23* im Großen und Ganzen
wide-ranging *69* breit gefächert
widowed *74* verwitwet
wild *146* wild
wildfire *175* Lauffeuer, Flächenbrand
willing, to **be ~ to do sth** *75* bereit sein, etw zu tun
wind, ~ farm *141* Windpark; **~ power** *135* Windkraft
wire *131* Draht
wish *114* Wunsch; **Best ~es** *120* *(Brief:)* Mit den besten Wünschen
to **withdraw** *129* *(Geld)* abheben
within *99* innerhalb, binnen
to **wonder** *81* sich fragen
wool *152* Wolle
work, to **~ hard** *68* hart arbeiten, fleißig sein; to **~ sth out** *116* etw herausfinden; *151* etw ausrechnen; **~ experience** *31* Praktikum; to **put in ~** *95* Arbeit leisten
worker, social ~ *65* Sozialarbeiter/in
workforce *69* Belegschaft; *190* Erwerbstätige, Erwerbsbevölkerung
working hours *pl* *65* Arbeitszeiten
working life *140* Betriebsdauer
workout *16* (Fitness-)Training
workplace *69* Arbeitsplatz
World Cup *13* Weltpokal
worldwide *16* weltweit
worried *17T* besorgt, beunruhigt
worries *pl* *143* Bedenken
worrying *137* besorgniserregend
worse, to **be ~ off** *94* schlechter dran sein; to **go from bad to ~** *62* immer schlimmer werden
worth, for what it's ~ *24* meiner (bescheidenen) Meinung nach
worthless (to sb) *145* wertlos (für jdn)
worthwhile *44* lohnend
worthy of sth *161* einer Sache würdig
wraparound skirt *156* Wickelrock
wrapped up *146* eingepackt
to **wreck** *40* demolieren
wrist *168* Handgelenk
to **write down** *18* aufschreiben
writer *31* Verfasser/in; *53* Autor/in, Schriftsteller/in; **~'s address** *76* Absenderanschrift
written *28* schriftlich
wrong, to **get sth ~** *62T* bei etw einen Fehler machen, etw falsch machen; to **go ~** *62T* schieflaufen

Y

yard, back ~ *124* Hinterhof
year, gap ~ *190* *das Jahr zwischen Schulabgang und Studienbeginn*
yearly *68* jährlich, Jahres-
years to come *196* die kommenden Jahre
yet, The best is ~ to come. *164* Das Beste kommt noch. Die besten Zeiten stehen uns noch bevor.
yield *190* Ertrag
youth *62* Jugend
Yuck! *24* Igitt! Bäh!

Z

zero *146* Null
zone, conflict ~ *126* Krisenregion, Konfliktzone

Abingdon ['æbɪŋdən] — Abingdon (Stadt an der Themse in Oxfordshire)

Accra ['ækrə] — Accra (Hauptstadt von Ghana)

Africa ['æfrɪkə] — Afrika
African ['æfrɪkən] — afrikanisch, Afrikaner/in
America [ə'merɪkə] — Amerika
American [ə'merɪkən] — amerikanisch, Amerikaner/in
Amsterdam ['æmstədæm] — Amsterdam
Anglo-Irish [,æŋɡləʊ 'aɪrɪʃ] — anglo-irisch
Antarctic [ænt'ɑːktɪk] — Antarktis, antarktisch
Arab ['ærəb] — arabisch, Araber/in
Arctic ['ɑːktɪk] — Arktis, arktisch
Asia ['eɪʃə] — Asien
Asian ['eɪʃn] — asiatisch, Asiate/-in
Australia [ɒ'streɪliə] — Australien
Australian [ɒ'streɪliən] — australisch, Australier/in
Austria ['ɒstriə] — Osterreich
Austrian ['ɒstriən] — österreichisch, Österreicher/in

Bangladesh [,bæŋɡlə'deʃ] — Bangladesch
Bangladeshi [,bæŋɡlə'deʃi] — bangladeschisch, Bangladescher/in
Bath [bɑːθ] — Bath (Stadt in Somerset)
Belgian ['beldʒən] — belgisch, Belgier/in
Belgium ['beldʒəm] — Belgien
Benin [be'niːn] — Benin
Birmingham ['bɜːmɪŋəm] — Birmingham
Black Forest [,blæk 'fɒrɪst] — Schwarzwald
Bosnia ['bɒzniə] — Bosnien
Brazil [brə'zɪl] — Brasilien
Brazilian [brə'zɪliən] — brasilianisch, Brasilianer/in
Bristol ['brɪstl] — Bristol (Stadt in Südwestengland)
Britain ['brɪtn] — Großbritannien
Briton ['brɪtn] — Brite/Britin
Brittany ['brɪtəni] — Bretagne
Brixton ['brɪkstən] — Brixton (Stadtteil im Süden Londons)
Brussels ['brʌslz] — Brüssel
Burkina Faso [bə,kiːnə 'fæsəʊ] — Burkina Faso
California [,kælə'fɔːniə] — Kalifornien
Canada ['kænədə] — Kanada
Central America [,sentrəl ə'merɪkə] — Mittelamerika
Chicago [ʃɪ'kɑːɡəʊ] — Chicago
China ['tʃaɪnə] — China
Chinese [tʃaɪ'niːz] — chinesisch, Chinese/-in
Cologne [kə'ləʊn] — Köln
Colombo [kə'lɒmbəʊ] — Colombo (Hauptstadt von Sri Lanka)
Columbia [kə'lʌmbiə] — Kolumbien
Dallas ['dæləs] — Dallas
Danish ['deɪnɪʃ] — dänisch, Däne/-in
Denmark ['denmɑːk] — Dänemark
Dublin ['dʌblɪn] — Dublin
East Ham [,iːst 'hæm] — East Ham (Stadtteil im Osten Londons)
Edinburgh ['edɪnbərə] — Edinburgh
Egypt ['iːdʒɪpt] — Agypten
England ['ɪŋɡlənd] — England
Eritrea [,erɪ'triə] — Eritrea
Eritrean [,erɪ'triən] — eritreisch, Eritreer/in
Ethiopia [,iːθi'əʊpiə] — Athiopien
Ethiopian [,iːθi'əʊpiən] — äthiopisch, Athiopier/in
Europe ['jʊərəp] — Europa

(the) Far East [,fɑːr 'iːst] — der Ferne Osten
Finland ['fɪnlənd] — Finnland
Florida ['flɒrɪdə] — Florida
France [frɑːns] — Frankreich
Germany ['dʒɜːməni] — Deutschland
Ghana ['ɡɑːnə] — Ghana
Ghanaian [ɡɑː'neɪən] — ghanaisch, Ghanaer/in
Glasgow ['ɡlɑːsɡəʊ] — Glasgow
Goa ['ɡəʊə] — Goa
Great Barrier Reef [,ɡreɪt 'bæriə riːf] — Großes Barriereriff
Greece [griːs] — Griechenland
Greek [griːk] — Grieche/Griechin, griechisch
Greenland ['griːnlənd] — Grönland
Guinea ['ɡɪni] — Guinea
Haiti ['heɪti] — Haiti
Hawaii [hə'waɪi] — Hawaii
Heathrow [,hiːθ'rəʊ] — Heathrow (Flughafen westlich von London)
Highgate ['haɪɡeɪt] — Highgate (Staddteil im Norden Londons)
Honolulu [,hɒnə'luːluː] — Honolulu (Haupstadt von Hawaii)
Hungary ['hʌŋɡəri] — Ungarn
Iceland ['aɪslənd] — Island
India ['ɪndiə] — Indien
Indian ['ɪndiən] — indisch, Inder/in
Indian Ocean [,ɪndiən 'əʊʃn] — Indischer Ozean
Indonesia [,ɪndəʊ'niːziə] — Indonesien
Iran [ɪ'rɑːn] — Iran
Iranian [ɪ'reɪniən] — iranisch, Iraner/in
Iraq [ɪ'rɑːk] — Irak
Ireland ['aɪələnd] — Irland
Irish ['aɪrɪʃ] — irisch, Ire/Irin
Italy ['ɪtəli] — Italien
Jamaica [dʒə'meɪkə] — Jamaika
Jamaican [dʒə'meɪkən] — jamaikanisch, Jamaikaner/in
Kenya ['kenjə] — Kenia
Kenyan ['kenjən] — kenianisch, Kenianer/in
Kilimanjaro [,kɪlɪmən'dʒɑːrəʊ] — Kilimandscharo
Korea [kə'rɪə] — Korea
Korean [kə'rɪən] — koreanisch, Koreaner/in
Kosovo ['kɒsəvəʊ] — Kosovo
Kosovian [kə'səʊviən] — kosovarisch, Kosovare/-in
Latin America [,lætɪn ə'merɪkə] — Lateinamerika
Latin American [,lætɪn ə'merɪkən] — lateinamerikanisch, Lateinamerikaner/in
London ['lʌndən] — London
Malawi [mə'lɑːwi] — Malawi
Mali ['mɑːli] — Mali
Manchester ['mæntʃɪstə] — Manchester
Massachusetts [,mæsə'tʃuːsɪts] — Massachusetts
Miami [maɪ'æmi] — Miami
Milan [mɪ'læn] — Mailand
(the) Netherlands ['neðələndz] — die Niederlande
New York [,njuː 'jɔːk] — New York
Niger ['naɪdʒə] — Niger
North America [,nɔːθ ə'merɪkə] — Nordamerika
North Sea [,nɔːθ 'siː] — Nordsee
Northern Ireland [,nɔːðən 'aɪələnd] — Nordirland
Oxford ['ɒksfəd] — Oxford

Geographical names

Oxford Circus	[ˌɒksfəd 'sɜːkəs]	Oxford Circus *(Platz und U-Bahn-Station in der Londoner Innenstadt)*
Pacific Ocean	[pəˌsɪfɪk 'əʊʃn]	Pazifischer Ozean
Pakistan	[ˌpækɪ'stɑːn]	Pakistan
Pakistani	[ˌpækɪ'stɑːni]	pakistanisch, Pakistaner/in
Panama	['pænəmɑː]	Panama
(the) Philippines	['fɪləpiːnz]	die Philippinen
Pittsburgh	['pɪtsbɜːg]	Pittsburgh *(Stadt in Pennsylvania)*
Poland	['pəʊlənd]	Polen
Polish	['pəʊlɪʃ]	polnisch, Pole/Polin
Portugal	['pɔːtʃʊgl]	Portugal
Portuguese	[ˌpɔːtʃu'giːz]	portugiesisch, Portugiese/-in
Red Sea	[ˌred 'siː]	Rotes Meer
River Clyde	[ˌrɪvə 'klaɪd]	der Clyde *(Fluss in Schottland)*
River Thames	[ˌrɪvə 'temz]	die Themse
Romania	[ruː'meɪniə]	Rumänien
Romanian	[ruː'meɪniən]	rumänisch, Rumäne/-in
Russia	['rʌʃə]	Russland
Russian	['rʌʃn]	russisch, Russe/Russin
Scotland	['skɒtlənd]	Schottland
Scot	[skɒt]	Schotte/-in
Scottish	['skɒtɪʃ]	schottisch, Schotte/-in
Shanghai	[ˌʃæŋ'haɪ]	Schanghai
Singapore	[ˌsɪŋə'pɔː]	Singapur
South Africa	[ˌsaʊθ 'æfrɪkə]	Südafrika
South America	[ˌsaʊθ ə'merɪkə]	Südamerika
South Carolina	[ˌsaʊθ ˌkærə'laɪnə]	South Carolina
South Pole	[ˌsaʊθ 'pəʊl]	Südpol
Spain	[speɪn]	Spanien
Spanish	['spænɪʃ]	spanisch, Spanier/in
Sri Lanka	[ˌsriː 'læŋkə]	Sri Lanka
Staffordshire	['stæfədʃə]	Staffordshire *(Grafschaft in Mittelengland)*
Staines	['steɪnz]	Staines *(Stadt in Surrey)*
sub-Saharan Africa	[sʌb səˌhɑːrən 'æfrɪkə]	Schwarzafrika
Sudan	[su'dɑːn]	Sudan
Sudanese	[ˌsuːdə'niːz]	sudanesisch, Sudanese/-in
Sweden	['swiːdn]	Schweden
Swede	[swiːd]	Schwede/-in
Swedish	['swiːdɪʃ]	schwedisch, Schwede/-in
Switzerland	['swɪtsələnd]	Schweiz
Swiss	[swɪs]	schweizerisch, Schweizer/in
Sydney	['sɪdni]	Sydney
Syria	['sɪriə]	Syrien
Tanzania	[ˌtænzə'niːə]	Tansania
Texas	['teksəs]	Texas
Tokyo	['təʊkiəʊ]	Tokio
Turkey	['tɜːki]	Türkei
Turkish	['tɜːkɪʃ]	türkisch, Türke/-in
Uganda	[ju'gændə]	Uganda
Ugandan	[ju'gændən]	ugandisch, Ugander/in
United Kingdom (UK)	[juˌnaɪtɪd 'kɪŋdəm]	Vereinigtes Königreich
United States (USA)	[juˌnaɪtɪd 'steɪts]	Vereinigte Staaten
Vancouver	[væn'kuːvə]	Vancouver
Wales	[weɪlz]	Wales
Welsh	[welʃ]	walisisch, Waliser/in
Warsaw	['wɔːsɔː]	Warschau
Wembley	['wembli]	Wembley *(Stadtteil im Nordwesten Londons)*
Wimbledon	['wɪmbldən]	Wimbledon *(Stadtteil im Süden Londons)*
Winchester	['wɪntʃɪstə]	Winchester *(Stadt im Süden Englands)*
Zambia	['sæmbiə]	Sambia

be	was/were	been	*sein*
beat	beat	beaten	*schlagen, besiegen*
become	became	become	*werden*
begin	began	begun	*anfangen, beginnen*
bend	bent	bent	*(sich) beugen*
blow	blew	blown	*wehen, blasen, ziehen*
break	broke	broken	*brechen*
breed	bred	bred	*sich vermehren, sich ausbreiten*
bring	brought	brought	*(mit)bringen*
build	built	built	*bauen*
burn	burnt/ burned	burnt/ burned	*(ver)brennen*
buy	bought	bought	*kaufen*
catch	caught	caught	*fangen, fassen, erreichen*
choose	chose	chosen	*(aus)wählen*
come	came	come	*kommen*
cost	cost	cost	*kosten*
cut	cut	cut	*schneiden*
deal (with)	dealt (with)	dealt (with)	*sich kümmern um, umgehen mit*
dig	dug	dug	*graben*
do	did	done	*tun, machen*
draw	drew	drawn	*zeichnen*
dream	dreamt/ dreamed	dreamt/ dreamed	*träumen*
drink	drank	drunk	*trinken*
drive	drove	driven	*fahren*
eat	ate	eaten	*essen*
fall	fell	fallen	*fallen*
feed	fed	fed	*füttern, ernähren*
feel	felt	felt	*(sich) fühlen, empfinden*
fight	fought	fought	*kämpfen*
find	found	found	*finden*
fit	fit/fitted	fit/fitted	*passen, anbringen, entsprechen*
fly	flew	flown	*fliegen*
forbid	forbade	forbidden	*verbieten*
forget	forgot	forgotten	*vergessen*
get	got	got (*AE* gotten)	*bekommen*
give	gave	given	*geben*
go	went	gone	*gehen, fahren*
grow	grew	grown	*wachsen*
hang	hung	hung	*hängen*
have	had	had	*haben*
hear	heard	heard	*hören*
hide	hid	hidden	*(sich) verstecken*
hit	hit	hit	*schlagen*
hold	held	held	*halten, festhalten*
hurt	hurt	hurt	*verletzen*
keep	kept	kept	*behalten*
know	knew	known	*kennen, wissen*
lay	laid	laid	*legen*
lead	led	led	*führen*
lean	leant/ leaned	leant/ leaned	*sich lehnen, sich beugen*
learn	learnt/ learned	learnt/ learned	*lernen*

leave	left	left	*abfahren, verlassen, weggehen*
let	let	let	*lassen*
lie	lay	lain	*liegen*
light	lit	lit	*anzünden, beleuchten*
lose	lost	lost	*verlieren*
make	made	made	*machen*
mean	meant	meant	*meinen, bedeuten*
meet	met	met	*treffen*
pay	paid	paid	*bezahlen*
put	put	put	*setzen, stellen, legen*
quit	quit/ quitted	quit/ quitted	*verlassen, aufhören*
read	read	read	*lesen*
ride	rode	ridden	*reiten, fahren*
ring	rang	rung	*anrufen, läuten*
rise	rose	risen	*(an)steigen*
run	ran	run	*laufen, rennen*
say	said	said	*sagen*
see	saw	seen	*sehen*
seek	sought	sought	*suchen*
sell	sold	sold	*verkaufen*
send	sent	sent	*senden, schicken*
set	set	set	*setzen, stellen*
shake	shook	shaken	*schütteln*
shine	shone	shone	*scheinen, glänzen*
show	showed	shown	*zeigen*
shrink	shrank	shrunk	*schrumpfen, zurückgehen*
shut	shut	shut	*schließen*
sing	sang	sung	*singen*
sink	sank	sunk	*sinken*
sit	sat	sat	*sitzen*
sleep	slept	slept	*schlafen*
slide	slid	slid	*(ab)rutschen, (ab)sacken*
smell	smelt/ smelled	smelt/ smelled	*riechen*
speak	spoke	spoken	*sprechen*
spell	spelt/ spelled	spelt/ spelled	*buchstabieren*
spend	spent	spent	*ausgeben, verbringen*
spread	spread	spread	*(sich) verbreiten*
stand	stood	stood	*stehen*
steal	stole	stolen	*stehlen*
swim	swam	swum	*schwimmen*
take	took	taken	*nehmen*
teach	taught	taught	*unterrichten, beibringen*
tell	told	told	*sagen, erzählen*
think	thought	thought	*denken*
throw	threw	thrown	*werfen*
understand	understood	understood	*verstehen*
wake	woke	woken	*aufwachen, -wecken*
wear	wore	worn	*tragen*
win	won	won	*gewinnen*
write	wrote	written	*schreiben*

Quellenverzeichnis

Bildrechte

Titelfoto: Shutterstock / Maxim Blinkov
S. 6/1–2: Shutterstock / sirtravelalot; **S. 6/3:** Corepics VOF / Tommy Lee Walker; **S. 6/4:** vario Images / PV productions; **S. 6/5:** vario Images / Fer Gregory; **S. 6/6:** vario Images / Meiry Peruch Mezari; **S. 8:** Shutterstock / Featureflash; S. 10/1-2: Shutterstock / racorn; **S. 12/1:** Shutterstock / Monkey Business Images; **S. 12/2:** Shutterstock / Carme Balcells; **S. 12/3:** Shutterstock / Andresr; **S. 12/4:** Shutterstock / Monkey Business Images; **S. 12/5:** Shutterstock / wavebreakmedia; **S. 14:** FOTOFINDER / PhotoAlto; **S. 18/1:** Shutterstock / Luciano Mortula; **S. 18/2:** Shutterstock / mikecphoto; **S. 21:** Shutterstock / Monkey Business Images; **S. 22:** Shutterstock / Monkey Business Images; **S. 23:** Shutterstock / Monkey Business Images; **S. 24:** Shutterstock / Monkey Business Images; **S. 25/1:** Shutterstock / Shane Gross; **S. 25/2:** Shutterstock / anthonymooney; **S. 25/3:** Shutterstock / auremar; **S. 25/4:** Shutterstock / merzzie; **S. 25/5:** Shutterstock / Rommel Canlas; **S. 25/6:** Shutterstock / Syda Productions; **S. 26:** Cartoonstock / Marty Bucella; **S. 27:** Glow Images / Blend Images LLC; **S. 29:** Shutterstock / Blend Images LLC; **S. 30:** Isobel Williams, Berlin; **S. 31:** Shutterstock / Minerva Studio; **S. 34:** Shutterstock / Minerva Studio; **S. 35/1:** Shutterstock / Syda Productions; **S. 35/2:** Shutterstock / Robert Kneschke; **S. 35/3:** Shutterstock / Leigh J; S. **35/4:** Shutterstock / gpointstudio; **S. 35/5:** Shutterstock / Antonio Guillem; **S. 35/6:** Shutterstock / RossHelen; **S. 35/7:** Shutterstock / Monkey Business Images; **S. 36:** Shutterstock / Photographee.eu; **S. 38/1:** Shutterstock / Photographee.eu; **S. 38/2:** Shutterstock / Agenturfotografin; **S. 40:** Shutterstock / Catherine Murray; **S. 43:** action press / SWNSaction press; **S. 44/1:** Fotolia / kasto; **S. 44/2:** Fotolia / kasahasa; **S. 44/3:** Cartoonstock / Kelly Kincaid; **S. 45/1:** Shutterstock / Evgeny Atamanenko; **S. 45/2:** Shutterstock / Syda Productions; **S. 45/3:** Shutterstock / Thinglass; **S. 45/4:** Shutterstock / rangizzz; **S. 45/5:** Shutterstock / michaeljung; **S. 45/6:** Shutterstock / Valentina Razumova; **S. 45/7:** Fotolia / Dirima; **S. 45/8:** Fotolia / Photocreo Bednarek ; **S. 45/9:** Electrolux Hausgeräte GmbH; **S. 46/1–2:** VW 2009 – DDB Stockholm; **S. 47:** VW 2009 – DDB Stockholm; **S. 51:** Mauritius Images / Alamy; **S. 54/1:** Shutterstock / Thomas M Perkins; **S. 54/2:** Shutterstock / szefei; **S. 54/3:** Shutterstock / Miriam Doerr; **S. 55/1:** Shutterstock / Goodluz; **S. 55/2:** Shutterstock / Rawpixel; **S. 55/3:** Shutterstock / qvist; **S. 55/4:** Shutterstock / mato; **S. 55/5:** Shutterstock / AntonioDiaz; **S. 55/6:** Shutterstock / Goodluz; **S. 55/7:** Shutterstock / wavebreakmedia; **S. 55/8:** Shutterstock / Mark Skalny; **S. 56/1:** Shutterstock / Alena Ozerova; **S. 56/2:** Monkey Business Images; **S. 57:** glow images / Stockbroker; **S. 60/1–6:** Oxford Designers & Illustrators; **S. 63/1:** Oxford Designers & Illustrators; **S. 63/2:** Shutterstock / wavebreakmedia; **S. 64/1:** Fotolia / Fabrice Beauchene; **S. 64/2:** Fotolia / dimbar76; **S. 65:** Oxford Designers & Illustrators; **S. 67/1:** Shutterstock / Adam Gregor; **S. 67/2:** Shutterstock / racorn; S. 67/3: glow images / GammaA; **S. 67/4:** glow images / Fancy; **S. 69:** Shutterstock - Ollyy; **S. 70:** Shutterstock / Gemenacom; **S. 74:** Oxford Designers & Illustrators; **S. 75:** Shutterstock / Minerva Studio; **S. 79/1:** Mauritius Images / Alamy; **S. 79/2:** Corbis / HillCreek Pictures/ROBIN UTRECHT FOTOGRAFIE; **S. 79/3:** Shutterstock / Olivier Juneau; **S. 79/4:** Photoshot / Xinhua; **S. 80/1–3:** Oxford Designers & Illustrators; **S. 81:** Oxford Designers & Illustrators; **S. 84/1:** Shutterstock / Daniel M Ernst; **S. 84/2:** Shutterstock / GSPhotography; **S. 84/3:** Shutterstock / dotshock; **S. 84/4:** Shutterstock / Nadino; **S. 89/1:** Shutterstock / Monkey Business Images; **S. 89/2:** Shutterstock / Panaspics; **S. 89/3:** Shutterstock / Monkey Business Images; **S. 89/4:** Shutterstock / wrangler; **S. 89/5:** glow images / Ariel Skelley/Blend Images LLC; **S. 89/6:** Shutterstock / Leremy; **S. 90/1:** Shutterstock / Leremy; **S. 90/2:** Shutterstock / Sylvie Bouchard; **S. 90/3:** Shutterstock / karelnoppe; **S. 90/4:** Shutterstock / Goodluz; **S. 90/5:** Shutterstock / bikeriderlondon; **S. 91:** Corbis / RICK WILKING/Reuters; **S. 92/1:** Shutterstock / spotmatik; **S. 92/2:** Shutterstock / scigelova; **S. 92/3:** Shutterstock / Levent Konuk; **S. 92/4:** Shutterstock / bikeriderlondon; **S. 94/1–2:** Bulls Press / Barcroft Media; **S. 96:** Shutterstock / Andresr; **S. 98/1:** Shutterstock / Dream Master; S. **98/2:** Shutterstock / Boguslaw Mazur; **S. 98/3:** Shutterstock / javi merino; **S. 98/4:** Shutterstock / aarows; **S. 98/5:** Shutterstock / murphy81; **S. 98/6:** Shutterstock / Nikola m; **S. 98/7:** Shutterstock / veronchick84; **S. 98/8:** Shutterstock / schab; **S. 98/9:** Shutterstock / Neyro; **S. 98/10:** Shutterstock / Okuneva; **S. 98/11:** Shutterstock / jorgen mcleman; **S. 99/1–2:** Oxford Designers & Illustrators; **S. 100/1:** Shutterstock / Sylvie Bouchard; **S. 100/2:** Shutterstock / mortalpious; **S. 100/3:** Shutterstock / Darryl Brooks; **S. 100/4:** Shutterstock / Stuart Jenner; **S. 102/1:** akg-images; **S. 102/2:** Visum / ANDIA / VISUM; **S. 103:** Cartoonstock / Hajo de Reijger; **S. 108:** Shutterstock / swissmacky; **S. 109/1:** action press / Patrik Österberg / AOP Sweden; **S. 109/2–4:** Oxford Designers & Illustrators; **S. 110:** Mauritius Images / Alamy; **S. 114/1:** Fotolia / Hunor Kristo; **S. 114/2:** Fotolia / Ermolaev Alexandr; **S. 117:** Shutterstock / Martina Ebel; **S. 118:** Shutterstock / CandyBox Images; **S. 119:** Shutterstock / Minerva Studio; **S. 123/1:** Shutterstock / arindambanerjee; **S. 123/2:** Shutterstock / Jonathan Nafzger; **S. 123/3:** Shutterstock / eldeiv; **S. 123/4:** Shutterstock / Pablo Hidalgo - Fotos593; **S. 123/5:** Shutterstock / alexmillos; **S. 123/6:** Shutterstock / withGod; **S. 123/7:** Shutterstock / Phatic-Photography; **S. 123/8:** Fotolia / Ingo Bartussek; **S. 124:** Shutterstock / fmua; **S. 126/1:** Shutterstock / Daniel M Ernst; **S. 126/2:** Shutterstock / Charlotte Purdy; **S. 126/3:** Shutterstock / racorn; **S. 126/4:** Shutterstock / Kinga; **S. 128:** Fotolia / beugdesign; **S. 131:** Photoshot / UPPA/Photoshot; **S. 132:** Shutterstock / Vasin Lee; **S. 133/1–2:** Shutterstock / Dubova; **S. 134:** Shutterstock / wavebreakmedia; **S. 135:** Oxford Designers & Illustrators; **S. 138:** Topic Media; **S. 140:** Oxford Designers & Illustrators; **S. 143:** Oxford Designers & Illustrators; **S. 144:** Mauritius Images / Alamy; **S. 146:** Shutterstock / Rob Hyrons; **S. 147/1:** The Christian Science Monitor - Bennett; **S. 147/2:** Cagle - Dario Castillejos ; **S. 147/3:** Oxford Designers & Illustrators; **S. 148:** Oxford Designers & Illustrators; **S. 151:** Shutterstock / StockCube; **S. 153:** Oxford Designers & Illustrators; **S. 155/1:** action press / KYODO NEWS; **S. 155/2:** Corbis / EDGAR SU/Reuters; **S. 156:** Mauritius Images / Alamy; **S. 158/1:** F1 online; **S. 158/2:** Laif / Anthony Asael/Hemis.fr; **S. 159/1:** Shutterstock / beboy; **S. 159/2:** Shutterstock / Dimedrol68; **S. 159/3:** Shutterstock / Dja65; **S. 159/4:** Fotolia / areeya_ann ; **S. 159/5:** Shutterstock / Somchai Som; **S. 159/6:** Shutterstock / kavione; **S. 159/7:** Shutterstock / Denis Dryashkin; **S. 159/8:** Shutterstock / catolla; **S. 159/9:** Shutterstock / Nikonaft; **S. 159/10:** Shutterstock / Mike Flippo; **S. 159/11:** Shutterstock / pzAxe; **S. 159/12:** Shutterstock / Anna Hoychuk; **S. 161:** Mauritius Images / Alamy; **S. 164:** Shutterstock / Mopic; **S. 166:** Shutterstock / Krivosheev Vitaly; **S. 168:** University of Birmingham; **S. 170/1:** Fotolia / magraphics.eu; **S. 170/2:** Shutterstock / Stephen VanHorn; **S. 170/3:** Shutterstock / Syda Productions; **S. 170/4:** Shutterstock / Warren Goldswain; **S. 171:** Shutterstock / Minerva Studio; **S. 175/1:** Fotolia / Jürgen Fälchle ; **S. 175/2:** Shutterstock / mimagephotography; **S. 176/1:** Shutterstock / Marusha Belle; **S. 176/2:** Shutterstock / losw; **S. 176/3:** Shutterstock / tuulijumala; **S. 178/1:** Leave our kids alone; **S. 178/2:** Oxford Designers & Illustrators; **S. 178/3:** Oxford Designers & Il-

lustrators; **S. 181:** Fotolia / Anelina ; **S. 184:** Shutterstock / AlexandreNunes; **S. 185:** Oregon Center for Nursing; **S. 186:** Cartoonstock / Jim Naylor; **S. 187/1:** Shutterstock / in Green; **S. 187/2:** Shutterstock / Olha Insight; **S. 187/3:** Shutterstock / Horst Petzold; **S. 187/4:** Shutterstock / Paul Stringer; **S. 187/5:** Shutterstock / Zurijeta; **S. 187/6:** Shutterstock / Globe Turner; **S. 187/7:** Fotolia / Aigars Reinholds; **S. 187/8:** Shutterstock / Olha Insight; **S. 187/9:** Shutterstock / Ivonne Wierink; **S. 187/10:** Shutterstock / Olha Insight; **S. 187/11 (unten):** Oxford Designers & Illustrators; **S. 188:** Fotolia / Amy Myers; **S. 189:** Imago / PEMAX; **S. 190/1:** Shutterstock / Kkulikov; **S. 190/2:** Shutterstock / Stephen Marques; **S. 190/3:** Shutterstock / KPG_Payless; **S. 190/4:** Fotolia / mihalec; **S. 192:** Shutterstock / Goodluz; **S. 193/1:** Shutterstock / Rido; **S. 193/2:** Shutterstock / Alexander Raths; **S. 196:** Shutterstock / bikeriderlondon; **S. 198:** Shutterstock / Lightspring; **S. 199/1:** Shutterstock / Neyro; **S. 199/2:** Jonathan Keenan, Manchester; **S. 200:** Colourbox / Sebastien JARRY; **S. 202/1:** Shutterstock / Balu; **S. 202/2:** Shutterstock / kanvag; **S. 202/3:** Shutterstock / wonderisland; **S. 202/4:** Shutterstock / BMJ; **S. 202/5:** Shutterstock / Payungkead Im-anong; **S. 202/6:** Shutterstock / Dudarev Mikhail; **S. 202/7:** Shutterstock / kwest; **S. 203:** Penguin Random House; S. 205/1: Fotolia / wjarek ; **S. 205/2:** Corbis / Jonathan Nicholson / Demotix; **S. 206/1–2:** picture-alliance / dpa; **S. 209/1:** Koninklijke Philips N.V.; **S. 209/2:** eone (www.eone-time.com); **S. 209/3:** toysf400; **S. 212/1–3:** Oxford Designers & Illustrators; **S. 215:** Shutterstock / Radu Razvan; **S. 222:** Shutterstock / michaeljung; **S. 226:** Shutterstock / bikeriderlondon; **S. 230:** Fotolia / govicinity; **S. 236:** Shutterstock / Tish1; **S. 237:** Cartoonstock / S. Haris

Textrechte

S. 27: Daily Mail Reporter, "Life's so unfair! Shopping mall sets 6pm curfew for teenagers – unless they bring their parents". http://www.dailymail.co.uk/news/article-2142964/Lifes-unfair-Shopping-mall-sets-6pm-curfew-forcing-teenagers-hang-parent-tow.html; Daily Mail Online, 11. Mai 2012;
S. 36–37: Pat Hurst, "Britons spend 62m hours a day on social media – that's an average one hour for EVERY adult and child". http://www.independent.co.uk/life-style/gadgets-and-tech/news/; The Independent, 27. Januar 2015;
S. 40: Mark Duell, "'Don't have any parties': Last words of mother leaving for holiday to her public schoolboy son, 17: days before drunken Facebook crashers trashed trashed her £1m house". http://www.dailymail.co.uk/news/article-2442337/Drunken-revellers-trash-1m-house-gatecrashing-Facebook-party.html; Daily Mail Online, 4. Oktober 2013;
S. 43: Sian Lloyd, "Cancer fundraiser Stephen Sutton dies aged 19". http://www.bbc.com/news/uk-england-27408818; BBC News, 14. Mai 2014;
S. 46: Kelsey Ramos, "Volkswagen brings the fun: Giant piano stairs and other 'Fun Theory' marketing. http://latimesblogs.latimes.com/money_co/2009/10/volkswagen-brings-the-fun-giant-piano-stairs-and-other-fun-theory-marketing.html#sthash.krm3bWiS.dpuf; Los Angeles Times, 15. Oktober 2009;
S. 54: Julia Bonstein,"Ethical Marketing: Selling Goods by Doing Good". http://www.spiegel.de/international/spiegel/ethical-marketing-selling-goods-by-doing-good-a-368038.html; Spiegel Online, 1. August 2005;
S. 69–70: Violet Johnstone, "'Mind how you move that chair – it's hot' Hot-desking is a growing trend, bringing a new culture writes Violet Johnstone". http://www.telegraph.co.uk/finance/4493463/Mind-how-you-move-that-chair-its-hot-Hot-desking-is-a-growing-trend-bringing-a-new-culture-writes-Violet-Johnstone.html; The Telegraph, 10. Oktober 2002;
S. 80–81: Benjamin Zephaniah, "Refugee Boy". Bloomsbury Publishing, 1. Auflage, 2001;
S. 90: Emily Buchanan, "What's it like to be a sponsored child?". http://www.bbc.com/news/world-13697855; BBC News World, 10. Juni 2011;
S. 90: Paul Abbott, "MicroLoan Foundation helps some of the poorest women". http://www.microloanfoundation.org.uk/what-we-do/; MicroLoan Foundation UK; Abruf September 2014;
S. 90: Elizabeth Scowcroft, "Benefits of volunteering for Samaritans". http://www.samaritans.org/volunteer-us/change-some-one's-life-your-own; Samaritans Volunteering Department, Abruf September 2014;
S. 90: The Salvation Army, "Donate now: £26 could pay for ...". https://www.salvationarmyappeals.org.uk/site/SPageServer/?pagename=home; The Salvation Army United Kingdom Territory Territorial Headquarters, Abruf September 2014;
S. 94: Orphans for Orphans. http://www.gandysflipflops.com/orphans-for-orphans;
S. 110–111: Georgia Leaker, "Pass it on: give Gen Y more than a foot in the door". http://www.smh.com.au/comment/pass-it-on-give-gen-y-more-than-a-foot-in-the-door-20130708-2pm8v.html; The Sydney Morning Herald, 9. Juli 2013;
S. 118: Philip Olterman, "Germany's 'multigeneration houses' could solve two problems for Britain". www.theguardian.com/world/2014/may/02/germany-multigeneration-house-solve-problems-britain; The Guardian, 2. Mai 2014;
S. 124: Jonathan R. White, "The Nature of Modern Terrorism". http://www.huffingtonpost.com/jonathan-r-white/confusion-about-boston_b_3128995.html; Huffington Post, 21. April 2013;
S. 131: George Orwell, "Nineteen Eighty-Four". Penguin Books, 1949;
S. 132: David Barrett, "One surveillance camera for every 11 people in Britain, says CCTV survey". http://www.telegraph.co.uk/technology/10172298/One-surveillance-camera-for-every-11-people-in-Britain-says-CCTV-survey.html; The Telegraph, 10. Juli 2013;
S. 134: Daily News, "Germany – Nursing Skills Shortage to Worsen". http://www.staffingindustry.com/eng/Research-Publications/Daily-News/Germany-Nursing-skills-shortage-to-worsen-25210; Staffing Industry Analysts, 3. April 2013;
S. 146: Rupert Neate, "Campfire Kids: Going Back to Nature with Forest Kindergartens?". http://www.spiegel.de/international/zeitgeist/forest-kindergartens-could-be-the-next-big-export-from-germany-a-935165.html; Spiegel Online, 22. November 2013;
S. 156–157: Tim Folger, "The Next Green Revolution". http://www.nationalgeographic.com/foodfeatures/green-revolution/; National Geographic Magazine, Oktober 2014;
S. 160–161: Jan Puhl, "Silicon Savannah: Africa's Transformative Digital Revolution". http://www.spiegel.de/international/world/silicon-savannah-how-mobile-phones-and-the-internet-changed-africa-a-936307.html; Spiegel Online International, 5. Dezember 2013;

S. 168–169: Michael Eyre, "Boris the robot can load up dishwasher". http://www.bbc.com/news/science-environment-29168675; BBC News Science, 11. September 2014;
S. 178: Jonathan Kent, "Leave our kids alone". http://www.leaveourkidsalone.org/aboutus.php; Leave Our Kids Alone, 2014;
S. 188–189: Claire Richardson, "Refugees Welcome is more than just a slogan in Germany". http://blogs.reuters.com/events/2014/09/18/refugees-welcome-is-more-than-a-slogan-in-germany/; Thomson Reuters, N.Y., 18. September 2014;
S. 190: "Volunteering in agriculture and farming in Jamaica". http://www.projects-abroad.org/volunteer-destinations/volunteer-jamaica/agriculture-and-farming/#overview; Projects Abroad, N.Y., 2014;
S. 190–191: "Organic farm volunteering in Togo". http://www.projects-abroad.org/volunteer-projects/agriculture-and-farming/volunteer-togo/; Projects Abroad, N.Y., 2014;
S. 196: Rachel Rickard Straus, "Today's kindergarten kids 'are already on the road to obesity' as the whole nation gets fatter". http://www.dailymail.co.uk/news/article-2065609/Todays-kindergarten-kids-road-obesity-nation-gets-fatter.html#ixzz3KwoLVUtR; DailyMail, 24. November 2011;
S. 199–200: Saba Salman, "'I am different, that is good': how an actor with Down's syndrome is changing perceptions". www.theguardian.com/social-care-network/2014/oct/14/sarah-gordy-downs-syndrome-changing-perceptions; The Guardian, 14. Oktober 2014
S. 202–203: Michael Foreman, "Dinosaurs and all that Rubbish". http://www.puffin.co.uk/books/dinosaurs-and-all-that-rubbish/9780140552607/; PUFFIN/Penguin Children's, 28. Oktober 1993;
S. 205: Ioanna Fotiadi, "A single man takes the initiative to feed the poor ". http://www.ekathimerini.com/4dcgi _w_articles_wsite6_1_10/02/2012_427206; International New York Times - Kathimerini English Edition, 10. Februar 2012;
S. 206: "Misereor: committed to fighting poverty". http://www.misereor.org/about-us.html; Bischöfliches Hilfswerk Misereor e. V., Aachen, Februar 2015;
S. 208: Ilya Pozin, "10 Health Tech Companies Changing The World". http://www.forbes.com/sites/ilyapozin/2014/06/01/10-health-tech-companies-changing-the-world/; Forbes, 6. Januar 2014;
S. 215: James Delay, "Pedestrians are the great menace to cyclists". http://www.independent.co.uk/environment/green-living/james-daley-pedestrians-are-the-great-menace-to-cyclists-887017.html; The Independent, 7. August 2008;
S. 241–242: Steve Doughty, "Changing face of the British family: One in three now has a step-child". http://www.dailymail.co.uk/news/article-2552650/Changing-face-British-family-One-three-step-child.html#ixzz3Dw5waM1L; Daily Mail Online, 6. Februar 2014